CONTENTS

JACQUELINE MARTIN
TONY STOREY

UNLOCKING
CRIMINAL LAW
SECOND EDITION

SERIES EDITORS:
JACQUELINE MARTIN & CHRIS TURNER

Hodder Education
A MEMBER OF HACHETTE LIVRE UK

Orders: please contact Bookpoint Ltd, 130 Milton Park, Abingdon, Oxon OX14 4SB. Telephone: (44) 01235 827720. Fax: (44) 01235 400454. Lines are open from 9.00-5.00, Monday to Saturday, with a 24 hour message answering service. You can also order through our website www.hoddereducation.co.uk

If you have any comments to make about this, or any of our other titles, please send them to educationenquiries@hodder.co.uk

British Library Cataloguing in Publication Data
A catalogue record for this title is available from the British Library

ISBN: 978 0 340 94199 7

First Edition Published 2004
This Edition Published 2007
Impression number   10 9 8 7 6 5 4 3 2
Year   2011 2010 2009 2008

Cover photo by Laurent Hamels/PhotoAlto/Getty Images
Typeset by Dorchester Typesetting Group Ltd.
Printed in Malta for Hodder Education, part of Hachette Livre UK, 338 Euston Road, London NW1 3BH

ACKNOWLEDGEMENTS ■

The books in this series are a departure from traditional law texts and represent one view of a type of learning resource that we feel is particularly useful to students. The series editors would therefore like to thank the publishers for their support in making the project a reality. In particular we would also like to thank Alexia Chan for her continued faith in the project from its first conception and Tessa Heath for all her hard work well above and beyond the call of duty.

The authors would like to thank Rebecca Huxley-Binns for her work in ensuring that the book is as accurate and readable as possible.

The authors and publishers would like to thank the following for permission to reproduce copyright material: extract on p 104 from 'Mistake and Strict Liability by John Beaumont from New Law Journal by permission of LexisNexis Butterworths; extracts on pp 95, 111 and 527 by permission of Sweet and Maxwell; pp 425, 432, 541 by permission of Oxford University Press. © Crown copyright material is reproduced with permission of the Controller of HMSO.

Every effort has been made to trace and acknowledge ownership of copyright. The publishers will be glad to make suitable arrangements with any copyright holders whom it has not been possible to contact.

PREFACE ∎

The *Unlocking the Law* series is an entirely new style of undergraduate law textbooks. Many student texts are very prose dense and have little in the way of interactive materials to help a student feel his or her way through the course of study on a given module.

The purpose of this series, then, is to try to make learning each subject area more accessible by focusing on actual learning needs, and by providing a range of different supporting materials and features.

All topic areas are broken up into 'bite size' sections with a logical progression and extensive use of headings and numerous sub-headings. Each book in the series will also contain a variety of charts, diagrams and key fact summaries to reinforce the information in the body of the text. Diagrams and flow charts are particularly useful because they can provide a quick and easy understanding of the key points, especially when revising for examinations. Key facts charts not only provide a quick visual guide through the subject but are useful for revision purposes also.

The books have a number of common features in the layout. Important cases are separated out for easy access and have full citation in the text as well as the table of cases for ease of reference. The emphasis of the series is on depth of understanding much more than breadth. For this reason each text also includes key extracts from judgments where appropriate. Extracts from academic comment from journal articles and leading texts are also included to give some insight into the academic debate on complex or controversial areas. In both cases these are indented to make them clear from the body of the text.

Finally, the books also include much formative 'self-testing', with a variety of activities ranging through subject specific comprehension, application of the law, and a range of other activities to help the student gain a good idea of his or her progress in the course.

Symbols used in this series:

> **J** This is a small extract from a judgment in a case. It may follow a case example or the case may be identified immediately above.

 This is a section from an Act.

 This is an Article of the EC Treaty or of the European Convention on Human Rights.

C This is a clause from the Draft Criminal Code.

> Where a paragraph is indented, this is an extract from an academic source such as
> an article or a leading textbook.

Note also that all incidental references to 'he', 'him', 'his', etc are intended to be gender neutral.

The first part of this book covers important concepts which underpin the criminal law. These include *actus reus*, *mens rea* and strict liability, participation in crime, capacity, inchoate offences and general defences. The second part covers the most important offences. These include fatal and non-fatal offences against the person, sexual offences, offences against property and the main offences against public order.

The book is designed to cover all of the main topics on undergraduate and professional criminal law syllabuses.

The law is stated as we believe it to be on 31st January 2007.

Jacqueline Martin
Tony Storey

TABLE OF CASES

TABLE OF STATUTES AND OTHER INSTRUMENTS

Statutes

Statutory Instruments

European Legislation

International Legislation

LIST OF FIGURES

PART I

CONCEPTS
IN CRIMINAL LAW ■

chapter 1 INTRODUCTION TO CRIMINAL LAW ■

AIMS AND OBJECTIVES

After reading this chapter you should be able to:

- Understand the basic origins and purposes of criminal law

- Understand the definitions and classifications of criminal law

- Understand the basic working of the criminal justice system

- Understand the basic concept of the elements of *actus reus* and *mens rea* in criminal law

- Understand the burden and standard of proof in criminal cases

- Understand how human rights law may have an affect on criminal law

This book deals with substantive criminal law: the actual law of what has to be proved for each criminal offence, including the general principles of intention and causation, the defences available and other general rules such as those on when participation in a crime makes the person criminally liable. It is not concerned with the rules of procedure or evidence or sentencing theory and practice. These are not 'substantive' law.

This first chapter, however, gives some background information on criminal law. The purpose of the criminal law is considered, as well as how we know what is recognised as a crime, and the sources of criminal law. There are also brief sections explaining the courts in which criminal offences are tried, and how offenders may be sentenced. The final section of this chapter explains the burden and standard of proof in criminal cases.

1.1 Purpose of criminal law

The purpose of criminal law has never been written down by Parliament and, as the criminal law has developed over hundreds of years, it is difficult to state the aims in any precise way. However, there is general agreement that the main purposes are to:

- protect individuals and their property from harm

- preserve order in society

- punish those who deserve punishment.

However, on this last point it should be noted that there are also other aims when a sentence is passed on an offender. These include incapacitation, deterrence, reformation and reparation.

In addition to the three main aims of the criminal law listed above, there are other points which have been put forward as purposes. These include:

- educating people about appropriate conduct and behaviour
- enforcing moral values.

The use of the law in educating people about appropriate conduct can be seen in the drink-driving laws. The conduct of those whose level of alcohol in their blood or urine was above specified limits has only been criminalised since 1967. Prior to that, it had to be shown that a driver was unfit to drive as a result of drinking. Since 1967 there has been a change in the way that the public regard drink-driving. It is now much more unacceptable and the main reason for this change is the increased awareness, through the use of television adverts, of people about the risks to innocent victims when a vehicle is driven by someone over the legal limit.

1.1.1 Should the law enforce moral values?

This is more controversial and there has been considerable debate about whether the law should be used to enforce moral values. It can be argued that it is not the function of criminal law to interfere in the private lives of citizens unless it is necessary to try to impose certain standards of behaviour. The Wolfenden Committee reporting on homosexual offences and prostitution (1957) felt that intervention in private lives should only be done:

- to preserve public order and decency
- to protect the citizen from what is offensive or injurious and
- to provide sufficient safeguards against exploitation and corruption of others, particularly those who are especially vulnerable.

Lord Devlin disagreed. He felt that 'there are acts so gross and outrageous that they must be prevented at any cost'. He set out how he thought it should be decided what type of behaviour be viewed as criminal by saying:

> 'How are the moral judgments of society to be ascertained . . . It is surely not enough that they should be reached by the opinion of the majority; it would be too much to require the individual assent of every citizen. English law has evolved and regularly uses a standard which does not depend on the counting of heads. It is that of the reasonable man. He is not to be confused with the rational man. He is not to be expected to reason about anything and his judgment may be largely a matter of feeling . . . for my purpose I should like to call him the man in the jury box . . .
>
> It is not nearly enough that to say that a majority dislike a practice: there must be a real feeling of reprobation . . . I do not think one can ignore disgust if it is

deeply felt and not manufactured. Its presence is a good indication that the bounds
of toleration are being reached.'

Lord Devlin, *The Enforcement of Morals* (Oxford University Press, 1965)

There are two major problems with this approach. The first is that the decision of what moral
behaviour is criminally wrong is left to each jury to determine. This may lead to inconsistent results,
as there is a different jury for each case. Secondly, Lord Devlin is content to rely on what may be
termed 'gut reaction' to decide if the 'bounds of toleration are being reached'. This is certainly not a
legal method nor a reliable method of deciding what behaviour should be termed criminal. Another
problem with Lord Devlin's approach is that society's view of certain behaviour changes over a period
of time. Perhaps because of the lack of agreement on what should be termed 'criminal' and the
difficulty of finding a satisfactory way of legally defining such behaviour, there is another problem in
that the courts do not approach certain moral problems in a consistent way. This can be illustrated by
conflicting cases on when the consent of the injured party can be a defence to a charge of assault. The
first is the case of *Brown* [1993] 2 All ER 75.

CASE EXAMPLE

Brown [1993] 2 All ER 75

Several men in a group of consenting adult sado-masochists were convicted of assault
causing actual bodily harm (s 47 Offences Against the Person Act 1861) and malicious
wounding (s 20 Offences Against the Person Act 1861) They had carried out in private
such acts as whipping and caning, branding, applying stinging nettles to the genital area,
and inserting map pins or fish hooks into the penises of each other. All of the men who
took part consented to the acts against them. There was no permanent injury to any of the
men involved and no evidence that any of them had needed any medical treatment. The
House of Lords considered whether consent should be available as a defence in these
circumstances. It took the view that it could not be a defence and upheld the convictions.

Lord Templeman said:

> 'The question whether the defence of consent should be extended to the
> consequences of sado-masochistic encounters can only be decided by consideration of
> policy and public interest . . . Society is entitled and bound to protect itself against a
> cult of violence. Pleasure derived from the infliction of pain is an evil thing. Cruelty is
> uncivilised.'

Two of the judges dissented and would have allowed the appeals. One of these judges, Lord Slynn, expressed his view by saying:

> J
> 'Adults can consent to acts done in private which do not result in serious bodily harm, so that such acts do not constitute criminal assaults for the purposes of the 1861 [Offences Against the Person] Act. In the end it is a matter of policy in an area where social and moral factors are extremely important and where attitudes could change. It is a matter of policy for the legislature to decide. It is not for the courts in the interests of paternalism or in order to protect people from themselves to introduce into existing statutory crimes relating to offences against the person, concepts which do not properly fit there.'

The second case is *Wilson* [1996] Crim LR 573, where a husband had used a heated butter knife to brand his initials on his wife's buttocks, at her request. The wife's burns had become infected and she needed medical treatment. He was convicted of assault causing actual bodily harm (s 47 Offences Against the Person Act 1861) but on appeal the Court of Appeal quashed the conviction. Russell LJ said:

> J
> '[W]e are firmly of the opinion that it is not in the public interest that activities such as the appellant's in this appeal should amount to a criminal behaviour. Consensual activity between husband and wife, in the privacy of the matrimonial home, is not, in our judgment, a proper matter for criminal investigation, let alone criminal prosecution . . . In this field, in our judgment, the law should develop upon a case by case basis rather than upon general propositions to which, in the changing times we live, exceptions may arise from time to time not expressly covered by authority.'

The similarities in the two cases are that both activities were in private and the participants were adults. In *Brown* there were no lasting injuries and no evidence of the need for medical treatment, whereas in *Wilson* the injuries were severe enough for Mrs Wilson to seek medical attention (and for the doctor to report the matter to the police). The main distinction which the courts relied on was that in *Brown* the acts were for sexual gratification, whereas the motive in *Wilson* was of 'personal adornment'. Is this enough to label the behaviour in *Brown* as criminal? (See 8.9.3 and 8.9.4 for further discussion of the decision in *Brown* and also the decision of the European Court of Human Rights in the case.)

The reference in Russell LJ's judgment to changing times acknowledges that society's view of some behaviour can change. There can also be disagreement about what morals should be enforced. Abortion was legalised in 1967, yet some people still believe it is morally wrong. A limited form of euthanasia has been accepted as legal with the ruling in *Airedale NHS Trust v Bland* [1993] 1 All ER 821, where it was ruled that medical staff could withdraw life support systems from a patient, who could breathe unaided but was in a persistent vegetative state. This ruling meant that they could withdraw the feeding tubes of the patient, despite the fact that this would inevitably cause him to die. Many people believe that this is immoral, as it denies the sanctity of human life.

All these matters show the difficulty of agreeing that one of the purposes of criminal law should be to enforce moral standards.

1.1.2 Example of the changing nature of criminal law

As moral values will have an effect on the law, what conduct is criminal may, therefore, vary over time and from one country to another. The law is likely to change when there is a change in the values of government and society. A good example of how views on what is criminal behaviour change over time can be seen from the way the law on consensual homosexual acts has changed.

- The Criminal Law Amendment Act 1885 criminalised consensual homosexual acts between adults in private. It was under this law that the playwright Oscar Wilde was imprisoned in 1895.

- The Sexual Offences Act 1967 decriminalised such behaviour between those aged 21 and over.

- The Criminal Justice and Public Order Act 1994 decriminalised such behaviour for those aged 18 and over.

- In 2000 the Government reduced the age of consent for homosexual acts to 16, though the Parliament Acts had to be used as the House of Lords voted against the change in the law.

We will now move on to consider where the criminal law comes from.

1.2 Sources of criminal law

The two main areas from which our criminal law is derived are case decisions (common law) and Acts of Parliament.

1.2.1 Common law offences

The courts have developed the criminal law in decisions over hundreds of years. In some instances offences have been entirely created by case law and precedents set by judges in those cases. An offence which is not defined in any Act of Parliament is called a common law offence. Murder is such an offence. The classic definition of murder comes from the seventeenth-century jurist, Lord Coke. This definition has continually been refined by judges, including some important decisions during the 1980s and 1990s. Other common law offences include manslaughter and assault and battery. Equally, some defences have been entirely created by the decisions of judges. The defences of duress, duress of circumstances, automatism and intoxication all come into this category.

One problem with common law offences is that they can be very vague. This is illustrated by the common law offence of outraging public decency. This offence has arisen so rarely that there have even been debates about whether it actually exists, but it was used in two separate cases in the 1990s. The first case was *Gibson and another* [1991] 1 All ER 439.

CASE EXAMPLE

***Gibson and another* [1991] 1 All ER 439**

In this the first defendant had created an exhibit of a model's head with earrings which were made out of freeze-dried real human foetuses. He intended to convey the message that women wear their abortions as lightly as they wear earrings. This model was put on public display in the second defendant's art gallery. Both men were convicted of outraging public decency and their convictions were upheld by the Court of Appeal.

The second case was very different. This was *Walker* [1995] Crim LR 44, where the defendant had exposed his penis to two girls in the sitting room of his own house. The Court of Appeal allowed the defendant's appeal against his conviction, as the place where the act occurred was not open to the public. The prosecution's choice of charge seems odd, but presumably the fact that there had been very few cases made it difficult for them to know whether it was necessary to prove only that other people had been outraged or whether, as decided by the Court of Appeal, it had to be in a place where there was a real possibility that members of the general public might witness the act. In fact in *Walker* there were other more suitable offences with which the defendant could have been charged, such as offences under the Indecency with Children Act 1960.

In some instances the courts will develop the law and then it will be absorbed into a statute. This happened with the defence of provocation (a defence to murder). It had been developed through case law but was then set out in the Homicide Act 1957. Even where there is a definition in an Act of Parliament, the courts may still have a role to play in interpreting that definition and drawing precise boundaries for the crime.

1.2.2 Statutory offences

Today the vast majority of offences are set out in an Act of Parliament or through delegated legislation. About 70 to 80 Acts of Parliament are passed each year. In addition there is a considerable amount of delegated legislation each year, including over 3,000 statutory instruments created by Government Ministers.

Most offences today are statutory ones. Examples include theft, robbery, burglary, obtaining property by deception and other related offences which are in the Theft Act 1968 and Theft Act 1978. Criminal damage is set out in the Criminal Damage Act 1971. The law on sexual offences is now largely contained in the Sexual Offences Act 2003.

1.2.3 Codification of the criminal law

One of the main problems in criminal law is that it has developed in a piecemeal way and it is difficult to find all the relevant law. Some of the most important concepts, such as the meaning of 'intention', still come from case law and have never been defined in an Act of Parliament. Other areas of the law rely on old Acts of Parliament, such as the Offences Against the Person Act which is nearly 150 years old. All these factors mean that the law is not always clear. In 1965 the Government created a full-time law reform body called the Law Commission. The Law Commission has the duty to review all areas of law, not just the criminal law. By s 3(1) of the Law Commissions Act 1965 the Commission was established to:

'... take and keep under review all the law ... with a view to its systematic development and reform, including in particular the codification of such law, the elimination of anomalies, the repeal of obsolete and unnecessary enactments, the reduction of the number of separate enactments and generally the simplification and modernisation of the law'.

The Law Commission decided to attempt the codification of the criminal law to include existing law and to introduce reforms to key areas. A first draft was produced in 1985 and this was followed by consultation which led to the publication of *A Criminal Code for England and Wales* (1989) (Law Com No 177).

The two main purposes of the code were regarded as:

- bringing together in one place most of the important offences
- establishing definitions of key fault terms such as 'intention' and 'recklessness'.

The second point would also have helped Parliament in the creation of any new offences as it would be presumed that, when using words defined by the code in a new offence, it intended the meanings given by the criminal code unless they specifically stated otherwise.

The Draft Criminal Code has never been made law. Parliament has not had either the time or the will for such a large-scale technical amendment to the law. Because of this the Law Commission has since 1989 tried what may be called a 'building-block' approach, under which it has produced reports and draft Bills on small areas of law in the hope that Parliament would at least deal with the areas most in need of reform. Law Commission reports for reform of the criminal law have included:

- *Legislating the Criminal Code: Offences Against the Person and General Principles* (1993) (Law Com No 218)
- *Legislating the Criminal Code: Intoxication and Criminal Liability* (1995) (Law Com No 229)
- *Legislating the Criminal Code: Involuntary Manslaughter* (1996) (Law Com No 237)
- *Legislating the Criminal Code: Fraud and Deception* (1999) (Law Com No 155)
- *Fraud* (2002) (Law Com No 276)
- *Partial Defences to Murder: Final Report* (2004) (Law Com No 290).

These reports deal with areas of law in which cases have highlighted problems. Although these are areas of law where reform is clearly needed Parliament has not, at the time of writing, enacted any of

the Law Commission's reports on reform of the substantive criminal law. However, in 2006 a Bill on Corporate Manslaughter was put before Parliament (see section 7.4.5).

It is worth noting that most European countries have a criminal code. France's *code pénal* was one of the earliest, being introduced by Napoleon in 1810, though there is now a new *code*, passed in 1992.

1.2.4 Reform of the law

Even if the law were codified, it would still be necessary to add to it from time to time. Modern technology can lead to the need for the creation of new offences. A recent example of this is that it is now a criminal offence to use a hand-held mobile phone when driving. Pressure for new laws comes from a variety of sources. The main ones are:

- government policy
- EU law
- Law Commission reports
- reports by other commissions or committees
- pressure groups.

It is also necessary since the passing of the Human Rights Act 1998 to ensure that new laws are compatible with the European Convention on Human Rights.

1.3 Defining a crime

As seen in section 1.1.2, it is difficult to know what standard to use when judging whether an act or omission is criminal. The only way in which it is possible to define a crime is that it is conduct forbidden by the state and to which a punishment has been attached because the conduct is regarded by the state as being criminal. This is the only definition which covers all crimes.

As the criminal law is set down by the state, a breach of it can lead to a penalty, such as imprisonment or a fine, being imposed on the defendant in the name of the state. Therefore, bringing a prosecution for a criminal offence is usually seen as part of the role of the state. Indeed, the majority of criminal prosecutions are conducted by the Crown Prosecution Service, which is the main state agency for criminal prosecutions. There are other state agencies which bring prosecutions for certain types of offence. For example, the Serious Fraud Office for large scale frauds, or the Environmental Agency for breaches of law affecting the environment.

It is also possible for a private individual or business to start a prosecution. Big shops often conduct their own prosecutions in shoplifting cases, and bodies like the RSCPA regularly bring prosecutions. However, it is unusual for an individual to bring a prosecution. Even where an individual brings a prosecution, the state still has control over the case by the CPS taking over the prosecution and then making the decision on whether to continue with the prosecution or not.

Alternatively the Attorney-General can stay (ie halt) the proceedings at any time by entering what is called a *nolle prosequi* without the consent of the prosecutor.

1.3.1 Conduct criminalised by the judges

Some conduct is criminalised not by the state but by the courts. This occurs where the courts create new criminal offences through case law. In modern times this only happens on rare occasions, because nearly all law is made by Parliament. An example of conduct criminalised by the courts is the offence of conspiracy to corrupt public morals. This offence has never been enacted by Parliament. Its creation was recognised in *Shaw v DPP* [1962] AC 220. In this case the defendant had published a *Ladies Directory*, which advertised the names and addresses of prostitutes with their photographs and details of the 'services' they were prepared to offer. In the House of Lords, Viscount Simonds asserted that the offence of conspiracy to corrupt public morals was an offence known to the common law. He also claimed:

> **J** '[T]here is in [the] court a residual power, where no statute has yet intervened to supersede the common law, to superintend those offences which are prejudicial to the public welfare. Such occasions will be rare, for Parliament has not been slow to legislate when attention has been sufficiently aroused. But gaps remain and will always remain since no one can foresee every way in which the wickedness of man may disrupt the order of society.'

Another offence which has been recognised in modern times by the judges is marital rape. This was declared a crime in *R v R* [1991] 4 All ER 481.

1.3.2 Retroactive effect of case law

It is argued that it is wrong for the courts to make law. It is Parliament's role to make the law, and the courts' role is to apply the law. One of the arguments for this view is that Parliament is elected while courts are not, so that law-making by courts is undemocratic.

The other argument involves the fact that judge-made law is retrospective in effect. This means that when courts decide a case, they are applying the law to a situation which occurred before they ruled on the law. At the time of the trial or appeal they decide, as a new point of law, that the conduct which the defendant did is criminal. That decision thus criminalises conduct which was not thought to be criminal when it was committed months earlier.

This point was considered in *R v R*, where a man was charged with raping his wife. The court in *R v R* had to decide whether, by being married, a woman automatically consented to sex with her husband. There had never been any statute law declaring that it was a crime for a man to have sexual intercourse with his wife without her consent. Old case law dating back as far as 1736 had taken the view that 'by their mutual matrimonial consent the wife hath given up herself in this to her husband, which she cannot retract'. In other words, once married, a woman was always assumed to consent and she could not go back on this. This view of the law had been confirmed as the law in *Miller* [1954] 2 QB 282, even though in that case the wife had already started divorce proceedings. In *R v R* the House of Lords ruled that that it was a crime of rape when a man had sexual intercourse with his wife without her consent, pointing out that:

'The status of women and the status of a married woman in our law have changed quite dramatically. A husband and wife are now for all practical purposes equal partners in marriage.'

Following the House of Lords' decision, the case was taken to the European Court of Human Rights in *CR v United Kingdom* (Case no 48/1994/495/577 [1996] FLR 434) claiming that there was a breach of art 7 of the European Convention on Human Rights. The article states:

'No one shall be held guilty of any criminal offence on account of any act or omission which did not constitute a criminal offence under national or international law at the time when it was committed.'

The European Court of Human Rights held that there had not been any breach, as the debasing character of rape was so obvious that to convict in these circumstances was not a variance with the object and purpose of art 7. In fact, abandoning the idea that a husband could not be prosecuted for the rape of his wife conformed with the one of the fundamental objectives of the Convention, that of respect for human dignity. (See section 1.9 for further discussion on human rights and criminal law.)

1.4 Classification of offences

There are many ways of classifying offences depending on the purpose of the classification. The main ways are:

- by source
- by police powers
- by type of offence
- by place of trial.

1.4.1 Classifying law by its source

As already explained in section 1.2, law comes from different sources. This distinction is important from an academic point of view. So law can be categorised as:

- common law (judge-made)
- statutory (defined in an Act of Parliament)
- regulatory (set out in delegated legislation).

1.4.2 Categories for purposes of police powers of detention

Police powers to detain a suspect who has been arrested depend on the category of offence. There are three categories:

- summary offences
- indictable offences
- terrorism offences.

Summary offences

Under s 24 PACE, as amended by s 110 of the Serious Organised Crime and Police Act 2005, an arrest can be made by a constable for any offence. However, an arresting officer can only arrest if he or she has reasonable grounds for believing that it is necessary to make the arrest for one of the following reasons:

- to enable the person's name or address to be ascertained
- to prevent the person:
  - causing physical injury to him or herself or any other person
  - suffering physical injury
  - causing loss of or damage to property
  - committing an offence against public decency where members of the public cannot reasonably be expected to avoid the person in question
  - causing an unlawful obstruction of the highway
- to protect a child or other vulnerable person
- to allow the prompt and effective investigation of the offence or of the conduct of the person
- to prevent any prosecution for the offence from being hindered by the disappearance of the person in question.

Where the offence is NOT one of terrorism or an indictable offence, the police can only detain a person for a maximum of 24 hours. They must also allow someone to be informed of the arrest and for the suspect to have legal advice as soon as possible after arrest.

Indictable offences

For these the police have the power to detain any person who has been arrested for an initial period of 24 hours. This can then be extended to 36 hours by an officer of the rank of superintendent or above under s 42(1) of the Police and Criminal Evidence Act 1984 (as amended). The police then

have the right to apply to a magistrate for permission to detain the suspect for up to a maximum of 96 hours.

In addition there are restrictions on the rights of the suspected person. The right to have someone informed of their arrest may be delayed for up to 36 hours (s 56 Police and Criminal Evidence Act 1984). The right to legal advice may also be delayed for up to 36 hours (s 58 Police and Criminal Evidence Act 1984).

Terrorism offences

Powers of detention for terrorism offences are controlled by the Terrorism Act 2000. Under Sch 8 of this Act, as amended by the Terrorism Act 2006, the police can detain a person arrested on suspicion of terrorism offences for 48 hours. After this they can apply to a judge to extend the period up to a maximum of 28 days. For extensions beyond 14 days the application has to be to a High Court Judge. The PACE Code of Practice H applies to those detained for a terrorism offence.

1.4.3 Classifying by the type of harm caused by the crime

When studying criminal law it is usual to study offences according to the type of harm caused. The main categories here are:

* offences against the person
* offences against property
* offences against public order.

1.4.4 Classification by where a case will be tried

One of the most important ways of classifying offences is by the categories that affect where and how a case will be tried. For this purpose offences are classified as:

1. *Indictable only offences*   These must be tried on indictment at the Crown Court (eg murder, manslaughter, rape).
2. *Triable either way offences*   These can be tried either on indictment at the Crown Court or summarily at the Magistrates' Court (eg theft, burglary, assault occasioning actual bodily harm).
3. *Summary offences*   These can only be tried at the Magistrates' Court (eg assaulting a policeman in the execution of his duty, common assault).

1.5 Criminal justice system

There are two courts which try criminal cases. These are:

* the Magistrates' Court
* the Crown Court.

As already seen in the section on classification of offences (section 1.4.4), the decision as to where the trial will take place depends on whether the offence is summary, triable either way or indictable.

1.5.1 Trials in the Magistrates' Court

Magistrates can try summary offences and any triable either-way offences where they accept jurisdiction and the defendant elects for the case to be tried in the Magistrates' Court. Cases are tried by a panel of two or three lay justices or by a District Judge (Magistrates' Court).

Lay justices have no legal qualifications, sit only part-time and are not paid a salary, although they are paid expenses. They are appointed from ordinary members of the community. The only qualifications they need are six key qualities:

- good character
- understanding and communication
- social awareness
- maturity and sound temperament
- sound judgement
- commitment and reliability.

Those appointed must be prepared to sit at least 26 half-days per year, although consideration is being given to making this 24 half-days, that is one day a month, in order to attract more people into the magistracy.

District Judges (Magistrates' Court) are qualified barristers or solicitors of at least seven years' standing. District Judges may hear cases on their own or they may form a panel with one or two lay magistrates.

Both lay magistrates and District Judges have dual roles. They hear the case and decided if the defendant is guilty or not guilty. Where the defendant is found guilty or has pleaded guilty, they pass sentence.

Magistrates' powers of sentencing were limited to a maximum of six months' imprisonment for one offence, or a total of 12 months' imprisonment for two or more offences. Under the Criminal Justice Act 2003 these powers will soon be increased to 12 months' imprisonment for one offence and 15 months' for two or more. Magistrates can also fine up to £5,000, though for some offences, such as causing pollution, the maximum fine is £20,000.

1.5.2 Trials in the Crown Court

The offences which can be tried at the Crown Court are all indictable only offences and any triable either-way offences where the magistrates have declined jurisdiction or the defendant has elected trial at the Crown Court.

Where the defendant pleads not guilty the case is heard by a judge and a jury of 12. The judge decides the law and sums up to the jury. The jury decide the facts and, accordingly, whether the defendant is guilty or not guilty. If the defendant is found guilty, it is then the role of the judge to pass sentence.

As the judge is the decider of law and the jury the decider of facts, the judge can decide at the end of the prosecution case that, as a matter of law, the prosecution has not proved the case, and he can direct that the defendant be acquitted. Statistics of trials in the Crown Court show that about 12 per cent are ended by a judge-directed acquittal.

Where the case continues, then, at the end of the whole case, the judge will direct the jury on any relevant points of law and they will then decide whether the defendant is guilty or not guilty. If they find the defendant not guilty, he is acquitted. Where they convict then the judge decides the appropriate sentence to impose on the defendant. If a defendant pleads guilty then the judge deals with the case on his own. There is no jury.

The use of a jury in the Crown Court is regarded as an important constitutional right and a way of protecting human rights. In the past few years Tony Blair's Labour Government has made three attempts to restrict the rights of defendants to trial by jury. In both 1999 and 2000 the Government tried to get a Bill passed which would have removed from offenders charged with triable either-way offences the right to choose jury trial. On both occasions the House of Lords voted against the Bill so that it was not made law. In 2003 the Criminal Justice Bill included two clauses which would have affected the defendant's right to trial by jury. The first gave the defendant the right to choose to be tried by a judge alone without a jury. This clause was defeated by the House of Lords. The other clause provided for the prosecution to apply for trial by a judge alone in complex fraud cases. The House of Lords voted against this, but eventually a compromise was reached so that the section was passed as part of the Criminal Justice Act 2003, but it is subject to an affirmative resolution which means that it cannot become law unless both the House of Commons and the House of Lords in the future vote in favour of this.

1.5.3 Appeals from the Magistrates' Court

There are two different appeal routes, as shown in Figure 1.1.

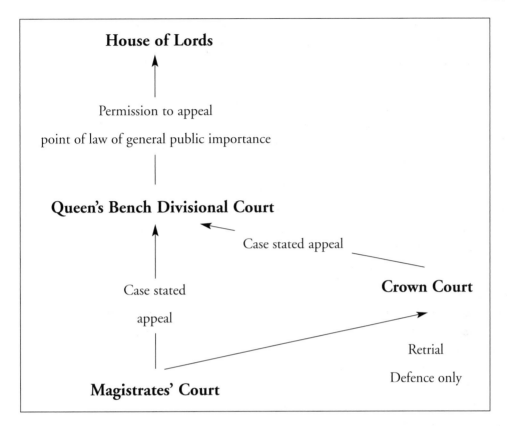

House of Lords

Permission to appeal

point of law of general public importance

Queen's Bench Divisional Court

Case stated appeal

Case stated

appeal

Crown Court

Retrial

Defence only

Magistrates' Court

■ *Figure 1.1 Appeal routes from the Magistrates' Court*

Case stated appeal to the Queen's Bench Divisional Court

This is used where the appeal is on a point of law. The magistrates are asked to state a case (finding of facts). This route is available for both the prosecution and the defence. The Divisional Court can quash the decision, confirm it or remit the case to the Magistrates' Court for a rehearing. Where reference is made to judgments of the Divisional Court or Queen's Bench Divisional Court in any textbook on criminal law, then the case must have originally been tried in the Magistrates' Court.

A further appeal is possible to the House of Lords. This must be on a point of law of general public importance and the House of Lords (or QBD) must give permission to appeal. Very few cases reach the House of Lords by this route: only about two or three per year.

Appeal to the Crown Court

This route is only available to the defendant. The appeal can be against sentence or conviction or both. The whole case is reheard at the Crown Court by a judge and two lay magistrates. They decide whether the defendant is guilty or not guilty and, if guilty, can pass any appropriate

sentence. There is no further appeal from the Crown Court, unless a point of law is involved when the appeal then goes to the QBD and House of Lords as above.

1.5.4 Appeals from trials in the Crown Court

House of Lords

↑

Need permission to appeal

point of law of general public importance

Court of Appeal

(Criminal Division)

↑

Crown Court

Figure 1.2 Appeals from the Crown Court

Appeals by the defendant

The defendant has the possibility of appealing against conviction and/or sentence to the Court of Appeal (Criminal Division). The rules on appeals are set out in the Criminal Appeal Act 1995 and in all cases the defendant must obtain leave to appeal from the Court of Appeal, or a certificate that the case is fit for appeal from the trial judge. On the hearing of an appeal the Court of Appeal can allow a defendant's appeal and quash the conviction. Alternatively it can vary the conviction to that of a lesser offence of which the jury could have convicted the defendant. So far as sentence is concerned, the court can decrease it, but cannot increase it on the defendant's appeal. Finally, the court can dismiss the appeal.

Appeals by the prosecution

Originally the prosecution had no right to appeal against either the verdict or sentence passed in the Crown Court. Gradually, however, some limited rights of appeal have been given to it by

Parliament. With one small exception, the prosecution cannot appeal against a finding of not guilty by a jury. The exception is for cases where the acquittal was the result of the jury being 'nobbled', that is where some jurors are bribed or threatened by associates of the defendant. In these circumstances, provided there has been an actual conviction for 'jury nobbling', the Criminal Procedure and Investigations Act 1996 allows the prosecution to appeal and the High Court can order a retrial.

However, the prosecution has a special referral right in cases where the defendant is acquitted. This is under s 36 of the Criminal Justice Act 1972, which allows the Attorney-General to refer a point of law to the Court of Appeal in order to get a ruling on the law. The decision by the Court of Appeal on that point of law does not affect the acquittal, but it creates a precedent for any future case involving the same point of law. When this has occurred, the reported case is cited in the form of *Attorney-General's Reference (No x of 2004)*.

Under the Criminal Justice Act 2003 it is also possible for a defendant who has been acquitted of certain serious offences to be tried a second time. This can only happen where the Court of Appeal decides that there is new and compelling evidence which justifies a second trial.

Appeals to the House of Lords

Both the prosecution and the defence may appeal from the Court of Appeal to the House of Lords, but it is necessary to have the case certified as involving a point of law of general public importance and to get leave to appeal, either from the House of Lords or from the Court of Appeal. Very few criminal appeals are heard by the House of Lords.

1.5.5 The hierarchy of the courts

This hierarchy of the appeal courts is important for judicial precedent. Decisions by the House of Lords on points of law are binding on all the other courts in England and Wales. The only exception to this is where there has been a decision by the European Court of Justice when lower courts have to follow this and not a House of Lords decision. Also, all courts have to take account of judgments of the European Court of Human Rights and may choose to follow such a decision.

The lower courts must also follow decisions of the Court of Appeal where there is no decision by the House of Lords. However, decisions made by the Court of Appeal can be overruled by the House of Lords. The Divisional Court is below the Court of Appeal in the hierarchy for the purposes of precedent, but lower courts are bound to follow any decisions made by the Divisional Court if there is no decision by either the Court of Appeal or the House of Lords.

1.6 Sentencing

1.6.1 Purposes of sentencing

It is recognised that sentencing can be aimed at different purposes, but for the first time the Government has set down the key aims in a statutory context. The Criminal Justice Act 2003 sets

out the purposes of sentencing for those aged 18 and over, saying that a court must have regard to:

- the punishment of offenders
- the reduction of crime (including its reduction by deterrence and by the reform and rehabilitation of offenders)
- the protection of the public and
- the making of reparation by offenders to persons affected by their offences.

The Act also states that 'in considering the seriousness of any offence, the court must consider the offender's culpability in committing the offence and the harm, or risk of harm, which the offence caused or was intended to cause'. Previous convictions are an aggravating factor if the court considers this so in view of the relevance to the present offence and the time which has elapsed since the previous conviction. Racially or religiously aggravated offences are viewed seriously and the Act allows for an increase in sentence in these situations. There can be a reduction in sentence for a guilty plea, particularly where made early in the proceedings.

1.7 Elements of a crime

For all crimes, except crimes of strict liability (see Chapter 4), there are two elements which must be proved by the prosecution. These are:

- *actus reus*
- *mens rea*.

These terms come from a Latin maxim, *actus non facit reum nisi mens sit rea*, which means 'the act itself does not constitute guilt unless done with a guilty mind'. Both an act (or omission) and a guilty mind must be proved for most criminal offences.

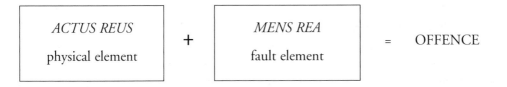

ACTUS REUS		MENS REA		
physical element	+	fault element	=	OFFENCE

■ *Figure 1.3 The elements of an offence*

Actus reus has a wider meaning than an 'act', as it can cover omissions or a state of affairs. The term has been criticised as misleading. Lord Diplock in *Miller* [1983] 1 All ER 978 preferred the term 'prohibited conduct', while the Law Commission in the Draft Criminal Code (1989) used the term 'external element'. *Actus reus* as a concept is considered fully in Chapter 2.

Mens rea translates as 'guilty mind', but this also is misleading. The Law Commission in the Draft Criminal Code (1989) used the term 'fault element'. The levels of 'guilty mind' required for different offences vary from the highest level, which is specific intention for some crimes, to much lower levels such as negligence or knowledge of a certain fact for less serious offences. The levels of *mens rea* are explained in detail in Chapter 3.

The *actus reus* and *mens rea* will be different for different crimes. For example, in murder the *actus reus* is the killing of a human being and the *mens rea* is causing the death with 'malice aforethought'. For theft the *actus reus* is the appropriation of property belonging to another, while the *mens rea* is doing this dishonestly and with the intention permanently to deprive the other of the property. The *actus reus* and the *mens rea* must be present together, but if there is an ongoing act, then the existence of the necessary *mens rea* at any point during that act is sufficient. This is explained fully in Chapter 3. Even where the *actus reus* and *mens rea* are present, the defendant may be not guilty if he has a defence.

There are some crimes which are an exception to the general rule that there must be both *actus reus* and *mens rea*. These are crimes of strict liability, where the prosecution need only prove the *actus reus*; no mental element is needed for guilt. (See Chapter 4 for strict liability.)

1.8 Burden and standard of proof

1.8.1 Presumption of innocence

An accused person is presumed innocent until proven guilty. The burden is on the prosecution to prove the case. This means that it must prove both the required *actus reus* and the required *mens rea*. The prosecution may also have to disprove a defence which the defendant raises. This was confirmed in the case of *Woolmington v DPP* [1935] AC 462.

CASE EXAMPLE

Woolmington v DPP [1935] AC 462

D's wife had left him and gone to live with her mother. D wanted her to return to him. He went to the mother's house and shot his wife dead. He claimed that he had decided to ask his wife to come back to him and, if she refused, to commit suicide. So he took with him a loaded sawn-off shotgun. He attached a piece of wire flex to the gun so he could put the flex over his shoulder and carry the gun underneath his coat. When his wife indicated that she would not return to him, he threatened to shoot himself and brought the gun out to show her he meant it. As he brought it across his waist it somehow went off, killing his wife. He claimed this was a pure accident.

The judge at the trial told the jury that the prosecution had to prove beyond reasonable doubt that the defendant killed his wife. He then went on to tell them that, if the prosecution satisfied them of that, the defendant had to show that there were circumstances which made that killing pure accident. This put the burden of proof on the defendant to prove the defence. In the House of Lords it was held that this was a misdirection.

Lord Sankey stated that:

> **J** 'Throughout the web of the English criminal law one golden thread is always to be seen – that it is that duty of the prosecution to prove the prisoner's guilt . . . if at the end of and on the whole of the case, there is a reasonable doubt, created by evidence given by either the prosecution or the prisoner, as to whether the prisoner killed the deceased with a malicious intention, the prosecution has not made out the case and the prisoner is entitled to an acquittal. No matter what the charge or where the trial, the principle that the prosecution must prove the guilt of the prisoner is part of the common law of England and no attempt to whittle it down can be entertained.'

This judgment makes several important points which the House of Lords regards as fixed matters on English law. These are:

- the prosecution must prove the case
- this rule applies to all criminal cases
- the rule must be applied in any court where there is a criminal trial (currently the Magistrates' Court and Crown Court)
- guilt must be proved beyond reasonable doubt
- a reasonable doubt can be raised by evidence from either the prosecution or the defence.

1.8.2 Raising a defence

If the defendant raises a defence then it is for the prosecution to negate that defence. In *Woolmington* the defendant stated that the gun had gone off accidentally, thus raising the defence of accident. The prosecution was obliged to disprove this if the defendant was to be found guilty.

For all common law defences, except insanity, the defendant only has to raise some evidence of the key points of the defence. This can be from evidence given by the defence or by the prosecution. If evidence of a defence is given at the trial, then even where the defendant has not specifically raised the defence, the prosecution must disprove at least one element of that defence. The trial judge must direct the jury to acquit unless they are satisfied that the defence has been disproved by the prosecution.

Reverse onus

For certain defences, the burden of proof is on the defendant. For example, if the defendant claims that he was insane at the time of the crime, the burden of proving this is on the defendant. This shifting of the burden of proof to the defendant is known as the 'reverse onus'. As well as the common-law defence of insanity, it applies to exceptions which have been created by statute. One of these is the defence of diminished responsibility in the Homicide Act 1957, where s 2(2) states:

 '2(2) On a charge of murder, it shall be for the defence to prove that the person
charged is by virtue of this section not liable to be convicted of murder.'

Where a statute places the burden of proof on the defendant to prove a defence, the standard is the civil one of balance of probabilities. This was decided in *Carr-Briant* [1943] 2 All ER 156, where the defendant was charged under the Prevention of Corruption Act 1916. Section 2 of the Act states that any money or other gift given by someone trying to get a contract with a government department or other public body to the holder of a public office 'shall be deemed to have been paid or given and received corruptly as such inducement or reward . . . unless the contrary is proved'.

The trial judge had directed the jury that this meant the defendant had to prove his innocence beyond reasonable doubt. On appeal the conviction was quashed on another ground, but the court went on to state that this direction was wrong:

> **J** 'In our judgment, in any case where, either by statute or at common law, some matter is presumed against an accused "unless the contrary is proved," the jury should be directed that it is for them to decide whether the contrary is proved; that the burden of proof is less than is required at the hands of the prosecution in proving the case beyond reasonable doubt; and that the burden may be discharged by evidence satisfying the jury of the probability of that which the accused is called upon to establish.'

There may be a breach of human rights when the defence have to prove a defence. (See section 1.9 for full discussion of this.)

1.8.3 Standard of proof

The standard of proof in order for a defendant to be found guilty is 'beyond reasonable doubt'. This is usually explained by the judge telling the jury that they should only convict if they are satisfied that they are sure of the defendant's guilt.

1.9 Criminal law and human rights

The Human Rights Act 1998 incorporated the European Convention on Human Rights into our law. Under s 3 of the Act all Articles of the Convention have to be taken into consideration by English courts. Much of the effect of the Convention is on evidence and procedure but it has also had an effect on substantive criminal law.

In criminal law the most relevant rights under the Convention are:

- the right to liberty (Art 5)
- the right to a fair trial (Art 6(1))
- the presumption of innocence (Art 6(2))
- that there should be no punishment without law (Art 7(1)).

However, challenges to our substantive criminal law have been made under other Articles. These include:

- the right not to be subjected to inhuman or degrading treatment (Art 3(1))
- the right of respect for a person's private life (Art 8)
- that, in the application of the Convention rights and freedoms, there should be no discrimination on the grounds of sex, race, religion or political opinion (Art 14).

1.9.1 The right to a fair trial

This right is contained in Art 6(1) of the European Convention.

 '6(1) Everyone is entitled to a fair trial and public hearing within a reasonable time by an independent and impartial tribunal established by law.'

In *G* [2006] EWCA Crim 821 it was held that the fact that the offence was one of strict liability did not render the trial unfair.

CASE EXAMPLE

G [2006] EWCA Crim 821

D was a boy aged 15 who had had sexual intercourse with a girl aged 12. He was charged under s 5 of the Sexual Offences Act 2003 (SOA) with rape of a child under 13. The facts accepted by the court were that V willingly agreed to have sexual intercourse and that D reasonably believed that V was 15 as she had told him this earlier. D pleaded guilty because he was advised that the offence is committed irrespective of:

- consent
- reasonable belief in consent
- a reasonable belief as to age.

On appeal it was argued that s 5 SOA 2003 breached Art 6 of the European Convention on Human Rights since the section created an absolute offence and could have consequences which are wholly unreasonable. In this case it made a 15 year old who had sexual intercourse with a consenting 12 year old, whom he reasonably believed to be 15, liable to a conviction for rape of a child. Such a conviction carries the stigma of being a sex offender and requires the defendant to notify police as to his whereabouts. The offence also carries a potential sentence of life imprisonment. The Court of Appeal upheld the conviction.

The Court of Appeal accepted that it was possible for an offence of strict liability to infringe other Articles of the Convention, but that it did not make the trial unfair. In his judgment, Lord Phillips CJ said:

J 'An absolute offence may subject a defendant to conviction in circumstances where he has done nothing blameworthy. Prosecution for such an offence and the imposition of sanctions under may well infringe articles of the Convention other than Article 6. The legislation will not, however, render the trial under which it is enforced unfair, let alone the presumption of innocence under Article 6(2).'

Lord Phillips did not specify which other Articles might be breached, but one of them was probably Art 8 respect for private life. The defence challenged the conviction under this Article as well as under Art 6, and although the Court of Appeal upheld the conviction they did indicate that in some circumstances there could be a breach of Art 8 (see section 1.9.4).

1.9.2 Burden of proof

Article 6(2) states that 'Everyone charged with a criminal offence shall be presumed innocent until proven guilty'.

This places the burden of proof on the prosecution and effectively makes the same provision for the standard of proof in a criminal trial as already exists in our legal system. The only potential conflict with human rights is where the defendant has to prove a defence. Defences which place the burden of proving the defence in the defendant may be in breach of Art 6(2).

In the conjoined appeals of *Attorney-General's Reference (No 4 of 2002)* and *Sheldrake v DPP* [2004] UKHL 43; [2005] 1 All ER 237 the House of Lords considered whether defences which require the defendant to prove them on the balance of probabilities were a breach of the presumption of innocence under Art 6(2) of the European Convention on Human Rights. The Lords came to the conclusion that in many cases the wording of the Act could be interpreted so that it did not create a legal burden to prove the defence as was held in *Attorney-General's Reference (No 4 of 2002)*. However, they held that even if a section did breach Art 6(2) it was permissible if it was 'justifiable, legitimate and proportionate'. This was the situation in the case of *Sheldrake v DPP*.

CASE EXAMPLE

Sheldrake v DPP [2004] UKHL 43; [2005] 1 All ER 237

Sheldrake was convicted of being in charge of a motor car in a public place while over the drink-drive limit, contrary to s 5(1)(b) of the Road Traffic Act 1988. Section 5(2) of the Act allows a defence if D can prove that there was no likelihood of his driving while he was over the limit. He was convicted but the Divisional Court quashed the conviction. The prosecution then appealed to the House of Lords.

The defence argued that s 5(2) infringed the presumption of innocence guaranteed by Art 6(2) as it imposed on the defendant a legal burden of proving innocence by proving a defence.

The House of Lords held that s 5(2) did impose a legal burden of proof on the defendant. However, they pointed there is an obvious risk that a person who is in charge of a car when unfit to drive, may drive and so risk causing death or serious injury. As a result, the Lords allowed the prosecution's appeal and reinstated the conviction.

CASE EXAMPLE

Attorney-General's Reference (No 4 of 2002) [2004] UKHL 43, [2005] 1 All ER 237

This case concerned s 11 of the Terrorism Act 2000. The defendant had been charged with counts (1) being a member of a proscribed organisation and (2) professing to be a member of a proscribed organisation, both contrary to s 11(1). The question was whether s 11(2) imposed a legal or evidential burden on the defendant.

Section 11(2) states:

'11(2) It is a defence for a person charged with an offence under subsection 11(1) to prove:
  (a) that the organisation was not proscribed on the last (or only) occasion on which he became a member or began to profess to be a member, and
  (b) that he has not taken part in the activities of the organisation at any time while it was proscribed.'

At the trial the judge ruled that there was no case to answer on the two counts. The Attorney-General referred the point of law for the opinion of the Court of Appeal, who ruled in the

Attorney-General's favour. The defence referred the matter to the House of Lords which ruled that s 11(2) could be read down as imposing an evidential instead of a legal burden.

Lord Bingham gave the leading speech in these conjoined cases. His judgment is particularly useful as he gave a review of reverse burden situations covering:

- the pre-Convention law of England and Wales
- the Convention and the Strasbourg jurisprudence and
- the leading United Kingdom cases since the Human Rights Act 1998.

After considering cases decided by the European Court of Human Rights, Lord Bingham said:

> **J** 'From this body of authority certain principles may be derived. The overriding concern is that a trial should be fair, and the presumption of innocence is a fundamental right directed to that end. The Convention does not outlaw presumptions of fact or law but requires that these should be kept within reasonable limits and should not be arbitrary.' (para 21.)

He went on to point out that:

> **J** 'Relevant to any judgment on reasonableness or proportionality will be the opportunity given to the defendant to rebut the presumption, maintenance of the rights of the defendant, flexibility in application of the presumption, retention by the court of a power to assess the evidence, the importance of what is at stake and the difficulty which a prosecutor may face in the absence of a presumption.' (para 21.)

UK decisions since the Human Rights Act 1998

Lord Bingham reviewed several cases. The most important being:

- *R v DPP, ex p Kebilene* [2000] 2 AC 326 regarding the provisions of the Prevention of Terrorism (Temporary Provisions) Act 1989, in which the majority of the Lords held that the relevant provision could be read down as imposing an evidential and not a legal burden.

- *Lambert* [2001] UKHL 37; [2002] 1 All ER 2 which concerned s 28(2) of the Misuse of Drugs Act 1971. The appeal failed because a majority of the Lords held that the Human Rights Act 1998 was not retrospective. Although the appeal failed on this ground the Lords did consider the presumption of innocence and a majority held that if s 28(2) of the Misuse of Drugs Act 1971 was read as imposing a legal burden on the defendant to prove lack of knowledge, then this undermined the presumption of innocence to an impermissible extent. However, they thought it could be read down as imposing only an evidential burden.

- *Johnstone* [2003] UKHL 28 concerning s 92(5) of the Trade Marks Act 1994. The Law Lords held that the section did impose a legal burden on the defendant and so derogated from the presumption of innocence. However, this could be justified if it was necessary to maintain a balance between the public interest and the interests of the defendant.

Lord Bingham pointed out that the first question the House of Lords had to consider in each case was whether the provision in question did, unjustifiably, infringe the presumption of innocence. In order to do this it was necessary to consider:

- did the provision make an inroad into Art 6, if so
- was an inroad justifiable, legitimate and proportionate?

If an inroad into Art 6 was justifiable, legitimate and proportionate, then a legal burden was placed on the defendant. If an inroad was unjustified, then a further question arose – could and should the provision be 'read down' in accordance with the courts' interpretative obligation under s 3 of the Human Rights Act 1998 so as to impose an evidential and not a legal burden on the defendant? 'Reading down' in this context means could the Act be interpreted to mean the lower level of an evidential burden of proof.

In *Sheldrake* the Law Lords decided that there was an inroad into Art 6 but that it was justifiable, legitimate and proportionate. In *Attorney-General's Reference (No 4 of 2002)* they decided that the provision could be read as imposing an evidential burden on the defendant.

1.9.3 No punishment without law

This is covered by Art 7 which states:

'7(1) No one shall be held guilty of any criminal offence on account of any act or omission which did not constitute a criminal offence under national or international law at the time when it was committed …

7(2) This article shall not prejudice the trial and punishment of any person for any act or omission which, at the time when it was committed, was criminal according to the general principles of law recognised by civilised nations.'

This Article was used to challenge the conviction in *CR v UK* (1996) 21 EHRR 363. D had been convicted of raping his wife. The argument was that such an offence did not exist until the conviction, so there was no law against it at the time of D's assault on his wife. The challenge was unsuccessful for two reasons. The first was that there had been earlier cases where such an offence was beginning to be recognised. The second was that the offence is one which supported fundamental objectives of the Convention. As a result it was not in breach of this Article.

Uncertainty

In other cases there have been challenges under Art 7 on the basis that the offence is too uncertain or lacks clarity. This happened in *Misra; Srivastava* [2004] EWCA Crim 2375; [2005] 1 Cr App R 21, where the defendants were charged with gross negligence manslaughter. The defence argued that the elements of this offence were not certain. They relied on the Law Commission's paper *Involuntary manslaughter* (Law Com No 237) in support of this argument. The paper had identified that the current test was circular and this circularity led to uncertainty. On this point the paper concluded:

'It is possible that the law in this area failed to meet the standard of certainty required by the European Convention on Human Rights.'

Involuntary manslaughter (Law Com No 237)

The Court of Appeal rejected the argument. They held that the elements of the offence of gross negligence manslaughter were made clear in *Adomako* [1995] 1 AC 171. They were:

- that a duty of care was owed

- that that duty had been broken

- that the breach of the duty of care amounted to gross negligence and

- that the negligence was a substantial cause of the death of the victim.

On the issue of risk it was clear from *Adomako* and subsequent cases that the risk must relate to death. It was not enough to show that there was risk of bodily injury or injury to health. (See section 9.4.2 for full details on gross negligence manslaughter.) As the elements of gross negligence manslaughter were clear, there was no breach of Art 7.

Another unsuccessful challenge on the basis of lack of clarity was in the case of *Goldstein* [2005] UKHL 63; [2005] 3 WLR 982 where D was charged with public nuisance.

CASE EXAMPLE

Goldstein [2005] UKHL 63; [2005] 3 WLR 982

Goldstein had sent an envelope containing salt through the post as a joke relating to kosher food and also to a public scare in the United States over anthrax. The salt spilled out of the envelope in a sorting office causing the evacuation of the building due to fears that it was anthrax. D was charged with causing a public nuisance contrary to the common law. The defence argued that this offence lacked precision and clarity of definition, the certainty and the predictability necessary to meet the requirements of Art 7.

The House of Lords held that the offence was defined by Sir James Stephens in *A Digest of Criminal Law* 1877 and subsequent cases so that it was clear, precise, adequately defined and based on a discernible rational principle. However, they allowed D's appeal as it had not been proved that he knew or ought to have known that the salt would escape from the envelope.

1.9.4 Other human rights

There have been challenges to the criminal law on the basis of other rights in the Convention. Article 3 states:

 '3 No one shall be subjected to torture or inhuman or degrading treatment or punishment.'

In *Altham* [2006] EWCA Crim 7, D argued that the refusal to allow him the defence of necessity in respect of his use of cannabis for extreme physical pain was a breach of Art 3.

CASE EXAMPLE

Altham [2006] EWCA Crim 7

D had been seriously injured in an accident some 15 years earlier in which he dislocated both hips and suffered a fracture of his pelvis. He subsequently had surgery but this was not successful, so, in 1997, his entire left hip was removed. Since then he had had chronic pain in his legs. He claimed that cannabis gave him more relief from pain than any prescribed drug and it also had fewer side-effects. He was charged with possession of a controlled drug. At the trial the judge ruled that the defence of necessity or duress of circumstances should not be left to the jury. Following this ruling D pleaded guilty and received an absolute discharge.

He appealed on the basis that Art 3 prohibits 'inhuman or degrading treatment' and there were circumstances where severe medical symptoms can amount to 'inhuman or degrading treatment'. If the State provides that the only way to avoid those symptoms is to break the criminal law and risk punishment up to an including imprisonment, then the State is subjecting that person to 'inhuman or degrading treatment'. The Court of Appeal dismissed the appeal holding that the state had done nothing to subject D to inhuman or degrading treatment.

Court of Appeal has also heard appeals in cases of breach of right to respect for private lives under Art 8.

'8(1) Everyone has the right to respect for his private and family life, his home and his correspondence.

8(2) There shall be no interference by a public authority with the exercise of this right except such as is in accordance with the law and is necessary in a democratic society in the interests of national security, public safety or the economic well-being of the country, for the prevention of disorder or crime, for the protection of health or morals, or for the protection of the rights and freedoms of others.'

In *Quayle* [2005] EWCA Crim 1415, the Court of Appeal heard appeals in five cases where the defendants claimed the defence of medical necessity for using cannabis. Ds argued that the refusal to allow them the defence of necessity in respect of use of cannabis for medical reasons was a breach of their right to respect for their private lives in under Art 8. This challenge failed.

In *E v DPP* (2005), *The Times*, 9th February 2005, D was a 15-year-old boy who was charged with unlawful sexual intercourse with a girl under the age of 16, contrary to s 6 of the Sexual Offences Act 1956 which has since been repealed. The girl was also aged 15 and was a willing participant. By prosecuting D, the State was criminalising his behaviour and treating the girl as victim, when this was not, in fact, the situation. At the trial it was argued that this was contrary to Art 6 (the right to a fair trial) and Art 14 (the right not to be discriminated against on the ground of sex). At the appeal in the Divisional Court the defence added the argument that it was also contrary to Art 8 (respect for D's private life).

The Divisional Court found there was no breach of Art 8(1). They further pointed out that even if there had been a breach, the State could assert a legitimate aim under Art 8(2), that of protection of health or morals. Since Art 14 does not create a free standing right, the fact that there was no breach of Art 8 meant there could not be a breach of Art 14. Even if there had been a breach of Art 14, the court stated that there would have been justification for the different treatment of males and females. That justification was to be found in the fact that females needed protection from the risk of pregnancy.

In *G* [2006] EWCA Crim 821, D was charged with rape of a child under 13 when he had had consensual sex with a 12-year-old girl, reasonably believing her to be 15 (see also section 1.9.4) Originally the girl had claimed she had been raped and D was charged under s 5 of the Sexual Offences Act 2003. D denied the charge and at the trial the prosecution agreed to proceed on the basis that there had been consent to sexual intercourse. However, as s 5 is one of strict liability D was still guilty, even though he reasonably believed the girl was 15. The defence argued that, once the prosecution agreed to proceed on the basis of consensual sexual intercourse, D should have been charged with unlawful sexual intercourse with a child under 13, contrary to s 13 of the Sexual

Offences Act 2003. The difference in the effect of these two sections was explained by Lord Phillips CJ in the judgment at para 43:

> J   'A conviction under s 5 labels the child a rapist, subjects him to notification
>   requirements as a sex offender and to a maximum sentence of detention for life.
>   Conviction under s 13 labels a child one who has had sexual activity with another child,
>   does not subject him to notification requirements unless sentenced to at least 12
>   months' imprisonment and is subject to a maximum sentence of five years' detention.'

The defence also pointed out that, during the passage of the Sexual Offences Bill through Parliament, Lord Falconer, the Lord Chancellor, made a statement to the effect that where sexual activity between minors took place by mutual consent prosecution would not be the inevitable outcome and one would not expect the full weight of the criminal law to be used against them. The continuation of the charge under s 5 rather than under s 13 meant that it was not proportionate to the behaviour. D was subjected to consequences so severe that the interference with his rights under Art 8(1) could not be justified under Art 8(2). It was accepted by the court that this might be so in some cases. Lord Phillips CJ said (para 46):

> J   'We accept the possibility that prosecution of a child under s 5 rather than under s 13,
>   or indeed prosecution at all, in relation to consensual sexual intercourse may, on the
>   particular facts, produce consequences that amount to an interference with the child's
>   Article 8(1) rights that are not justified under Article 8(2). Where, however, as here no
>   criticism can be made of an initial charge of breach of s 5, we do not consider that it
>   follows that the judge must necessarily substitute an alternative charge of breach of
>   s 13 if transpires that the sexual activity was, or must be treated as, consensual.'

The Court of Appeal upheld D's conviction. However, the sentence imposed on him was reduced from 12 months' detention and training order (of which he had already served five months) to a conditional discharge for a period of 12 months. The court pointed out that this would mean that the notification requirements as a sexual offender would cease at the end of the period of the conditional discharge; also that, if D did not re-offend during that same period, then he would no longer be deemed to have had a conviction.

Although the court did not rule that there had been a breach of human rights in this case, it is clear from their judgment that there may be future cases in which a breach is found.

Article 10

This gives the right to freedom of expression. Many laws restrict our freedom of expression but are justified on the basis that it is necessary for national security, or to prevent crime or disorder. In *Dehal v DPP* [2005] EWHC 2154 (Admin) it was held there was a breach of Art 10 by bringing a criminal prosecution where it was more suitable to deal with the matter under civil law.

CASE EXAMPLE

Dehal v DPP [2005] EWHC 2154 (Admin)

D entered a temple and placed a notice stating that the preacher at the temple was 'a hypocrite'. D was convicted of an offence under s 4A of the Public Order Act 1986. D argued that his right to freedom of expression was infringed by being prosecuted for his action. The Divisional Court quashed his conviction. They held that the criminal law should not be invoked unless the conduct amounted to such a threat to public order that it required the use of the criminal law and not merely the civil law.

Keys facts on human rights and the criminal law

KEY FACTS

Article	Right	Comment/case
3	Right not to be subjected to inhuman or degrading treatment or punishment	Refusal to allow defence of necessity to charge of possessing cannabis was not a breach *Altham* (2006).
5	Right to liberty	Important in law on arrests and detention.
6 (1)	Right to a fair trial	Strict liability offences are not a breach *G* (2006).
6(2)	Presumption of innocence	Reverse burdens of proof can be a breach of this Article but may be justified. *Attorney-General's Reference (No 4 of 2002)* and *Sheldrake v DPP* (2004).

Article	Right	Comment/case
7	Can only be convicted if the offence existed and was sufficiently certain	*CR v UK* (1996). *Misra; Srivastava* (2004). *Goldstein* (2005).
8	Right to respect for private life	No breach for failure to allow defence of necessity to charge of possessing cannabis *Quayle* (2005). Possible breach if consequences of offence of strict liability are out of proportion *G* (2006).
9	Freedom of thought, conscience and religion	This could affect the law of blasphemy.
10	Freedom of expression	*Dehal v DPP* (2005) criminal law should not be invoked unless the conduct amounted to such a threat to public order that it was required.
11	Freedom of peaceful assembly	Restriction can be justified where it is necessary for national security, public safety or prevention of disorder or crime, such as regulations limiting demonstrations outside the Houses of Parliament. Also this freedom does not extend to purely social gatherings, eg a group hanging about in a shopping centre *Anderson & others v UK* (1997) 25 EHRR CD 172.
14	Right not be discriminated against on basis of sex or race, religion, political or other opinion, property, birth or other status	Can only be invoked if there is an infringement of another right *E v DPP* (2005). As well as race, the Article includes that there should be no discrimination on the basis of colour, language, national origin or association with a national minority.

1.9.5 Human rights and criminal procedure

One of the main effects of human rights has been on the procedure for trying child defendants, where they are charged with a very serious offence. Such offences must be tried in the Crown Court. However, the procedure and formality of the Crown Court can mean that a child defendant is unable to understand what is happening. In *T v UK: V v UK* (1999) 7 EHRR 659 the European Court of Human Rights held there was a breach of Art 6 the right to a fair trial, as the defendants were unable to participate effectively in the trial. Following this decision by the European Court of Human Rights, special arrangements must be made whenever a child is tried at the Crown Court, to ensure that he or she understands what is happening.

ACTIVITY

Self-test questions

1. What are the main purposes of criminal law?

2. How is it possible to define a crime?

3. What are the main sources of criminal law?

4. What is the burden of proof on the prosecution?

5. In the exceptional cases where the defence has to adduce evidence of a defence, what is the standard of proof on the defence?

Further reading

Ashworth, A, 'Is the Criminal Law a Lost Cause?' (2000) 116 LQR 223.
Ashworth, A, 'The Human Rights Act and Substantive Law' [2000] Crim LR 564.
Devlin, Lord, 'The Conscience of the Jury' (1991) 107 LQR 398.
Wells, C, 'Reversing the burden of proof' (2005) NLJ 183 (4 Feb).

Internet links

www.parliament.gov.uk – for all draft Bills before Parliament and for all debates in *Hansard*.

www.opsi.gov.uk – for all Acts of Parliament from 1988 onwards and for all Statutory Instruments from 1987 onwards.

www.lawcom.gov.uk – for the work of the Law Commission and their reports.

www.sentencing-guidelines.gov.uk – for the guidelines of the Sentencing Guidelines Council.

chapter 2 ACTUS REUS ■

AIMS AND OBJECTIVES

After reading this chapter you should be able to:

■ Understand when liability can be imposed for a failure to act (an omission)

■ Understand the rules on factual causation, the 'but for' test

■ Understand the rules on legal causation

■ Analyse critically the laws on omissions and causations

■ Apply the law to factual situations to determine whether there is liability for a failure to act or whether there has been a break in the "chain of causation"

This chapter examines the physical elements that are required to be proved for liability to be imposed. The Latin phrase '*actus reus*' is used as a convenient shorthand for describing all the physical elements that go to make up different criminal offences.

2.1 The physical element

The majority of criminal offences considered in this textbook require as a starting point some physical element on the part of the defendant (D). Precisely what that physical element is depends on the criminal offence. To give some examples:

• Murder and manslaughter require, in most cases, that D does an act which causes the death of the victim (V) (see Chapter 9).

• Battery requires that D applies unlawful force to the body of the victim. The crime of malicious wounding requires that D does some act which cuts the skin of the victim (see Chapter 10).

• Rape requires that D 'penetrates' the vagina, anus or mouth of the victim with his penis and without V's consent (see Chapter 11).

• Theft requires that D 'appropriates' 'property' which 'belongs to another' person (see Chapter 12).

2.1.1 Conduct and consequences

You will see that the physical element in murder actually sub-divides into two elements: an act (conduct) and death (consequence). The act part could be, for example, aiming a gun at V and pulling the trigger; stabbing V with a knife; strangling V with a piece of cord; pushing V from the top of a tall building (no doubt you can think of plenty of other examples). The consequence that must follow from D's act, namely the death of V, is also part of the physical element. In most cases death follows fairly swiftly after D's act but, in some cases, there may be a delay of minutes, hours, days or even longer. Has D caused V's death if he strangles her, leaving her in a coma as a result of hypoxia (loss of oxygen to the brain) from which she eventually dies six months later? It is impossible to give a definite answer to this question; it is a question of fact for a jury. However, there are a number of legal principles which exist to help a jury in such cases and these will be examined below.

With malicious wounding, the conduct and consequence could be regarded as inseparable: the act of stabbing or slashing at V with a knife, broken bottle, etc (conduct) must cause V's skin to be cut (consequence). In battery, the physical element requires conduct (applying force to V's body) but there is no consequence requirement. Similarly, in rape there is a conduct requirement (penetration) but no consequence is required. Theft is another example: there is a conduct element (D must 'appropriate', which means to assume rights over, property) but there is no consequence requirement.

2.1.2 Circumstances

Some criminal offences require certain circumstances to exist in addition to the conduct/ consequence elements. One of the physical elements required in rape is that V must not have consented. This is a circumstance that must exist at the time D penetrates V's vagina, anus or mouth, and without it there is no crime. Similarly, in theft, in addition to the conduct element of appropriating, there must be 'property' that 'belonged to another' at the time of the appropriation. D, a vagrant, might assume rights of ownership over an old, worn-out shoe that he finds lying in the street, but this would probably not be enough to satisfy all the physical elements in the crime of theft, as it is likely that the shoe has been abandoned and hence is ownerless.

2.1.3 The physical element alone is not a crime

Look again at the conduct elements of the crimes above. In none of the cases does it automatically follow that D has committed a crime. In most rape cases, the conduct element is penetration of V's vagina or anus by D's penis, which are, generally speaking, perfectly lawful activities (subject to V having attained the age of consent, which in England is 16 (Sexual Offences (Amendment) Act 2000)). In theft, the conduct element is 'appropriating' property, an act which does not imply any wrongdoing. If you are reading this book whilst sitting at a desk in a library, you are 'appropriating' the seat and the desk because you are assuming rights of ownership over them (albeit temporarily). What prevents this performance of the physical element from amounting to a criminal offence is, in some cases, the lack of other physical elements. Thus, for D to use his penis to penetrate V's vagina, anus or mouth is, generally speaking, not the crime of rape, because V consents. In other cases, all the physical elements (whether conduct, consequences and circumstances) may be present, but still the crime may not be committed because the mental element of the crime is missing. Thus, in order to commit theft, it is necessary that D has the 'intention to permanently deprive' the owner of their property and that D was 'dishonest'. Someone sitting innocently at a library

desk does not have either the requisite intent nor the dishonesty. There are exceptions to this rule, however. Some criminal offences may be committed with no, or a very little, mental element. These crimes are known as 'absolute' or 'strict' liability offences, and will be examined in Chapter 4.

2.1.4 Omissions

It was stated above that, in murder and manslaughter, 'in most cases' D must do some act which causes death. The exception is where D does nothing to prevent V's death. In certain circumstances, D may be under a duty to take positive steps to assist V, and failing to take them can amount to the physical element of the crimes of murder and manslaughter. This topic will be examined below.

2.2 Voluntary conduct

In *Bratty v Attorney-General of Northern Ireland* [1963] AC 386, Lord Denning said that: 'The requirement that [the act of the accused] should be a voluntary act is essential . . . in every criminal case. No act is punishable if it is done involuntarily.' An example of this might be if the defendant, D, were to push a bystander, E, so that E lost his balance and knocked a second bystander, V. If V loses his balance and falls to the ground, fracturing his leg, has E committed the *actus reus* of battery or even assault occasioning actual bodily harm? The *actus reus* of battery requires the unlawful application of physical force to the body of the victim; the *actus reus* of actual bodily harm is the same plus the infliction of some hurt or injury to the victim. The answer is that E is not guilty of any crime: although E was the immediate cause of V's falling to the ground and hence his injuries, in no sense can E be said to have 'acted'. Moreover, even if E could be said to have performed an 'act' in the above scenario, it was clearly not 'voluntary' in the sense of being a deliberate or willed 'act' on his behalf. (These are the facts of *Mitchell* [1983] QB 741. V, aged 89, died of a pulmonary embolism caused by thrombosis, which in turn was caused by the fracture. In the event, D (and not E) was charged and convicted of her manslaughter.)

2.3 Omissions

Originally, the English criminal law only punished those who caused a prohibited result by a positive act. But it came to accept that it should also punish those who fail to act, when a duty to act could be implied, with the result that the prohibited result ensued. Nevertheless, on the whole, the position is still that there is no general duty to act. There may well be a *moral* obligation on someone to be a 'Good Samaritan', but there is not a *legal* one. There are two requirements:

- the crime has to be capable of being committed by omission (known as result crimes) and

- D must be under a duty to act.

2.3.1 Commission by omission

Generally speaking, the crime must be capable of being committed by omission. Nearly all of the leading cases involve murder or gross negligence manslaughter. Other crimes capable of being committed by omission are arson (*Miller* [1983] 2 AC 161, which will be discussed below) and assault and battery. This was decided in *DPP v Santana-Bermudez* [2003] EWHC 2908.

CASE EXAMPLE

DPP v Santana-Bermudez [2003] EWHC 2908

V, a female police officer, asked D to turn out all his pockets, which he did. V asked him if he had removed everything; he replied 'Yes'. She then asked 'Are you sure that you do not have any needles or sharps on you?'. D said 'No'. V commenced her search but when she put her hand into one pocket she pricked her finger on a hypodermic needle. V noticed that D was smirking. D was convicted of assault by magistrates, but appealed to the Crown Court, successfully arguing that it was legally impossible to commit an assault by omission. The prosecution appealed to the Divisional Court, which allowed the appeal.

Conversely, a crime that is incapable of being committed by omission is constructive manslaughter (a positive act is always required, according to *Lowe* [1973] QB 702; see Chapter 9). Sometimes the definition of the *actus reus* makes it clear that a positive act is required. For example, burglary (s 9 of the Theft Act 1968 requires D to 'enter' into a building; see Chapter 13), and making off without payment (s 3 of the Theft Act 1978 requires D to 'make off'; see also Chapter 13). The definition of rape in s 1(1) of the Sexual Offences Act 2003 makes clear that the offence is committed only when D 'penetrates the vagina, anus or mouth of another person with his penis'. Section 79(2) of the same Act states that 'penetration is a continuing act …'. This would seem to rule out any possibility of committing rape by omission (although see the discussion of the cases of *Kaitamaki* [1984] 2 All ER 435 and *Cooper and Schaub* [1994] Crim LR 531 on this point in Chapter 11). Another example is the offence of 'throwing missiles' (s 2 Football Offences Act 1991). In *Ahmad* [1986] Crim LR 739, D, a landlord, was convicted of 'doing acts calculated to interfere with the peace and comfort of a residential occupier with intent to cause him to give up occupation of the premises', contrary to the Protection from Eviction Act 1977. The relevant acts had been done without the requisite intent; D had then deliberately refrained from rectifying the situation. The Court of Appeal quashed the conviction; D had not 'done acts' with the requisite intent.

One problem with the imposition of liability for failing to act in 'result' crimes, such as murder and gross negligence manslaughter, which the courts have not really acknowledged, is the requirement of causation. Suppose D, a professional lifeguard on duty, sees a small child fall into a

pool, but simply stands and watches while she struggles and eventually drowns. No-one else is present. There is little doubt that D is under a duty to save the girl (because of contractual responsibility; see below) and failure to do so could well be murder (if D intends death or serious injury) or gross negligence manslaughter. But did D 'cause' the girl to die? She would almost certainly have died in exactly the same way – the same 'result' would have occurred – had she been completely alone and D had not been there. The Law Commission tackles this when it provides in its Draft Criminal Code (1989), clause 17(1), that 'a person causes a result … when … (b) he omits to do an act which might prevent its occurrence and which he is under a duty to do according to the law relating to that offence'.

2.3.2 Imposition of a duty of care

The most important factor is that D must be under a duty, recognised by the law, to act or intervene in the circumstances. In *Khan and Khan* [1998] EWCA Crim 971; [1998] Crim LR 830, the Court of Appeal quashed manslaughter convictions of two drug dealers because the judge had made no ruling as to whether the facts were capable of giving rise to any relevant duty, nor had he directed the jury in relation to that issue.

CASE EXAMPLE

Khan and Khan [1998] EWCA Crim 971; [1998] Crim LR 830

D and E were drug dealers in Birmingham. V, a 15-year-old prostitute, went to a flat where they supplied her with heroin. She ingested a large amount, lapsed into a coma and was obviously in need of medical assistance. However, D and E left the flat, leaving V alone to die. They were charged with murder but were convicted of manslaughter. The Court of Appeal quashed their convictions. The Crown's case was that the appellants' omission to summon medical assistance formed the basis of their liability. However, the Court of Appeal decided that, in such circumstances, before they could convict, the jury had to be sure that D was criminally responsible, and this required that D be standing in such a relation to the victim that he is under a duty to act.

It should be noted that the above case does not decide that no duty was (or could be) owed on the facts; rather that it must be left to the jury to decide whether, on the facts, a duty was in fact owed. Such a duty may be owed in a variety of situations, as the following cases illustrate.

Duty arising out of contractual liability

Where failure to fulfil a contract is likely to endanger lives, the criminal law will impose a duty to act. The duty is owed to anyone who may be affected, not just the other parties to the contract. The leading cases are *Pittwood* (1902) 19 TLR 37 and *Adomako* [1995] 1 AC 171. In *Pittwood*, D was a signalman employed by the railway company to look after a level crossing and ensure the gate was shut when trains were due. D left the gate open and was away from his post, with the result that someone crossing the line was hit and killed. D was convicted of manslaughter. The court rejected D's argument that his duty was owed simply to the railway company: he was paid to look after the gate and protect the public. This duty will be held by members of the emergency services, lifeguards, etc. In *Adomako*, a duty to act was imposed on a hospital anaesthetist (see Chapter 9). In *Singh* [1999] EWCA Crim 460; [1999] Crim LR 582, a duty to act was imposed on a landlord. D, who helped his father run a lodging house, was convicted of manslaughter after carbon monoxide poisoning from a defective fire killed one of the tenants. On appeal he contended that no duty of care had arisen: whether as rent collector, maintenance man, or anything else. However, the Court of Appeal decided that, as it was D's responsibility to maintain the flat, a duty of care was imposed on him to deal with any danger by calling in expert help.

Duty arising out of a relationship

Parents are under a duty to their children (*Gibbins and Proctor* (1918) 13 Cr App R 134) and spouses owe a duty to each other (*Smith* [1979] Crim LR 251: see *Hood* [2003] EWCA Crim 2772 below).

Duty arising from the assumption of care for another

A duty will be owed by anyone who voluntarily undertakes to care for another person, whether through age, infirmity, illness, etc. The duty may be express but is more likely to be implied from conduct. Thus in *Nicholls* (1874) 13 Cox CC 75, D, a grandmother who took her granddaughter into her home after the girl's mother died was held to have undertaken an express duty of care. In *Instan* [1893] 1 QB 450, D moved in with her elderly aunt, who became ill and for the last 12 days of her life was unable to care for herself or summon help. D did not give her any food or seek medical assistance, but continued to live in the house and eat the aunt's food. Eventually the aunt died and D was convicted of manslaughter. In *Gibbins and Proctor*, the court found that the deliberate non-performance of a legal duty to act could result in liability for murder being imposed on D, who had voluntarily undertaken responsibility to care for a child.

CASE EXAMPLE

Gibbins and Proctor (1918) 13 Cr App R 134

G was the father of several children, including a seven-year-old daughter, Nelly. His wife had left him and he was living with a lover, P. They kept Nelly separate from the other children and deliberately starved her to death. Afterwards they concocted a story about how Nelly had 'gone away'; in fact G had buried her in the brickyard where he worked. Both adults were convicted of murder and the Court of Criminal Appeal upheld the convictions. G owed Nelly a duty as her father; P was held to have undertaken a duty.

The leading case is now *Stone and Dobinson* [1977] QB 354.

CASE EXAMPLE

Stone and Dobinson [1977] QB 354

S lived with his mistress, D. In 1972, S's sister, Fanny, aged 61, came to live with them. Fanny was suffering from anorexia nervosa and although initially capable of looking after herself, her condition deteriorated. Eventually, in 1975, she was confined to bed in the small front room where she remained until her death, refusing to eat anything other than biscuits. S was then 67, partly deaf, nearly blind and of low intelligence. D was 43 but was described as 'ineffectual' and 'somewhat inadequate'. Both were unable to use a telephone. They had tried to find Fanny's doctor but failed; eventually a local doctor was called, but by this point it was too late. Fanny had died, weighing less than 5½ stone, in an excrement- and urine- soiled bed with two large, maggot-infested ulcers on her right hip and left knee, and bone clearly visible. The Court of Appeal upheld S and D's manslaughter convictions. They had assumed a duty of care to Fanny, and their pathetically feeble efforts to look after her amounted to gross negligence.

Question

Would Stone and Dobinson have been better off simply ignoring Fanny after she became bedbound?

Duty arising from the creation of a dangerous situation

Where D inadvertently, and without the requisite *mens rea*, does an act which creates a dangerous situation then, on becoming aware of it, he is under a duty to take all such steps as lie within his power to prevent or minimise the harm. If he fails to take such steps with the appropriate *mens rea*, then he will be criminally liable. This situation arose in *Miller*.

CASE EXAMPLE

Miller [1983] 2 AC 161

D, a vagrant, was squatting in a house in Birmingham. He had fallen asleep one night but awoke to find that a cigarette he had been smoking had set fire to the mattress. He did nothing to extinguish the fire, but moved to another room and went back to sleep. The house caught fire, and £800 damage was caused. The House of Lords upheld his conviction, on the basis that his inadvertent creation of a dangerous situation imposed a duty on him to take steps to minimise that danger as soon as he realised what he had done. What those steps are will depend on what is reasonable in the circumstances. At the least, D might have been expected to try to put out the fire or, if it was beyond control, call the fire brigade.

Two recent cases have seen the *Miller* principle discussed.

- In *Matthews and Alleyne* [2003] EWCA Crim 192; [2003] Crim LR 553 (the full facts of which appear in the next chapter in the context of intention) the trial judge suggested that D and E could have been convicted of murder if, having pushed V into a river, they subsequently realised that he was unable to swim and (with intent that he should die or suffer serious injury) took no steps to rescue him. The appellants and V were strangers to each other prior to this event, so the basis on which D and E owed V a duty to act could be regarded as similar to that in *Miller*.

- In *Santana-Bermudez*, the facts of which were given above, the Divisional Court expressly applied *Miller* as the basis for finding D's duty of care to V. The court held that, when D gave V a dishonest assurance about the contents of his pockets, he exposed her to a reasonably foreseeable risk of injury. His subsequent failure to inform her of the presence of needles in his pockets constituted an evidential basis for a finding that the *actus reus* of assault occasioning actual bodily harm had occurred.

The Draft Criminal Code (1989), clause 23, also endorses the *Miller* principle:

'23 Where it is an offence to be at fault in causing a result, a person who lacks the fault required when he does an act that causes or may cause the result nevertheless commits the offence if –

(a) he has become aware that he has done the act and that the result had occurred and may continue, or may occur; and

(b) with the fault required, he fails to do what he can reasonably be expected to do that might prevent the result continuing or occurring; and

(c) the result continues or occurs.'

Clause 31 of the Draft Criminal Law Bill (1993) is to similar effect.

Release from duty to act

One issue that has troubled the courts is whether D, having undertaken a duty or having had one imposed on him, may be released from it. In *Smith* (1979), D's wife had given birth to a stillborn child at home. She hated doctors and would not allow D to call one. When she finally gave D permission it was too late, she died and D was charged with manslaughter. The judge directed the jury 'to balance the weight that it is right to give to his wife's wish to avoid calling a doctor against her capacity to make rational decisions. If she does not appear too ill it may be reasonable to abide by her wishes. On the other hand, if she appeared desperately ill then whatever she may say it may be right to override'. The jury was unable to agree and D was discharged. The principle that, provided V is rational, she may release D from a duty of care, was confirmed in *Re B (Consent to Treatment: Capacity)* [2002] EWHC 429 (Fam); [2002] 2 All ER 449. Here, the High Court held that, when a competent patient gives notice that they wish life-preserving treatment to be discontinued, anyone responsible up to that point for providing such treatment (in this case doctors) would be obliged to respect that notice.

Cessation of duty to act

In *Airedale NHS Trust v Bland* [1993] AC 789 (like *Re B*, a civil case), the House of Lords provided guidance on the issue of when a duty to act ceases. Bland, who had been suffocated during the Hillsborough Stadium tragedy in 1989, had been in a persistent vegetative state in hospital for over three years. When the hospital authorities applied for judicial authority to discontinue treatment in the form of artificial feeding and hydration, the House of Lords held that, on the facts, it was permissible to do so. Lord Goff, giving the leading judgment, stated that there was no absolute rule that a patient's life had to be prolonged regardless. The fundamental principle was the sanctity of life, but respect for human dignity demanded that the quality of life be considered. The principle of 'self-determination' meant that an adult patient of sound mind could refuse treatment. Doctors (or other persons responsible for the patient) would have to respect that. In *Bland*, the House of Lords was careful to characterise the withdrawal of life support as an omission (a failure to continue treatment). The case does not stand as an authority for the proposition that doctors may take positive steps to end a patient's life. Euthanasia, therefore, remains illegal in England and Wales.

The crime of assisting another's suicide is also unaffected by the *Bland* decision. This was demonstrated in *R (on the application of Pretty) v DPP* [2001] UKHL 61; [2002] 1 AC 800. P was suffering from motor neurone disease which she knew would eventually lead to her suffocating to death. She applied to the courts for a judicial declaration that, if her husband assisted her to commit suicide, he would not be prosecuted (her physical condition having deteriorated to such an extent by this point that she was unable to take her own life unassisted). This request was denied by the High Court and confirmed by the Court of Appeal and House of Lords. Assisting another person to commit suicide seems, inevitably, to amount to a positive act. A final appeal to the European Court of Human Rights also failed, the Court in Strasbourg ruling that English law did not infringe P's human rights.

In *Re A (Children) (Conjoined Twins: Surgical Separation)* [2000] EWCA Civ 254; [2000] 4 All ER 961, the Court of Appeal (Civil Division) confirmed that a surgical procedure to separate two baby girls who were born joined together at the abdomen was a positive act and not an omission. Therefore, because the doctors knew that the procedure would inevitably lead to the death of one girl, the doctors had both the *actus reus* and *mens rea* of murder. However, they were able to apply the defence of necessity (not operating would lead to both girls' deaths) and held that the procedure was lawful (see Chapter 8 for further discussion of this case).

2.3.3 Breach of duty to act

It should also be noted that there is a range of crimes (mostly statutory) which can be committed simply by failing to act. Examples include:

- failing to provide a police officer with a specimen of breath when required to do so is an offence under s 6 of the Road Traffic Act (RTA) 1988;

- failing to stop and provide a name and address to any person reasonably requiring it when your vehicle has been involved in an accident where there has been injury to another person or damage to another vehicle is an offence under s 170 of the RTA 1988;

- failing to disclose to the police information that another person has committed certain terrorist offences is an offence under s 19 of the Terrorism Act 2000.

One such offence exists at common law, and a conviction for it was upheld by the Court of Appeal in *Dytham* [1979] QB 722.

CASE EXAMPLE

Dytham [1979] QB 722

D, a police officer, was on duty near a nightclub at about 1 am. He was standing about 30 yards from the door when a bouncer ejected V from the club. A noisy fight ensued in which a large number of men participated. Three men eventually kicked V to death, all of which was clearly audible and visible to D. However, he took no steps to intervene and, when the incident was over, adjusted his helmet and drove off, telling two people nearby that he was going off duty. D was convicted of the common law offence of misconduct whilst acting as an officer of justice, in that he had wilfully omitted to take any steps to carry out his duty to preserve the Queen's Peace or to protect V or to arrest or otherwise bring to justice his assailants. The Court of Appeal upheld his conviction.

Interestingly, PC Dytham was not charged with manslaughter, a result crime, although it could well be argued that, on the facts, he owed a duty of care to V to intervene and assist him, this duty arising from D's contractual obligations. The reason that D was not charged with the more serious crime may be because of the difficulties in proving that he had actually made a causative contribution to V's death.

2.3.4 Reform

Advocates of reform of this area suggest that where rescue of the victim would not pose a danger to D, then liability should be imposed for failing to act, even where there was no pre-existing legal duty on D (A Ashworth, 'The Scope of Criminal Liability for Omissions' (1989) 105 LQR 424). There are, however, serious moral and practical objections:

- Definition of when it would be easy for D to attempt a rescue.

- Moral objection to forcing citizens to watch out for and protect each other, especially as most citizens already pay (through taxes) for highly trained and well-equipped professionals (police, fire brigade officers, lifeboat crew, paramedics etc) to do that job on our behalf.

- Possibility that D may (genuinely and/or reasonably) misjudge the situation and either fail to attempt a rescue when it was in fact easy (D thinking it would be dangerous) or attempt a dangerous rescue (D thinking it was actually easy). In the former scenario, D faces potential liability for homicide if V is killed. In the latter scenario, D's own life is put at risk and genuine rescuers (police etc) now have two people to rescue (D and V) instead of just V.

- Possible imposition of liability on large numbers of people. For example, when a train platform is crowded with commuters and all fail to come to the aid of V who has slipped and fallen onto the tracks and is lying unconscious, despite the fact that no train is due for several minutes, should all the commuters be held liable? Alternatively, what about all the sunbathers on a crowded beach who all choose to ignore V who is clearly drowning 20 yards from shore?

2.4 Causation

When D is charged with any result crime, the Crown must prove that his acts or omissions caused the prohibited consequence. For example, in murder or manslaughter (see Chapter 9), it is necessary to prove that D, by his or her acts or omissions, caused V's death. If V dies because of some other cause, then the offence has not been committed even though all the other elements of the offence, including the *mens rea*, are present. D may of course be liable for attempt instead (*White* [1910] 2 KB 124; see below and see Chapter 6 for discussion of attempts). Similarly, if D is charged with causing grievous bodily harm with intent, contrary to s 18 of the Offences Against the Person Act (OAPA) 1861, the Crown must prove that D's acts or omissions caused V to suffer serious injuries. The issue of causation is for the jury to decide. The judge should direct them as to the elements of causation, but it is for them to decide if the causal link between D's act and the prohibited consequence has been established. Usually it will be sufficient to direct the jury (*per* Robert Goff LJ in *Pagett* [1983] Crim LR 393): 'simply that in law the accused's act need not be the sole cause, or even the main cause, of the victim's death, it being enough that his act contributed significantly to that result.' When a problem arises, as occasionally happens, then it is for the judge to direct the jury in accordance with the legal principles which they have to apply. There are two main principles:

- the jury must be satisfied that D's conduct was a factual cause of V's death or injuries
- the jury must also be satisfied that D's conduct was a legal cause of V's death or injuries.

2.4.1 Factual causation

This is determined using the 'but for' test; that is, it must be established that the consequence would not have occurred as and when it did *but for* D's conduct. If the consequence would have happened anyway, there is no liability. The leading example of this is *White* [1910] 2 KB 124.

CASE EXAMPLE

White [1910] 2 KB 124

D put potassium cyanide into his mother's drink. He had direct intent to kill, in order to gain under her will. Later V was found dead, sitting on the sofa at her home. Although she had drunk as much as a quarter of the poisoned drink, medical evidence established that she had died of a heart attack, not poisoning. In any event D had not used enough cyanide for a fatal dose. D was acquitted of murder: he had not caused her death. (He was, however, convicted of attempted murder.)

Factual causation on its own is insufficient for liability. To give one well-known example, if D invites V to his house for a party and, on the way there, V is accidentally run over and killed, D would not face prosecution for any form of homicide. Although D has caused V's death as a matter of fact, there is no *actus reus* of either murder or manslaughter. The missing element is legal causation.

2.4.2 Legal causation

Factual causation alone is not enough. It is essential that legal causation is established as well. This is again a question for the jury: the question is whether the consequence (death, serious injury, as the case may be) can fairly be said to be D's **fault**. In an early case, *Dalloway* (1847) 2 Cox CC 273, D was acquitted because, although V's death would not have occurred but for D's driving a horse and cart over him, the jury was not convinced that D was to blame.

CASE EXAMPLE

Dalloway (1847) 2 Cox CC 273

D was driving a horse and cart without holding the reins, which were lying loose on the horse's back. A child, V, ran in front of the cart, was struck by one of the wheels and killed. D was charged with manslaughter but the jury acquitted. It appeared from the evidence that, even if D had been holding the reins, he could not have stopped the cart in time. Hence the death was not D's fault.

This principle was seen in *Marchant and Muntz* [2003] EWCA Crim 2099; [2004] 1 WLR 442, a case of causing death by dangerous driving. V, a motorcyclist, impaled himself on a metre-long spike (called a tine) attached to the front of an agricultural vehicle being driven on a public road. There was no suggestion that D's driving was dangerous; rather, the allegation was that simply having the vehicle on the road at all was dangerous. Although D was convicted, the Court of Appeal quashed the conviction. Expert evidence at trial indicated that the spike could have been 'covered by some sort of guard', but Grigson J concluded that 'even had such a guard been in place, it would not have prevented the collision. The consequences to anyone striking a tine *or the guard* at speed would have been very severe, if not fatal' (emphasis added). In other words, D had not caused V's death.

Minimal causes may be discounted

If D's act or omission provides only a minimal contribution to V's death or injuries, then it may be discounted under the *de minimis* principle (the law ignores trivialities). Perkins and Boyce in *Criminal Law* (3rd edn, 1982) give the following example, where V has suffered two stab wounds from different defendants:

'Suppose one wound severed the jugular vein whereas the other barely broke the skin of the hand, and as the life blood gushed from the victim's neck one drop oozed from the bruise on his finger . . . metaphysicians will conclude that the extra drop of blood hastened the end by the infinitesimal fraction of a second. But the law . . . will conclude that death be imputed only to the severe injury in such an extreme case as this.'

It is sometimes said that D's act must be a 'substantial' cause of death; this probably states the case too favourably for D. What is required is that D's act provides something more than minimal contribution. Thus, in *Kimsey* [1996] Crim LR 35, a case of causing death by dangerous driving, the trial judge told the jury that they did not have to be sure that D's driving 'was the principal, or a substantial cause of the death, as long as you are sure that it was a cause and that there was something more than a slight or trifling link'. On appeal, it was argued that it was wrong to say that D's driving did not have to be a 'substantial cause'. The Court of Appeal dismissed the appeal; reference to 'substantial cause' was not necessary and moreover might encourage the jury to attach too much importance to D's driving. Reference to 'more than a slight or trifling link' was permissible and a useful way of avoiding the term '*de minimis*'.

Multiple causes

D's act or omission need not, therefore, be the sole or even the main cause of V's death or injuries. It is sufficient that D's act or omission provides a more than minimal cause. Other contributory causes may be the acts of others, or even of V themselves.

Actions of third parties

The early case of *Benge* (1865) 4 F & F 504 provides a good example. D, the foreman of a track-laying crew, misread the railway timetable, so that the track was up at the time the train was due. He realised his error, and placed a signalman with a flag 540 yards up the line, although statutory regulations specified a distance of at least 1,000 yards. However, the train driver was not keeping proper lookout and failed to stop. Several deaths were caused. Thus, the deaths were a combination of:

- D's misreading of the train timetable
- the signalman's failure to stand 460 yards further up the line
- the train driver's failure to keep a proper lookout.

Nevertheless, the jury were directed to convict D if they were satisfied that his conduct mainly or substantially caused the deaths (they were so satisfied, and D was convicted).

A slightly different approach is required in cases where D's act or omission triggers some further act by a third party, and it is the latter act or omission which is the immediate cause of death. D is clearly a factual cause of death, but to what extent can D also be regarded as the legal cause? The

leading case is *Pagett*, where Goff LJ said that, where the third party's act is a reasonable response to D's initial act, the chain will not be broken. D did not escape liability where a third party, forced into reasonable self-defence by D, inadvertently caused V's death.

CASE EXAMPLE

Pagett [1983] Crim LR 393

Several police officers were trying to arrest D for various serious offences. He was hiding in his first-floor flat with his 16-year-old girlfriend, V, who was pregnant by him. D armed himself with a shotgun and, against her will, used V's body as a shield. He fired at two officers, who returned fire; three bullets fired by the officers hit V. She died from the wounds. D was convicted of manslaughter; his appeal was dismissed.

It is crucial that the question of causation is left to the jury to decide. If it is not, convictions may be quashed. A good example is *Watson* [1989] 2 All ER 865 (examined in detail in Chapter 9). D was convicted of manslaughter on the basis that his act of burgling V's home had triggered a fatal heart attack 90 minutes later. However, D's conviction was quashed on the ground of causation: the heart attack may have been caused by the arrival of the police or council workmen to board up the window. There is now a considerable body of case law on the application of these principles to cases where the third parties are medical personnel dealing with injuries inflicted by D. These cases raise special considerations of public policy and will be dealt with separately below.

Actions of the victim: fright or flight

In some cases, V brings about his own death or injuries through attempting to escape from a threat (whether real or imagined) posed by D. However, D may remain responsible for those outcomes. The courts have devised a test which involves establishing a 'chain of causation' between D's original act or omission and V's ultimate death or injury. If V's actions in trying to escape from a threat posed by D are regarded by the jury as 'daft' (or 'unexpected' or 'unreasonable') then the 'chain' is broken and D escapes liability. If V's actions are not regarded as 'daft' then D remains liable. The question of 'daftness', which is one for the jury to answer, is particularly important in cases where D contends that V has misinterpreted his act or omission and (possibly in a state or confusion and/or panic) has overreacted. *Marjoram* [2000] Crim LR 372 provides a recent example.

CASE EXAMPLE

Marjoram [2000] Crim LR 372

D, who had been shouting abuse and kicking V's hostel room door, forced open the door, at which point V fell, or possibly jumped, from the window. V sustained serious injury in the fall. D maintained that he had broken down the door because he had heard the window being opened and had intended to rescue V from what he thought was a suicide bid. Nevertheless, D was convicted of inflicting grievous bodily harm, contrary to s 20 OAPA 1861. The Court of Appeal dismissed D's appeal. The jury were entitled to find that V's reaction to having D forcing open their door was not daft.

Similarly, in *Corbett* [1996] Crim LR 594, the Court of Appeal rejected D's appeal that V had overreacted and upheld his manslaughter conviction. D had punched and head-butted V, who had run off, tripped and fallen into the path of a passing car. D argued on appeal that it should have to be proved that what happened was the natural consequence of D's act. The Court of Appeal, however, confirmed that the jury had been properly directed that only by a 'daft' reaction by V was capable of breaking the chain. The criterion of V's reaction being 'daft' stems from *Roberts* [1972] Crim LR 242, in which D was convicted of assault occasioning actual bodily harm (contrary to s 47 OAPA 1861) after the girl passenger in his car jumped out after he allegedly had tried to remove her coat. He appealed on the ground that causation had not been established. The Court of Appeal dismissed the appeal. Stephenson LJ said:

> **J** 'The test is: was [V's reaction] the natural result of what [D] said and did, in the sense that it was something that could reasonably have been foreseen as the consequence of what [D] was saying or doing? . . . If of course [V] does something so "daft" . . . or so unexpected . . . that no reasonable man could be expected to foresee it, then it is only in a very remote and unreal sense a consequence of [D's] assault, it is really occasioned by a voluntary act on the part of [V] which could not reasonably be foreseen and which breaks the chain of causation between the assault and harm or injury.'

If the jury agrees that V's reaction was 'daft' and the chain of causation broken, it is common to refer to this reaction using the latin term *'novus actus interveniens'*, literally 'new intervening act'. Thus, in the words of Stuart-Smith LJ in *Williams and Davis* [1992] 2 All ER 183:

> J 'V's conduct [must] be something that a reasonable and responsible man in D's shoes would have foreseen . . . The nature of the threat is of importance in considering . . . the question whether V's conduct was proportionate to the threat, that is to say that it was within the ambit of reasonableness and not so daft as to make it his own voluntary act which amounted to a *novus actus interveniens* and consequently broke the chain of causation.'

CASE EXAMPLE

Williams and Davis [1992] 2 All ER 183

D and E had given a lift to a hitchhiker, V. After some five miles, V opened a rear door and jumped out to his death. The Crown alleged that V had leaped out to escape being robbed. The defendants were convicted of robbery and manslaughter. The Court of Appeal quashed the latter convictions because of a lack of any direction on the question of causation. The jury should have been asked whether V's reaction in jumping from the moving car was 'within the range of responses' which might be expected from a victim placed in the situation in which V was. The jury should also have been told to bear in mind the fact that 'in the agony of the moment he may act without thought and deliberation'.

The accused must take the victim as they find them

D cannot complain if V is particularly susceptible to physical injury, eg haemophilia causing death, or brittle bones leading to worse injuries. In *Martin* (1832) 5 C & P 128, Parke J said: 'It is said that [V] was in a bad state of health; but that is perfectly immaterial, as, if [D] was so unfortunate as to accelerate her death, he must answer for it.' It was accepted in *Towers* (1874) 12 Cox CC 692 that, because children are particularly susceptible to fright and shock, D may frighten a child to death. D violently assaulted a young girl who was holding V, a four-month-old baby, in her arms. The girl screamed, frightening V so much that it cried until its face turned black. V died a month later and D was convicted of manslaughter. The implication of this ruling was that it would not be possible to frighten an adult to death. However, this implication was rejected in *Hayward* (1908) 21 Cox CC 692.

CASE EXAMPLE

Hayward (1908) 21 Cox CC 692

D, in a state of 'violent excitement', was heard to say that he was going to give 'his wife something' when she returned home. When she did so, an argument ensued and D chased her from the house using violent threats. She collapsed in the road and died. Medical evidence was such that she was suffering from an abnormal condition that might be exacerbated by any combination of physical exertion with strong emotion or fright. The trial judge directed the jury that proof of death from fright alone, caused by some illegal conduct such as the threats of violence, would suffice.

The principle that D must take their victim as they find them is not confined to pre-existing physical or physiological conditions. In *Blaue* [1975] 3 All ER 446, it was extended to religious beliefs. Lawton LJ said:

> J 'It has long been the policy of the law that those who use violence on other people must take their victim as they find them. This in our judgment means the whole man, not just the physical man. It does not lie on the mouth of the assailant to say that the victim's religious beliefs which inhibited him from accepting certain kinds of treatment were unreasonable. The question for decision is what caused her death. The answer is the stab wound. The fact that the victim refused to stop this end coming about did not break the causal connection between the act and death.'

CASE EXAMPLE

Blaue [1975] 3 All ER 446

D had approached his female victim, V, and asked for sex. When she refused he produced a knife and stabbed her four times, one wound penetrating a lung. She was admitted to hospital and told that a blood transfusion was necessary to save her life. As she was a Jehovah's Witness (to whom blood transfusions are regarded as contrary to the teachings of the Bible), she refused and died within a few hours of internal bleeding. Medical evidence indicated she would have survived had she accepted the transfusion. D was charged with murder, but was convicted of manslaughter (the jury having accepted his plea of diminished responsibility: see Chapter 9). On appeal against that conviction, he argued that her refusal was unreasonable and broke the chain of causation. This was rejected.

Question

Suppose V had been stabbed in a remote place and had died before medical assistance could reach her. Then D's liability would certainly have been manslaughter. Why should D be allowed to escape a manslaughter conviction on the ground that V declined medical assistance?

Self-neglect

If V mistreats or neglects to treat his injuries, this will not break the chain of causation. In a very early case, *Wall* (1802) 28 State Tr 51, D, the governor of a British colony was convicted of the murder of V, a soldier whom he had sentenced to an illegal flogging of 800 lashes, even though V had aggravated the injuries by drinking spirits in hospital. MacDonald LCB said that D was 'not at liberty to put another into such perilous circumstances as these, and to make it depend upon [V's] own prudence, knowledge, skill or experience', whether he escaped liability or not. In a slightly later example, *Holland* (1841) 2 Mood & R 351, D cut V on the finger with a piece of metal. The wound became infected, but V ignored medical advice that he should have the finger amputated or risk death. The wound caused lockjaw, and although the finger was then amputated, V died. The trial judge directed the jury that it made no difference whether the wound was instantly mortal, or became so by reason of V not seeking medical help. The jury convicted. Although medical science has advanced hugely since the early nineteenth century, it is still no answer to a homicide charge that V refuses treatment. D must accept that V may be irrational, stupid or afraid of hospitals. *Holland* was in fact followed in *Blaue* in the 1970s and the principles can be seen in use in the most recent case, *Dear* [1996] Crim LR 595.

CASE EXAMPLE

Dear [1996] Crim LR 595

D had slashed at V several times with a Stanley knife, severing an artery. V died from blood loss two days later. At his trial for murder, D pleaded provocation, claiming that he had only just discovered that V had been sexually interfering with his (D's) 12-year-old daughter. (See Chapter 9 for discussion of provocation as a defence to murder.) An alternative defence was that the chain of causation had been broken in that V had committed suicide by either (a) deliberately reopening the wounds, or (b) the wounds having reopened themselves, from failing to take steps to staunch the blood flow. The judge directed the jury that they were entitled to find D guilty of murder if V's wounds remained an 'operating' and 'substantial' cause of death. The jury convicted.

Medical treatment

A number of cases have arisen where doctors have been accused of causing death. The cases divide into two types:

- Where doctors are treating patients with naturally occurring diseases, and administer drugs to alleviate pain (palliative care). If a side-effect of this treatment is to accelerate death, should the doctor face liability for homicide (murder or manslaughter, depending on the doctor's *mens rea*)?

- Where doctors are treating patients who have been rushed in for emergency surgery having (typically) been stabbed or shot by D. The treatment is imperfect and the patient dies. Should (a) the doctor face liability for the death; (b) the doctor's mistreatment relieve D of liability for the death?

Where doctors are providing patients with palliative care

Adams [1957] Crim LR 365 was a case involving a doctor who, in treating a terminally ill patient, may have contributed to her death through the administration of drugs. On trial for murder, the trial judge directed the jury that it did not matter that the victim's death was inevitable, nor that her days were numbered. He said, 'If her life were cut short by weeks or months it was just as much murder as if it was cut short by years.' However, he went on to say:

> **J** 'That did not mean that a doctor who was aiding the sick and dying had to calculate in minutes, or even in hours, and perhaps not in days or weeks, the effect upon a patient's life of the medicines which he administers or else be in peril of a charge of murder. If the first purpose of medicine, the restoration of health, can no longer be achieved there is still much for a doctor to do, and he is entitled to do all that is proper and necessary to relieve pain and suffering, even if the measures he takes may incidentally shorten life. . . .'

Where doctors provide medical mistreatment

Two question were posed above. The first question, whether doctors who inadvertently (as opposed to deliberately) mistreat patients during surgery resulting in death may themselves face liability for homicide, will be dealt with in Chapter 9, specifically the section on gross negligence manslaughter (see in particular the case of *Adomako*). The answer to the second question, whether medical mistreatment provided to the victims of gunshots or stab wounds may relieve the original perpetrator of liability, is, generally speaking, no. In *Smith (Thomas)* [1959] 2 QB 35, Lord Parker CJ said:

> **J** 'If at the time of death the original wound is still an operating cause and a substantial cause, then the death can properly be said to be the result of the wound, albeit that some other cause of death is also operating. Only if it can be said that the original wounding is merely the setting in which another cause operates can it be said that the death did not result from the wound. Putting it another way, only if the second cause is so overwhelming as to make the original wound merely part of the history can it be said that the death does not flow from the wound.'

CASE EXAMPLE

Smith (Thomas) [1959] 2 QB 35

D was a British soldier. During the course of a barrack-room fight he stabbed V, another soldier, twice with a bayonet. One of the wounds had pierced a lung. V eventually died of a haemorrhage (internal bleeding) but, before his death, the following had occurred: (a) another soldier carried V to the medical station and dropped him – twice; (b) the medics, who were under pressure, failed to realise that V had suffered serious injuries because D had been stabbed in the back; (c) the medics gave him treatment which, in the light of this, was described as 'thoroughly bad and might well have affected [V's] chances of recovery'. D was convicted of murder at a court-martial, and the Court-Martial Appeal Court dismissed his appeal.

In *Cheshire* [1991] 3 All ER 670, Beldam LJ proposed a new test, asking not whether the wound was still 'operating' but rather whether D's act or omission could still be said to have 'contributed significantly' to V's death. Approaching the same question from the opposite direction, he indicated that only if the medical treatment could be classed as 'independent' of D's original act, would D escape liability. This new test is very important as it allows the jury to impose liability on D even in cases where V survives, perhaps on a life-support machine, for a long enough time after the original assault such that the gun shot wounds or stab wounds have healed. Beldam LJ said:

> **J** '[D] need not be the sole cause or even the main cause of death, it being sufficient that his acts contributed significantly to that result. Even though negligence in the treatment of [V] was the immediate cause of his death, the jury should not regard it as excluding the responsibility of [D] unless the negligent treatment was so independent of [D's] acts, and in itself so potent in causing death, that they regard the contribution made by [D's] acts as insignificant.'

Beldam LJ also suggested that it was only in the most extraordinary and unusual case that medical treatment would break the chain of causation. He said that 'Treatment which falls short of the standard expected of the competent medical practitioner is unfortunately only too frequent in human experience for it to be considered abnormal in the sense of extraordinary'.

CASE EXAMPLE

Cheshire [1991] 3 All ER 670

On 9th December, D and V got into an argument which culminated in D shooting V twice with a handgun, in the thigh and stomach. The second wound was the more serious and required an extensive bowel resection in hospital. Respiratory problems then ensued, necessitating a tracheotomy. By 8th February, however, V was recovering, although he began to complain of breathing difficulties. Various doctors who saw him around this time thought that his respiratory problems were caused by 'anxiety'. In fact his condition deteriorated rapidly on the night of 14th February and he died of cardio-respiratory arrest, as a result of his windpipe becoming narrow and eventually obstructed; a rare but not unknown side-effect of the tracheotomy. By this time, the gunshot injuries had healed to the point where they were no longer life-threatening. D was convicted of murder, and the Court of Appeal upheld the conviction.

Beldam LJ's test in *Cheshire* has been followed since. In *Mellor* [1996] 2 Cr App R 245, V, a 71-year-old man, was attacked by a gang including D. V was taken to hospital suffering facial bruising and complaining of chest pain and a pain in his right shoulder. He died in hospital two days later. D tried to avoid liability by claiming the hospital failed to give V sufficient oxygen in time, as a result of which V had developed bronchopneumonia (the medical cause of death). However, the Court of Appeal upheld D's conviction of manslaughter. Schiemann LJ noted that, where the victim of a violent assault does not die immediately, 'supervening events' are quite likely to occur which may have some causative effect leading to the victim's death. He listed some examples: a delay in the arrival of the ambulance; a delay in resuscitation; V's reaction to medical or surgical treatment; the quality of medical, surgical and nursing care. In all cases, however, Schiemann LJ said that it was a question for the jury to decide, bearing in mind the gravity of the 'supervening event', whether the injuries inflicted by the defendant remained a 'significant' cause of death. It should be pointed out that the 'operating' and 'substantial' factor test, first devised in *Smith* in the 1950s, has never been overruled, so it would not be a misdirection for a judge in an appropriate case to refer to it. Indeed in *Malcherek, Steel* [1981] 2 All ER 422, the Court of Appeal used the same words. However, it seems that, following the more recent *Cheshire* and *Mellor*, trial judges today are more likely to ask juries to consider whether the original injuries inflicted by D have made a 'significant' contribution to V's death.

In *Warburton & Hubbersty* [2006] EWCA Crim 627, the Court of Appeal confirmed that the law as stated in *Cheshire* and *Mellor* was correct, namely 'did the acts for which the defendant is responsible significantly contribute to the victim's death'?

The cases above all emphasise that it is ultimately a question for the jury to decide. They allow for the possibility that medical mistreatment could be so extreme as to relieve D from liability for V's death. In *Jordan* (1956) 40 Cr App R 152, this possibility duly occurred. The case remains unique, but that is not to imply that it is wrongly decided. Every rule has an exception and, if the rule is that generally speaking hospital mistreatment does not absolve D of liability, this is the exception to it. Indeed, in *Blaue*, Lawton LJ distinguished *Jordan* on the ground that it was 'a case decided on its own special facts' and in *Malcherek, Steel*, which will be discussed below, the Court of Appeal described *Jordan* as 'a very exceptional case'. You will note that neither court stated that *Jordan* was wrongly decided.

CASE EXAMPLE

Jordan (1956) 40 Cr App R 152

D had stabbed V with a knife, the wound penetrating the intestine in two places. V was rushed to hospital where the wound was stitched. Eight days later, however, he died, and D was convicted of murder. On appeal, fresh evidence was adduced which showed that, at the time of V's death, the wound had mainly healed. Doctors had given V a drug called terramycin to prevent infection, but he had shown intolerance to a previous injection. Defence experts described this treatment as 'palpably wrong'. Furthermore, large quantities of liquid had been administered intravenously, which had caused V's lungs to become waterlogged. This was also described as 'wrong' by the defence doctors. As a result of the waterlogging, V developed pulmonary oedema which led inevitably to bronchopneumonia, which was the medical cause of death. The Court of Criminal Appeal quashed D's conviction: if the jury had heard this evidence, they 'would have felt precluded from saying that they were satisfied that death was caused by the stab wound'.

Life support machines

A particular problem concerns victims of violence who have been placed on life-support machines. If there is no prospect of recovery, and the doctors switch off the machinery, how (if at all) does this affect D's responsibility? In *Malcherek, Steel*, it was argued on appeal that in just such a case it was the doctors who had caused death. The Court of Appeal rejected the argument, describing it as 'bizarre'. Lord Lane CJ said:

J 'Where a medical practitioner adopting methods which are generally accepted comes *bona fide* to the conclusion that the patient is for practical purposes dead, and that such vital functions as exist – for example, circulation – are being maintained solely by mechanical means, and therefore discontinues treatment, that does not prevent the person who inflicted the initial injury from being responsible.'

CASE EXAMPLE

Malcherek [1981] 2 All ER 422

On 26th March, Malcherek stabbed his estranged wife, C, nine times. She was admitted to hospital, where over 1½ litres of blood were removed from her abdominal cavity. She seemed to be recovering, but on 1st April she suffered a pulmonary embolism. Her condition deteriorated, and her heart stopped. During open-heart surgery a massive blood clot was removed, at which point her heart restarted. However, 30 minutes had elapsed and severe brain damage had been caused, from which she never recovered. The doctors carried out five of the six tests recommended by the Royal College for establishing brain death (omitting the 'gag reflex' test), and on the strength of this switched off the life support. She was certified dead on 5th April.

CASE EXAMPLE

Steel [1981] 2 All ER 422

On 10th October, Steel attacked W, a random stranger, in the street. He battered her about the head with a large stone, causing severe head injuries, and left her for dead. She was rushed to hospital and placed on life support immediately. However, she never recovered consciousness, and the system was withdrawn two days later after four of the six Royal College tests proved negative (the 'corneal reflex' – where the eyeball is touched with cotton wool – and the 'vestibulo-ocular' – where ice-cold water is dripped into the ear – tests were omitted). She was certified dead on 12th October.

Thus, both victims had life-support equipment switched off after some, but not all, of the Royal College tests indicated brain death. With the equipment switched off, the victims ceased breathing, their hearts stopped and 'conventional' death, that is, cessation of heartbeat, occurred. Malcherek and Steel were both convicted of murder, at Winchester and Leeds Crown Courts respectively. The Court of Appeal, which heard both cases together, rejected both appeals. The same principles apply if V is not brain dead but is in a persistent vegetative state (PVS). In *Airedale NHS Trust v Bland* (1993) (discussed above), Lord Goff said that in discontinuing treatment a doctor was 'simply allowing the patient to die in the sense that he [is] desisting from taking a step which might prevent his patient from dying as a result of his pre-existing condition'.

ACTIVITY

1. Consider whether the "chain of causation" would be broken in the following example:

   V had been taken to hospital having been poisoned by D, his wife. At the hospital V is treated by Dr Young, an inexperienced doctor who is also very tired having spent the previous 36 hours on duty. Dr Young prescribes an antidote for the poison but, in his tired and confused state, tells the nurse to administer a dose 10 times stronger than required. V suffers a massive heart attack and dies.

2. Consider the liability of D in this scenario:

   D, a middle-aged man, has been prescribed powerful pain-killers in tablet form for chronic back pain. One day he discovers his teenage daughter, V, and her friend, W, slumped, unconscious, on V's bedroom floor. It is obvious that the girls have taken D's tablets from the medicine cabinet in the bathroom as the bottle is lying on the bedroom floor, empty. D panics because his doctor had warned him to keep the tablets out of the reach of any children in the house. He goes to the living room to fix himself a large drink to calm his nerves. Eventually he calls for an ambulance but by the time it arrives V has lapsed further into unconscious and dies in the ambulance. W survives but is left severely brain-damaged. D has now been charged with the manslaughter of V and with causing grievous bodily harm to W. The prosecution's case is that both girls might have survived and made full recoveries had D acted immediately on discovering them in the bedroom.

Further reading

Beynon, H, 'Causation, Omissions and Complicity' [1987] Crim LR 539.

Elliott, D W, 'Frightening a Person into Injuring Himself' [1974] Crim LR 15.

Norrie, A, 'A Critique of Criminal Causation' (1991) 54 MLR 685.

Tur, R, 'Legislative Technique and Human Rights: the Sad Case of Assisted Suicide' [2003] Crim LR 3.

Williams, G, 'Finis for Novus Actus?' (1989) 48 CLJ 391.

Williams, G, 'Criminal Omissions – the Conventional View' (1991) 107 LQR 86.

MENS REA ■──────────────────────

AIMS AND OBJECTIVES □ □ □

After reading this chapter you should be able to:

■ Understand the law of intention, both direct and oblique

■ Understand the law of recklessness

■ Understand the principles of transferred malice and coincidence

■ Analyse critically the law on intention and recklessness

3.1 The mental element

It was noted at the start of the previous chapter that the physical element alone is, generally speaking, not enough to constitute criminal liability. The presence of some mental element is usually required. This allows the courts to impose punishment on those who acted with, at least, some awareness of what they were doing. As a general rule, courts in England are reluctant to apportion blame and impose punishment on those who acted inadvertently, that is, without awareness of the conduct, circumstances and consequence elements that make up the *actus reus*. As with the physical elements discussed in Chapter 2, a different mental element is required for each crime. Some criminal offences require one mental element; some require two, either in addition to each other or as alternative states. Some examples are as follows.

• In murder the *mens rea* is intention only (see Chapter 9).

• In theft one mental element is intention; however, there is an additional element of dishonesty.

• In criminal damage and most non-fatal offences against the person, such as assault and battery, the *mens rea* is intention or recklessness (see Chapters 15 and 10).

• In one form of manslaughter, the mental element is recklessness only, while in a different form of manslaughter, the mental element is 'gross negligence' (see Chapter 9).

3.2 Intention

As noted above, in many offences, the *mens rea* required is an 'intention'. However, intention does not exist as an abstract concept: there must be proof of an intention to cause a particular result. The following examples illustrate this.

- Murder requires as its mental element intention to kill or cause grievous bodily harm (see Chapter 9).

- The criminal offence found in s 18 of the Offences Against the Person Act (OAPA) 1861 requires as its mental element an intention to cause grievous bodily harm (see Chapter 10).

- In theft, the mental element is an intention permanently to deprive another person of their property, plus dishonesty (see Chapter 12).

However, whichever crime is charged, the meaning of 'intent' is the same. In criminal law, there are two types of intent:

- Direct intent – this refers to someone's aim, purpose or desire.

- Indirect or oblique intent – this is much harder to define. The question whether D intends a consequence of his actions when he believes that it is *virtually certain*, or *very probable*, is one that has greatly troubled English courts for the last 30 years. The House of Lords has dealt with the problem on five occasions, all murder cases, the most recent in 1998.

3.2.1 Direct intention

As indicated above, **direct intention** refers to the situation when D desires an outcome. For example:

- D is a hired professional killer (an example is *Calhaem* [1985] 1 QB 808: see Chapter 6) who aims a loaded gun at V's heart and pulls the trigger. Clearly D has direct intent to kill. The fact that D's desire is motivated by cash is irrelevant: D still wanted to kill V.

- D is a sadistic psychopath who enjoys torturing and killing people. He strangles V to death and then cuts up the body (as in *Byrne* [1960] 2 QB 396: see Chapter 9). Clearly D again has direct intent to kill. The fact that D's desire is motivated by his abnormal mental condition is irrelevant to the question of intent: D still wanted to kill V.

An example of a situation where D does not desire a consequence but may still be said to have intended it might be where D sees a child trapped in a locked car, towards which a runaway lorry is heading at speed. D grabs a brick and smashes the windscreen to rescue the child. D's desire here was to save the child but in doing so he had to cause criminal damage to the car (see Chapter 15). If D were prosecuted for the offence of intentional criminal damage to the windscreen, it seems that the prosecution could establish the elements of the offence. (It is extremely unlikely that the Crown Prosecution Service would prosecute on these facts; even if they did, D would almost certainly be found not guilty by pleading duress of circumstances, see Chapter 8.)

3.2.2 Oblique intention

As indicated above, indirect or **oblique intention** occurs where D does not necessarily desire an outcome but realises that it is almost (but not quite) inevitable. However, this scenario invites problems. What *degree of probability* is required before an undesired consequence, but one which D has foreseen, can be said to have been intended? Some would argue none – that once one steps away from foresight of something as *100 per cent certain to happen,* then one is dealing with *risk,* and that means *recklessness,* not intent. Others would argue that very high probability would suffice. A good place to start an examination of 'intent' is the Criminal Justice Act 1967, which states that:

> **S** '8 A court or jury in determining whether a person has committed an offence (a) shall not be bound in law to infer that he intended or foresaw a result of his actions by reason only of its being a natural and probable consequence of those actions; but (b) shall decide whether he did intend or foresee that result by reference to all the evidence, drawing such inferences from the facts as appear proper in the circumstances.'

This provision was passed in order to reverse the decision of the House of Lords in *DPP v Smith* [1961] AC 290. The Law Lords had declared that there was an irrebuttable presumption of law that a person foresaw and intended the 'natural consequences' of his acts. Proof that D did an act, the natural consequence of which was death, was proof that D intended to kill. Further, the test of what was a natural consequence was purely objective: 'not what [D] contemplated, but what the ordinary reasonable man would in all the circumstances of the case have contemplated as the natural and probable result'. None of this is now good law. The leading case is now that of *Woollin* [1998] UKHL 28; [1998] 3 WLR 382. Lord Steyn (with whom the other members of the House of Lords agreed) laid down a model direction, for trial judges to use in cases where D's intention is unclear, as follows:

> **J** 'Where the charge is murder . . . the jury should be directed that they are not entitled [to find] the necessary intention, unless they feel sure that death or serious bodily harm was a virtual certainty (barring some unforeseen intervention) as a result of [D]'s actions and that [D] appreciated that such was the case.'

CASE EXAMPLE

Woollin [1998] UKHL 28; [1998] 3 WLR 382

D had killed his three-month-old son by throwing him against a wall, fracturing his skull. D did not deny doing this, but claimed that it was not intended. He claimed that he had picked the child up after he began to choke and shaken him, then, in a fit of rage or frustration, had thrown him with some considerable force towards a pram four or five feet away. The trial judge directed the jury that they might infer intention if satisfied that when D threw the child, he had appreciated that there was a 'substantial risk' that he would cause serious harm to the child. D was convicted of murder and appealed on the basis that the phrase 'substantial risk' was a test of recklessness, not of intent, and that the judge should have used 'virtual certainty'. The Court of Appeal dismissed the appeal but the House of Lords unanimously reversed that court's decision, quashed D's murder conviction and substituted one of manslaughter.

You will note that in the 1967 Act there is a verb, 'to infer'. This word was faithfully used by trial judges and the appeal courts until *Woollin*. But in that case the Law Lords agreed that juries would more easily understand the verb 'to find'. It appears that the Law Lords simply intended to substitute one word for another, although academics argue that the words have slightly different meanings. Prior to *Woollin*, the most oft-quoted statement of the law of intent was found in *Nedrick* [1986] 3 All ER 1. This was a Court of Appeal case, in which Lord Lane CJ attempted to, as he put it, 'crystallise' the various speeches made in the House of Lords in two cases from the early 1980s: *Moloney* [1985] AC 905 and *Hancock and Shankland* [1986] AC 455. Lord Lane stated:

> **J** 'It may be advisable first of all to explain to the jury that a man may intend to achieve a certain result whilst at the same time not desiring it to come about . . . if the jury are satisfied that at the material time [D] recognised that death or serious harm would be virtually certain (barring some unforeseen intervention) to result from his voluntary act, then that is a fact from which they may find it easy to infer that he intended to kill or do serious bodily harm, even though he may not have had any desire to achieve that result. Where a man realises that it is for all practical purposes inevitable that his actions will result in death or serious harm, the inference may be irresistible that he intended that result, however little he may have desired or wished it to happen. The decision is one for the jury to be reached on a consideration of all the evidence.'

Directions on intention not always necessary

Most of the cases mentioned above reached the appeal courts because the trial judge unnecessarily confused the issue by raising indirect intent in the first place. When this happens it invites an appeal on the basis that the jury has been unnecessarily confused. As Lord Bridge put it in *Moloney*:

> **J** 'The golden rule should be that . . . the judge should avoid any elaboration or paraphrase of what is meant by intent, and leave it to the jury's good sense to decide whether the accused acted with the necessary intent, unless the judge is convinced that, on the facts and having regard to the way that case has been presented . . . some further explanation or elaboration is strictly necessary to avoid misunderstanding.'

The case of *Fallon* [1994] Crim LR 519 provides a perfect example. D was charged with attempted murder (this requires proof of an intent to kill). He had shot a police officer in the leg. The prosecution alleged that he intended to kill; D argued that the gun had gone off accidentally when the officer tried to grab the gun, which D was trying to hand over. The trial judge directed the jury on intent, referring to *Moloney* and *Nedrick* and introducing the concept of virtual certainty. Unsurprisingly, the jury asked for clarification, and the judge gave them further direction, also based on *Nedrick*. After the jury convicted D of murder, the Court of Appeal allowed his appeal (although they instead substituted a conviction under s 18 OAPA 1861, of causing grievous bodily harm with intent to resist arrest). The prosecution accepted that the judge's directions were unnecessary and confusing; he had ignored Lord Bridge's 'golden rule'. The jury simply had to decide whether they believed the prosecution or the defence version of events. If they were sure the prosecution's version was correct, then they should convict (D had direct intent); if they thought the defence might be correct, then acquit (the shooting was an accident, D did not intend to do the officer any harm at all).

In *Wright* [2000] EWCA Crim 28; [2000] Crim LR 928, the Court of Appeal rejected D's appeal against a murder conviction based on the ground that the judge had *not* directed the jury according to *Nedrick* and *Woollin*. At the time of the killing, D and V were sharing a prison cell (D was on remand). One morning V was found lying on the cell floor, unconscious and with a piece of bedsheet tied round his neck. He died a week later. D denied murder, claiming that, while he (D) was asleep, V had hanged himself. Upholding the murder conviction, Beldam LJ said that in simply giving 'the straightforward direction on intention' – that is, by just directing the jury to consider direct intent – the judge was 'directing the jury to the real question they had to determine and steering them away from the chameleon-like concepts of purpose, foresight of consequence and awareness of risk'. This must be correct. The prosecution case was that D wanted to kill V – that is, he had direct intent; the defence case was that D had nothing to do with V's death at all. There was no need for any direction based on oblique intent; indeed, had the jury been directed to consider D's foresight of consequences it would only have served to have distracted them from the key question: did they believe the prosecution's version of the facts, or the defence's version?

Foresight is not intention but evidence of intention

All the courts agree on one thing: foresight of a consequence, even of a virtually certain consequence, is <u>not</u> intent, but is simply evidence from which intention may be found. It will therefore be a misdirection for the judge to equate foresight with intention. The jury must be left to 'find' intent from foresight. For example, in *Scalley* [1995] Crim LR 504, D was convicted of murder but on appeal his conviction was reduced to manslaughter. The problem was that the judge had directed the jury that if they found that D had foreseen death or serious injury as virtually certain, then he had intended it. However, this is somewhat confusing. If the jury are agreed that D foresaw a consequence as virtually certain, then they are entitled to 'find' that D intended that consequence. Equally, they are not compelled to do so. So when should a jury 'find' intention based on evidence that D foresaw a virtually certain consequence (and convict D), and when should it not (and acquit D)? The courts have failed to give any clues as to when, or how, juries are to take this step. It has been said that there is a 'logical gap' between foresight and intention (G Williams, 'Oblique Intention' (1987) 46 CLJ 417).

Nevertheless, the proposition that foresight of a consequence is not intention but evidence of it was confirmed in *Matthews and Alleyne* [2003] EWCA Crim 192; [2003] 2 Cr App R 461.

CASE EXAMPLE

Matthews and Alleyne [2003] EWCA Crim 192; [2003] 2 Cr App R 461

D and E had pushed V from a bridge over the River Ouse (despite the fact he had told them he could not swim) where he fell about 25 feet and drowned. D and E were convicted of murder (among other offences including robbery and kidnapping) after the trial judge told the jury that if 'drowning was a virtual certainty and [D and E] appreciated that . . . they must have had the intention of killing him'. D and E appealed on the basis that this direction went beyond what was permitted by *Nedrick/Woollin* and equated foresight with intention. The Court of Appeal rejected the appeal. Although the judge had gone further than he was permitted (and had equated foresight with intention), the court thought that, on the particular facts of the case, if the jury were sure that D and E had appreciated the virtual certainty of V's death when they threw him into the river, it was 'impossible' to see how they could not have drawn the inference that D and E intended V's death.

Criticism

Some academics take the view that intention should be limited to direct intention (desire, aim or purpose). As Finnis has pointed out ('Intention and Side-Effects' (1993) 109 LQR 329), in ordinary English we would not say that 'someone who hangs curtains knowing that the sunlight will make them fade' intends that they will fade – and yet according to the House of Lords, a jury

would be entitled to 'find' that they did intend exactly that. Finnis described the definition of indirect or oblique intent as the 'Pseudo-Masochistic Theory of Intention – for it holds that those who foresee that their actions will have painful effects upon themselves intend those effects'.

Question

Tony celebrates his birthday by drinking five glasses of red wine. He knows from previous, bitter experience that drinking anything more than two or three glasses of red wine will give him a terrible hangover in the morning. According to the *Nedrick/Woollin* definition, does Tony intend to have a terrible hangover?

The *Nedrick/Woollin* test fails to provide a clear distinction between intention and recklessness. How is it possible to distinguish a consequence foreseen as 'virtually certain' (which might be evidence of intent) from one foreseen as 'highly probable' (which would be evidence of recklessness)? There is no obvious cut-off point, and yet this is the dividing line between murder and manslaughter. There are also strong moral justifications for distinguishing D who acts in order to achieve V's death because that is what he wants to happen, and D who has one goal but foresees that V's death is certain to happen, although he desperately hopes it will not.

Reform proposals

The Law Commission's Draft Criminal Code (1989) defined intention as follows: 'a person acts . . . intentionally with respect to . . . a result when he acts either in order to bring it about or being aware that it will occur in the ordinary course of events'. In its Commentary, the Commission observed that acting 'in order to bring about a result' was 'the standard case', but added that a definition of 'intention' had to refer to 'the means as well the end and the inseparable consequences of the end as well as the means.' This has the obvious advantage of dispensing with references to virtual certainty, and juries 'finding' intention from evidence.

The late Professor Sir John Smith suggested a slightly different version ('A Note on Intention' [1990] Crim LR 85), which was adopted by the Law Commission in its Draft Criminal Law Bill (1993). This definition provides that 'a person acts intentionally with respect to a result' when:

(i) it is his purpose to cause it, or

(ii) although it is not his purpose to cause it, he knows that it would occur in the ordinary course of events if he were to succeed in his purpose of causing some other result.

The American Law Institute's Model Penal Code takes a narrower approach. According to the Code, a person acts intentionally when it is his 'conscious object to engage in conduct of that nature or to cause such a result'. As to the mental state of foresight of virtual certainty, under the Code this forms a special category of *mens rea*, between intention and recklessness, namely knowledge. The Code states that: 'A person acts knowingly with respect to a material element of an offense when . . . (ii) if the element involves a result of his conduct, he is aware that it is practically certain that his conduct will cause such a result.'

3.3 Recklessness

Recklessness generally involves D taking an unjustifiable risk of a particular *consequence* occurring, with awareness of that risk. Sometimes, however, the question is whether D was reckless as to the existence of a particular set of *circumstances*, such as whether or not V was consenting to sex with D.

Recklessness is the *mens rea* state sufficient for many crimes, some very serious, including manslaughter, rape, malicious wounding, inflicting grievous bodily harm, and assault occasioning actual bodily harm. The question that has troubled the appeal courts for the last quarter century is whether recklessness should be assessed 'subjectively' – that is, by looking at the case from the defendant's perspective, or 'objectively' – that is, looking at the case from the perspective of the reasonable man. It will be seen that the courts have gone on a long, circular journey. After starting with a subjective test, in 1981 an objective test was introduced. For a short time in the early 1980s it seemed that the objective test would replace the subjective test, but the original test began a comeback in the mid-1980s and continued to reassert itself throughout the 1990s. Finally, in 2003, the objective test was banished to the pages of history.

3.3.1 The *Cunningham* test

The original case on the definition of recklessness is *Cunningham* [1957] 2 QB 396. Here the court gave us the classic, subjective test for recklessness. The question for the Court of Criminal Appeal was actually what was meant by the word 'maliciously' (in s 23 OAPA 1861: see Chapter 10). The judge had directed the jury that it meant 'wickedly'. The Court of Criminal Appeal did not agree. In quashing the conviction, the court approved a definition given by Professor Kenny in 1902:

> 'In any statutory definition of a crime, "malice" must be taken not in the old vague sense of wickedness in general but as requiring either (i) an actual intention to do the particular kind of harm that in fact was done or (ii) recklessness as to whether such harm should occur or not (ie the accused has foreseen that the particular kind of harm might be done, and yet has gone on to take the risk of it).'

CASE EXAMPLE

Cunningham [1957] 2 QB 396

D ripped a gas meter from the cellar wall of a house in Bradford, in order to steal the money inside. He left a ruptured pipe, leaking gas, which seeped through into the neighbouring house, where V (actually the mother of D's fiancée) inhaled it. He was charged with maliciously administering a noxious substance so as to endanger life, contrary to s 23 OAPA 1861, and convicted. The crux of the matter was whether D had foreseen the risk; in this case, of someone inhaling the gas.

This definition was subsequently applied throughout the OAPA 1861 (for example *Venna* [1976] QB 421, a case of assault occasioning actual bodily harm contrary to s 47) and to other statutes, such as the Malicious Damage Act 1861 (MDA), whenever the word 'malicious' was used. In 1969, the Law Commission was working on proposals to reform the law of property damage. In its final *Report on Criminal Damage*, it recommended the replacement of the MDA with what became the Criminal Damage Act 1971 (CDA). The Law Commission considered that the mental element, as stated in *Cunningham*, was properly defined, but that for simplicity and clarity the word 'maliciously' should be replaced with 'intentionally or recklessly'. Unfortunately, the Act does not define 'reckless' anywhere; it is left to the courts to interpret. Hence, after 1971 the courts defined 'recklessness' by referring to D's awareness of the consequences of his actions. In *Stephenson* [1979] QB 695, for example, Lane LJ said:

> **J** 'A man is reckless when he carries out the deliberate act appreciating that there is a risk that damage to property may result from his act . . . We wish to make it clear that the test remains subjective, that the knowledge or appreciation of risk of some damage must have entered the defendant's mind even though he may have suppressed it or driven it out.'

CASE EXAMPLE

Stephenson [1979] QB 695

D was a schizophrenic; he was also homeless. One November night he had decided to shelter in a hollowed-out haystack in a field. He was still cold, and so lit a small fire of twigs and straw in order to keep warm. However, the stack caught fire and was damaged, along with various pieces of farming equipment. D was charged under s 1(1) of the CDA. Evidence was given that schizophrenia could have the effect of depriving D of the ability of a normal person to foresee or appreciate the risk of damage. The judge directed the jury that D was reckless if he closed his mind to the obvious fact of risk, and that schizophrenia could be the reason for D closing his mind. The Court of Appeal quashed his conviction. What mattered was whether D himself had foreseen the risk.

3.3.2 The *Caldwell* years: 1981–2003

In 1981, the House of Lords in *Metropolitan Police Commissioner v Caldwell* [1982] AC 341, a criminal damage case, introduced an objective form of recklessness. That is, recklessness was to be determined according to what the 'ordinary, prudent individual' would have foreseen, as opposed to the *Cunningham* test of what the defendant actually did foresee. Lord Diplock, with whom Lords Keith and Roskill concurred, said:

> **J** 'A person charged with an offence under s 1(1) of the Criminal Damage Act 1971 is "reckless as to whether or not any such property be destroyed or damaged" if (1) he does an act which in fact creates an obvious risk that property will be destroyed or damaged and (2) when he does the act he either has not given any thought to the possibility of their being any such risk or has recognised that there was some risk involved and has nonetheless gone on to do it. That would be a proper direction to the jury . . .'.

Because *Caldwell* was a criminal damage case it meant that, while *Stephenson* would be overruled, other areas of law were still subject to the *Cunningham* definition. However, in *Lawrence* [1982] AC 510, the House of Lords gave an objective definition to 'recklessness' in the context of the crime of causing death by reckless driving. A year later, in *Seymour* [1983] 2 AC 493, a reckless manslaughter case, the House of Lords applied the objective test here too. Their Lordships also indicated that the *Caldwell/Lawrence* definition of 'recklessness' was 'comprehensive'. Lord Roskill said that 'Reckless should today be given the same meaning in relation to all offences which involve "recklessness" as one of the elements unless Parliament has otherwise ordained'.

This marked the high-water point for the *Caldwell/Lawrence* objective test. During the late 1980s and continuing into the 1990s the courts began a gradual movement to reject *Caldwell* and return to the *Cunningham* subjective test. In *DPP v K (a minor)* [1990] 1 All ER 331, the Divisional Court had applied *Caldwell* to s 47 OAPA 1861 (assault occasioning actual bodily harm), but almost immediately the Court of Appeal in *Spratt* [1991] 2 All ER 210 declared that *DPP v K* was wrongly decided. D had been convicted of the s 47 offence after firing his air-pistol through the open window of his flat, apparently unaware that children were playing outside. One was hit and injured. At his trial, D pleaded guilty (on the basis that he had been reckless in that he had failed to give thought to the possibility of a risk that he might cause harm) and appealed. The Court of Appeal quashed his conviction. McCowan LJ pointed out that Lord Roskill's dictum in *Seymour* was clearly *obiter* and could not have been intended to overrule *Cunningham*. McCowan LJ added:

> **J** 'The history of the interpretation of [the OAPA 1861] shows that, whether or not the word "maliciously" appears in the section in question, the courts have consistently held that the *mens rea* of every type of offence against the person covers both intent and recklessness, in the sense of taking the risk of harm ensuing with foresight that it might happen.'

Shortly afterwards the House of Lords dealt with a joint appeal involving both s 47 and s 20 OAPA 1861. In *Savage, DPP v Parmenter* [1992] AC 699, Lord Ackner, giving the unanimous decision of the House of Lords, said that: 'in order to establish an offence under s 20 the

prosecution must prove either that [D] intended or that he actually foresaw that his act would cause harm.' *Seymour* was effectively overruled by the House of Lords in *Adomako* [1995] 1 AC 171. Lord Mackay pointed out that, to the extent that *Seymour* was concerned with the statutory offence of causing death by reckless driving, it was no longer relevant as that offence had been replaced with a new statutory crime of causing death by dangerous driving (see Chapter 9). As far as manslaughter was concerned, Lord Mackay decided that objective recklessness set too low a threshold of liability for such a serious crime and restored the test based on gross negligence (see below).

3.3.3 Back to *Cunningham*: *G and another*

In October 2003, the House of Lords completed the circle begun 22 years earlier by overruling *Caldwell*. In *G and another* [2003] UKHL 50; [2003] 3 WLR 1060, their Lordships unanimously declared that the objective test for recklessness was wrong and restored the *Cunningham* subjective test for criminal damage. The case itself involved arson, as had *Caldwell*. The certified question from the Court of Appeal was:

> **J** 'Can a defendant properly be convicted under s 1 of the CDA 1971 on the basis that he was reckless as to whether property would be destroyed or damaged when he gave no thought to the risk, but by reason of his age and/or personal characterisitics the risk would not have been obvious to him, even if he had thought about it?'

In a number of earlier cases, this question had been answered 'yes': see *Elliott v C (a minor)* [1983] 1 WLR 939; *R (Stephen Malcolm)* (1984) 79 Cr App R 334; and *Coles* [1995] 1 Cr App R 157. All of those cases involved teenagers committing arson and being convicted because, under the *Caldwell* test, it was irrelevant that they had failed to appreciate the risk of property damage created by starting fires, because that the risk would have been obvious to the ordinary prudent adult. However, in *G and another* the House of Lords held that the certified question should be answered 'no'. According to Lord Bingham the question was simply one of statutory interpretation, namely, what did Parliament mean when it used the word 'reckless' in s 1 of the 1971 Act? He concluded that Parliament had not intended to change the meaning of the word from its *Cunningham* definition. The majority of the Law Lords in *Caldwell*, specifically Lord Diplock, had 'misconstrued' the 1971 Act. There were four reasons for restoring the subjective test:

1. As a matter of principle, conviction of a serious crime should depend on proof that D had a culpable state of mind. While it was 'clearly blameworthy' to take an obvious risk, it was not clearly blameworthy to do something involving a risk of injury (or property damage) if D genuinely did not perceive that risk. While such a person might 'fairly be accused of stupidity or a lack of imagination', that was insufficient for culpability.

2. The *Caldwell* test was capable of leading to 'obvious unfairness'. It was neither 'moral nor just' to convict any defendant, but least of all a child, on the strength of what someone else would have appreciated.

3. There was significant judicial and academic criticism of *Caldwell* and the cases that had followed it. In particular, Lords Wilberforce and Edmund Davies had dissented in *Caldwell* itself and Goff LJ in *Elliott v C* had followed *Caldwell* only because he felt compelled to do so because of the rules of judicial precedent. That could not be ignored.

4. The decision in *Caldwell* was a misinterpretation of Parliament's intention. Although the courts could leave it to Parliament to correct that misinterpretation, because it was one that was 'offensive to principle and was apt to cause injustice', the need for the courts to correct it was 'compelling'.

Lord Bingham also observed that there were no compelling public policy reasons for persisting with the *Caldwell* test. The law prior to 1981 revealed no miscarriages of justice with guilty defendants being acquitted.

CASE EXAMPLE

G and another [2003] UKHL 50; [2003] 3 WLR 1060

One night in August 2000 the two defendants, G and R, then aged 11 and 12, entered the back yard of a shop. There they found bundles of newspapers, some of which they set alight using a lighter they had brought with them. They threw the burning paper under a large, plastic wheelie-bin and left the yard. Meanwhile, the fire had set fire to the wheelie-bin. It then spread to another wheelie-bin, then to the shop and its adjoining buildings. Damage estimated at approximately £1 million was caused. G and R were charged with arson (that is, damaging or destroying property by fire, being reckless as to whether such property would be destroyed or damaged). At trial, they said that they genuinely thought the burning newspapers would extinguish themselves on the concrete floor of the yard. Hence, looking at the case <u>subjectively</u>, neither of them appreciated a risk that the wheelie-bins, let alone the shop and its adjoining buildings, would be destroyed or damaged by fire. The judge, however, directed the jury according to the *Caldwell* test. The jury, looking at the case <u>objectively</u>, was satisfied that the ordinary prudent adult would have appreciated that risk, and therefore convicted the two boys. The Court of Appeal dismissed their appeal but certified the question for appeal to the House of Lords.

The Court of Appeal has confirmed the development in *G & another* on two occasions, in *Cooper* (2004) and *Castle* (2004), both aggravated arson cases. These cases will be examined in Chapter 15 on criminal damage (see section 15.2.4).

There is a supreme irony to all this: on the facts of the *Caldwell* case itself, D would have been found guilty without any need for the objective test. D had been very drunk when he started a fire in a hotel. When charged with reckless arson, he argued that his extreme intoxication prevented him from foreseeing the consequences of his actions, and was therefore not guilty. However, the House of Lords had dealt with this very problem and very similar arguments only four years earlier. In *DPP v Majewksi* [1977] AC 443, Lord Elwyn-Jones LC stated that when D is intoxicated and carries out the *actus reus* of a crime for which the *mens rea* state is recklessness, then his very intoxication:

> J   'supplies the evidence of *mens rea*, of guilty mind certainly sufficient for crimes of basic intent. It is a reckless course of conduct and recklessness is enough to constitute the necessary *mens rea* in assault cases . . . The drunkenness is itself an intrinsic, an integral part of the crime'.

This case and the public policy arguments underpinning it will be looked at in detail in Chapter 8. Returning to *G and another*, it is worth noting that the House of Lords did give consideration to arguments from the Crown that the *Caldwell* definition could be modified. There were two possibilities, both of which were rejected.

1. That *Caldwell* be adapted for cases involving children and mentally handicapped adults. Thus, according to the Crown, a teenage defendant could be convicted if he had failed to give any thought to a risk which would have been obvious to a child of the same age. The House of Lords rejected this, on the basis that it was just as offensive to the above principles. It would also 'open the door' to 'difficult and contentious arguments concerning the qualities and characteristics to be taken into account for the purposes of comparison'.

2. That *Caldwell* be adapted so that D would be reckless if he had failed to give thought to an obvious risk which, had he bothered to think about it at all, would have been equally obvious to him. This argument was rejected because it had the potential to over-complicate the jury's task. It was inherently speculative to ask a jury to consider whether D would have regarded a risk as obvious, had he thought about it. Lord Bingham thought that the simpler the jury's task, the more reliable its verdict would be.

It should finally be noted that, in addition to *Caldwell*, a significant number of Court of Appeal cases following *Caldwell* have, by necessity, been overruled too. As well as the cases cited above – *Elliott v C*; *R (Stephen Malcolm)* and *Coles* – the following have also been overruled: *Chief Constable of Avon v Shimmen* (1986) Cr App R 7 and *Merrick* [1995] Crim LR 802. It is safe to assume that the Law Commission will welcome the House of Lords' decision in *G and another*. In both the Draft Criminal Code (1989) and the Draft Criminal Law Bill (1993) the Commission defined 'recklessness' in a subjective sense. The late Professor Sir John Smith would also have welcomed the House of Lords' ruling. A well-known objector to *Caldwell*, he commented in the Criminal Law Review of the Court

of Appeal's decision to refer the *G and another* case to the House of Lords that 'the law would be better without all the unnecessary complexity [*Caldwell*] introduced' ([2002] Crim LR at 928).

3.4 Negligence

Negligence is the mental element that must be proved in order to impose liability on defendants in some forms of civil litigation. In that context, it typically means that D is liable if he or she fails to appreciate circumstances or consequences that would have been appreciated by the reasonable man. This mental element is rarely found in mainstream criminal law, with one exception, because it is seen as too low a threshold to justify imposing punishment on the defendant. (In civil litigation, if liability is imposed on D, he or she is required to compensate the victim but is not otherwise punished.) The exception is a form of manslaughter – however, it should be noted that the mental element is 'gross' negligence. The leading case now is *Adomako*, but the position is perfectly summed up by Lord Atkin in the early House of Lords case of *Andrews v DPP* [1937] AC 576, who said:

> **J** 'Simple lack of care as will constitute civil liability is not enough. For purposes of the criminal law there are degrees of negligence, and a very high degree of negligence is required to be proved before the [crime] is established.'

Gross negligence manslaughter will be considered in depth in Chapter 9.

3.5 Knowledge

This form of *mens rea* does not feature as heavily in the criminal law as intention or recklessness. One criminal offence dealt with in this book that uses knowledge as a *mens rea* state is rape. The focus of the inquiry in rape is into D's awareness of a circumstances (whether V is consenting to sex), as opposed to a consequence, so it is inappropriate to use intention as a *mens rea* state (we would not talk about intending a circumstance). Section 1 of the Sexual Offences Act 2003 provides that D has the *mens rea* of rape if he 'does not reasonably believe that B consents' to sex (see Chapter 11 for a full definition of the offence). Clearly, if D <u>knows</u> that V is not consenting (because she is struggling or screaming, for example) he cannot 'reasonably believe' that she is consenting. However, knowledge is not essential for a rape conviction. If D honestly (but unreasonably, perhaps because he has been drinking) thinks that V is consenting, he cannot simultaneously know that she is not consenting. Nevertheless D has the *mens rea* as defined in s 1 of the 2003 Act.

3.6 Transferred malice

If D, with the *mens rea* of a particular crime, does an act that causes the *actus reus* of that crime, then he faces liability. It is no excuse to say that the way in which the *actus reus* was carried out was not exactly as D intended it. Suppose that D, intending to punch V, swings his fist in the direction

of V who ducks so that D's fist connects with W who is standing immediately behind V. Should D be allowed to plead not guilty to the battery on W, on the basis that he had intended to punch V? The answer is no. This scenario is an example of the doctrine of transferred malice. Something very similar to those facts occurred in one of the leading cases, *Latimer* (1886) 17 QBD 359.

CASE EXAMPLE

Latimer (1886) 17 QBD 359

D was involved in a disagreement with V. He took off his belt and swung it at V. The belt glanced off V, and W, who was nearby, received virtually the full impact of the blow. She was badly wounded and D was charged with malicious wounding under s 20 OAPA 1861. At trial, the jury found that the injuries to W were 'purely accidental' and could not reasonably have been expected. However, the doctrine of transferred malice rendered this irrelevant, and D was convicted.

Latimer was followed and applied in the more recent case of *Mitchell* [1983] QB 741, the facts of which were given in Chapter 2. You may recall that D pushed E, who lost his balance and knocked V to the ground, where she broke her leg and eventually died of her injuries. D was convicted of V's manslaughter. In *Attorney-General's Reference (No 3 of 1994)* [1997] 3 WLR 421, Lord Mustill explained the transferred malice doctrine as follows:

> **J** 'The effect of transferred malice . . . is that the intended victim and the actual victim are treated as if they were one, so that what was intended to happen to the first person (but did not happen) is added to what actually did happen to the second person (but was not intended to happen), with the result that what was intended and what happened are married to make a notionally intended and actually consummated crime.'

CASE EXAMPLE

Attorney-General's Reference (No 3 of 1994) **[1997] 3 WLR 421**

D had stabbed his girlfriend, V, who was between five and six months pregnant. She subsequently recovered from the wound but, some seven weeks later, gave birth prematurely. Subsequently, the child, W, died some four months after birth. It was clear the stab wound had penetrated W whilst in the womb and this was the cause of death. D was charged with W's murder, but was formally acquitted after the judge held that the facts did not disclose a homicide against the child. The case was referred to the Court of Appeal, which held the trial judge was wrong and that, applying the doctrine of transferred malice, a murder conviction was possible. Unusually, a further reference was made to the House of Lords, where it was decided that, at most, manslaughter was possible. The Law Lords took exception to the Court of Appeal's use of the transferred malice doctrine, holding that the 'transferee' had to be in existence at the time that D was proven to have formed the mental element. Lord Mustill said that it would 'overstrain the idea of transferred malice by trying to make it fit the present case'.

Meanwhile, if D, with the *mens rea* of one crime, does an act which causes the *actus reus* of *some different* crime, he cannot, generally speaking, be convicted of either crime. This is illustrated by the facts of *Pembliton* (1874) LR 2 CCR 119.

CASE EXAMPLE

Pembliton **(1874) LR 2 CCR 119**

D was involved in a fight involving some 40–50 people, outside a pub in Wolverhampton. D separated himself from the group, picked up a large stone and threw it in the direction of the others. The stone missed them and smashed a large window. D was convicted of malicious damage but his conviction was quashed on appeal. The jury had found that he intended to throw the stone at the people but did not intend to break the window.

Criticism

Although a useful, practical device for obtaining convictions, the doctrine has not gone uncriticised. Professor Williams argued that the doctrine is a 'rather arbitrary exception to normal principles' ('Convictions and Fair Labelling' (1983) CLJ 85). Considering the situation where D intends to kill V but misses and instead kills W, Professor Williams commented that because the indictment

would actually charge D with killing W, strictly speaking it should be necessary to prove that D intended to kill (or seriously injure) W. However, this view has not attracted support from the courts.

Reform

The Law Commission, in both the Draft Criminal Code (1989) and the Draft Criminal Law Bill (1993), accepted the need to preserve the transferred malice doctrine. Clause 32(1) of the 1993 Bill provides as follows:

> '32(1) In determining whether a person is guilty of an offence, his intention to cause, or his awareness of a risk that he will cause, a result in relation to a person or thing capable of being the victim or subject-matter of the offence shall be treated as an intention to cause or, as the case may, an awareness of a risk that he will cause, that result in relation to any other person or thing affected by his conduct.'

3.7 Coincidence of *actus reus* and *mens rea*

Suppose that D, the victim of domestic violence, forms a vague intention to kill her husband, V, at some convenient moment in the future if it should present itself, perhaps by pushing him off a set of ladders while he is cleaning leaves from the roof gutter. Ten minutes later, D reverses her car from the garage, oblivious of the fact that V is sitting in the driveway attempting to repair the lawnmower, and runs him over, killing him instantly. Is D guilty of V's murder? The answer would be 'no', because of the requirement that the *actus reus* of any crime must be accompanied at that precise moment in time by the *mens rea* of the same crime. Although D did cause death, and had formed an intention to do so, the various elements were separated in time. There are certain exceptions to this doctrine, however. First, where the *actus reus* takes the form of a continuing act, it has been held that it is sufficient if D forms *mens rea* at some point during the duration of the act. In *Fagan v Metropolitan Police Commissioner* [1969] 1 QB 439 James J said:

> 'We think that the crucial question is whether, in this case, [D's act] can be said to be complete and spent at the moment of time when the car wheel came to rest on the foot, or whether his act is to be regarded as a continuing act operating until the wheel was removed. In our judgment, a distinction is to be drawn between acts which are complete, though results may continue to flow, and those acts which are continuing . . . There was an act constituting a battery which at its inception was not criminal because there was no element of intention, but which became criminal from the moment the intention was formed to produce the apprehension which was flowing from the continuing act.'

CASE EXAMPLE

Fagan v Metropolitan Police Commissioner **[1969] 1 QB 439**

D was being directed to park his car by a police officer. D accidentally drove his car onto the officer's foot, who shouted at D to move the car. At this point, D refused and even switched off the engine. The officer had to repeat his request several times until D eventually acquiesced. D was charged with battery (physical element: the application of unlawful force; mental element: intent or recklessness). The magistrates were not convinced that D had deliberately driven onto the officer's foot; however, they were satisfied that he had intentionally allowed the wheel to remain there afterwards. D was therefore convicted on the basis that allowing the wheel to remain on the officer's foot constituted a continuing act, and the Divisional Court dismissed D's appeal.

The second exception is where the *actus reus* is itself part of some larger sequence of events, it may be sufficient that D forms *mens rea* at some point during that sequence. The leading case is the Privy Council decision (hearing an appeal from South Africa) in *Thabo Meli and others* [1954] 1 All ER 373.

CASE EXAMPLE

Thabo Meli and others **[1954] 1 All ER 373**

The appellants, in accordance with a pre-arranged plan, took V to a hut where they beat him over the head. Believing him to be dead, they rolled his body over a low cliff, attempting to make it look like an accidental fall. In fact, V was still alive at this point in time but eventually died from exposure. The appellants were convicted of murder and the Privy Council dismissed their appeals, which had been based on an argument that the *actus reus* (death from exposure) was separated in time from the *mens rea* (present during the attack in the hut but not later, because they thought V was dead). Lord Reid stated that it was:

> 'Impossible to divide up what was really one series of acts in this way. There is no doubt that the accused set out to do all these acts in order to achieve their plan, and as part of their plan: and it is much too refined a ground of judgment to say that, because they were at a misapprehension at one stage and thought that their guilty purpose was achieved before it was achieved, therefore they are to escape the penalties of the law.'

This dictum appears to suggest that the judgment might have been different if the acts were not part of a pre-arranged plan. *Thabo Meli* was, indeed, distinguished on this ground in New Zealand (*Ramsay* [1967] NZLR 1005) and, at first, in South Africa (*Chiswibo* 1960 (2) SA 714). However, the Court of Appeal in England has followed *Thabo Meli*, in two cases where there was no antecedent plan. In *Church* [1965] 2 All ER 72, D got into a fight with a woman and knocked her unconscious. After trying unsuccessfully for 30 minutes to wake her, he concluded she was dead, panicked and threw her body into a nearby river. V drowned. The jury convicted D of manslaughter, after a direction that they could do so 'if they regarded [D]'s behaviour from the moment he first struck her to the moment when he threw her into the river as a series of acts designed to cause death or GBH'. D's conviction was upheld. A more recent case is *Le Brun* [1991] 4 All ER 673, where the Court of Appeal dismissed an appeal based on the significant time lapse that had occurred between the original assault (when D had *mens rea*) and V's eventual death (when he did not). Lord Lane CJ said that:

> J 'Where the unlawful application of force and the eventual act causing death are parts of the same sequence of events, the same transaction, the fact that there is an appreciable interval of time between the two does not serve to exonerate [D] from liability. That is certainly so where [D's] subsequent actions which caused death, after the initial unlawful blow, are designed to conceal his commission of the original unlawful assault.'

CASE EXAMPLE

Le Brun [1991] 4 All ER 673

D had a row with his wife as they made their way home late one night. Eventually he punched her on the chin and knocked her unconscious. While attempting to drag away what he thought was her dead body he dropped her, so that she hit her head on the kerb and died. The jury was told that they could convict of murder or manslaughter (depending on the mental element present when the punch was thrown), if D accidentally dropped V while (i) attempting to move her against her wishes and/or (ii) attempting to dispose of her 'body' or otherwise cover up the assault. He was convicted of manslaughter. The Court of Appeal upheld the conviction.

ACTIVITY

Consider the following scenario (described by Lord Bridge in *Moloney*). Does the terrorist have *mens rea* for murder and, if so, is it direct or oblique intent?

- D, a terrorist, plants a time bomb in a public building and gives timely warning to enable the public to be evacuated. D knows that, following evacuation, it is virtually certain that a bomb squad will attempt to defuse the bomb. In the event the bomb explodes, killing the bomb disposal expert.

Further reading

Duff, R A, 'The Obscure Intentions of the House of Lords' [1986] Crim LR 771.

Goff, Lord, 'The Mental Element in the Crime of Murder' (1988) 104 LQR 30.

Horder, J, 'Transferred Malice and the Remoteness of Unexpected Outcomes from Intentions' (2006) Crim LR 383.

Lacey, N, 'A Clear Concept of Intention: Elusive or Illusory?' (1993) 56 MLR 621.

Norrie, A, 'After Woollin' [1999] Crim LR 532.

Pedain, A, 'Intention and the Terrorist Example' [2003] Crim LR 579.

Simester, A P, 'Murder, Mens Rea and the House of Lords – Again' (1999) 115 LQR 17.

Sullivan, G R, 'Contemporaneity of Actus Reus and Mens Rea' (1993) 52 CLJ 487.

Williams, G, 'Oblique Intention' (1987) 46 CLJ 417.

Williams, G, 'The Mens Rea for Murder: Leave it Alone' (1989) 105 LQR 387.

Wilson, W, 'Doctrinal Rationality after Woollin' (1999) 62 MLR 448.

UNLOCKING
CRIMINAL
LAW

chapter
4 STRICT LIABILITY ■

AIMS AND OBJECTIVES □□□

After reading this chapter you should be able to:

■ Understand the basic concept of strict liability in criminal law

■ Understand the tests the courts use to decide whether an offence is one of strict liability

■ Be able to apply the tests to factual situations to determine the existence of a strict liability

■ Understand the role of policy in the creation of strict liability offences

■ Analyse critically the concept of strict liability

The previous chapter explained the different types of *mens rea*. This chapter considers those offences where *mens rea* is not required in respect of at least one aspect of the *actus reus*. Such offences are known as strict liability offences. The 'modern' type of strict liability offences was first created in the mid-nineteenth century. The first known case on strict liability is thought to be *Woodrow* (1846) 15 M & W 404. In that case the defendant was convicted of having in his possession adulterated tobacco, even though he did not know that it was adulterated. The judge, Parke B, ruled that he was guilty even if it needed a 'nice chemical analysis' to discover that the tobacco was adulterated.

The concept of strict liability appears to contradict the basis of criminal law. Normally criminal law is thought to be based on the culpability of the accused. In strict liability offences there may be no blameworthiness on the part of the defendant. The defendant, as in *Woodrow*, is guilty simply because he has done a prohibited act.

A more modern example demonstrating this is *Pharmaceutical Society of Great Britain v Storkwain Ltd* [1986] 2 All ER 635.

CASE EXAMPLE

Pharmaceutical Society of Great Britain v Storkwain Ltd [1986] 2 All ER 635

This case involved s 58(2) of the Medicines Act 1968, which provides that no person shall supply specified medicinal products except in accordance with a prescription given

82

by an appropriate medical practitioner. D had supplied drugs on prescriptions which were later found to be forged. There was no finding that D had acted dishonestly, improperly or even negligently. The forgery was sufficient to deceive the pharmacists. Despite this the House of Lords held that the Divisional Court was right to direct the magistrates to convict D. The pharmacists had supplied the drugs without a genuine prescription and this was enough to make them guilty of the offence.

For nearly all strict liability offences it must be proved that the defendant did the relevant *actus reus*. In *Woodrow* this meant proving that he was in possession of the adulterated tobacco. For *Storkwain* this meant proving that they had supplied specified medicinal products not in accordance with a prescription given by an appropriate medical practitioner. In these cases it also had to be proved that the doing of the *actus reus* was voluntary. However, there are a few rare cases where the defendant has been found guilty even though they did not do the *actus reus* voluntarily. These are known as crimes of absolute liability.

4.1 Absolute liability

Absolute liability means that no *mens rea* at all is required for the offence. They involve status offences; that is, offences where the *actus reus* is a state of affairs. The defendant is liable because they have 'been found' in a certain situation. Such offences are very rare. To be an absolute liability offence the following conditions must apply:

*   the offence does not require any *mens rea* and
*   there is no need to prove that the defendant's *actus reus* was voluntary.

The following two cases demonstrate this. The first is *Larsonneur* (1933) 24 Cr App R 74.

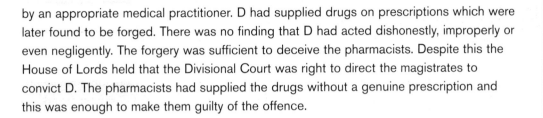

CASE EXAMPLE

Larsonneur (1933) 24 Cr App R 74

The defendant, who was an alien, had been ordered to leave the United Kingdom. She decided to go to Eire, but the Irish police deported her and took her in police custody back to the UK, where she was put in a cell in Holyhead police station. She did not want to return to the UK. She had no *mens rea*; her act in returning was not voluntary. Despite this she was found guilty under the Aliens Order 1920 of 'being an alien to whom leave to land in the United Kingdom has been refused' was 'found in the United Kingdom'.

The other case is *Winzar v Chief Constable of Kent, The Times*, 28th March, 1983; Co/1111/82 (Lexis), QBD.

CASE EXAMPLE

Winzar v Chief Constable of Kent, The Times, 28th March 1983

D was taken to hospital on a stretcher, but when he was examined by doctors they found that he was not ill but was drunk. D was told to leave the hospital, but was later found slumped on a seat in a corridor. The police were called and they took D to the roadway outside the hospital. They formed the opinion he was drunk so they put him in the police car, drove him to the police station and charged him with being found drunk in a highway contrary to s 12 of the Licensing Act 1872. The Divisional Court upheld his conviction.

As in *Larsonneur*, the defendant had not acted voluntarily. He had been taken to the highway by the police. In the Divisional Court Goff LJ justified the conviction, pointing out:

> '[L]ooking at the purpose of this particular offence, it is designed . . . to deal with the nuisance which can be caused by persons who are drunk in a public place. This kind of offence is caused quite simply when a person is found drunk in a public place or highway. . . . [A]n example . . . illustrates how sensible that conclusion is. Suppose a person was found drunk in a restaurant and was asked to leave. If he was asked to leave, he would walk out of the door of the restaurant and would be in a public place or in a highway of his own volition. He would be there of his own volition because he had responded to a request. However, if a man in a restaurant made a thorough nuisance of himself, was asked to leave, objected and was ejected, in those circumstances he would not be in a public place of his own volition because he would have been put there. . . . It would be nonsense if one were to say that the man who responded to the plea to leave could be said to be found drunk in a public place or in a highway, whereas the man who had been compelled to leave could not.
>
> This leads me to the conclusion that a person is "found to be drunk or in a public place or in a highway", within the meaning of those words as used in the section, when he is perceived to be drunk in a public place. It is enough for the commission of the offence if (1) a person is in a public place or a highway, (2) he is drunk, and (3) in those circumstances he is perceived to be there and to be drunk.'

It is not known how Winzar came to be taken to the hospital on a stretcher, but commentators on this case point out that there may an element of fault in Winzar's conduct. He had become drunk, and in order to have been taken to hospital must have either been in a public place when the ambulance collected him and took him to hospital, or he must have summoned medical assistance when he was not ill but only drunk.

ACTIVITY

Discuss whether the law should impose liability where there is no *mens rea* and no
voluntary act of the defendant.

4.2 Strict liability

For all offences there is a presumption that *mens rea* is required. The courts will always start with
this presumption, but if they decide that the offence does not require *mens rea* for at least part of
the *actus reus*, then the offence is one of strict liability. This idea of not requiring *mens rea* for part
of the offence is illustrated by two cases, *Prince* (1875) LR 2 CCR 154 and *Hibbert* (1869) LR 1
CCR 184. In both these cases the charge against the defendant was that he had taken an
unmarried girl under the age of 16 out of the possession of her father against his will, contrary to
s 55 of the Offences Against the Person Act 1861.

Prince knew that the girl he took was in the possession of her father but believed, on reasonable
grounds, that she was aged 18. He was convicted, as he had the intention to remove the girl from
the possession of her father. *Mens rea* was required for this part of the *actus reus* and he had the
necessary intention. However, the court held that knowledge of her age was not required. On this
aspect of the offence there was strict liability. In *Hibbert* the defendant met a girl aged 14 on the
street. He took her to another place where they had sexual intercourse. He was acquitted of the
offence as it was not proved that he knew the girl was in the custody of her father. Even though the
age aspect of the offence was one of strict liability, *mens rea* was required for the removal aspect
and, in this case, the necessary intention was not proved.

As already stated, the *actus reus* must be proved
and the defendant's conduct in doing the *actus
reus* must be voluntary. However, a defendant can
be convicted if his voluntary act inadvertently
caused a prohibited consequence. This is so even
though the defendant was totally blameless in
respect of the consequence, as was seen in *Callow
v Tillstone* (1900) 83 LT 411. A butcher asked a
vet to examine a carcass to see if it was fit for
human consumption. The vet assured him that it
was all right to eat, and so the butcher offered it
for sale. In fact it was unfit and the butcher was
convicted of the offence of exposing unsound
meat for sale. It was a strict liability offence and,
even though the butcher had taken reasonable
care not to commit the offence, he was still guilty.

4.2.1 No due diligence defence

For some offences the statute provides a defence of 'due diligence'. In other words the defendant will not be liable if he can adduce evidence that he did all that was within his power not to commit the offence. There does not seem, however, to be any sensible pattern for when Parliament decides to include a due diligence defence and when it does not. It can be argued that such a defence should always be available for strict liability offences. If it was, then the butcher in the above case would not have been guilty. By asking a vet to check the meat he had clearly done all that he could not to commit the offence.

Another example where the defendants took all reasonable steps to prevent the offence but were still guilty, as there was no due diligence defence available, is *Harrow LBC v Shah and Shah* [1999] 3 All ER 302.

CASE EXAMPLE

Harrow LBC v Shah and Shah [1999] 3 All ER 302

The defendants owned a newsagent's business where lottery tickets were sold. They had told their staff not to sell tickets to anyone under 16 years old. They also told their staff that if there was any doubt about a customer's age, the staff should ask for proof of age, and if still in doubt should refer the matter to the defendants. In addition there were clear notices up in the shop about the rules and staff were frequently reminded that they must not sell lottery tickets to underage customers. One of their staff sold a lottery ticket to a 13-year-old boy without asking for proof of age. The salesman mistakenly believed the boy was over 16 years old. D1 was in a back room of the premises at the time: D2 was not on the premises.

D1 and D2 were charged with selling a lottery ticket to a person under 16, contrary to s 13(1)(c) of the National Lottery etc Act 1993 and the relevant Regulations. Section 13(1)(c) provides that 'Any other person who was a party to the contravention shall be guilty of an offence'. This subsection does not have any provision for a due diligence defence, although s 13(1)(a), which makes the promoter of the lottery guilty, does contain a due diligence defence. Both these offences carry the same maximum sentence (two years' imprisonment, a fine or both) for conviction after trial on indictment. The magistrates dismissed the charges. The prosecution appealed by way of case stated to the Queen's Bench Divisional Court.

The Divisional Court held the offence to be one of strict liability. They allowed the appeal and remitted the case to the magistrates to continue the hearing. The Divisional Court held that the offence did not require any *mens rea*. The act of selling the ticket to someone who was actually under 16 was enough to make the defendants guilty, even though they had done their best to prevent this happening in their shop.

4.2.2 No defence of mistake

Another feature of strict liability offences is that the defence of mistake is not available. This is important as, if the defence of mistake is available the defendant will be acquitted when he made an honest mistake. Two cases which illustrate the difference in liability are *Cundy v Le Cocq* (1884) 13 QBD 207 and *Sherras v De Rutzen* [1895] 1 QB 918. Both of these involve contraventions of the Licensing Act 1872.

In *Cundy* the defendant was charged with selling intoxicating liquor to a drunken person, contrary to s 13 of the Act. This section enacts:

'13 If any licensed person permits drunkenness or any violent quarrelsome or riotous conduct to take place on his premises, or sells any intoxicating liquor to any drunken person, he shall be liable to a penalty . . . '

The magistrate trying the case found as a fact that the defendant and his employees had not noticed that the person was drunk. The magistrate also found that while the person was on the licensed premises he had been 'quiet in his demeanour and had done nothing to indicate insobriety; and that there were no apparent indications of intoxication'. However, the magistrate held that the offence was complete on proof that a sale had taken place and that the person served was drunk and convicted the defendant. The defendant appealed against this but the Divisional Court upheld the conviction. Stephen J said:

> **J** 'I am of the opinion that the words of the section amount to an absolute prohibition of the sale of liquor to a drunken person, and that the existence of a bona fide mistake as to the condition of the person served is not an answer to the charge, but is a matter only for mitigation of the penalties that may be imposed.'

CASE EXAMPLE

Sherras v De Rutzen [1895] 1 QB 918

In *Sherras* the defendant was convicted by a magistrate of an offence under s 16(2) of the Licensing Act 1872. This section makes it an offence for a licensed person to 'supply any liquor or refreshment' to any constable on duty. There were no words in the section requiring the defendant to have knowledge that a constable was off duty. The facts were that local police when on duty wore an armband on their uniform. An on-duty police officer removed his armband before entering the defendant's public house. He was served by the defendant's daughter in the presence of the defendant. Neither the defendant or his daughter made any enquiry as to whether the policeman was on duty. The defendant thought that the constable was off duty because he was not wearing his armband. The Divisional Court quashed the conviction. They held that the offence was not one of strict liability and accordingly a genuine mistake provided the defendant with a defence.

When giving judgment in the case Day J stated:

J 'This police constable comes into the appellant's house without his armlet, and with every appearance of being off duty. The house was in the immediate neighbourhood of the police station, and the appellant believed, and had very natural grounds for believing, that the constable was off duty. In that belief he accordingly served him with liquor. As a matter of fact, the constable was on duty; but does that fact make the innocent act of the appellant an offence? I do not think it does. He had no intention to do a wrongful act; he acted in the bona fide belief that the constable was off duty. It seems to me that the contention that he committed an offence is utterly erroneous.'

It is difficult to reconcile this decision with the decision in *Cundy*. In both cases the sections in the Licensing Act 1872 were expressed in similar words. In *Cundy* the offence was 'sells any intoxicating liquor to any drunken person', while in *Sherras* the offence was 'supplies any liquor . . . to any constable on duty'. In each case the publican made a genuine mistake. Day J justified his decision in *Sherras* by pointing to the fact that although s 16(2) did not include the word 'knowingly', s 16(1) did, for the offence of 'knowingly harbours or knowingly suffers to remain on his premises any constable during any part of the time appointed for such constable being on duty'. Day J held this only had the effect of shifting the burden of proof. For s 16(1) the prosecution had to prove that the defendant knew the constable was on duty, while for s 16(2) the prosecution did not have to prove knowledge, but it was open to the defendant to prove that he did not know.

The other judge in the case of *Sherras*, Wright J, pointed out that if the offence was to be made one of strict liability then there was nothing the publican could do to prevent the commission of the crime. No care on the part of the publican could save him from a conviction under s 16(2), since it would be as easy for the constable to deny that he was on duty when asked as to remove his armlet before entering the public house. It is more possible to reconcile the two cases on this basis as in most cases the fact of a person being drunk would be an observable fact, so the publican should be put on alert and could avoid committing the offence.

4.2.3 Summary of strict liability

So where an offence is held to be one of strict liability the following points apply:

- the defendant must be proved to have done the *actus reus*
- this must be a voluntary act on his part
- there is no need to prove *mens rea* for at least part of the *actus reus*
- no due diligence defence will be available
- the defence of mistake is not available.

These factors are well-established. The problem lies in deciding which offences are ones of strict liability. For this the courts will start with presuming that *mens rea* should apply. This is so for both common law and statutory offences.

4.3 Common law strict liability offences

Nearly all strict liability offences have been created by statute. Strict liability is very rare in common law offences. Only four common law offences have been held to be ones of strict liability. These are:

- public nuisance
- criminal libel
- blasphemous libel
- criminal contempt of court.

Public nuisance and criminal libel probably do not require *mens rea*, but there are no modern cases. There has been a relatively recent case on blasphemous libel which confirmed that it is a strict liability offence. This was *Lemon and Whitehouse v Gay News* [1979] 1 All ER 898, where a poem had been published in *Gay News* describing homosexual acts done to the body of Christ after his crucifixion and also describing his alleged homosexual practices during his lifetime. The editor and publishers were convicted of blasphemy. On their appeal to the House of Lords, the Law Lords held that it was not necessary to prove that the defendants intended to blaspheme. Lord Russell said:

> J
>
> 'Why then should the House, faced with a deliberate publication of that which a jury with every justification has held to be a blasphemous libel, consider that it should be for the prosecution to prove, presumably beyond reasonable doubt, that the accused recognised and intended it to be such. . . . The reason why the law considers that the publication of a blasphemous libel is an offence is that the law considers that such publications should not take place. And if it takes place, and the publication is deliberate, I see no justification for holding that there is no offence when the publisher is incapable, for some reason particular to himself, of agreeing with a jury on the true nature of the publication.'

Criminal contempt of court was a strict liability offence at common law. It is now a statutory offence and Parliament has continued it as a strict liability offence.

4.4 Statutory strict liability offences

The surprising fact is that about half of all statutory offences are strict liability. This amounts to over 3,500 offences. Most strict liability offences are regulatory in nature. This may involve such matters as regulating the sale of food and alcohol and gaming tickets, the prevention of pollution and the safe use of vehicles.

In order to decide whether an offence is one of strict liability, the courts start by assuming that *mens rea* is required, but they are prepared to interpret the offence as one of strict liability if Parliament has expressly or by implication indicated this in the relevant statute. The judges often have difficulty in deciding whether an offence is one of strict liability or not. The first rule is that where an Act of Parliament includes words indicating *mens rea* (eg 'knowingly', 'intentionally', 'maliciously' or 'permitting'), the offence requires *mens rea* and is not one of strict liability. However, if an Act of Parliament makes it clear that *mens rea* is not required, the offence will be one of strict liability. An example of this is the Contempt of Court Act 1981.

However, in many instances a section in an Act of Parliament is silent about the need for *mens rea*. Parliament is criticised for this. If they made clear in all sections which create a criminal offence whether *mens rea* was required or not, then there would be no problem. As it is, where there are no express words indicating *mens rea* or strict liability, the courts have to decide which offences are ones of strict liability.

4.4.1 The presumption of *mens rea*

Where an Act of Parliament does not include any words indicating *mens rea*, the judges will start by presuming that all criminal offences require *mens rea*. This was made clear in the case of *Sweet v Parsley* [1969] 1 All ER 347.

CASE EXAMPLE

Sweet v Parsley [1969] 1 All ER 347

D rented a farmhouse and let it out to students. The police found cannabis at the farmhouse and the defendant was charged with 'being concerned in the management of premises used for the purpose of smoking cannabis resin'. The defendant did not know that cannabis was being smoked there. It was decided that she was not guilty as the court presumed that the offence required *mens rea*.

The key part of the judgment was when Lord Reid said:

J '. . . there has for centuries been a presumption that Parliament did not intend to make criminals of persons who were in no way blameworthy in what they did. That means that, whenever a section is silent as to *mens rea*, there is a presumption that, in order to give effect to the will of Parliament, we must read in words appropriate to require *mens rea* . . . it is firmly established by a host of authorities that *mens rea* is an ingredient of every offence unless some reason can be found for holding that it is not necessary.'

This principle has been affirmed by the House of Lords in *B (a minor) v DPP* [2000] 1 All ER 833 where the House of Lords reviewed the law on strict liability. The Law Lords quoted with approval what Lord Reid had said in *Sweet v Parsley* (see section 4.4.8 for full details of *B v DPP*).

Although the courts start with the presumption that *mens rea* is required, they look at a variety of points to decide whether the presumption should stand or if it can be displaced and the offence made one of strict liability.

4.4.2 The *Gammon* tests

In *Gammon (Hong Kong) Ltd v Attorney-General of Hong Kong* [1984] 2 All ER 503 the appellants had been charged with deviating from building work in a material way from the approved plan, contrary to the Hong Kong Building Ordinances. It was necessary to decide if it had to be proved that they knew that their deviation was material or whether the offence was one of strict liability on this point. The Privy Council started with the presumption that *mens rea* is required before a person can be held guilty of a criminal offence, but went on to give four others factors to be considered. These were stated by Lord Scarman to be that:

- The presumption in favour of *mens rea* being required before D can be convicted applies to statutory offences and can be displaced only if this is clearly or by necessary implication the effect of the statute.

- The presumption is particularly strong where the offence is 'truly criminal' in character.

- The only situation in which the presumption can be displaced is where the statute is concerned with an issue of social concern; public safety is such an issue.

- Even where the statute is concerned with such an issue, the presumption of *mens rea* stands unless it can be shown that the creation of strict liability will be effective to promote the objects of the statute by encouraging greater vigilance to prevent the commission of the prohibited act.

4.4.3 Looking at the wording of an Act

As already stated, where words indicating *mens rea* are used, the offence is not one of strict liability. If the particular section is silent on the point then the courts will look at other sections in the Act. Where the particular offence has no words of intention, but other sections in the Act do, then it is likely that this offence is a strict liability offence. In *Pharmaceutical Society of Great Britain v*

Storkwain the relevant section, s 58(2) of the Medicines Act 1968, was silent on *mens rea*. The court looked at other sections in the Act and decided that, as there were express provisions for *mens rea* in other sections, Parliament had intended s 58(2) to be one of strict liability.

However, the fact that other sections specifically require *mens rea* does not mean that the courts will automatically make the offence without express words of *mens* rea one of strict liability. In *Sherras*, even though s 16(1) of the Licensing Act 1872 had express words requiring knowledge, it was held that *mens rea* was still required for s 16(2), which did not include the word 'knowingly'. This point was reinforced in *Sweet*, when Lord Reid stated:

> **J** 'It is also firmly established that the fact that other sections of the Act expressly require *mens rea*, for example because they contain the word "knowingly", is not of itself sufficient to justify a decision that a section which is silent as to *mens rea* creates an absolute offence. In the absence of a clear intention in the Act that an offence is intended to be an absolute offence, it is necessary to go outside the Act and examine all relevant circumstances in order to establish that this must have been the intention of Parliament.'

Where other sections allow for a defence of no negligence but another section does not, then this is another possible indicator from within the statute that the offence is meant to be one of strict liability. In *Harrow LBC v Shah and Shah* the defendants were charged under s 13(1)(c) of the National Lottery etc Act 1993. The whole of s 13 reads:

'13(1) If any requirement or restriction imposed by regulations made under section 12 is contravened in relation to the promotion of a lottery that forms part of the National Lottery,

(a) the promoter of the lottery shall be guilty of an offence, except if the contravention occurred without the consent or connivance of the promoter and the promoter exercised all due diligence to prevent such a contravention,

(b) any director, manager, secretary or other similar officer of the promoter, or any person purporting to act in such a capacity, shall be guilty of an offence if he consented to or connived at the contravention or if the contravention was attributable to any neglect on his part, and

(c) any other person who was a party to the contravention shall be guilty of an offence.

(2) A person guilty of an offence under this section shall be liable

(a) on summary conviction, to a fine not exceeding the statutory maximum;

(b) on conviction on indictment, to imprisonment not exceeding two years, to a fine or to both.'

The subsection under which the defendants were charged, (1)(c), contains no words indicating either that *mens rea* is required or that it is not, nor does it contain any provision for a defence of due diligence. However, subs (1)(a) clearly allows a defence of due diligence. In addition it contains an element of *mens rea* as it provides for the defendant be not guilty if the contravention was not done with his consent or connivance. Subsection (1)(b) clearly requires *mens rea*, as it only makes the accused guilty if he 'consented to or connived at the contravention or if the contravention was attributable to any neglect on his part'. The inclusion of a due diligence defence in part of s 13 but not in the section under which the defendants were charged was an important point in the Divisional Court coming to the decision that s 13(1)(c) was an offence of strict liability. Mitchell J said:

> **J** 'Section 13 has two important features. First, whereas in subsection (1) paragraphs (a) and (b) the liability of the promoter and the promoter's directors, managers and the like is tempered by the provision of a statutory defence. In subsection (1)(c) the liability of "any other person" who was a party to the contravention of the regulations is not expressed to be subject to a statutory defence.'

In fact this statement by Mitchell J that both in both paragraphs (1)(a) and (1)(b) liability is tempered by the provision of a statutory defence is not accurate. Only s 13(1)(a) has such a provision. But despite this, the case illustrates how the courts will look at the wording of other relevant provisions in the statute in deciding whether or not to impose strict liability.

4.4.4 Quasi-criminal offences

In *Gammon* the Privy Council stated that the presumption that *mens rea* is required is particularly strong where the offence is 'truly criminal' in character. Offences which are regulatory in nature are not thought of as being truly criminal matters and are, therefore, more likely to be interpreted as being of strict liability. This idea of offences which are 'not criminal in any real sense, but are acts which in the public interest are prohibited under penalty' was a category mentioned by Wright J in *Sherras* as being an exception to the presumption of *mens rea* where the courts would hold that the offence was one of strict liability. Regulatory offences are usual classed as being 'not truly criminal'. In *Wings Ltd v Ellis* [1984] 3 All ER 584 the House of Lords were considering the Trade Descriptions Act 1968, which creates offences aimed at consumer protection. Lord Scarman pointed out that this Act was 'not a truly criminal statute. Its purpose is not the enforcement of the criminal law but the maintenance of trading standards'.

Regulatory offences are also referred to as 'quasi crimes'. They affect large areas of everyday life. They include offences such as breaches of regulations in a variety of fields, such as:

- selling food, as in *Callow*
- the selling of alcohol, as in *Cundy*

- building regulations, as occurred in *Gammon*

- sales of lottery tickets to an under-age child, as in *Harrow LBC*

- regulations prevent pollution from being caused, as in *Alphacell Ltd v Woodward* [1972] 2 All ER 475.

In the *Alphacell* case the company was charged with causing polluted matter to enter a river, contrary to s 2(1)(a) of the Rivers (Prevention of Pollution) Act 1951, when pumps which it had installed failed, and polluted effluent overflowed into a river. There was no evidence either that the company knew of the pollution or that it had been negligent. The offence was held by the House of Lords to be one of strict liability and the company found guilty. Lord Salmon stated:

> **J** 'It is of the utmost public importance that rivers should not be polluted. The risk of pollution . . . is very great. The offences created by the Act of 1951 seem to me to be prototypes of offences which are "not criminal in any real sense, but are acts which in the public interest are prohibited under penalty". . . . I can see no valid reason for reading the word "intentionally", "knowingly" or "negligently" into section 2(1)(a) . . . this may be regarded as a not unfair hazard of carrying on a business which may cause pollution on the banks of a river.'

Penalty of imprisonment

Where an offence carries a penalty of imprisonment it is more likely to be considered 'truly criminal' and so less likely to be interpreted as an offence of strict liability. In *B v DPP* the offence was the commission of gross indecency with or towards a child under 14 which, at the time the offence was committed, carried a maximum penalty of two years' imprisonment. Lord Nicholls pointed out that this was a serious offence and this was important since 'the more serious the offence, the greater was the weight to be attached to the presumption [of *mens rea*], because the more severe was the punishment and the graver the stigma that accompanied a conviction'.

However, some offences carrying imprisonment have been made strict liability offences. In *Gammon* the offence carried a penalty of HK$250,000 and imprisonment for three years. The Privy Council admitted that this penalty was a 'formidable argument' against strict liability, but went on to hold that there was nothing inconsistent with the purpose of the Ordinance in imposing severe penalties for offences of strict liability. It said 'the legislature could reasonably have intended severity to be a significant deterrent, bearing in mind the risks to public safety arising from some contraventions of the ordinance'. Similarly, in *Storkwain* the offence carried a maximum sentence of two years' imprisonment, but this fact did not persuade the House of Lords not to impose strict liability for the offence.

In both these cases the defendant was a corporation, so there was no question of a penalty of imprisonment actually being used. However, in *Howells* [1977] QB 614 the defendant was charged with possession of a firearm without a firearm certificate, contrary to s 1(1)(a) of the Firearms Act 1968. The maximum penalty for this offence was five years' imprisonment. Despite this the Court of Appeal held that the offence was one of strict liability. It thought that the wording of the Act and the danger to the public from the unauthorised possession of firearms outweighed the fact of the severity of the maximum sentence in deciding whether to impose strict liability.

It appears unjust that an individual should be liable to imprisonment even though the offence does not require proof of some fault on the behalf of the defendant. Some writers take the view that it is wrong to impose *any* penalty on a person where they are not blameworthy. Peter Brett, writing in 1963, put this view forward:

> 'Let us now consider what ought to be the future of the doctrine of strict liability. There are those who believe that there is no great objection to it, and even that it serves a useful and proper social purpose. Sayre's general conclusion ("Public Welfare Offences", 33 Col L Rev 55 (1933)) was that the doctrine was applicable only to the minor public welfare offences, despite his recognition of its applicability in some other fields, which he attempted to distinguish on special grounds. In his view there is no objection to applying strict liability so long as only a light penalty is involved; but it ought not to be applied to "true crimes". This seems rather like saying that it is all right to be unjust so long as you are not too unjust. My own position is that any doctrine which permits the infliction of punishment on a morally innocent man is reprehensible.'

> P Brett, *An Inquiry into Criminal Guilt* (Sweet & Maxwell, 1963), p 114

4.4.5 Strict liability and human rights

Where a defendant is at risk of being sentenced to imprisonment, the question of whether this is a breach of human rights is also raised. In Canada, s 7 of their Charter of Human Rights states that 'everyone has the right to life, liberty and security of the person and the right not to be deprived thereof except in accordance with the fundamental principles of justice'. In 1986 the Supreme Court of Canada held that the fundamental principles of justice precluded strict liability where the offence was one which carried a penalty of imprisonment. They said that the 'combination of imprisonment and absolute liability violates s 7 irrespective of the nature of the offence'.

In England and Wales the Human Rights Act 1998 incorporated the European Convention on Human Rights into our law from October 2000. The right to liberty is contained in art 5 of the Convention, and the right to a fair trial in art 6. These are not as broadly worded as the Canadian Charter of Human Rights. They state:

'5(1) Everyone has the right to liberty and security of person. No one shall be deprived of his liberty save as in the following cases and in accordance with a procedure prescribed by law:

(a) the lawful detention of a person after conviction by a competent court . . .

6(2) Everyone charged with a criminal offence shall be presumed innocent until proved guilty according to law.'

Unlike the Canadian Charter, this wording does not make any reference to 'fundamental principles of justice'. Instead, art 5 focuses on the procedure being 'prescribed by law' and provided the procedure is lawful and carried out by a competent court then there is no breach of the Convention. With art 6 the focus is on a fair trial, though art 6.2 maintains the need for the prosecution to prove guilt. However, guilt can be proved by proving that the defendant did the prohibited act.

In *K* [2001] 3 All ER 897 the Court of Appeal had to consider whether a genuine mistake was a defence to s 14 of the Sexual Offences Act 1956. It held that the offence was one of strict liability, but that this was not incompatible with art 6. The Court of Appeal's ruling that the offence was one of strict liability was overruled by the House of Lords (see section 4.4.6), so the human rights implication was not a necessary part of the House of Lords' judgment. The Court of Appeal relied on a decision of the European Court of Human Rights in *Salabiaku v France* (1988) 13 EHRR 379, in which it had been said:

> **J** 'Article 6(2) does not therefore regard the presumptions of fact or of law provided for in the criminal law with indifference. It requires states to confine them within reasonable limits which take into account the importance of what is at stake and maintain the rights of the defence.'

The House of Lords considered the effect of art 6 in *DPP, ex parte Kebilene* [1999] 4 All ER 801 and Lord Hope said of the provisions of the Convention: 'As a matter of general principle therefore a fair balance must be struck between the demands of the general interest of the community and the protection of the fundamental rights of the individual.'

The question of whether a strict liability offence may be a breach of the right to a fair trial was considered again in *G* [2006] EWCA Crim 821.

CASE EXAMPLE

G [2006] EWCA Crim 821

D was a boy aged 15 who had had sexual intercourse with a girl aged 12. He was charged under s 5 of the Sexual Offences Act 2003 (SOA) with rape of a child under 13. The girl was actually 12, but D believed on reasonable grounds that she was 15. She had told him so on an earlier occasion. D was held to be guilty as the offence is one of strict liability and may be committed irrespective of:

- consent
- reasonable belief in consent
- a reasonable belief as to age.

The Court of Appeal held that the fact that s 5 was an offence of strict liability did not breach human rights.

All this leads to the conclusion that, provided the state can show that the law is a fair balance, no challenge could be made to the imposition of strict liability for an imprisonable offence.

4.4.6 Issues of social concern

The type of crime and whether it is 'truly criminal' is linked to another condition laid down by the case of *Gammon*; that is the question of whether the crime involves an issue of social concern. The Privy Council ruled that the only situation in which the presumption of *mens rea* can be displaced is where the statute is concerned with an issue of social concern. This echoed what had been said in *Sweet*, when Lord Diplock stated:

J

'Where the subject-matter of a statute is the regulation of a particular activity involving potential danger to public health, safety or morals, in which citizens have a choice whether they participate or not, the court may feel driven to infer an intention of Parliament to impose, by penal sanctions, a higher duty of care on those who choose to participate and to place on them an obligation to take whatever measure may be necessary to prevent the prohibited act, without regard to those considerations of cost or business practicability which play a part in the determination of what would be required of them to fulfil the ordinary common law duty of care.'

This allows strict liability to be justified in a wide range of offences as issues of social concern can be seen to cover any activity which is a 'potential danger to public health, safety or morals'. Regulations covering health and safety matters in relation to food, drink, pollution, building and road use are obviously within the range, but other issues such as possession of guns are also regarded as matters of public safety. It is recognised that even sexual offences may come within its ambit where the law is aimed at protecting children or other vulnerable people.

Even transmitting an unlicensed broadcast has been held to be a matter of social concern. This was in *Blake* [1997] 1 All ER 963, where the defendant was a disc jockey who was convicted of using a station for wireless telegraphy without a licence, contrary to s 1(1) of the Wireless Telegraphy Act 1949. His defence was that he believed he was making a demonstration tape and did not know he was transmitting. He was convicted on the basis that the offence was one of strict liability. He appealed to the Court of Appeal, but his appeal was dismissed. Hirst J said:

> **J** '[S]ince throughout the history of s 1(1), an offender has potentially been subject to a term of imprisonment, the offence is "truly criminal" in character, and . . . the presumption in favour of *mens rea* is particularly strong. However, it seems to us manifest that the purpose behind making the unlicensed transmissions a serious criminal offence must have been one of social concern in the interests of public safety . . . since undoubtedly the emergency services and air traffic controllers were using radio communications in 1949, albeit in a much more rudimentary form than nowadays. . . . Clearly, interference with transmissions by these vital public services poses a grave risk to wide sections of the public . . . [T]he imposition of an absolute offence must surely encourage greater vigilance on the part of those establishing or using a station, or installing or using the apparatus, to avoid committing the offence, eg in the case of users by carefully establishing whether they are on air; it must also operate as a deterrent. . . . In these circumstances we are satisfied that s 1(1) does create an absolute offence.'

Key facts on the factors affecting strict liability

KEY FACTS

Law	Comment	Case
The presumption is that the offence has a *mens rea* requirement.	This is an important presumption at common law and also applies to statutory offences.	*Sweet v Parsley* (1969) *B v DPP* (2000)
The presumption can only be displaced if this is clearly or by necessary implication the effect of the statute.	This can occur if there are clear words stating that no *mens rea* is required. If the Act is silent on *mens rea*, then the courts will look at words in other relevant sections.	*Gammon (Hong Kong) Ltd v Att-Gen of Hong Kong* (1984) *Pharmaceutical Society v Storkwain* (1986): strict liability as other sections had express provision for *mens rea* *R v K* (2001): no strict liability as sections were not part of a 'coherent legislative scheme'
The presumption is particularly strong where the offence is 'truly criminal'.	The graver the offence the less likely strict liability will be imposed. Where the potential penalty is a long term of imprisonment, the offence is unlikely to be one of strict liability. Some imprisonable offences are strict liability.	*B v DPP* (2000) *Sweet v Parsley* (1969) *Howells* (1977)
The only time strict liability should be imposed is where the issue one of social concern.	These are issues where there is a potential danger to public health, safety or morals.	*Sweet v Parsley* (1969) *Blake* (1997): unauthorised radio transmission posed 'a grave risk'
The court should also be sure that strict liability will be effective in promoting the law.	If strict liability does not do this then it should not be imposed.	*Lim Chin Aik v The Queen* (1963)

4.4.7 Promoting enforcement of the law

In *Gammon,* the final point in considering whether strict liability should be imposed, even where the statute is concerned with an issue of social concern, was whether it would be effective to promote the objects of the statute by encouraging greater vigilance to prevent the commission of the prohibited act. If the imposition of strict liability will not make the law more effective, then there is no reason to make the offence one of strict liability.

In *Lim Chin Aik v The Queen* [1963] AC 160, the appellant had been convicted under s 6(2) of the Immigration Ordinance of Singapore of remaining (having entered) in Singapore when he had been prohibited from entering by an order made by the Minister under s 9 of the same Ordinance. The Ordinance was aimed at preventing illegal immigration. However, the appellant had no knowledge of the prohibition and there was no evidence that the authorities had even tried to bring it to his attention. The Privy Council thought that it was not enough to be sure that the statute dealt with a grave social evil in order to infer strict liability. It was also important to consider whether the imposition of strict liability would assist in the enforcement of the regulations. Lord Evershed said:

> **J** 'It is pertinent also to inquire whether putting the defendant under strict liability will assist in the enforcement of the regulations. That means there must be something he can do, directly or indirectly, by supervision or inspection, by improvement of his business methods or by exhorting those whom he may be expected to influence or control, which will promote the observance of the regulations. Unless this is so, there is no reason in penalising him, and it cannot be inferred that the legislature imposed strict liability merely in order to find a luckless victim . . .
>
> Where it can be shown that the imposition of strict liability would result in the prosecution and conviction of a class of persons whose conduct could not in any way affect the observance of the law, their Lordships consider that, even where the statute is dealing with a grave social evil, strict liability is not likely to be intended.'

ACTIVITY

Essay writing

Critically discuss the factors the courts take into account when considering whether an offence is one of strict liability or not.

4.4.8 Recent cases

In 2000 and 2001 the House of Lords considered the principles of strict liability in two important cases. These were *B v DPP* and *K*. In both they continued the trend, which started with *Sweet*, against the imposition of strict liability. In *B v DPP* the Lords reviewed the law on strict liability.

CASE EXAMPLE

B v DPP [2000] 1 All ER 833

B was a boy aged 15. He sat next to a 13-year-old girl on a bus and asked her to give him a 'shiner', meaning by that to have oral sex with him. He believed she was over the age of 14. He was charged with inciting a child under the age of 14 to commit an act of gross indecency. This is an offence under s 1(1) of the Indecency with Children Act 1960. This states: 'Any person who commits an act of gross indecency with or towards a child under 14 [subsequently raised to 16] or who incites a child under that age to such an act with him or another . . . is guilty of an offence'.

The question for the House of Lords was whether B's mistake about the girl's age gave him a defence to the charge. If the offence was one of strict liability then he could not use the defence of mistake. Lord Nicholls gave the leading judgment. He started by pointing out that the section says nothing about the mental element required for the offence. In particular, it says nothing about what the position should be if the person who commits or incites the act of gross indecency honestly but mistakenly believed that the child was 14 or over.

He then reviewed the major elements which have to be considered in deciding whether the offence is one of strict liability. These were:

- the presumption of *mens rea*
- the lack of words of intention
- whether that presumption was negatived by necessary implication
- the severity of the punishment
- the purpose of the section
- evidential problems
- effectiveness of strict liability.

What was said on each of these points will now be briefly examined.

Presumption of *mens rea*

Lord Nicholls said that the starting point was the presumption that *mens rea* was intended and he approved what Lord Reid had said in *Sweet* (see section 4.4.1), that it was firmly established that *mens rea* is an essential ingredient of every offence unless some reason can be found for holding that it is not necessary.

Lack of words of intention

The section had no words referring to the need for *mens rea*. Nor had Parliament expressly stated that there was no need for a mental element in the offence. This meant that the court had to consider whether the need for a mental element was negatived by necessary implication.

Necessary implication

Looking at the factors to be examined in considering whether Parliament's intention was to impose strict liability by 'necessary implication', Lord Nicholls pointed out that, in view of the presumption of *mens rea*, any necessary implication could only be satisfied by an implication that was 'compellingly clear'. He said that such an implication may be found in 'the language used, the nature of the offence, the mischief sought to be prevented and other circumstances that might assist in determining what intention was properly to be attributed to Parliament'. In this case he thought that the position was relatively straightforward. The section had created an entirely new offence which was set out in simple and straightforward language. A major feature was the penalty it attracted.

Severity of punishment

A conviction under s 1 originally (when the offence in the case had been committed) had a maximum penalty of two years' imprisonment. This had been increased to a maximum of 10 years' imprisonment. In addition, all offenders convicted of this offence, regardless of their age, were placed on the sex offenders' register and required to notify their movements to the police. Lord Nichols felt that these factors reinforced the application of the presumption of *mens rea*. The offence carried a severe penalty and also the stigma of being a sex offender.

Purpose of the section

Even though the purpose of s 1(1) of the 1960 Act was to protect children, this factor did not, of itself, lead to the conclusion that liability was intended to be strict so far as the age element was concerned.

Evidential problems

The fact that it might sometimes be difficult for the prosecution to prove that the defendant had not known that the child was under 14, or that the defendant had been recklessly indifferent about the child's age, was not enough to make the offence one of strict liability. Lord Nicholls quoted from an Australian case, *Thomas v R* (1937) 44 ALR 37 on this point:

> '[A] lack of confidence in the ability of a tribunal to estimate evidence of states of mind and the like can never be sufficient ground for excluding from inquiry the most fundamental element in a rational and humane code.'

Effectiveness of strict liability

On whether strict liability would promote the purpose of s 1(1) more effectively than if *mens rea* were required, Lord Nicholls simply pointed out that there was no general agreement that strict liability was necessary to the enforcement of the law protecting children in sexual matters. In fact the Draft Criminal Code proposed by the Law Commission in 1989 included a defence of belief that the child was over 16 on similar offences.

Effect of *Prince*

The final point considered was whether the decision in *Prince*, where it had been held that the defendant could not use a genuine belief that a girl was over 16 for an offence of removing her from her father's custody, should be followed. The prosecution submitted that the law had been settled since the case of *Prince* (1875) (ie that a mistaken belief about age was no defence) and that as the Sexual Offences Act 1956 had not been intended to change this, so the same was true of the 1960 Act. In addition, the prosecution argued that when Parliament intended belief as to age to be a defence, this was stated expressly. He cited as an example s 6(3) of the 1956 Act, where a belief that a girl was 16 or over was a defence to a defendant under 24 on a charge of unlawful sexual intercourse with a girl under 16.

Lord Nicholls rejected these arguments because:

- the reasoning in *Prince* has been subjected to sustained criticism
- the offences gathered into the Sexual Offences Act 1956 displayed no overall consistent pattern and therefore the compelling guidance that another statute would have to give to the present one under consideration was simply not there.

Conclusion

The Law Lords reached the conclusion that there was nothing to displace the common law presumption that *mens rea* was required. This is the modern approach which reinforces the need for *mens rea* and shows the courts' reluctance to declare an offence which is 'truly criminal' to be one of strict liability. However, it should be noted that the House of Lords did not specifically overrule the decision in *Prince* as it pointed out that the case concerned a different offence.

Commentators disagreed on the importance of this decision in *B v DPP*. Professor Sir John Smith, in a commentary on the case in [2000] Criminal Law Review 404, suggested it would have far-reaching

consequences, whereas the editors of *Archbold* thought that this was 'significantly overstating its significance because it is far from clear what it decides other than in relation to the particular offence'. John Beaumont also highlighted the fact that it did not necessarily lay down general principles:

> '[T]he case does not really make any progress to solve the general problem of when strict liability should be imposed. The various considerations that are said by the House to be relevant in this context amount to no more than a restatement of the principles set out in earlier cases, such as *Sweet v Parsley*. They suffer from the same defect as all such attempts, that it they leave the law in this area in an uncertain state.'

John Beaumont, 'Mistake and Strict Liability' (2000) New Law Journal 382 and 433

Law reform

Finally, the case also highlighted the need for reform of the law and a consistent approach by Parliament on whether offences required *mens rea*. Lord Hutton said it was to be regretted that Parliament had not taken account of the expert advice that it had received over the years from bodies such as the Law Commission and the Criminal Law Reform Committee regarding the need to state clearly in all criminal offences whether or not *mens rea* is required.

K

One year after *B v DPP* the use of strict liability offences was again considered by the House of Lords, in *K*. In this case it had to consider whether s 14(1) of the Sexual Offences Act 1956 was a strict liability offence. The defendant was a 26-year-old man who had taken part in consensual sexual activity with a 14-year-old girl. He honestly believed that she was aged 16 or over and the point in the case was whether this could be a defence to s 14(1). The whole section provides:

'14(1) It is an offence, subject to the exception mentioned in subsection (3) of the section, for a person to make an indecent assault on a woman.

(2) A girl under the age of 16 cannot in law give any consent which would prevent an act being an assault for the purposes of this section.

(3) Where a marriage is invalid under section two of the Age of Marriage Act 1929 (the wife being a girl under the age of 16), the invalidity does not make the husband guilty of any offence under this section by reason of her incapacity to consent while under that age, if he believes her to be his wife and has reasonable cause for the belief.

(4) A woman who is a defective cannot in law give any consent which would prevent an act being an assault for the purposes of this section, but a person is only to be treated as guilty of an indecent assault on a defective by reason of that incapacity to consent, if that person knew of had reason to suspect her to be a defective.'

As in *B v DPP*, there are no words at all referring to *mens rea* contained in subs (1). However, there is a difference, in that there are two situations in which a mistake as to a fact (of a valid marriage or of being a defective) can provide a defence. At the trial, a preliminary issue was raised as to whether the prosecution had to prove that at the time of the incident K did not honestly believe that the girl was 16 or over. The trial judge ruled that the prosecution did have to prove that the defendant had an absence of genuine belief on this point. The prosecution appealed against this ruling and the Court of Appeal allowed the appeal holding that an absence of belief did not have to be proved. The Court of Appeal certified the following point of law of general public importance for the consideration of the House of Lords:

> **J**
>
> **'a** Is a defendant entitled to be acquitted of the offence of indecent assault on a complainant under the age of 16 years, contrary to s 14(1) of the Sexual Offences Act 1956, if he may hold an honest belief that the complainant in question was aged 16 years or over?
>
> **b** If yes, must the belief be held on reasonable grounds?'

The House of Lords reversed the decision of the Court of Appeal and held that an honest belief was a defence to the charge. It considered the language of the section and concluded that they could not place any reliance on the structure of s 14. It said it was not part of a 'single coherent legislative scheme', but rather of a 'rag-bag nature'. In fact it had been a consolidation Act with offences being brought together from several earlier Acts. Lord Bingham pointed out that, within s 14, each subsection had its origins in different Acts:

- s 14(1) derived from s 52 of the Offences Against the Person Act 1861
- s 14(2) had its origins in the Criminal Law Amendment Act 1880 when the age was 13 and this had been changed by the Criminal Law Amendment Act 1922 to the age of 16
- s 14(3) had its origins in the Age of Marriage Act 1929
- s 14(4) derives from s 56(3) of the Mental Deficiency Act 1913.

It could not, therefore, be said from looking at the structure of the section that Parliament had intended ss 14(1) and 14(2) to impose strict liability in relation to a situation where the defendant had made an honest mistake about the girl's age. They relied on the fact that there was no express exclusion of the need to prove an absence of genuine belief on the part of the defendant as to the age of an under-age victim.

The Law Lords also thought that it was right to look at the Act involved in *B v DPP*, the Indecency with Children Act 1960, as the Lords in that case had been invited to treat the Acts as part of a single code. As absence of genuine belief as to the age of an under-age victim had to be proved against a defendant under s 1 of the 1960 Act, it would create a 'glaring anomaly' if the same rule was not to be applied to s 14 of the 1956 Act. There was also a persistent and

unacceptable anomaly within the 1956 Act, by which a defendant could plead the 'young man's defence' to a charge under s 6 of sexual intercourse with a girl under the age of 16, but could not rely on any similar argument in respect of a charge of indecent assault arising out of that sexual intercourse.

The Lords concluded that the presumption of *mens rea* had been underlined in *Sweet v Parsley* and again recently in *B v DPP*. In a statutory offence the presumption of *mens rea* could only be excluded by express words or by necessary implication. In s 14 there were no express words, and the 'rag-bag' nature of the Act, together with the anomaly arising from the young man's defence, made it impossible to find the necessary implication.

Although, as with *B v DPP*, this case does not expressly overrule *Prince*, the Lords in *R v K* referred to it as being 'discredited' and it appears to have been impliedly overruled.

The decisions in *B v DPP* and *K* were followed in *Kumar* [2004] EWCA Crim 3207 where the Court of Appeal held that buggery of a boy under the age of 16 (an offence under s 12 of the Sexual Offences Act 1956, now repealed) was not one of strict liability.

CASE EXAMPLE

***Kumar* [2004] EWCA Crim 3207**

D, aged 34, picked up V, a 14-year-old boy at a recognised gay club. The club had a policy of admitting only those aged 18 or over. The evidence was that V looked about 17. V willingly went to D's flat and consensual sexual activity took place, including penetration of V's anus by D. The trial judge ruled that the offence was one of strict liability in regard to the age of V. D then pleaded guilty. He appealed on the ground that the judge was wrong in holding that the offence was one of strict liability and that an honest belief as to the age of V should be allowed as a defence. The Court of Appeal allowed the appeal.

In this case the Court of Appeal relied on the judgment in *B v DPP* [2000] Cr App R 65. They referred to several passages in it starting with Lord Nicholls when he said:

> J 'As habitually happens with statutory offences, when enacting this offence Parliament
> defined the prohibited conduct solely in terms of the prescribed physical acts. ...
>
> In these circumstances the starting point for a court is the established common law
> presumption that a mental element, traditionally labelled *mens rea*, is an essential
> ingredient unless Parliament has indicated a contrary intention either expressly or by
> necessary implication. The common law presumes that, unless Parliament indicated
> otherwise, the appropriate mental element is an unexpressed ingredient of every
> statutory offence.'

They also considered the judgment of another judge in *B v DPP*, Lord Steyn, who explained the
principle in a slightly different way:

> J 'The language is general and nothing on the face of s 1(1) [of the Indecency with
> Children Act 1960] indicates one way or the other whether s 1(1) creates an offence of
> strict liability. In enacting such a provision Parliament does not write on a blank sheet.
> The sovereignty of Parliament is the paramount principle of our constitution. But
> Parliament legislates against the background of the principle of legality.'

To explain the point of the principle of legality, Lord Steyn quoted from the judgment of Lord
Hoffmann in *R v Secretary of State for the Home Department, ex p Simms* [1999] 3 WLR 328 where
he said:

> J 'But the principle of legality means that Parliament must squarely confront what it is
> doing and accept the political cost. Fundamental rights cannot be overridden by
> general or ambiguous words. This is because there is too great a risk that the full
> implications of their unqualified meaning may have passed unnoticed in the democratic
> process. In the absence of express language or necessary implication to the contrary,
> the courts therefore presume that even the most general words were intended to be
> subject to the basic rights of the individual.'

The Court of Appeal concluded that very similar considerations to those in *B v DPP* and *K* applied
in *Kumar*. The mental element had not been excluded from s 12 of the Sexual Offences Act 1956
by necessary implication. Consequently an honest belief that V was over 16 was a defence.

Cases where strict liability has been found

Although the above cases demonstrate an unwillingness to declare an offence one of strict liability, there have been other recent cases where the courts have been prepared to rule that the offence was one of strict liability. For example in *Muhamad* [2002] EWCA Crim 1865 the Court of Appeal held that the offence of materially contributing to insolvency by gambling under s 362(1)(a) of the Insolvency Act 1986 was an offence of strict liability even though it carried a maximum sentence of two years' imprisonment. They held that it was not necessary to prove that D knew or was reckless as to whether his act of gambling would materially contribute to his insolvency.

The Sexual Offences Act 2003 (SOA) has created several offences of strict liability in respect of belief in the age of a willing participant in sexual activity. In *G* [2006] EWCA Crim 821 the defence accepted that s 5 of the SOA 2003 (rape of a child under 13) created a strict liability offence, even where the defendant honestly and reasonably believed that the child was over 13 and the child was a willing participant. The defence accepted this as other sections in the Act have express references to reasonable belief that a child is over 16, whereas s 5 has no allowance for a reasonable belief as to age. Despite the fact that this offence is one of strict liability, it carries a maximum penalty of imprisonment for life.

APPLYING THE LAW   ☐☐☐

Read the following sections of the Food Safety Act 1990 and apply them to the situations below to decide whether an offence has been committed or not.

'14. Selling food not of the nature or substance or quality demanded

(1) Any person who sells to the purchaser's prejudice any food which is not of the nature or substance or quality demanded by the purchaser shall be guilty of an offence.

(2) In subsection (1) above the reference to sale shall be construed as a reference to sale for human consumption: and in proceedings under that subsection it shall not be a defence that the purchaser was not prejudiced because he bought for analysis or examination.'

'21. Defence of due diligence

(1) In any proceedings for an offence under any of the preceding provisions of this Part, it shall . . . be a defence for the person charged to prove that he took all reasonable precautions and exercised all due diligence to avoid the commission of the offence by himself or by a person under his control.

(2) Without prejudice to the generality of subsection (1) above, a person charged with an offence under section 8, 14 or 15 above who neither:

(a) prepared the food in respect of which the offence is alleged to have been committed; nor

(b) imported it into Great Britain,

shall be taken to have established the defence provided by that subsection if he satisfies the requirements of subsection (3) or (4) below.

(3) A person satisfies the requirements of this subsection if he proves:

(a) that the commission of the offence was due to an act or default of another person who was not under his control, or to reliance on information supplied by such a person;

(b) that he carried out all such checks of the food in question as were reasonable in all the circumstances, or that it was were reasonable in all the circumstances for him to rely on checks carried out by the person who supplied the food to him; and

(c) that he did not know and had no reason to suspect at the time of commission of the alleged offence that his act or omission would amount to an offence under the relevant provision.'

Situations

1. Grant owns a pizza parlour. He buys toppings to put on pizzas from Home Foodies Ltd. When he bought the latest batch, he told the sales representative of Home Foodies that he did not want any of the toppings to contain nuts. The sales rep assured him that all their products were 'nut-free'. Halouma bought a pizza and suffered a severe allergic reaction, which was found to be because the topping contained traces of nuts.

2. Tanya owns a sandwich bar. Unknown to her, Wesley, one of the sandwich makers, used Edam cheese to make sandwiches described as 'cheddar cheese and chutney'. These sandwiches were sold in the sandwich bar.

3. Kylie, who is a trained nutritionist, owns a restaurant. On the menu certain meals as described as 'low-calorie'. Kylie has given the chefs a list of suitable ingredients to be used in these meals. This includes using low-fat yogurt instead of cream in making sauces. One evening a chef uses cream instead of the yogurt in a 'low-calorie' dish served to one of the diners.

4.5 Justification for strict liability

The main justification is that given in *Sweet*, that strict liability offences help protect society by regulation of activities 'involving potential danger to public health, safety or morals'. The imposition of strict liability promotes greater care over these matters by encouraging higher standards in such matters as hygiene in processing and selling food, or in obeying building or transport regulations. It makes sure that businesses are run properly. This reason for justifying the use of strict liability was put by Kenny:

> 'The application of strict liability can be justified in special cases: particularly with regard to the conduct of a business. In such a case, even a strict liability statute makes an appeal to the practical reasoning of the citizens: in this case, when the decision is taken whether to enter the business the strictness of the liability is a cost to be weighed. Strict liability is most in place when it is brought to bear on corporations. In such cases there may not be, in advance, any individual on whom an obligation of care rests which would ground a charge of negligence for the causing of the harm which the statute wishes to prevent: the effect of the legislation may be to lead corporations to take the decision to appoint a person with the task of finding out how to prevent the harm in question.'

A Kenny, *Free Will and Responsibility* (Routledge, 1978), p 93

As failure to comply with high standards may cause risk to the life and health of large numbers of the general public, there is good reason to support this point of view. However, some opponents of strict liability argue that there is no evidence that that strict liability leads to business taking a higher standard of care. Some even argue that strict liability may be counter-productive. If people realise that they could be prosecuted even though they have taken every possible care, they may be tempted not to take any precautions.

Other justifications for the imposition of strict liability include that:

- it is easier to enforce, as there is no need to prove *mens rea*
- it saves court time, as people are more likely to plead guilty
- Parliament can provide a no-negligence defence where this is thought appropriate
- lack of blameworthiness can be taken into account when sentencing.

As there is no need to prove *mens rea* it is clear that enforcement of the law is more straightforward. In addition, rather than prosecute for minor regulatory breaches, the Health and Safety Executive and local trading standards officers are more likely to serve improvement notices or prohibition notices in the first instance. This can help ensure that the law is complied with, without the need for a court hearing. When a case is taken to court, the fact that only the act has to be proved saves time and also leads to many guilty pleas.

The use of due diligence defence (or a no negligence defence) can temper the law on strict liability. In many instances Parliament provides such a defence in the statute creating the offence. If the inclusion of such defences was done in a consistent way, then many of the objectors to the imposition of strict liability would be satisfied. However, the use of due diligence clauses in Acts often seems haphazard. For example in *Harrow LBC v Shah and Shah* the relevant section allowed a due diligence defence for promoters of the lottery but not for those managing a business in which lottery tickets were sold (see section 4.4.2).

The final justification for strict liability is that allowances for levels of blameworthiness can be made in sentencing. Baroness Wootton wrote:

> 'Traditionally, the requirement of the guilty mind is written into the actual definition of a crime. No guilty intention, no crime, is the rule. Obviously this makes sense if the law's concern is with wickedness: where there is no guilty intention, there can be no wickedness. But it is equally obvious, on the other hand, that an action does not become innocuous merely because whoever performed it meant no harm. If the object of the criminal law is to prevent the occurrence of socially damaging actions, it would be absurd to turn a blind eye to those which were due to carelessness, negligence or even accident. The question of motivation is in the first instance irrelevant. But only in the first instance. At a later stage, that is to say, after what is now known as a conviction, the presence or absence of guilty intention is all-important for its effect on the appropriate measures to be taken to prevent a recurrence of the forbidden act.'

> Baroness Wootton, *Crime and the Criminal Law* (2nd edn, 1981)

4.5.1 Arguments against strict liability

Although there are sound justifications for imposing strict liability, there are also equally persuasive arguments against its use. The main argument against strict liability is that it imposes guilt on people who are not blameworthy in any way. Even those who have taken all possible care will found guilty and can be punished. This happened in the case of *Harrow LBC v Shah and Shah*, where they had done their best to prevent sales of lottery tickets to anyone under the age of 16. Another case where all possible care had been taken was *Callow*. In this case even the use of an expert (a vet) was insufficient to avoid liability.

Although an important reason for imposition of strict liability is the maintenance of high standards so that health and safety are not put in jeopardy, there is, as already mentioned earlier, no evidence that it improves standards. Finally, the imposition of strict liability where an offence is punishable by imprisonment is contrary to the principles of human rights.

ACTIVITY

Self-test questions

1. Explain what is meant by 'absolute liability'. How does this differ from 'strict liability'?

2. Explain with examples which defence is not available to a defendant charged with a strict liability offence.

3. What are the *Gammon* tests for deciding when a statutory offence will be construed as an offence of strict liability?

4. Give examples of matters which are considered to be of 'social concern' and, therefore, more likely to be construed as strict liability offences.

5. Explain the arguments for and against strict liability.

Further reading

Beaumont, J, 'Mistake and Strict Liability' (2000) NLJ 382 and 433.

Horder, J, 'Strict Liability, Statutory Construction and the Spirit of Liberty' (2002) 118 LQR 458.

Smith, J C, 'Commentary on the Case of *B v DPP*' [2000] Crim LR 404.

chapter 5 PARTIES TO A CRIME ■

AIMS AND OBJECTIVES □□□

After reading this chapter you should be able to:

■ Understand the law of secondary liability – aiding, abetting, counselling or procuring

■ Understand the law of joint enterprise

■ Understand when secondary liability can be avoided by withdrawing

■ Analyse critically the rules on secondary liability and joint enterprise

■ Apply the law to factual situations to determine whether there is liability either as an accessory or for a joint enterprise

5.1 Principal offenders

The person who directly and immediately causes the *actus reus* of the offence is the 'perpetrator' or 'principal', while those who assist or contribute to the *actus reus* are 'secondary parties', or 'accessories'. Just because two (or more) parties are involved in the commission of a criminal offence, it does not mean that one of them must be principal and the other their accessory. They may be both (or all) principals, provided that each has *mens rea* and together they carry out the *actus reus* (see below). If D and E plant a bomb, which explodes killing V, then they are both liable as principals for homicide. This often happens where D and E carry out a robbery or burglary together, which is referred to as a 'joint enterprise', although it is possible to conceive of a situation whereby D and E, for example, independently attack V and the combined effect is serious injury or death. Each would be guilty of assault as principal offenders.

5.1.1 Difficulties in identifying the principal

In some cases it may be obvious that a crime has been committed by one or both of two people but it may not be clear either who is the principal or whether the other was an accessory. In such a case, both may escape liability. There is a particular problem when a child has died whilst being looked after by two parents or carers. Thus, in *Lane and Lane* (1986) 82 Cr App R 5, CA, evidence showed that the Lanes' child was killed between 12 noon and 8.30 pm. Each parent had been present for some of this time and absent for some of this time. It could not be proved that one was the principal nor could it be proved that the other must have been an accessory. Both had to be acquitted of manslaughter.

This problem has now been addressed by Parliament. Section 5(1) of the Domestic Violence, Crime & Victims Act 2004 provides as follows:

'5(1)   A person ("D") is guilty of an offence if:

(a) a child or vulnerable adult ("V") dies as a result of the unlawful act of a person who:

(i) was a member of the same household as V, and

(ii) had frequent contact with him,

(b) D was such a person at the time of that act,

(c) at that time there was a significant risk of serious physical harm being caused to V by the unlawful act of such a person, and

(d) either D was the person whose act caused V's death or:

(i) D was, or ought to have been, aware of the risk mentioned in paragraph (c),

(ii) D failed to take such steps as he could reasonably have been expected to take to protect V from the risk, and

(iii) the act occurred in circumstances of the kind that D foresaw or ought to have foreseen.'

The first conviction under s 5 occurred in June 2006. Sandra Mujuru, 21, was convicted at the Old Bailey of what the Crown Prosecution Service described as 'familial homicide'. She had gone to work leaving her live-in partner, Jerry Stephens, alone with her four-month-old daughter, Ayesha, despite knowledge of his history of violence against his ex-girlfriend, that woman's son, and Ayesha. On a previous occasion, Stephens had caused Ayesha a broken arm and a brain injury, probably caused by violent shaking. On the fateful day itself, Stephens killed Ayesha either by striking her head with an instrument or by slamming her head into a hard surface. Stephens was convicted of murder and Mujuru was convicted under s 5 of the 2004 Act.

Meanwhile, if it can be proved that D, being one of two or more parties to a crime, *must* have been guilty as either principal or accessory, then he may be convicted. In *Giannetto* [1997] 1 Cr App R 1, D was convicted of the murder of his wife, V. According to the prosecution's case, V was murdered either by D or by a hired killer on his behalf. D appealed on the ground that, if the prosecution could not prove whether he had murdered V himself or someone else had done it, he was entitled to an acquittal. The Court of Appeal dismissed the appeal. Provided, in either case, that D had the requisite *actus reus* and *mens rea* (as principal, this is causing death with intent to kill or cause really serious injury; for secondary parties, see below), then it did not matter whether he had killed her himself or encouraged another to do so.

5.2 Innocent agents

Where the perpetrator of the *actus reus* of a crime is an 'innocent agent', someone without *mens rea*, or not guilty because of a defence such as infancy or insanity, then the person most closely connected with the agent is the principal. So if D, an adult, employs his eight-year-old son to break in to houses and steal, the child is an innocent agent, and the father liable as principal. A well-known example of an 'innocent agent' acting without *mens rea* would be a postman unknowingly delivering a letter bomb. An example comes from the case of *Cogan and Leak* [1976] QB 217. L terrorised his wife into having sex with another man, C. C's conviction for rape was quashed because his plea that he honestly believed L's wife was consenting had not been left to the jury. L's rape conviction was upheld on the basis that he had procured (caused) the crime to happen (see below). The Court of Appeal also considered, *obiter*, that L may alternatively have committed the offence as principal through the doctrine of an innocent agency. Lawton LJ said that, 'had [L] been indicted as a principal offender, the case against him would have been clear beyond argument'.

5.3 Secondary parties

5.3.1 *Actus reus* of secondary parties: aiding, abetting, counselling or procuring

The law for indictable offences is set out in s 8 of the Accessories and Abettors Act 1861, (s 44 of the Magistrates' Courts Act 1980 provides the same for summary offences): 'Whosoever shall aid, abet, counsel or procure the commission of any indictable offence . . . is liable to be tried, indicted and punished as a principal offender.' This is a very wide definition. It should also be noted that it is possible for a secondary party to be held liable for committing an offence which they could not commit as principal. For example, a woman may commit rape as an accessory, although women cannot commit rape as principal offender (*DPP v K & C* [1997] Crim LR 121: see Chapter 11). A secondary party will be charged with 'aiding, abetting, counselling or procuring' the particular offence (murder, robbery, theft etc.) and is liable to be convicted provided that it can be proved that he participated in at least one of the four ways. The Court of Appeal has held that the words should simply bear their ordinary meaning. In *Attorney-General's Reference (No 1 of 1975)* [1975] 2 All ER 684, Lord Widgery CJ said:

> J 'We approach s 8 of the 1861 Act on the basis that the words should be given their ordinary meaning, if possible. We approach the section on the basis also that if four ordinary words are employed here – aid, abet, counsel or procure – the probability is that there is a difference between each of those four words and the other three, because, if there were no such difference, then Parliament would be wasting time in using four words where two or three would do.'

There is considerable overlap between the four words, and it is quite possible for A to participate in more than one ways.

<table>
<tr><td colspan="2" align="center">KEY FACTS</td></tr>
</table>

Aiding	Helping or assisting the principal; whether prior to, or at the time of, the commission of the *actus reus* by the principal. Typical examples: supplying information or equipment; keeping watch; acting as getaway driver.
Abetting	Encouraging the principal at the time of the offence. An example might involve a crowd of onlookers shouting encouragement to the perpetrators of an assault or rape.
Counselling	Encouraging the principal prior to the commission of the *actus reus*. Also advising, suggesting or instigating an offence. The best-known English case involves hiring a 'hitman' to carry out a murder.
Procuring	Used to mean 'to produce by endeavour'. More modern cases indicate that it is enough for D to make some causal contribution to the performance by the principal of the *actus reus*.

'Aiding'

As indicated above, this means to provide some assistance before or during the commission of a crime by the principal. The scope of aiding is demonstrated by the case of *Bland* [1988] Crim LR 41. D shared a room with her co-accused, E, who was convicted of drugs possession. D was also convicted of the offence, because she was living with E. However, the Court of Appeal quashed D's conviction. The fact that D and E lived together in the same room was not sufficient evidence from which the jury could draw an inference that D had provided assistance. Although assistance could be passive, it required more than mere knowledge.

'Abetting'

The threshold of involvement is very low. The Court of Appeal in *Giannetto* [1996] Crim LR 722 stated that 'any involvement from mere encouragement upwards would suffice' for a conviction of abetting. In turn, 'encouragement' could be 'as little as patting on the back, nodding, saying "Oh goody"'. Although it is not essential for D to be present at the scene of the crime if charged with aiding, it seems that it is essential for abetting. A number of cases have raised the issue whether mere presence at the scene of the crime (as opposed to presence combined with some actions: shouting, gesticulating, etc) will suffice for the *actus reus* of abetting. In *Coney and others* (1882) 8 QBD 534, three onlookers at an illegal bare-knuckle fight were convicted of abetting assault. The Court of Criminal Appeal quashed their convictions following misdirections to the jury. The court held that, although presence alone may suffice for the *actus reus*, it must be combined with the culpable mental element for it to amount to the offence of abetting. Hawkins J said:

> **J** 'A man may unwittingly encourage another in fact by his presence, by misinterpreted words, or gestures, or by his silence . . . or he may encourage intentionally by expressions, gestures or actions intended to signify approval. In the latter case he aids and abets, in the former he does not. It is no criminal offence to stand by, a mere passive spectator of a crime . . . But the fact that a person was voluntarily and purposely present witnessing the commission of a crime and offered no opposition to it . . . or at least to express his dissent might under some circumstances afford cogent evidence upon which a jury would be justified in finding that he wilfully encouraged and so aided and abetted.'

There have been a number of cases since. The law now is that D may be guilty of abetting via presence alone if:

- his presence provided encouragement in fact and
- he intended to provide encouragement through his presence.

In *Allan* [1965] 1 QB 130, there was no actual encouragement in fact. D was present at an affray. He was totally passive, though he had a secret intention to join in to help his 'side' if need be. The Court of Appeal quashed his conviction of abetting a public order offence. To hold otherwise would be tantamount to convicting D for his thoughts alone. Meanwhile, in *Clarkson and others* [1971] 1 WLR 1402 there was no evidence of an intention to encourage. The appellants were soldiers at a British Army barracks in Germany who had witnessed the gang-rape by at least three soldiers of an 18-year-old girl. Other soldiers had clearly aided and abetted the rape by holding the girl down, but there was no evidence that two of the appellants did anything other than just watch. However, both elements were present in *Wilcox v Jeffrey* [1951] 1 All ER 464.

CASE EXAMPLE

Wilcox v Jeffrey [1951] 1 All ER 464

Coleman Hawkins, a famous American saxophonist, appeared at a concert in London, illegally (the terms of his entry into the UK being that he did not take up employment). D was the owner of a magazine, *Jazz Illustrated*, who had met Hawkins at the airport, attended the concert and then written a very positive review of the concert in the magazine. D's conviction for abetting Hawkins' illegal concert was upheld, based on his voluntary presence in the crowd.

Abetting by omission

If D has knowledge of the actions of the principal, plus the duty or right to control them, but deliberately chooses not to, then he may be guilty of aiding or abetting by omission. In *Du Cros v Lambourne* [1907] 1 KB 40 and *Rubie v Faulkner* [1940] 1 KB 571, the defendants were the owners of cars who had allowed the principal to drive their cars carelessly, whilst they sat in the passenger seat. Both defendants were convicted of abetting road traffic offences. Presence in the vehicle, combined with (at least) the right to tell the driver what to do, was sufficient for liability. The principle is not limited to road traffic cases, as *Tuck v Robson* [1970] 1 WLR 741 illustrates. D, a pub landlord, had failed to get late drinkers out of his pub after closing time. D was convicted of aiding and abetting three customers to consume intoxicating liquor out of licensed hours, contrary to the Licensing Act 1964. His presence in the pub combined with his failure to take steps to ensure the drinkers drank up and left on time was enough for liability.

Du Cros v Lambourne was confirmed in the recent case of *Webster* [2006] EWCA Crim 415. D was convicted of abetting his friend, E, in causing death by dangerous driving. E, who had been drinking all day, drove D's car erratically and at high speed before losing control, leaving the road and crashing in a field. V, a rear seat passenger, was thrown out of the car and killed. E pleaded guilty to the substantive offence and D, who had pleaded not guilty, was convicted of abetting him by allowing him to drive his car, when E was obviously drunk. The Court of Appeal held that the crucial issue was whether D had an opportunity to intervene once he realised (because of the speed at which he was going) that E was driving dangerously. (D's conviction was subsequently quashed because of a misdirection concerning *mens rea* – see section 5.3.2 below.)

'Counselling'

In *Calhaem* [1985] 1 QB 808, Parker LJ said that, 'we should give to the word "counsel" its ordinary meaning, which is . . . "advise", "solicit", or something of that sort . . .'. Although this is a wide definition, the scope of 'counselling' is subject to some limitations. In *Calhaem*, Parker LJ added that 'there must clearly be, first, contact between the parties and, second, a connection between the counselling and the [offence committed]. Equally, the act done must . . . be done within the scope of the authority or advice and not, for example, accidentally'.

CASE EXAMPLE

Calhaem [1985] 1 QB 808

D wanted a woman, V, killed. She hired a hitman, Z, to murder V and paid a down-payment of £5,000. Subsequently, Z changed his mind about the killing but nevertheless went to V's house armed with a hammer, knife and a loaded shotgun with the intention of pretending to kill V so that he would not forfeit his down-payment. When V answered the door, Z apparently 'went berserk', hit V several times with the hammer and then stabbed her in the neck. Z pleaded guilty to murder and D was convicted of counselling. On appeal, she argued that the causal connection between her instigation of the crime and Z's killing was broken when Z decided to kill V of his own accord. This was rejected and her conviction was upheld.

'Procuring'

In *Attorney-General's Reference (No 1 of 1975)* (1975), Lord Widgery CJ said that 'to procure means to produce by endeavour. You procure a thing by setting out to see that it happens and taking the appropriate steps to produce that happening'. A good example is provided by the facts of *Cogan and Leak* (1976), above: L clearly procured the crime of rape by terrorising his wife into having sex with C. However, recent cases have suggested that all that seems to be required now is a causal connection between D's act and the principal's commission of the offence. This is not inconsistent with the *Attorney-General's Reference*, above, where Lord Widgery said that, 'you cannot procure an offence unless there is a causal link between what you do and the commission of the offence'. Hence procuring means 'causing'. In *Millward* [1994] Crim LR 527, D, a farmer, had given his employee, E, instructions to drive a tractor and trailer on a public road. The tractor was poorly maintained and the trailer became detached, hit a car and killed V, a passenger in the car. E was acquitted of causing death by reckless driving (there being no suggestion that his driving was to blame), but D was convicted of procuring the offence and the Court of Appeal upheld the conviction. It could hardly be said that D produced V's death through endeavour.

In *Marchant and Muntz* [2003] EWCA Crim 2099; [2004] 1 WLR 442, another farmer was convicted of procuring the offence of causing death by dangerous driving after instructing an employee, E, to take an agricultural vehicle onto a public road. A motorcyclist collided with the vehicle and was killed and it was alleged that simply driving the vehicle itself on a public road was dangerous. Here D's conviction was quashed: the vehicle was authorised for use on a public road and D had not caused the motorcyclist's death simply by sending D out onto the public road in

the vehicle, which was properly maintained. (This case is discussed further in Chapter 9.) In the *Attorney-General's Reference* case, above, Lord Widgery CJ also said that 'It may . . . be difficult to think of a case of aiding, abetting or counselling when the parties have not met and have not discussed in some respects the terms of the offence which they have in mind. But we do not see why a similar principle should apply to procuring . . .'. This proposition is still correct. D may be found guilty of procuring an offence by going against the principal's wishes, as the facts of the *Attorney-General's Reference* illustrate.

CASE EXAMPLE

Attorney-General's Reference (No 1 of 1975) [1975] QB 773

D surreptitiously added alcohol to the principal's soft drink, apparently for a joke. When the latter drove home he was arrested and charged with driving under the influence of alcohol. D was charged with procuring the offence. D's addition of alcohol to the principal's drink was the direct cause of the offence, and would, the Court of Appeal thought, amount to procuring.

What if the principal lacks *mens rea*, or has a defence?

The accessory may be liable here: what is crucial is the performance of the *actus reus* by the principal. This was seen in *Cogan and Leak*, above. Lawton LJ said that C's act of having sex with L's wife without her consent 'was the *actus reus*; it had been procured by L who had the appropriate *mens rea*', namely an intention that C should have sex with her without her consent. The Court of Appeal upheld L's conviction on the basis that he simply procured the *actus reus* of rape (C's lack of *mens rea* – he honestly thought L's wife was consenting – was irrelevant to the question of L's liability). The same principle was used in *Millward*, above. The hapless driver of the tractor-and-trailer on the occasion of the fatality was not convicted (he had not driven recklessly), but the owner of the machinery was found guilty of procuring the offence of causing death by reckless driving. Similarly, where the principal has committed both the *actus reus* and the *mens rea* of the offence but has a defence, D remains liable. In *Bourne* (1952) 36 Cr App R 125, D forced his wife on two occasions to commit buggery with a dog. His conviction of aiding and abetting the offence was upheld, even though the principal, his wife, could not be convicted (had she been prosecuted), because of his duress. The *actus reus* (and *mens rea*) of buggery had been carried out.

5.3.2 *Mens rea* of secondary parties

The accessory must:

- intend to assist, encourage, etc., the principal to commit the offence and
- have knowledge of the circumstances which constitute the offence.

Intention

D must have intended to participate in the commission of the offence. As was noted in Chapter 3, intention is a legal concept which includes desire; foresight of consequences as virtually certain to happen is strong evidence of intent. It is enough that D intends to, for example, supply the principal with a gun; it is no defence that D is utterly indifferent as to whether the principal commits the offence or not. In *National Coal Board v Gamble* [1959] 1 QB 11, an abetting case, Devlin J said:

> 'An indifference to the result of the crime does not of itself negative abetting. If one man deliberately sells to another man a gun to be used for murdering a third, he may be indifferent about whether the third man lives or dies and interested only in the cash profit to be made out of the sale, but he can still be an aider and abetter. To hold otherwise would be to negative the rule that *mens rea* is a matter of intent only and does not depend on desire or motive.'

This gives accessorial liability a very wide scope. The House of Lords discussed this issue in *Gillick v West Norfolk and Wisbech AHA* [1986] AC 112, a civil case.

CASE EXAMPLE

Gillick v West Norfolk and Wisbech AHA [1986] AC 112

G was seeking a declaration that it would be unlawful for a doctor to give contraceptive advice to a girl under 16, because this would amount to aiding and abetting the girl's boyfriend to commit the offence of unlawful sexual intercourse with a girl under 16. (This offence was found in s 6 of the Sexual Offences Act 1956, which has since been replaced by s 9 of the Sexual Offences Act 2003; see Chapter 11.) The House of Lords thought that the doctor would not be acting illegally, provided what he did was 'necessary' for the physical, mental and emotional health of the girl. Lord Scarman said that the '*bona fide* exercise by a doctor of his clinical judgment must be a complete negation of the guilty mind which is an essential ingredient of the criminal offence of aiding, abetting the commission of unlawful sexual intercourse'.

Subsequently, Lord Hutton approved this decision in *English* [1999] AC 1; [1997] 4 All ER 545; [1997] UKHL 45, saying that 'I consider that a doctor exercising his clinical judgment cannot be regarded as engaging in a joint criminal enterprise with the girl'.

Question

These *dicta* of Lords Scarman and Hutton suggest that motive can be relevant and that a 'good' motive provides a defence. Traditionally, however, motive is regarded as irrelevant to the imposition of criminal liability. Motive apart, what difference – in terms of liability for aiding and abetting – is there between the gun salesman interested only in cash and the doctor interested only in the girl's best interests?

Knowledge of the circumstances

D must have knowledge of the circumstances that constitute the offence. In *Johnson v Youden and others* [1950] 1 KB 544, Lord Goddard CJ said:

> **J** 'Before a person can be convicted of aiding and abetting the commission of an offence he must at least know the essential matters which constitute that offence. He need not actually know that an offence has been committed, because he may not know that the facts constitute an offence and ignorance of the law is not a defence.'

Johnson v Youden was followed in *Webster* [2006] EWCA Crim 415, the facts of which were given above. The Court of Appeal allowed D's appeal because the judge had invited the jury to consider whether D knew *or ought to have realised* that E was drunk. The Court of Appeal decided that this posed an objective standard instead of a purely subjective standard for D's *mens rea*. The judge compounded this error by inviting the jury to consider whether D realised (or ought to have realised) that allowing E to drive was dangerous. This was not the correct question, which should have been whether D realised that E was likely to drive dangerously.

Question

What does the 'essential matters which constitute that offence' mean?

Suppose D supplies the principal with a gun – what else does D have to know before he can be held liable as an accessory to murder? The law has developed a 'contemplation' principle. In *Bainbridge* [1960] 1 QB 129, Lord Parker CJ said that it was not necessary to prove that D had 'knowledge of the precise crime' or 'knowledge of the particular crime'. Conversely, it was insufficient for the prosecution to prove simply that D knew that 'some illegal venture' was intended. Rather, a middle ground test was devised, according to which D is liable if he had knowledge of 'the type of crime that was in fact committed'.

CASE EXAMPLE

Bainbridge [1960] 1 QB 129

D had acquired some oxygen-cutting equipment for the principal, E, who subsequently used it to carry out a break-in at a bank. The equipment was left behind and it was subsequently traced back to D. He was convicted of aiding and abetting burglary and the Court of Criminal Appeal upheld his conviction. So what 'knowledge' did D need to have?

- Not enough: if D was aware that S was to use the equipment in some illegal venture, D would not be guilty.

- More than enough: the prosecution would not need to prove that D knew the details of the crime (eg the date, time of the break-in; the address of the bank, etc).

- Enough: liability would depend on the prosecution proving that D knew that a crime of the same 'type' as burglary was to be committed.

In *DPP of Northern Ireland v Maxwell* [1978] 1 WLR 1350, the House of Lords extended the *Bainbridge* principle. Lord Fraser said that the 'possible extent of [D's] guilt was limited to the range of crimes any of which he must have known were to be expected that night'. Lord Scarman said:

> J 'A man will not be convicted of aiding and abetting any offence his principal may commit, but only one which is within his contemplation. He may have in contemplation only one offence, or several; and the several which he contemplates he may see as alternatives. An accessory who leaves it to his principal to choose is liable, provided always the choice is made from the range of offences from which the accessory contemplates the choice will be made.'

5.3.3 Joint enterprise

In *Stewart and Schofield* [1995] 3 All ER 159, the Court of Appeal drew a clear distinction between participation in a 'joint enterprise' and secondary participation. Hobhouse LJ said that joint enterprise entailed taking part 'in the execution of a crime'. Conversely, 'a person who is a mere aider or abettor, etc, is truly a secondary party to the commission of whatever crime it is that the principal has committed.' The late Professor Sir John Smith was an outspoken critic of this approach. He argued that joint enterprise should be regarded as an example of aiding and abetting. In his view, the use of the expression invited confusion because it implied different principles

applied, which was not the case. However, senior judges in the House of Lords and the Law Commission, among others, have adopted the phrase. Assuming 'joint enterprise' does exist, it typically involves two parties, D and E, together taking part in a crime (murder, burglary, etc). They both attack V, or burgle V's house, so that it is difficult to say that one is helping or encouraging the other.

Mens rea of joint enterprise

The cases that have arisen before the appeal courts tend to involve the same issues. Typically, D and E have set out to commit burglary. They disturb the householder, V, and E produces a knife and stabs V to death. Is D liable for burglary and murder, or just burglary? The basic proposition is that D is liable for all crimes committed by E as a result of carrying out the joint enterprise, provided that D foresaw or 'contemplated' them in advance. This means that D must have foreseen that E would commit a criminal offence; in other words, that E might perform the *actus reus* with the requisite *mens rea*. In the above scenario, it would not be enough that D foresaw that E might stab V with a knife; D would only be liable for murder if he foresaw that E might stab V with the intent to kill or cause really serious harm. (The scenario is based on the Privy Council case of *Chan Wing-Siu and others* [1985] 1 AC 168, which will be considered below.) In the leading House of Lords case, *English*, Lord Hutton, with whom the rest of the House of Lords agreed, said:

> **J** 'There is a strong line of authority that where two parties embark on a joint enterprise to commit a crime and one party foresees that in the course of the enterprise the other party may commit, with the requisite *mens rea*, an act constituting another crime, the former is liable for that crime if committed by the latter in the course of the enterprise.'

CASE EXAMPLE

English [1997] UKHL 45; [1999] AC 1; [1997] 4 All ER 545

D and E took part in a joint enterprise to attack a police officer, V, with wooden posts. In the course of the attack, E produced a knife with which he killed V. There was a reasonable possibility that D did not know that E was armed with the knife. The trial judge nevertheless directed the jury to convict D of murder if they believed that D knew that E might cause really serious injury <u>with the wooden post</u>. He also directed them to convict if they believed that D had participated in the attack realising that there was a substantial risk that in the attack E might kill or cause serious injury. The Court of Appeal upheld E's conviction but, on further appeal, the House of Lords quashed D's conviction. Because D knew that E intended to attack V with one weapon but actually attacked him with another, the jury should have received further direction from the judge on this point.

Lord Hutton accepted D's argument that the use of a knife was 'fundamentally different' to the use of a wooden post. However, he went on to say, *obiter*, that if the weapon used by the principal was different to, but equally as dangerous as, the weapon which the secondary party contemplated he might use, the secondary party should not escape liability for murder because of the difference in weapon. Lord Hutton gave as an example a case where D foresaw that the principal 'might use a gun to kill and the latter used a knife to kill or *vice versa*.' *English* confirmed a long line of cases in both the Court of Appeal and Privy Council involving joint enterprise situations.

- *Chan Wing-Siu and others* [1985] 1 AC 168. D participated in an armed robbery during which one of his accomplices stabbed the householder to death. The trial judge directed the jury that D might be convicted of murder if, when he took part in the robbery, he contemplated that one of his accomplices might use a knife with the intention of inflicting serious injury. The jury convicted and the Privy Council rejected the appeal.

- *Slack* [1989] 3 WLR 513. D and E were on a joint enterprise to commit burglary. The householder, V, a 78-year-old widow, was in the house. E asked D to find him a knife, ostensibly in order to threaten V if she came round and started screaming. Instead, E used it to kill V. D was convicted and the Court of Appeal upheld the conviction following *Chan Wing-Sui*.

- *Hyde, Sussex and Collins* [1991] 1 QB 134. The three appellants kicked a man into unconsciousness in a pub car park. He later died, one kick to the forehead having been fatal. Although they denied joint enterprise, they were convicted of murder after the jury was directed that each man was guilty either because he delivered the fatal blow (with intent to cause at least serious injury) or he foresaw that one of the others might do so. The Court of Appeal upheld the convictions.

- *Hui Chi-Ming* [1992] 1 AC 34. Six men including D set off to attack V, who had upset the girlfriend of one of the six. V was struck over the head with a metal pipe and died. D was convicted of murder after the trial judge directed the jury to convict if satisfied that D had contemplated that, during the assault, one of the others might use the pipe with the intention of causing at least really serious bodily injury. The Privy Council upheld the conviction approving *Chan Wing-Siu* and *Hyde*.

- *Perman* [1996] 1 Cr App R 24. D and E were engaged on a joint enterprise to rob a newsagent's shop. E was carrying a loaded sawn-off shotgun, with which he shot V, a friend of the newsagent. D was convicted of robbery and manslaughter; he appealed against the latter conviction on the basis that, although he knew E had the gun, he did not know it was loaded and thought that it would be used only to frighten. The Court of Appeal quashed the manslaughter conviction because the jury had not been directed to consider the exact nature of D's contemplation of what E might do.

In all of these cases the appellants have challenged murder convictions, although the facts giving rise to those convictions have varied. Nevertheless, in *Roberts* [1993] 1 All ER 583, Lord Taylor CJ confirmed that the 'contemplation' principles were the same whether:

- the object of the enterprise was to cause physical injury or to do some other unlawful act, eg burglary or robbery

- weapons were carried or not.

He added that it would 'be easier for the Crown to prove that [D] participated in the venture realising that [E] might wound with murderous intent if weapons are carried or if the object is to attack the victim or both. But that is purely an evidential difference, not a difference in principle.' The contemplation principle also represents the law in Australia (*McAuliffe* (1995) 183 CLR 108, High Court of Australia). In *Uddin* [1998] EWCA Crim 999; [1998] 2 All ER 744, Beldam LJ attempted to encapsulate the law on joint enterprise where a death has occurred into seven principles:

- Where several persons join to attack V in circumstances which show that they intend to inflict serious harm and, as a result of the attack, the victim sustains fatal injury, they are jointly liable for murder but, if such injury inflicted with that intent is shown to have been caused solely by the actions of one participant of a type entirely different from actions which the others foresaw as part of the attack, only that participant is guilty of murder.

- In deciding whether the actions are of such a different type, the use by that party of a weapon is a significant factor. If the character of a weapon, eg its propensity to cause death, is different from any weapon used or contemplated by the others and if it is used with a specific intent to kill, the others are not responsible for the death unless it is proved that they knew or foresaw the likelihood of the use of such a weapon.

- If some or all of the others are using weapons which could be regarded as equally likely to inflict fatal injury, the mere fact that a different weapon was used is immaterial.

- If the jury conclude that the death of the victim was caused by the actions of one participant which can be said to be of a completely different type to those contemplated by the others, they are not to be regarded as parties to the death, whether it amounts to murder or manslaughter. They may nevertheless by guilty of offences of wounding or inflicting GBH with intent which they individually commit.

- If, in the course of the concerted attack, a weapon is produced by one of the participants and the others, knowing that he has it in circumstances where he may use it in the course of the attack, participate or continue to participate in the attack, they will be guilty of murder if the weapon is used to inflict a fatal wound.

- In a case in which, after a concerted attack, it is proved that the victim died as a result of a wound with a lethal weapon, eg a stab wound, but the evidence does not establish which of the participants used the weapon then, if its use was foreseen by the participants in the attack, they will be guilty of murder – notwithstanding that this particular participant who administered the fatal blow cannot be identified. If, however, the circumstances do not show that the participants foresaw the use of a weapon of this type, none of them will be guilty of murder though they may, individually, have committed offences in the course of the attack.

- The mere fact that, by attacking the victim together, each of them had the intention to inflict serious harm on the victim is insufficient to make them responsible for the death of the victim caused by the use of a lethal weapon used by one of the participants with the same or shared intention.

CASE EXAMPLE

Uddin [1998] EWCA Crim 999; [1998] 2 All ER 744

D was one of a group of at least six men who attacked and killed V. They beat him with parts of a snooker cue and he was also kicked. The medical evidence, however, was that death was caused by a single stab wound from a flick-knife to the base of the skull which penetrated the brain. The man who used the knife, E, was convicted of murder. D was also convicted of murder on the basis of joint enterprise in July 1996 (that is, before the House of Lords gave judgment in *English*). D denied knowledge of E being armed. The Court of Appeal, hearing the case after *English*, quashed the conviction. The jury's attention had not been 'specifically focussed' on whether D was aware that E had a knife and also whether D foresaw that he might use it with intent to cause serious harm or death.

However, there was nevertheless evidence that a jury, directed in accordance with *English*, could have concluded that D was aware that one of the others had a knife and was prepared to use it and would thus be guilty of murder. Alternatively, it was open to the jury to say that the use of the knife was not so different from the concerted actions of hitting V with the snooker cue and kicking him that the actions of E went beyond what had been contemplated. The court therefore ordered a retrial.

Justification of the contemplation principle

One of the grounds of appeal in *English* was that it was anomalous that a less culpable form of *mens rea* is required for a secondary party to a joint enterprise. Specifically, it is enough for D to be guilty of murder if he **foresaw the possibility** (albeit not a remote possibility) of the principal committing murder, whereas in the case of the principal the law insists on proof of **intention** to kill or cause really serious harm. Lord Steyn took a forthright view of the implied criticism of the contemplation principle:

> **J** 'The answer to this supposed anomaly . . . is to be found in practical and policy considerations. If the law required proof of the specific intention on the part of a secondary party, the utility of the accessory principle would be gravely undermined. It is just that a secondary party who foresees that the primary offender might kill with intent sufficient for murder, and assists and encourages the primary offender in the criminal enterprise on this basis, should be guilty of murder. He ought to be criminally liable for harm which he foresaw and which in fact resulted from the crime he assisted and encouraged.'

The reasons for this stance were twofold.

- First, the difficulty in proving that D had the requisite intention. Lord Steyn thought that it would 'almost invariably be impossible for a jury to say that the secondary party wanted death to be caused or that he regarded it as virtually certain'.

- Secondly, the desirability of controlling gangs: Lord Styen said that 'The criminal justice system exists to control crime. A prime function of that system must be to deal justly but effectively with those who join with others in criminal enterprises. Experience has shown that joint criminal enterprises only too readily escalate into the commission of greater offences. In order to deal with this important social problem the accessory principle is needed and cannot be abolished or relaxed.'

In *Concannon* [2001] EWCA Crim 2607; [2002] Crim LR 213, D and E had embarked on a joint enterprise to commit robbery of V, a drug dealer, but when they reached the latter's home E produced a knife and stabbed V to death. D was convicted of murder following a trial at which the judge had relied on *English*. D appealed, arguing that the principles of joint enterprise were in breach of art 6 of the European Convention on Human Rights, in that they denied him a 'fair trial'. The appeal was dismissed. Professor Sir John Smith, commenting in the *Criminal Law Review*, observed as follows:

> 'Some lawyers would agree that the law of joint enterprise is unfair and many more would agree that mandatory penalties requiring the imposition of the same sentence on persons of widely varying culpability is unfair. But to allow the substantive law to be challenged on such grounds would throw the whole system into uncertainty and chaos.'

Remoteness

You should note that, according to Lord Hutton in *English*, it is sufficient that the Crown proves that D foresaw that E 'may' commit murder. It is not necessary to prove that D foresaw that E would do so (a point made expressly by the Court of Appeal in *O'Brien* [1995] Crim LR 734).

This begs the question, could D be held liable for any highly improbable crimes committed by his accomplices that he had, nevertheless, foreseen? This point was addressed by the Privy Council in *Chan Wing-Siu and others*. Sir Robin Cooke said that there was a remoteness principle:

> J
>
> 'It is right to allow for a class of case in which the risk was so remote as not to make [D] guilty of a murder . . . But if [D] knew that lethal weapons, such as a knife or a loaded gun, were to be carried on a criminal expedition, the defence should succeed only very rarely . . . Various formulae have been suggested – including a substantial risk, a real risk, a risk that something might well happen . . . What has to be brought home to the jury is that occasionally a risk may have occurred to an accused's mind but may genuinely have been dismissed by him as altogether negligible.'

Liability of principal and accessories/members of joint enterprise for different offences

In all of the above murder cases the accessory/member of the joint enterprise was either found guilty of murder along with the principal on the basis that he had foreseen that the principal might kill with intent to do at least serious harm (*Chan Wing-Siu*; *Slack*; *Hyde, Sussex and Collins*; *Hui Chi-Ming*) or found not guilty of any offence, on the basis that the principal had unforeseeably departed from the agreed plan (*English*; *Uddin*). Other cases with a similar outcome to that in *English* are *Anderson and Morris* [1966] 2 QB 110 (during a joint enterprise to assault V, E produced a knife and killed V. D denied knowledge that E was armed, but was convicted of manslaughter. The Court of Appeal quashed the conviction) and *Lovesey and Peterson* [1970] 1 QB 352 (during a joint enterprise to commit robbery, E unexpectedly used extensive force and killed V. D and E were convicted of murder. The Court of Appeal held that this went beyond the scope of the joint enterprise and thus D was not guilty of any homicide offence). This suggests that accessorial/joint enterprise liability is an 'all-or-nothing' situation. However, there is another line of case law, which holds that D might be liable for manslaughter even though the principal has been convicted of murder (*Betty* (1964) 48 Cr App R 6; *Reid* (1975) 62 Cr App R 109). In *Stewart and Schofield*, a joint enterprise case, Hobhouse LJ explained how this was possible:

> J
>
> 'The question whether the relevant act was committed in the course of carrying out the joint enterprise in which [D] was a participant is a question of fact not law. If the act was not so committed then the joint enterprise ceases to provide a basis for a finding of guilt against [D]. He ceases to be responsible for the act. This is the fundamental point illustrated by *Anderson and Morris* and *Lovesey and Peterson*. But it does not follow that a variation in the intent of some of the participants at the time the critical act is done precludes the act from having been done in the course of carrying out the joint enterprise, as is illustrated by *Betty* and *Reid*.'

CASE EXAMPLE

Stewart and Schofield [1995] 3 All ER 159

D, E and a man called Lambert, were engaged on a joint enterprise to rob a delicatessen. While D kept watch outside, E (who was armed with a knife) and Lambert (who was carrying a scaffolding pole) entered the shop. There, Lambert viciously beat the 60-year-old owner, V, with the pole, fatally injuring him. The three fled with £100. At their trial, Lambert pleaded guilty to robbery and murder. D and E pleaded guilty to robbery but not guilty to murder and were convicted of manslaughter after the judge directed the jury that they were guilty if they had realised or, if they had thought about it, must have realised, that Lambert 'might strike a blow intended to inflict some bodily injury'. They appealed, arguing that the vicious killing had gone beyond the scope of the joint enterprise. In particular, they claimed that Lambert was racially motivated (V was Pakistani). However, the Court of Appeal upheld their convictions.

In *Gilmour* [2000] 2 Cr App R 407, D drove E to a house in Ballymoney in the early hours of the morning. E threw a large petrol bomb (a 1¾ litre whiskey bottle containing petrol) into the house, starting a major fire which killed three of the six occupants, all young boys. Both D and E were convicted of murder but the Northern Ireland Court of Appeal quashed D's murder conviction and substituted a conviction of manslaughter. The court was satisfied that E, in throwing such a large bomb into a house in the middle of the night, intended to cause at least serious harm. With respect to D, however, the court decided that he did not have awareness of the size of the bomb and could not therefore be said to have appreciated that E intended to cause serious harm (most petrol bombs, apparently, do not cause death). Carswell LCJ said that 'It would be difficult to attribute to [D] an intention that the attack should result in more than a blaze which might do some damage, put the occupants in fear and intimidate them into moving from the house'. However, the court held that D was guilty of manslaughter. Carswell LCJ held that cases as *Anderson and Morris, Lovesey and Peterson* and *English* were distinguishable. He said:

> J
>
> 'The line of authority represented by such cases as *Anderson and Morris* deals with situations where the principal departs from the contemplated joint enterprise and perpetrates a more serious act of a different kind unforeseen by the accessory. In such cases it is established that the accessory is not liable at all for such unforeseen acts. It does not follow that the same result should follow where the principal carries out the very act contemplated by the accessory, though the latter does not realise that the principal intends a more serious consequence from the act. We do not consider that we

> are obliged by authority to hold that the accessory in such a case must be acquitted of manslaughter as well as murder . . . We do not . . . see any convincing policy reason why a person acting as an accessory to a principal who carries out the very deed contemplated by both should not be guilty of the degree of offence appropriate to the intent with which he so acted.'

The English Court of Appeal adopted similar principles in *Day, Day and Roberts* [2001] EWCA Crim 1594; [2001] Crim LR 984. D, E and F jointly attacked V and killed him. The cause of death was a brain haemorrhage caused by a kick to the side of the head. All three were charged with murder. However, the jury convicted D of manslaughter while E and F were convicted of murder. D appealed, arguing that if he was not guilty of murder then he should be acquitted altogether. The Court of Appeal dismissed D's appeal. Laws LJ said that there was 'a joint enterprise at least to inflict some harm' involving all three men, which was not negated by 'the larger intentions' of E and F to inflict serious harm. Simester and Sullivan in *Criminal Law Theory and Doctrine* (2nd edn, 2003) support this view: 'In principle it seems possible for [D] to be guilty of manslaughter in circumstances where [E] is guilty of murder.'

5.4 Withdrawal from participation

5.4.1 Pre-planned criminal activity

An accessory, or a member of a joint enterprise, may withdraw, and escape liability for the full offence. The principles appear to be identical in either case, as follows:

- mere repentance without action is not enough

- D must communicate his withdrawal to E in such a way as to 'serve unequivocal notice upon the other party to the common unlawful cause that if he proceeds upon it he does so without the further aid and assistance of those who withdraw' (according to Dunn LJ in *Whitefield* (1984) 79 Cr App R 36)

- D must take active steps to prevent the offence (this depends on how advanced the crime is). McDermott J in *Eldredge v United States* 62 F 2d 449 (1932) said: 'A declared intent to withdraw from a conspiracy to dynamite a building is not enough, if the fuse has been set; he must step on the fuse'.

These principles are demonstrated in *Becerra and Cooper* (1975) 62 Cr App R 212.

CASE EXAMPLE

Becerra and Cooper (1975) 62 Cr App R 212

D and E were engaged on a joint enterprise to commit burglary of a flat. They got into a confrontation with the householder and the commotion disturbed her neighbour upstairs, V, who came down to investigate. At this point D shouted 'Come on, let's go', climbed out of the window and ran off. E tried to escape but was prevented from doing so by V. There was a struggle and E, who had a knife, stabbed V to death. D and E were convicted of murder. D appealed on the ground that, by the time E stabbed V, he had withdrawn from the joint enterprise. The Court of Appeal upheld the convictions. Roskill LJ said that something 'vastly different and vastly more effective' was required from D before he could be said to have withdrawn.

The communication of withdrawal must be 'unequivocal'. Thus, simply failing to turn up on the day that the joint enterprise was due to take place does not constitute an effective withdrawal. This was demonstrated in *Rook* [1993] 2 All ER 955. A contract killing had been arranged and D was supposed to participate. However, on the appointed day he simply failed to appear. His accomplices carried out the murder without him. D was convicted and the Court of Appeal rejected his appeal. Lloyd LJ said that D's absence 'could not possibly' amount to unequivocal communication of his withdrawal. Although D had made it quite clear 'to himself' that he did not want to be there, he did not make it clear to the others. Thus, the 'minimum necessary for withdrawal from the crime' was not established. This was confirmed in *Baker* [1994] Crim LR 444. Three men including D had taken V to some waste ground and stabbed him to death. D's own evidence was that he had reluctantly stabbed V three times before handing the knife to E, stating 'I'm not doing it', moving a short distance away and turning his back while the others finished the job (death was caused by 48 stab wounds). D was convicted of murder and appealed on the basis that he had withdrawn from the joint enterprise before the other 45 stab wounds were inflicted. The Court of Appeal dismissed his appeal – he had not unequivocally withdrawn from the joint enterprise. His words, 'I'm not doing it', were quite capable of meaning no more than 'I will not myself strike any more blows.'

5.4.2 Spontaneous criminal activity

In *Mitchell and King* [1998] EWCA Crim 2444; [1999] Crim LR 496, the Court of Appeal held that communication of withdrawal from a joint enterprise was only a necessary condition for disassociation from pre-planned violence. This was not the case where the violence is spontaneous. In such cases, it was possible to withdraw from the enterprise merely by walking away.

CASE EXAMPLE

Mitchell and King [1998] EWCA Crim 2444; [1999] Crim LR 496

D, E and F were together in an Indian take-away. There was a fight involving other customers, and damage was caused to the take-away. The three men then left, followed by some of the staff. Fighting broke out between all the men. Eventually D, E and F walked off, but F returned and inflicted fatal injuries on one of the staff who had been lying on the ground. F was subsequently convicted of murder. The prosecution case against D and E was that they were involved in a joint enterprise. There was a question as to whether D and E had withdrawn from the enterprise at the time when the fatal blows were struck. The judge told the jury that there had to be effective communication and, as there was no evidence of that, D and E were convicted of murder. However, their appeals were allowed.

5.5 Assisting an offender

The above rules (whether on aiding, abetting, counseling and procuring or joint enterprise) only apply to assistance given to the principal offender either <u>before</u> or <u>during</u> the commission of a crime. However, a person may be held criminally liable for assisting an offender <u>after</u> the commission of an offence. Section 4(1) of the Criminal Law Act 1967 states:

'4(1) Where a person has committed an arrestable offence, any other person who, knowing or believing him to be guilty of the offence or of some other arrestable offence, does without lawful authority or reasonable excuse any act with intent to impede his apprehension or prosecution shall be guilty of an offence.'

5.6 Reform

In 1993, the Law Commission published a Consultation Paper, *Assisting and Encouraging Crime* (Law Com No 131). The Commission proposed the abolition of the present law of aiding, abetting, counselling and procuring and its replacement with two substantive offences:

* assisting the commission of an offence
* encouraging the commission of an offence.

The Commission regarded joint enterprise as a separate issue and so it would not have been abolished were the other proposals to be implemented. Professor Sir John Smith noted in the 10th edition of *Smith and Hogan's Criminal Law* (2001) that 'the proposals have many attractive features but involve serious practical difficulties'. He also described the suggestion that aiding, abetting, etc,

133

were different from joint enterprise as 'a dangerous theory'. In December 2003, the Law Commission website (www.lawcom.gov.uk) carried a statement that 'The doctrine [of secondary liability] is complicated, uncertain and anomalous, particularly that part related to "joint enterprise".'

In July 2006, the Commission published a long-awaited report, entitled *Inchoate Liability for Assisting and Encouraging Crime*. The report is extensive, at over 100 pages, and includes a draft *Crime (Encouraging & Assisting) Bill*. In the Bill, the Commission proposes a new criminal offence, intentionally encouraging or assisting the doing of a criminal act. The new proposed offence in clause 1 of the Bill would be committed by D if:

'(a) he does an act capable of encouraging, or assisting the doing, of a criminal act in relation to an offence ("the principal offence"), and

(b) he intends to encourage or assist the doing of that criminal act.'

Under clause 2, an offence would be committed if D:

'(a) does an act capable of encouraging or assisting the doing of a criminal act (the "act in question"), and

(b) he believes (i) that the act in question will be done, and (ii) that his act will encourage or assist the doing of the act in question.'

Thus, clause 1 focuses on those who encourage or assist crime intentionally, while in clause 2 the focus is on those who assist or encourage crime without necessarily intending that the act be committed but believing that it will be. Clause 3 makes clear that liability under the new offences may be imposed 'whether or not the principal offence is committed'. In terms of punishment, clause 12(2) provides that if D has encouraged or assisted murder, he becomes liable to life imprisonment. For other crimes, clause 12(3) states that 'unless an enactment provides otherwise [D] is liable to any penalty for which he would be liable on conviction of the principal offence'.

The main thrust of the reform was a perceived loophole in the present law of aiding and abetting which allows certain defendants, such as drug dealers and people-traffickers, to escape liability. Under the present law, a person (D) who helps someone else (E) to commit a crime cannot be charged with an offence *if the crime is never actually carried out*. Under the proposed new offence, D could simply be charged with 'doing an act capable of assisting the doing of a criminal act'.

Meanwhile, those who encourage a crime which is never actually carried out could be convicted of the 'inchoate offence of incitement' (see Chapter 6). Under the proposed new offence, D would be charged with 'doing an act capable of encouraging the doing of a criminal act'. There would therefore be an overlap between the two offences – hence, clause 13 of the Bill states that 'the common law offence of inciting the commission of another offence is abolished'.

The Law Commission website also promised that 'A second, and final, report, dealing with secondary liability, is due to be published in the week beginning 19th March 2007, together with a draft bill'.

ACTIVITY

1. In the 10th edition of *Smith and Hogan's Criminal Law* (2001), Professor Sir John Smith argued that 'retaining joint enterprise while abolishing aiding, abetting, etc . . . is impossible'. Do you agree?

2. Despite the best efforts of the courts, the meaning and scope of the *actus reus* elements of secondary participations is ambiguous and confused. The Law Commission's recommendation to replace the existing verbs 'aid, abet, counsel or procure' with 'assist or encourage' should be implemented. Discuss.

3. The 'contemplation' principle is too wide in that it is capable of imposing, for example, liability for murder on those who simply foresaw death or serious injury as a possible outcome of their involvement in a joint enterprise. Discuss.

4. D and E have agreed a plan to burgle a house known to be the home of V, a well-known MP. D thinks that the house will be empty on the night they plan to burgle it. E, however, is aware that Parliament will not be sitting that day and that there is a strong possibility that the MP will be at home. E is fundamentally opposed to V's stance on a number of political issues and has often spoken to D of how he would like to 'finish off' V. D is unsure whether this means to kill V or just to destroy his political career. On the night of the burglary D sees E putting a sharp-looking knife into his pocket. D asks what this is for and E says it will only be used in an emergency to 'warn off anyone who comes snooping around'. D is satisfied with this explanation. When they reach the house at 2 am it is in darkness. They break in through a rear window and start looking for a safe or any valuables. In fact, V is at home and is disturbed by the noise. He comes down to investigate. D hears footsteps coming down the stairs and shouts to E 'I'm off!', before climbing back out of the window. E waits behind and, when V enters the living room, stabs him in the neck, killing him. D and E are arrested soon after. At trial, E pleads guilty to aggravated burglary and murder. D pleads guilty to burglary but denies liability for murder.

   Discuss D's liability for murder or manslaughter.

Further reading

Clarkson, C M V, 'Complicity, Powell and Manslaughter' [1988] Crim LR 556.

Duff, R A, 'Can I Help You? Accessorial Liability and Intention to Assist' (1990) 10 Legal Studies 165.

Lanham, D J, 'Accomplices and Withdrawal' (1981) 97 LQR 575.

Smith, J C, 'Secondary participation in Crime: Can we do Without it?' (1994) 144 New Law Journal 679.

Smith, J C, 'Criminal Liability of Accessories: Law and Law Reform' (1997) 113 LQR 453.

Smith, K J M, 'The Law Commission Consultation Paper on Complicity: A Blueprint for Rationalism' [1994] Crim LR 239.

Smith, K J M, 'Withdrawal in Complicity: A Restatement of Principles' [2001] Crim LR 769.

Sullivan, G, 'Complicity for First Degree Murder and Complicity in Unlawful Killing' (2006) Crim LR 502.

Sullivan, G R, 'Fault Elements and Joint Enterprise' [1994] Crim LR 252.

Toczek, L, 'Manslaughter and Accomplices' (2000) 150 New Law Journal 1368.

Williams, G, 'Complicity, Purpose and the Draft Code' [1990] Crim LR 4.

Internet links

Law Commission, *Children: Their Non-Accidental Death or Serious Injury (Criminal Trials)* (Law Com No 282), available at www.lawcom.gov.uk.

Law Commission, *Inchoate Liability for Assisting and Encouraging Crime* (Law Com No 300), available at www.lawcom.gov.uk.

chapter 6

INCHOATE OFFENCES ■

AIMS AND OBJECTIVES

After reading this chapter you should be able to:

■ Understand the law on attempts

■ Understand the law on conspiracy

■ Understand the law on incitement

■ Understand the rules on impossibility

■ Analyse critically the rules on inchoate liability

■ Apply the law to factual situations to determine whether there is liability for an inchoate offence

6.1 Inchoate offences

Inchoate offences refers to those offences where D has not actually committed a 'substantive' crime, such as murder, rape, theft or burglary, but D has done one of the following three things:

- Made an **attempt** to do so (that is, D has tried to commit the crime but has failed, for some reason, to complete it).

- Entered into a **conspiracy** with at least one other person to do so (that is, D has entered into an agreement that a criminal offence will be committed).

- Tried to encourage or persuade someone else to commit a crime: this is **incitement**.

'Inchoate' literally means 'at an early stage'. Inchoate offences are designed to allow for liability to be imposed on those who have taken some steps towards the commission of an offence (whether the crime would have been committed by them personally or by someone else). It allows the police to intervene at an early stage and make arrests before a substantive crime has occurred, thus making a significant contribution towards public safety. Of course, where no substantive offence has been committed, obtaining sufficient evidence that an attempt, a conspiracy or an incitement has actually occurred can be difficult. As we shall see, the point at which D can be regarded as having committed an attempt has troubled courts in England for many years (and the issue cannot be said to be completely settled even now). Moreover, in a modern democracy where freedom of expression is protected by law (art 10 of the European Convention on Human Rights, incorporated into

English law by the Human Rights Act 1998), the criminal law has to strike the appropriate balance between the individual's right to free speech and society's interest in ensuring that those who make agreements with or encourage others to commit crimes (conspiracy and incitement respectively) are punished.

6.2 Attempt

The offence of attempt existed at common law but is now regulated by statute, the Criminal Attempts Act 1981.

 '1(1) If, with intent to commit an offence to which this section applies, a person does an act which is more than merely preparatory to the commission of the offence, he is guilty of attempting to commit the offence.'

6.2.1 *Actus reus* of attempt

The 1981 Act imposes liability on those who do 'an act which is more than merely preparatory to the commission of the offence'. Although the judge must decide whether there is evidence on which a jury could find that there has been such an act, the test of whether D's acts have gone beyond the merely preparatory stage is essentially a question of fact for the jury (s 4(3) of the 1981 Act). If the judge decides there is no such evidence, he must direct them to acquit; otherwise he must leave the question to the jury, even if he feels the only possible answer is guilty.

'More than merely preparatory'

What does this phrase mean? The first thing to note is that the test looks <u>forward</u> from the point of preparatory acts to see whether D's acts have gone beyond that stage. Prior to the 1981 Act there were a number of common law tests, one of which, the 'proximity' test, looked <u>backwards</u> from the complete substantive offence to see whether D's act were so 'immediately connected' to the *actus reus* to justify the imposition of liability for an attempt. Thus, in *Eagleton* (1855) Dears 515, it was said that:

> J 'Some act is required and we do not think that all acts towards committing a [criminal offence] are indictable. Acts remotely leading towards the commission of the offence are not to be considered as attempts to commit it, but acts immediately connected with it are.'

In the years immediately following the 1981 Act, the courts tended to refer back to some of the common law tests (which were not expressly excluded by the 1981 Act and so had persuasive value). Hence, in *Widdowson* (1986) 82 Cr App R 314, the Court of Appeal adopted Lord

Diplock's 'Rubicon' test formulated in *DPP v Stonehouse* [1978] AC 55 as representing the law under the Act. Lord Diplock had said:

> J 'Acts that are merely preparatory to the commission of the offence, such as, in the instant case, the taking out of insurance policies are not sufficiently proximate to constitute an attempt. They do not indicate a fixed irrevocable intention to go on to commit the complete offence unless involuntarily prevented from doing so. [D] must have crossed the Rubicon and burnt his boats.'

Shortly afterwards, in *Boyle and Boyle* [1987] Crim LR 111, the Court of Appeal referred to a test devised by Stephen known as the 'series of acts' test. According to this test, 'an attempt to commit a crime is an act done with intent to commit that crime, and forming part of a series of acts which would constitute its actual commission if it were not interrupted'. As a result the Court of Appeal upheld the appellants' convictions of attempted burglary (they had been found by a policeman standing near a door, the lock and one hinge of which were broken). However, in *Gullefer* [1990] 3 All ER 882, Lord Lane CJ tried to devise a new test that incorporated elements of the proximity, Rubicon and series of acts tests. According to this test D has committed an attempt when he has 'embarked on the crime proper'. Lord Lane said:

> J 'The words of the Act seek to steer a midway course. They do not provide . . . that the *Eagleton* test is to be followed, or that, as Lord Diplock suggested, [D] must have reached a point from which it was impossible for him to retreat before the *actus reus* of an attempt is proved. On the other hand, the words give perhaps as clear a guidance as is possible in the circumstances on the point of time at which Stephen's "series of acts" begins. It begins when the merely preparatory acts have come to an end and [D] embarks upon the crime proper. When that is will depend of course upon the facts in any particular case.'

CASE EXAMPLE

Gullefer [1990] 3 All ER 882

D had placed an £18 bet on a greyhound race. Seeing that his dog was losing, he climbed onto the track in front of the dogs, waving his arms and attempting to distract them, in an effort to get the stewards to declare 'no race', in which case he would get his stake back. D was unsuccessful in this endeavour but he was prosecuted for attempted theft and convicted. The Court of Appeal quashed his conviction: D's act was merely preparatory. In order to have 'embarked on the crime proper' the Court thought that D would have to go to the bookmakers and demand his money back.

Question

Do you agree with the decision of the Court of Appeal to quash the conviction in *Gullefer* (1990)?

In *Jones* [1990] 3 All ER 886, Taylor LJ agreed with Lord Lane CJ in *Gullefer* (1990).

 ASE EXAMPLE ────────────────────────

Jones [1990] 3 All ER 886

D had been involved for some time in a relationship with a woman, X. When he discovered that she had started seeing another man, V, and that she no longer wanted to continue their relationship, D bought a shotgun and shortened the barrel. One morning, he went to confront V as the latter dropped his daughter off at school. D got into V's car, wearing overalls and a crash helmet with the visor down and carrying a bag. He took the sawn-off shotgun (which was loaded) from the bag and pointed it at V. He said, 'You are not going to like this'. At this point, V grabbed the end of the gun and pushed it sideways and upwards. There was a struggle during which V threw the gun out of the window. D was charged with attempted murder. He was convicted and the Court of Appeal upheld his conviction. Taylor LJ said that obtaining the gun, shortening the barrel, loading the gun, and disguising himself were clearly preparatory acts. However, once D had got into V's car and pointed the loaded gun, then there was sufficient evidence to leave to the jury.

In the light of the expansive approach seen in *Gullefer* (1990) and *Jones* (1990), the next Court of Appeal judgment, *Campbell* [1991] Crim LR 268, may be regarded as somewhat narrow. D had been arrested by police when, wearing a motorcycle crash helmet and armed with an imitation gun, he had approached to within a yard of a post office door. The Court of Appeal quashed his conviction for attempted robbery. Watkins LJ thought that there was no evidence on which a jury could 'properly and safely' have concluded that his acts were more than merely preparatory. Too many acts remained undone and those that had been performed – making his way from home, dismounting from his motorbike and walking towards the post office door – were clearly acts which were 'indicative of mere preparation'.

Questions

What should the police have done in order to ensure D's conviction for attempted robbery? Wait until D had entered the post office? Wait for him to approach the counter? Wait for him to make a demand for money?

The next case was *Attorney-General's Reference (No 1 of 1992)* [1993] 2 All ER 190. D had been charged with the attempted rape of a young woman, V, but had been acquitted after the trial judge directed the jury to acquit. The Court of Appeal, however, held that there was sufficient evidence on which the jury could have rightly convicted. Lord Taylor CJ stated:

> J
>
> 'It is not, in our judgment, necessary, in order to raise a *prima facie* case of attempted rape, to prove that D . . . had necessarily gone as far as to attempt physical penetration of the vagina. It is sufficient if . . . there are proved acts which a jury could properly regard as more than merely preparatory to the commission of the offence. For example, and merely as an example, in the present case the evidence of V's distress, of the state of her clothing, and the position in which she was seen, together with D's acts of dragging her up the steps, lowering his trousers and interfering with her private parts, and his answers to the police, left it open to a jury to conclude that D had the necessary intent and had done acts which were more than merely preparatory. In short that he had embarked on committing the offence itself.'

In *Geddes* [1996] Crim LR 894, a case of attempted false imprisonment, the Court of Appeal offered another formulation for identifying the threshold, by postulating the following question: was D 'actually trying to commit the full offence'? Lord Bingham CJ stated:

> J
>
> 'The line of demarcation between acts which are merely preparatory and acts which may amount to an attempt is not always clear or easy to recognise. There is no rule of thumb test. There must always be an exercise of judgment based on the particular facts of the case. It is, we think, an accurate paraphrase of the statutory test and not an illegitimate gloss upon it to ask whether the available evidence, if accepted, could show that [D] has done an act which shows that he has actually tried to commit the offence in question, or whether he has only got himself in a position or equipped himself to do so.'

CASE EXAMPLE

Geddes [1996] Crim LR 894

D was discovered by a member of staff in the boys' toilet of a school. He ran off, leaving behind a rucksack, in which was found various items including string, sealing tape and a knife. He was charged with attempted false imprisonment of a person unknown. The judge ruled that there was evidence of an attempt and the jury convicted. On appeal, the conviction was quashed. Although there was no doubt about D's intent, there was serious doubt that he had gone beyond the mere preparation stage. He had not even tried to make contact with any pupils.

More recent cases have continued to apply the test in *Geddes* (1996). In *Tosti and White* [1997] EWCA Crim 222; [1997] Crim LR 746, D and E provided themselves with oxy-acetylene equipment, drove to a barn which they planned to burgle, concealed the equipment in a hedge, approached the door and examined the padlock using a light, as it was nearly midnight. They then became aware that they were being watched and ran off. D claimed that they had gone to the barn to try to find water because their car engine was overheating; E admitted that they were on a reconnaissance mission with a future aim to burgle the barn. The Court of Appeal, applying *Geddes* (1996), upheld their convictions of attempted burglary. There was evidence that D and E were trying to commit the offence. Beldam LJ said that the question was whether D and E 'had committed acts which were preparatory, but not merely so – so that it could be said the acts of preparation amounted to acts done in the commission of the offence. Essentially the question is one of degree: how close to, and necessary for, the commission of the offences were the acts which it was proved that they had done'.

In *Nash* [1998] EWCA Crim 2392; [1999] Crim LR 308, D left three letters addressed to 'Paper boy' in a street in Portsmouth. When opened, two were found to contain invitations to engage in mutual masturbation and/or oral sex with the author; the third, signed 'JJ', purported to offer work with a security company. At the instigation of the police a paper boy went to meet the writer of the third letter in a local park. There he met D, who asked him if he was looking for 'JJ'. D was arrested and convicted of three counts of attempting to procure an act of gross indecency. On appeal, it was argued that there was no case to answer with regard to the third letter, which was merely a preparatory act. The Court of Appeal confirmed the conviction with respect to the first two letters but allowed the appeal, following *Geddes* (1996), with respect to the third. Otton LJ said that the third letter 'was not sufficiently approximate to the act of procurement to amount to an attempt'. Otton LJ described *Geddes* (1996) as a 'helpful decision [that] illustrates where and how the line should be drawn'.

In *Bowles & Bowles* [2004] EWCA Crim 1608, D was accused of attempting to:

> 'make a false instrument, namely a Last Will and Testament in the name of
> Catherine Grew with the intention of using it to induce another to accept it as
> genuine'.

D was a neighbour of Mrs Grew, an elderly widow with dementia. After his arrest on other
matters, an unsigned will was found in D's house, under the terms of which Mrs Grew would leave
her house to D. Mrs Grew had already created a will, leaving her estate to charity. D was convicted
but, on appeal, the Court of Appeal quashed the conviction. Holland J said that:

> **J** 'The document was found in July 2001: it had seemingly lain fallow since the preceding
> November and there was no evidence of any interim steps to have it executed, whether
> by Mrs Grew or by someone else ... The Crown's evidence disclosed no more than
> preparatory acts.'

More than merely preparatory to what?

It is important to be clear exactly what it is that D needs to have gone beyond preparing for. This
entails a clear understanding of the *actus reus* as opposed to the *mens rea* of the substantive offence.
In *Toothill* [1998] Crim LR 876, D unsuccessfully appealed against his conviction of attempted
burglary. V had seen D standing in her garden at approximately 11 pm, apparently masturbating.
She called the police and D was arrested. A knife and a glove were found in V's garden and a
condom was found in D's pocket. D admitted knocking on V's door but claimed that he was lost
and seeking directions. D was convicted and appealed on the ground that evidence of an attempt
to enter V's home was insufficient; there had to be evidence of an attempt to commit rape as well.
The Court of Appeal dismissed the appeal. The *actus reus* of burglary in s 9(1)(a) of the Theft Act
1968 is simply entering a building as a trespasser: there is no requirement in the *actus reus* that D
actually rape anyone (indeed there is no requirement that anyone actually be in the building). The
actus reus of attempted burglary was therefore doing an act which was more than merely
preparatory to that entry. On the facts, there was evidence that D had gone beyond the preparatory
stage, by actually knocking on V's door.

More than merely preparatory: key facts

KEY FACTS

Case	Year	Offence attempted	Test proposed
Gullefer (1990)	1990	Theft	'embarks upon the crime proper' – Lord Lane CJ
Jones (1990)	1990	Murder	–
Campbell (1991)	1991	Robbery	–
Att-Gen's Ref (No 1 of 1992) (1993)	1992	Rape	'embarked on committing the offence itself' – Lord Taylor CJ
Geddes (1996)	1996	False imprisonment	'actually tried to commit the offence in question' – Lord Bingham CJ
Tosti and White (1997)	1997	Burglary	'had started upon the commission of the offence' – Beldam LJ
Nash (1999)	1999	Procuring gross indecency	–

Reform

The Draft Criminal Code (1989), cl 49(1), preserves the wording of the 1981 Act, stating that 'A person who, intending to commit an indictable offence, does an act that is more than merely preparatory to the commission of the offence is guilty of attempt to commit the offence'.

6.2.2 *Mens rea* of attempt

The essence of the *mens rea* in attempt cases is D's intention. In *Whybrow* (1951) 35 Cr App R 141, the Court of Appeal held that, although on a charge of murder, an intention to cause GBH would suffice, where attempted murder was alleged, nothing less than an intent to kill would do: 'the intent becomes the principal ingredient of the crime'. The *Nedrick* [1986] 3 All ER 1/*Woollin* [1998] 3 WLR 382 direction on when a jury may find that D intended a result based on D's foresight of virtually certain consequences has been applied to attempts by the Court of Appeal in *Walker and Hayles* [1990] Crim LR 44.

Conditional intent

Attempted theft and burglary cases have caused difficulties when it comes to framing the indictment. The problem is that most burglars, pickpockets, etc. are opportunists who do not have something particular in mind. The case of *Easom* [1971] 2 All ER 945 illustrates the problem. D had been observed rummaging in a handbag belonging to a plain-clothes police woman. He did not take anything and was subsequently charged with the theft of the handbag and its contents (a purse, notebook, tissues, cosmetics and a pen). He was convicted, but the Court of Appeal quashed his conviction following a misdirection. The Court also declined to substitute a conviction of attempted theft of those articles: there was no evidence that D intended to steal those specific items. In *Attorney-General's Reference (Nos 1 and 2 of 1979)* [1979] 3 All ER 143, the Court of Appeal provided a solution to the problem: in such cases D should be charged with an attempt to steal 'some or all of the contents' of the handbag.

Relevance of recklessness

Where an attempt is charged, it may be possible to obtain a conviction even though D was reckless as to some of the elements of the *actus reus*. This is illustrated in *Attorney-General's Reference (No 3 of 1992)* [1994] 2 All ER 121.

CASE EXAMPLE

Attorney-General's Reference (No 3 of 1992) [1994] 2 All ER 121

A petrol bomb had been thrown from a moving car, narrowly missing a parked car in which four men were sitting and two other men standing nearby, and smashing into a wall. Those responsible for throwing the bomb were charged with attempted aggravated arson, the court alleging that, while the criminal damage was intentional, they had been reckless as to whether life would be endangered. At the end of the Crown case, the judge ruled no case to answer. He ruled that an attempted crime could not be committed without intent; it was impossible to intend to be reckless; therefore it had to be shown D both intended to damage property *and* to endanger life. The Court of Appeal held this was wrong: it was enough that D intended to damage property, being reckless as to whether life would be endangered.

In *Khan* [1990] 2 All ER 783, four men had been convicted of the attempted rape of a 16-year-old girl. All four had tried to have sex with her, unsuccessfully. Their convictions were upheld despite the trial judge's direction that, on a charge of attempted rape, it was only necessary for the Crown to prove that they had intended to have sex, knowing that the girl was not consenting, or not caring whether she consented or not.

6.2.3 Impossibility

If a crime is impossible, obviously no one can be convicted of actually committing it; but it does not follow that no one can be convicted of attempting to commit it. There may be an attempt where D fails to commit the substantive crime, because he makes a mistake or is ignorant as to certain facts. The crime may be:

* physically impossible (for example, D attempts to pick V's pocket but, unknown to D, the pocket is in fact empty; D attempts to murder V by stabbing him with a dagger but, unknown to D, V died that morning of natural causes); or

* legally impossible (for example, D handles goods, believing them to be stolen, when they are not in fact not stolen).

There are also situations where the crime is physically and legally possible but, in the actual circumstances, because of the inadequate methods D plans to use, or does use, it is impossible to commit the substantive offence (eg D attempts to break into a three-inch-thick titanium steel safe using a plastic spoon). At common law, there was no liability for attempt if the crime attempted was physically or legally impossible; only if D used methods that were simply inadequate to commit the substantive offence, could D be liable. This was seen in *White* [1910] 2 KB 124, where D was convicted of attempted murder after giving his mother an insufficient dose of poison. (Had he given her sugar instead, he would have been acquitted.) This rule was confirmed as recently as 1975 by the House of Lords in *Haughton v Smith* [1975] AC 476. However, s 1 of the Criminal Attempts Act 1981 was intended to make all three examples of impossibility capable of leading to liability:

'1 . . . (2) A person may be guilty of attempting to commit an offence to which this section applies even though the facts are such that the commission of the offence is impossible.

(3) In any case where –

(a) apart from this subsection a person's intention would not be regarded as having amounted to an intention to commit an offence; but

(b) if the facts of the case had been as he believed them to be, his intention would be so regarded,

then, for the purposes of subsection (1) . . . he shall be regarded as having had an intention to commit an offence.'

However, despite the new provisions above, in *Anderton v Ryan* [1985] AC 560 the House of Lords decided that the 1981 Act had not been intended to affect the situations of physical impossibility.

Lord Roskill said that 'if the action is innocent and [D] does everything he intends to do, s 1(3) does not compel the conclusion that erroneous belief in the existence of facts which, if true, would have made his completed act a crime makes him guilty of an attempt to commit that crime'. This decision was overruled less than a year later. In *Shivpuri* [1987] AC 1, Lord Bridge said that:

> **J** 'The concept of "objective innocence" is incapable of sensible application in relation to the law of criminal attempts. The reason for this is that any attempt to commit an offence which involves "an act which is more then merely preparatory to the commission of the offence" but which for any reason fails, so that in the event no offence is committed, must *ex hypothesi*, from the point of view of the criminal law be 'objectively innocent'. What turns what would otherwise . . . be an innocent act into a crime is the intent of the actor to commit an offence.'

CASE EXAMPLE

Shivpuri [1987] AC 1

D was persuaded to act as a drugs courier. He was given instructions to receive drugs and transport them somewhere else. D duly collected a suitcase which he believed contained either heroin or cannabis. The suitcase contained several packages of white powder, one of which D took to the delivery point. There, he was arrested and was subsequently charged with attempting to be 'knowingly concerned in dealing in prohibited drugs'. This was despite the fact that the white powder was not drugs at all but perfectly legal snuff or some similar harmless vegetable matter. D was nevertheless convicted and the Court of Appeal and House of Lords upheld his conviction.

It has been argued that, in such cases, D is being punished solely for his intention. However, it should not be forgotten that the law of attempt does not punish D for his thoughts alone: there must always be the 'more than preparatory act'. Defendants like those in *Shivpuri* (1987) (who did not actually commit a substantive crime) clearly intended to deal in prohibited drugs and are therefore just as dangerous as those who do commit the substantive crime. D's prosecution and conviction can be seen to be in the public interest. In many cases, the 'objectively innocent' nature of the acts means that the attempt will not come to light. But in those cases where it does, D should not escape punishment.

Reform

The Draft Criminal Code (1989), cl 50(1), confirms that impossibility is no defence to a charge of attempt. The provision states that 'a person may be guilty of . . . attempt to commit an offence although the commission of the offence is impossible, if it would be possible in the circumstances which he believes or hopes exist or will exist at the relevant time'.

6.2.4 Excluded offences

Section 1(4) of the 1981 Act excludes attempts to commit the following:

- conspiracy
- aiding, abetting, counselling or procuring the commission of an offence (except where this amounts to a substantive offence, eg complicity in another's suicide contrary to s 2(1) Suicide Act 1961).

Moreover, there must be 'an act', so it is impossible to attempt to commit a crime which can only be committed by omission (eg failing to provide a breath test), or to attempt to commit a result crime by omitting to act when under a duty to act solely on that basis. However, in most cases there would presumably be some act to which liability could be attached.

Because intent is essential, where a crime cannot be committed intentionally, such as gross negligence manslaughter and reckless manslaughter (see Chapter 9), D cannot be liable for an attempt to commit it. There is therefore no offence in English law of 'attempted manslaughter'.

Reform

The Law Commission, in the Draft Criminal Code (1989), cl 61, propose the creation of attempted manslaughter. This would be committed where:

- D attempts to kill V but fails and
- D would have been able to successfully plead provocation, diminished responsibility or use of excessive force in self-defence had the attempt been successful.

Under the present law, provocation and diminished responsibility are defences to murder only. Thus, if D is provoked into losing his self-control and making an unsuccessful attempt on V's life, he is still liable for attempted murder (*Pears* [1972] Crim LR 678: see Chapter 9). Meanwhile, the use of excessive force in self-defence is no defence at all under the present law (*Clegg* [1995] 1 AC 482; *Martin* [2002] 2 WLR 1: see Chapter 8). Thus, if D is placed in a position where he is justified in using some force (but not fatal force) to defend himself from an assault but uses more force than is reasonable and tries to kill V, he is still liable for attempted murder.

Question

Do you agree with the Law Commission that English law should be reformed in order to create an offence of 'attempted manslaughter'?

6.2.5 Successful attempts

Is failure essential to successful conviction for attempt? A doctrine of 'merger' existed at common law, whereby an attempt blended in with the substantive crime, if committed. This was abolished, for indictable offences, by s 6(4) Criminal Law Act 1967. Now D may be convicted of an attempt, notwithstanding that he is also shown to be guilty of the completed offence.

6.3 Conspiracy

Until 1977, the law of conspiracy was a matter of common law. Since then, although certain conspiracies continue to exist as common law offences (agreements to defraud and, possibly, to corrupt public morals: see below), the law is regulated by the Criminal Law Act 1977. Section 1(1) provides that a person is guilty of conspiracy if he 'agrees with any other person or persons that a course of conduct shall be pursued which, if the agreement is carried out in accordance with their intentions . . . (a) will necessarily amount to or involve the commission of any offence or offences by one or more of the parties to the agreement'. Despite the statutory framework under the 1977 Act, judicial reference may be (and is) made to pre-1977 case law in order to help clarify the meaning and scope of the statutory provisions.

6.3.1 *Actus reus* of statutory conspiracy

'Agreement'

There is no conspiracy unless the parties have reached agreement to commit the same offence. Sometimes this is not as straightforward as it appears. For example, in *Barnard* (1980) 70 Cr App R 28, D agreed to assist what he thought was a conspiracy to commit theft. In fact, the others had agreed to commit robbery. The Court of Appeal quashed D's conviction on the basis that an agreement to commit theft was not equivalent to an agreement to commit robbery (significantly, theft is less serious than robbery). This was also seen in *Taylor (Robert John)* [2002] Crim LR 205. The Court of Appeal decided that an agreement to import class B drugs was not equivalent to an agreement to import class A drugs (again, importing class B drugs is less serious than importing class A drugs). Conversely, because the greater includes the lesser, if D agrees to commit a more serious crime than his co-conspirators, he may be held liable. For example:

- D agrees to commit robbery while E and F have agreed to commit theft. D is guilty of conspiracy to commit theft.

- D agrees to import class A drugs (eg cocaine or heroin) while E and F have agreed to import class B drugs. D is liable for conspiracy to import class B drugs.

If the parties have reached general agreement to commit an offence, then the courts may be prepared to overlook disagreements as to the details. Thus, in *Broad* [1997] Crim LR 666, D and E were convicted of a conspiracy to produce a class A drug. The fact that D thought they had agreed to produce heroin while E thought they had agreed to produce cocaine was irrelevant. A conspiracy comes into existence as soon as there is an agreement between two or more conspirators, although the agreement continues until the substantive offence is either performed, abandoned or frustrated (*DPP v Doot* [1973] AC 807); this means that further parties may join a subsisting conspiracy at any time until then.

'With any other person or persons'

Where more than two parties are involved, it is still a conspiracy even if all the conspirators never meet each other. This could happen in the following situations:

- A 'wheel' conspiracy exists where there is a co-ordinating party, D, who communicates separately with E and F, but E and F never meet.
- A 'chain' conspiracy exists where D communicates with E, E communicates with F and F communicates with G.

What is essential is that there is a common purpose or design, and that each alleged conspirator has communicated with at least one other (*Scott* (1979) 68 Cr App R 164). D must agree with someone, although no one need be identified (*Philips* (1987) 86 Cr App R 18). Certain parties are excluded by virtue of the 1977 Act. Section 2(2), as amended by the Civil Partnership Act 2004, specifically provides there is no conspiracy if D agrees with (a) his spouse or civil partner; (b) a person under the age of criminal responsibility; or (c) the intended victim.

Spouse or civil partner

The exclusion of D's spouse was a pre-existing common law rule. Thus, in *Lovick* [1993] Crim LR 890, Mrs Lovick's conviction was quashed because it had not been established that anyone other than she and Mr Lovick were involved. However, if a third party *is* involved, spouses may face liability for conspiracy. This was seen in *Chrastny* [1992] 1 All ER 189. There was evidence that Mrs Chrastny had conspired with her husband (to supply cocaine) and that she knew he had conspired with others. The Civil Partnership Act 2004 amended the 1977 Act so that D cannot conspire with his or her civil partner.

A person under the age of criminal responsibility

This means under D cannot conspire with E if E is under 10 years of age.

The intended victim

'Victim' is not defined in the Act. It may be restricted to victims of offences created specifically to protect that person, as in *Tyrrell* [1894] 1 QB 710. Here, D, a girl under 16 years old, had allowed

E to have intercourse with her. D was subsequently convicted of aiding and abetting the offence of unlawful sexual intercourse contrary to s 5 of the Criminal Law Amendment Act 1885. On appeal, her conviction was quashed: the purpose of the statute was to protect 'women and young girls against themselves', according to Lord Coleridge, and the policy of the courts is that statutes should be construed so that they do not criminalise those they were designed to protect. It follows that, on the facts of *Tyrrell*, there was no conspiracy to commit unlawful sexual intercourse either, because D was the victim of the offence. However, the word 'victim' could be defined in a broader sense. If D, a sadist, agrees with V, a masochist, that D will whip V, is this a conspiracy to commit assault? If V is a 'victim', then the answer is 'no'.

6.3.2 *Mens rea* of statutory conspiracy

The parties must:

- agree . . . that a course of conduct shall be pursued which,
- if the agreement is carried out in accordance with their intentions,
- will necessarily amount to or involve the commission of any offence or offences by one or more of the parties to the agreement.

'Course of conduct'

In *Siracusa* (1989) 90 Cr App R 340, the Court of Appeal decided that the *mens rea* sufficient to support the substantive offence would not necessarily be sufficient to support a charge of conspiracy. The offence charged was a conspiracy to import heroin, contrary to s 170(2) of the Customs and Excise Management Act 1979, which prohibits the importation of various classes of drugs, with various penalties attached. As far as the *mens rea* of the substantive offence is concerned, an intention to import <u>any</u> prohibited drug suffices. The question for the Court of Appeal was whether the same *mens rea* sufficed for the conspiracy. O'Connor LJ said that if the prosecution charged a conspiracy to import heroin, then the prosecution must prove that the agreed course of conduct was the importation of heroin. 'This is because the essence of the crime of conspiracy is the agreement and, in simple terms, you do not have an agreement to import heroin by proving an agreement to import cannabis.'

'In accordance with their intentions'

If D and E agree to commit a crime but D, secretly, has no intention of seeing it through, is there a conspiracy? Prior to the 1977 Act, the courts had held that D was not liable for conspiracy unless he intended that the agreement be seen through to its completion (*Thompson* (1965) Cr App R 1). However, in *Anderson* [1986] AC 27; [1985] 2 All ER 961, the House of Lords unanimously held

that it was **not** necessary that D intend to see through the commission of the offence. Lord Bridge, giving judgment for the House, stated:

> J
>
> 'I am clearly driven by consideration of the diversity of roles which parties may agree to play in criminal conspiracies to reject any construction of the statutory language which would require the prosecution to prove an intention on the part of each conspirator that the criminal offence or offences which will necessarily be committed by one or more of the conspirators if the agreed course of conduct is fully carried out should in fact be committed . . . In these days of highly organised crime the most serious statutory conspiracies will frequently involve an elaborate and complex agreed course of conduct in which many will consent to play necessary but subordinate roles, not involving them in any direct participation in the commission of the offence or offences at the centre of the conspiracy. Parliament cannot have intended that such parties should escape conviction of conspiracy on the basis that it cannot be proved against them that they intended that the relevant offence or offences should be committed.'

CASE EXAMPLE

Anderson [1986] AC 27; [1985] 2 All ER 961

D agreed with E and F, for a fee of £20,000, to purchase and supply diamond wire (capable of cutting through prison bars) which would be used to enable F's brother, X, who was on remand in Lewes Prison awaiting trial on charges of serious drug offences, to escape. D was also to provide rope and a ladder, transport and safe accommodation where X could hide out. D was charged with conspiracy to effect the escape of a prisoner, but argued that he had no intention of seeing the plan through to its conclusion. He claimed that he hoped to collect most of the £20,000 after supplying the diamond wire. He would then use the money to travel to Spain and would take no further part in the escape plan. Finally, he doubted that the escape plan would succeed. Therefore, he had no 'intention' to see X escape from prison. Despite all of this, D's conviction was upheld by the House of Lords.

The issue raises particular difficulty for police officers working undercover trying to infiltrate drug smuggling operations. It is perhaps inevitable that these officers will make agreements with criminals in order to lend credence to their undercover story. Do the officers intend to smuggle drugs? The Privy Council has dealt with such arguments on two occasions. In *Somchai Liangsiriprasert* [1991] AC 225, the Privy Council left open the question whether US drug enforcement officers were guilty of conspiracy when they infiltrated a plot to import drugs into the USA with the object of trapping the dealers. Then in *Yip Chiu-Cheung* [1995] 1 AC 111; [1994] 2 All ER 924, which involved a drug smuggling operation between Hong Kong and Australia, the Privy Council held that a conspiracy between D and E, an undercover agent working for the United States drugs enforcement agency, had been committed. A plan had been agreed upon, whereby E would fly from Australia to Hong Kong, collect the drugs from D and return to Australia with them. D was convicted of conspiracy and appealed, unsuccessfully. The Privy Council ruled that the fact that E would not be prosecuted did not mean that he did not intend to form an agreement with D to transport drugs.

Intention to take part?

In *Anderson* (1986) Lord Bridge also said, *obiter*, that 'beyond the mere fact of agreement, the necessary *mens rea* of the crime is, in my opinion, established if, and only if, it is shown that the accused, when he entered into the agreement, intended to play some part in the agreed course of conduct in furtherance of the criminal purpose which the agreed course of conduct was intended to achieve. Nothing less will suffice; nothing more is required'. This statement seems to suggest that it is necessary for the Crown to prove that any particular conspirators actually intended to play some physical part in the commission of the offence. If so, it would undermine what Lord Bridge said earlier in his speech (quoted above) when he explained that the policy of the 1977 Act was to allow for the prosecution of those with minor roles in the conspiracy, 'not involving them in any direct participation in the commission of the offence'. More seriously, it would prevent the prosecution for conspiracy of gang leaders or 'crimelords' who reach agreements with their subordinates but who deliberately distance themselves from physical participation in criminal activity.

This prompted the Court of Appeal in *Siracusa* (1989) (the facts of which were given above) to explain what Lord Bridge had, apparently, meant to say. The defendant in *Siracusa* (1989) had reached an agreement with others to smuggle drugs but it could not be proven that he intended to play any physical part in the operation. Nevertheless, the Court of Appeal upheld his conviction of conspiracy. O'Connor LJ said that D's 'intention to participate [was] established by his failure to stop the unlawful activity. Lord Bridge's *dictum* does not require anything more'.

'If the agreement is carried out': conditional intent

If D and E agree to rob a bank if it is quiet when they get there, have they agreed on a course of conduct, which will <u>necessarily</u> amount to the commission of an offence? The answer, according to the High Court in *Reed* [1982] Crim LR 819, would be 'yes'.

CASE EXAMPLE

Reed [1982] Crim LR 819

D and E agreed that E would visit people contemplating suicide. He would then, depending on his assessment of the most appropriate course of action, either provide faith healing, consolation and comfort whilst discouraging suicide, or actively help them to commit suicide. They were both convicted of several counts of conspiracy to aid and abet suicide. On appeal it was argued that, if the agreement is capable of being successfully completed without a crime being committed, there is no conspiracy; moreover, in the present case, the agreement was capable of execution without the law being broken, and therefore they were wrongly convicted. The court rejected the argument and upheld the convictions.

In *Jackson* [1985] Crim LR 442, D and E agreed with V to shoot V in the leg if V, who was then on trial for burglary, was convicted (in order to encourage the judge to sentence him more leniently). They were convicted of conspiracy to pervert the course of justice. The Court of Appeal held that:

> **J** 'Planning was taking place for a contingency and if that contingency occurred the conspiracy would necessarily involve the commission of an offence. "Necessarily" is not to be held to mean that there must inevitably be the carrying out of the offence; it means, if the agreement is carried out in accordance with the plan, there must be the commission of the offence referred to in the conspiracy count.'

'Will necessarily amount to or involve the commission of any offence or offences'

A conspiracy may involve an agreement to commit one offence, or several offences. Thus, in *Roberts* [1998] 1 Cr App R 441, the prosecution alleged a single conspiracy against several defendants to commit both aggravated and simple criminal damage. This does not mean that the prosecution cannot allege more than one conspiracy deriving from the same agreement. In *Lavercombe* [1988] Crim LR 435, D and E were convicted of conspiracy to <u>import</u> cannabis into the UK from Thailand. The Court of Appeal upheld their convictions, despite the fact that they had already been convicted of conspiracy to <u>possess</u> cannabis by a court in Thailand.

Until quite recently, a conspiracy had to involve an agreement to commit an offence in England. However, the Criminal Justice (Terrorism and Conspiracy) Act 1998 inserted a new s 1A into the

1977 Act, allowing for conspiracies made in England to commit crimes in other jurisdictions to fall within the offence. Thus, for example, 'an agreement made in Birmingham to rob a bank in Brussels' is now a conspiracy contrary to English law and triable in English courts.

Reform

The Draft Criminal Code (1989), cl 48(1), contains a definition of 'conspiracy', as follows:

'48(1) A person is guilty of conspiracy to commit an offence or offences if (a) he agrees with another or others that an act or acts shall be done which, if done, will involve the commission of the offence or offences by one of the parties to the agreement; and (b) he and at least one other party to the agreement intend that the offence or offences shall be committed.'

6.3.3 Common law conspiracy

The Criminal Law Act 1977 abolished the offence of conspiracy at common law, except for conspiracies:

* to corrupt public morals or to outrage public decency
* to defraud.

Conspiracy to corrupt public morals or outrage public decency

This is defined (by s 5(3) of the Criminal Law Act 1977, but preserving the common law nature of the offence) as an agreement 'to engage in conduct which (a) tends to corrupt public morals or outrages public decency; but (b) would not amount to or involve the commission of an offence if carried out by a single person otherwise than in pursuance of an agreement'. These types of common law conspiracy were retained because it was unclear at the time (1977) whether corrupting public morals or outraging public decency constituted substantive crimes. However, in *Gibson and another* [1990] 2 QB 619, the Court of Appeal held that outraging public decency was a substantive offence in its own right. Conspiracy to outrage public decency therefore now falls under the statutory offence.

CASE EXAMPLE

Gibson and another [1990] 2 QB 619

D and E submitted an exhibition to a commercial art gallery, entitled 'Human Earrings'. This consisted of a model human head attached to which were earrings made out of freeze-dried human fetuses. The gallery was open to, and was visited by, members of the public. D and E were convicted of outraging public decency and the Court of Appeal upheld the convictions.

The position regarding corruption of public morals is still slightly ambiguous (there have been no cases since 1977). In *Shaw v DPP* [1962] AC 220, D had published a magazine entitled *Ladies Directory* containing the names and addresses of prostitutes and certain details of sexual perversions which they were willing to practise. The Court of Criminal Appeal held that corrupting public morals was a substantive offence but, when the case went on appeal, the House of Lords did not address the question (the House upheld D's conviction for conspiracy to corrupt public morals instead). However, following *Gibson* (1990), it is certainly arguable that both these heads of common law conspiracy have now been transferred to the statutory offence (this is the position of Simester and Sullivan, *Criminal Law Theory and Doctrine* (2nd edn, 2003)).

Corruption of public morals

In *Knuller (Publishing, Printing & Promotions) Ltd v DPP* [1973] AC 439, the House of Lords held that a finding that conduct was liable to corrupt public morals was not to be lightly reached. It was not enough that it is liable to 'lead morally astray'. Lord Simon said that the words 'corrupt public morals' suggested 'conduct which a jury might find to be destructive of the very fabric of society'.

Outraging public decency

In *Knuller* (1973), Lord Simon said that 'It should be emphasised that "outrage" . . . is a very strong word. "Outraging public decency" goes considerably beyond offending the susceptibilities of, or even shocking, reasonable people'. He added that the offence was 'concerned with recognised minimum standards of decency, which are likely to vary from time to time'. As to the meaning of 'public', he said that 'the jury should be invited . . . to remember that they live in a plural society, with a tradition of tolerance towards minorities, and that this atmosphere of toleration is itself part of public decency'.

In *Rose v DPP* [2006] EWHC 852 (Admin), the High Court quashed a conviction of outraging public decency on the basis that only one person had seen the allegedly outrageous act, and that was insufficient to establish the 'public' element of the crime. D was observed on CCTV in the foyer of a Sheffield branch of Lloyds TSB bank by the bank manager shortly before 1 am. His penis was exposed and an unidentified woman was performing oral sex. D was convicted of the offence but his conviction was quashed because no-one other than the bank manager had seen the act and therefore the act did not outrage 'public' decency. This makes D's acquittal a matter of pure chance: he was in a public place – the bank foyer was open 24 hours a day for the public to use to ATM machines, it was well lit and the interior was visible from the street. However, no-one else could be proven to have seen D's act other than the bank manager and, according to the High Court, a single person does not constitute the 'public'.

Conspiracy to defraud

This offence does still exist purely at common law. Simester and Sullivan, *Criminal Law Theory and Doctrine* (2nd edn, 2003) state that 'it is incontrovertibly the case that forms of dishonest conduct which would not otherwise be criminal are rendered criminal by virtue of the common law conspiracy'.

Actus reus

In *Scott v MPC* [1975] AC 818, Viscount Dilhorne said 'it is clearly the law that an agreement by two or more persons by dishonesty to deprive a person of something which is his or to which he is, or would be, entitled, and an agreement by two or more by dishonesty to injure some proprietary right of his, suffices to constitute the offence of conspiracy to defraud'.

Mens rea

There are two elements: D must intend to defraud, and must do so dishonestly.

Intention

In *Scott* (1975), Lord Diplock stated that the 'purpose of the conspirators must be to cause the victim economic loss'. However, it is doubtful whether many conspirators had as their *purpose* causing economic loss to anyone. Typically, defendants involved in fraud operations operate out of greed, not spite. D's purpose is almost inevitably to make profit for himself although, in many cases, he will recognise that it is an inevitable consequence that loss will be caused to V. This is illustrated in *Cooke* [1986] 2 All ER 985. D, a British Rail steward, was charged, along with a number of his colleagues, with conspiracy to defraud British Rail. The allegation was that they had taken their own supplies of tea, coffee powder, cheese and beefburgers into the buffet car crew of a Penzance to Paddington train, intending to sell these to passengers as if they were BR's products and pocketing the proceeds. Although the others were acquitted, D was convicted and the House of Lords upheld the conviction. D's fraud involved fraudulent conduct going 'substantially' beyond cheating British Rail's passengers; the Crown was entitled to charge him with conspiracy to defraud.

Dishonesty

In *Ghosh* [1982] 2 All ER 689 the Court of Appeal held that the test was the same as in theft. The standard is that of ordinary decent people; if D knows he is acting contrary to that standard, he is dishonest (see Chapter 12).

6.3.4 Impossibility

At common law, impossibility was a defence to a charge of conspiracy **except** where it was down to D and E's choice of method being inadequate. This was seen in *DPP v Nock* [1978] AC 979.

CASE EXAMPLE

DPP v Nock [1978] AC 979

D and E resolved to extract cocaine from a powder, which they believed was a mixture of cocaine and lignocaine. In fact the powder was pure lignocaine hydrochloride, an anaesthetic used in dentistry, which contains no cocaine at all. Their convictions for conspiracy to produce a controlled drug were quashed: it was physically impossible to extract cocaine from the powder.

Now, however, s 1(1) of the Criminal Law Act 1977 (as amended by the Criminal Attempts Act 1981) provides that a person is guilty of statutory conspiracy even if it would be impossible for the agreement to be carried out as intended. You will recall that the Act states that a person is guilty of conspiracy if he agrees with at least one any other person that a course of conduct shall be pursued which (a) will necessarily amount to the commission of an offence. Section 1(1)(b) goes on to provide 'or would do so but for the existence of facts which render the commission of the offence or any of the offences impossible'.

Reform

The Draft Criminal Code (1989), cl 50(1), confirms that impossibility is no defence to a charge of conspiracy. The provision states that 'a person may be guilty of . . . conspiracy . . . to commit an offence although the commission of the offence is impossible, if it would be possible in the circumstances which he believes or hopes exist or will exist at the relevant time'.

6.4 Incitement

Incitement is primarily a common law offence, involving an allegation that D incited E to (for example) commit theft, robbery, or rape. However, Parliament has also created various statutory offences of incitement. For example, it is an offence to incite:

* another person to commit murder (Offences Against the Person Act (OAPA) 1861, s 4)
* another person to commit various offences involving the production, possession or supply of controlled drugs (Misuse of Drugs Act 1971, s 19)
* another person to commit rape outside the United Kingdom (Sexual Offences (Conspiracy and Incitement) Act 1996, s 2)
* a child to engage in sexual activity (Sexual Offences Act (SOA) 2003, s 10)
* a child family member to engage in sexual activity (SOA 2003, s 26)
* a person with a mental disorder to engage in sexual activity (SOA 2003, s 31)

- another person to become a child prostitute or to be involved in child pornography (SOA 2003, s 48)

- another person to become a prostitute (SOA 2003, s 52).

In *Hinton-Smith* [2005] EWCA Crim 2575, D was convicted under the new statutory crime of 'inciting a child to engage in sexual activity contrary to s 10(1) of the Sexual Offences Act 2003'.

CASE EXAMPLE

Hinton-Smith [2005] EWCA Crim 2575

In 2003, D became the musical director of 'The Majorettes' dancing troupe comprising a number of girls aged 3 to 17 years, of which V was a member. Over a period of time, D and V developed the habit of texting each other on their mobile phones. By the summer of 2004, when V was 14, the passing of text messages from D to V became both increasingly frequent and increasingly sexual in nature and content. In the end they were ranging from attempts to persuade V to perform acts of masturbation upon D or to engage in full sexual intercourse with him. Eventually, V's mother found the text messages on her daughter's mobile phone and called the police. D was convicted under s 10.

6.4.1 *Actus reus* of incitement

Section 4 OAPA 1861 (soliciting another person to commit murder), provides a useful list of verbs that help to convey the scope of incitement. The section states that 'whosoever shall solicit, encourage, persuade, or endeavour to persuade, or shall propose to any person to murder any other person' is guilty of an offence. In *Goldman* [2001] Crim LR 894, the Court of Appeal approved the following definition of an 'inciter' given by a South African judge, Holmes JA, in *Nkosiyana* 1966 (4) SA 655, as anyone who:

J 'reaches and seeks to influence the mind of another to the commission of a crime. The machinations of criminal ingenuity being legion, the approach to the other's mind may take various forms, such as suggestion, proposal, request, exhortation, gesture, argument, persuasion, inducement, goading or the arousal of cupidity.'

Incitement also extends to threats or pressure, according to Lord Denning MR in *Race Relations Board v Applin* [1973] 2 All ER 1190. This was a decision of the Court of Appeal (Civil Division) and is thus, as a matter of precedent, of persuasive value only for criminal courts. Members of the National Front had written threatening letters to a white foster couple, seeking to dissuade them

from taking in black children. The Race Relations Board sought a declaration that this activity amounted to inciting the couple to commit an unlawful act (a breach of s 12 of the Race Relations Act 1968, which prohibits discrimination in the public provision of services) and the Court of Appeal agreed. In *Marlow* [1997] EWCA Crim 1833; [1997] Crim LR 897, the trial judge directed the jury using phrases 'may encourage or persuade' and 'is capable of encouraging or persuading'. On appeal it was argued that this set the standard too low; that it was the test of whether there was a case to answer, not whether D was guilty. However, the Court of Appeal dismissed the appeal. Potter LJ described the use of the word 'encourages' as representing 'as well as any modern word can the concept involved'.

The width of the *actus reus* of incitement was seen in *Goldman* (2001), where D responded to an advertisement placed by E offering to sell indecent photographs of children. The Court of Appeal upheld D's conviction of inciting E to distribute indecent photographs of children, contrary to s 1 of the Protection of Children Act 1978. The *actus reus* of the offence is committed as soon as the incitement occurs; there is no requirement that D's encouragement, persuasion, etc, have any effect. This was seen recently in *DPP v Armstrong* [2000] Crim LR 379, where the incitee was an undercover police officer. (If this were not the case then D's liability would depend on the chance factor of whether the incitee was influenced by D or not. It would also force the prosecuting authorities to charge D in such circumstances with attempted incitement, a double inchoate offence.)

D will usually give incitement to an individual, but it is not necessary that this occurs. D may incite the general public to commit an offence. This was demonstrated in *Invicta Plastics Ltd v Clare* [1976] Crim LR 131.

CASE EXAMPLE

Invicta Plastics Ltd v Clare [1976] Crim LR 131

Magistrates had convicted the defendant company of inciting the readers of *What Car?* magazine to commit the offence of using unlicensed apparatus under s 1(1) of the Wireless Telegraphy Act 1949 by advertising a device, 'Radatec', which they claimed could give drivers advance warning of the police using radar speed traps. The High Court upheld the conviction.

Similarly, in *Marlow* (1997), D was convicted under s 19 of the Misuse of Drugs Act 1971 of inciting members of the public to produce cannabis (an offence under s 4 of the 1971 Act). He had written a book about the cultivation of cannabis and advertised for it in various magazines, including *Private Eye* and *Viz*. The Court of Appeal saw no difficulty in upholding D's conviction. Potter LJ said that 'open incitement that the law should be broken regardless remains a serious offence'.

The act incited must constitute an *actus reus*

If D persuades E to do an act, he is only liable for incitement if that act would constitute the *actus reus* of an offence. This is illustrated by *Whitehouse* [1977] 3 All ER 737. D was convicted of inciting his 15-year-old daughter to commit incest with him, contrary to s 10 of the Sexual Offences Act 1956 (subsequently replaced by s 25 of the Sexual Offences Act 2003). Had intercourse taken place, he would have been guilty of incest. However, the girl would have committed no offence (because of a provision in the 1956 Act, which provided that girls under 16 could not commit the offence). Thus, D had incited his daughter to do something which (as far as she was concerned) was not a crime. D's conviction was therefore quashed on appeal. Although Parliament very quickly intervened to deal with the loophole in the law exposed by *Whitehouse* (1977) (s 54 of the Criminal Law Act 1977 now makes it a specific statutory offence for a man to incite a girl under 16 whom he knows to be his daughter (or granddaughter or sister) to have sex with him), the principle of the case remains valid.

However, it is not necessary that the act incited amount to a full offence. That is, D is nevertheless guilty of incitement by persuading E to commit the *actus reus* of an offence even though E lacks *mens rea* or has a defence (such as duress). In *Pickford* [1995] 1 Cr App R 420, D pleaded guilty to a charge of inciting his stepson, E, to commit incest with E's mother. However, as E was under 14 and, under the then law, conclusively presumed to be incapable of sexual intercourse, the Court of Appeal held that the act incited did not constitute the *actus reus* of an offence. However, the Court of Appeal did not quash D's conviction. The court reasoned that, if he had been charged with inciting E's mother to commit incest instead, then he would have been rightly convicted on the basis that she performed the *actus reus* of incest. This was so even though neither son nor mother was 'remotely a willing party to the events which took place. They were both forced to the act of intercourse by this appellant'. That is, had the mother been charged with incest, she would have had the defence of duress.

6.4.2 *Mens rea* of incitement

D must actually intend that the offence incited be committed (*Invicta Plastics* (1976)). This means that:

- D must also intend any consequences required by the *actus reus*. Thus, if D incites E to 'knee-cap' V by shooting him in the knee (a form of punishment used by certain terrorist and gangland organisations), D would be liable for incitement to wound and/or incitement to cause GBH – but would not be liable for incitement to murder should V happen to suffer unexpected blood loss and die.

- D must also have knowledge, or at least belief, that any consequences required by the *actus reus* will also exist at the time when V carries out the offence.

- Finally, D must also intend, or believe, that E will act with the *mens rea* required.

Question

In *Invicta Plastics* (1976) and *Marlow* (1997), did the defendants intend anything other than to make money through the sale of the Radatec device and book respectively? Should their convictions have been quashed on the basis of lack of *mens rea*?

Reform

The Draft Criminal Code (1989), cl 47(1), states:

> '47(1) A person is guilty of incitement to commit an offence or offences if (a) he incites another to do or cause to be done an act or acts which, if done, will involve the commission of the offence or offences by the other; and (b) he intends or believes that the other, if he acts as incited, shall or will do so with the fault required for the offence or offences.'

It appears from this definition, particularly the words 'if he acts as intended', that there would be no requirement that D need to have intended the offence actually be committed by E.

6.4.3 Impossibility

Incitement is still governed by the common law. Hence, impossibility is a defence **except** where it relates to the adequacy of the methods to be used. If D incites E to break into a safe using a screwdriver which, unknown to them, will never work, D should be guilty of inciting theft. Otherwise it appears that D will have a defence. In *Fitzmaurice* [1983] 1 All ER 189, the Court of Appeal stated *obiter* that the principles in *Haughton v Smith* (1975) (attempt) and *DPP v Nock* (1978) (conspiracy) should apply to incitement. Thus, if D incites E to kill V but, unknown to them both, V has recently died of natural causes, then D is not guilty of inciting murder. (Of course, if D and E agree that E will kill V, then both are guilty of conspiracy to commit murder, for which impossibility is not a defence.)

Question

Why does impossibility remain a defence to incitement?

Reform

The Draft Criminal Code (1989), cl 50(1), would change the law so that impossibility would provide no defence to a charge of incitement. The provision states that 'a person may be guilty of incitement . . . to commit an offence although the commission of the offence is impossible, if it would be possible in the circumstances which he believes or hopes exist or will exist at the relevant time'. This would rationalise the rules on impossibility across all the inchoate offences and is a welcome reform suggestion.

Summary of impossibility and inchoate offences

□□□□□□ KEY FACTS □□□□□□

Inchoate offence	Impossibility a defence?	Authority
Attempt	No	Criminal Attempts Act 1981; *Shivpuri* (1987)
Conspiracy	No	Criminal Law Act 1977 (as amended)
Incitement	Yes	*Fitzmaurice* (1983)

ACTIVITY

1. D is an expert in bank security systems, now retired. E is a former racing driver. They are both in need of cash having lost heavily on the stock market and gambling, respectively. They agree to form a team to steal money from a bank: D will provide the knowledge required to get past the bank's security systems and into the safe; E will be the getaway driver in the event that a high-speed escape is required. D is reluctant to actually enter the bank himself and E must wait outside in the getaway car. They therefore 'advertise' their plan in underworld circles, and invite a third party to join them to do the physical task of entering the bank and stealing from the safe. F, who has recently been released from prison having served eight years for armed robbery, responds to their 'advertisement'. F believes that D and E plan to carry out an armed robbery in broad daylight; D and E actually intend to quietly break into the bank during the night.

   At this point, consider whether D and E, and F, have committed conspiracy and, if so, conspiracy to commit which offence(s)?

2. The police, who have been tipped off, think they know what D, E and F are plotting and set up observation of the bank. The police observe F walk up to a bank in the early hours of the morning. F, who is dressed all in black and carrying a black holdall, stops next to a rear window of the bank and is examining it when the police rush from their hiding place and arrest him. D and E are also arrested in a car parked nearby. Diagrams showing the position of security cameras and alarms for the bank are found in the car. D, E and F do not deny that they planned to burgle the bank but insist that they intended to carry out the burglary the next night and that F was simply making a reconnaissance trip.

Consider whether D, E and F have committed attempted burglary. (If necessary, refer back to Chapter 5 for a reminder of the principles of secondary participation/joint enterprise.)

3. F was also found to have a loaded firearm hidden in an inside jacket pocket. He admits to police that he would have used this to shoot any security guard who might have been in the bank when the burglary went ahead.

Consider whether D, E and F have committed conspiracy to murder.

Note: For the purposes of the above activities, <u>theft</u> is the dishonest appropriation of property belonging to another; <u>burglary</u> involves entering a building as a trespasser with intent to steal; <u>robbery</u> is theft with the use of or threat or force; <u>murder</u> is causing the death of another human being with intent to kill or cause serious harm.

Further reading

Dennis, I, 'The Rationale of Criminal Conspiracy' (1977) 93 LQR 39.

Elliott, D W, '*Mens Rea* in Statutory Conspiracy' [1978] Crim LR 202.

Smith, J C, 'Conspiracy under the Criminal Law Act 1977' [1977] Crim LR 598 and 638.

Smith, K J M, 'Proximity in Attempt: Lord Lane's Midway Course' [1991] Crim LR 576.

Williams, G, 'The Lords and Impossible Attempts' [1986] CLJ 33.

Williams, G, 'Wrong Turnings on the Law of Attempt' [1991] Crim LR 416.

chapter 7 CAPACITY ■

AIMS AND OBJECTIVES

After reading this chapter you should be able to:

■ Understand the limitations on liability of children in criminal law

■ Understand the effects a person's mental state may have on their criminal liability

■ Understand the concept and basic principles of vicarious liability in the criminal law

■ Analyse critically the concept of vicarious liability

■ Understand the basic principles of corporate liability in the criminal law

■ Analyse critically the need for corporate liability and the tests used in establishing it

There are some circumstances in which the law rules that a person is not capable of committing a crime. The main limitations are on:

• children under the age of 10

• mentally ill persons

• corporations.

On the other hand, there are some circumstances in which a person may be liable for the actions of another under the principle of vicarious liability.

Capacity to commit a crime is important, as one of the principles of justice is that only those who are blameworthy should be liable for their crimes. Without capacity to understand or be responsible for his actions, a person has no moral blame. For this reason English law recognises categories of those without capacity and they are generally not held to be not criminally responsible for their actions. This means that if, for example, a five-year-old child takes some sweets from a counter in a shop, he cannot be guilty of theft. He has done the *actus reus* of theft (appropriation of property belonging to another), but the law automatically assumes that he is not capable of forming the necessary *mens rea*.

7.1 Children

7.1.1 Children under the age of 10

The age of criminal responsibility in England and Wales is 10. This age was set by the Children and Young Persons Act 1933, which states in s 50 that:

'50 It shall be conclusively presumed that no child under the age of ten years can be guilty of any offence.'

This is known as the *doli incapax* presumption. Children under the age of 10 cannot be criminally liable for their acts. This conclusive presumption that a child under 10 cannot commit a crime means that those who use children to do the act of an offence are liable as principals, rather than as secondary participants in the offence. For example, if two teenage boys get a child aged eight to enter into a house through a small window and bring out to them money or other valuables, the eight-year-old cannot be guilty of burglary. Normally anyone who waited outside during a burglary would be a secondary participant in the offence, but in this case the teenagers are guilty as principal offenders.

Prior to the Children and Young Persons Act 1933 the age of criminal responsibility in England and Wales was eight. This was thought to be too low. The age of 10 is now the lowest age of criminal responsibility in any Western European country, and many critics think that it should be increased to 12. In fact as long ago as 1960 the Ingelby Committee, Cmnd 1911 (1960) recommended that it should be increased to 12 in England and Wales.

The age limit of 10 for criminal responsibility is also extended into quasi-criminal areas, such as anti-social behaviour orders under s 1 of the Crime and Disorder Act 1998. Anti-social behaviour orders cannot not be made against any child under the age of 10.

Children under 10 who have committed criminal-type behaviour can be dealt with in other ways. The local authority can bring proceedings in the family court under s 31 of the Children Act 1989 asking for an order that the child be placed in the care of the local authority or for an order placing the child under the supervision of the local authority or a probation officer. Such an order will only be made if it is in the interests of the child's welfare and the court is satisfied under s 31(2) of the Children Act 1989:

31(2)(a) that the child concerned is suffering, or is likely to suffer, significant harm; and

    (b) that harm, or the likelihood of harm, is attributable to –

        (i) the care given to the child, or likely to be given to him if the order were not made, not being what it would be reasonable to expect a parent to give to him; or

        (ii) the child's being beyond parental control.'

7.1.2 Child safety orders

The other area where the law does now allow orders to be made in respect of children under 10 is in respect of child safety orders under s 11 of the Crime and Disorder Act 1998. This focuses on behavioural problems of the child and an order can be made if:

- the child has committed an act which, if he had been aged 10 or over, would be an offence or
- a child safety order is necessary to prevent the child committing an act which, if he had been aged ten or over, would be an offence or
- the child has broken a curfew order imposed under s 14 of the Crime and Disorder Act 1998; or the child has acted in a manner that caused or was likely to cause harassment, alarm or distress to one or more person not of the same household as himself.

The local authority has to apply to a Magistrates' Family Proceedings Court for an order. If it is granted the magistrates can place the child under the supervision of a social worker or a member of a youth offending team for a period of up to three months. This period can be extended to 12 months if the court is satisfied that the circumstances of the case are exceptional. The magistrates can also add on conditions which they think are desirable in securing that the child receives appropriate care, protection and support and is subject to proper control or to prevent any repetition of the kind of behaviour which led to the child safety order being made.

These powers are aimed at preventing children from becoming criminal offenders when they are older. It is also probable that a parenting order will be made at the same time requiring the parents of the child to comply with requirements thought necessary and/or attend at counselling or guidance sessions.

7.1.3 Children aged 10 and over

In the legal system there are different terms for different age groups. These are:

- those aged 10 but under 14 are known as 'children'
- those aged 14 but under 17 are known as 'young persons'
- those offenders aged 14 but under 21 are known as 'young offenders'.

Until 1998 there was a rebuttable presumption that those aged 10 to 13 inclusive were *doli incapax*. This meant that they were presumed not to be capable of committing an offence but the prosecution could rebut this presumption by bringing evidence that the child knew that what he did was seriously wrong. The need for such a presumption was challenged by the Queen's Bench Divisional Court in *C v DPP* [1995] 2 All ER 43.

CASE EXAMPLE

C v DPP [1995] 2 All ER 43

D a boy aged 12 was seen tampering with a motorcycle and, when challenged, ran away. The prosecution relied on the fact that he had run away as evidence that he knew that what he was doing was seriously wrong. The Divisional Court held that this was insufficient to rebut the presumption of *doli incapax*, as it could show mere naughtiness rather than a realisation that what he was doing was seriously wrong.

However, they thought that the presumption was out of date and should no longer be part of our law. Mann LJ said:

> J 'Whatever may have been the position in any earlier age, when there was no system of universal compulsory education and when perhaps children did not grow up as quickly as they do nowadays, this presumption at the present time is a serious disservice to our law . . . it is unreal and contrary to common sense.'

Although the Divisional Court rejected the presumption, the case was appealed to the House of Lords. They held that it was not the judges' role to abolish such a long-standing law and that if the Government thought it should be abolished, then they could do so democratically through Parliament. The Government did take action and s 34 Crime and Disorder Act 1998 abolished the rebuttable presumption that a child aged 10 to 13 is incapable of committing an offence.

Not everyone agreed that the presumption should be abolished. One view is that it means that a child aged 10 and over is considered to be 'as responsible for his actions as if he were 40'. This was particularly so for offences in which the concept of objective recklessness used to apply the standards of the reasonable adult and the fact that the defendant was a child was ignored. However, since *G and another* [2003] UKHL 50, in which the House of Lords effectively abolished the concept of objective recklessness at least as far as criminal damage is concerned, this objection is no longer valid. The prosecution have to prove the relevant *mens rea* for the offence charged, so a child defendant will only be found guilty if he or she is proved to have had the necessary intent. If a child, because of lack of understanding, does not have the necessary intent, they will be acquitted.

Rape cases

There was also an irrebutable presumption that boys under the age of 14 were incapable of having sexual intercourse and therefore incapable of committing as principal the offence of rape or any other offence requiring proof of sexual penetration. This presumption was felt to be out of date due to the fact that physical development can be much earlier and it seemed unjust to have a rule which prevented prosecution for such serious offences. The presumption was eventually abolished by s 1 of the Sexual Offences Act 1993 and over the past decade there have been a number of convictions.

Trial

One way in which child defendants are dealt with differently to older offenders is that, for all but the most serious offences, children and young persons are tried in the Youth Court. The procedure here is more informal and in private. For some very serious offences, including murder, manslaughter and rape, a child defendant must be tried in the Crown Court. It is also possible for them to be sent for trial at the Crown Court where the offence would, if the defendant was an adult, carry a maximum penalty of 14 years' imprisonment. Where a child or young person is being tried in the Crown Court, special arrangements must be made to allow him to participate effectively in the trial. In *T v UK; V v UK* (1999) 7 EHRR 659 it was held that if this is not done, there may be a breach of art 6 of the European Convention on Human Rights.

There are also different sentencing powers for child offenders and young offenders compared to those for adults. Most sentences for children are aimed at reforming their behaviour. However, for serious offences or for repeat offenders, custodial sentences can be imposed.

KEY FACTS

Age	Law	Comment
Under 10	They are *doli incapax*, that is deemed incapable of committing a crime (s 50 Children and Young Persons Act 1933).	Is 10 the right age? Should it be raised to 12?
	Liable to a child safety order (s 11 Crime and Disorder Act 1998).	Is the use of a child safety order merely a way round the *doli incapax* rule?
		Or does it serve a useful purpose in preventing young children from becoming criminal offenders when they are older?
10–13 inclusive	Now fully responsible for their actions (s 34 Crime and Disorder Act 1998).	Is it right that the level of responsibility for their actions be the same as for an adult?
	Previously there was a rebuttable presumption that they were *doli incapax*.	Should the rebuttable presumption have been abolished?
14–17 inclusive	Fully responsible for their actions.	Allowance for their age can be made in sentencing.

7.2 Mentally ill persons

The defendant's mental capacity is relevant at three different stages in the criminal justice process. These are:

- at the point of the commission of the offence
- at the time of trial
- when the defendant is sentenced.

There is also a special defence to murder of diminished responsibility, where the defendant's mental state may provide a partial defence so that the offence is reduced to manslaughter.

7.2.1 Unfitness to plead

Even before the trial, there are procedures for dealing with mentally ill defendants. Under the Mental Health Act 1983 it is possible for a defendant who has been refused bail to be detained in a mental hospital, instead of on remand in prison. This can only occur where the Home Secretary has reports from at least two medical practitioners and is satisfied that the defendant is suffering from mental illness or severe mental impairment The Home Secretary will only exercise this power:

> 'where the prisoner's condition is such that immediate removal to a mental hospital
> is necessary, that it would not be practicable to bring him before a court, or that
> the trial is likely to have an injurious effect on his mental state.'

> *Report of the Royal Commission on Capital Punishment*, Cmd 8932 (1953)

If the Home Secretary uses this power, then the defendant will still be brought to trial when he is well enough.

At the trial

When the defendant is brought up for trial the court may consider the question of whether he is fit to plead. This can occur whether or not the accused has been sent to a mental hospital under the power above. The court is concerned with whether the defendant is able to understand the charge and the difference between a plea of guilty and not guilty; whether he is able to instruct lawyers and follow the evidence. Where he is unable to defend himself properly because of his mental state the Criminal Procedure (Insanity) Act 1964, as amended by the Criminal Procedure (Insanity and Unfitness to Plead) Act 1991 and the Domestic Violence, Crime and Victims Act 2004, allows him to be found unfit to plead.

The issue is decided by a judge without a jury. There must be evidence of at least two medical practitioners, at least one of whom is approved by the Home Office as having special experience in the field of mental disorder.

Burden of proof

If the defence raise the issue that the defendant is unfit to plead, then the burden of proof is on the defence, but it need only prove it to the civil standard of the balance of probabilities (see Chapter 1, section 1.8.2). If the prosecution raises the issue then it must prove it beyond reasonable doubt.

Finding of unfitness to plead

If the defendant is found unfit to plead then a jury must be sworn in to decide whether the defendant 'did the act or made the omission charged against him'. This provision is in the Criminal Procedure (Insanity) Act 1964 as amended. In *Antoine* [2000] 2 All ER 208 it was decided that the words 'did the act or made the omission' mean that the jury only have to consider the *actus reus* of the offence. It is not necessary for the jury to consider the mental element of the crime. If the jury find that the defendant did not do the *actus reus,* then the defendant cannot be held under any criminal law provision, though he may still be detained in a mental hospital if his condition warrants this under the Mental Health Act 1983.

When a defendant is found unfit to plead and the jury decide that he or she did do the relevant *actus reus*, the judge has the power to make one of the following orders:

• a hospital order (with or without a restriction order)

• a supervision order, or

• an absolute discharge.

If the offence is one for which the sentence is fixed by law, for example murder where there is a mandatory sentence of life imprisonment and the court have the power to make a hospital order, then the judge must make a hospital order with a restriction order.

7.2.2 Insanity at time of offence

Where a person is fit to plead but is found to be insane at the time he committed the offence, a special verdict of 'Not guilty by reason of insanity' is given by the jury. The rules on insanity come from the M'Naghten Rules (see Chapter 8). Where the verdict is 'Not guilty by reason of insanity', the judge has the same powers of disposal under the Criminal Procedure (Insanity and Unfitness to Plead) Act 1991 as set out above in section 7.2.1.

7.2.3 Diminished responsibility

This is a partial defence which is only available on a charge of murder. It is set out in s 2 Homicide Act 1957 and operates where a person suffers from an abnormality of the mind which substantially impairs his mental responsibility for his acts or omissions in doing or being a party to the killing (see Chapter 9 for full discussion of the defence). If the defence is successful the charge of murder is reduced to manslaughter.

7.2.4 Sentencing mentally ill offenders

As well as the normal range of custodial and community penalties there are also special powers available to the courts when dealing with mental ill people who have been convicted of an offence. The aim is to provide treatment and help for such people while at the same time balancing the need for society to be protected from any danger posed by the person. The main additional powers available to the courts are:

- a community sentence with a treatment requirement
- a hospital order
- a restriction order under s 41 of the Mental Health Act 1983.

This last order can only be made in the Crown Court when the offender is considered to be danger to the community. The order means that the offender is sent to a secure hospital for a set period or, where necessary, for an indefinite period.

ACTIVITY

Self-test questions

1. What is the *doli incapax* presumption and at what age does it cease to apply in England and Wales?
2. What other differences are there in the way children and young people are dealt with in the criminal justice system?
3. What is the purpose of the unfitness to plead procedure?
4. What safeguards are there for defendants when the unfitness to plead procedure is used?
5. Apart from the unfitness to plead procedure when is the mental health of the defendant a relevant matter in criminal proceedings?

7.3 Vicarious liability

There is a rule in the law of torts that one person can be liable for the torts committed by another. This is known as vicarious liability. It usually occurs in the employer/employee relationship where the employer is liable for any torts committed by an employee in the course of his employment. However, in criminal law the normal rule is that one person is not liable for crimes committed by another. This was illustrated nearly 300 years ago in *Huggins* (1730) 2 Strange 883, where the warden of Fleet prison was acquitted of the murder of a prisoner who had been placed in an unhealthy cell by one of the turnkeys (gaolers). The warden did not know that this had been done. Raymond CJ in this 1730 case pointed out the difference between civil and criminal law when he said:

J 'It is a point not to be disputed but that in criminal cases the principal is not answerable for the act of the deputy as he is in civil cases; they must each answer for their own acts and stand or fall by their own behaviour. All the authors that treat of criminal proceedings proceed on the foundation of this distinction; that to affect the superior by the act of the deputy there must be command of the superior which is not found in this case.'

However, there are some situations in criminal law where one person can be liable for the acts or omission of another. These are:

- common law crimes of public nuisance and criminal libel
- statutory offences where a statute imposes vicarious liability.

At common law the principle expressed in *Huggins* nearly always applies. The only exceptions are the offences of public nuisance and criminal libel where the actions of an employee can make his employer vicarious liability. Causing a public nuisance on the highway can be disruptive to the general public and a reason for having vicarious liability for public nuisance is that it is likely to encourage employers to take steps to prevent their employees from creating the nuisance.

In statute law Parliament can make any offence it thinks appropriate one of vicarious liability by including such words as 'person, himself or by his servant or agent' in the offence. As well as having clear wording imposing vicarious liability it also imposed in two other ways. These are:

- through the extended meanings of words
- under the principle of delegation.

Who can be vicariously liable?

The main categories of people who can be vicariously liable are:

- principals, including corporations, for acts of their agents
- employers, including corporations, for acts of their employees
- licensees for acts of others employed in the business for which the licensee holds the licence where they have delegated control of the business. This is so even though the licensee may himself be an employee of the brewer or other owner of the premises which are licensed.

Vicarious liability can make principals responsible for the actions of their agents. In *Duke of Leinster* [1924] 1 KB 311 the Duke was a bankrupt. He was convicted of obtaining credit without disclosing his bankrupt status. In fact it was his agent who, contrary to the Duke's instructions, had obtained the credit without disclosing the facts. The Duke was guilty because he was vicariously liable for his agent's failure to disclose the bankruptcy.

The main area in which vicarious liability exists is where employers are liable for the actions of their employees.

7.3.1 Extended meaning of words

Words such as 'sell' and 'use' are usually taken to include the employer (or principal or licensee), even though the actual sale or use is by an employee. These are strict liability offences where there is no need to prove any mental element. In such a case the act of the employee (selling, using etc) is the act of the employer. However, vicarious liability can only occur where an employee is doing an act which he is employed or authorised to do. Where the employee is not authorised to carry out the act then the employer is not liable. In *Adams v Camfoni* [1929] 1 KB 95 D was a licensee who was charged with selling alcohol outside the hours permitted by the licence. The sale had been made by a messenger boy who had no authority to sell anything. D was held to be not guilty.

If the employee is carrying out an authorised act then the employer will be liable even though the employee does it in a way which has not been authorised. This was seen in *Coppen v Moore (No 2)* [1898] 2 QB 306 where a sales assistant sold ham which she wrongly described as 'Scotch ham' against instruction of the employer. The employer was liable because the assistant was authorised to sell the item.

Vicarious liability still exists even where the employer has taken steps to ensure that such an offence is not committed. In *Harrow LBC v Shah and Shah* [1999] 3 All ER 302 the Shahs were newsagents who were convicted of selling a lottery ticket to a boy under 16. They had instructed their staff not to sell ticket to under-age children and also told the staff that if they were not sure, they should ask the Shahs to check that it was all right to sell a ticket. An employee sold a ticket to a boy whom he reasonably thought was 16 or over, when the boy was in fact under 16. One of the Shahs was on the premises, though not in the shop when the sale was made. Despite these facts the Shahs were still held to be vicariously liable for the sale.

7.3.2 Delegation principle

Where an offence requires proof of *mens rea* then vicarious liability can only exist if the principal has delegated responsibility. In such instances the acts and intention of the person to whom responsibility has been delegated are imputed to the principal. This was demonstrated in *Allen v Whitehead* [1930] 1 KB 211.

CASE EXAMPLE

Allen v Whitehead [1930] 1 KB 211

The defendant owned a café which was run by a manager. He was charged under s 44 of the Metropolitan Police Act 1839 with the offence of knowingly permitting or suffering prostitutes to meet together and remain in a place where refreshments are sold and consumed. D had been warned by the police that prostitutes were meeting in his café and had instructed his manager not to allow this. D also had a notice displayed on the wall of the café forbidding prostitutes to meet at the café. He visited the café once or twice a week and there was no evidence that there had been any breach of the 1839 Act while he was on the premises. However, the manager allowed prostitutes to stay at the café for several hours on eight consecutive days. D was charged and it was held by the Divisional Court that both the acts and knowledge of his manager were to be imputed to D. The fact that he did not know of the breach was not a defence. He had delegated the management of the café to the manager and this made D liable.

In *Linnett v Metropolitan Police Commissioner* [1946] 1 All ER 380 the same principle was used to make a co-licensee liable for the acts of his fellow co-licensee. He had delegated the management of a refreshment house to his co-licensee and was absent from the premises but was still held guilty of 'knowingly permitting disorderly conduct', even though he personally had no knowledge of it.

There must be complete delegation for the principal to be vicariously liable, as seen in the case of *Vane v Yiannopoullos* [1964] 3 All ER 820.

CASE EXAMPLE

Vane v Yiannopoullos [1964] 3 All ER 820

D was the licensee of a restaurant. He had given instructions to the waitress in the restaurant not to serve alcoholic drinks to people unless they ordered a meal as well. While D was on another floor of the building a waitress served alcohol to two youths who did not order a meal. D was charged with the offence of 'knowingly selling intoxicating liquor to person to whom he was not entitled to sell', contrary to s 22 of the Licensing Act 1961, but acquitted. The prosecution appealed against this but the Divisional Court dismissed the appeal. The prosecutor appealed to the House of Lords. The Lords dismissed the appeal, holding that there had not been sufficient delegation to make D vicariously liable for the employee's actions.

The House of Lords pointed out that the principle had never been extended to cover the case where the whole of the authority has not been transferred to another. In fact Lord Reid appeared to confine the principle to situations in which the licensee was not on the premises but had left someone else in charge. However, in *Howker v Robinson* [1972] 2 All ER 786 the Divisional Court found that the magistrates had correctly decided that a licensee was guilty when an illegal sale was made by a barman in the lounge, even though the licensee was present (and working) in the public bar of the business. This decision is contrary to the House of Lords' judgment in *Vane* and is unlikely to be followed in future cases. Indeed, in the later case of *Bradshaw v Ewart-Jones* [1983] 1 All ER 12, the Divisional Court did not apply the doctrine but held that the master of a ship was not liable for breach of statutory duty when he had delegated performance of the duty to his chief officer. The master was still on board the ship and in command, so the delegation was only partial.

Should delegation impose liability?

In most of the offences where the delegation principle is used there is no provision for making the servant himself liable to prosecution. So, unless the licensee is made liable, it would be impossible to enforce the law adequately. The main problem comes where the particular offence includes the word 'knowingly'. If the licensee does not know the relevant facts, should the knowledge of the person to whom he has delegated control by imputed to him? In *Vane v Yiannopoullos* (1964) the

House of Lords was unhappy about the use of the delegation principle where the offence charged included the word 'knowingly'. Lord Reid, who gave the leading judgment, pointed out that there had been only four cases in the 60 years before *Vane* in which the offence used the word 'knowingly'. Two of these were *Allen v Whitehead* (1930) and *Linnett v Metropolitan Police Commissioner* (1946), which are explained above. Lord Reid; in *Vane*, said:

> **J** '[T]he courts adopted a construction which on any view I find hard to justify. They drew a distinction between acts done by a servant without the knowledge of the licence holder while the licence holder was on the premises and giving general supervision to his business, and acts done without the knowledge of the licence holder but with the knowledge of a person whom the license holder had left in charge of the premises. In the latter case they held that the knowledge of the person left in charge must be imputed to the licence holder . . . If this were a new distinction recently introduced by the courts I would think it necessary to consider whether a provision that the licence holder shall not knowingly sell can ever make him vicariously liable by reason of the knowledge of some other person; but this distinction has now been recognised and acted on by the courts for over half a century. It may have been unwarranted in the first instance, but I would think it now too late to upset so long-standing a practice.'

ACTIVITY

Discuss whether Lord Reid's view that the practice was long-standing justifies imposing liability on a licence holder when he has no knowledge of the offence and its circumstances.

7.3.3 Reasons for vicarious liability

The main reason for vicarious liability is that it makes it easier to enforce regulations about such matters as selling food and alcohol and using vehicles. Modern regulatory legislation in these areas is aimed at protecting consumers and promoting public health and safety and preventing pollution. If employers were not liable for the acts of their employees then it would be virtually impossible to enforce such legislation. It is fair and just that those who make the profits from a business should also pay for any breaches of standards in that business. Without the principle of vicarious liability, it would be difficult to convict those responsible for the business. By imposing liability on the principal, employer, or licensee this will make him do all he can to prevent breaches of the legislation by his agents, servants of delegates. Employers are more likely to train and control staff properly and the principle of delegation makes a licensee retain proper control over his business even when he is not there.

Key facts on vicarious liability

KEY FACTS

	Law	Cases
Who can be vicariously liable?	Principals for acts of their agents.	*Duke of Leinster* (1924)
	Employers for acts of their employees.	*Coppen v Moore (No 2)* (1898)
	Licensees for acts of those to whom they delegate responsibility.	*Allen v Whitehead* (1930)
When does vicarious liability exist?	Common law offences of public nuisance and criminal libel.	Very rare
	Extended meaning of words in statutory offences where an employee is acting within the scope of his employment.	*Coppen v Moore (No 2)* (1898) owner of business was liable for a sale made by employee
	Delegation principle.	*Allen v Whitehead* (1930)
The extended meanings of words	An employer is liable even though the employee is disobeying instructions.	*Coppen v Moore (No 2)* (1898)
	An employer is not liable if the employee is not acting within the scope of his employment.	*Adams v Camfoni* (1929)
The delegation principle	A licensee is liable where there is full delegation.	*Allen v Whitehead* (1930)
	A licensee is not liable where there is partial delegation.	*Vane v Yiannopoullos* (1964)

7.3.4 Criticisms of vicarious liability

The main criticism is that it is unjust to penalise someone for the actions of another. This is especially so where the principal has taken steps to ensure that no offence is committed. For example in *Coppen* (1898) the sales assistant had disobeyed the instructions of her employer and yet the employer was still liable. Also in *Duke of Leinster* (1924) the agent had acted contrary to the Duke's instructions when he obtained credit without disclosing the bankruptcy. Again in *Harrow LBC* (1999) the owners of the newsagent business had done all that was within their power to prevent the sale of lottery tickets to under-age children yet were still convicted of the offence.

These criticisms would be avoided if a defence of 'due diligence' were available for all regulatory offences. Some statutes do contain this defence which can be used if the employer can show that he exercised all due diligence in the management of the business and that there was nothing more that could reasonably have done to prevent a breach.

Where an offence requires *mens rea* it is even more unjust to convict someone who had no knowledge of the offence. This is the effect of the delegation principle as illustrated in the cases of *Allen* (1930) and *Linnett* (1946). In both those cases the licensee had no knowledge of the offence but was convicted of 'knowingly permitting' it. It should also be considered that the rules of vicarious liability have not been created by Parliament; they are judge-made. In some cases where Parliament has used the word 'knowingly' in an offence, the concept of vicarious liability appears to be contrary to the intentions of Parliament.

ACTIVITY

Self-test questions

1. Who can be held vicariously liable for a criminal offence?
2. Explain with examples the two ways in which vicarious liability may be imposed for statutory offences.
3. What problems have the courts identified with the use of the delegation principle in vicarious liability?
4. Why is vicarious liability used in criminal law?

7.4 Corporate liability

A corporation is a legal person. Corporations include limited companies, public corporations and local authorities. It was established in *Salomon v Salomon & Co Ltd* [1897] AC 22 that on incorporation, a company acquires a separate legal personality from its members.

As a corporation is a legal person, it can be criminally liable even though it has no physical existence. This ability to be liable for statutory offences is set out in the Interpretation Act 1978, which provides that in every Act, unless the contrary intention appears, 'person' includes a body of persons, corporate

or unincorporate. This rule has existed for over a hundred years as it existed in the previous Interpretation Act of 1889. In fact the interpretation is even wider than making corporations liable, as it also includes unincorporated bodies such as a partnership. As well as being liable for statutory offences the common law also recognises that a corporation can be criminally liable for common law offences such as manslaughter. The issue of whether a corporation could be convicted of manslaughter was resolved in *P & O European Ferries (Dover) Ltd* (1991) 93 Cr App R 72 (see section 7.4.5).

There are three different principles by which a corporation may be liable. These are:

- the principle of identification
- vicarious liability
- breach of statutory duty.

These are considered separately in sections 7.4.2, 7.4.3 and 7.4.4.

7.4.1 Exceptions to the general rule of liability

There are two general exceptions to corporate liability for criminal offences. Firstly, a corporation cannot be convicted of an offence where the only punishment available is physical, such as imprisonment or community service. Effectively the only offence that is currently eliminated by this rule is murder, which carries a mandatory sentence of life imprisonment. Corporations can be liable for any offence which has a discretionary maximum penalty of life imprisonment, since for these the judge can impose alternative penalties such as a fine.

Secondly a corporation cannot be liable as a principal for crimes such as bigamy, rape, incest or perjury, which by their physical nature can only be committed by a real person. A corporation, however, may be liable as a secondary participant in such offences. J C Smith in *Criminal Law: Cases and Materials* (8th edn) puts forward the example that a corporation could be liable as a secondary participant for bigamy if the managing director of an incorporated marriage advisory bureau were to arrange a marriage which he knew to be bigamous.

In *Robert Millar (Contractors) Ltd* [1971] 1 All ER 577 a company was convicted of being a secondary participant to the offence of causing death by dangerous driving. The managing director of the company had sent a lorry on a long journey, knowing that it had a seriously defective tyre. The tyre burst and the lorry crashed causing six deaths. The driver was convicted as principal of six offences of causing death by dangerous driving and the managing director and the company were convicted of counselling and procuring those offences.

7.4.2 The principle of identification

Where an offence requires *mens rea* it is necessary to show that the corporation had the required *mens rea*. As a corporation has no body and no mind this causes problems in making corporations liable. In order to hold corporations liable the courts have sought to identify a person (or persons) within the company structure whose mind is the 'directing mind and will' of the corporation. This phrase was first used in *Lennard's Carrying Co Ltd v Asiatic Petroleum Co Ltd* [1915] AC 705, but the identification principle was really established by three cases in 1944. These were:

- *DPP v Kent and Sussex Contractors Ltd* [1944] KB 146

- *ICR Haulage Ltd* [1944] KB 551

- *Moore v I Bresler Ltd* [1944] 2 All ER 515.

In each case one or more senior members of the management of the company were identified as the directing mind and will, so that their intent was deemed to be the intent of the company. For example in *DPP v Kent and Sussex Contractors Ltd* (1944) the offence required an intent to deceive, and the courts held that the intent of the transport manager of the company was the intent of the company. It could, however, be argued that a transport manager is not sufficiently senior for his intent to be the intent of the company. In *ICR Haulage Ltd* (1944) the company was convicted of a common law conspiracy to defraud. The act and the intent of the managing director were held to be the act and intent of the company. In *Moore v I Bresler Ltd* (1944) the company was convicted of making false returns with intent to deceive, contrary to the Finance (No 2) Act 1940. The returns had been made by the company secretary and a branch sales manager. There is no doubt that a company secretary is an official whose acts and intent will be viewed as the company's acts and intent. However, this case can be criticised for including a branch sales manager in the category of the directing mind and will of the company.

As a corporation has no physical existence it is always necessary to identify those people within the corporation who can be considered as the directing mind and will of the company. In *H L Bolton (Engineering) Co. Ltd v TJ Graham & Sons Ltd* [1956] 3 All ER 624 Denning LJ pointed out that:

> **J** 'A company may in many ways be likened to a human body. It has a brain and a nerve centre which controls what it does. It also has hands which hold the tools and act in accordance with directions from the centre. Some of the people in the company are mere servants and agents who are nothing more than hands to do the work and cannot be said to represent the mind or will. Others are directors and managers who represent the directing mind and will of the company and control what it does. The state of mind of these managers is the state of mind of the company and is treated by the law as such.'

This concept was used by the courts in subsequent cases, but in very large companies with several layers of management, there can be difficulties in deciding who exactly is the 'brain', in Lord Denning's analogy, as against those who are 'nothing more than hands to do the work'. For example, in *Tesco Supermarkets Ltd v Nattrass* [1972] AC 153 Tesco advertised packs of washing powder in the shop window of one of their stores at a reduced price. An employee failed to tell the store manager when all the packs were sold, so that the advertisement continued even though there were no reduced packs left. A shopper who tried to buy a reduced priced pack was told that the only packets left were full price. The shopper complained to the Inspector of Weights and Measures, and Tesco was prosecuted under s 11 of the Trade Descriptions Act 1968, which provides that:

'11 If any person offering to supply any goods gives, by whatever means, any indication likely to be taken as an indication that the goods are being offered at a price less that that at which they are in fact being offered he shall . . . be guilty of an offence.'

Tesco accepted that this had happened, but claimed a defence under s 24(1) of the Trade Descriptions Act, that the fault was due to another person. As it was the fault of the manager for not adequately supervising the employee who had failed to check the packs, the question for the courts to decide was whether the store manager was identified as the company, or whether he was 'another person' for the purpose of s 24(1). Tesco was convicted and appealed. The Divisional Court held that the store manager was 'the embodiment of the company' and dismissed the appeal. The case was then appealed to the House of Lords, who ruled that a store manager was not sufficiently senior for his acts to be the acts of the company.

Lord Reid started his judgment by considering the nature of corporate personality. He said:

> J
>
> 'A living person has a mind which can have knowledge or intention or be negligent and he has hands to carry out his intentions. A corporation has none of these; it must act through living persons, though not always one or the same person. Then the person who acts is not speaking or acting for the company. He is acting as the company and his mind which directs his acts is the mind of the company. There is no question of the company being vicariously liable. He is not acting as a servant, representative, agent or delegate. He is an embodiment of the company or, one could say, he hears and speaks through the persona of the company, within his appropriate sphere, and his mind is the mind of the company. If it is a guilty mind then that guilt is the guilt of the company.'

Lord Reid also referred to Lord Denning's comparison of a company to a human body in *H L Bolton (Engineering) Co Ltd* (1956). He pointed out that there had been attempts to apply Lord Denning's words to all servants of a company whose work was brain work or who exercised some managerial discretion under the direction of superior officers of the company. Lord Reid felt that this was not what had been intended. Lord Denning had limited the category to those 'who represent the directing mind and will of the company and control what it does'. For this reason the manager of a local store could not be identified with the company and so, for the purposes of s 24(1) of the Trade Descriptions Act 1968, the manager was 'another person'. Effectively this case decided that only those in senior positions or those who have been given power to act as the company can be considered as the 'controlling mind' of a corporation.

Lord Reid thought that those who would be the embodiment of the company were:

> **J** 'the board of directors, the managing director and perhaps other superior officers of a company [who] carry out the functions of management and speak and act as the company.'

However, other judges in the House of Lords gave slightly different definitions. Viscount Dilhorne thought that it was a person:

> **J** 'who is in actual control of the operations of a company or of part of them and who is not responsible to another person in the company for the manner in which he discharges his duties in the sense of being under orders.'

Lord Diplock thought that it was necessary to identify:

> **J** 'those natural persons who by the memorandum and articles of association or as a result of action taken by the directors or by the company in general meeting pursuant to the articles are entrusted with the exercise of the powers of the company.'

Apart from deciding who exactly can be identified as being the company, the principle of identification causes problems in the following three areas.

1. The bigger the company and the more layers of management, the less likely it is that a senior officer will have made a decision (or have the required *mens rea*) to make the company liable. This means that bigger companies are more likely to avoid prosecution.

2. The principle of identification does not work where there are several people who have combined to create a dangerous situation, but individually they have not got the required *mens rea*. This was seen in *P & O European Ferries (Dover) Ltd* (1991) where there were several failures by different levels of staff which resulted in the cross-channel ferry, the *Herald of Free Enterprise*, leaving the port of Zeebrugge with her bow doors open. As a result the ship sank and 187 people were killed. The company was not criminally liable for the deaths as there was no individual whose negligence could be identified as the negligence of the company. It can be argued that the faults of different people should be aggregated to prove the guilty mind of the company. The opposite view was put by Devlin J in *Armstrong v Strain* [1952] 1 All ER 139, when he said that:

> **J** 'You cannot add an innocent state of mind to an innocent state of mind and get as a result a dishonest state of mind.'

3. The principle in *Tesco v Nattrass* (1972) could lead to companies being found not guilty of regulatory offences and this would make regulation ineffective against big companies. However, in *Tesco v Brent LBC* [1993] 2 All ER 718 this result was avoided by the Divisional Court. In this case Tesco was convicted of supplying a pre-recorded video with an 18 rating to someone under the age of 18, contrary to s 11(1) of the Video Recordings Act 1984. The Act allowed a defence if the defendant 'neither knew nor had reasonable grounds to believe that the person concerned had not attained that age'. Tesco argued that the directing minds of the company, in other words the board and managing director, would have no way of knowing the age of the purchaser. They would not be present at the store, but worked from the London headquarters of the company. The Divisional Court dismissed Tesco's appeal. They held it was impracticable to suppose that those who controlled a large company would have any knowledge or information about the age of a purchaser. The only person who could have that knowledge was the cashier who served the purchaser. As the magistrates had been satisfied that the cashier had reasonable grounds to believe that the purchaser was under 18, then that was enough to make the company liable. This can be viewed as an extension of the principle of vicarious liability where a company is responsible for the acts of its employees (see section 7.4.3).

In addition to the above problems, Lord Denning's analogy in *H L Bolton (Engineering)* (1956) has been criticised by the Privy Council in *Meridian Global Funds Management Asia Ltd v Securities Commission* [1995] 3 All ER 918.

CASE EXAMPLE

Meridian Global Funds Management Asia Ltd v Securities Commission [1995] 3 All ER 918

The chief investment officer and the senior portfolio manager of Meridian used funds managed by the company to acquire shares in a public issue. They did not give notice as required by s 20 of the New Zealand Securities Amendment Act 1988. The board of directors and managing director were not aware of the purchase or the failure to give notice. The trial judge found the company guilty of a breach of s 20 as he held that the knowledge of the chief investment officer and the senior portfolio manager was to be attributed to the company. On appeal to New Zealand's Court of Appeal the conviction was upheld on the basis that the chief investment officer was the directing mind and will of the company. The case was then appealed to the Privy Council.

In the Privy Council Lord Hoffmann pointed out that the phrase 'directing mind and will' had first been used by Viscount Haldane in *Lennard's Carrying Co Ltd* (1915) in a very specific circumstance. Lord Hoffmann said of Denning LJ's comments:

> J 'But this . . . by the very power of the image, distracts attention from the purpose for which Viscount Haldane said he was using the notion of the directing mind and will, namely to apply the attribution rule derived from s 502 [of the Merchant Shipping Act 1894] to the particular defendant in the case:
>
> "For if Mr Lennard was the directing mind of the company, then his action must, unless a corporation is not to be liable at all, have been an action which was the action of the company itself within the meaning of section 502." '

Instead of using the identification principle, the Privy Council relied on the idea of the 'rules of attribution'. Lord Hoffmann explained what was meant when he said:

> J 'Any proposition about a company necessarily involves a reference to a set of rules. A company exists because there is a rule (usually in a statute) which says that a *persona ficta* [fictional person] shall be deemed to exist and to have certain of the powers, rights and duties of a natural person. But there would be little sense in deeming such a *persona ficta* to exist unless there were also rules to tell one what acts were to count as acts of the company. It is therefore a necessary part of corporate personality that there should be rules by which acts are attributed to the company. These may be called "the rules of attribution".
>
> The company's primary rules of attribution will generally be found in its constitution, typically the articles of association, and will say things such as "for the purpose of appointing members of the board, a majority vote of shareholders shall be a decision of the company" or "the decisions of the board in managing the company's business shall be the decisions of the company" . . .
>
> The company's primary rules of attribution together with the general principles of agency, vicarious liability and so forth are usually sufficient to enable one to determine its rights and obligations.'

Lord Hoffmann did accept that there would be exceptional cases where these rules would not provide an answer. In these cases he thought that the normal rules of interpretation would provide the answer:

> J 'Given that it was intended to apply to a company, how was it intended to apply? Whose act (or knowledge, or state of mind) was *for this purpose* intended to count as the act etc of the company? One finds the answer to this question by applying the usual canons of interpretation, taking into account the language of the rule (if it is a statute) and its contents and policy.'

The main problem with this is that it appears to ignore common law offences where there is no written version of the offence to be interpreted. A major area where very few prosecutions have succeeded against corporations is for the common law offence of involuntary manslaughter. In view of the difficulty of establishing liability for manslaughter, the Law Commission recommended a new offence of corporate killing where a management failure is the cause (or one of the causes) of death, and that failure constitutes conduct falling far below what can reasonably be expected (see section 7.4.5 for further discussion on corporate manslaughter).

7.4.3 Vicarious liability

As already seen in section 7.3 the law recognises situations where one person may be liable for offences committed by another under the principles of vicarious liability. The principles of vicarious liability apply equally to corporations. So corporations may be vicariously liable for the acts of their employees in the same way as a natural person may be liable for his employee or agent. Liability of corporations by way of vicarious liability was first recognised many years ago in *Great North of England Railway Co* (1846) 9 QB 315.

Corporations can be liable where a statute imposes vicarious liability or, in rare instances, under the common law, for example the offence of creating a public nuisance.

Examples of corporations being vicariously liable include *Coppen v Moore (No 2)* (1898), where a sales assistant sold ham which she wrongly described as 'Scotch ham', against instruction of the employer. The employer was convicted of selling goods to which a false trade description applied because the assistant. The court pointed out that:

> J 'It cannot be doubted that the appellant sold the ham in question, although the transaction was carried our by his servants. In other words he was the seller, although not the salesman.'

Another example is *National Rivers Authority v Alfred McAlpine Homes (East) Ltd* (1994) 158 JP 628, in which employees of the company were constructing a water feature on the site. In doing this they discharged wet cement into it. The company was convicted of polluting a river. The judge said:

> J 'to make an offence an effective weapon in the defence of environmental protection, a company must, by necessary implication, be criminally liable for the acts and omissions of its servant or agents during activities being done for the company. I do not find that this affects our concept of a just or fair criminal justice system, having regard to the magnitude of environmental pollution.'

Distinction between the identification principle and vicarious liability

The liability of corporations under vicarious liability is quite different from the way in which liability arises under the identification principle. This was explained in *HM Coroner for East Kent, ex parte Spooner* (1989) 88 Cr App R 10 by Bingham LJ when he distinguished between the identification principle and a company being vicarious liable, saying:

> J 'A company may be vicariously liable for the negligent acts and omissions of its servants and agents, but for a company to be criminally liable for manslaughter it is required that *mens rea* and *actus reus* should be established not against those who acted for or in the name of the company but against those who were to be identified with the embodiment of the company itself.'

So for liability by the principle of identification it is necessary to prove *mens rea* and *actus reus* in someone who can be considered the company, whereas under the principles of vicarious liability the acts and omissions of employees or agents can make the company liable.

7.4.4 Breach of statutory duty

A statute or regulation can make a corporation liable for offences. In particular this can happen where the statute (or regulation) makes the occupier liable. If the corporation is the occupier of premises then it is liable for offences committed in relation to those premises. Equally a law may make an employer liable. If the corporation is the employer then it is liable. An important statute is the Health and Safety at Work etc Act 1974. In *Attorney-General's Reference (No 2 of 1999)* [2000] 3 All ER 187, where a train crash killed seven people, the company was found not guilty of manslaughter. However, the company pleaded guilty to a breach of statutory duty under the Health and Safety at Work etc Act 1974 and was fined £1.5 million.

This rule of liability for statutory breach also applies to unincorporated bodies if they are the occupier or employer. This was seen in *Clerk to the Croydon Justices, ex parte Chief Constable of Kent* [1989] Crim LR 910, where the Queen's Bench Divisional Court held that if an unincorporated body was the 'registered keeper' of a vehicle then it was liable for fixed penalties for illegal parking under the Transport Act 1982.

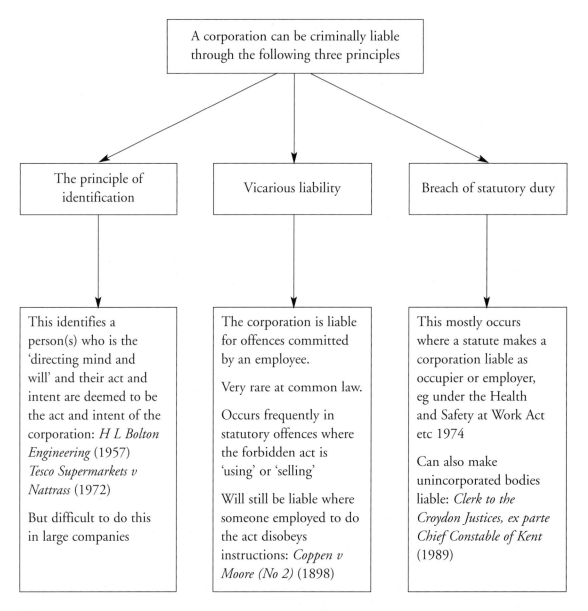

A corporation can be criminally liable through the following three principles

The principle of identification

Vicarious liability

Breach of statutory duty

This identifies a person(s) who is the 'directing mind and will' and their act and intent are deemed to be the act and intent of the corporation: *H L Bolton Engineering* (1957) *Tesco Supermarkets v Nattrass* (1972)

But difficult to do this in large companies

The corporation is liable for offences committed by an employee.

Very rare at common law.

Occurs frequently in statutory offences where the forbidden act is 'using' or 'selling'

Will still be liable where someone employed to do the act disobeys instructions: *Coppen v Moore (No 2)* (1898)

This mostly occurs where a statute makes a corporation liable as occupier or employer, eg under the Health and Safety at Work Act etc 1974

Can also make unincorporated bodies liable: *Clerk to the Croydon Justices, ex parte Chief Constable of Kent* (1989)

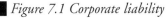 *Figure 7.1 Corporate liability*

7.4.5 Corporate manslaughter

In the past few years there have been a number of high-profile disasters in which people have died as a result of poor practice by a corporation. These have included:

- the *Herald of Free Enterprise* disaster in 1987, in which 192 people died
- the King's Cross fire in 1987, in which 31 people were killed
- the Clapham rail crash in 1988 when 35 people died and nearly 500 others were injured
- the Southall rail crash in 1997 when seven people were killed and 150 injured.

Initially it was thought that a corporation could not be liable for manslaughter. However, this was resolved in *P & O European Ferries (Dover) Ltd* (1991) when, following the *Herald of Free Enterprise* disaster, P & O (who had taken over Townsend Car Ferries Ltd, the operators the ferry at the time of the disaster) were charged with manslaughter.

CASE EXAMPLE

> ### *P & O European Ferries (Dover) Ltd* (1991) 93 Cr App R 72
>
> The car ferry sailed from Zeebrugge harbour with its inner and outer bow doors (through which the cars were loaded) still open. The assistant bosun should have closed the doors but he failed to do so because he had overslept. The Chief Officer who was in charge of loading the car deck was responsible for checking that the doors were closed, but in practice he interpreted this as checking that the assistant bosun was at the controls. The Master of the day was responsible for the safety of the ship on that sailing, but he merely followed the system approved by the Senior Master who had overall responsibility for co-ordinating the practice of all crews and Masters who worked in the *Herald of Free Enterprise*. Shore management had not provided any instructions on this aspect of ship safety.

The causes of the disaster were investigated by the Sheen Inquiry. This reached the conclusion that the immediate cause of the sinking was the Chief Officer's failure to ensure that the doors were closed. It also concluded that the Senior Master should have introduced a 'fail-safe system' so that the Master of the day knew when the doors were closed and it was safe to sail. However, the Sheen Report also found that the company's management had failed in their duties. The Report stated:

> 'At first sight the faults which led to this disaster were the . . . errors of omission on the part of the Master, the Chief Officer and the assistant bosun, and also the failure by Captain Kirby [Senior Master] to issue and enforce clear orders. But a full investigation into the circumstances of the disaster leads inexorably to the

conclusion that the underlying or cardinal faults lay higher up in the Company. The Board of Directors did not appreciate their responsibility for the safe management of their ships. They did not apply their minds to the question: What orders should be given for the safety of our ships? The directors did not have any proper comprehension what their duties were . . . All concerned in the management, from the members of the board down to junior superintendents, were guilty of fault in that all must be regarded as sharing responsibility for the failure of management. From the top to the bottom the body corporate was infected with the disease of sloppiness. The failure on the part of the shore management to give proper and clear directions was a contributory cause of the disaster.'

Para 14.1 The Sheen Report (Department of Transport, Report of the Court No 8074, 1987)

The Report went on to highlight three management failures. The first was that, although a proposal had been made by Masters that a warning light should be fitted on the bridge so that the Master on duty would know when the bow doors were shut, the management had failed to give this proposal serious consideration. Secondly there had been five or six previous incidents when ferries had sailed with doors open but these incidents had not been documented and collated. If they had been then the management of the company would have been alerted to the risk of disaster. Thirdly there was a lack of any proper system within the company to ensure that their ships were operated in accordance with the highest standards of safety.

The company and seven individuals were charged with manslaughter. At the start of the trial the company submitted that the counts for manslaughter should be quashed for two reasons. First, that English law did not recognise the offence of corporate manslaughter, and secondly, that manslaughter could only be committed by a natural person. The trial judge ruled that it was possible through the principle of identification for a corporation to be liable for manslaughter. He rejected the argument that manslaughter could only be committed by a natural person, pointing out that the old definitions of 'homicide' which use the words a killing by a *human being* were formulated when corporations did not exist. He held that where a corporation, through the controlling mind of one of its agents, did an act which fulfilled the definition of manslaughter, then the corporation could properly be indicted for the offence.

Although this case established that a corporation could be liable for manslaughter there have been only a very small number of prosecutions and even fewer convictions. This is because the way the principle of identification works makes it difficult to obtain a conviction against a corporation for manslaughter. For example, in the Clapham rail crash no prosecution was brought even though an inquiry into the matter criticised British Rail for allowing working practices which were 'positively dangerous'. Again, in the King's Cross fire no prosecution was brought because no one person had responsibility for fire precautions.

In the *P & O* case, although the company was prosecuted and the judge ruled that the case could go ahead, the charge was eventually dismissed by the judge because it was not possible to identify one person who was the controlling mind and will of the company and who had been grossly negligent. The disaster had occurred because of errors by a number of people, some of whom were very junior. The judge dismissed the case against all the defendants except the bosun and the Chief Officer. The prosecution then withdrew the charges against these two.

A prosecution was also brought in the Southall rail crash, where a high speed train collided with a freight train, causing the deaths of seven people. There was evidence that two safety devices on the train which would have prevented the train from passing a signal at danger were switched off. The driver failed to see a sequence of signals (green, double yellow, yellow and red) until it was too late to avoid the collision. He gave evidence that he remembered seeing the green signal and the next signal he could recall was the red one. There was no second driver in the cab. The judge ruled that to establish a charge for gross negligence manslaughter it was necessary to prove a guilty mind. Where the defendant was a company it could only be convicted if a person with whom it was identified had the necessary guilty mind. As no such person could be identified (the train driver was too junior for his mind to embody the mind and will of the company), the judge dismissed the case against the company.

Following the judge's ruling, the Attorney-General referred two questions of law to the Court of Appeal (*Attorney-General's Reference (No 2 of 1999)* [2000] 3 All ER 187). These were:

J

'**a** Can a defendant be properly convicted of manslaughter by gross negligence in the absence of evidence as to that defendant's state of mind?

b Can a non-human defendant be convicted of the crime of manslaughter by gross negligence in the absence of evidence establishing the guilt of an identified human individual for the same crime?'

The Court of Appeal answered the first question 'yes' and the second question 'no'. For corporate liability, it is the answer to the second question that is important. The Court of Appeal affirmed the identification principle and refused to follow the decision of the Privy Council in *Meridian Global Funds Management Asia Ltd* (1995) (see section 7.4.2 above). It rejected the aggregation theory for manslaughter, even though the company had pleaded guilty to breaches of health and safety legislation. There has been considerable criticism of this decision. This criticism is focused on the fact that gross negligence manslaughter is not an offence requiring *mens rea*. It involves the jury deciding whether the defendant's conduct was so grossly negligent as to amount to a crime. The company's breaches of health and safety legislation might have come within this category. The Court of Appeal appeared to have ignored the leading decision of *Adomako* [1994] 3 All ER 79 on

gross negligence and to have relied on cases prior to it which are no longer applicable. Indeed Rose LJ stated:

> **J** 'unless an identified individual's conduct, characterisable as gross criminal negligence, can be attributed to the company, the company is . . . not liable for manslaughter. Civil negligence rules . . . are not apt to confer criminal liability on a company.'

This statement on civil liability ignores Lord Mackay's judgment in *Adomako*, when he said that 'the ordinary principles of the law of negligence apply to ascertain whether or not the defendant has been in breach of a duty of care towards the victim who died'. If a breach is established it is that for the jury to decide if that breach caused the victim's death and if so, the jury then go on to consider whether that breach of duty should be characterised as gross negligence. However, Rose LJ pointed out that the decision the Court of Appeal came to in *Attorney-General's Reference (No 2 of 1999) (2000)* was consistent with the Law Commission's analysis of the law in its report *Legislating the Criminal Code: Involuntary Manslaughter* (Law Com No 237) (1996). The Law Commission's conclusions were that, in the present state of the law, a corporation could only be liable for manslaughter on the principle of the identification. This was why the Law Commission had drafted a Bill which, if enacted, would base liability on management failure.

Small companies

It is noticeable that the few successful convictions of a corporation for manslaughter have all involved small companies where it has been easier to identify an individual as the directing mind and will of the company. There have been at least four successful prosecutions. The first was *Kite and OLL, The Independent*, 9th December 1994, where four teenagers died in a canoeing tragedy because of the risks taken by the leisure company who organised the activity. The company was a one-man outfit run by Kite. His gross negligence was attributed to the company and both he and the company were convicted of manslaughter. More recently another small company, *Roy Bowles Transport Ltd, The Times*, 11th December 1999, was convicted of manslaughter. While the courts maintain the identification principle it is unlikely that a large company will ever be successfully prosecuted for manslaughter. This effect of the application of the law appears unjust on small companies.

Reform

The problems highlighted in the *P & O* (1991) case led to the Law Commission considering corporate manslaughter in a general review of the law on manslaughter. The Law Commission consulted on the problems before producing its report: *Legislating the Criminal Code: Involuntary Manslaughter* (Law Com No 237) (1996). It was noticeable that the Health and Safety Executive put in a response to the consultations and commented that death or personal injury resulting from a major disaster is rarely due to the negligence of a single individual. In the majority of cases the

disaster is caused as a result of the failure of systems controlling the risk with the carelessness of individuals being a contributing factor.

The Law Commission's main proposals for corporate liability were that:

- There should be a special offence of corporate killing and this should broadly correspond to the Law Commission's proposal of a new offence of killing by gross carelessness.

- The offence would be committed only where the corporation's conduct in causing death fell far below what could reasonably be expected.

- A death should be regarded as having been caused by the conduct of the corporation if it is caused by a 'management failure'. A management failure is described as occurring if the way in which its activities are managed or organised fails to ensure the health and safety of persons employed in or affected by its activities.

- Such a failure would be regarded as a cause of a person's death even if the immediate cause is the act or omission of an individual.

- Individuals within a company could still be liable for offences of reckless killing and killing by gross carelessness (which the Law Commission had recommended should replace the current offence of manslaughter but has never done so) as well as the company being liable for the offence of corporate killing.

The Law Commission's report was published in 1996. It was not until 2000 that the Government issued a consultation paper, *Reforming the Law on Involuntary Manslaughter: The Government's Proposals* on the matter. Finally, in 2005, the Government issued a draft Bill. This draft Bill was jointly scrutinised by the Home Affairs Committee and the Work and Pensions Committee. Their report, issued in December 2005, was very critical of aspects of the draft Bill. In particular they thought that the use of the civil concept of negligence was not appropriate as the basis for a criminal offence. Also they pointed out that using a test of management failure by senior managers, as set out in the draft Bill, would simply re-introduce some of the problems of the identification principle, which exist under the present law (see discussion at section 7.4.2).

The Government replied to this report in *The Government Reply to the First Joint Report from the Home Affairs Work and Pensions Committees* (Session 2005-06 High Court 540). The Government accepted some of the criticisms and, in 2006, laid another Bill, the Corporate Manslaughter and Corporate Homicide Bill, before Parliament. This Bill, which may become law in 2007 or 2008, addresses some of the concerns of the joint committees, but not all.

7.4.6 Corporate Manslaughter and Corporate Homicide Bill

The offence of corporate manslaughter is set out in cl 1(1) of the Bill. (Note that corporate homicide is the name of the offence to be introduced into Scottish law.) Clause 1(1) states:

> '1(1)   An organisation to which this section applies is guilty of an offence if the way in which any of its activities are managed or organised by its senior managers:
>
> (a) causes a person's death, and
>
> (b) amounts to gross breach of a relevant duty of care owed by the organisation to the deceased.'

The difficulty of wording the offence of corporate manslaughter in a clear and satisfactory way was highlighted by the fact that the wording of this clause was subjected to various amendments during the passage of the Bill through Parliament. The House of Commons amended it to read:

> (1) An organisation to which this section applies is guilty of an offence if:
>
> (a) the way in which any of its activities are managed or organised:
>
> (i) causes a person's death,
>
> (ii) amounts to a gross breach of a relevant duty of care owed by the organisation to the deceased, and
>
> (b) the gross breach could have been prevented had all reasonable precautions been taken and all due diligence been exercised by those at a senior manager level within the organisation.'

This version was wider than the original clause as the activities do not have to be managed or organised by those at senior manager level. The duty placed on the senior managers is to take all reasonable precautions and exercise due diligence. This wider test would appear to be more likely to lead to a finding of corporate manslaughter in situations such as the *P & O* case. However, this clause was amended yet again (in Standing Committee) to read:

> '1(1)   An organisation to which this section applies is guilty of an offence if the way in which its activities are managed or organised:
>
> (a) causes a person's death, and
>
> (b) amounts to gross breach of a relevant duty of care owed by the organisation to the deceased.
>
> . . .
>
> 1(3)   An organisation is guilty of an offence under this section only if the way in which its activities are managed or organised by its senior management is a substantial element in the breach referred to in subsection (1).'

Senior manager/management

Senior manager/management is defined as being persons who plays a significant role in:

- the making of decisions about how the whole or a substantial part of its activities are to be managed or organised, or

- the actual managing or organising of the whole or a substantial part of those activities.

This definition is an effort to prevent the problems that have arisen over identification of the 'brain' of a corporation. However, the Bill does not provide for individual senior managers to be liable as secondary parties to corporate manslaughter as proposed by the Law Commission.

Relevant duty of care

The relevant duty of care means any of the following duties owed under the law of negligence:

- a duty owed to employees or to other persons working for the organisation or performing services for it

- a duty owed as occupier of premises

- a duty owed in connection with:

    (i)   the supply by the organisation of goods and services (whether for consideration or not)

    (ii) the carrying on by the organisation of any construction or maintenance operations

    (iii) the carrying on by the organisation of any other activity on a commercial basis, or

    (iv) the use or keeping by the organisation of any plant, vehicle or other thing.

Gross breach

Once a relevant duty of care has been established, then, under cl 9(1)(b), the jury decide if there has been a gross breach.

Clause 9 then sets out matters that the jury *must* consider and those which they *may* consider.

'9(2) The jury must consider whether the evidence shows that the organisation failed to comply with any health and safety legislation that relates to the alleged breach, and if so:

(a) how serious that failure was,

(b) how much of a risk of death it posed.

9(3) The jury may also:

(a) consider the extent to which the evidence shows that there were attitudes, policies, systems or accepted practices within the organisation

that were likely to have encouraged any failure as is mentions in subsection (2), or to have produced tolerance of it,

(b) have regard to any health and safety guidance that relates to the alleged breach.'

The jury is not limited to considering only the matters in subclauses (2) and (3), and (4) states that the clause does not prevent the jury from having regard to any other matters they consider relevant.

The factors in 9(3) are an attempt to cover situations such as the *Herald of Free Enterprise* case. (See *P & O European Ferries (Dover)* (1991) 93 Cr App R 72 at section 7.4.5.)

Penalties

The Bill provides that corporations found guilty of corporate manslaughter can be fined an unlimited amount. In addition, it gives the court power to order the corporation to take specific steps to remedy the gross breach of a relevant duty of care or any other matter that appears to have resulted from that breach and been a cause of the death.

7.4.7 Why make corporations criminally liable?

It is sometimes argued that it is pointless making a corporation criminally liable. After all, the act and the intention are those of a human person within the corporation. Since that person can be prosecuted as an individual, why is it necessary to prosecute the corporation as well? For example, in *Kite and OLL* (1994) the managing director was convicted of manslaughter and he was given a prison sentence. Was it necessary or worthwhile to prosecute the company in addition? Imposing criminal liability on a corporation can be justified for three main reasons:

* Many of the recent disasters have not been caused by one individual; the poor practices throughout the company have contributed; in such circumstances it is just that the company should be liable.

* Many offences involve breaches of laws relating to health and safety; companies should be encouraged to take their responsibilities in these areas seriously and not to put profits before health and safety.

* The public perceive large companies as being above the law; when there has been a death though poor practice, relatives of victims want to see the company 'named and shamed'.

ACTIVITY

Self-test questions

1. What exceptions are there to the general rule that a corporation can be criminally liable?

2. What difficulties are there in using the principle of identification to decide whether or not a corporation is criminally liable?

3. Apart from the principle of identification, in what other two ways can a corporation be criminally liable?

4. What problems are there in trying to establish corporate liability for manslaughter?

5. Why is it considered necessary to be able to make corporations liable for manslaughter?

APPLYING THE LAW

In each of the following situations, explain whether the law will operate to impose criminal liability.

1. Crazy Golf Club is a members' club with a management committee of seven members. The club has a bar and employs a full-time steward and two part-time stewards to work there. The club has a licence to sell alcohol to members only. One of the part-time stewards sells an alcoholic drink to a non-member. Can the club be held criminally liable for the sale?

2. Getupandgo Ltd is a company which owns and operates leisure and activity centres. The company has a board of directors and a managing director. In addition, each centre has a manager. The board operates very tight financial controls over the amount to be spent at each centre on general maintenance and centre managers who overspend know that they will face dismissal. Many of the activity centres have climbing walls. The board of directors has never issued any directions about safety or the level of supervision for the use of these climbing walls. At one of the centres there have been no maintenance checks on the climbing wall and it has become unsafe. Safety helmets are provided for climbers but the centre manager has not instructed the staff to ensure that they are used. Harry, aged 14, climbs the wall without using a safety helmet. When he is near the top, part of the wall becomes detached, causing him to fall and be killed. The problem with wall would have been discovered if there had been a maintenance check.

The company faces prosecution for:

a manslaughter of Harry

b breach of safety legislation as the occupier of the building.

3. Den owns a newsagents' shop. He employs Ella as a sales assistant and Freddy as a cleaner. Cigarettes are sold in the shop and Den has told Ella that she must not sell these to anyone under the age of 16, and if she is not sure then she must ask for proof of age. Ella sells a packet to a boy who looks at least 18. She is so convinced that he is over 16 she does not ask him for proof of his age. Later in the day Ella cuts her finger and needs to leave the till. As she does not want to leave it unattended she asks Freddy to mind it for her. During the time that Ella is absent Freddy sells a packet of cigarettes to a girl aged 12.

Will liability be imposed on Den for:

a the sale by Ella

b the sale by Freddy?

Further reading

Forlin, G, 'A softly, softly approach' [2006] NLJ 907.

Jefferson, M, 'Corporate Liability in the 1990s' (2000) 64 JCL 106.

Sullivan, R, 'Corporate Killing – Some Government Proposals' [2001] Crim LR 31.

Walker, H, 'Criminalising Companies – Will Corporate Killing Make a Difference?' [2001] NLJ 1494.

Internet Links

www.lawcom.gov.uk for Law Commission reports.

www.parliament.gov.uk for draft Bill on Corporate Manslaughter.

AIMS AND OBJECTIVES ☐☐☐

After reading this chapter you should be able to:

■ Understand the law on insanity and automatism

■ Understand the law on intoxication

■ Understand the law on duress, necessity and marital coercion

■ Understand the law on mistake

■ Understand the law on self-defence

■ Understand the law on consent

■ Analyse critically the scope and limitations of the general defences, and the reform proposals for the general defences

■ Apply the law to factual situations to determine whether liability can be avoided by invoking a defence

8.1 Insanity

Although the insanity defence is rarely used and is therefore of little real practical significance, it nevertheless raises fundamental questions about criminal responsibility and the role of criminal law in dealing with violent people. Its importance had been much reduced, particularly in murder cases, by two developments:

• the introduction of the diminished responsibility defence in 1957 (see Chapter 9)

• the abolition of the death penalty in 1965.

It is a general defence and may be pleaded as a defence to any crime requiring *mens rea* (including murder), whether tried on indictment in the Crown Court or summarily in the magistrates' court (*Horseferry Road Magistrates' Court, ex parte K* [1996] 3 All ER 719). However, it is not, apparently, a defence to crimes of strict liability (see Chapter 4). In *DPP v H* [1997] 1 WLR 1406, the High Court held that insanity was no defence to a charge of driving with excess alcohol contrary to s 5 of the Road Traffic Act 1988. Medical evidence that D was suffering manic depressive psychosis with symptoms of distorted judgment and impaired sense of time and of morals at the time of the offence was, therefore, irrelevant.

8.1.1 Procedure

Often D does not specifically raise the defence of insanity, but places the state of his mind in issue by raising another defence such as automatism. The question whether such a defence, or a denial of *mens rea*, really amounts to the defence of insanity is a question of law to be decided by the judge on the basis of medical evidence (*Dickie* [1984] 3 All ER 173). Whether D, or even his medical witnesses, would call it insanity or not is irrelevant. According to Lord Denning in *Bratty v Attorney-General of Northern Ireland* [1963] AC 386, in such cases the prosecution may – indeed must – raise the issue of insanity.

Importance of medical evidence

If the judge decides that the evidence does support the defence, then he should leave it to the jury to determine whether D was insane (*Walton* [1978] 1 All ER 542). In practice, the evidence of medical experts is critically important. Section 1 of the Criminal Procedure (Insanity and Unfitness to Plead) Act 1991 provides that a jury shall not return a special verdict (see below) except on the written or oral evidence of two or more registered medical practitioners, at least one of whom is approved as having special expertise in the field of medical disorder.

8.1.2 The special verdict

If D is found to have been insane at the time of committing the *actus reus* then the jury should return a verdict of 'not guilty by reason of insanity' (s 1 Criminal Procedure (Insanity) Act 1964), otherwise referred to as the *special verdict*. Until quite recently this verdict obliged the judge to order D to be detained indefinitely in a mental hospital. In many cases the dual prospect of being labelled 'insane' and indefinite detention in a special hospital such as Broadmoor or Rampton discouraged defendants from putting their mental state in issue. In some cases it led to guilty pleas to offences of which defendants were probably innocent (*Quick* [1973] QB 910; *Sullivan* [1984] AC 156; *Hennessy* [1989] 1 WLR 287, all of which will be considered below).

The Criminal Procedure (Insanity and Unfitness to Plead) Act 1991

The position described above was modified by the 1991 Act. The Act made a number of changes but, most significantly, substituted a new s 5 into the Criminal Procedure (Insanity) Act 1964. The new section allowed the judge considerable discretion with regard to disposal on a special verdict being returned. That section has since been replaced by another version of s 5 following the enactment of the Domestic Violence, Crime and Victims Act 2004. Now, following a special verdict, the judge may make either:

a   a hospital order (with or without a restriction order)

b   a supervision order, or

c   an order for his absolute discharge.

This is particularly useful where the offence is trivial and/or the offender does not require treatment. The new power was first utilised in *Bromley* (1992) 142 NLJ 116.

This new power does not, however, apply to murder cases when indefinite hospitalisation is unavoidable. However, as noted above, defendants charged with murder are far more likely to plead diminished responsibility under s 2 of the Homicide Act 1957 than insanity.

This much broader range of disposal options should make the insanity defence more attractive. Nevertheless, the 1991 Act does not tackle the definition of insanity, and so the stigma of being labelled 'insane' remains. This issue will be addressed below.

8.1.3 The M'Naghten Rules

The law of insanity in England is contained in the M'Naghten Rules, the result of the deliberations of the judges of the House of Lords in 1843. Media and public outcry at one Daniel M'Naghten's acquittal on a charge of murder led to the creation of rules to clarify the situation. Lord Tindal CJ answered on behalf of himself and 13 other judges, while Maule J gave a separate set. The Rules are not binding as a matter of strict precedent. Nevertheless, the Rules have been treated as authoritative of the law ever since (*Sullivan* (1984)). The Rules state as follows:

> 'The jurors ought to be told in all cases that every man is presumed to be sane,
> and to possess a sufficient degree of reason to be responsible for his crimes, until
> the contrary be proved to their satisfaction; and that to establish a defence on the
> ground of insanity it must be clearly proved that, at the time of the committing of
> the act, the party accused was labouring under such a defect of reason, from
> disease of the mind, as not to know the nature and quality of the act he was doing,
> or, if he did know it, that he did not know he was doing what was wrong.'

The Rules can be broken down into three distinct elements, all of which must be established:

- defect of reason
- disease of the mind
- not knowing what D was doing or not knowing that it was 'wrong'.

Because of the presumption of sanity, the burden of proof is on the defence (albeit on the lower standard, the balance of probabilities).

Defect of reason

The phrase 'defect of reason' was explained in *Clarke* [1972] 1 All ER 219 by Ackner J, who said that:

J ‘The M'Naghten Rules relate to accused persons who by reason of a "disease of the mind" are deprived of the power of reasoning. They do not apply and never have applied to those who retain the power of reasoning but who in moments of confusion or absent-mindedness fail to use their powers to the full.'

CASE EXAMPLE

Clarke [1972] 1 All ER 219

D went into a supermarket. She placed various items, including a pound of butter, a jar of coffee and a jar of mincemeat into her own bag and left the supermarket without paying for them. At her trial for theft she claimed to have lacked the intention to permanently deprive on the basis of absent-mindedness caused by diabetes and depression. She claimed to have no recollection of putting the items into her bag. The trial judge ruled that this amounted to a plea of insanity, at which point D pleaded guilty. The Court of Appeal quashed her conviction: she had not been deprived of her powers of reasoning but had simply failed to use them.

Disease of the mind

'Disease of the mind' is a legal term, not a medical term. In *Kemp* [1957] 1 QB 399, D suffered from arteriosclerosis (hardening of the arteries) which restricted the flow of blood to the brain, causing blackouts. In this condition he committed the *actus reus* of grievous bodily harm (he hit his wife with a hammer). The question arose whether arteriosclerosis supported the defence of automatism or insanity. Devlin J decided that it was a case of insanity. He stated:

J ‘The law is not concerned with the brain but with the mind, in the sense that 'mind' is ordinarily used, the mental faculties of reason, memory and understanding. If one read for "disease of the mind" "disease of the brain", it would follow that in many cases pleas of insanity would not be established because it could not be proved that the brain had been affected in any way, either by degeneration of the cells or in any other way. In my judgment the condition of the brain is irrelevant and so is the question whether the condition is curable or incurable, transitory or permanent.'

Thus, if D suffers from a condition (not necessarily a condition of the brain) which affects his 'mental faculties' then this amounts to the defence of insanity. The problem is, how to distinguish such cases from situations when D suffers some temporary condition (for example, concussion following a blow to the head). In the latter situation, D loses his 'mental faculties' but the problem is extremely unlikely to repeat itself and so ordering hospitalisation or treatment would be pointless. Hence, in such cases the true defence is automatism (see below). In order to distinguish cases of insanity from cases of automatism, the courts have adopted a test based on whether the cause of D's 'defect of reason' was internal or external (such as the blow to the head example). First employed by the New Zealand Court of Appeal in *Cottle* [1958] NZLR 999, it was approved by the English Court of Appeal in *Quick* (1973). Lawton LJ said:

> **J** 'Our task has been to decide what the law now means by the words "disease of the mind". In our judgment the fundamental concept is of a malfunctioning of the mind caused by disease. A malfunctioning of the mind of transitory effect caused by the application to the body of some external factor such as violence, drugs, including anaesthetics, alcohol and hypnotic influences cannot fairly be said to be due to disease.'

The implications of this decision have been profound and not without criticism. In *Quick* (1973) itself, D was a diabetic who had taken prescribed insulin to control his blood sugar levels. However, he had forgotten to eat afterwards, with the result that he subsequently suffered a condition known medically as hypoglycaemia (low blood-sugar). Whilst in this condition he physically assaulted V and was charged accordingly. At his trial, he testified that he could not remember what he had done. However, the judge ruled that the evidence only supported a plea of insanity. At this point, D changed his plea to guilty and appealed. The Court of Appeal quashed his conviction. The cause of D's lack of awareness was not his diabetes, but his insulin overdose; this was an external factor; and so the proper defence was automatism.

This case should be contrasted with that of *Hennessy* (1989).

CASE EXAMPLE

Hennessy [1989] 1 WLR 287

In this case D, another diabetic, had forgotten to take his insulin. He suffered what is known medically as hyperglycaemia (high blood-sugar). In this condition he was seen by police officers driving a car that had been reported stolen. D was charged with two counts of taking a motor vehicle without consent and driving a motor vehicle while disqualified. Like the defendant in *Quick* (1973), he testified that he could not remember taking the car and driving it away. Again the trial judge declared that the evidence supported a defence of insanity. Again, D changed his plea to guilty and appealed. However, distinguishing *Quick* (1973), the Court of Appeal confirmed that hyperglycaemia was caused by an internal factor, namely diabetes, and was therefore a disease of the mind. The correct verdict was insanity.

Two criticisms may be made here:

- a relatively common medical condition (diabetes) is regarded by the criminal law as supporting a defence of insanity, with all the negative implications that that label conveys
- this is only the case in certain situations, namely when D suffers hyperglycaemia.

According to the Diabetes UK website, 1.4 million people in the UK (that is, three in every 100 people) have been diagnosed with diabetes (and another 1 million people are estimated to have the condition without realising it). Does the decision in *Hennessy* (1989) mean that nearly 2.5 million people in the UK are legally insane? For more information refer to the 'Internet links' section at the end of this chapter. The problem associated with diabetes is not the only one created by the decision in *Quick* (1973). According to the House of Lords, epileptics who suffer *grand mal* seizures and inadvertently assault someone nearby are also to be regarded as insane. This was seen in two cases: *Bratty* (1963) and *Sullivan* (1984). In the latter case, Lord Diplock stated:

> **J** 'It matters not whether the aetiology of the impairment is organic, as in epilepsy, or functional, or whether the impairment itself is permanent or is transient and intermittent, provided that it subsisted at the time of the commission of the act. The purpose of the . . . defence of insanity . . . has been to protect society against recurrence of the dangerous conduct. The duration of a temporary suspension of the mental faculties . . . particularly if, as in Sullivan's case, it is recurrent, cannot . . . be relevant to the application by the courts of the *M'Naghten* Rules.'

CASE EXAMPLE

Sullivan [1984] AC 156

D had suffered from epilepsy since childhood. He occasionally suffered fits. One day he was sitting in a neighbour's flat with a friend, V. The next thing D remembered was standing by a window with V lying on the floor with head injuries. D was charged with assault. The trial judge ruled that the evidence that D had suffered a post-epileptic seizure, amounted to a disease of the mind. To avoid hospitalisation, D pleaded guilty and appealed. Both the Court of Appeal and House of Lords upheld his conviction.

According to the Epilepsy Action website, 440,000 people in the UK have epilepsy (this corresponds to one in every 133 people). In the event that any one of these people commits the *actus reus* of a crime, are they to be regarded as legally insane too? For more information, refer to the 'Internet links' section at the end of this chapter. Thus, diabetics (sometimes) and epileptics are regarded as 'insane' by English criminal law. What about someone who carries out the *actus reus* of a crime, such as assault, whilst sleepwalking? This was a question for the Court of Appeal in *Burgess* [1991] 2 QB 92. There was a persuasive precedent for deciding that this amounted to automatism (*Tolson* (1889) 23 QBD 168) but the Court of Appeal held that, after *Quick* (1973) and *Sullivan* (1984), it had to be regarded as insanity. Lord Lane CJ stated that sleepwalking was 'an abnormality or disorder, albeit transitory, due to an internal factor'.

CASE EXAMPLE

Burgess [1991] 2 QB 92

D and his friend, V, were in D's flat watching videos. They both fell asleep but, during the night, D attacked V while she slept, hitting her with a wine bottle and a video recorder. She suffered cuts to her scalp which required sutures. To a charge of unlawful wounding contrary to s 20 OAPA 1861, D pleaded automatism, but the trial judge ruled he was pleading insanity and the jury returned the special verdict. The Court of Appeal dismissed D's appeal.

According to an American website, www.sleepdoctor.com, some 18 per cent of the population are predisposed to sleepwalking. With the UK population in excess of 59 million, this equates to nearly 11 million people in the UK. It is useful to note at this point that in Canada (which also uses the M'Naghten Rules), the Supreme Court has diverged from English law on this point. In *Parks* (1992) 95 DLR (4d) 27, D had carried out a killing and an attempted killing whilst asleep. However, the Supreme Court found that his defence was automatism. During the trial the defence had called expert witnesses in sleep disorders, whose evidence was that sleepwalking was not regarded as a neurological, psychiatric or any other illness, but a sleep disorder, very common in children but also found in 2–2.5 per cent of adults. Furthermore, aggression while sleepwalking was quite rare, and repetition of violence almost unheard of. Using this evidence, the Canadian

Chief Justice, Lamer CJC, said that 'Accepting the medical evidence, [D's] mind and its functioning must have been impaired at the relevant time but sleepwalking did not impair it. The cause was the natural condition, sleep'.

Another possible basis for an insanity plea is dissociation, most commonly referred to now as post-traumatic stress disorder. If D suffers this condition (which is triggered by experiencing and/or witnessing extremely traumatic events) and carries out the *actus reus* of a crime whilst in this state, does it amount to a plea of insanity or automatism? In *T* [1990] Crim LR 256, the Crown Court decided that it could support a plea of automatism.

CASE EXAMPLE

_T_ [1990] Crim LR 256

D had been raped three days prior to carrying out a robbery and causing actual bodily harm. She was diagnosed as suffering post-traumatic stress disorder, such that at the time of the alleged offences she had entered a dissociative state. The trial judge allowed automatism to be left to the jury, noting that 'such an incident could have an appalling effect on any young woman, however well-balanced normally'.

In Canada, meanwhile, a plea of dissociation was regarded as one of insanity. The difference was that in that case, the traumatic events leading up to the alleged dissociative state were much less distressing. In *Rabey* (1980) 114 DLR (3d) 193, D had developed an attraction towards a girl. When he discovered that she regarded him as a 'nothing', he hit her over the head with a rock and began to choke her. He was charged with causing bodily harm with intent to wound, and pleaded automatism, based on the psychologically devastating blow of being rejected by the girl. The trial judge accepted that D had been in a complete dissociative state. The prosecution doubted that D was suffering from such a state (the reality being that he was in an extreme rage), but that *if he were* then his condition was properly regarded as a disease of the mind. The trial judge ordered an acquittal based on automatism, but the appeal court allowed the prosecution appeal. The Supreme Court of Canada upheld that decision – the defence was insanity.

To summarise the law on 'disease of the mind', the following conditions have been held to support a plea of insanity (in England):

- arteriosclerosis (*Kemp* (1957))
- epilepsy (*Sullivan* (1984))
- hyperglycaemia (high blood-sugar: *Hennessy* (1989)) but not hypoglycaemia (low blood-sugar: *Quick* (1973))
- sleepwalking (*Burgess* (1991)).

And in Canada, post-traumatic stress disorder caused by a relatively mundane event such as rejection by a prospective girlfriend (*Rabey* (1980)). In Australia, meanwhile, although the M'Naghten Rules have been adopted there, the internal/external factor test in *Quick* (1973) has not. The leading case there is *Falconer* (1990) 171 CLR 30. Toohey J described the internal/external factor theory as 'artificial' and said that it failed to pay sufficient regard to 'the subtleties surrounding the notion of mental disease'. In Australia, therefore, the distinction between insanity and automatism is found by identifying whether D's mental state at the time of the *actus reus* was either:

- 'the reaction of an *unsound mind* to its own delusions, or to external stimuli, on the one hand', which is insanity or

- 'the reaction of a *sound mind* to external stimuli including stress-producing factors on the other hand', which is automatism.

ACTIVITY

> Applying the Australian sound/unsound mind test, as opposed to the English internal/external factor test, would the defendants in *Sullivan* (1984), *Hennessy* (1989) and *Burgess* (1991) have been found to be sane or insane?

Nature and quality of the act

It seems there will be a good defence provided that when D acted he was not aware of, or did not appreciate, what he was actually doing, or the circumstances in which he was acting, or the consequences of his act. D's lack of knowledge must be fundamental. Two famous old examples used to illustrate this point are:

- D cuts a woman's throat but thinks (because of his 'defect of reason') that he is cutting a loaf of bread

- D chops off a sleeping man's head because it would be amusing to see him looking for it when he wakes up.

Obviously, in both these situations D does not know what he is doing and is entitled to the special verdict. If, on the other hand, D kills a man whom he believes, because of a paranoid delusion, to be possessed by demons, then he is still criminally responsible and not insane – his delusion has not prevented him from understanding that he is committing murder.

The act was wrong

What is meant here by 'wrong'? Does it mean wrong as in 'contrary to the criminal law', or wrong as in 'morally unacceptable' – or perhaps both? In *M'Naghten* (1843) the Law Lords said that if D knew at the time of committing the *actus reus* of a crime that he 'was acting contrary to law; by which expression we understand your lordships to mean the law of the land' then he would not have the defence. This clearly suggested D will have the defence if he does not realise that he is committing a crime. The Court of Criminal Appeal in *Windle* [1952] 2 QB 826 confirmed this view of the word 'wrong'. D had poisoned his wife and, on giving himself up to the police, said, 'I suppose they will hang me for this?' Despite medical evidence for the defence that he was suffering from a medical condition known as *folie à deux*, this statement showed that D was aware of acting unlawfully. D was convicted of murder. Lord Goddard CJ said:

> **J** 'Courts of law can only distinguish between that which is in accordance with law and that which is contrary to law . . . The law cannot embark on the question and it would be an unfortunate thing if it were left to juries to consider whether some particular act was morally right or wrong. The test must be whether it is contrary to law . . . [T]here is no doubt that in the M'Naghten Rules "wrong" means contrary to the law, and does not have some vague meaning which may vary according to the opinion of one man or of a number of people on the question of whether a particular act might or might not be justified.'

The position, therefore, is that if D knew his act was illegal, then he has no defence of insanity. This is the case even if he is suffering from delusions which cause him to believe that his act was morally right. This position has, however, been criticised. In 1975, the Royal Committee on Mentally Abnormal Offenders (Butler Committee) stated that the *Windle* (1952) definition of 'wrong' was 'a very narrow ground of exemption since even persons who are grossly disturbed generally know that murder and arson, for instance, are crimes'.

In *Stapleton* (1952) 86 CLR 358, the High Court of Australia refused to follow *Windle* (1952). That Court decided that morality, and not legality, was the concept behind the use of 'wrong'. Thus in Australia (which as noted above has adopted the M'Naghten Rules) the insanity defence is available if 'through the disordered condition of the mind [D] could not reason about the matter with a moderate degree of sense and composure'. The same is true in Canada (which also uses the M'Naghten Rules). The leading case there is *Chaulk* (1991) 62 CCC (3d) 193, where D had been charged with murder. Medical evidence showed that he suffered paranoid delusions such that he believed he had power to rule the world, and that the killing had been a necessary means to that end. D believed himself to be above the law (of Canada). Finally, he deemed V's death appropriate because he was a 'loser'. The Supreme Court stated that 'It is possible that a person may be aware that it is ordinarily wrong to commit a crime but, by reason of a disease of the mind, believes that it would be "right" according to the ordinary standards of society to commit the crime in a particular context. In this situation, [D] would be entitled to be acquitted by reason of insanity'.

8.1.4 Situations not covered by the Rules

Irresistible impulse

Until the early twentieth century, a plea of irresistible impulse was a good defence under the M'Naghten Rules. In *Fryer* (1843) 10 Cl & F, the jury was directed that if D was deprived of the capacity to control his actions, it was open for them to find him insane. By 1925, however, the fact that D was unable to resist an impulse to act was held to be irrelevant, if he was nonetheless aware that his act was wrong. In *Kopsch* (1925) 19 Cr App R 50, D confessed to strangling his aunt with a necktie, apparently at her request. Upholding his conviction, Lord Hewart CJ described the defence argument, that a person acting under an uncontrollable impulse was not criminally responsible as a 'fantastic theory', which if it were to become part of the law, 'would be merely subversive'. The reluctance of the courts to recognise a defence of irresistible impulse appears to be based on two grounds:

- the difficulty of distinguishing between an impulse caused by insanity, and one motivated by greed, jealousy or revenge
- the view that the harder an impulse is to resist, the greater is the need for a deterrent.

In 1953 the Royal Commission on Capital Punishment suggested, as an alternative to replacing the Rules altogether, adding a third limb, ie that D should be considered insane if at the time of his act he 'was incapable of preventing himself from committing it . . .'. This was not taken up. However, irresistible impulse may support a defence of diminished responsibility (*Byrne* [1960] 2 QB 396). Thus, if D is charged with murder and claims that he could not resist killing V he may avoid a murder conviction. But the same defendant who fails to kill V and is charged with attempted murder will have neither insanity nor diminished responsibility available.

8.1.5 Reform

The Draft Criminal Code (1989) replaced the term 'insanity' with 'mental disorder'. Clause 35(1) of the Code provides as follows:

> '35(1) A mental disorder verdict shall be returned if the defendant is proved to have committed an offence but it is proved on the balance of probabilities (whether by the prosecution or by the defendant) that he was at the time suffering from severe mental illness or severe mental handicap.'

Clause 34 provides definitions for these new terms, as follows.

- 'Mental disorder' is defined as '(a) severe mental illness; or (b) a state of arrested or incomplete development of mind; (c) a state of automatism (not resulting only from intoxication) which is a feature of a disorder, whether organic or functional and whether continuing or recurring, that may cause a similar state on another occasion'.
- 'Severe mental illness' is defined as 'a mental illness which has one or more if the following characteristics (a) lasting impairment of intellectual functions shown by failure of memory,

orientation, comprehension and learning capacity; (b) lasting alteration of mood of such degree as to give rise to delusional appraisal of the defendant's situation, his past or his future, or that of others, or lack of any appraisal; (c) delusional beliefs, persecutory, jealous or grandiose; (d) abnormal perceptions associated with delusional misinterpretation of events; (e) thinking so disordered as to prevent reasonable appraisal of the defendant's situation or reasonable communication with others'.

- 'Severe mental handicap' is defined as 'a state of arrested or incomplete development of mind which includes severe impairment of intelligence and social functioning'.

You will note that the Law Commission's definition would remove from the law all references to such ambiguous phrases as 'defect of reason' and 'disease of the mind'. It also dispenses with reference to D's knowledge of whether his or her act was 'wrong'. However, the M'Naghten Rules would not be consigned entirely to history: the phrase 'a disorder, whether organic or functional and whether continuing or recurring, that may cause a similar state on another occasion' is clearly inspired by Lord Diplock's *dictum* in *Sullivan* (1984).

Key facts on insanity as a defence

KEY FACTS

Elements	Comment	Cases
Defect of reason	To be deprived of the power of reasoning.	*Clarke* (1972)
Disease of the mind	Not concerned with the brain but with the mind. Must derive from an internal source.	*Kemp* (1957) *Quick* (1973)
Examples	Arteriosclerosis Epilepsy Hyperglycaemia Sleepwalking	*Kemp* (1957) *Bratty* (1963), *Sullivan* (1984) *Hennessy* (1989) *Burgess* (1991)
Not knowing what D was doing or not knowing that it was 'wrong'	'Wrong' means legally wrong.	*Windle* (1952)
Burden of proof	It is for the defence to prove on the balance of probabilities.	
Effect of defence	Defendant is not guilty 'by reason of insanity' (the special verdict).	Unless charge was murder, judge has a variety of disposal options: hospital order, supervision order; absolute discharge. If charge was murder, judge must order indefinite hospitalisation in a special hospital.

211

8.2 Automatism

8.2.1 What is automatism?

'Automatism' is a phrase that was introduced into the criminal law from the medical world. There, it has a very limited meaning, describing the state of unconsciousness suffered by certain epileptics. In law it seems to have two meanings. According to Lord Denning in *Bratty* (1963):

> J
>
> 'Automatism . . . means an act which is done by the muscles without any control by the mind such as a spasm, a reflex action or a convulsion; or an act done by a person who is not conscious of what he is doing such as an act done whilst suffering from concussion or whilst sleepwalking.'

Conscious but uncontrolled

Here D is fully aware of what is going on around him, but is incapable of preventing his arms, legs, or even his whole body from moving. In this sense, automatism is incompatible with *actus reus:* D is aware of what his body is doing but there is no voluntary act.

Impaired consciousness

In *Bratty* (1963), Lord Denning arguably gave 'automatism' too narrow a definition in referring to D being 'not conscious'. While automatism certainly includes unconsciousness, it is suggested that is should also include states of 'altered', 'clouded' or 'impaired' consciousness. If correct, this analysis suggests that automatism is a defence because it is incompatible with *mens rea*: D is not aware (or not fully aware) of what he is doing.

8.2.2 The need for an evidential foundation

If D wishes to plead automatism it is necessary for him to place evidence in support of his plea before the court. The reasoning behind this rule was explained by Devlin J (as he then was) in *Hill v Baxter* [1958] 1 QB 277:

> J
>
> 'It would be quite unreasonable to allow the defence to submit at the end of the prosecution's case that the Crown had not proved affirmatively and beyond a reasonable doubt that the accused was at the time of the crime sober, or not sleepwalking or not in a trance or black-out. I am satisfied that such matters ought not to be considered at all until the defence has provided at least *prima facie* evidence.'

The evidence of D himself will rarely be sufficient, unless it is supported by medical evidence, because otherwise there is a possibility of the jury being deceived by spurious or fraudulent claims. In *Bratty* (1963), Lord Denning stated that it would be insufficient for D to simply say 'I had a black-out' because that was 'one of the first refuges of a guilty conscience and a popular excuse'. He continued:

> J   'When the cause assigned is concussion or sleep-walking, there should be some evidence from which it can reasonably be inferred before it should be left to the jury. If it is said to be due to concussion, there should be evidence of a severe blow shortly beforehand. If it is said to be sleep-walking, there should be some credible support for it. His mere assertion that he was asleep will not suffice.'

8.2.3 Extent of involuntariness required

Must D's control over his bodily movements be totally destroyed before automatism is available? How unconscious does D have to be before he can be said to be an automaton? It seems that the extent of involuntariness required to be established depends on the offence charged. There are two categories.

Crimes of strict liability

As we saw in Chapter 4, when D is charged with a strict liability offence, denial of *mens rea* is no defence, so a plea that D was unconscious would seem doomed to failure. D must therefore provide evidence that he was incapable of exercising control over his bodily movements. If, despite some lack of control, he was still able to appreciate what he was doing and operate his body to a degree, then the defence is not made out. The majority of cases in this area involve driving offences. In *Isitt* (1978) 67 Cr App R 44, Lawton LJ said:

> J   'The mind does not always operate in top gear. There may be some difficulty in functioning. If the difficulty does not amount to either insanity or automatism, is the accused entitled to say, "I am not guilty because my mind was not working in top gear"? In our judgment he is not . . . it is clear that the appellant's mind was working to some extent. The driving was purposeful driving, which was to get away from the scene of the accident. It may well be that, because of panic or stress or alcohol, the appellant's mind was shut to the moral inhibitions which control the lives of most of us. But the fact that his moral inhibitions were not working properly . . . does not mean that the mind was not working at all.'

In *Isitt* (1978), D was convicted of dangerous driving after he drove off following an accident, evading a police car and road block in the process. Medical evidence suggested that he was in a dissociative state. The Court of Appeal, however, held that this did not amount to a defence. Other cases with similar facts and legal outcomes include:

- *Hill v Baxter* [1958] 1 QB 277. Although D claimed to have become unconscious as a result of being overcome by a sudden illness, the High Court found that the facts showed that D was 'driving', in the sense of controlling the car and directing its movements, and D's plea of automatism was rejected.

- *Watmore v Jenkins* [1962] 2 QB 572. D, a diabetic, suffered a hypoglycaemic episode while driving. He was able to drive some five miles before crashing. He was charged with, inter alia, dangerous driving, but was acquitted on the basis of automatism. On appeal, this decision was reversed. There was not 'such a complete destruction of voluntary control as could constitute in law automatism'. There had to be some evidence to raise a reasonable doubt that D's bodily movements were 'wholly uncontrolled and uninitiated by any function of conscious will'.

- *Broome v Perkins* [1987] Crim LR 271. D, charged with driving without due care and attention, after he had been observed driving erratically for some miles, pleaded a loss of consciousness. The Court of Appeal, however, found that he was only intermittently an automaton: although he was not in full control, there was evidence that his mind was controlling his limbs enough to allow him to avoid crashing by veering away from other traffic or braking violently.

These decisions may be explained on the ground that the automatism must be of such a degree that D cannot be said to have performed the *actus reus* voluntarily. But they do seem harsh. The defendant who retains some control over his actions faces conviction. The Law Commission, in its Commentary to the Draft Criminal Code (1989), stated: 'Finding it necessary to choose between the authorities, we propose a formula under which we expect (and indeed hope) that a person in the condition of the defendant in *Broome v Perkins* (1987) would be acquitted (subject to the question of prior fault).' The Commission therefore proposed that, for any crime, D should have an automatism defence when no longer in 'effective control' of his acts (see below).

Crimes of *mens rea*

In this category the degree of automatism is, or should be, much reduced. D will have a good defence provided he was prevented from forming *mens rea*. In a New Zealand case, *Burr* [1969] NZLR 736, North P said:

> 'I think it should be made plain that when Lord Denning [in *Bratty*] speaks of 'an act which is done by the muscles without any control by the mind', he does not mean that the accused person must be absolutely unconscious because you cannot move a muscle without a direction given by the mind. What his Lordship in my opinion was saying is that all the deliberative functions of the mind must be absent so that the accused person acts automatically.'

The leading case in England is *T* (1990). D was charged with robbery and assault occasioning actual bodily harm. These are crimes which require at least subjective recklessness. However, the prosecution claimed, *inter alia*, that D's opening of the blade of a pen-knife had required a 'controlled and positive action', that following *Broome v Perkins* (1987) and *Isitt* (1978) this was a case of partial loss of control only and that automatism was not, therefore, available. However, those cases were distinguished by the trial judge, who held that D was 'acting as though in a dream'.

However, comments made by the Court of Appeal in *Narbrough* [2004] EWCA Crim 1012 seriously undermine the value of *R v T* as a precedent. D had been convicted of wounding with intent to do GBH contrary to s 18 OAPA 1861 after stabbing V with a Stanley knife. On appeal, he argued that psychiatric evidence that he had been seriously sexually abused as an 8 to 12-year-old child had left him suffering post-traumatic stress disorder, with flashbacks, so that he sometimes confused the past and the present. He claimed that, during the attack on V, he had suffered such a flashback and had acted 'like a zombie'. In other words, the evidence supported a plea of automatism, but the trial judge had declared it to be inadmissible. The Court of Appeal, however, rejected the appeal. Zucker J said that the defence psychiatrist had not referred:

> **J** 'to any authority or to any research which supports the conclusion that a post-traumatic stress disorder can so affect a person's normal mental processes that his mind is no longer in control of his actions or that he behaves as an automaton. We have no doubt that the evidence . . . was rightly ruled by the judge to be inadmissible.'

8.2.4 Self-induced automatism

Where the automatism was due to D's consumption of alcohol and/or drugs, then the rules of intoxication apply (*Lipman* [1970] 1 QB 152, approved in *DPP v Majewski* [1977] AC 443). These rules will be explained fully in the next section of this chapter but, essentially, they state that D cannot rely on evidence that he was intoxicated in order to deny having appreciated the consequences of his actions. This principle could apply whenever automatism is self-inflicted. A driver who suffers an epileptic fit whilst driving may still be held liable, depending on the degree and frequency of epileptic attacks that he has suffered in the past. Similarly, the driver who feels drowsy but continues to drive, then falls asleep (*Kay v Butterworth* (1945) 173 LT 191).

8.2.5 Reflex actions

In *Ryan v R* (1967) 40 ALJR 488, an Australian case, a defence of reflex action was advanced. D had shot and killed a petrol station attendant, V, during an armed robbery. D claimed that as he was tying V up the latter moved and, startled, D had pulled the trigger of the shotgun he was carrying. He was convicted of manslaughter and the High Court of Australia upheld the conviction. Windeyer J stated that, even assuming D's act was 'involuntary' in a dictionary sense, it

was incapable of absolving him from criminal responsibility. The judge added that there were only two legally recognised categories of involuntary actor: those which were involuntary because 'by no exercise of the will could the actor refrain from doing it', such as convulsions or an epileptic seizure; and those which were involuntary 'because he knew not what he was doing', such as the sleepwalker or a person rendered unconscious for some other reason. However, reflex actions did not bear any true analogy to either category:

> **J** 'Such phrases as "reflex action" and "automatic reaction" can, if used imprecisely and unscientifically, be, like "blackout", mere excuses. They seem to me to have no real application to the case of a fully conscious man who has put himself in a situation in which he has his finger on the trigger of a loaded rifle levelled at another man. If he then presses the trigger in immediate response to a sudden threat or apprehension of danger, as is said to have occurred in this case, his doing so is, it seems to me, a consequence probable and foreseeable of a conscious apprehension of danger, and in that sense a voluntary act.'

8.2.6 Reform

The Draft Criminal Code (1989), cl 33, provides the following definition of an automatism defence.

> **S** '33(1) A person is not guilty of an offence if (a) he acts in a state of automatism, that is, his act (i) is a reflex, spasm or convulsion; or (ii) occurs while he is in a condition (whether of sleep, unconsciousness, impaired consciousness or otherwise) depriving him of effective control of his act; and (b) the act or condition is the result neither of anything done of omitted with the fault required for the offence nor of voluntary intoxication.
>
> (2) A person is not guilty of an offence by virtue of an omission to act if (a) he is physically incapable of acting in the way required; and (b) his being so incapable is the result neither of anything done or omitted with the fault required for the offence nor of voluntary intoxication.'

ACTIVITY

The Draft Criminal Code pre-dates the Court of Appeal ruling in *Burgess* (1991) that evidence of sleepwalking can only be regarded as the defence of insanity. Do you agree with the Law Commission that sleepwalking should give rise to the defence of automatism, or do you think that the Court of Appeal was correct to rule that it really amounts to the defence of insanity?

8.3 Intoxication

Intoxication as a defence in English law is a means of putting doubt into the minds of the
magistrates or jury as to whether D formed the necessary *mens rea*. It is an area governed
exclusively by case law. Although the majority of those cases involve alcohol, the defence potentially
applies to any case where D has consumed a substance (or cocktail of substances) which is capable
of affecting D's ability to intend or foresee the consequences of their actions. It follows that if,
despite the intoxication, D forms the necessary *mens rea* required for the crime in question
(whether it be intention or recklessness, or some other state of mind such as dishonesty) then the
defence is not available. Alcohol and many other drugs, most notably hallucinogenic drugs such as
LSD and tranquilisers, are obviously capable of affecting a person's perception of their
surroundings. But if D, having consumed several pints of lager, is still sufficiently aware of what is
going on when he gets involved in a fight, his intoxication would provide no defence to any
charges of actual bodily harm or malicious wounding that may result.

But does it also necessarily follow that if D, because of intoxication, failed to form *mens rea*, then
he is automatically entitled to be acquitted, regardless of what he may have actually done whilst in
the intoxicated condition? Logically, the answer is 'yes' and, indeed, courts in other common law
jurisdictions such as Australia and New Zealand are content to leave the matter there. In the
leading Australian case on intoxication, *O'Connor* (1980) ALR 449, the Australian High Court
decided that if the prosecution is unable to prove that D formed *mens rea* because of intoxication,
then D must be acquitted. This reflected the earlier decision of the New Zealand Court of Appeal
in *Kamipeli* [1975] 2 NZLR 610. South African courts have reached the same conclusion (*Chrétien*
1981 (1) SA 1097).

In England, however, the courts have decided that this logical conclusion would send out
dangerous signals. As a matter of public policy there is clearly a need to discourage anti-social
behaviour caused by excessive drinking or drug consumption. In the leading English case, *DPP v
Majewksi* (1977), Lord Simon expressed the concern that, without special rules on intoxication, the
public would be 'legally unprotected from unprovoked violence where such violence was the
consequence of drink or drugs having obliterated the capacity of the perpetrator to know what he
was doing or what were its consequences'. The result in England has been an uneasy compromise
between the logical conclusion reached in Australia and New Zealand (on the one hand) and the
public policy demands of discouraging violent crime (on the other). The law in England can be
summarised as follows:

- intoxication is no defence if, despite the intoxication, D formed *mens rea*

- where D was involuntarily intoxicated and failed to form *mens rea*, D is entitled to be
  acquitted

- where D was voluntarily intoxicated and failed to form *mens rea*, D is entitled to be acquitted if
  the offence charged is one of 'specific intent'. If the offence charged is one of 'basic intent' then
  the jury must consider whether D would have formed *mens rea* had he been sober.

8.3.1 Intoxication is no defence if D still formed *mens rea*

According to the Court of Appeal in *Sheehan* [1975] 1 WLR 739, where D raises intoxication in an attempt to show lack of *mens rea*, the jury should be directed that:

> **J** 'The mere fact that the defendant's mind was affected by drink so that he acted in a way in which he would not have done had he been sober does not assist him at all, provided that the necessary intention was there. A drunken intent is nevertheless an intent.'

The leading case on this point is now *Kingston* [1995] 2 AC 355. D had been convicted by a jury of indecent assault. The prosecution had satisfied the jury that D, despite being involuntarily intoxicated at the time, had enough appreciation of his surroundings to have formed *mens rea*. However, the Court of Appeal allowed D's appeal on the basis that D was not at fault in becoming intoxicated in the first place. Lord Taylor CJ said that, if a 'drink or a drug, surreptitiously administered, causes a person to lose his self-control and for that reason to form an intent which he would not otherwise have formed . . . the law should exculpate him because the operative fault is not his'. The prosecution appealed against this ruling to the House of Lords, which allowed the appeal and reinstated D's conviction.

CASE EXAMPLE

Kingston [1995] 2 AC 355

D was a middle-aged businessman. He had admitted paedophiliac, homosexual tendencies, which he was able to control whilst sober. This presented an opportunity for former business associates of his to blackmail him. As part of the set-up, both D and a 15-year-old boy were lured, separately, to a flat and drugged. While the boy fell asleep, D was intoxicated but not unconscious. In this condition D was encouraged to abuse the boy, which he did, and was photographed and tape-recorded doing so. In the prosecution's view there was evidence that D, despite the effects of the drugs, intended to touch the boy in circumstances of indecency, and the jury agreed.

In *O'Connell* [1997] Crim LR 683, D appealed against his murder conviction on the basis that halcion, a sleeping drug that he was taking, may have prevented him from forming the *mens rea* for murder. The appeal was dismissed, however, because of lack of any evidence that the drug had prevented D from forming the intent.

8.3.2 Involuntary intoxication

If D was involuntarily intoxicated such that the prosecution cannot prove *mens rea*, then D is then entitled to an acquittal. Involuntary intoxication refers to any situation where D consumes alcohol or some other drug unintentionally. The following is a non-exhaustive examination of the circumstances where intoxication will be regarded as involuntary.

'Lacing'

Intoxication is involuntary when D's non-alcoholic drink has been drugged or 'laced' without his knowledge. The surreptitious drugging of D's coffee in *Kingston* (1995), above, is one example. It is, however, crucial that D thought he was consuming a non-alcoholic drink. The mere fact that D's alcoholic drink (or drug) has a stronger effect than he expected is not enough to render the intoxication involuntary. In *Allen* [1988] Crim LR 698, D had been given some home-made wine. Unknown to him it was particularly strong wine. As a result he became extremely drunk and in that state carried out a serious sexual assault. He was convicted of buggery and indecent assault and the Court of Appeal upheld the convictions. There was no evidence that D's drinking was anything other than voluntary. This is obviously correct. D knew he was drinking alcohol, and therefore took the risk as to its strength. Moreover, it is common knowledge that home-made alcohol is often much stronger than the conventional pub-strength, and D ought to have realised this. If intoxication through alcohol was deemed to be voluntary only if D knew <u>exactly</u> what he was drinking, including in terms of strength, that would severely undermine the public policy argument advanced in *Majewski* (1977) because it would enable D to escape liability simply because he had failed to appreciate the strength of his drinks.

In *Allen* (1988), D was drinking wine and knew he was drinking wine; it just happened to be stronger than he realised. But what about D who drinks alcohol surreptitiously laced with another (much stronger) drug? This may be regarded as involuntary intoxication. In *Eatch* [1980] Crim LR 650, D at a party had drunk from a can of beer to which another, stronger drug had been added without his knowledge. The judge directed the jury that it was up to them to decide whether D's condition was 'due solely to voluntary intoxication'. This seems correct: although D had taken one intoxicating substance voluntarily, he was unaware, through no fault of his own, of the additional substance. To similar effect are the cases of *Ross v HM Advocate* 1991 SLT 564 (Scotland) and *People v Cruz* 83 Cal App 3d 308 (1978) (California), in both of which intoxication caused by the surreptitious addition of LSD to beer was deemed to be involuntary. However, a different conclusion was reached in *People v Velez* 175 Cal App 3d 785 (1985) (California), where D had voluntarily smoked marijuana at a party, apparently unaware that PCP, a much stronger drug, had been added to it. D was held to be voluntarily intoxicated after the court pointed out that the effect of marijuana consumption was itself unpredictable.

What about the defendant who consumes a substance that he knows is an intoxicant, but does not know exactly what it is or how strong it is? There is no English case law on this point, but the public policy approach laid down in *Majewski* (1977) would dictate that such conduct be deemed voluntary intoxication. In *Hanks v State* 542 SW 2d 413 (1976) (Texas), where D knew that a drug had been placed in his drink but did not necessarily know what it was, this was nevertheless deemed be voluntary intoxication.

Drugs taken under medical prescription

In *Majewski* (1977), Lord Elwyn Jones LC specifically included those who take 'drugs not on medical prescription' within the scope of voluntary intoxication; by implication, therefore, we can say that those who *do* take drugs under medical prescription will be deemed to be involuntarily intoxicated.

CASE EXAMPLE

Bailey [1983] 1 WLR 760

D had been charged with malicious wounding. His defence was that he was a diabetic and had taken insulin (which had been medically prescribed for him). However, because he had forgotten to eat afterwards, the insulin had triggered a hypoglycaemic episode and this had prevented him from fully appreciating what he was doing.

The Court of Appeal held that a distinction should be drawn between intoxication arising from alcohol and 'certain sorts of drugs to excess', on the one hand, and the unexpected side-effects of therapeutic substances, on the other. It was 'common knowledge' that those who took alcohol and certain drugs could become 'aggressive or do dangerous or unpredictable things'. Griffiths LJ stated:

'The question in each case will be whether the prosecution have proved the necessary element of recklessness. In cases of assault, if [D] knows that his actions or inaction are likely to make him aggressive, unpredictable or uncontrolled with the result that he may cause some injury to others and he persists in the action or takes no remedial action when he knows it is required, it will be open to the jury to find that he was reckless.'

In most cases D who takes prescribed medicines will be quite unaware of potential side-effects. However, where D *is* aware of the effect of a prescribed drug, and takes it anyway, then he is in the same position as D who drinks alcohol. The exception is likely to be rarely applicable to alcohol, though it might apply where brandy is administered to D after an accident. In *Johnson v Commonwealth* 135 Va 524 (1923) a court in Virginia held that D who drank whisky to relieve pain was doing so voluntarily because no medical advice was involved; the implication being that had medical advice been given to drink whisky, then his drinking could be classified as involuntary.

'Soporific or sedative' drugs

A third example of involuntary intoxication involves drugs that are said to have a soporific or sedative influence, as opposed to an inhibition-lowering or mind-expanding effect. In *Burns* (1974) 58 Cr App R 364, D had consumed, *inter alia*, morphine tablets (not medically prescribed) for a stomach complaint, before committing an offence. The Court of Appeal quashed his conviction. The jury should have been directed to acquit if they believed that Burns did not appreciate that morphine was likely to produce unawareness. The leading case is now *Hardie* [1985] 1 WLR 64, where D had taken valium tablets (not medically prescribed) before committing acts of criminal damage, Parker LJ said:

> J 'There was no evidence that it was known to [D] or even generally known that the taking of valium in the quantity taken would be liable to render a person aggressive or incapable of appreciating risks or have other side effects such that its self-administration would itself have an element of recklessness . . . [T]he drug is . . . wholly different in kind from drugs which are liable to cause unpredictability or aggressiveness . . . if the effect of a drug is merely soporific or sedative the taking of it, even in some excessive quantity, cannot in the ordinary way raise a conclusive presumption against the admission of proof of intoxication . . . such as would be the case with alcoholic intoxication or incapacity or automatism resulting from the self-administration of dangerous drugs . . . [The jury] should have been directed that if they came to the conclusion that, as a result of the valium, [D] was, at the time, unable to appreciate the risks to property and persons from his actions they should consider whether the taking of the valium was itself reckless.'

CASE EXAMPLE

Hardie [1985] 1 WLR 64

D was depressed at having been asked to move out of the South London flat he had shared with his girlfriend, V, for some years. He reluctantly agreed to leave and packed. Before he left, however, he took one of V's prescription valium tablets from her medicine cabinet. During the course of the day he took more of the pills, moved some of his possessions out and returned that evening. Shortly after, he started a fire in the wardrobe in the bedroom. His defence was that he did not know what he was doing because of the valium. The jury convicted of arson after being directed to ignore the effects of the valium. However, D's conviction was quashed.

Identifying 'soporific and sedative' drugs

One problem in this area is how to draw a distinction between 'dangerous' drugs on one hand, and 'soporific and sedative' drugs on the other, if indeed such a distinction is possible. Marijuana, depending on the circumstances, may be a sedative or a hallucinogen. Heroin is presumably a 'dangerous' drug but it has undeniably 'soporific' effects. Much depends on several variables: the user himself; the amount taken; how much has been taken before; how the drug is taken (injecting generally produces more dramatic effects than smoking or eating); the surroundings in which the drug is taken; even what the user expects or hopes will happen. The same person may take the same drug at different times with markedly different consequences. Uncertainty in predicting the effect of taking a single drug becomes much more complicated when two or more drugs are taken at the same time, because of the likelihood of interaction. A common example is the enhancing effect of alcohol on the sedative qualities of tranquilisers. The courts in England have yet to address these questions, but you should recall the importance placed on public policy by the House of Lords in *Majewski* (1977). It is suggested that where there is doubt about whether a drug is 'dangerous' or 'soporific', such as heroin, the courts could deem it to be both, and therefore ingestion of it would be regarded as voluntary.

Intoxication under duress

Although there is no English case law on this point, there is American authority for the proposition that 'intoxication under duress' should be regarded as involuntary. In *Burrows v State* 38 Ariz 99, 297 (1931) (Arizona), where D, an 18-year-old boy, had killed his adult victim only after the latter had vehemently insisted the boy drink several bottles of beer and some whisky, the court held that it was possible for this to be regarded as involuntary.

8.3.3 Voluntary intoxication

In the leading English case, *Majewksi* (1977), D was charged with, *inter alia*, assault occasioning actual bodily harm, a crime requiring subjective recklessness, ie awareness of risk. But this is a modest standard; even fleeting awareness will suffice for a conviction. It follows that D's intoxication must be extreme in order to remove altogether the ability to appreciate the risks created by his actions (a point acknowledged by the Court of Appeal in *Stubbs* (1989) 88 Cr App R 53). Moreover, the defence medical evidence in *Majewski* (1977) was to the effect that his intoxication was more likely to have produced amnesia *afterwards*, rather than inducing a state of intoxication *during*, the assaults. In shouting 'You pigs, I'll kill you all', D was obviously aware that (a) he was assaulting someone, and (b) the people whom he was assaulting were police officers.

CASE EXAMPLE

Majewski [1977] AC 443

D had consumed a combination of barbiturates, amphetamines, and alcohol, beginning on a Sunday morning and continuing until Monday night, when he was involved in a pub brawl and assaulted a customer, the manager and police officers sent to deal with him. He was charged with three offences of assault contrary to s 47 of the Offences Against the Person Act (OAPA) 1861 and three offences of assaulting a police officer in the execution of his duty. His defence was that he was suffering the effects of the alcohol and drugs at the time. He was convicted, after the trial judge directed the jury that they could ignore the effect of drink and drugs as being in any way a defence to assault. The Court of Appeal and House of Lords upheld his convictions.

Of course the public must be protected from violent drunkards, no one denies that. But it must surely be in very rare cases that D's capacity has been 'obliterated' such that he must be acquitted? So, were the matter simply to be left to the jury, the number of cases where D might escape conviction would be very few. This reasoning underpins the approach of the courts in the Australia, New Zealand and South Africa, as mentioned in the introduction to this section. The result of this approach, moreover, has not been a proliferation of acquittals (G Orchard, 'Surviving without *Majewski* – a View from Down Under' [1993] Crim LR 426). The English judiciary, however, does not possess such confidence in the jury's ability to reject intoxication in all but a handful of cases. In England, to reiterate this point, the law states that when intoxication is voluntary and D has failed to form *mens rea*:

- D will have a defence if the offence charged is one of 'specific intent'
- where the offence charged is one of 'basic intent', the magistrates or jury must consider whether D would have formed *mens rea* had he been sober.

To understand this approach it is necessary to appreciate its historical origins. Until the mid-nineteenth century, voluntary intoxication was not regarded as any form of defence at all. Instead intoxicated defendants were treated as more culpable. But in the early twentieth century, the courts began to relax the strict approach. In *Meade* [1909] 1 KB 895, Lord Coleridge J said: 'if the mind at the time is so obscured by drink, if the reason is dethroned and the man is incapable of forming the intent, it justifies the reduction of the charge from murder to manslaughter.' This proposition of law (which is still true in the early twenty-first century) was confirmed in *DPP v Beard* [1920] AC 479. Lord Birkenhead emphasised that intoxication was merely a means of demonstrating that D lacked, on a particular charge, the mental element necessary:

> J 'Where a specific intent is an essential element in the offence, evidence of a state of drunkenness rendering the accused incapable of forming such an intent should be taken into consideration in order to determine whether he had in fact formed the intent necessary to constitute the particular crime. If he was so drunk that he was incapable of forming the intent required he could not be convicted of a crime which was committed only if the intent was proved.'

This principle has remained largely unchanged since, though it is now firmly accepted that D need not be *incapable* of forming intent; it is sufficient if he *does not in fact do so* (*Pordage* [1975] Crim LR 575; *Cole* [1993] Crim LR 300).

Basic and specific intent

It seems highly probable that in that in *Beard* Lord Birkenhead was using the word 'specific' to mean 'particular'. The rest of his speech shows that he was not proposing an exceptional rule for 'specific' intent crimes, but was simply pointing out that where a particular crime required a particular intent to be proven, then the case was not made out until that was achieved: 'a person cannot be convicted of a crime unless the *mens* was *rea*.' At no point did Lord Birkenhead refer to anything called 'basic intent' (that concept seems to be attributed to Lord Simon in *DPP v Morgan* [1976] AC 182). Nevertheless, legal doctrine has developed over the last century to the present situation, according to which all crimes divide into two categories for the purposes of the voluntary intoxication defence. In *Bratty*, Lord Denning said:

> J 'If the drunken man is so drunk that he does not know what he is doing, he has a defence to any charge, such as murder or wounding with intent, in which a specific intent is essential, but he is still liable to be convicted of manslaughter or unlawful wounding for which no specific intent is necessary, see *Beard's case*.'

Distinguishing basic and specific intent offences

The division of crimes into specific and basic intent is now well established in English criminal law (and has been adopted in most American states and Canada too). It is obviously crucial to demonstrate which offences belong in which category. Over the years there have been a number of attempts at an explanation:

- The '**purposive element**' argument. A purposive element is some identifiable result desired by D. This possibility was suggested by Lord Simon in *Majewski* (1977). But not all specific intent offences contain a purposive element. For example, murder is beyond argument a crime of specific intent, but can be committed where D only intends to cause GBH. Conversely, some basic intent crimes, eg rape, require purpose (it is essential for liability that D had the purpose of having sex).

- The '**fallback**' argument. Specific intent crimes are those where D, were he to be acquitted because of intoxication, would only convict himself of some lesser offence of basic intent. Many specific intent offences do have this fallback, eg murder has a basic intent fallback (manslaughter), as does s 18 OAPA 1861 (s 20 OAPA 1861); however, some specific intent crimes have no fallback, eg theft.

- The '**ulterior intent**' argument. This proposal received the support of Lord Elwyn-Jones LC in *Majewski* (1977), and was the first to gain broad acceptance. Ulterior intent crimes are those where the mental element goes beyond the *actus reus*. A good example is theft, where the *actus reus* is complete as soon as D appropriates property belonging to another. However, the *mens rea* goes beyond this in requiring that D have the intention to permanently deprive V of his property. However, murder is, as already noted, unquestionably a crime of specific intent, yet it is not a crime of ulterior intent. The *actus reus* is causing the death of a human being; the *mens rea* (malice aforethought) is intent to cause death (or even intent to cause serious harm).

- The **recklessness** argument. This theory holds that basic intent crimes are those offences that may be committed recklessly. This argument has now gained widespread acceptance. In *Metropolitan Police Commissioner v Caldwell* [1982] AC 341, Lord Diplock stated that *Majewski* (1977) is authority for the proposition that self-induced intoxication is no defence to a crime in which recklessness is enough to constitute the necessary *mens rea*.

The various definitions perhaps illustrate the need for statutory clarification. The lack of any definitive test could pose problems for trial judges faced with a new crime (such as those introduced by Parliament in the Sexual Offences Act 2003). Nevertheless, the courts have now assigned most crimes to one category or another, as follows.

Crimes of specific intent

- Murder (*Beard* (1920))
- wounding or causing GBH with intent (*Bratty* (1963); *Pordage* (1975))
- theft (*Ruse v Read* [1949] 1 KB 377)
- obtaining property by deception, robbery and burglary (as a corollary of theft)
- handling stolen goods (*Durante* [1972] 3 All ER 962)
- arson/criminal damage with intent to do so and/or with intent to endanger life (*Metropolitan Police Commissioner v Caldwell* (1982); *Bennett* [1995] Crim LR 877)
- any attempt to commit one of these.

Crimes of basic intent

- Manslaughter, in all its forms (*Beard* (1920); *Lipman* (1970))

- rape (*Woods* (1981) 74 Cr App R 312; *Fotheringham* (1989) 88 Cr App R 206)

- malicious wounding or infliction of GBH, s 20 OAPA 1861 (*Aitken and others* [1992] 1 WLR 1006)

- assault occasioning ABH, s 47 OAPA 1861 (*Majewski* (1977))

- common assault

- arson/criminal damage being reckless whether property would be damaged or destroyed (*Jaggard v Dickinson* [1980] 3 All ER 716)

- arson/criminal damage, being reckless whether property would be damaged or destroyed, and being reckless whether life would be endangered thereby (*Bennett* (1995)).

Intoxication and basic intent

If D is charged with, for example, murder, he may plead intoxication as a means of denying that he formed the intent to kill or cause grievous bodily harm. But what if D is charged with a basic intent offence, such as manslaughter? Is there any point in pleading intoxication? There are suggestions by some of the Law Lords in *Majewski* (1977) that were D to do this he would, in effect, be pleading guilty. For example, Lord Elwyn-Jones LC said that D who voluntarily reduced himself to an intoxicated condition

> **J** 'supplies the evidence of *mens rea*, of guilty mind certainly sufficient for crimes of basic intent. It is a reckless course of conduct and recklessness is enough to constitute the necessary *mens rea* in assault cases . . . The drunkenness is itself an intrinsic, an integral part of the crime'.

That is to say, voluntary intoxication was to be regarded, in law, as a form of recklessness. This somewhat harsh view may not represent the law today. Another view which has been adopted in some cases is that, when faced with a defendant pleading intoxication to a basic intent offence, the magistrates or jury are required to consider whether D would have formed the requisite *mens rea* had he been sober. An early indication of the newer approach was seen in *Aitken and others* (1992) 95 Cr App R 304, which will be examined below in the section on consent. The judge advocate (this was a court martial) had directed the jury that they had to be 'satisfied . . . that each defendant, when he did the act, either foresaw that it might cause some injury . . . or would have foreseen that the act might cause some injury, had he not been drinking'. The Courts-Martial Appeal Court, although quashing the conviction on other grounds, confirmed that the judge advocate's direction was correct. *Aitken and others* (1992) was followed in *Richardson and Irwin* [1998] EWCA Crim 3269; [1999] 1 Cr App R 392.

CASE EXAMPLE

Richardson and Irwin [1998] EWCA Crim 3269; [1999] 1 Cr App R 392

The appellants and V were students at Surrey University. They had each consumed about
five pints of lager before indulging in 'horseplay' – something they did regularly – during
the course of which V was lifted over the edge of a balcony and dropped at least 10 feet,
suffering injury. D and E were charged with inflicting GBH contrary to s 20 OAPA 1861.
The prosecution case was that they had both foreseen that dropping V from the balcony
might cause him harm but, nevertheless, took that risk. Their defence was that V had
consented to the horseplay and/or that his fall was an accident. On the question of *mens
rea* the jury was directed to consider each man's foresight of the consequences on the
basis of what a reasonable, sober man would have foreseen. They were convicted, but the
Court of Appeal quashed the conviction. The question was not what the reasonable,
sober man would have foreseen, but what these particular men would have foreseen had
they not been drinking. Clarke LJ memorably said that, 'the defendants were not
hypothetical reasonable men, but University students'.

Obviously this poses a hypothetical question for the magistrates or jury. Nevertheless, if there is
evidence of factors which might cast doubt on whether D would have formed *mens rea*, such as
fatigue or illness, then these must be taken into account. In *Majewski* (1977) one of the grounds of
appeal was that the denial of intoxication as a defence in basic intent offences was irreconcilable
with s 8 of the Criminal Justice Act 1967, which requires a jury to consider 'all the evidence' before
deciding whether D intended or foresaw the result of his conduct. The view of Lord Elwyn-Jones
LC was forthright:

> **J** 'In referring to "all the evidence" [s 8] meant all the *relevant* evidence. But if there is a
> substantive rule of law that in crimes of basic intent, the factor of intoxication is
> irrelevant (and such I hold to be the substantive law), evidence with regard to it is
> irrelevant.'

The evidential burden

In all cases – whether specific or basic intent – D is required to adduce evidence of intoxication
before the matter becomes a live issue. D's evidence must go to the degree of intoxication, and not
just to the fact of intoxication. The strength of evidence needed to discharge the evidential burden
will differ from one situation to the next, depending on the nature of the crime and the

circumstances. The mere assertion that D was drinking all day prior to the commission of the alleged offence will not, generally, suffice in itself. The question of whether D's intoxication is sufficient is a question of law for the judge. If the evidence is insufficient to raise a doubt that D possessed *mens rea*, the trial judge must remove the matter from the jury's consideration. This point was made clear in *Groark* [1999] EWCA Crim 207; [1999] Crim LR 669.

CASE EXAMPLE

Groark [1999] EWCA Crim 207; [1999] Crim LR 669

D had struck V whilst wearing a knuckleduster. He was charged with wounding under s 18 and s 20 OAPA 1861. At trial he gave evidence that he had drunk 10 pints of beer but that he knew what he had done and that he had acted in self-defence. The judge did not direct the jury as to intoxication and D was convicted of the s 18 offence. He appealed, arguing that there was a duty on the judge to direct the jury on intoxication. However, the Court of Appeal dismissed the appeal: there was no obligation on the judge to direct the jury.

This was confirmed in *McKnight* [2000] EWCA Crim 33; *The Times*, 5th May 2000. D, charged with murder, also claimed to have acted in self-defence. She admitted being drunk, but not 'legless'. In summing-up to the jury, the trial judge did not direct them as to the possibility of intoxication providing a defence. The jury rejected the plea of self-defence and convicted of murder. The Court of Appeal upheld the conviction. On her arrest, D had given a full account of the incident and there was nothing to suggest that her perceptions were such that she could not appreciate what she was doing. In those circumstances there was no sufficient basis in the evidence before the jury which would have entitled them to have concluded that D might not have formed the intention to kill or cause GBH because she had been so drunk, and accordingly it would have been wrong and confusing for the judge to have left the matter to the jury.

8.3.4 'Dutch courage'

A special rule applies in the situation whereby D, having resolved to commit an offence requiring specific intent whilst sober, or at least when not intoxicated, then deliberately becomes intoxicated in order to provide himself with 'Dutch courage' before carrying out the offence. The situation remains theoretical. In *Attorney-General of Northern Ireland v Gallagher* [1963] AC 349, Lord Denning said:

> J 'If a man, whilst sane and sober, forms an intention to kill and makes preparation for it knowing it is a wrong thing to do, and then gets himself drunk so as to give himself Dutch courage to do the killing, and whilst drunk carries out his intention, he cannot rely on this self-induced drunkenness as a defence to murder, not even as reducing it to manslaughter. He cannot say he got himself into such a stupid state that he was incapable of an intent to kill . . . The wickedness of his mind before he got drunk is enough to condemn him, coupled with the act which he intended to do and did do.'

CASE EXAMPLE

Gallagher [1963] AC 349

D, having decided to kill his wife, bought a knife and a bottle of whisky. He drank much of the whisky, then killed her with the knife. His defence was that he was either insane, or too drunk to be able to form the intent at the time of the stabbing. He was convicted, but the NI Court of Appeal quashed his conviction, holding that the judge's directions to the jury required them to consider insanity at the time D started drinking, not when he killed his wife. The Lords agreed that this *would* have been a misdirection, but found that the judge had directed the jury to consider D's state of mind at the time of the killing. The jury having found that D had *mens rea* at that time, there was no need to consider the question of intoxication. Lord Denning, however, ventured the opinion that even if D had been found to be lacking *mens rea* at the time of the killing, he would still have no defence even for murder.

8.3.5 Intoxication and insanity

Where intoxication produces insanity as defined in the M'Naghten Rules, then those latter rules apply. In *Davis* (1881) 14 Cox CC 563, where D claimed that a history of alcohol abuse had caused *delirium tremens*, and based his defence on insanity, Stephen J directed the jury that:

> J 'Drunkenness is one thing and disease to which drunkenness leads are different things; and if a man by drunkenness brings on state of disease which causes such a degree of madness, even for a time, which would have relieved him from responsibility if it had been caused in any other way, then he would not be criminally responsible.'

8.3.6 Intoxication and automatism

An act done in a state of (non-insane) automatism will negative criminal liability except where the automotive state is self-induced. This is most obviously the case where the automotive state is due to intoxication. *Lipman* (1970) is the clearest example of this.

CASE EXAMPLE

Lipman [1970] 1 QB 152

D and his girlfriend had both taken LSD. During the subsequent 'trip', D believed that he had descended to the centre of the earth and the girl was a snake. He proceeded to kill the girl by stuffing 8 inches of bedsheet down her throat. Although clearly lacking intent to kill the girl, and so not guilty of the specific intent crime of murder, D was convicted of the basic intent offence of manslaughter.

In Canada, meanwhile, a new policy has emerged. Until fairly recently, the law concerning intoxication in England and Canada was (minor differences aside) identical. However, in *Daviault* (1995) 118 DLR (4d) 469 the Supreme Court of Canada created a new rule, recognising a defence of intoxication when a person charged with a basic intent offence was <u>incapable</u> of forming basic intent. D bears the burden of proving, on the balance of probabilities, that his intoxication had reached this extreme level. The new rule was confirmed in *Levy* (1996) 104 CCC (3d) 423. D had consumed cocaine and alcohol before allegedly assaulting his own mother. Evidence was given at the trial that taking cocaine (a stimulant) followed by alcohol (a depressant) could intoxicate someone very quickly indeed (the cocaine initially defers the effect of the alcohol but, when the cocaine wears off, the full effects of the alcohol consumption are felt). The trial judge, however, ruled that D had not proved that he was so intoxicated as to be incapable of forming the basic intent required for assault. D was convicted and appealed, arguing that it should be sufficient for the defence to establish a reasonable doubt as to whether he was capable of forming the *mens rea*. The appeal court rejected his appeal, confirming that it was necessary for D to show the requisite degree of intoxication on the balance of probabilities.

8.3.7 Intoxicated mistakes

An intoxicated defendant is sometimes actually pleading mistake. As will be seen in section 8.7 below, when a (sober) defendant pleads the defence of mistake, he is entitled to be judged on the facts as he genuinely perceived them to be. However, when D is intoxicated, this changes and D is subjected to the normal *Majewski* (1977) rules. He will be assumed to be aware of any circumstances and consequences of which he would have been aware had he been sober. A good example is the *Fotheringham* (1989) rape case. The Court of Appeal held that self-induced intoxication was no defence, whether the issue was intention, consent or mistake as to the identity of the victim.

CASE EXAMPLE

Fotheringham (1989) 88 Cr App R 206

D had been out with his wife one evening and had been drinking heavily. When they returned home, D climbed into the marital bed where the baby-sitter, V, was asleep. Under the mistaken impression that V was his wife, he had sex with her without her consent. At the time, the fact that D was married meant he could not be convicted of rape if he genuinely believed D was his wife. However, the judge directed the jury to disregard intoxication. He was convicted and the Court of Appeal upheld the conviction.

Statutory exceptions

Fotheringham (1989) represents the common law position. There is one significant statutory exception, found in s 5(2) of the Criminal Damage Act 1971. This provides that a person charged with criminal damage shall have a lawful excuse in two situations: belief in consent and belief in the need to damage property in order to protect other property. Section 5(3) provides that 'it is immaterial whether a belief is justified or not, provided it is honestly held'. In *Jaggard v Dickinson* (1980), Donaldson LJ in the High Court refused to allow the *Majewski* (1977) rule to override the express words of Parliament by introducing a qualification that 'the honesty of the belief is not attributable only to self-induced intoxication'.

CASE EXAMPLE

Jaggard v Dickinson [1980] 3 All ER 716

D's friend, H, had invited her to treat his house at no 67 as if it were her own. One night, when drunk, D ordered a taxi and asked to be taken to H's house. Instead, she was dropped off outside no 35, which looked identical. She assumed it was H's house and entered the garden. She was ordered to leave by the occupier, V. Rather than leaving, D broke in by breaking the window in the back door, damaging a net curtain in the process. Charged with criminal damage, D relied upon the statutory defence. She contended that, at the time she broke into no 35, she had a genuine belief she was breaking into no 67 and that her relationship with D was such that she had his consent to break into his house. Hence, s 5(2) afforded her a defence to the charge. The magistrates ruled that she was unable to rely upon the defence because of her self-induced intoxication, and she was convicted. On appeal, the High Court accepted that, although criminal damage is a basic intent offence, s 5(2) and (3) meant that D's intoxication had to be considered, resulting in her acquittal. Donaldson LJ said that her intoxication 'helped to explain what would otherwise have been inexplicable, and hence lent colour to her evidence about the state of her belief.'

Intoxication, mistake and self-defence

A drunken belief in the need to use force in self-defence is no defence, at least to a basic intent offence, such as manslaughter or assault. The leading case is *O'Grady* [1987] QB 995. Lord Lane CJ was concerned that, because self-defence is a good defence to all crimes in the case of the sober defendant, were this to be applied to the drunken one, dangerous harm-doing could go unpunished. He said:

> J 'This brings us to the question of public order. There are two competing interests. On the one hand the defendant who has only acted according to what he believed to be necessary to protect himself, and on the other hand that of the public and the victim in particular who probably through no fault of his own, has been injured or perhaps killed because of the defendant's drunken mistake. Reason recoils from the conclusion that in such circumstances a defendant is entitled to leave the court without a stain on his character.'

CASE EXAMPLE

O'Grady [1987] QB 995

D and his friend V had been drinking heavily when they fell asleep in the former's flat. D, who claimed that he awoke when V began hitting him with a piece of glass, picked up an ashtray and hit V with it, killing him. The judge's direction suggested that D would have a defence if his intoxication caused him to believe he was under attack; but not if his intoxication caused him to use unreasonable force. He was convicted of manslaughter. The Court of Appeal held that this direction in fact erred in favour of D. Instead, they concluded that where the jury is satisfied that D was mistaken either that any force, or the force which he in fact used, was necessary and, further, that the mistake was caused by intoxication, the defence must fail.

Interestingly, however, the court also refused to draw the usual distinction between crimes of specific and basic intent. Lord Lane CJ thought that 'the question of mistake can and ought to be considered separately from the question of intent'. If D was mistaken in his belief that any force, or the amount of force in fact used, was necessary to defend himself, and this mistake was caused by self-induced intoxication, then he would not have a good defence, even for murder. However, would D be 'entitled to leave the court without a stain on his character'? The answer is, almost certainly not. While the sober D is entitled to an acquittal, the intoxicated one is not, for either of two reasons:

- his intoxication supplies the *mens rea* for the basic intent offence of unlawful and dangerous act manslaughter, following *Lipman* (1970), approved in *Majewski* (1977) or

- his drunken mistake, though honest, is surely grossly negligent, leading to gross negligence manslaughter.

Lord Lane's opinion in *O'Grady* that a drunken mistake is no basis for a defence of self-defence to murder is strictly *obiter* because the appeal concerned a conviction for manslaughter. But the Court of Appeal in *O'Connor* [1991] Crim LR 135 treated it as binding. Consequently where D raises self-defence to a specific intent offence, the jury should be directed (a) to consider intoxication in deciding whether he formed the necessary intent, but (b) to ignore intoxication in deciding whether he believed he was acting in self-defence. This could lead to bizarre consequences:

- Where D, through alcoholic confusion, shoots a man whom he mistakenly thought was a wild animal, and hence fails to form the intention to kill another human being, he is entitled to have his intoxication considered by the jury (this is subject to the *Majewski* rules).

- Where D, again through alcoholic confusion, forms a mistaken belief that he is under attack and kills another human being in self-defence, he is entitled to no defence at all (this is the *O'Grady* rule).

Despite these criticisms, the Court of Appeal confirmed the *O'Grady* decision in *Hatton* [2005] EWCA Crim 2951; [2006] 1 Cr App R 16. At D's trial for murder the defence suggested that V may have attacked D under the erroneous impression that he was homosexual and D, in his drunken condition, may have believed that V was an SAS officer who was attacking him with a sword. The trial judge, however, ruled that a mistaken belief in the need to use force in self-defence, where the mistake was due to intoxication, provided no defence – even to murder. The jury convicted D of murder and the Court of Appeal upheld his conviction. Referring to *O'Grady*, Lord Phillips CJ stated:

> **J** 'We do not believe that upon a proper application of the law of precedence we can treat the general principle that was the reason for this court's decision as being mere *obiter dicta* so far as the law of murder is concerned. We are obliged to follow *O'Grady* and to reject [counsel's] contention that the judge should have directed the jury to consider whether the appellant's drunkenness might have led him to make a mistake as to the severity of any attack to which he may have been subjected by [V].'

Lord Phillips did acknowledge the academic criticism that had been made of *O'Grady*, but concluded that 'whether or not the law is soundly based must be decided elsewhere' (meaning either the House of Lords or in Parliament). The Court of Appeal in *Hatton* did certify a question for the House of Lords, namely 'Is a defendant who raises the issue of self-defence to a charge of murder entitled to be judged upon the basis of what he mistakenly believed to be the situation

when that mistaken belief was brought about by self-induced intoxication by alcohol or drugs?', but leave to appeal to the House was subsequently refused.

CASE EXAMPLE

Hatton **[2005] EWCA Crim 2951; [2006] 1 Cr App R 16; [2006] Crim LR 353**

One night D battered V to death with a sledgehammer. The pair had only met that evening, at a nightclub, before returning to D's flat. During the evening V, who was a manic depressive, had been behaving 'strangely', falsely representing that he had been an SAS officer, striking martial art poses and exhibiting a hatred of homosexuals. After D's arrest he claimed to have no recollection of the killing because he had been drinking heavily beforehand (some 20 pints of beer according to his own evidence). However, he did claim to have a 'vague recollection of being involved in an altercation' with V, and that he may have been acting in self-defence. A stick, which had been fashioned into the shape of a samurai sword, belonging to D was found under V's body, provided the basis for D's claim that he may have been attacked by V. D's murder conviction was upheld.

8.3.8 Reform

A number of proposals have been made to reform the English rules on intoxication.

Codification

The Draft Criminal Code (1989), cl 22(1), provides that 'Where an offence requires a fault element of recklessness (however described), a person who was voluntarily intoxicated shall be treated – (a) as having been aware of any risk of which he would have been aware had he been sober'. The Draft Criminal Law Bill (1993), cl 21, is virtually identical although it substitutes 'not been intoxicated' for 'been sober'. After a period in the early 1990s when the Law Commission supported the idea of abolishing the *Majewski* rules (see below), it returned to the theme of codification in a 1995 Report, *Legislating the Criminal Code: Intoxication and Criminal Liability* (Law Com No 229). The draft Bill attached to the report essentially endorsed the *Majewski* rules. For discussion see J Horder, 'Sobering Up? The Law Commission on Criminal Intoxication' (1995) 58 MLR 534; E Paton, 'Reformulating the Intoxication Rules: The Law Commission's Report' [1995] Crim LR 382; and S Gough, 'Intoxication and Criminal Liability: The Law Commission's Proposed Reforms' (1996) 112 LQR 335.

Simple abolition

Abolishing the *Majewski* rules would not be unduly drastic – it would bring English law into line with several other common law jurisdictions, including Australia, New Zealand and South Africa. It would have the useful side-effect of removing all arguments about the distinction between

'specific' and 'basic' intent plus the implications of pleading voluntary intoxication as a defence to a basic intent offence. The distinction between voluntary and involuntary intoxication would also disappear (except where relevant in sentencing).

Key facts on intoxication

KEY FACTS

	Specific intent crimes	Basic intent crimes
Voluntary intoxication	If defendant has *mens rea* he is guilty (*Gallagher* (1963)). If defendant has no *mens rea* he is not guilty (*Beard* (1920)).	The defendant is probably guilty of the offence. Becoming intoxicated may be deemed to be a reckless course of conduct (*Majewski* (1977)). D will be deemed to have appreciated any risk he would have appreciated had he been sober (*Richardson and Irwin* (1999)).
Involuntary intoxication	If defendant has *mens rea* he is guilty (*Kingston* (1995)). If defendant has no *mens rea* he is not guilty (*Hardie* (1985)).	If defendant has *mens rea* he is guilty (*Kingston* (1995)). The defendant has not been reckless in becoming intoxicated, so if he has no *mens rea* he is not guilty (*Bailey* (1983)).
Drunken mistake	If the mistake negates *mens rea* the defendant is not guilty (*Lipman* (1970)). If the mistake is about the need to defend oneself it is not a defence. The defendant will be guilty (*O'Grady* (1987); *Hatton* (2005)).	This is a reckless course of conduct, so the defendant is guilty (*Fotheringham* (1989)). Unless the mistake concerns belief in owner's consent to criminal damage (*Jaggard v Dickinson* (1980)).

Abolition and creation of a new offence

As indicated above, in a 1993 Consultation Paper, *Intoxication and Criminal Liability* (Law Com No 127), the Law Commission recommended the abolition of the *Majewski* rules coupled with the adoption of a new offence, known as 'criminal intoxication'. D would be entitled to plead intoxication as a defence to any crime and, if the magistrates or jury were not satisfied as to whether D had formed *mens rea*, they would acquit. However, they would then go on to convict D of the new offence if satisfied that he had committed the *actus reus* of the original crime charged and at the time of doing so 'his awareness, understanding or control was substantially impaired by his being deliberately intoxicated'. Similar proposals had been made on several occasions in the past. In 1961, Professor Glanville Williams suggested an offence of being 'drunk and dangerous'. In 1975, the Royal Committee on Mentally Abnormal Offenders (Butler Committee) recommended the creation of an offence called 'dangerous intoxication' (Cmnd 6244). In 1980, a majority of the Criminal Law Revision Committee's 14th Report, *Offences Against the Person* (Cmnd 7844), objected to the idea of a new offence on the ground that it was too crude because it categorised together people who had committed an assault whilst drunk with those who had killed whilst drunk. The Law Commission's 1993 proposals were opened up to consultation but the feedback was so negative that the Law Commission dropped them two years later. For discussion refer to G Virgo, 'Reconciling Principle with Policy' [1993] Crim LR 415.

8.4 Duress

With this defence, D is claiming that he committed the *actus reus* of the offence, with *mens rea*, but that he did so because he had no effective choice, being faced with threats of serious injury or death, or with similar threats against others close to him. The defence is not a denial of *mens rea*, like intoxication, nor a plea that D's act was justified, as is the case with self-defence. Rather D is seeking to be excused. There is a possible analogy to automatism, except that when D pleads duress, his actions are morally, as opposed to physically, involuntary. In *Lynch v DPP of Northern Ireland* [1975] AC 653, Lord Morris said:

> **J** 'It is proper that any rational system of law should take fully into account the standards of honest and reasonable men . . . If then someone is really threatened with death or serious injury unless he does what he is told is the law to pay no heed to the miserable, agonising plight of such a person? For the law to understand not only how the timid but also the stalwart may in a moment of crisis behave is not to make the law weak but to make it just.'

8.4.1 Sources of the duress

Duress comes in two types:

- **Duress by threats**: here, D is threatened by another person to commit a criminal offence. For example, D is ordered at gunpoint to drive armed robbers away from the scene of a robbery or he will be shot.

- **Duress of circumstances** (sometimes referred to as 'necessity', but in this chapter necessity will be dealt with separately): here, the threat does not come from a person, but the circumstances in which D finds himself.

The principles applying are identical in either case of duress. The principles were originally established in duress by threats cases and subsequently applied to duress of circumstances.

8.4.2 The seriousness of the threat

The threats must be of death or serious personal injury (*Hudson and Taylor* [1971] 2 QB 202). A threat to damage or destroy property is insufficient (*M'Growther* (1746) Fost 13). In *Lynch* (1975), Lord Simon said: 'The law must draw a line somewhere; and as a result of experience and human valuation, the law draws it between threats to property and threats to the person.' Threats to expose sexual immorality are insufficient (*Singh* [1974] 1 All ER 26; *Valderrama-Vega* [1985] Crim LR 220). In *Baker and Wilkins* [1996] EWCA Crim 1126; [1997] Crim LR 497, a duress of circumstances case, the Court of Appeal refused to accept an argument that the scope of the defence should be extended to cases where D believed the act was immediately necessary to avoid serious psychological injury as well as death or serious physical injury. Although there must be a threat of death or serious personal injury, it need not be the sole reason why D committed the offence with which he is charged. This was seen in *Valderrama-Vega*.

CASE EXAMPLE

Valderrama-Vega [1985] Crim LR 220

D claimed that he had imported cocaine because of death-threats made by a Mafia-type organisation. But he also needed the money because he was heavily in debt to his bank. Furthermore, he had been threatened with having his homosexuality disclosed. His conviction was quashed by the Court of Appeal: the jury had been directed he only had a defence if the death-threats were the sole reason for acting.

ACTIVITY

In the light of the House of Lords' decision in *Ireland, Burstow* [1998] AC 147 to extend the scope of the phrase 'bodily harm' in the context of ss 20 and 47 OAPA 1861, to include psychological harm, discuss whether the Court of Appeal's decision in *Baker and Wilkins* is justifiable.

8.4.3 Threats against whom?

At one time it seemed that, in cases of duress by threats, the threat had to be directed at D personally. However, in *Ortiz* (1986) 83 Cr App R 173, D had been forced into taking part in a cocaine-smuggling operation after he was told that, if he refused, his wife and children would 'disappear'. At his trial, D pleaded duress by threats, but the jury rejected the defence. The trial judge had directed them that 'duress is a defence if a man acts solely as a result of threats of death or serious injury to himself or another'. The Court of Appeal did not disapprove of the inclusion in the direction of 'threats . . . to another'. The view that the threats could be directed at someone other than D was confirmed in the early duress of circumstances cases, *Conway* [1988] 3 All ER 1025 and *Martin* [1989] 1 All ER 652. In the former case, the defence was allowed when D's passenger in his car was threatened and in the latter case D's wife threatened to harm herself. It is now well established that the threats can be directed towards members of D's immediate family, or indeed to 'some other person, for whose safety D would reasonably regard himself as responsible', according to Kennedy LJ in *Wright* [2000] Crim LR 510.

CASE EXAMPLE

Wright [2000] Crim LR 510

D had been arrested at Gatwick Airport with four kilos of cocaine worth nearly £½ million hidden under her clothing, having just flown in from St Lucia. She was charged with trying to import unlawful drugs and pleaded duress. She claimed that she had flown to St Lucia in order to bring back the drugs under threat of violence from her drug dealer, to whom she was £3,000 in debt. In St Lucia, D was threatened with a gun and told that her boyfriend Darren (who had flown out to join her) would be killed if she did not go through with the trip; she was also told that Darren would only be allowed to return to the UK once she had reached Gatwick. This meant that when she was arrested at Gatwick she was still fearful for Darren's life. However, she was convicted after the trial judge directed the jury that duress was only available if a threat was directed at D herself or at a 'member of her immediate family'. He reminded the jury that D did not live with Darren and was not married to him. D was convicted but the Court of Appeal allowed her appeal (although it ordered a retrial). Kennedy LJ said that 'it was both unnecessary and undesirable for the judge to trouble the jury with the question of Darren's proximity. Still less to suggest, as he did, that Darren was insufficiently proximate'. The question for the jury should simply have been whether D had good cause to fear that if she did not import the drugs, she or Darren would be killed or seriously injured.

ACTIVITY

1. D is accosted in his car by armed robbers who direct him to drive them away, or they will shoot randomly into a group of schoolchildren at a bus stop. Should D have a defence of duress if charged with aiding and abetting armed robbery?

2. This question was posed by Professor Sir John Smith in his commentary on *Wright* in the Criminal Law Review: could a fan of Manchester United be reasonably expected to resist a threat to kill the team's star player if he did not participate in a robbery?

8.4.4 Imminence of the threat, opportunities to escape and police protection

Imminence of the threat

The threat must have been operative on D, or other parties, at the moment he committed the offence. In *Hudson and Taylor* [1971] 2 QB 202, Lord Widgery CJ said:

> 'When . . . there is no opportunity for delaying tactics and the person threatened must make up his mind whether he is to commit the criminal act or not, the existence at that moment of threats sufficient to destroy his will ought to provide him with a defence even though the threatened injury may not follow instantly but after an interval.'

CASE EXAMPLE

Hudson and Taylor [1971] 2 QB 202

D, aged 17, and E, aged 19, were the principal prosecution witnesses at the trial of a man called Jimmy Wright. He had been charged with malicious wounding. Both D and E had been in the pub where the wounding was alleged to have occurred and gave statements to the police. At the trial, however, the girls failed to identify Wright and, as a result, he

was acquitted. In due course, the girls were charged with perjury (lying in court). D claimed that another man, F, who had a reputation for violence, had threatened her that if she 'told on Wright in court' she would be cut up. She passed this threat on to E, and the result was that they were too frightened to identify Wright (especially when they arrived in court and saw F in the public gallery). The trial judge withdrew the defence of duress from the jury because the threat of harm could not be immediately put into effect when they were testifying in the safety of the courtroom. Their convictions were quashed.

In *Abdul-Hussain and Others* [1999] Crim LR 570, confirmed in *Safi and Others* [2003] EWCA Crim 1809, the Court of Appeal decided that, for the defence of duress to be available, the threat to D (or other persons) had to be believed by D to be 'imminent' but not necessarily 'immediate'. This led the Court of Appeal to quash hijacking convictions in both cases because the trial judge had directed the jury to disregard the threat to the defendants unless the threat was believed by D to be 'immediate'. However, when the House of Lords came to examine this issue, in *Hasan* [2005] UKHL 22; [2005] 2 AC 467, that court decided that the correct test was that the threat had to be believed by D to be 'immediate' or 'almost immediate'. Giving the leading judgment, Lord Bingham said:

> **J** It should be made clear to juries that if the retribution threatened against the defendant or his family or a person for whom he reasonably feels responsible is not such as he reasonably expects to follow immediately or almost immediately on his failure to comply with the threat, there may be little if any room for doubt that he could have taken evasive action, whether by going to the police or in some other way, to avoid committing the crime with which he is charged.

The *Hasan* case will be examined in more detail below.

Opportunities to escape, and police protection

D will be expected to take advantage of any reasonable opportunity that he has to escape from the duressor and/or contact the police. If he fails to take it, the defence may fail. This was illustrated in *Gill* [1963] 2 All ER 688. D claimed that he had been threatened with violence if he did not steal a lorry. The Court of Criminal Appeal expressed doubts whether the defence was open, as there was a period of time in which he could have raised the alarm and wrecked the whole enterprise. In *Pommell* [1995] 2 Cr App R 607, Kennedy LJ accepted that 'in some cases a delay, especially if unexplained, may be such as to make it clear that any duress must have ceased to operate, in which case the judge would be entitled to conclude that . . . the defence was not open'.

CASE EXAMPLE

Pommell [1995] 2 Cr App R 607

Police found D at 8 am lying in bed with a loaded gun in his hand. He claimed that, during the night, a man called Erroll had come to see him, intent on shooting some people who had killed E's friend. D had persuaded E to give him the gun, which he took upstairs. This was between 12.30 am and 1.30 am. D claimed that he had intended to hand the gun over to the police the next day. D was convicted of possessing a prohibited weapon, contrary to the Firearms Act 1968, after the trial judge refused to allow the defence of duress to go to the jury. This was on the basis that, even if D had been forced to take the gun, he should have gone immediately to the police. The Court of Appeal allowed the appeal on the basis that this was too restrictive, and ordered a retrial.

In *Hudson and Taylor* (1971), the Crown contended that D and E should have sought police protection. Lord Widgery CJ rejected this argument, which, he said 'would, in effect, restrict the defence . . . to cases where the person threatened had been kept in custody by the maker of the threats, or where the time interval between the making of the threats and the commission of the offence had made recourse to the police impossible'. Although the defence had to be kept 'within reasonable grounds', the Crown's argument would impose too 'severe' a restriction. He concluded that 'in deciding whether [an escape] opportunity was reasonably open to the accused the jury should have regard to his age and circumstances and to any risks to him which may be involved in the course of action relied upon'.

8.4.5 Duress does not exist in the abstract

It is only a defence if the defendant commits some specific crime which was nominated by the person making the threat. This was seen in *Cole* (1993), where money-lenders were pressurising D for money. They had threatened him, as well as his girlfriend and child, and hit him with a baseball bat. Eventually, D robbed two building societies. To a charge of robbery he pleaded duress, but the judge held that the defence was not available and withdrew it from the jury. D's conviction was upheld by the Court of Appeal: the defence was only available where the threats were directed to the commission of the particular offence charged. The duressors had not said 'Go and rob a building society or else . . .'.

8.4.6 Voluntary exposure to risk of compulsion

D will be denied the defence if he voluntarily places himself in such a situation that he risks being threatened with violence to commit crime. This may be because he joins a criminal organisation. In *Fitzpatrick* [1977] NI 20, D pleaded duress to a catalogue of offences, including murder, even though he was a voluntary member of the IRA. The trial judge rejected the defence, stating that 'If

a man chooses to expose himself and still more if he chooses to submit himself to illegal compulsion, it may not operate even in mitigation of punishment'. Any other conclusion he said 'would surely be monstrous'. The Northern Ireland Court of Appeal dismissed the appeal. In *Sharp* [1987] 3 All ER 103, Lord Lane CJ said:

> J
>
> 'Where a person has voluntarily, and with knowledge of its nature, joined a criminal organisation or gang which he knew might bring pressure on him to commit an offence and was an active member when he was put under such pressure, he cannot avail himself of the defence.'

CASE EXAMPLE

Sharp [1987] 3 All ER 103

D and two other men had attempted an armed robbery of a sub-post office, but were thwarted when the sub-postmaster pressed an alarm. As they made their escape one of the others fired a shotgun in the air to deter pursuers. Three weeks later they carried out a second armed robbery, which resulted in the murder of the sub-postmaster. D claimed that he was only the 'bagman', that he was not armed and only took part in the second robbery because he had been threatened with having his head blown off by one of the others if he did not co-operate. The trial judge withdrew the defence, and D was convicted of manslaughter, robbery and attempted robbery. The Court of Appeal upheld the convictions. The Court treated it as significant that D knew of the others' violent and trigger-happy nature several weeks before he attempted to withdraw from the enterprise.

This principle has been confirmed, and extended, in a number of subsequent cases. It is now firmly established that D does not necessarily have to have joined a criminal organisation (as in *Lynch* (1975) or *Sharp* (1987)). Voluntarily associating with persons with a propensity for violence (typically, by buying unlawful drugs from suppliers) may well be enough to deny the defence.

- *Ali* [1995] Crim LR 303 and *Baker and Ward* [1999] EWCA Crim 913; [1999] 2 Cr App R 335, both concerned drug-users who pleaded duress to robbery, having become indebted to their supplier and having then been threatened with violence if they did not find the money. In each case the Court of Appeal confirmed the defence would be denied in situations where D voluntarily placed himself in a position where the threat of violence was likely.

- In *Heath* [1999] EWCA Crim 1526; [2000] Crim LR 109, D was a drug-user who had become heavily indebted to a man with a reputation for violence and who had threatened D with violence if he did not deliver a consignment of 98 kilos of cannabis from Lincolnshire to

Bristol. D was caught and charged with being in possession of cannabis. He pleaded duress, but the defence was denied and he was convicted. The Court of Appeal rejected his appeal. D had voluntarily associated himself with the drugs world, knowing that in that world, debts are collected *via* intimidation and violence.

- *Harmer* [2001] EWCA Crim 2930; [2002] Crim LR 401, was factually very similar to *Heath*. D had been caught at Dover docks trying to smuggle cocaine into the UK hidden inside a box of washing-up powder. At his trial D pleaded duress on the basis that his supplier had forced him to do it or suffer violence. D admitted that he had knowingly involved himself with criminals (he was a drug addict and had to have a supplier to get drugs) and knew that his supplier might use or threaten violence. However, he said that he had not appreciated that his supplier would demand that he get involved in crime. The defence was denied and D was convicted; the Court of Appeal upheld his conviction, following *Heath* (1999). Voluntary exposure to unlawful violence was enough to exclude the defence.

Professor Sir John Smith was critical of the decision in *Harmer*. He wrote in the commentary to the case in the Criminal Law Review that 'the joiner may know that he may be subjected to compulsion, but compulsion to pay one's debts is one thing, compulsion to commit crime is quite another.' Given the judicial uncertainty and academic criticism of the law, it was perhaps inevitable that the House of Lords would eventually be asked to clarify the position regarding the availability of duress when D voluntarily associates himself with a criminal gang or organisation. In *Hasan* [2005] UKHL 22; [2005] 2 AC 467, the Court of Appeal had quashed D's conviction of aggravated burglary but certified a question for the consideration of the House of Lords, seeking to establish whether the defence of duress is excluded when, as a result of the accused's voluntary association with others:

(i) he foresaw (or possibly should have foreseen) the risk of being then and there subjected to *any compulsion* by threats of violence; or

(ii) only when he foresaw (or should have foreseen) the risk of being subjected to compulsion to *commit criminal offences*; and, if the latter

(iii) only if the offences foreseen (or which should have been foreseen) were of the *same type* (or possibly the same type and gravity) as that ultimately committed.

The Lords reinstated D's conviction after taking the view that option (i) above correctly stated the law. By a 4:1 majority, the Lords confirmed that it was sufficient if D should have foreseen the risk of being subjected to 'any compulsion'. Lord Bingham stated:

> **J** 'The defence of duress is excluded when as a result of the accused's voluntary association with others engaged in criminal activity he foresaw or ought reasonably to have foreseen the risk of being subjected to any compulsion by threats of violence.'

Only Baroness Hale departed from the majority: she would have preferred to take option (ii). None of the five judges chose option (iii). The case of *Baker and Ward* [1999] EWCA Crim 913, in which the Court of Appeal had decided that D had to foresee that he would be compelled to commit offences of the type with which he was charged (that is, option (iii)), was therefore overruled. However, the judgments in the other Court of Appeal cases, including *Heath* and *Harmer*, have now been confirmed.

CASE EXAMPLE

Hasan [2005] UKHL 22; [2005] 2 AC 467

Z, a driver and minder for Y, a prostitute, had been threatened by Y's boyfriend, X, who had a reputation as a violent gangster and drug-dealer, to carry out a burglary. Z attempted to burgle a house, armed with a gun, but was scared off by the householder. Z was charged with aggravated burglary and pleaded duress. The trial judge directed the jury that the defence was not available if Z had voluntarily placed himself in a position in which threats of violence were likely. Z was convicted, and although the Court of Appeal quashed his conviction, it was reinstated by the House of Lords.

One case in which the defence of duress succeeded, despite D voluntarily associating himself with a criminal gang, is *Shepherd* [1987] Crim LR 686. The decision in *Hasan* confirms that this case, too, was correctly decided. In *Shepherd* [1987] Crim LR 686, D had joined a gang of apparently non-violent shoplifters. When charged with theft, D had pleaded duress on the basis that when he tried to leave the gang one of the other members had threatened him and his family with violence. The trial judge had refused to put the defence to the jury and D was convicted. The Court of Appeal allowed his appeal. Mustill LJ said:

> J 'Common sense must recognise that there are certain kinds of criminal enterprises the joining of which, in the absence of any knowledge of propensity to violence on the part of one member, would not lead another to suspect that a decision to think better of the whole affair might lead him into serious trouble. The logic which appears to underlie the law of duress would suggest that if trouble did unexpectedly materialise and if it put the defendant into a dilemma in which a reasonable man might have chosen to act as he did, the concession to human frailty should not be denied to him.'

8.4.7 Should D have resisted the threats?

The defence is not available just because D reacted to a threat; the threat must be one that the ordinary man would not have resisted. In *Graham* [1982] 1 All ER 801, Lord Lane CJ laid down the following test to be applied by juries in future cases whenever duress was pleaded:

> J 'The correct approach on the facts of this case would have been as follows: (1) Was [D], or may he have been, impelled to act as he did because, as a result of what he reasonably believed [the duressor] had said or done, he had good cause to fear that if he did not so act [the duressor] would kill him or . . . cause him serious physical injury? (2) If so, have the prosecution made the jury sure that a sober person of reasonable firmness, sharing the characteristics of [D], would not have responded to whatever he reasonably believed [the duressor] said or did by taking part in the killing?

CASE EXAMPLE

Graham [1982] 1 All ER 801

D was a practising homosexual living in a 'bizarre *ménage à trois*' with his wife, V, and another man, E. D, according to medical evidence, was particularly susceptible to bullying. E was a violent and jealous man. Eventually E suggested killing V and together D and E strangled her to death. At D's trial he claimed he only participated in the killing because he was afraid of E. The Court of Appeal, however, upheld his murder conviction.

In *Howe and Bannister* [1987] AC 417, the House of Lords approved the *Graham* test. It is clear that the same test applies (with appropriate modification to the wording to indicate the source of the threats) to duress of circumstances. The test is carefully framed in such a way to ensure the burden of proof remains on the prosecution at all times (although D must raise evidence of duress). If the jury believes that D may have been threatened, and that the reasonable man might have responded to it, then they should acquit.

The first question

The first question, relating to D's belief, is essentially (if not entirely) subjective. That is, if the jury is satisfied that D reasonably believed he faced a threat of death or serious injury, and that the belief gave him 'good cause', then the first question is answered in D's favour. This issue was examined by the Court of Appeal in *Nethercott* [2001] EWCA Crim 2535; [2002] Crim LR 402. D had been convicted of attempting to dishonestly obtain jewellery in May 1999. At his trial he

had pleaded duress, relying on evidence that his co-accused, E, had stabbed him (a separate offence for which E had been charged with attempted murder) and that he therefore reasonably believed that if he did not take part in the crime, he had good cause to fear death or serious injury. The only problem for D was that the stabbing took place in August 1999 – three months <u>after</u> the alleged attempt. The trial judge refused to admit this evidence and D was convicted. However, the Court of Appeal quashed his conviction. Evidence that E had stabbed D in August <u>was</u> relevant to the question whether, in May, he reasonably believed that E might kill or seriously injure him. It must be emphasised that there is no requirement that what D feared actually existed. This point was made clear in *Cairns* [1999] EWCA Crim 468; [1999] 2 Cr App R 137, a duress of circumstances case.

CASE EXAMPLE

Cairns [1999] EWCA Crim 468; [1999] 2 Cr App R 137

V, who was inebriated, stepped out in front of D's car, forcing him to stop. V climbed onto the bonnet and spread-eagled himself on it. D drove off with V on the bonnet. A group of V's friends ran after the car, shouting and gesticulating (they claimed later that they just wanted to stop V, not do any harm to D). D had to brake in order to drive over a speed bump, V fell off in front of the car, and was run over, suffering serious injury. D was convicted of inflicting grievous bodily harm with intent contrary to s 18 OAPA 1861, after the trial judge ruled that the defence of duress of circumstances was only available when 'actually necessary to avoid the evil in question'. However, the Court of Appeal quashed the conviction. It was not necessary that the threat (or, in the judge's words, 'evil in question') was, in fact, real.

The principle that it is D's <u>belief</u> in the existence of a threat, as opposed to its existence in fact, was confirmed in the recent case of *Safi and others* (2003). The appellants in this case had hijacked a plane in Afghanistan and ordered it to be flown to the UK, in order to escape the perceived threat of death or injury at the hands of the Taliban. (The facts of the case occurred in February 2000, that is, before the overthrow of the Taliban regime by American-led military forces in 2002.) At their trial for hijacking, false imprisonment (relating to the appellants' failure to release the other passengers after the plane's arrival in the UK until three days had elapsed) and other charges, the appellants pleaded duress of circumstances. This was disputed by the Crown and the jury at the first trial failed to agree. At the retrial, the trial judge told the jury to examine whether the appellants were in imminent peril (as opposed to whether they reasonably believed that they were in imminent peril). The Court of Appeal allowed the appeal and quashed the convictions. Longmore LJ suggested that, if public policy demanded the existence of an actual threat, as opposed to a reasonably perceived one, it was for Parliament to change the law.

The subjective limb as defined in *Graham* (1982) and approved in *Howe and Bannister* (1987) does have two objective aspects. First, D's belief must have been reasonable. Thus, if D honestly (but unreasonably) believes that he is being threatened and commits an offence, the defence is not available. Hence, if D's belief was based purely on his own imagination, it would not be difficult for a jury to conclude that his (honest) belief was unreasonable. This may be contrasted with the position in self-defence. There, if D believes he is being attacked and reacts in self-defence, he is entitled to be judged as if the facts were as he (honestly) believed them to be (*Williams* (*Gladstone*) [1987] 3 All ER 411). One rationale for this difference could be that self-defence is a justification, while duress is 'only' an excuse. After a period of doubt on this point, in *Hasan* [2005] UKHL 22; [2005] 2 AC 467 the House of Lords confirmed that D's belief must be reasonable. Giving the leading judgment, Lord Bingham said that 'It is of course essential that the defendant should genuinely, that is actually, believe in the efficacy of the threat by which he claims to have been compelled. But there is no warrant for relaxing the requirement that the belief must be reasonable as well as genuine'.

The second objective aspect is that D's belief must have given him 'good cause' to fear death or serious injury. Thus, even if D genuinely (and reasonably) believed that death or serious injury would be done to him but, objectively (that is, in the opinion of the jury), death or serious injury was unlikely, then the defence fails.

The second question

This question is objective, although certain characteristics of D will be attributed to the reasonable person. In *Graham* (1982), Lord Lane CJ said:

> **J** 'As a matter of public policy, it seems to us essential to limit the defence of duress by means of an objective criterion formulated in terms of reasonableness . . . The law [of provocation] requires a defendant to have the self-control reasonably to be expected of the ordinary citizen in his situation. It should likewise require him to have the steadfastness reasonably to be expected of the ordinary citizen in his situation.'

Thus, if the ordinary person, sharing the characteristics of D, would have resisted the threats, the defence is unavailable. Despite the analogy drawn with provocation, the courts have been reluctant to attribute characteristics to the reasonable man in duress cases as freely as they have done in provocation cases (a good example being the characteristic allowed in *Morhall* [1996] AC 90 – glue sniffing; see Chapter 9). The relevant characteristics will include age and sex and, potentially at least, other permanent physical and mental attributes which would affect the ability of D to resist pressure and threats. In *Hegarty* [1994] Crim LR 353, however, the Court of Appeal held that the trial judge had correctly refused to allow D's characteristic of being in a 'grossly elevated neurotic state', which made him vulnerable to threats, to be considered as relevant. Similarly, in *Horne*

[1994] Crim LR 584, the Court of Appeal agreed that evidence that D was unusually pliable and vulnerable to pressure, did not mean that these characteristics had to be attributed to the reasonable man. In *Bowen* [1996] Crim LR 577, the Court of Appeal said that the following characteristics were obviously relevant:

- age: a young person may not be so robust as a mature one

- pregnancy: where there was an added fear for the unborn child

- serious physical disability: as that might inhibit self-protection

- recognised mental illness or psychiatric condition: such as post-traumatic stress disorder leading to learnt helplessness. Psychiatric evidence might be admissible to show that D was suffering from such condition, provided persons generally suffering them might be more susceptible to pressure and threats. It was not admissible simply to show that in a doctor's opinion D, not suffering from such illness or condition, was especially timid, suggestible or vulnerable to pressure and threats.

Finally, D's gender might possibly be relevant, although the court thought that many women might consider they had as much moral courage to resist pressure as men. The Court of Appeal dismissed D's appeal holding that a low IQ – falling short of mental impairment or mental defectiveness – could not be said to be a characteristic that made those who had it less courageous and less able to withstand threats and pressure. The decision in *Bowen* (1996) to allow evidence of post-traumatic stress disorder leading to learnt helplessness as a characteristic is interesting, and not particularly easy to reconcile with the earlier decisions of *Hegarty* (1994) and *Horne* (1994). A jury faced with the question, 'Would the defendant, displaying the firmness reasonably to be expected of a person of that age and sex suffering from learnt helplessness have yielded to the threat?' are almost certain to answer in the affirmative, except if the threat was very trivial indeed.

8.4.8 The scope of the defence

Duress (either by threats or circumstances or both) has been accepted as a defence to manslaughter (*Evans and Gardiner* [1976] VR 517, an Australian case); causing grievous bodily harm with intent (*Cairns* (1999)); criminal damage (*Crutchley* (1831) 5 C & P 133); theft (*Gill* (1963)); handling stolen goods (*Attorney-General v Whelan* [1934] IR 518) and obtaining property by deception (*Bowen* (1996)). It has also been accepted as a defence to the following: perjury (*Hudson and Taylor* (1971)); drugs offences (*Valderrama-Vega* (1985)); firearms offences (*Pommell* (1995)); driving offences (*Willer* (1986) 83 Cr App R 225; *Conway* (1988); *Martin* [1989] 1 All ER 652); hijacking (*Abdul-Hussain* (1999) and *Safi and others* (2003)); kidnapping (*Safi and others*); breach of the Official Secrets Act (*Shayler* [2001] EWCA Crim 1977; [2001] 1 WLR 2206: see below). Indeed, it seems that duress (both forms) will be accepted as a defence to any crime except murder and attempted murder (and possibly some forms of treason).

Murder

The Victorian case of *Dudley and Stephens* (1884) 14 QBD 273 is often cited as authority for the proposition that necessity is not a defence to murder (a view not accepted by the Court of Appeal (Civil Division) in *Re A (Children) (Conjoined Twins: Surgical Separation)* [2000] EWCA Civ 254; [2000] 4 All ER 961, a case which will be discussed in section 8.5 below). *Dudley and Stephens* was, however, relied upon by Lords Hailsham, Griffiths and Mackay in *Howe and Bannister* (1987) as authority for the proposition that the defence of duress by threats was also unavailable to those charged with murder.

CASE EXAMPLE

Dudley and Stephens (1884) 14 QBD 273

D and S had been shipwrecked in a boat with another man and a cabinboy. After several days without food or water, they decided to kill and eat the boy, who was the weakest of the four. Four days later they were rescued. On the murder trial, the jury returned a special verdict, finding that they would have died had they not eaten the boy (although there was no greater necessity for killing the boy than anyone else). Lord Coleridge CJ agreed with the last point, adding that as the mariners were adrift on the high sea, killing any one of them was not going to guarantee their safety and thus it could be argued it was not necessary to kill anyone. D and S were sentenced to hang, but this was commuted to six months' imprisonment after Queen Victoria intervened and exercised the Royal Prerogative.

In *Howe and Bannister* (1987), the Lords gave a variety of reasons for withdrawing the defence of duress by threats from those charged with murder:

- The ordinary man of reasonable fortitude, if asked to take an innocent life, might be expected to sacrifice his own. Lord Hailsham could not 'regard a law as either "just" or "humane" which withdraws the protection of the criminal law from the innocent victim, and casts the cloak of protection on the cowards and the poltroon in the name of a concession to human frailty'.

ACTIVITY

Discuss whether the law should require heroism. Refer back to Lord Lane's test in *Graham* (1982) (approved in *Howe and Bannister* (1987)) which sets a standard of the 'sober person of reasonable firmness'. If the reasonable man would have killed in the same circumstances, why should D be punished – with a life sentence for murder – when he only did what anyone else would have done?

- One who takes the life of an innocent cannot claim he is choosing the lesser of two evils (*per* Lord Hailsham).

This may be true if D alone is threatened; but what if D is told to kill V and that if he does not a bomb will explode in the middle of a crowded shopping centre? Surely that is the lesser of two evils? The situation where D's family are threatened with death if D does not kill a third party is far from uncommon.

- The Law Commission had recommended in 1977 that duress be a defence to murder. That recommendation was unimplemented; that suggested Parliament was happy with the law as it was.

Parliament's lack of legislative activity in various aspects of criminal law, despite numerous promptings from the Law Commission and others, is notorious (eg failure to reform non-fatal offences, discussed in Chapter 10). So its failure to adopt one Law Commission proposal should not be taken to indicate Parliament's satisfaction instead of its intransigence.

- Hard cases could be dealt with by not prosecuting, or by action of the Parole Board or exercise of the Royal Prerogative of Mercy in ordering D's early release.

But D still faces being branded as, in law, a 'murderer', and a morally innocent man should not have to rely on an administrative decision for his freedom.

- To recognise the defence would involve overruling *Dudley and Stephens* (1884). According to Lord Griffiths, the decision was based on 'the special sanctity that the law attaches to human life and which denies to a man the right to take an innocent life even at the price of his own or another's life'.

The *ratio* of *Dudley and Stephens* (1884) is in fact far from clear.

- Lord Griffiths thought the defence should not be available because it was 'so easy to raise and may be difficult for the prosecution to disprove'.

This argument applies to most defences! It also ignores the fact that in *Howe and Bannister* (1987) itself, the jury had rejected the defence and convicted. Indeed, Lord Hailsham said that 'juries have been commendably robust' in rejecting the defence on other cases.

- Lord Bridge thought that it was for Parliament to decide the limits of the defence.

Why should this be? Duress is a common law defence, so the judges should decide its scope.

CASE EXAMPLE

Howe and Bannister [1987] AC 417

D, aged 19, and E, aged 20, together with two other men, one aged 19, and the other, Murray, aged 35, participated in the torture, assault, and then strangling of two young male victims at a remote spot on the Derbyshire moors. At their trial on two counts of murder and one of conspiracy to murder, they pleaded duress, arguing that they feared for their lives if they did not do as Murray directed. He was not only much older than the others but had appeared in court several times before and had convictions for violence. D and E were convicted of all charges, and their appeals failed in the Court of Appeal and House of Lords.

Duress and attempted murder

In *Howe and Bannister* (1987), Lord Griffiths said, *obiter,* that the defence of duress was not available to charges of attempted murder. This was confirmed in *Gotts* [1991] 2 All ER 1, where Lord Jauncey said that he could 'see no justification in logic, morality or law in affording to an attempted murderer the defence which is withheld from a murderer'. D, aged 16, had been threatened with death by his father unless he tracked his mother down to a refuge and killed her. D did as directed but, although seriously injured, his mother survived. The trial judge withdrew the defence and D was convicted. The Court of Appeal and House of Lords upheld his conviction.

ACTIVITY

D1, with intent to do serious harm, attacks and kills V. He appears to be guilty of murder and would have no defence of duress to murder (*Howe and Bannister* (1987)) and would face life imprisonment. D2, with intent to do serious harm, attacks V and causes serious injury but not death. He could plead duress to a charge under s 18 OAPA 1861 (*Cairns* (1999)) and, if successful, would receive an acquittal. (D2 could not be convicted of attempted murder because this requires proof of an intent to kill.) D1 and D2 have the same *mens rea*, but one is labelled a murderer and faces a long prison term; the other escapes with no punishment at all. Is this justifiable? Bear in mind that the difference between the two cases is simply whether or not V survives, which is subject to a number of variables (V's age and state of health, the quality of medical treatment available, etc).

Reform

The Draft Criminal Code (1989) preserved the defence essentially unchanged from the common law as it then was. More recently, in the Draft Criminal Law Bill (1993), cl 25(1), the Law Commission proposed a codification of the defence as follows:

'25(1) A person does an act under duress by threats if he does it because he knows or believes –

(a) that a threat has been made to cause death or serious injury to himself or another of the act is not done, and

(b) that the threat will be carried out immediately if he does not do the act or, if not immediately, before he or that other can obtain effective police protection, and

(c) that there is no other way of preventing the threat being carried out,

and the threat is one which in all the circumstances (including any of his personal characteristics that affect its gravity) he cannot reasonably be expected to resist.'

Clause 25(4) preserved the exception established in cases such as *Sharp* (1987). The relevant provision states that the defence would not apply to a 'person who knowingly and without reasonable excuse exposed himself to the risk of the threat made or believed to have been made'.

8.4.9 The development of duress of circumstances

Duress of circumstances has really only received official recognition from the appellate courts in the last 20 years. The first cases all, coincidentally, involved driving offences:

* *Willer* (1986). D was forced to drive his car on the pavement in order to escape a gang of youths who were intent on attacking him and his passenger. The Court of Appeal allowed D's appeal against a conviction for reckless driving, on the basis of duress of circumstances. Watkins LJ said that D was 'wholly driven by force of circumstance into doing what he did and did not drive the car otherwise than under that form of compulsion, ie under duress.'

* *Conway* (1988). D again successfully appealed against a conviction for reckless driving. He had driven his car at high speed to escape what he thought were two men intent on attacking his passenger (in fact they were police officers).

* *Martin* (1989). D's conviction for driving whilst disqualified was quashed. He had only driven his car after his wife became hysterical and threatened to kill herself if D did not drive his stepson to work.

- *DPP v Bell* [1992] Crim LR 176. D's conviction for driving with excess alcohol was quashed. He had only got into his car and driven it (a relatively short distance) in order to escape a gang who were pursuing him.

- *DPP v Davis; DPP v Pittaway* [1994] Crim LR 600. Both appellants had convictions for driving with excess alcohol quashed on the basis that they had only driven to escape perceived violence from other people.

In *Conway*, Woolf LJ (as he then was) spelled out the ingredients of the new defence as follows:

> **J** 'Necessity can only be a defence . . . where the facts establish "duress of circumstances", that is, where [D] was constrained to act by circumstances to drive as he did to avoid death or serious bodily injury to himself or some other person . . . This approach does no more than recognise that duress is an example of necessity. Whether "duress of circumstances" is called "duress" or "necessity" does not matter. What is important is that it is subject to the same limitations as the "do this or else" species of duress.'

In *Martin* (1989), Simon Brown J said that English law did 'in extreme circumstances recognise a defence of necessity. Most commonly this defence arises as duress [by threats]. Equally however it can arise from other objective dangers threatening the accused or others. Arising thus it is conveniently called "duress of circumstances".' For a time there was a perception that duress of circumstances might be limited to driving offences, but in *Pommell* (1995), the Court of Appeal confirmed that the defence was of general application. It has subsequently been pleaded (not necessarily successfully) in cases of hijacking (*Abdul-Hussain* (1999), *Safi and others* (2003)) and breach of the Official Secrets Act 1989 (*Shayler* (2001)).

Duress of circumstances and necessity: are they the same thing?

You will have noted that in several of the above cases the courts have tended to describe duress of circumstances and necessity as the same thing. You are referred in particular to Lord Woolf's comments in *Conway* (1988) and more recently in *Shayler* (2001). In the latter case D, a former member of the British Security Service (MI5), was charged (and ultimately convicted of) disclosing confidential documents in breach of the Official Secrets Act 1989. Unusually, his defence (whether it is properly regarded as duress of circumstances or necessity is perhaps a moot point) was considered both by the Court of Appeal and the House of Lords <u>before</u> the actual trial. Lord Woolf CJ, giving judgment in the Court of Appeal, gave a very strong indication that duress of circumstances and necessity were interchangeable. He stated:

J 'The distinction between duress of circumstances and necessity has, correctly, been by and large ignored or blurred by the courts. Apart from some of the medical cases like *Re F* [1990] 2 AC 1, the law has tended to treat duress of circumstances and necessity as one and the same.'

However, in this book they will be regarded as separate defences. There are two reasons for this:

• It is clear that duress, whether by threats or of circumstances, cannot be a defence to murder (or attempted murder). However, according to the case of *Re A (Children) (Conjoined Twins)* (2000), discussed in section 8.5, 'necessity' may be a defence to murder.

• Duress (again whether by threats or of circumstances) exists only where D or someone he is responsible for is in danger of death or serious injury. This is not necessarily the case in necessity, a point for which *Re A* is again authority.

8.4.10 Reform

The Draft Criminal Code (1989) preserved the defence of duress of circumstances, again essentially unchanged from the common law as it then was (and indeed still is). More recently, in the Draft Criminal Law Bill (1993), cl 26(2), the Law Commission proposed a codification of the defence as follows:

C '26(2) A person does an act under duress of circumstances if (a) he does it because he knows or believes that it is immediately necessary to avoid death or serious injury to himself or another, and (b) the danger that he knows or believes to exist is such that in all the circumstances (including any of his personal characteristics that affect its gravity) he cannot reasonably be expected to act otherwise.'

Clause 26(4) would introduce an exception that has not as yet been encountered in the common law, providing that the defence would be unavailable to a person who 'knowingly and without reasonable excuse exposed himself to the danger known or believed to exist'.

Key facts on duress

Elements	Comment	Cases
Source of duress	• By threats • By circumstances	*Lynch* (1975) *Willer* (1986), *Conway* (1988), *Martin* (1989)
Degree of duress	Threat or danger posed must be of death or serious personal injury. This means physical injury not psychological injury. Threat of exposure of sexual immorality insufficient.	*Hudson and Taylor* (1971) *Baker and Wilkins* (1997) *Valderrama-Vega* (1985)
Duress against whom?	Usually D personally. Also includes duress against family. Even persons for whom defendant reasonably feels responsible.	*Graham* (1982), *Cairns* (1999) *Ortiz* (1986), *Conway* (1988), *Martin* (1989) *Wright* (2000)
Imminence	Threat or danger must be believed to be immediate or almost immediate. Defendant should alert police as soon as possible; delay in doing so does not necessarily mean defence fails.	*Hasan* (2005) *Gill* (1963), *Pommell* (1995)

Association with Crime	Voluntarily joining a violent criminal gang means defendant may not have the defence.	*Fitzpatrick* (1977), *Sharp* (1987)
	Voluntary association with violent criminals has the same effect.	*Ali* (1995), *Baker and Ward* (1999), *Heath* (2000)
	But only if the defendant foresaw (or possibly should have foreseen that he may be subjected to duress.	*Shepherd* (1987), *Hasan* (2005)
Reasonable man test	Defendant must have reasonably believed that a threat/danger existed.	*Cairns* (1999), *Safi* (2003), *Hasan* (2005)
	Defence fails if a sober person of reasonable firmness would have resisted the threats.	*Graham* (1982), *Howe and Bannister* (1987)
	The reasonable man shares some of D's characteristics, such as age and physical disability.	*Bowen* (1996)
Availability	Defence available to most crimes except murder . . .	*Howe and Bannister* (1987)
	. . . and attempted murder.	*Gotts* (1991)
Burden of proof	It is for the prosecution to **disprove** beyond reasonable doubt.	
Effect of defence	Defendant is not guilty.	

8.5 Necessity

Ammunition for the proposition that 'necessity' is a separate defence comes from *Re A* (2000). There, Brooke LJ said: 'In cases of pure necessity the actor's mind is not irresistibly overborne by external pressures. The claim is that his or her conduct was not harmful because on a choice of two evils the choice of avoiding the greater harm was justified.' He went on to summarise the position as follows, by stating that 'there are three necessary requirements for the application of the doctrine of necessity':

- the act is needed to avoid inevitable and irreparable evil
- no more should be done than is reasonably necessary for the purpose to be achieved
- the evil inflicted must not be disproportionate to the evil avoided.

This definition is very different to that regarded as the classic test for duress of circumstances, which requires that D must have acted in order to avoid a perceived threat of imminent death or serious injury and with no reasonable opportunity for escaping from the threat or contacting the authorities.

CASE EXAMPLE

Re A (Conjoined Twins: Surgical Separation) [2000] EWCA Civ 254; [2000] 4 All ER 961

J and M were conjoined twin girls; that is, they were physically joined at the lower abdomen. J was capable of independent existence; M was not. An operation to separate the twins was deemed appropriate in order to give J a chance of a separate life. This operation would inevitably result in the death of M, who was alive only because of a common artery, through which J's stronger heart circulated enough oxygenated blood for both of them. Both girls would die, within six months at the outside, if the operation did not take place, because J's heart would eventually lack strength to pump blood around both bodies. However, the girls' parents, who were both Catholics, refused to give their consent. The hospital authorities therefore applied for a declaration that the proposed operation would be lawful. The Court of Appeal (Civil Division) found that the operation was a positive act and therefore had to be justified to prevent the surgeons facing liability for murder. Justification came in the form of the necessity defence. The operation was carried out successfully, in that J survived (M died) and was released from hospital shortly afterwards.

Strictly speaking, as a matter of precedent, this case involved a decision of the Civil Division of the Court of Appeal and is only persuasive on criminal courts. In *Shayler* (2001), a decision of the Criminal Division of the Court of Appeal, Lord Woolf CJ gave a definition of the ingredients of

'necessity' in exactly the same terms as Brooke LJ in *Re A* (2000) (although, as noted above, he regarded necessity and duress of circumstances as interchangeable).

In *Quayle & Others* [2005] EWCA Crim 1415; [2005] 1 WLR 3642, however, a defence of necessity was recognised, although the appeals were rejected, by the Court of Appeal (Criminal Division). The appellants had been charged with a variety of offences relating to the 'cultivation, production, importation and possession' of cannabis. They were convicted and appealed, claiming that, because they used cannabis not as a recreational drug but for the purposes of relieving painful symptoms of conditions such as multiple sclerosis, a defence of necessity should be available. The Court of Appeal dismissed the appeals. Mance LJ said that whatever benefits there might be (real or perceived) for any individual patients, such benefits were regarded by Parliament as outweighed by disbenefits 'of sufficient strength to require a general prohibition in the national interest'. The suggested defence of 'necessitous medical use' on an individual basis was in conflict with the purpose of the legislation, for two reasons:

(1) no such use was permitted under the legislation, even on doctor's prescription, except for medical research trials and

(2) it would involve unqualified individuals prescribing cannabis to themselves as patients or assuming the role of unqualified doctors by obtaining, prescribing and supplying it to other individual 'patients'.

Mance LJ summarised the judgment as follows:

> **J** 'The law has to draw a line at some point in the criteria which it accepts as sufficient to satisfy any defence of duress or necessity. Courts and juries have to work on evidence. If such defences were to be expanded in theory to cover every possible case in which it might be felt that it would be hard if the law treated the conduct in question as criminal, there would be likely to be arguments in considerable numbers of cases, where there was no clear objective basis by reference to which to test or determine such arguments. It is unlikely that this would lead overall to a more coherent result, or even necessarily to a more just disposition of any individual case. There is, on any view, a large element of subjectivity in the assessment of pain not directly associated with some current physical injury. The legal defences of duress by threats and necessity by circumstances should in our view be confined to cases where there is an imminent danger of physical injury.'

CASE EXAMPLE

Quayle & Others [2005] EWCA Crim 1415; [2005] 1 WLR 3642

The case involved five appellants. Barry Quayle (a 38-year-old amputee who was still in considerable pain), Reay Wales (a 53-year-old man who suffered from a variety of back injuries and illnesses which led to him becoming depressed and alcoholic and which in turn led to a condition called pancreatitis which left him in 'chronic' pain) and Graham Kenny (a 25-year-old man who had injured his back at work) had all been convicted of cultivating cannabis for their own use, contrary to the Misuse of Drugs Act 1971. Anthony Taylor, the manager of *Tony's Holistic Clinic* in London, a treatment centre for people with HIV and AIDS, had been stopped by customs officers at Luton Airport returning from Switzerland and Taylor was found to be carrying 20½ kilos of cannabis worth £35,000, an offence under the Customs & Excise Management Act 1979. A month later, one of Taylor's employees, May Po Lee, was also caught at Luton Airport returning from Switzerland with just over 5 kilos of cannabis. At trial, the judge refused to allow any of the accused a defence of 'medical necessity' to be left to the jury and all were convicted. The Court of Appeal dismissed their appeals.

Quayle & Others was followed in *Altham* [2006] EWCA Crim 7; [2006] 2 Cr App R 8.

CASE EXAMPLE

Altham [2006] EWCA Crim 7; [2006] 2 Cr App R 8

D had been involved in a road traffic accident some 15 years earlier which left him with both hips dislocated; subsequently, his left hip had to be surgically removed altogether leaving him 'in chronic pain in his lower limbs ever since'. After several pain-relieving strategies including acupuncture and prescribed antidepressants had failed, D turned to cannabis, which apparently provided the first form of pain relief since his accident. However, he was eventually prosecuted for and convicted of possessing a controlled drug.

The Court of Appeal upheld his conviction, relying heavily upon the judgment in *Quayle & Others*. In addition, the Court held that a person who used cannabis for pain relief could not raise

a defence of necessity by relying on Article 3 of the *European Convention on Human Rights* (the prohibition of inhuman or degrading treatment or punishment). Baker LJ stated:

> **J** 'In our judgment the state has done nothing to subject the appellant to either inhuman or degrading treatment and thereby engage the absolute prohibition in Article 3. If the true position is that, absent a defence of necessity, the appellant will either break the criminal law or continue to suffer degrading treatment, the state is not in breach of its Article 3 obligation . . .We do not think that this is a case in which . . . the state is properly to be regarded as responsible for the harm inflicted on the appellant. Nor do we think that Article 3 requires the state to take any steps to alleviate the appellant's condition.'

It is submitted that the cases of *Quayle & Others* and *Altham* are authority for the proposition that 'necessity' exists as a defence in English law separate from 'duress of circumstances'. In his commentary in the Criminal Law Review on the former case, Professor David Ormerod argues that the case could be regarded as one of 'pure necessity' (*Quayle & Others* [2006] Crim LR 149). He refers to the 'general principles of necessity' identified by Brooke LJ in *Re A* (2000) and adds that:

> 'Applying those criteria it would come as no surprise if a jury, having heard expert evidence of the genuine nature and severity of pain being avoided, regarded the action of breaking the law as justified. A plea of necessity avoids many of the restrictions which constrain duress of circumstances: there is no requirement of a threat of death or serious injury ... the defence is potentially available to all crimes, even murder, and there is no requirement of immediacy ... Clarification from the House of Lords as to the elements of the defence of necessity, its rationale, and its relationship with duress of circumstances is urgently needed. If necessity is to be subsumed within duress of circumstances it should, it is submitted, only be by express pronouncement of the House.'

It follows that older cases which indicated that it did not exist should not now be relied upon. For example, in *Buckoke v GLC* [1975] Ch 655, Lord Denning stated, *obiter*, that the driver of a fire engine who crossed a red traffic light to rescue a man from a blazing building on the other side of the junction would commit an offence against the road traffic regulations.

ACTIVITY

> If the circumstances described by Lord Denning in *Buckoke* (1975) did occur, discuss whether the driver would have a defence of necessity under the criteria laid down by Brooke LJ in *Re A* (2000).

Note: this particular issue is now a moot point, as reg 33(1)(b) of the Traffic Signs Regulations and General Directions (SI 1994 No. 1519) 1994 provides that fire brigade, ambulance or police vehicles may cross red lights if stopping 'would be likely to hinder the use of that vehicle for the purpose for which it is being used'. However, the vehicle must not cross the red light 'in a manner or at a time likely to endanger any person' or cause another vehicle 'to change its speed or course in order to avoid an accident'.

In *Southwark LBC v Williams* [1971] Ch 734, a civil case, it was held that the defence of necessity did not apply to enable the homeless to enter and occupy empty houses owned by the local authority. Lord Denning MR justified the rule on the ground that:

> **J** 'If hunger were once allowed to be an excuse for stealing, it would open a door through which all kinds of lawlessness and disorder would pass . . . If homelessness were once admitted as a defence to trespass, no one's house could be safe. Necessity would open a door which no man could shut. It would not only be those in extreme need who would enter. There would be others who would imagine that they were in need, or would invent a need, so as to gain entry.'

ACTIVITY

Would homeless people seeking shelter in empty properties now be able to satisfy the criteria for necessity laid down by Brooke LJ in *Re A* (2000)? What other information might you wish to have in order to be able to answer this question?

8.6 Marital coercion

The defence exists at common law, where it provided a presumption that any crime committed by a married woman in the presence of her husband was done under 'coercion'. The presumption was abolished by Parliament in the Criminal Justice Act 1925, s 47, but the defence itself survives. Now a woman must prove, albeit on the balance of probabilities, that:

- she was married to her husband at the time; and

- her will was overborne by her husband so that she committed the offence unwillingly.

Neither physical force nor threat are required, so the defence is clearly much wider than that of duress. This point was made in *Shortland* [1996] 1 Cr App R 116, involving the offence of procuring a passport by deception, and recently confirmed in *Cairns* [2002] EWCA Crim 2838; [2003] 1 WLR 796. D had been convicted along with two others of conspiracy to supply heroin.

Her defence of marital coercion was rejected after the trial judge gave the jury an ambiguous direction which seemed to suggest that force or the threat of force was required in addition to her will being overborne. The Court of Appeal allowed her appeal – there is no requirement that physical force, or the threat of it, was required. Instead, according to Keene LJ, 'moral force or emotional threats' would suffice, provided that D's will was overborne.

If threats of physical violence have occurred, then there is nothing to prevent a wife from relying upon duress, where the burden of proof is on the prosecution. This was the case in *Bourne* (1952) 36 Cr App R 125, where the Court of Criminal Appeal stated that a wife who was forced into committing buggery with a dog would be entitled to the defence of duress on the basis that she had been forced into the act by her husband.

Marriage

In *Ditta* [1988] Crim LR 43, Lord Lane CJ doubted whether an Islamic polygamous marriage was sufficient for the defence. This view was questioned by the late Professor Sir John Smith in the 10th edition of *Smith and Hogan's Criminal Law* (2001). He argued that such a marriage should be assimilated with a 'monogamous' marriage, as indeed should an unmarried woman who lives as the partner of a man.

Moreover, in the 11th edition of the same book, David Ormerod writes about the judgment in *Ditta* that:

> 'There are obvious difficulties with such a discriminatory definition of the defence.
> It is questionable whether it would be regarded as compatible with Article 14 of
> the ECHR (the non-discrimination provision) if D was convicted and imprisoned
> (therefore suffering deprivation of liberty) or suffering some other penalty
> infringing her right to respect for private life (Article 8) . . . The defence seems to
> be restricted to the "wife" but ought to be available to a party in a civil partnership
> under the Civil Partnerships Act 2004.'

Reform

In 1989 the Law Commission in the Draft Criminal Code, cl 42(6), recommended the abolition of marital coercion as a separate defence, although it would preserve the right of a married woman to rely on duress by threats when the facts supported it.

8.7 Mistake

8.7.1 Mistakes of fact

'Mistake of fact' is a defence in a similar way to intoxication: it prevents the prosecution from establishing that D possessed the relevant *mens rea* at the time of the offence. At one time only mistakes of fact that were reasonably made could operate to negate liability. However, that was changed by the leading case, *DPP v Morgan* [1976] AC 182, where it was held that mistakes of fact may negate liability provided they were honestly made. Lord Hailsham said:

> J
>
> 'Either the prosecution proves that [D] had the requisite intent, or it does not. In the former case it succeeds, and in the latter it fails. Since honest belief clearly negatives intent, the reasonableness or otherwise of that belief can only be evidence for or against the view that the belief and therefore the intent was actually held.'

Morgan (1976) was a rape case, but the proposition of Lord Hailsham, above, extends to most criminal offences. It was followed in the indecent assault case of *Kimber* [1983] 3 All ER 316, a Court of Appeal judgment concerning D's mistaken belief that V was consenting. In a supreme irony, *Morgan* (1976) has now been overruled by Parliament's enactment of the Sexual Offences Act 2003, which restores a requirement that, in rape cases, D's belief as to whether or not V was consenting to sexual intercourse must be a reasonable one (see Chapter 11). However, the principle stated above remains applicable to other crimes and, therefore, D will have a good defence if he honestly believed in a mistaken set of facts such that that he did not have the *mens rea*. A good example of the continuing legacy of *Morgan* (1976) is any case where D is charged with murder, manslaughter or some non-fatal offence and claims to have acted in self-defence, having used force in the mistaken belief about the need to use (a) any force; or (b) the amount of force he did in fact use. In *Williams* (1987), the Court of Appeal held that D had a good defence provided his belief that he was under attack was honestly held. Lord Lane CJ said:

> J
>
> 'The mental element necessary to constitute guilt is the intent to apply unlawful force to the victim. [The] question is, does it make any difference if the mistake of [D] was . . . an unreasonable mistake? . . . The reasonableness or unreasonableness of [D]'s belief is material to the question of whether the belief was held by [D] at all. If the belief was in fact held, its unreasonableness, so far as guilt or innocence is concerned, is neither here nor there. It is irrelevant.'

CASE EXAMPLE

Williams [1987] 3 All ER 411

D was charged with an assault occasioning ABH on a man called Mason. His defence was that he was preventing Mason from assaulting and torturing a black youth. D claimed that he had seen Mason dragging the youth along and repeatedly punching him. The youth was struggling and calling for help. D approached Mason to ask him what on earth he was doing; Mason replied that he was arresting the youth for mugging an old lady (which was true) and that he was a police officer (which was not true). D asked to see Mason's warrant card, which was of course not forthcoming, at which point a struggle broke out between them. As a result of this altercation Mason sustained injuries to his face, loosened teeth and bleeding gums. D did not deny punching Mason but claimed that he did so in order to save the youth from further beatings and torture. The jury was directed that D only had a defence if he believed *on reasonable grounds* that Mason was acting unlawfully. The Court of Appeal quashed his conviction.

In *Beckford* [1988] AC 130, in which D was accused of murder but pleaded honest mistaken belief in the need to act in self-defence, the Privy Council approved both *Morgan* (1976) and *Williams* (1987). Lord Griffiths said that 'If then a genuine belief, albeit without reasonable grounds, is a defence to rape because it negatives the necessary intention, so also must a genuine belief in facts which if true would justify self-defence be a defence to a crime of personal violence because the belief negates the intent to act unlawfully.'

Intoxicated mistakes

An intoxicated defendant is often really pleading mistake. If this is the case then the rules described above do not apply; instead the intoxication rules as set out in *Majewski* (1977) (described earlier in this chapter) apply instead.

8.7.2 Mistakes of law

It is no defence for D who causes the *actus reus* of an offence with *mens rea* to say that he did not know the *actus reus* was an offence, ignorance of the law being no excuse. Thus, in *Esop* (1836) 7 C & P 456, D, from Iraq, buggered a man on board a ship lying in an English port. Buggery was not illegal in Iraq and D assumed it was lawful in England. He was convicted. In *Lee* [2000] Crim LR 991, D was convicted of two offences of assault with intent to resist arrest (contrary to s 38 OAPA 1861). He had given a roadside breathalyser test which the two police officers had said was positive. D said it was not clear that the crystals had changed colour beyond the red line. There was no doubt he had assaulted the officers; the question was whether he had the *mens rea*, the intent to resist arrest. The defence case was that, because he thought the test was negative, the officers had no power of arrest and therefore he could not have intended to resist arrest. However, under s 6(5) of the Road Traffic Act 1988, a power of arrest arises provided that the police officer, as a result of a breath test, 'has reasonable cause to suspect' that D was over the limit. He was convicted. On appeal it was submitted that the trial judge should have directed the jury to acquit unless sure that D had no honest belief that he had passed the breathalyser test. However, the Court of Appeal dismissed the appeal, distinguishing *Morgan* (1976), *Williams* (1987) and *Beckford* (1988). D's mistake was not one of fact but one of law, that is, the lawfulness of his arrest. Once the lawfulness of his arrest was established (and it was conceded on appeal that there was evidence on which the jury could conclude that the officers were acting lawfully), then the *mens rea* required was an intent to resist arrest with knowledge that the person was seeking to arrest him.

8.8 Self-defence

Causing injury or even death to other persons may be justified if the force was reasonably used in self-defence or to protect another person. The term 'self-defence' will be used in this section, although it should be remembered that D may use force to defend others (the term 'private defence' is sometimes used instead for this reason). Self-defence is a common law defence. It overlaps to some extent with the prevention of crime defence, which is covered by s 3 of the Criminal Law Act 1967, which provides:

'3(1) A person may use such force as is reasonable in the circumstances in the prevention of crime, or in effecting or assisting in the lawful arrest of offenders or suspected offenders or of persons unlawfully at large.'

Section 3(2) of the 1967 Act adds that s 3(1) 'shall replace the rules of common law on the question when force used for a purpose mentioned in the subsection is justified by that purpose'. Despite that, the courts have accepted that self-defence remains and that the two justifications operate in parallel (*Cousins* [1982] QB 526). Where there is evidence of self-defence, this must be left to the jury (*DPP v Bailey* [1995] 1 Cr App R 257). However, there must be evidence before the court on which a jury might think it was reasonably possible that D was acting in self-defence. If it was 'a mere fanciful and speculative matter', the judge could withdraw the defence (*Johnson* [1994] Crim LR 376). Self-defence or the s 3 defence are usually raised to charges of homicide or non-fatal offences against the person, but are not confined to them. Thus the s 3 defence was pleaded to a charge of reckless driving in *Renouf* [1986] 2 All ER 449 (D had driven his car at speed in attempting to prevent people who had assaulted him from escaping in another vehicle). Self-defence was pleaded to a charge of dangerous driving in *Symonds* [1998] Crim LR 280 (D had driven away in his car at speed to escape from someone whom he thought was trying to attack him).

8.8.1 The necessity of force

The use of any force is not justified if it is not necessary. This is a question for the jury. However, in determining whether the use of force was necessary, the jury must place themselves in the position that D honestly perceived to exist. It does not matter if D wrongly imagined that a threat existed. Moreover, there is no requirement that D's mistaken belief be based on reasonable grounds. Thus, if D is walking alone along a road late at night and sees what he <u>thinks</u> is a large man about to attack him with a club, the jury should readily conclude that it was necessary for D to use force to defend himself. If, in reality, D had made a foolish mistake and the 'large man' was in fact an elderly woman and the 'club' was actually an umbrella, the jury's conclusion should be unchanged. It therefore follows that D can use force to repel what is in fact perfectly lawful behaviour, provided D honestly thinks that force is necessary. This was made explicit in the case of *Re A (Children) (Conjoined Twins)* (2000), discussed above in the context of necessity. Ward LJ adopted a different approach from that of Brooke LJ, although he reached the same conclusion. Ward LJ equated M's dependence on blood from J's heart as, in effect, a potentially fatal attack upon J, which entitled doctors to intervene and use force to save her.

In *Rashford* [2005] EWCA Crim 3377; [2006] Crim LR 547, the Court of Appeal decided that – in principle at least – it was possible to plead self-defence to a charge of murder, even though D admitted that he had gone out looking for revenge. Dyson LJ stated that:

> **J** 'The mere fact that a defendant goes somewhere in order to exact revenge from the victim does not of itself rule out the possibility that in any violence that ensues self-defence is necessarily not available as a defence. It must depend on the circumstances. It is common ground that a person only acts in self-defence if in all the circumstances he honestly believes that it is necessary for him to defend himself and if the amount of force that he uses is reasonable.'

In the event, the Court of Appeal upheld D's murder conviction on the basis that, according to his own testimony, he had not actually been placed in a position where it was necessary to use force at the time when he stabbed V through the heart.

Pre-emptive strike

It is not necessary for there to be an attack in progress; it is sufficient if D apprehends an attack. In *Beckford* (1988), Lord Griffiths said: 'A man about to be attacked does not have to wait for his assailant to strike the first blow or fire the first shot; circumstances may justify a pre-emptive strike.' In *DPP v Bailey* [1995] 1 Cr App R 257, Lord Slynn said: 'Self-defence as a concept embraces not only aggressive action such as a pre-emptive strike or aggressive reaction but applies equally to a wholly defensive posture . . .'. It follows that it will be permissible for D to issue threats of force, even death, if that might prevent an attack upon himself or prevent a crime from taking place (*Cousins* (1982)).

Preparing for an attack

Where D apprehends an attack upon himself, may he make preparations to defend himself, even where that involves breaches of the law? In *Attorney-General's Reference (No 2 of 1983)* [1984] QB 456, Lord Lane CJ answered this question in the affirmative:

> J 'D is not left in the paradoxical position of being able to justify acts carried out in self-defence but not acts immediately preparatory to it. There is no warrant for the submission . . . that acts of self-defence will only avail [D] when they have been done spontaneously . . . [A person] may still arm himself for his own protection, if the exigency arises, although in doing so he may commit other offences.'

CASE EXAMPLE

Attorney-General's Reference (No 2 of 1983) [1984] QB 456

D's shop had been attacked and damaged by rioters. Fearing further attacks, he made petrol bombs. D was charged with possessing an explosive substance in such circumstances as to give rise to a reasonable suspicion that he did not have it for a lawful object, contrary to s 4(1) of the Explosive Substances Act 1883. He pleaded self-defence and the jury acquitted. The Court of Appeal accepted that this was correct.

A duty to retreat?

At one time, it had been thought that the law required D to retreat as far as possible before resorting to violence (*Julien* [1969] 1 WLR 839). However, this is no longer the test. In *Bird* [1985] 2 All ER 513, D was convicted after the trial judge directed the jury that it was necessary for D to have demonstrated by her actions that she did not want to fight. The Court of Appeal, allowing the appeal, made it clear that this direction 'placed too great an obligation' on D. In particular, it was going too far to say that it was 'necessary' for her to demonstrate a reluctance to fight. Lord Lane CJ said:

> J 'If [D] is proved to have been attacking or retaliating or revenging himself, then he was not truly acting in self-defence. Evidence that [D] tried to retreat or tried to call off the fight may be a cast-iron method of casting doubt on the suggestion that he was the attacker or retaliator or the person trying to revenge himself. But it is not by any means the only method of doing that.'

CASE EXAMPLE

Bird [1985] 2 All ER 513

D was at a house party when a former boyfriend of hers, V, arrived. An argument broke out between D and V which became heated; eventually V slapped D. At this D lunged forward with her hand, which held an empty glass. The glass broke in V's face and gouged his eye out. At D's trial for malicious wounding, the prosecution claimed that she knew she had a glass; the defence claimed that it was self-defence. D's conviction was quashed on appeal.

8.8.2 The reasonableness of force

This is again a question for the jury. The general principle is that only such force may be used as is reasonable in the circumstances. However, as with the question of whether any force was necessary, it is critical that the jury put themselves in the circumstances which D perceived (whether reasonably or not) to exist. In *Palmer* [1971] AC 814, Lord Morris said:

> **J** 'If there has been attack so that defence is reasonably necessary it will be recognised that a person defending himself cannot weigh to a nicety the exact measure of his necessary defensive action. If a jury thought that in a moment of unexpected anguish a person attacked had only done what he honestly and instinctively thought was necessary that would be most potent evidence that only reasonable defensive action had been taken.'

The Court of Appeal affirmed this proposition in *Shannon* (1980) Cr App R 192, where a conviction of murder was quashed after the trial judge told the jury simply to consider whether or not D had used more force than was necessary in the circumstances, neglecting to remind them to consider this from D's perception of events. Similarly, in *Whyte* [1987] 3 All ER 416, Lord Lane CJ held that 'where the issue is one of self-defence, it is necessary and desirable that the jury should be reminded that [D]'s state of mind, that is his view of the danger threatening him at the time of the incident, is material. The test of reasonableness is not . . . a purely objective test.'

In *Scarlett* [1993] 4 All ER 629, D, a pub landlord, had been convicted of the manslaughter of V, a large, drunken man that he had ejected from the pub. The prosecution case was that D had used excessive force in bundling V out of the pub and, therefore, committed an assault; when V died from his injuries D was prosecuted for constructive manslaughter. The jury was directed to convict if they thought that the degree of force used was excessive. The Court of Appeal quashed the conviction because the jury had not been directed specifically to look at the events from D's perspective. Regrettably, Beldam LJ's judgment was slightly ambiguous. At one point he said that D ought not to be convicted unless the jury was satisfied that the degree of force used was plainly more than was called for 'by the circumstances as he believed them to be'. This is perfectly clear and consistent with earlier authorities. However, Beldam LJ then added that 'provided he believed the circumstances called for the degree of force used, he is not to be convicted even if his belief was unreasonable'. This seemed to suggest that D was entitled to be judged purely subjectively – which contradicts what had been said in *Palmer* (1971), *Shannon* (1980) and *Whyte* (1987). In *Owino* [1996] 2 Cr App R 128, however, Collins LJ pointed out that when Beldam LJ's judgment was read as a whole, all he had said was the traditional rule, namely that D was entitled to be judged according to the circumstances as he believed them to be. Collins LJ then summarised the law as follows:

> **J** 'The essential elements of self-defence are clear enough. The jury have to decide whether [D] honestly believed that the circumstances were such as required him to use force to defend himself from attack or threatened attack. In this respect [D] must be judged in accordance with his honest belief, even though that belief may have been mistaken. But the jury must then decide whether the force used was reasonable in the circumstances as he believed them to be.'

Relevance of D's characteristics

In *Martin (Anthony)* [2001] EWCA Crim 2245; [2002] 2 WLR 1, the Court of Appeal held that psychiatric evidence that caused D to perceive much greater danger than the average person was irrelevant to the question of whether D had used reasonable force. In a case of self-defence the question was whether the amount of force used was (objectively) reasonable, according to what D (subjectively) believed. Lord Woolf CJ said that the jury is entitled to take into account D's physical characteristics (this might have an impact on D's perception of events). However, he said that the Court did not accept that it was 'appropriate . . . in deciding whether excessive force has been used to take into account whether [D] is suffering from some psychiatric condition'. The Court distinguished self-defence from the approach taken by the House of Lords in what was (at the time) the leading provocation case, *Smith (Morgan)* [2001] 1 AC 146. Lord Woolf CJ justified this difference in approach for two reasons:

- Provocation provides only a partial defence to murder, whereas self-defence is capable of providing a complete defence. This would justify a more flexible approach for provocation than for self-defence.

- Self-defence is typically raised in cases of minor assaults and it would be 'wholly disproportionate to encourage medical disputes in cases of that sort'.

CASE EXAMPLE

Martin (Anthony) [2001] EWCA Crim 2245; [2002] 2 WLR 1

D lived alone at a remote farmhouse in Norfolk. One night two men, V and W, broke into D's farmhouse. D was awakened by the break-in and, armed with a pump-action shotgun, went downstairs to investigate. There was a dispute about exactly what happened next, but what is undisputed is that D fired the shotgun three times, hitting both men. V was wounded in the legs and W, who had been shot in the back, died shortly afterwards. D was convicted of murder and wounding after the jury rejected his plea of self-defence. On appeal, he argued (amongst other things) that psychiatric evidence had emerged after the trial showing that he suffered from a paranoid personality disorder with recurrent bouts of depression. This meant that he may have genuinely (but mistakenly) thought he was in an extremely dangerous situation on the night in question. The Court rejected his appeal on the basis of self-defence, for the reasons given above, but did quash the murder conviction (substituting one of manslaughter), on the basis that the evidence would instead have supported a plea of diminished responsibility at his trial.

Question

Do you agree with the Lord Chief Justice that D's characteristics are irrelevant to the issue of reasonable force?

In *Canns* [2005] EWCA Crim 2264, the Court of Appeal followed *Martin (Anthony)* (2001) in holding that, when deciding whether D had used reasonable force in self-defence, it was not appropriate to take into account whether D was suffering from some psychiatric condition (in the present case, paranoid schizophrenia, which may have produced delusional beliefs that he was about to be attacked), except in 'exceptional circumstances which would make the evidence especially probative'. The Court held that, generally speaking, it was for the jury, considering all the circumstances – but not evidence of D's psychiatric condition – to set the standards of reasonableness of force.

8.8.3 Should excessive force in homicide reduce murder to manslaughter?

Where D has caused grievous bodily harm with intent, contrary to s 18 OAPA 1861, and his plea of self-defence fails only because the jury decided that he used excessive force, then the judge can reflect this in sentencing. Where D has committed murder there is no such option. It has been argued that the use of excessive force in self-defence should, like provocation and diminished responsibility, reduce murder to manslaughter. However, in *Palmer* [1971] AC 814, Lord Morris said that if the prosecution proves that D had used excessive force in self-defence, then 'that issue is eliminated from the case'. He added that 'self-defence either succeeds so as to result in an acquittal

or it is disproved in which case as a defence it is rejected'. *Clegg* [1995] 1 AC 482, considered the question of whether a killing resulting from the excessive use of force in self-defence led to murder or manslaughter. On the facts of the case, the Lords found that, as the danger had passed, the issue of excessive force did not, strictly speaking, arise. The Lords nevertheless reviewed the authorities on the use of excessive force in self-defence. Their speeches, although *obiter*, are obviously very persuasive. According to Lord Lloyd, if excessive force is used in self-defence, this did not justify reducing liability from murder to manslaughter.

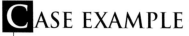

CASE EXAMPLE

Clegg [1995] 1 AC 482

D, a soldier of the Parachute Regiment, was on duty at a checkpoint in West Belfast one night. The purpose of the checkpoint was to catch joyriders, although this had not been explained to D. A car (which turned out to be stolen) approached D's section of patrol at speed with its headlights full on. Someone from a different section shouted to stop the car. All four members of D's section fired at the car. D fired three shots through the windscreen as the car approached, and a fourth at the car as it passed. This last shot hit a female passenger in the back, and killed her. Forensic evidence showed that the last shot was fired after the car had passed and would already have been 10 yards away on the road to Belfast. On trial for murder of the passenger and the attempted murder of the driver, D pleaded self-defence of himself and a fellow soldier. He was convicted after the trial judge found that this last shot was fired with the intention of causing death or serious harm, and that D could not have fired in self-defence because, once the car had passed, none of the soldiers were in any danger. The Northern Ireland Court of Appeal upheld the conviction, on the basis that the last shot was a 'grossly excessive and disproportionate' use of force. The House of Lords rejected D's appeal.

Reform

The 'all-or-nothing' position regarding the use of force in self-defence cases where D has killed V (guilty of murder or acquittal) has led to frequent criticism and reform proposals. The Australian courts used to apply a principle that excessive self-defence reduces murder to manslaughter (*Howe* (1958) 100 CLR 448) but, in *Zekevic* (1987) 61 ALJR 375, the High Court of Australia reversed this decision. In England, both the Criminal Law Revision Committee (14th Report, Cmnd 7844) in 1980 and the Select Committee of the House of Lords on Murder and Life Imprisonment (HL Paper 78-1) in 1989, recommended that the use of excessive force in self-defence should reduce what would otherwise be murder to manslaughter. Clause 59 of the Draft Criminal Code (1989) provides that a person who causes death using force that he believed was necessary and reasonable would not be

guilty of murder. However, where 'the force exceeds that which is necessary and reasonable in the circumstances which exist or (where there is a difference) in those circumstances which he believes to exist' then, under cl 55, a person in such circumstances would be guilty of manslaughter.

Following *Clegg* (1995), the then Home Secretary announced a review of the position. The subsequent report expressed the view that a verdict of manslaughter where excessive force in self-defence had been used 'might assist in a comparatively small number of cases', but did not consider that the availability of such an option 'would enable the court or jury to achieve a result which would necessarily always be seen as just' (*Report of the Inter-Departmental Review of the Law on the Use of Lethal Force in Self-Defence or the Prevention of Crime*, Home Office (1996)). The report concluded that a change in this area alone would be difficult 'without taking a more fundamental look at the scope and operation of the law on, and the penalty for, murder'. A 'more fundamental look at murder' has now taken place. In December 2005, the Law Commission published a paper entitled '*A New Homicide Act?*' (Consultation Paper No 177), in which it proposed that excessive force in self-defence should become a partial defence to first degree murder, reducing liability to second degree murder. (The Law Commission also proposes that murder be split into first and second degree murder. This aspect of the Report will be examined in Chapter 9.) However, this would not be a separate defence but would instead be brought within a redefined provocation defence (see also Chapter 9). The defence would be made out if D acted in response to 'fear of serious violence towards the defendant or another' provided that 'a person of the defendant's age and of ordinary temperament, that is, ordinary tolerance and self-restraint, in the circumstances of the defendant might have reacted in the same or in a similar way'. The Law Commission essentially repeated this proposal in its Final Report, published in November 2006, entitled *Murder, Manslaughter and Infanticide* (Law Com No 304).

8.9 Consent

Consent is a defence to, in theory at least, all non-fatal offences and even homicides. The onus of proving lack of consent rests on the prosecution (*Donovan* [1934] 2 KB 498). Is consent a defence, or is lack of consent an element of the offence? In the leading House of Lords case, *Brown and others* [1994] 1 AC 212, the majority (Lords Templeman, Lowry and Jauncey) assumed that all physical contact is assault unless a specific defence (here consent) applied; the minority assumed that it is a prerequisite of assault that there is no consent.

8.9.1 Consent must be real

The fact that V apparently consents to D's act does not mean that the law will treat that consent as valid. If V is a child, or mentally retarded, this apparent consent may not suffice (*Howard* [1965] 3 All ER 684). The question is whether V was able to comprehend the nature of the act. Thus, in *Burrell v Harmer* [1967] Crim LR 169, D was convicted of assault occasioning ABH after tattooing two boys aged 12 and 13, the result being that their arms became inflamed and painful. The court held there was no consent, as the boys did not understand the nature of the act. Presumably they understood what a tattoo was, but they would not have understood the level of pain involved.

8.9.2 Consent and fraud

Fraud does not necessarily negative consent. It only does so if it deceives V as to the identity of the person or the 'nature and quality' of the act. In *Clarence* (1888) 22 QBD 23, D had sexual intercourse with his wife (with her consent), having failed to reveal to her the fact that he was infected with gonorrhoea, a sexually transmittable disease. D was convicted of inflicting grievous bodily harm and actual bodily harm but, on appeal, these convictions were quashed. Stephen J said:

> **J** 'Is the man's concealment of the fact that he was infected such a fraud as vitiated his wife's consent to his exercise of marital rights and converted the act of connection into an assault? It seems to me the proposition that fraud vitiates consent in criminal matters is not true if taken to apply in the fullest sense of the word and without qualification . . . If we apply it . . . to the present case, it is difficult to say that the prisoner was not guilty of rape, for the definition of rape is having connection with a woman without her consent; and if fraud vitiates consent, every case in which a man infects a woman . . . is also a case of rape.'

On similar reasoning there was no assault committed in the following cases:

- *Bolduc and Bird* (1967) 63 DLR (2d) 82. D, a doctor, by falsely telling V that E was a medical student, obtained her consent to the latter's presence at a vaginal examination. In fact E was a musician. The Supreme Court of Canada held that there was no assault because the fraud was not as to the 'nature and quality' of what was to be done.

- *Mobilio* [1991] 1 VR 339. D was charged with three counts of rape. On three separate occasions, while employed as a radiographer, he had inserted an 'ultrasound transducer' (a medical probe) into the vagina of the female patient, ostensibly for diagnostic purposes. In fact D was acting for sexual gratification. He was convicted, but the Court of Criminal Appeal of Victoria, Australia, allowed his appeal. Each of the three women had either expressly or by their conduct consented to the insertion of the probe into their vagina by D and that was exactly what had happened. The fact that D had inserted the probe for the purpose of sexual gratification instead of diagnostic reasons did not vitiate those consents.

- *Richardson* [1998] EWCA 1086; [1998] 2 Cr App R 200. D was a dentist until August 1996 when the General Dental Council suspended her from practice. However, she continued to treat patients. She was subsequently charged with six counts of ABH following treatment given to six patients in September 1996. She was convicted, but the Court of Appeal allowed the appeal. The Court held that, where the patients' consent to treatment was procured only by a failure to inform them that she was no longer qualified to practice, she could not be guilty of an assault. The Court confirmed that fraud only negatived consent to an assault if V was deceived as to the identity of the person concerned or the 'nature and quality' of the act performed. The concept of 'identity of the person', moreover, could not be extended to cover D's qualifications or other attributes.

However, in *Tabassum* [2000] 2 Cr App R 328, the Court of Appeal distinguished both *Clarence* (1888) and *Richardson* (1998). The Court of Appeal drew a distinction between consent to the 'nature' of a touching and consent as to its 'quality'. Rose LJ said that the victims were 'consenting to touching for medical purposes not to indecent behaviour, that is, there was consent to the nature of the act but not its quality.'

CASE EXAMPLE

Tabassum [2000] 2 Cr App R 328

D had a degree in chemistry, and postgraduate qualifications on the use of IT in training doctors. However, he had no medical training or qualifications. Over a period of some months in 1997 he examined the breasts of three women, in two cases using his hands and on the third and final occasion with a stethoscope. He obtained their consent on the pretext that the examinations were part of a survey he was conducting, leading ultimately to the production of a computer software package for sale to doctors, to assist in the diagnosis of breast cancer. He did not actually tell them that he was medically qualified, although he did tell two of the women that he had worked at Christie's cancer hospital in Manchester and was a breast cancer specialist. When arrested he denied touching the women's breasts for sexual gratification but had done it in order to show them how to do it for themselves. He also denied acting or pretending to be a doctor. The prosecution case was that all three women would not have consented, had they known the truth about D. The defence case was that the women had all consented to D touching their breasts; he had touched their breasts; but he had done nothing for which he had not been given consent. He was convicted on three counts of indecent assault (an offence which has since been abolished by the Sexual Offences Act 2003; see Chapter 11)), and the Court of Appeal upheld all three convictions. As the women were only consenting for medical purposes, they had been deceived as to the 'quality' of D's act, and hence there was no consent.

Commentating on the case ([2002] Crim LR at 688), Professor Sir John Smith described the drawing of a distinction between the 'nature' of an act and the 'quality' of that act as 'new and highly suspect'. He pointed out that, previously, the inquiry had always been whether V had consented to the 'nature and quality' of the act (ie this was a single question), as opposed to whether she had consented to its 'nature' and 'quality' (ie two separate questions). He further argued that, if the distinction was correct, then *Clarence* (1888) was wrongly decided, on the basis that 'an act of sexual intercourse with a man suffering a dangerous contagious disease is surely an act of a different quality from an act of intercourse with a healthy man'. This would negate Mrs Clarence's consent, rendering D guilty of assault (it would now be rape). Professor Smith concluded that Parliament's intervention was 'urgently needed'.

Support for the decision in *Tabassum* (2000) comes from the Supreme Court of Canada. In *Cuerrier* [1998] 2 SCR 371, D had unprotected sex with two women, despite knowing that he had contracted HIV and despite having been warned by a nurse to always use a condom when having sexual intercourse. He obtained their consent, but did not tell either woman of his condition (he actually told one of the women that he was not HIV positive when she asked him). Both women testified in court that they would never have consented to unprotected sex with D had they known of his condition. By a majority, the court ruled that *Clarence* (1888) was distinguishable and that, on the facts, it was possible that D had committed a form of aggravated assault. Justifying the decision, L'Heureux-Dubé J said that 'those who know they are HIV-positive have a fundamental responsibility to advise their partners of their condition and to ensure that their sex is as safe as possible'.

The doctrine of informed consent

The decisions in *Cuerrier* (1998) and *Tabassum* (2000) suggested that the decision in *Clarence* was open to review. In *Dica* [2004] EWCA Crim 1103; [2004] QB 1257, the Court of Appeal confirmed that *Clarence* was, indeed, wrongly decided. In *Dica*, the facts of which are virtually identical to *Cuerrier*, D was convicted of two counts of inflicting 'biological' GBH contrary to s 20 OAPA 1861 and, although his convictions were quashed by the Court of Appeal because of a judicial misdirection, the Court took the opportunity to overrule *Clarence*. Judge LJ held as follows:

> **J** 'The effect of this judgment . . . is to remove some of the outdated restrictions against the successful prosecution of those who, knowing that they are suffering HIV or some other serious sexual disease, recklessly transmit it through consensual sexual intercourse, and inflict GBH on a person from whom the risk is concealed and who is not consenting to it. In this context, *Clarence* has no continuing relevance. Moreover, to the extent that *Clarence* suggested that consensual sexual intercourse of itself was to be regarded as consent to the risk of consequent disease, again, it is no longer authoritative.'

CASE EXAMPLE

Dica [2004] EWCA Crim 1103; [2004] QB 1257

Mohammed Dica had been diagnosed with HIV in 1995. Despite this knowledge, he had unprotected sex on a number of occasions with two women, V and W, who had been willing to be sexual partners with D but were unaware of his condition at the time. V claimed that D insisted that they have unprotected sex because he had had a vasectomy.

According to V, each time they had sex, D said 'Forgive me in the name of God'. After some time V noticed that her glands were swollen; she went to hospital and was diagnosed with HIV. W's story was similar. D was charged with two offences of inflicting GBH, contrary to s 20 OAPA 1861. He denied the offences contending that any sexual intercourse which had taken place had been consensual. The trial judge made two legal rulings: (a) that it was open to the jury to convict D of the charges, notwithstanding the decision in *Clarence*; (b) that any consent by V and W was irrelevant and provided no defence, because of the serious nature of the disease. D was convicted in October 2003. The Court of Appeal allowed D's appeal, but only on the basis that the trial judge had erred in withdrawing the issue of consent from the jury. If V and/or W had consented to the risk, that continued to provide a defence under s 20. However, the Court confirmed that *Clarence* was no longer good law. Finally, the Court ordered a retrial.

At Dica's retrial in March 2005, he was again convicted of inflicting 'biological' GBH and sentenced to four-and-a-half years in prison. He then appealed against that conviction and sentence, unsuccessfully, to the Court of Appeal (*Dica* [2005] EWCA Crim 2304). The *Dica* (2004) ruling was relied on shortly afterwards in the similar case of *Konzani* [2005] EWCA Crim 706; [2005] 2 Cr App R 14.

CASE EXAMPLE

Konzani [2005] EWCA Crim 706; [2005] 2 Cr App R 14

Feston Konzani, a 28-year-old asylum seeker from Malawi living in Middlesbrough, was convicted of inflicting 'biological' GBH on the three women – a 15-year-old virgin called Dawn whom he kept prisoner at his home, a 27-year-old African student who had a child by him, and a 26-year-old voluntary worker – over a three-year period between 2000 and 2003. The jury rejected his plea that the victims all consented to the risk of catching HIV because they agreed to have unprotected sex with him. The judge directed the jury as follows: 'If a little bird had whispered in the ear of one of the women as she was about to have unprotected sex with [D], "Would you be doing this if you knew he was HIV infected?", would she reply "No I wouldn't", or would she reply "It doesn't matter, I'll be all right."? If it's the former you have to find him guilty, if it's the latter you must find him not guilty.' D was given a 10-year prison sentence to be followed by deportation. The Court of Appeal dismissed his appeal. The Court said that D had 'deceived' the three women and there was 'not the slightest evidence, direct or indirect, from which a jury could begin to infer that [D] honestly believed that [the victims] consented to that specific risk (of contracting HIV)'.

Although *Cuerrier*, *Dica* and *Konzani* all involved HIV, the decisions in those cases could be applied to any life-threatening sexually transmitted disease.

In the 1st edition of this book, a question was posed whether the defendant in *Dica* could be guilty of rape, on the basis that the victims in that case had not consented to the 'quality' of the act in question, namely sex. That question has now been answered by the Court of Appeal. The answer is 'no'. In *B* [2006] All ER (D) 173 (Oct), D – who had previously been diagnosed as HIV positive – was charged with rape contrary to s 1 of the Sexual Offences Act 2003 (see Chapter 11) after having sex with V without disclosing his medical condition. The prosecution's case was that D had subjected V to a prolonged assault; this was denied by D who claimed that V had consented to sex. The prosecution therefore pursued an alternative argument that, notwithstanding V's consent to the physical act of sex, she had not consented to the risk of contracting a potentially fatal disease. This lack of consent meant that D was guilty of rape. The trial judge allowed this argument to go to the jury, and D was convicted of rape, but the Court of Appeal allowed his appeal (although it confirmed that the facts could support a conviction of inflicting grievous bodily harm contrary to s 20 OAPA 1861, following *Dica*, and ordered a retrial on that charge).

Latham LJ added that the question whether or not the facts of the *B* case could amount to rape was a matter requiring debate not in a court of law but as a matter of public and social policy, bearing in mind all the facts concerning, *inter alia*, 'questions of personal autonomy in delicate personal relationships'. In other words, that was a matter for Parliament to decide.

The cases of *Cuerrier*, *Dica*, *Konzani* and now *B* all involved the situation where D had unprotected sex with V, knowing that he had a sexually transmittable disease beforehand. This knowledge appears to be essential in order for the prosecution to establish subjective recklessness, the minimum *mens rea* state for all non-fatal offences. It follows that, if D did not know (or even suspect) that he was HIV positive, no charge could be brought against him for assaulting V. Authority for this proposition comes from the Supreme Court of Canada case of *Williams* [2003] 2 SCR 134. Here, D had unprotected sex with V despite his knowledge that he was HIV positive. After she contracted the disease as well, D was prosecuted but his conviction of aggravated assault was quashed because the couple had been having unprotected sex for six months *prior to* D learning of his HIV status. Binnie J (with whom the rest of the Supreme Court of Canada agreed) said that, although D had shown a 'shocking level of recklessness and selfishness', the prosecution could not prove that D's conduct after he learned of his condition had harmed V, because at that point she was possibly, and even probably, already HIV positive herself. The Court accepted medical evidence that a single act of unprotected sex carried a 'significant risk' of HIV transmission. It was therefore at least doubtful that V was free of HIV infection on the date when D learned of his condition. However, the Court convicted D of an *attempted* aggravated assault (for the law on attempt in English law, see Chapter 6). It is therefore quite possible that, should a case on similar facts occur in England, the court would be required to distinguish *Dica* and *Konzani* but could follow *Williams* and convict D of attempted ABH, attempted GBH – or even attempted murder.

8.9.3 The scope of consent

There are limits to anyone's right to consent to the infliction of harm upon themselves. Consensual killing is still murder (or possibly manslaughter on the ground of diminished responsibility), or euthanasia as it is popularly known. According to Lord Mustill in *Brown and others* [1994] 1 AC 212, 'The maintenance of human life is "an overriding imperative".' However, V may consent to a high *risk* of injury, or even death, if justified by the purpose of D's act. This depends on the social utility of the act. Where the act has some social purpose, it is a question of balancing the degree of harm which will or may be caused, against the value of D's purpose. In *Attorney-General's Reference (No 6 of 1980)* [1981] 2 All ER 1057, two youths, aged 17 and 18, decided to settle an argument with a bare-knuckle fist fight. One had sustained a bloody nose and a bruised face. Following acquittals, the Court of Appeal held that the defence of consent was not available in this situation. Lord Lane CJ said:

> **J** 'It is not in the public interest that people should try to cause or should cause each other actual bodily harm for no good reason . . . Nothing we have said is intended to cast doubt on the accepted legality of properly conducted games and sports, lawful chastisement or correction, reasonable surgical interference, dangerous exhibitions etc. These apparent exceptions can be justified as involving the exercise of a legal right, in the case of chastisement or correction, or as needed in the public interest, in the other cases.'

In *Brown and others* [1994] 1 AC 212, the majority's view was that consent was a defence to a charge of common assault, but not to any offence under s 47, s 20 or s 18 OAPA 1861 <u>unless</u> a recognised exception applied. These, according to Lord Templeman, related to 'lawful activities' which carried a risk of harm. He listed the following examples:

- contact sports, including boxing
- surgery
- ritual circumcision
- tattooing
- ear-piercing.

The appellants argued for a different test altogether. They suggested that GBH should always be unlawful, but that the infliction of wounds or actual bodily harm would not be unlawful, provided there was consent. The majority rejected the argument, holding that precedent drew the line below ABH. The majority seemed concerned that if the law was drawn too high, it might encourage more serious behaviour, with the attendant risk that even more serious harm might occur. Lord Jauncey said: 'An inflicter who is carried away by sexual excitement or by drink or drugs could very easily inflict pain and injury beyond the level to which the receiver had consented.'

Contact sports

No prosecutions have ever been brought in respect of boxing matches conducted within the Queensberry Rules. The high entertainment value and popularity of the sport is taken to justify V's consent to D trying to inflict serious injury potentially amounting to GBH. The enormously popular 'sport' of professional wrestling is regarded in the same light. However, fights conducted outside the scope of the Rules (sometimes referred to as 'prize fights') are not regarded as justifying V's consent. Any entertainment value they may have is far outweighed by the risk of injury to the fighters. Thus, in *Coney* (1882) 8 QBD 534, prosecutions were brought against various spectators at a bare-knuckle prize fight, for aiding and abetting the unlawful activities. One question for the court was whether the consent of the participants negated the unlawful element of assault. Cave J said:

> **J** 'The true view is that a blow struck in anger, or which is likely or is intended to do corporal hurt, is an assault, but that a blow struck in sport, and not likely, nor intended to cause bodily harm, is not an assault, and that, an assault being a breach of the peace and unlawful, the consent of the person struck is immaterial. If this view is correct, a blow struck in a prize-fight is clearly an assault; but . . . wrestling [does] not involve an assault, nor does boxing with gloves in the ordinary way.'

With other contact sports such as football, rugby and ice-hockey, a clear distinction must be drawn between two situations. An off-the-ball incident is in principle no different to any other assault, involving as it does the deliberate use of unlawful force. There is no suggestion that players consent, impliedly or otherwise, to the use of force in such situations. This is shown by *Billinghurst* [1978] Crim LR 553.

CASE EXAMPLE

Billinghurst [1978] Crim LR 553

D punched V in an off-the-ball incident during a rugby union match, fracturing his jaw in two places. He was convicted of inflicting GBH. The only defence was consent. D gave evidence that on previous occasions he had been punched and had himself punched opponents on the rugby field. The trial judge directed the jury that rugby was a contact sport involving the use of force and that players are deemed to consent to force 'of a kind which could reasonably be expected to happen during a game'. He went on to direct them that a rugby player has no unlimited licence to use force and that 'there must obviously be cases which cross the line of that to which a player is deemed to consent'. A distinction that the jury might regard as decisive was that between force used in the course of play and force used outside the course of play. The jury convicted.

The commentary to *Billinghurst* (1978) gives another example, contrasting a batsman in cricket being accidentally hit on the head by a 'fast' delivery (no assault, regardless of the seriousness of the injury) and another batsman being hit on the head after the bowler picked up a 'dead' ball and deliberately threw it at his head (assault). Problems arise where the alleged assault occurs on-the-ball, during play. The players in modern contact sports impliedly consent to D doing what the rules of the particular game permit. The rules themselves only provide a guide as to what has been consented to. In *Bradshaw* (1878) 14 Cox CC 83 and *Moore* (1898) 14 TLR 229, it was said that 'no rules or practice of any game whatever can make lawful that which is unlawful by the law of the land.' Therefore where an alleged criminal assault has occurred during play, this should be assessed independently of the rules. Lord Mustill in *Brown and others* (1994) referred to a series of Canadian decisions on ice-hockey, including *Ciccarelli* (1989) 54 CCC (3d) 121. There the courts accept that all the players consent to a certain level of violence. Each particular case should be treated on its facts: could V be said to have tacitly accepted a risk of violence at the level that actually occurred? The Canadian courts have provided a helpful list of criteria to determine the scope of implied consent in sport, including:

- the nature of the game played, whether amateur or professional league and so on
- the nature of the particular acts(s) and their surrounding circumstances
- the degree of force employed
- the degree of risk of injury
- the state of mind of the accused.

Ice hockey is a particularly violent sport, and in one Canadian case, *Moloney* (1976) 28 CCC (2d) 323, the judge ruled that ice hockey players impliedly consented to 'body contacts, boardings [ie being shoved into the boards around the rink] and maybe even a fight if it is two players consenting to the fight with each other.' In another case, *Gray* (1981) 24 CR (3d) 109, the judge said that 'it might well be that it would be extremely difficult to convict any hockey player of a common assault for his play during a game'. The position is obviously different if the referee's whistle has been blown to stop play <u>before</u> the alleged assault occurred. In *Ciccarelli* (1989), D was a professional ice hockey player with the Minnesota North Stars. He was convicted of assaulting V, a player with the Toronto Maple Leafs, during a game. The whistle had blown for offside against D when V, who had been skating across to block D, was unable to stop and they collided. D retaliated, using his stick to hit V over the head three times. The officials intervened to separate the pair but D punched out at them too. D was convicted of assault and his appeal dismissed.

In *Barnes* [2004] EWCA Crim 3246; [2005] 1 WLR 910, the Court of Appeal held that prosecutions should only be brought against a player who injured another player in the course of a sporting event if his conduct was 'sufficiently grave to be properly categorised as criminal', where what had occurred had gone beyond what the injured player could reasonably be regarded as having accepted by taking part in the sport.

CASE EXAMPLE

Barnes [2004] EWCA Crim 3246; [2005] 1 WLR 910

Mark Barnes was convicted of inflicting GBH under s 20 OAPA 1861 following a tackle in the course of an amateur football match. The prosecution alleged that it was the result of a 'late, unnecessary, reckless and high crashing tackle'. D claimed that the tackle was a fair, if hard, challenge in the course of play and that any injury caused was accidental. The Court of Appeal allowed the appeal.

Lord Woolf CJ said that the starting point was the fact that most organised sports had their own disciplinary procedures for enforcing their particular rules and standards of conduct. There was also the possibility of an injured player obtaining damages in a civil action. A criminal prosecution should be reserved for situations where the conduct was sufficiently grave to be properly categorised as criminal. In all contact sports, the participants impliedly consent to the risk of certain levels of harm. However, according to Lord Woolf, what was implicitly accepted in one sport would not necessarily be covered by the defence in another sport. In highly competitive sports, such as rugby, football and ice hockey conduct outside the rules could be expected to occur in the 'heat of the moment' and, even if the conduct justified a warning or a sending off, it still might not reach the threshold level required for it to be criminal. That level was an objective one and did not depend upon the views of individual players.

The type of sport, the level at which it was played, the nature of the act, the degree of force used, the extent of the risk of injury and D's state of mind were all likely to be relevant in determining whether D's actions went beyond the threshold. Whether conduct reached the required threshold to be criminal would therefore depend on all the circumstances. There would be cases that fell within a 'grey area' and then the tribunal of fact would have to make its own determination as to which side of the line the case fell. In such a situation the jury would need to ask themselves, among other questions, whether the contact was so 'obviously late and/or violent' that it could not be regarded as 'an instinctive reaction, error or misjudgment in the heat of the game'.

Surgery

With 'reasonable surgical interference' there is really no issue of consent as a defence to bodily harm, given that no *harm* is caused or inflicted. But in surgery there is certainly a 'wounding', and the patient must consent to that. Consent to any recognised surgical procedure is effective; this includes sex-change operations (*Corbett v Corbett* [1971] P 83) and probably cosmetic surgery and organ transplants. In *Bravery v Bravery* [1954] 3 All ER 59, which concerned the legality of a sterilisation operation, Denning LJ stated:

> **J** 'When it is done with the man's consent for a just cause, it is quite lawful, as, for instance, when it is done to prevent the transmission of an hereditary disease. But when it is done without just cause or excuse, it is unlawful, even though the man consents to it. Take a case where a sterilisation operation is done so as to enable a man to have the pleasure of sexual intercourse without shouldering the responsibilities attaching to it. The operation is then injurious to the public interest.'

The point was reversed by the National Health Service (Family Planning) Amendment Act 1972, but the view of the court and the influence of public policy is nevertheless interesting.

Horseplay

Society accepts that community life, such as in the playground, may involve a mutual risk of deliberate physical contact, and that the criminal law may distance itself. Honest belief, even if based on unreasonable grounds, that the others consent, will negative recklessness. In *Jones and others* [1987] Crim LR 123, some boys were injured having been tossed into the air by schoolmates. Despite not consenting to being thrown in the air at all, never mind the height at which they were thrown, the Court of Appeal held that there was no assault. In *Aitken and others* [1992] 1 WLR 1006, all those involved were RAF officers who attended a party where they all became drunk and engaged in an 'initiation ceremony' which involved setting fire to V's fire-resistant suit. The appellants overcame V's resistance and poured a large quantity of white spirit onto his suit before igniting it. He was severely burned. Nevertheless, the Courts-Martial Appeal Court quashed convictions of grievous bodily harm on the basis that the question of whether or not the appellants genuinely believed V to be consenting had not been put to the court.

Sexual activity

In *Boyea* [1992] Crim LR 574, D inserted his hand into V's vagina, and twisted it causing injuries consistent with the use of force. He was convicted of indecent assault and the Court of Appeal dismissed his appeal, which was based on his belief that V was consenting. The court held that V's consent to an assault was irrelevant if the jury was satisfied that the assault was intended to, or likely to, cause harm, provided the injury was not 'transient or trifling'. In *Slingsby* [1995] Crim LR 570, the question was whether D had committed an unlawful act for the purposes of constructive manslaughter (see Chapter 9). D had met the deceased, V, at a nightclub, and later had vaginal and anal intercourse with her, with her consent. Subsequently, also with her consent, he had penetrated her vagina and rectum with his hand. V suffered internal cuts caused by a ring on D's hand. She was unaware how serious these were and, although she was eventually admitted to hospital, she died of septicaemia. The trial judge held that it was clearly established that the deliberate infliction of bodily harm on another without good reason was unlawful. Furthermore, the infliction of violence for the purposes of sexual gratification, whether that be the gratification of either party, is unlawful (relying on *Boyea* (1992) and

Brown and others (1994)). However, in this case it was clear that all the activities were consented to by V; consequently, there was no assault and therefore D was not guilty of manslaughter.

Tattooing and other forms of branding

Consent is a valid defence to tattooing. The majority of the Lords in *Brown and others* (1994) accepted that much. The Court of Appeal confirmed and extended this proposition in *Wilson* [1997] 3 WLR 125, saying that branding was no more hazardous than a tattoo.

ASE EXAMPLE

Wilson [1997] 3 WLR 125

D had branded his initials, 'A' and 'W', onto his wife's buttocks using a hot blade. She regarded the branding as 'a desirable personal adornment', and had apparently originally requested that the branding be on her breasts. It was D who persuaded her to have the branding on her buttocks instead. The matter only came to light when her doctor reported the incident to the police. Wilson was convicted of assault occasioning ABH, and appealed. The Court of Appeal allowed the appeal.

Sado-masochism is beyond acceptable limits

As seen above, the courts do accept that injury accidentally inflicted during the course of sexual activity between consenting adults does not amount to assault (even where one of the parties dies). However, the law does not tolerate the idea of consent being a defence to injuries inflicted for the sexual gratification of either party. This was shown by *Donovan* [1934] 2 KB 498.

ASE EXAMPLE

Donovan [1934] 2 KB 498

D had been convicted of common and indecent assault. He had, apparently for his own sexual gratification, beaten a 17-year-old prostitute on the buttocks with a cane 'in circumstances of indecency'. A doctor examined her two days later and concluded that she had had a 'fairly severe beating'. D's convictions were quashed but only because the trial judge had failed to direct the jury that the issue of disproving consent was on the Crown.

In *Brown and others* (1994), when the case was still in the Court of Appeal, Lord Lane CJ said: 'It is not in the public interest that people should try to cause or should cause each other actual bodily harm for no good reason.' And when the case reached the House of Lords, Lord Templeman said:

> **J** 'In my opinion sado-masochism is not only concerned with sex. Sado-masochism is also concerned with violence . . . The violence of sado-masochistic encounters involves the indulgence of cruelty by sadists and the degradation of victims. Such violence is injurious to the participants and unpredictably dangerous.'

CASE EXAMPLE

Brown and others [1994] 1 AC 212

The appellants belonged to a group of sado-masochistic homosexuals who, over a 10-year period, willingly and enthusiastically participated in acts of violence against each other for sexual pleasure. Many of these acts took place in rooms designed as torture-chambers. The activities included branding with wire or metal heated by a blow-lamp, use of a cat o'nine tails, and genital torture. All the activities were carried out in private with the consent of the passive partner or 'victim'. There were no complaints to the police, no medical attention was ever sought and no permanent injury suffered. The police discovered the activities by accident. All members were charged with various offences, including wounding contrary to s 20 and assaults contrary to s 47 OAPA 1861. They were convicted and their appeals dismissed by the Court of Appeal and House of Lords (albeit by a three to two majority).

Justifying their decision, the majority referred to the risk of infection and the possible spread of AIDS. They did not comment about the role the criminal law should play in tackling the spread of AIDS; rather, no doubt, it was raised in order to make it even harder for the appellants to argue that their activities were a justifiable exception in the public interest. Lord Lowry commented that homosexual sado-masochism could not be regarded as a 'manly diversion', nor were they 'conducive to the enhancement of enjoyment of family life or conducive to the welfare of society'. For Lord Jauncey the corruption of young men was a real danger to be considered. This harks back to the 1957 Wolfenden Report (*Committee on Homosexual Offences and Prostitution*), which commented that the criminal law in relation to homosexual behaviour was designed 'to preserve public order and decency, to protect the citizen from what is offensive or injurious, and to provide sufficient safeguards against exploitation and corruption of others, particularly those who are especially vulnerable because they are young, weak in body or mind, inexperienced, or in a state of special, physical, official or economic dependence.'

ACTIVITY

Do you agree that the activities in *Brown and others* (1994) can be described as 'offensive or injurious'? Bear in mind everything took place in private; no one was induced or coerced into the activities; there was no evidence that anyone was 'exploited' or 'corrupted'.

The minority (Lords Mustill and Slynn), meanwhile, treated the question as whether the particular activities should be treated as included within the offences charged, and concluded that they should not. Lord Mustill said: 'This is not a case about the criminal law of violence. In my opinion it should be about the criminal law of private sexual relations, if about anything at all.' After analysing the authorities, the minority found that there were none binding the House, which was therefore free to decide. Both Law Lords decided that a victim's consent to the infliction of GBH was ineffective, but that consent was not necessarily ineffective to the occasioning of ABH. They were clear about what they were being asked to decide. Despite their disgust at the conduct, and their disapproval of it, the only issue was whether the activities were criminal. Lord Mustill identified the specific policy considerations that might point towards criminal liability:

- First, the risk of infection and septicaemia. This was, Lord Mustill said, greatly reduced by modern medicine.

- Secondly – contrary to what Lord Jauncey said about risks of more serious harm – Lord Mustill thought that the possibility that things might get out of hand with grave results was no reason for criminalising the appellants' conduct. If grave results did occur, however, then they would, of course, attract criminal sanctions.

- Thirdly, the evidence adduced in the case did <u>not</u> support the risk of the spread of AIDS. Such evidence as there was suggested that consensual buggery was the main cause of transmission, and this was, of course, legal.

- Fourthly, the possibility of corrupting the young was already provided for by existing legislation.

Key facts on consent

KEY FACTS

Elements	Comment	Cases
Scope of defence	There is implied consent available to all batteries.	*Collins v Wilcock* (1984)
	For ABH, GBH and wounding, consent is only available when there is a 'good reason'.	*Attorney-General's Reference (No 6 of 1980)*
	Consent may be a defence to manslaughter . . .	*Slingsby* (1995)
	. . . but not deliberate killing.	*Pretty* (2002) (see Chapter 2)
Good reasons	• Sport (including boxing) is a good reason, but not if defendant is involved in 'off-the-ball' incident.	*Billinghurst* (1978), *Barnes* (2004)
	• Horseplay is a good reason, whether involving children or adults.	*Jones and others* (1987), *Aitken and others* (1992)
	• Surgery is a good reason, as is tattooing and branding.	*Wilson* (1997)
	• Sexual contact is a good reason.	*Slingsby* (1995)
Reasons which are not good	Boxing is good but street-fighting is not a good reason.	*Coney* (1882), *Attorney-General's Reference (No 6 of 1980)*
	Sadomasochistic behaviour is not a good reason.	*Donovan* (1934), *Brown and others* (1994), *Emmett* (1999)
Consent and fraud	Victim must have consented to the nature and quality of the defendant's act.	*Clarence* (1888), *Bolduc and Bird* (1967), *Mobilio* (1991), *Richardson* (1998)
	'Nature' and 'quality' are separate elements and victim must have consented to both of them.	*Cuerrier* (1998), *Tabassum* (2000), *Dica* (2004), *Konzani* (2005)

Defences (including diminished responsibility, provocation and suicide pact (discussed in Chapter 9)): summary

KEY FACTS

Defence	Definition	Comments on scope and limitations	Burden of proof	Role of defence
Insanity	*M'Naghten* (1843)	Defence to all crimes, but results in 'special verdict'.	Defence	Denial of *mens rea*.
Automatism	*Bratty* (1961)	Full defence to all crimes.	Prosecution	Denial of *actus reus*.
Intoxication (voluntary)	*Majewski* (1977)	Partial defence to crimes of 'specific intent', such as murder, s 18 OAPA 1861 and theft. No defence to crimes of 'basic intent' such as assault, s 47 and s 20 OAPA 1861 and rape.	Prosecution	Denial of *mens rea*.
Intoxication (involuntary)	*Kingston* (1995)	Full defence to all crimes.	Prosecution	Denial of *mens rea*.
Duress by threats	*Howe* (1995)	Full defence to all crimes except murder and attempted murder.	Prosecution	Excuse
Duress of circumstances	*Martin* (1989)	Full defence to all crimes except murder and attempted murder.	Prosecution	Excuse
Necessity	*Re A* (2000)	Full defence to all crimes.	Prosecution	Justification
Marital coercion	CJA 1925, s 47	Full defence to all crimes.	Defence	Excuse
Mistake	*Morgan* (1976)	Full defence to all crimes.	Prosecution	Denial of *mens rea*.
Self-Defence	*Beckford* (1988)	Full defence to all crimes.	Prosecution	Justification

Prevention of crime	Criminal Law Act 1967, s 3	Full defence to all crimes.	Prosecution	Justification
Consent	*Brown* (1994)	Full defence to all crimes depending on circumstances.	Prosecution	Excuse
Diminished responsibility	Homicide Act 1957, s 2	Partial defence to murder only. (Reduces liability to manslaughter.)	Defence	Excuse
Provocation	Homicide Act 1957, s 3	Partial defence to murder only. (Reduces liability to manslaughter.)	Prosecution	Excuse
Suicide pact	Homicide Act 1957, s 4	Partial defence to murder only. (Reduces liability to manslaughter.)	Defence	Excuse

Lord Slynn thought that the whole area was for Parliament to decide. In *Wilson* (1997), the Court of Appeal distinguished *Brown and others* (1994) on its facts but in *Emmett*, [1999] EWCA Crim 1710; *The Times* 15th October 1999, the Court of Appeal applied the House of Lords' judgment. D and his girlfriend, G, enjoyed sado-masochistic sex. On one occasion D had placed a plastic bag over G's head and tied it tightly around her neck. As a result of lack of oxygen, she nearly lost consciousness, suffered bruising to the neck and ruptured blood vessels in her eyes. On another occasion D poured lighter fluid over G's left breast and ignited it. As a result of that injury, D persuaded her to go to the doctor, who informed the police. D was charged with two counts of s 47 ABH. D was convicted and appealed. He sought to rely on *Jones and others* (1986), but the Court of Appeal dismissed the appeal. The acts in the present case could not be construed as 'rough and undisciplined love-play'.

8.9.4 The impact of the European Convention on Human Rights (1950) and the Human Rights Act 1998

In *Laskey v UK* (1997) 24 EHRR 39, the European Court of Human Rights in Strasbourg upheld the judgment of the majority in *Brown and others* (1994). It had been argued before the Strasbourg Court that the imposition of criminal punishment constituted a breach of art 8(1) of the European Convention, which provides that 'Everyone has the right to respect for his private and family life, his home and his correspondence'. However, the Strasbourg court applied art 8(2), which justifies interference by the State in the art 8(1) rights which 'is necessary in a democratic society . . . for the protection of health or morals'. The court ruled that, once conduct had gone beyond a potential risk with a sufficient degree of seriousness, it could not possibly amount to a breach of art 8(1). The Court of Appeal in *Emmett* (1999) reached the same conclusion.

Note: in all the defences where the burden of proof is on the prosecution, D is expected to make the defence a 'live' issue by producing evidence to support it (referred to as the 'evidential burden'). Sometimes evidence of a defence is introduced inadvertently, eg D pleads automatism but the evidence actually supports insanity; D pleads self-defence but the evidence actually supports provocation, etc.

Role of the reasonable man and characteristics: summary

D is expected to comport with 'reasonable' standards in four defences. However, the courts have adopted different policies when analysing the extent to which D's characteristics can be taken into account.

KEY FACTS

Defence	Role of characteristics
Duress by threats	Certain characteristics may be attributed such as age, sex, physical disability and serious mental conditions (*Bowen* (1996)) but not vulnerability (*Hegarty* (1994), *Horne* (1994)).
Duress of circumstances	Presumably the same as duress by threats (*Shayler* (2001)).
Self-defence	Not relevant (*Martin (Anthony)* (2002)).
Provocation	Apparently no characteristics are excluded, except perhaps pugnacity (*Smith (Morgan)* (2001)). However, characteristics (other than age and sex) are only relevant is assessing the gravity of the provocation, not the standard of self-control to be expected (*Camplin* (1978); *Holley* (2005)).

ACTIVITY

1. The defence of voluntary intoxication represents an uneasy compromise between principle and public policy. But experience in Australia and New Zealand shows that these public policy considerations are overstated. The *Majewski* rules should be scrapped. Discuss.

2. D, aged 18, goes to her friend's birthday party one evening. She has a driving test in the morning and does not want to get drunk, so she tells her friend that she won't be drinking alcohol. However, her friend decides that D won't enjoy herself if she is completely sober and so pours a measure of vodka into D's coke. D does not notice the alcohol and, over the course of the evening, becomes drunk as her friend repeats this subterfuge on several occasions. At around midnight D stands up to leave but sways unsteadily on her feet. One of the other party guests, V, tried to help. In her drunken state D interprets V's gesture as an attack and kicks V in the shins. D then makes her way into the hallway and picks up what she thinks is her coat. In fact it is W's. D puts on W's coat and goes home.

   a Discuss D's liability for battery on V and for theft of W's coat.

   b What difference, if any, would it make to your answers if D had knowingly been drinking vodka 'n' coke all night?

3. The meaning and scope of the insanity defence is in urgent need of legislative overhaul. Discuss.

4. Five years ago D was involved in a serious train crash. Although she herself suffered only minor physical injuries, other passengers were killed and D was subsequently diagnosed as suffering a form of post-traumatic stress disorder. Six months ago D discovered that she was expecting a baby. Last week she was sitting in her car at a junction when the passenger door was opened and a complete stranger, E, jumped in. He pointed a handgun at her and told her to drive, which she did. After a mile he told her to park outside a jeweller's shop. E said that she had to wait while he went inside 'to do a job', then drive him to a safe location after which he would let her go. E threatened her that if she drove off or called for help on her mobile she would 'regret it'. He added that if, when he came out of the shop, she had gone, he would shoot the first person he saw. At that, E went into the jeweller's shop while D waited outside. Some five minutes later he emerged clutching a bag and got in. D drove off and kept going until eventually E told her to stop in a country lane where he got out and ran off.

   Consider whether D would be entitled to rely on duress in the event of her being charged with aiding an armed robbery.

5. The parameters of the consent defence are vague and lead to inconsistency in the courts – for example, compare *Brown and others* (1994) with *Wilson* (1996) and compare *Richardson* (1998) with *Tabassum* (2000). Legislative action is required to bring clarity. Discuss.

Further reading

Baker, E, 'Human Rights, McNaghten and the 1991 Act' [1994] Crim LR 84.

Barlow, N L A, 'Drug Intoxication and the Principle of *Capacitas Rationalis*' (1984) 100 LQR 639.

Dingwall, G, 'Intoxicated Mistakes about the Need for Self-Defence' [2007] 70 MLR 127.

Elliott, D W, 'Necessity, Duress and Self-Defence' [1989] Crim LR 611.

Gardner, S, 'Direct Action and the Defence of Necessity' (2005) Crim LR 371.

Gardner, S, 'The Importance of *Majewski*' (1994) 14 OJLS 279.

Gough, S, 'Surviving Without *Majewski*?' [2002] Crim LR 719.

Gunn, M J and Ormerod, D, 'The Legality of Boxing' (1995) 15 Legal Studies 181.

Horder, J, 'Pleading Involuntary Lack of Capacity' [1993] CLJ 298.

Huxtable, R, 'Separation of Conjoined Twins: Where next for English Law?' [2002] Crim LR 459.

Jones, T H, 'Insanity, Automatism and the Burden of Proof on the Accused' (1995) 111 LQR 475.

Leverick, F, 'Is English self-defence law incompatible with Article 2 of the ECHR?' [2002] Crim LR 347; 'The Use of Force in Public and Private Defence and Article 2: A Reply to Professor Smith' [2002] Crim LR 963.

Mackay, R D, 'Intoxication as a Factor in Automatism' [1982] Crim LR 146.

Mackay, R D and Kearns, G, 'The Continued Underuse of Unfitness to Plead and the Insanity Defence' [1994] Crim LR 576.

Mackay, R D and Kearns, G, 'More Facts about the Insanity Defence' [1999] Crim LR 714.

Mackay, R, Mitchell, B and Howe, L, 'Yet More Facts about the Insanity Defence' [2006] Crim LR 399.

Milgate, H P, 'Intoxication, Mistake and the Public Interest' [1987] CLJ 381.

Ryan, S, 'Reckless Transmission of HIV: Knowledge and Culpability' [2006] Crim LR 981.

Smith, J C, 'The Use of Force in Public and Private Defence and Article 2' [2002] Crim LR 958.

Smith, K J M, 'Duress and Steadfastness: In Pursuit of the Unintelligible' [1999] Crim LR 363.

Spencer, J, 'Liability for Reckless Infection' (2004) NLJ 384, 448.

Sullivan, G R, 'Involuntary Intoxication and Beyond' [1994] Crim LR 272; 'Violent Self-help' (1983) 46 MLR 78.

Ward, A R, 'Making Sense of Self-induced Intoxication' [1986] CLJ 247.

Weait, M, 'Criminal Law and the Sexual Transmission of HIV: *R v Dica*' (2005) 68 MLR 121; 'Knowledge, Autonomy and Consent: *R v Konzani*' [2005] Crim LR 763.

Wilson, W, Ebrahim, I, Fenwick, P & Marks, R, 'Violence, Sleepwalking and the Criminal Law: (2) The Legal Aspects' [2005] Crim LR 614.

Internet links

Diabetes UK: www.diabetes.org.uk.

Epilepsy Action: www.epilepsy.org.uk.

Law Commission, *Partial Defences to Murder* (Law Com No 173), available at www.lawcom.gov.uk.

PART II

SPECIFIC
OFFENCES

AIMS AND OBJECTIVES □□□

After reading this chapter you should be able to:

■ Understand the law of murder

■ Understand the law of diminished responsibility

■ Understand the law of provocation

■ Understand the law of involuntary manslaughter (constructive, gross negligence and reckless manslaughter)

■ Analyse critically the law on homicide, including reform proposals

■ Apply the law to factual situations to determine whether there is liability for murder or manslaughter

9.1 *Actus reus* of homicide

The *actus reus* elements of murder are as follows:

• causing death of a human being

• under the King or Queen's Peace

• within any county of the realm.

The *actus reus* is fundamentally the same for manslaughter. Causation was dealt with in Chapter 2.

9.1.1 Human being: birth

A foetus that is killed in the womb cannot be a victim of homicide, though there are other (statutory) offences (see below). When does a foetus become a person in being? It appears that the child must be wholly expelled from the mother (*Poulton* (1832) 5 C & P 329) and have a separate existence from her (*Enoch* (1833) 5 C & P 539). That requirement creates its own problems: for example, it is now accepted that a foetus in the womb has an independent circulation within two months of conception. Where a foetus has been born alive but dies afterwards from injuries inflicted whilst in the womb, this may be manslaughter but not murder (*Attorney-General's Reference (No 3 of 1994)* [1997] 3 WLR 421, considered in Chapter 3).

9.1.2 Human being: death

A person who is already dead cannot be the victim of homicide. But the legal definition of death has proved elusive. There is conventional death, when the heartbeat and breathing stop. But there is also brain death, when through artificial means the heart continues to beat and air circulates in the lungs. Brain death is recognised by the British Medical Association and is the point when life-support machinery will be switched off. In *Malcharek, Steel* [1981] 2 All ER 422 (the facts of which were discussed in Chapter 2), the Court of Appeal adverted to this test, although they did not have to decide the point. It is likely that if the question arose squarely, then the courts would adopt the brain death test (or strictly <u>tests</u>, as there are six of them). Thus, if D stabs V who has been certified brain dead but whose functions are being maintained on a ventilating machine, it is unlikely that the Court of Appeal would uphold a murder conviction.

9.1.3 Under the King or Queen's Peace

This serves to exclude from the scope of homicide enemy soldiers killed in the course of war.

9.1.4 Within any county of the realm

The limitations in this phrase have now all but disappeared. Murder (and manslaughter) committed by a British citizen outside of the UK may be tried in England (ss 9 and 10, Offences Against the Person Act (OAPA) 1861; s 3, British Nationality Act 1948). Murder committed on a British aircraft may be tried in the UK (s 92, Civil Aviation Act 1982). Murder committed on a foreign aircraft coming to the UK may also be tried in England (Civil Aviation (Amendment) Act 1996). The War Crimes Act 1991 confers jurisdiction on English courts over offences of murder (and manslaughter) committed as war crimes in Germany or German-occupied territory during the Second World War.

9.1.5 The year and a day rule

Until 1996 there was a further element: that V had to die within a year and a day. This rule was originally justified because of the difficulty in establishing causation where there was a long interval between the original wound, injury etc and V's death. The net result was that if D stabbed, shot, strangled or otherwise fatally injured V, but V was kept alive for at least 367 days on a life support machine before death, D could not be guilty of homicide (see *Dyson* [1908] 2 KB 454). However, over time, medical science developed to such an extent that the original justification was no longer valid and it was abolished by Parliament in 1996. The main impetus for change was public perception of 'murderers' escaping conviction for murder because the victim had been kept alive for more than 366 days. In the case of gross negligence manslaughter, there was not even an alternative offence for which D might be held liable if V survived the 367 days.

ˈLaw Reform (Year and a Day Rule) Act 1996

1 The rule known as the "year and a day rule" (that is, the rule that, for the purposes of offences involving death and of suicide, an act or omission is conclusively presumed not to have caused a person's death if more than a year and a day have elapsed before he died) is abolished for all purposes.

2(1) Proceedings to which this section applies may only be instituted by or with the consent of the Attorney-General.

(2) This section applies to proceedings against a person for a fatal offence if (a) the injury alleged to cause death was sustained more than three years before the death occurred, or (b) the person has previously been convicted of an offence committed in circumstances alleged to be connected with the death.

(3) In subsection (2) "fatal offence" means (a) murder, manslaughter, infanticide or any other offence of which one of the elements is causing a person's death, or (b) the offence of aiding, abetting, counselling or procuring a person's death.'

The consent of the Attorney-General is required in two circumstances. First, where several years had passed since the original incident, it was thought to be undesirable to have the history of the case trawled over again in a homicide trial. It would mean some defendants having to live for years with the threat of a murder change hanging over them. Second, where D has already been convicted of a non-fatal offence, or attempt, on the same set of facts. This encourages the prosecution to bring assault or wounding charges earlier, while V is still alive, rather than wait for years to see whether V dies or not.

9.2 Murder

The *actus reus* elements of murder have been dealt with above. The only remaining element is that of *mens rea*, 'with malice aforethought'. This is a legal term – potentially very misleading – which requires neither ill-will nor premeditation. A person who kills out of compassion to alleviate suffering (a so-called 'mercy killing') almost certainly acts with malice aforethought. Proof of malice aforethought means that a jury is satisfied that, at the time of killing V, D either (*Moloney* [1985] AC 905):

- intended to kill (express malice); or

- intended to cause grievous bodily harm (implied malice).

Thus, it is possible for D to be convicted of murder when he intends some serious injury but does not contemplate that V's life be endangered. This has generated some controversy and calls for reform (see below).

9.2.1 Intention

All of the leading cases on the meaning and scope of intention have involved murder. You should refer back to the discussion of these cases – especially *Woollin* [1998] 3 WLR 382 – in Chapter 2, for a reminder of the principles.

9.2.2 Grievous bodily harm

The meaning of the phrase 'grievous bodily harm' is the same as when the phrase is used in the context of ss 18 and 20 OAPA 1861 (see Chapter 10). In *DPP v Smith* [1961] AC 290, a murder case, Viscount Kilmuir, with whom the rest of the Lords agreed, held that there was no reason to give the words any special meaning. Thus, he said, bodily harm 'needs no explanation' while 'grievous' means no more and no less than 'really serious'. Subsequently, in the context of s 20 OAPA 1861, the Court of Appeal held that the omission of the word 'really' when a judge was directing a jury was not significant (*Saunders* [1985] Crim LR 230). This was confirmed in the context of murder in *Janjua and Choudury* [1998] EWCA Crim 1419; [1998] Crim LR 675. The Court of Appeal dismissed the defendants' argument on appeal that the word 'really' had to be used in every single murder case.

9.2.3 Procedure in murder trials

In *Coutts* [2006] UKHL 39; [2006] 1 WLR 2154, the House of Lords allowed an appeal against a murder conviction on the basis that the jury was not allowed to consider manslaughter as an alternative verdict. D had pleaded not guilty, his defence being that Jane's death was a tragic accident, but the jury rejected that version of events and therefore convicted him of murder. Lord Rodger explained as follows:

> J 'The jury were told that they had to choose between convicting the appellant of murder and acquitting him on the ground that the victim had died as a result of an accident. On that basis they chose to convict of murder. But the jury should also have been told that, depending on their view of the facts, they could convict him of manslaughter . . .The reality is that, in the course of their deliberations, a jury might well look at the overall picture, even if they eventually had to separate out the issues of murder, manslaughter and accident. So, introducing the possibility of convicting for manslaughter could have changed the way the jury went about considering their verdict.'

CASE EXAMPLE

Coutts [2006] UKHL 39; [2006] 1 WLR 2154

D was convicted of the murder of Jane Longhurst. He admitted having what is described in the judgment as 'consensual asphyxial sex' with Jane, meaning that he had – with her consent – 'tied a pair of tights round her neck and tied a knot in them'. At some point D had closed his eyes and released the tights, but by that time Jane had died. D said that he did not know how she had died. The prosecution alleged murder, and adduced evidence that D visited pornographic websites 'showing extreme violence towards women' under headings such as 'asphyxiation' and 'strangulation'. The Crown also contended that he had visited Jane's body in various places where he had stored it for five weeks post-mortem before dumping it in woodland and setting it alight; this was suggestive of 'necrophiliac propensities'. At his trial, D claimed that Jane's death was a complete accident but the jury convicted him of murder and he was sentenced to 30 years' imprisonment.

Reform

The Draft Criminal Code (1989), cl 54(1), defines murder as follows: 'A person is guilty of murder if he causes the death of another (a) intending to cause death; or (b) intending to cause serious personal harm and being aware that he may cause death.' This would narrow the *mens rea* of murder from its present common law definition. See also the discussion in section 9.8 below.

ACTIVITY

1. Should the definition of murder be amended so as to impose a requirement that, if D did not intend to cause death but did intend to cause serious injury, he also had an awareness that death may be caused?

2. Consider the following scenario. D is a 'loan shark'. One of his clients, V, is in considerable debt to D but cannot afford to repay it. D decides to physically punish V in such a way that D's other clients will be left in no doubt as to the consequences if they fail to repay their debts. D specifically wants V to survive the punishment, to provide a long-term reminder of the implications of failing to repay D's loans. One night D ambushes V and shoots him in the leg with a handgun. The idea is to leave V with a permanent limp. However, the bullet hits an artery and, within minutes, V bleeds to death. Is D guilty of murder:

   a under the present common law definition

   b under the Draft Criminal Code?

9.3 Voluntary manslaughter

9.3.1 Diminished responsibility

The defence of diminished responsibility (DR) evolved at common law in the courts of Scotland and was introduced into English law by the Homicide Act 1957:

S '2(1) Where a person kills or is party to a killing of another, he shall not be convicted of murder if he was suffering from such abnormality of mind (whether arising from a condition of arrested or retarded development of mind or any inherent causes or induced by disease or injury) as substantially impaired his mental responsibility for his acts and omissions in doing or being party to the killing.'

DR is a 'special' defence in that it is purely a defence to murder. In *Campbell* [1997] Crim LR 495, it was unsuccessfully argued that DR should be allowed as a defence to attempted murder. In *Antoine* [2000] UKHL 20; [2001] 1 AC 340, the House of Lords held that evidence of DR is not relevant when a jury is deciding whether or not D is fit to stand trial on a charge of murder. D had been charged with murder. He was found unfit to plead under the Criminal Procedure (Insanity) Act 1964, and another jury was brought in to determine whether he had done 'the act . . . charged against him'. He sought to rely upon DR but the judge ruled that it was unavailable. The jury duly found that he had done the act charged, and the judge ordered indefinite hospitalisation. The Court of Appeal and House of Lords dismissed the appeal.

Procedure

D bears the burden of proving DR (Homicide Act 1957, s 2(2)) on the balance of probabilities (*Dunbar* [1958] 1 QB 1). A successful defence results in a verdict of not guilty to murder but guilty of manslaughter (Homicide Act 1957, s 2(3)). This allows the judge full discretion on sentencing. Some defendants may receive an absolute discharge, others probationary or suspended sentences, while in appropriate circumstances some will receive hospital or guardianship orders under s 37(1) of the Mental Health Act 1983. Others may still face imprisonment, with some receiving life sentences for manslaughter (about 15 per cent of cases). If D raises the defence, and the prosecution has evidence that he is insane then, under s 6 Criminal Procedure (Insanity) Act 1964, evidence may be adduced to prove this. Here, the burden remains on the prosecution to prove insanity. The converse situation is also allowed by s 6, that is, if D raises insanity, then the prosecution may argue it is really a case of DR. Where this happens, the burden is on the prosecution to prove DR beyond reasonable doubt (*Grant* [1960] Crim LR 424).

Pleading guilty to manslaughter on grounds of DR

Originally, the courts took the view that DR had to be proved to the jury in every case and could not be accepted by a trial judge. However, it is now accepted that D may plead guilty to a charge of manslaughter on the ground of DR. Such a plea would be proper 'where the medical evidence available, in the possession of the prosecution as well as the defence, showed perfectly plainly that the plea' was one that could properly be accepted (*Cox* [1968] 1 WLR 308). In *Vinagre* (1979) 69 Cr App R 104 the Court of Appeal said that pleas of guilty to manslaughter on the ground of DR should only be accepted where there was 'clear evidence' of mental imbalance. The plea was refused in the following cases:

- *Ahmed Din* (1962) 46 Cr App R 270. D attacked and killed a man whom he believed was having an affair with his wife, stabbing him several times and almost severing V's head. After death, D cut off V's penis. D pleaded DR, based on paranoia induced by an unreasonable belief in his wife's infidelity. Two medical experts supported the plea; the prosecution was prepared to accept it. However, the judge insisted on leaving the defence to the jury, which returned a verdict of guilty of murder. D's appeal was dismissed. Lord Parker CJ said that the case was 'a very good illustration of what for long has been apparent', namely, that the prosecution were 'only too ready to fall in with and to support' a defence of DR.

- *Walton* (1978) 66 Cr App R 25. D shot a random stranger, a 16-year-old girl. Charged with murder, he pleaded DR. Two defence medical experts described D as 'retarded in certain respects', suffering from 'an extremely immature personality' and 'having an inadequate personality enhanced by emotional immaturity and low tolerance level'. The jury, however, rejected the defence. The Privy Council rejected D's appeal. Lord Keith said that the jury was entitled to regard the medical evidence as 'not entirely convincing'.

Where D pleads DR but it is rejected by the jury, the Court of Appeal may, if it believes the murder conviction to be unsupported by the evidence, quash it and substitute one of manslaughter. This happened in the following cases:

- *Matheson* [1958] 2 All ER 87. D killed a 15-year-old boy. The medical experts agreed that D was suffering an abnormality of mind but the jury rejected the defence. D's murder conviction was quashed on appeal. Lord Goddard CJ said that where there was 'unchallenged' evidence of abnormality of mind and substantial impairment of mental responsibility, and 'no facts or circumstances appear that can displace or throw doubt on that evidence' then the Court was 'bound' to say that the conviction was unsafe.

- *Bailey* [1961] Crim LR 828. D battered V, a 16-year-old girl, to death with an iron bar. Three medical experts agreed that D suffered from epilepsy, that he had suffered a fit at the time of the killing, and that it had substantially impaired his mental responsibility at that time. The jury rejected the defence. D appealed and his murder conviction was quashed.

According to research (S Dell, 'Diminished Responsibility Reconsidered' [1982] Crim LR 809) in practice 80 per cent of pleas of guilty to manslaughter are accepted. Where the case does go to trial (usually because the prosecution disputes the defence), there is about a 60 per cent chance of conviction for murder. Thus the overall failure rate of the defence is quite small, around 10 per cent. Where there was a dispute between the prosecution and defence medical experts, about half

concerned the question of whether D suffered an abnormality of mind, and about half the question of whether D's responsibility was substantially impaired (Dell, above). These two disputes raise quite different issues. The question of whether or not D was suffering an abnormality of mind is a psychiatric one; a question on which experts might be expected to have differing views. However, the other question is essentially a legal/moral issue, strictly for the jury, and it is odd that pleas of guilty to manslaughter could be refused on this ground because medical 'experts' disagreed on moral principles.

Importance of medical evidence

Medical evidence is crucial to the success of the defence. In *Byrne* [1960] 2 QB 396 it was said that, while there is no statutory requirement that a plea be supported by medical evidence, the 'aetiology of the abnormality of mind . . . does, however, seem to be a matter to be determined on expert evidence'. Thus, where D was suffering a condition that was not, at the time of the trial, regarded by psychiatrists as a mental condition the defence will be unavailable but, if the condition subsequently becomes so regarded, a conviction may be quashed. This was the outcome in *Hobson* [1998] 1 Cr App R 31.

CASE EXAMPLE

Hobson [1998] 1 Cr App R 31

In January 1992, D stabbed her abusive, alcoholic partner, V, to death during an argument. At her murder trial in October 1992, D described the abuse she had endured for 18 months. The trial judge left self-defence (which had been relied on by the defence) and provocation (which had not) to the jury, but not DR. The jury rejected self-defence and provocation and D was convicted. In May 1997 she appealed on the ground that the evidence disclosed a DR defence, based on battered woman syndrome (BWS), which should have been left to the jury. D's appeal was allowed and a retrial ordered. The Court of Appeal noted that BWS was not regarded as an abnormality of mind until 1994, two years after her trial.

The Court of Appeal in *Dix* (1982) 74 Crim LR 302, declared that medical evidence was a 'practical necessity if the defence is to begin to run at all'. The jury were not, however, bound to accept that evidence if there was other material, which, in their opinion, conflicted with and outweighed the medical evidence. Occasionally, the jury may be faced with conflicting medical evidence. They are then required to weigh up and choose between the different opinions.

Operation of the defence

Section 2(1) breaks down into three components:

- an abnormality of mind
- arising from certain specified causes
- which substantially impairs mental responsibility.

There are no further requirements nor exceptions. In *Matheson* (1958) it was accepted that the fact that a killing was premeditated did not destroy a plea of DR. Initially, it was thought that the judge's task was simply to read s 2 and leave it up to the jury. Now it is clear the judge must direct the jury as to the meaning of s 2. Thus, in *Gomez* (1964) 48 Cr App R 310, where the judge declined to direct the jury on the meaning of the section, with the result being a murder conviction, D's appeal was successful. Trial judges should attempt to tailor the direction to fit the facts of the case. In most cases it would not be particularly unhelpful for the judge to direct the jury by simply reading out s 2(1) in full (*Sanderson* [1993] Crim LR 857).

'Abnormality of mind'

Although medical evidence is important, whether or not D was suffering an 'abnormality of mind' is ultimately a question for the jury. In the leading case, *Byrne* [1960] 2 QB 396, Lord Parker CJ said:

> **J** 'Abnormality of mind . . . means a state of mind so different from that of ordinary human beings that the reasonable man would term it abnormal. It appears to us to be wide enough to cover the mind's activities in all its aspects, not only the perception of physical acts and matters, and the ability to form a rational judgment as to whether an act is right or wrong, but also the ability to exercise will-power to control physical acts in accordance with that rational judgment.'

CASE EXAMPLE

Byrne [1960] 2 QB 396

D, a sexual psychopath, suffered violent, perverted sexual desires, which he found difficult, if not impossible, to control. He strangled a girl and then mutilated the body. The trial judge directed the jury that this was not enough of its own to bring the defendant within s 2. He was convicted of murder and appealed. His conviction was quashed.

The definition of 'abnormality of mind' is therefore much wider than that of 'disease of the mind' under the M'Naghten Rules (see Chapter 8). An inability, or even difficulty, to control impulses could amount to an abnormality of mind. The 'irresistible impulse' defence, long denied under the M'Naghten Rules, has thus been recognised, albeit only as a defence to murder. In *Byrne* (1960), the Court of Criminal Appeal approved the medical witnesses' description of D's condition as amounting to 'partial insanity'. Earlier cases had used the expressions 'bordering on, though not amounting to insanity' (*HM Advocate v Braithwaite* (1945) JC 55, a Scottish case) and 'not quite mad but a borderline case' (*Spriggs* [1958] 1 QB 270). Unsurprisingly, these directions created a risk of confusion with the insanity defence. This problem was finally resolved in *Seers* (1984) 79 Cr App R 261, where D was suffering chronic reactive depression. The trial judge had directed the jury that DR was available to those who were 'partially insane' or 'on the borderline of insanity'. The jury convicted of murder and D appealed. The Court of Appeal held that a depressive illness could amount to an abnormality of mind, although no one would consider it to be on the 'borderline of insanity'. The judge should have kept to Lord Parker's statement and avoided references to 'insanity' altogether.

The causes specified in s 2(1)

D's abnormality of mind should be attributable to at least one of the causes listed in s 2(1). The courts have tended to allow a wide range of mental conditions to provide a basis for DR pleas. Some factors, especially transient external influences like alcohol or drugs, are certainly supposed to be excluded; however, in some cases, such factors have supported the defence, eg jealousy (*Miller*, *The Times*, 16th May 1972) and rage (*Coles* (1980) 144 JPN 528). In *Seers* (1984), noted above, reactive (as opposed to endogenous) depression was accepted as the basis of a DR plea. Mercy killers not infrequently receive verdicts of not guilty to murder on grounds of DR, with the only evidence adduced in support of mental abnormality being reactive depression (S Dell, *Murder into Manslaughter: The Diminished Responsibility Defence in Practice* (1984)).

In many cases there will be more than one alleged cause of D's abnormality of mind. Where that is the case, then there is no requirement that any one of the causes be sufficient to qualify in its own right as such an abnormality. It should be sufficient that together they constitute an abnormal state of mind (*Dietschmann* [2003] UKHL 10; [2003] 1 AC 1209, which will be discussed in detail below). This was also the decision of the Queensland Court of Appeal in *Whitworth* (1987) 31 A Crim R 453, applying legislation similar to the Homicide Act 1957. The jury was left to consider whether D's abnormality of mind was induced by a psychological injury caused by childhood trauma, or by physical injuries to the brain, or a combination of both. There is nothing in the 1957 Act to indicate that the 'abnormality of mind' has to have any degree of permanence. It should suffice that it existed at the time of the killing and that it substantially diminished D's responsibility (*Tumanako* (1992) 64 A Crim R 149).

'Any inherent cause'

The words 'any inherent cause' clearly have a wide scope. The following have all been accepted as inherent causes:

- psychopathy (*Byrne* (1960); *Turnbull* (1977) 65 Cr App R 242)
- mental deficiency (*Speake* (1957) 41 Cr App R 222)
- paranoia (*Simcox* [1964] Crim LR 402)
- epilepsy (*Price* [1963] 2 QB 1)
- depression (*Bathurst* [1968] 2 QB 99; *Seers* (1984) 79 Cr App R 261; *Ahluwalia* [1992] 4 All ER 869)
- pre-menstrual tension (*Reynolds* [1988] Crim LR 679)
- battered woman syndrome (*Hobson* (1998)).

The word 'inherent' in s 2 certainly does not require that the condition be an inherited one (see a decision from New South Wales, *McGarvie* (1986) 5 NSWLR 270). Nor need it have been present from birth (*Gomez* (1964)).

In *Jama* [2004] EWCA Crim 960, the Court of Appeal held that Asperger's syndrome (AS), a neurobiological disorder in which sufferers have 'grave difficulty in developing relationships' and are 'self-centred and [do] not empathise with other people', constituted an 'abnormality of mind' for the purposes of DR. Yonis Omar Jama was convicted of murdering his friend, Steven Siewlal, by stabbing him with two 'quite large' knives. There were two grounds of appeal (one involving alleged provocation arising from an argument that the pair had had over a Playstation game), the other based on DR. The Court allowed the appeal, on both grounds, substituting a manslaughter conviction. Hooper LJ said that there was 'no dispute' that psychiatric evidence of Asperger's syndrome supported a defence of DR. The same evidence would also have been relevant as a characteristic for the purposes of the objective limb of provocation (see below).

'Disease'

'Disease' is wide enough to cover mental, as well as physical, diseases. In *Sanderson* (1993), D was convicted of murder after the judge's direction to the jury to the effect that the defence had to show injury to the brain. On appeal, he argued that 'disease' covered mental illnesses that were functional, as well as organic. The Court of Appeal accepted that the defence did not have to show some organic or physical injury. The physical condition of the brain, though not irrelevant, was a question for evidence only. In any event, 'any inherent cause' would cover functional mental illness.

'Injury'

In *Whitworth* (1987), the Queensland Court of Appeal gave a wide meaning to 'injury'. Although it will usually be a result of physical violence, it could be inflicted by 'violent or dramatic

psychological stress' as well as by 'slow, merciless factors, little by little, and with hopelessness'. In each case it would be a question of degree whether a true injury had been caused. It could also be a combination of physical injury and psychological injuries.

'Substantially impaired mental responsibility'

The expression 'diminished responsibility' does not actually appear in s 2 itself; rather it is used in the marginal note. Instead, s 2 uses the phrase 'substantially impaired mental responsibility'. In *Byrne* (1960), the Court of Appeal said that the question of whether D's impairment could be described as 'substantial' was a question of degree and, hence, although medical evidence was not irrelevant, one for the jury. In *Lloyd* [1967] 1 QB 175, the trial judge, Ashworth J, directed the jury as follows:

> J 'Substantial does not mean total, that is to say, the mental responsibility need not be totally impaired, so to speak, destroyed altogether. At the other end of the scale substantial does not mean trivial or minimal. It is something in between and Parliament has left it to you and other juries to say on the evidence, was the mental responsibility impaired and if so, was it substantially impaired?'

This clearly gives juries a wide discretion. Sympathy/empathy for the defendant is crucial. On one hand, it is not uncommon for manslaughter verdicts to be returned in cases with little evidence of abnormality but where D has reacted to situations of extreme grief or stress. Thus mercy-killers, or killings committed by the severely depressed, receive convictions for manslaughter instead of murder. Conversely, murder convictions have been returned in cases when the psychiatrists all agreed that D was suffering severe mental abnormality but whose actions evoked little or no jury sympathy (the classic example being the Yorkshire Ripper, Peter Sutcliffe).

Diminished responsibility and intoxication

This can be a difficult area of law. There is often conflicting medical evidence, which can create confusion in the mind of the jury – and sometimes of the judge! The case of *Sanderson* illustrates some of the difficulties in this area. D was a regular user of cocaine and heroin. He admitted killing his girlfriend; the only issue was whether he was guilty of murder or manslaughter. The defence psychiatrist stated that D was suffering paranoid psychosis which was already present, irrespective of his drug abuse, and was therefore an 'inherent cause'. The prosecution psychiatrist, meanwhile, stated that there was no long-standing psychosis. Instead, D was suffering from paranoia caused purely by his cocaine abuse, which falls outside of the parameters of s 2. D was convicted of murder and appealed. The Court of Appeal quashed the conviction because of contradictions in the judge's summing-up which might have confused the jury. It is not difficult to see how the jury would have struggled to reach a verdict in this case, with such conflicting evidence presented to them.

First, it is clear that a plea of DR may not be supported with evidence of intoxication. In *Fenton* (1975) 61 Cr App R 261, Lord Widgery CJ said that: 'We do not see how self-induced intoxication can of itself produce an abnormality of mind due to inherent causes.' Where the evidence suggests that D was intoxicated and was suffering from at least one of the causes within s 2, then the judge should direct the jury to ignore the effects of the intoxication and consider whether the admissible cause(s) on its own would have been enough to amount to an abnormality of mind so as substantially to impair D's mental responsibility. This was the decision in *Gittens* [1984] 3 All ER 252, where D was suffering depression and had, on the night in question, consumed a large amount of drink and anti-depressant pills. In this state he clubbed his wife to death with a hammer and then raped and strangled his 15-year-old stepdaughter. At his murder trial, the judge directed the jury that if they decided that the substantial cause of D's conduct was his depression, then DR was available; if they decided it was a combination of the drink and anti-depressant pills then DR was not available. The jury convicted of murder and D appealed. The appeal was allowed: the references to 'substantial causes' was confusing.

In *Egan* [1992] 4 All ER 470, the Court of Appeal said that 'the vital question' for the jury in such cases was to ask, 'was the appellant's abnormality of mind such that he would have been under diminished responsibility, drink or no drink?' In this case D was described as suffering intellectual impairment with some psychopathy. On the day in question he been drinking very heavily all day; he had consumed 15 pints of beer plus some gin and tonics prior to bludgeoning to death a 79-year-old woman. D pleaded guilty to manslaughter but the Crown rejected his plea and he was tried for murder. A majority of the medical witnesses were of the opinion that D's underlying condition was enough of itself to substantially diminish D's responsibility. However, the jury convicted and D's appeal was dismissed. The jury had been properly directed.

Imposition of a causal requirement?

A serious problem was caused by Lord Lane CJ's model jury direction in *Atkinson* [1985] Crim LR 314, where he said that the jury should be asked: 'Has D satisfied you . . . that, if he had not taken drink, (i) he would have killed as he in fact did? and (ii) he would have been under diminished responsibility when he did so?' According to this test, the jury should convict D of murder unless satisfied that the killing would not have taken place but for D having taken drink. But to direct a jury that they must be satisfied that D would not have killed had he not taken drink is to impose a causal requirement unsupported by the 1957 Act. This point has now been recognised in *Dietschmann* (2003), where *Atkinson* (1985) was overruled on this point. Lord Hutton suggested the following model direction for future juries:

J

'Assuming that the defence have established that [D] was suffering from mental abnormality as described in s 2, the important question is: did that abnormality substantially impair his mental responsibility for his acts in doing the killing? . . . Drink cannot be taken into account as something which contributed to his mental abnormality and to any impairment of mental responsibility arising from that abnormality. But you may take the view that both [D]'s mental abnormality and drink played a part in impairing his mental responsibility for the killing and that he might not have killed if he had not taken drink. If you take that view, then the question for you to decide is this: has [D] satisfied you that, despite the drink, his mental abnormality substantially impaired his mental responsibility for his fatal acts, or has he failed to satisfy you of that? If he has satisfied you of that, you will find him not guilty of murder but you may find him guilty of manslaughter. If he has not satisfied you of that, the defence of diminished responsibility is not available to him.'

CASE EXAMPLE

Dietschmann [2003] UKHL 10; [2003] 1 AC 1209

D killed V by punching him and kicking him in the head in a savage attack. At the time of the killing, D was heavily intoxicated, in addition to suffering from an 'adjustment disorder', a 'depressed grief reaction' to the recent death of his girlfriend. At his trial for murder D relied on DR. The expert evidence for D was that, as well as the adjustment disorder, he had suffered a 'transient psychotic episode' at the time of the incident so that, even if he had been sober, he would still probably have killed V. The Crown's case was that the alcohol had been a significant factor as a disinhibitor and that, if D had been sober, he would probably have exercised self-control. The judge directed the jury according to *Atkinson*, and the jury convicted. D appealed and although the Court of Appeal dismissed the appeal, he was successful in the House of Lords.

Dietschmann was followed by the Court of Appeal in *Hendy* [2006] EWCA Crim 819; [2006] 2 Cr App R 33. D admitted killing V while intoxicated on alcohol. At his trial for murder, evidence was adduced that D had brain damage, possibly caused by a head injury as a child, and a psychopathic disorder. D was convicted of murder but the Court of Appeal allowed the appeal on the basis that the jury had not been directed in accordance with Lord Hutton's model direction (above) on the interplay between underlying mental abnormality and intoxication.

Intoxication causing an abnormality of mind

In the above cases, D was intoxicated in addition to having some underlying abnormality. Different rules apply where it is suggested that D's 'abnormality of mind' was itself caused by intoxication. This may happen in two situations. First, where D's long-term alcohol and/or drug abuse has actually led to brain damage or psychosis, this would almost certainly be held to amount to an 'injury' within s 2. In *Veen (No 2)* (1988) 164 CLR 465, the High Court of Australia accepted a plea of DR on the basis of brain damage due to alcohol abuse. The leading English case is the Court of Appeal judgment in *Tandy* [1989] 1 All ER 267, where Watkins LJ said that

> **J** 'If . . . alcoholism had reached the level at which [D's] brain had been injured by the repeated insult from intoxicants so that there was gross impairment of . . . judgment and emotional responses, then the defence was available.'

For obvious reasons, the immediate effects of taking alcohol or drugs cannot be classed as an 'injury'. This is seen in *Di Duca* (1959) 43 Cr App R 167, where it was unsuccessfully argued that the toxic effect of alcohol on the brain was an 'injury' for the purposes of s 2. This decision was confirmed in *O'Connell* [1997] Crim LR 683. There, it had been argued that a sleeping drug that D was taking (Halcion) may have caused a temporary malfunctioning of the brain, a temporary 'injury' for the purposes of s 2. The Court of Appeal rejected the appeal. If the temporary effects of the sleeping drug were to be characterised as an 'injury' then there was no reason why the effects of alcohol should not be similarly characterised. The Court of Appeal thought that it could not have been Parliament's intention that the transient effects of drink and drugs should have been regarded as giving rise to the possibility of constituting 'injury' within s 2.

The second situation in which the ingestion of intoxicants may be relevant is where alcoholism and/or drug addiction may be considered to be a 'disease'. Evidence suggests that there are many causes of alcoholism, one of which may be genetic (that is, some people are predisposed towards addiction). Alcoholism may be connected with, or arise from, some earlier or deeper illness or condition such as depression. In other cases, alcoholism aggravates the symptoms of such deeper illness. Thus, it is often not clear whether a patient with a history of depression drinks because he is depressed, or is depressed because he drinks too much. However, the courts in England have been reluctant to accept that simply being an alcoholic suffices. In *Fenton* (1975), Lord Widgery CJ in the Court of Appeal envisaged the possibility that a craving for drink or drugs could produce an abnormality of mind. However, in *Tandy* (1989), Watkins LJ added a very important *caveat*, holding that alcoholism on its own would not suffice for a plea of DR. Instead, it would have to be established (by the defence) that D's 'drinking had become involuntary, that is to say she was no longer able to resist the impulse to drink'.

CASE EXAMPLE

Tandy [1989] 1 All ER 267

D, according to her own evidence and that of her first husband, was a long-term alcoholic. Crucially (as it turned out) she usually drank only barley wine or Cinzano. However, over the course of the day in question she drank 90 per cent of a bottle of vodka, which is significantly stronger than either barley wine or Cinzano. The medical evidence indicated that this level of alcohol would be lethal for a normal person but that alcoholics, because of their persistent abuse of alcohol, develop a tolerance. Later she strangled her 11-year-old daughter, Amanda, after she told her mother that D's second husband, Amanda's stepfather, had sexually interfered with her. D was convicted of murder and appealed. The appeal was dismissed. First, D had not shown that her brain had actually been injured. Second, she had failed to prove that her first drink was 'involuntary'.

This has been criticised on the basis that it unduly limits the scope of the defence. One commentator has argued that 'very few, if any, alcoholics will be permanently in a condition where the immediate consumption of alcohol is required to prevent or assuage the symptoms of withdrawal from alcohol' (G R Sullivan, 'Intoxicants and Diminished Responsibility' [1994] Crim LR 156). Another commentator has also criticised the *Tandy* (1989) rule that the first drink must be 'involuntary' before alcoholism can amount to an abnormality of mind. He points out that, under the rule, 'the symptoms of the disease are seen in isolation from the disease itself, leaving the idea of "disease" devoid of meaning' (J Goodliffe '*Tandy* and the Concept of Alcoholism as a Disease' (1990) 53 MLR 809). Despite this criticism, in *Inseal* [1992] Crim LR 35, the Court of Appeal followed *Tandy*. In that case D, an alcoholic, had killed his girlfriend whilst in a drunken stupor. He claimed that he was either too drunk to have the intent to kill (the intoxication defence; see Chapter 8) or, if he did have the intent, his alcoholism was an 'abnormality of mind' within s 2. The jury convicted and the Court of Appeal dismissed the appeal. The jury must have been satisfied that D could have resisted the temptation to take the first and subsequent drinks and that 'accordingly' any abnormality of mind was not induced by alcoholism.

Reform of diminished responsibility

In October 2003, the Law Commission published a Consultation Paper, 'Partial Defences to Murder' (Law Com No 173), which explores a number of proposals that have been made to change the wording of s 2 of the Homicide Act.

The Butler Report, 1975

The 1975 Report of the Royal Committee on Mentally Abnormal Offenders (Cmnd 6244), the Butler Committee, contained the following, alternative formula for DR (paragraph 19.17):

> 'Where a person kills or is party to the killing of another, he shall not be convicted of murder if there is medical or other evidence that he was suffering from a form of mental disorder . . . and if, in the opinion of the jury, the mental disorder was such as to be an extenuating circumstance which ought to reduce the offence to manslaughter.'

The definition of 'mental disorder' that would be used here is found in s 1 of the Mental Health Act 1983, which refers to 'mental illness, arrested or incomplete development of mind, psychopathic disorder and any other disorder or disability of mind'.

The Criminal Law Revision Committee (CLRC), 1980

The Committee, comprising the leading criminal law academics of the time, and including Professors John Smith and Glanville Williams, published a report entitled *Offences Against the Person* (Cmnd 7844) in 1980, suggesting a very similar formulation. The only difference was in the effect of the 'mental disorder'. In the Committee's formulation, the mental disorder had 'to be a substantial enough reason to reduce the offence to manslaughter'.

The Draft Criminal Code, 1989

Clause 56 of the Law Commission's Draft Criminal Code (1989) adopted the formulation of the CLRC, although it substituted the words 'mental abnormality' for 'mental disorder'. Neither Butler, the CLRC nor the Law Commission, therefore, felt that there should necessarily be any requirement that the mental disorder/abnormality stem from a specified cause. This would broaden the scope of the defence – although this may be a tacit acceptance of accepted practice under s 2 in any event.

The New South Wales Law Reform Commission, 1997

The Commission published a report, *Partial Defences to Murder: Diminished Responsibility* (Report 82) in 1997, suggesting a significantly different formulation. D would have a defence if at the time of causing V's death his/her 'capacity to (a) understand events; or (b) judge whether [his/her] actions were right or wrong; or (c) control himself or herself, was so substantially impaired by an abnormality of mental functioning arising from an underlying condition as to warrant reducing murder to manslaughter'. 'Underlying condition' is defined as a 'pre-existing mental or psychological condition other than that of a transitory kind'. This formulation retains the requirement in s 2 that D's mental abnormality derive from a specified cause. In other respects it is quite radical: the notion that D might plead DR because of an impaired capacity to judge what is right or wrong is certainly novel (although it does create a potential overlap with the M'Naghten Rules).

Professor Mackay, 2000

Another formulation has been suggested by Professor Mackay ('Diminished Responsibility and Mentally Disordered Killers'). Under his formulation, D would have a defence if, at the time of the killing, 'his mental functioning was so aberrant and affected his criminal behaviour to such a substantial degree that the offence ought to be reduced to manslaughter'.

Law Commission, 2004

In the Law Commission's *Partial Defences to Murder* Final Report, published in August 2004, the Commission suggested a formulation to replace s 2 of the Homicide Act 1957, based very closely on the New South Wales Law Reform Commission's 1997 suggestion. The formulation requires that:

A person, who would otherwise be guilty of murder, is not guilty of murder but of manslaughter if, at the time of the act or omission causing death (1) that person's capacity to (a) understand events; or (b) judge whether his actions were right or wrong; (c) or control himself, was substantially impaired by an abnormality of mental functioning arising from an underlying condition and (2) the abnormality was a significant cause of the defendant's conduct in carrying out or taking part in the killing. 'Underlying condition' means a pre-existing mental or physiological condition other than of a transitory kind.

The latter point about the defence being based on a pre-existing condition other than those of a 'transitory kind' was designed to exclude 'a transitory disturbance of the mind reflecting a temporary state of heightened emotions, for example extreme anger arising out of a typical case of road rage'. On the other hand, the defence would 'in principle' be available to those suffering 'post-traumatic stress disorder and severe depression'.

The Commission repeated this formulation in its 2005 Consultation Paper, *A New Homicide Act for England & Wales?*

Law Commission 2006

However, the Law Commission revised its position after consultation. The latest reform proposal, in the Commission's Final Report entitled *Murder, Manslaughter and Infanticide* (Law Com No 304), published in November 2006, is as follows:

'(a) A person, who would otherwise be guilty of 1st degree murder, is guilty of 2nd degree murder if, at the time he or she played his or her part in the killing, his or her capacity to:

  (i)   understand the nature of his or her conduct; or

  (ii) form a rational judgment; or

  (iii) control him or herself,

was substantially impaired by an abnormality of mental functioning arising from a recognised medical condition, developmental immaturity in a D under the age of 18, or a combination of both;

and

   (b)   the abnormality, the developmental immaturity, or the combination of both provides an explanation for the defendant's conduct in carrying out or taking part in the killing.'

Points to note

- The Law Commission has also proposed to split murder into 1st and 2nd degree murder, with DR operating as a defence to the former only. This point will be addressed below (see section 9.8)

- The reference to 'abnormality of mind' in the present s 2 would be replaced by 'abnormality of mental functioning'

- The reference to 'arrested or retarded development of mind' in the present s 2 would be replaced by 'developmental immaturity'. The Commission state that D should be able to bring a plea of DR based on developmental immaturity 'through appeal either to biological factors (such as poor frontal lobe development), or to social and environmental factors, or to a combination of both'.

- Between its 2005 Consultation Paper and 2006 Report, the Commission was persuaded to drop references to D's capacity to 'understand events' and to 'judge whether his actions were right or wrong'. The former wording was dropped because the Commission wanted to ensure that D's lack of understanding of 'global political events' was <u>not</u> relevant to a plea of DR. The latter wording was changed following feedback from the Royal College of Psychiatrists. It also avoids a potentially confusing overlap with the M'Naghten Rules on insanity (see Chapter 8).

Abolition of diminished responsibility

The Law Commission's 2003 Paper, *Partial Defences to Murder* (Law Com No 173), even suggested abolishing DR altogether, for five reasons:

1. It is anomalous because it is only a defence to murder.

2. It is an 'ill-defined compromise' that would not exist were it not for the limited scope of the insanity defence.

3. It would be better to abolish the mandatory life sentence for murder and allow the 'variety of circumstances' which may give rise to DR to be taken into account as mitigating factors.

4. Its existence encourages defendants to plead guilty to manslaughter instead of insanity, which would lead to an acquittal.

5. It is open to manipulation, for example in cases of mercy killing where it has been accepted despite D suffering no mental abnormality.

The Law Commission acknowledged that there are arguments in favour of retaining the defence:

1. Without it, the only mental disorder defence to murder would be insanity, which is very limited in scope.

2. Defendants who could not plead insanity but who did suffer a mental disorder would be convicted of murder. Abolishing the mandatory sentence for murder would allow judges to

reflect the defendant's diminished culpability in a lower sentence, but the 'label' of murderer would be unavoidable.

3. If the provision that those who successfully plead insanity as a defence to murder face mandatory indefinite detention in a secure hospital was abolished, more defendants would plead that instead of guilty to manslaughter.

4. Generally speaking, the defence has worked in practice. The fact that 'it is sometimes used in a benign way' to accommodate mercy killers is not enough reason to abolish it.

ACTIVITY

Should DR be abolished? If not, should it be reworded? If so, what formulation would you choose?

Key facts chart on diminished responsibility

KEY FACTS

	Law	Section/Case
Definition	• suffering from an abnormality of mind; • caused by arrested or retarded development of mind, an inherent cause, disease or injury; • which substantially impaired his mental responsibility for the killing.	s 2(1) Homicide Act 1957
Abnormality of mind	A state of mind so different from that of ordinary human beings that the reasonable man would term it abnormal.	*Byrne* (1960)
Substantially impaired	A question of degree for the jury to decide. Substantial does not mean total nor trivial or minimal but something in between.	*Byrne* (1960) *Lloyd* (1967)

Examples of abnormality of mind	• Psychopathy	*Byrne* (1960)
	• Paranoia	*Simcox* (1964)
	• Epilepsy	*Price* (1963)
	• Depression	*Seers* (1984)
	• Battered woman syndrome	*Hobson* (1998)
Effect of intoxication	Transient effect of drink or drugs on brain is not an injury.	*Di Duca* (1959), *O'Connell* (1997)
	Alcoholism is only a defence if drinking is involuntary or brain has been damaged.	*Tandy* (1989)
	Where the defendant has a pre-existing mental disorder, intoxication does not prevent him using the defence; the abnormality of mind does not have to be the sole cause of the defendant doing the killing.	*Gittens* (1984), *Egan* (1992), *Dietschmann* (2003), *Hendy* (2006)
Burden of proof	It is for the defence to prove on the balance of probabilities.	s 2(2) Homicide Act 1957
Effect of defence	The charge of murder is reduced to manslaughter.	s 2(3) Homicide Act 1957

315

9.3.2 Provocation

Like diminished responsibility, provocation is only a partial defence to murder. In *Pears* [1972] Crim LR 678, it was held that the defence is not available to a charge of attempted murder. Even when D successfully pleads provocation as a defence to murder, it only reduces liability to manslaughter. The defence existed at common law (indeed it still does), although it is now regulated by the Homicide Act 1957, s 3 of which provides as follows:

> '3 Where on a charge of murder there is evidence on which the jury can find that the person charged was provoked (whether by things done or by things said or by both together) to lose his self-control, the question whether the provocation was enough to make a reasonable man do as he did shall be left to the jury; and in determining that question the jury shall take into account everything both done and said according to the effect it would have on a reasonable man.'

Procedure

If D wishes to rely on the defence, they must provide evidence of provocation. The onus is then on the prosecution to prove that D was <u>not</u> provoked (*Cascoe* [1970] 2 All ER 833). If there is evidence of provocation, the judge must direct the jury to consider it. Failure to do so, resulting in the jury returning a murder conviction, will almost certainly lead to the Court of Appeal quashing a murder conviction (*Rossiter* [1994] 2 All ER 752; *Cambridge* [1994] 2 All ER 760). In such circumstances the Court of Appeal has a choice: either substituting a manslaughter conviction (giving the defendant the benefit of the doubt) or ordering a retrial. This is the case even if the defence does not plead provocation but instead relies on some other defence, typically self-defence (this is often a deliberate, tactical move, because a successful plea of self-defence results in an acquittal whereas a successful plea of provocation leads to conviction of manslaughter).

Further examples of this occurrence include *Burgess and McLean* [1995] Crim LR 425; *Stewart* [1995] 4 All ER 999; and *Dhillon* [1997] Crim LR 295. The late professor Sir John Smith commented on the latter case that 'the result was that D was able to have his cake at trial and eat it on appeal'. Nevertheless there must be some evidence of provocation to bring the judicial duty into play. According to Lord Steyn, giving judgment for the House of Lords in *Acott* [1997] UKHL 5; [1997] 1 All ER 706, if there is no evidence of provocation, it is not up to the judge to direct the jury on what would be a 'speculative possibility'.

CASE EXAMPLE

Acott [1997] UKHL 5; [1997] 1 All ER 706

D was convicted of the murder of his 78-year-old mother at the home they shared. His unsuccessful defence at trial was that she had fallen and her injuries were the result of

316

this plus his unskilled efforts to resuscitate her, but on appeal he argued that the Crown had made provocation a live issue by repeatedly suggesting in cross-examination that he had lost self-control after his mother continually treated him like a little boy. However, the defence had not been left to the jury. He now argued that her injuries were evidence of a frenzied attack indicative of loss of self-control. The Court of Appeal rejected the appeal and the House of Lords unanimously agreed. There was no evidence of provocation, and suggestions by Crown counsel during cross-examination could not in themselves raise the defence where the evidence, even on the most favourable view for D, did not raise such an issue. Because s 3 of the 1957 Act requires that provocation must be by things done or said, Lord Steyn said that there must be 'some evidence of *what* was said or *what* was done to provoke the homicidal reaction'.

This ruling was applied in *Miao* [2003] EWCA Crim 3486. D admitted killing his partner, V, one night at the home they shared together but denied doing so intentionally. According to the prosecution, cause of death was strangulation. D claimed that V had accused him of having an affair and had slapped and kicked him. D said that, to stop her shouting, he had put his hand over her mouth, but when she bit his hand he had put it on her throat. As a result she had died, but D denied that he had intended to kill her or cause serious harm. The judge was invited by both counsel for the Crown and for the defence to leave provocation to the jury, but declined to do so as the evidence was 'minimal' and provocation was no more than a speculative possibility. D was convicted of murder and the Court of Appeal, following *Acott*, upheld his conviction.

What can amount to provocation?

Prior to the 1957 Act, violence was required and words alone would not suffice. However, after the 1957 Act, provocation need not be something illegal, or wrongful. It simply has to be something 'done' or 'said'. This is shown in *Doughty* (1986) 83 Cr App R 319, where the Court of Appeal quashed D's murder conviction on the ground that provocation should have been left to the jury. He had killed his 19-day-old son after the child would not stop crying. The Court of Appeal held that it was open to the jury to find that was provocation by 'things done'.

Indirect provocation

Provocation may come from third parties. This is seen in *Davies* [1975] QB 691. D had shot his wife, V, dead. He was convicted of murder and appealed on the basis that the judge had excluded from the jury's consideration provocation from any source other than from V. Specifically, D contended that his wife's lover might also have provoked him. The Court of Appeal allowed the appeal. Provocation may also have been directed at a third party but, if it has the effect of provoking D, it can be relied upon. This was seen in *Pearson* [1992] Crim LR 193.

CASE EXAMPLE

Pearson [1992] Crim LR 193

Two brothers, Malcolm (16) and William (17), killed their violent, abusive father by taking it in turns to beat him over the head with a sledgehammer. M had suffered worst, being abused for eight years, during which time W had largely been abroad. However, W had returned home to protect M. M was convicted of manslaughter, but W of murder. On appeal, this was also reduced to manslaughter, on the ground that the judge failed to direct the jury to take account of the provocative effect on W of the father's treatment of M, even when W had been away.

Self-induced provocation

The fact that D has done something to V, which made the latter react to and in turn provoke D, does not preclude the defence. In *Edwards* [1973] AC 648, Lord Pearson had suggested that 'a blackmailer cannot rely on the predictable results of his own blackmailing conduct as constituting provocation'. However, in *Johnson* [1989] 1 WLR 740, the Court of Appeal disapproved of this limitation. Watkins LJ said that, given the 'express wording' of the 1957 Act, it was 'impossible to accept that the mere fact that [D] caused a reaction in others, which in turn led him to lose his self-control, should result in the issue of provocation being kept outside a jury's consideration'.

The subjective and objective questions

Once the judge had decided there was evidence of provocation, there are two questions to be answered by the jury:

- did the defendant lose his or her self-control?
- might the reasonable man have done as the defendant did?

The former, because it focuses on what the defendant did, is referred to as the 'subjective' question or limb of the defence, the latter, focussing on the reasonable man, is referred to as the 'objective' question or limb.

The subjective question

The first question for the jury is: was D provoked to lose his self-control? If he or she was not, then it is unnecessary to consider the objective limb. If D is unusually emotionless and retained his cool when the reasonable man would have lost his, then the defence is not available. In addition, the loss of self-control must be, in the words of Devlin J in *Duffy* [1949] 1 All ER 932n 'sudden and temporary . . . rendering the accused so subject to passion as to make him or her for the moment not the master of his mind'. This qualification on the subjective question pre-dates the 1957 Act, but any suggestion that it was overruled by the statute was dispelled by the Court of Appeal in *Ibrams and Gregory* (1981) 74 Cr App R 154, which confirmed that it was still part of the law of provocation. Lawton LJ said:

> **J** 'Circumstances which induce a desire for revenge are inconsistent with provocation, since the conscious formulation of a desire for revenge means that a person has had time to think, to reflect, and that would negative a sudden temporary loss of self-control, which is the essence of provocation.'

CASE EXAMPLE

Ibrams and Gregory (1981) 74 Cr App R 154

D was sharing a flat with his fiancée, A. An ex-boyfriend of hers, John Monk, regularly visited the flat to bully and terrorise the pair of them. On some occasions a friend of the couple, E, was also at the flat. Eventually the three met on 10th October and agreed a plan for dealing with Monk, which was to get him drunk and encourage him to go to bed with A. D and E would then burst in and attack Monk while he was in bed. The plan was carried out two days later, and D and E killed Monk. The Court of Appeal upheld their murder convictions. There was no evidence that Monk had done anything after 7th October to provoke either them. The time delay between the last act of provocation and Monk's death, plus the pre-formulated plan, negatived their claims of loss of self-control.

More recently, the Court of Appeal has confirmed that a time delay is not necessarily fatal to a successful provocation plea. Rather, the principle is that, the longer the period after the provoking event or words, the weaker the plea becomes and the less likely it is that the defence will succeed. This was seen in *Baillie* [1995] Crim LR 739.

CASE EXAMPLE

Baillie [1995] Crim LR 739

D had shot and killed a drug-dealer, M, who was supplying D's three teenage sons with drugs. D's youngest son had told him that M had threatened them with violence. D fetched his shotgun from the attic, and a cut-throat razor, and drove around to M's house. There was an altercation, where M grappled for the gun. M was cut severely by the razor and attempted to flee, whereupon D shot and killed him. D pleaded provocation, based on being told of the threats by his son, or alternatively by M's grappling for the gun. The judge directed the jury only to consider the latter act, because any sudden and temporary loss of self-control induced earlier 'must have ceased' by the time of the fatal act. The Court of Appeal allowed the appeal. The question whether D had lost his self-control at the time of the shooting was entirely one for the jury.

Cumulative provocation

Provocation is not confined to the last act or word before the killing. There may have been previous acts or words which, when added together, cause the defendant to lose self-control. The issue of cumulative provocation was recognised by the Court of Appeal in *Humphreys* [1995] 4 All ER 1008 and by the Privy Council in *Luc Thiet Thuan* [1997] AC 131, where Lord Goff said:

> J 'It may be open to a defendant to establish provocation in circumstances in which the act of the deceased, though relatively non-provocative if taken in isolation, was the last of a series of acts which finally provoked the loss of self-control by the defendant and so precipitated his extreme reaction which led to the death of the deceased.'

'Slow burn'

The defence of provocation developed from traditional, male ideas of reacting instantly to violence with violence. Consequently, there have been difficult cases when it is a woman who kills, typically as the result of domestic violence cases. When a woman who has suffered years of violence and abuse and, finally, out of desperation, seizes the opportunity when her husband or partner is asleep or drunk or both, to kill him, she may not be reacting to any particular act or incident, but rather to the accumulation of years of abuse. The *Duffy* test of a 'sudden and temporary' loss of self-control does not fit this situation comfortably. The result has been that battered women who kill face life sentences for murder. Leading cases are *Thornton (No 1)* [1992] 1 All ER 306 and *Ahluwalia* (1992).

CASE EXAMPLE

Thornton (No 1) [1992] 1 All ER 306

The Thorntons' marriage was an unhappy one, with D suffering physical abuse from her husband, V, who was a heavy drinker, jealous and possessive. One night, D returned home to find V lying on the sofa. He allegedly called her a 'whore', at which point she went into the kitchen to find something with which to defend herself if he attacked her. She found a bread-knife and sharpened it before returning to the living room, where V allegedly said that he would kill her when she was asleep. D then fatally stabbed him in the stomach. She was convicted of murder and her appeal on the ground of provocation was dismissed on the basis that, at the crucial time of using the knife, she was not suffering a 'sudden and temporary loss of self-control'. The fact she had gone to the kitchen to fetch, and sharpen, the knife, were crucial factors.

ASE EXAMPLE

Ahluwalia [1992] 4 All ER 869

D had an arranged marriage, which had been violent for many years. Her husband, V, had frequently assaulted D and had also threatened to kill her. One night he told her that, unless she paid a bill the next day, he would beat her. Later, when he was asleep, she doused him in petrol and set him alight. He died six days later and D was convicted of murder. She appealed on the grounds of DR and provocation, but the Court of Appeal rejected the latter ground. (Her appeal was allowed on the former ground and she was convicted of manslaughter at a retrial.)

The objective question

The jury must be satisfied that the reasonable man would (1) have lost self-control, and (2) done as D did.

Who is the 'reasonable man'?

Prior to the 1957 Act, the common law rule was that the reasonable man was 'purely' objective – that is, he was an adult, with normal physical and mental attributes. This had the capability of producing some very harsh decisions. The best example is the notorious case of *Bedder v DPP* [1954] 2 All ER 801. Here, D was provoked about his impotence and killed his provoker. The House of Lords dismissed his appeal, which had been based on the ground that the jury had been told to consider the effect of V's provocation on a reasonable man who was not impotent. It was hardly surprising that the jury convicted – taunts about impotence would, presumably, have little or no effect on a man who is not impotent. In *DPP v Camplin* [1978] AC 705, however, the House of Lords held that *Bedder* (1954) had been overruled by s 3 of the 1957 Act. In allowing words to constitute evidence of provocation, it followed that Parliament intended that the reasonable man should be endowed with those of D's characteristics that would have a bearing on his or her reaction to those words. Lord Diplock, giving a model direction with which the rest of the House concurred, concluded that:

J   'A proper direction to a jury . . . should state . . . that the reasonable man . . . is a person having the power of self-control to be expected of an ordinary person of the sex and age of the accused, but in other respects sharing such of the accused's characteristics as they think would affect the gravity of the provocation to him; and that the question is not merely whether such a person would in like circumstances be provoked to lose his self-control but also whether he would react to the provocation as the accused did.'

CASE EXAMPLE

DPP v Camplin [1978] AC 705

V, a middle-aged man, had buggered D, a 15-year-old boy, and then laughed at him. At this, D had lost his self-control and hit V over the head with a chapati-pan with fatal consequences. The trial judge directed the jury to consider the effect that V's provocation may have had on the reasonable man, as opposed to a reasonable 15-year-old boy. The jury convicted, but the Court of Appeal and the House of Lords allowed the appeal.
The jury should have been told to assess the impact of the provocation on a reasonable 15-year-old boy.

The *Camplin* distinction (1978–2000)

Thus, *Camplin* allowed juries to take account of D's characteristics when deciding whether the reasonable man may have lost self-control. Lord Diplock's direction divides the objective question into two separate and distinct issues:

- The **gravity of the provocation:** theoretically, any of D's characteristics may be relevant.

- The **power of self-control:** this remained a 'purely' objective standard (only D's sex and age were relevant).

This distinction was confirmed by the House of Lords in *Morhall* [1996] AC 90 and by a majority of the Privy Council in *Luc Thiet Thuan*. In *Smith (Morgan)* [2000] UKHL 49; [2001] 1 AC 146, however, a majority of the House of Lords (Lords Clyde, Hoffmann and Slynn), decided that the objective test should not be divided up in the way suggested by Lord Diplock.

The majority's view

A majority of the Law Lords in *Smith (Morgan)* (2000) decided that to draw a distinction between the two parts of the objective test would be very difficult for juries and thus probably unworkable. Lord Hoffmann described the effect of the distinction as requiring the jury to perform 'mental gymnastics'.

The minority's view

Lord Millett and Lord Hobhouse dissented, and their decisions were described by Professor Sir John Smith as 'completely convincing'. He argued that allowing juries to consider evidence of a depressive illness when deciding on the standard of self-control possessed by the reasonable man effectively eliminated the objective element altogether. The minority view also represents the law in both Canada and Australia. In *Hill* (1986) 25 CCC (3d) 322, the Supreme Court of Canada decided that, whilst certain characteristics of the accused could be attributed to the reasonable man for the purposes of determining the gravity of the provocation, the standard of self-control should be determined simply according to the reasonable man of D's age and sex. This distinction existed 'in order to ensure that in the evaluation of the provocation defence there is no fluctuating standard of self-control against which accused are measured'. To similar effect see the High Court of Australia in *Stingel* (1990) 65 ALJR 141 and *Masciantonio* (1995) 69 ALJR 598.

CASE EXAMPLE

Smith (Morgan) [2000] UKHL 49; [2001] 1 AC 146

D and his old friend, V, had an argument, concerning some tools belonging to D which had gone missing. The argument became heated and, suddenly, D stabbed V in the chest with a kitchen knife. At trial, D pleaded provocation. The trial judge directed the jury that evidence that D suffered a depressive illness was a characteristic that was relevant to the gravity of the provocation but was not relevant to standard of self-control to be expected of the reasonable man. D was convicted of murder and appealed. The Court of Appeal quashed the conviction and a three to two majority of the House of Lords dismissed the Crown's appeal. The question of D's characteristics was relevant not only in assessing the gravity of the provocation, but also the power of self-control to be expected of the reasonable man.

Attributing characteristics to the 'reasonable man'

In *Camplin* (1978), Lord Diplock said that the reasonable man shared 'such of the accused's characteristics as [the jury] think would affect the gravity of the provocation'. Ever since, there has been a constant flow of cases through the Court of Appeal and House of Lords examining this question. Bear in mind as you look at these cases that they were all decided after *Camplin* (1978) and before *Smith (Morgan)* (2000), so the issue was whether the characteristics were capable of affecting the gravity of the provocation (but not whether they were capable of affecting the level of self-control to be expected). The key cases are as follows.

- *Ahluwalia* (1992) (which was considered above in the context of the subjective question). The Court of Appeal considered that battered woman syndrome, a psychological condition caused by years of domestic violence, could be a relevant characteristic because a battered woman might well perceive threats of violence more seriously than a woman who had never suffered physical violence before.

- *Dryden* [1995] 4 All ER 987. The Court of Appeal considered that D's eccentricity and obsessiveness were relevant characteristics which could well have exacerbated the provocation that he had suffered (local government planning officers had attempted to demolish D's self-built bungalow).

- *Humphreys* (1995). The Court of Appeal thought that D's immaturity and attention-seeking traits were relevant characteristics which might have worsened the gravity of the provocation that she had experienced (taunting from V, D's partner and pimp, concerning D's unsuccessful suicide attempt).

- *Morhall* (1996). The House of Lords decided that characteristics may **not** be withdrawn from the jury's consideration simply because they were self-induced (such as, in this case, addiction to glue-sniffing). Lord Goff, with whom the rest of the House agreed, said that the reasonable man shared whichever of D's characteristics were capable of affecting the gravity of the provocation.

You will note that in the first three cases in the above list the characteristics were of a psychological (as opposed to physical) quality. A majority of the Privy Council in *Luc Thiet Thuan* (1997) were highly critical of these decisions because, in their view, it invited confusion between the defences of provocation and diminished responsibility. However, that view did not prevail and the correctness of allowing psychological characteristics to be deemed relevant in provocation was confirmed in *Smith (Morgan)* (2000). This area will be examined below in more detail.

The death of the 'reasonable man'?

As well as abolishing the *Camplin* (1978) distinction, a majority of the House of Lords in *Smith (Morgan)* (2000) made another very significant (and very controversial) change in the law. They held that it was no longer necessary to refer to the reasonable man at all. Lord Clyde said that although s 3 'expressly refers to a reasonable man it does not follow that in directing a jury on provocation a judge must in every case use that particular expression. The substance of the section may well be conveyed without necessarily importing the concept of a reasonable man'. In the same case, Lord Hoffmann said that 'judges should not be required to describe the objective element in the provocation defence by reference to a reasonable man, with or without attribution of personal characteristics'. He added that 'if judges are freed from the necessity of invoking the formula of the reasonable man equipped with an array of unreasonable "eligible characteristics", they will be able to explain the principles in simple terms.' He set out the following guidance for trial judges in future cases (Lord Hoffmann's emphasis):

> **J** 'The general principle is that the same standards of behaviour are expected of everyone, regardless of their individual psychological make-up. In most cases, nothing more will need to be said. But the jury should in an appropriate case be told, in whatever language will best convey the distinction, that this is a principle and not a rigid rule. It may sometimes have to yield to a more important principle, which is to do justice in the particular case. So the jury may think that there was some characteristic of the accused, whether temporary or permanent, which affected the degree of control which society could reasonably have expected of <u>him</u> and which it would be unjust not to take into account. If the jury take this view, they are at liberty to give effect to it.'

Lord Slynn also adopted a formulation which did not refer to 'the reasonable man'. He said that s 3 'requires that the jury should ask what could reasonably be expected of a person with the accused's characteristics'. The Court of Appeal in *Weller* [2003] EWCA Crim 815; [2003] Crim LR 724 developed this new policy. Mantell LJ said that 'there are two elements to the defence of provocation. For present purposes they may be identified as follows: (a) whether [D] lost his self-control; (b) whether he should reasonably have controlled himself'.

ACTIVITY

> Is asking the question 'whether he should reasonably have controlled himself' (Mantell LJ in *Weller*) (2003) the same as asking 'whether the provocation was enough to make a reasonable man do as he did' (Homicide Act 1957, s 3)?

The resurrection of the 'reasonable man' and the restoration of the *Camplin* distinction (2005)

In June 2005, in *Attorney-General for Jersey v Holley* [2005] 2 AC 580; [2005] UKPC 23, an unusually large nine-member Privy Council gave judgment in an appeal from the Court of Appeal of Jersey. The statutory defence of provocation there (Art 4 Homicide (Jersey) Law 1986) is identical to that in the Homicide Act 1957. A majority of the Board (Lords Bingham, Hoffmann and Carswell dissenting) disagreed with *Morgan Smith* (2000) and instead confirmed that the decision in *Luc Thiet Thuan* (1997) was correct. Referring to the majority's view in *Morgan Smith*, Lord Nicholls said:

J 'This majority view ... is one model which could be adopted in framing a law relating to provocation. But their Lordships consider there is one compelling, overriding reason why this view cannot be regarded as an accurate statement of English law ... However much the contrary is asserted, the majority view does represent a departure from the law as declared in s 3 of the Homicide Act 1957. It involves a significant relaxation of the uniform, objective standard adopted by Parliament. Under the statute the sufficiency of the provocation ("whether the provocation was enough to make a reasonable man do as [the defendant] did") is to be judged by one standard, not a standard which varies from defendant to defendant. Whether the provocative act or words and the defendant's response met the "ordinary person" standard prescribed by the statute is the question the jury must consider, not the altogether looser question of whether, having regard to all the circumstances, the jury consider the loss of self-control was sufficiently excusable. The statute does not leave each jury free to set whatever standard they consider appropriate in the circumstances by which to judge whether the defendant's conduct is "excusable". On this short ground their Lordships, respectfully but firmly, consider the majority view expressed in the *Morgan Smith* case is erroneous.'

CASE EXAMPLE

***Attorney-General for Jersey v Holley* [2005] 2 AC 580; [2005] UKPC 23**

D, a chronic alcoholic, lived with his longstanding girlfriend, V, also an alcoholic, in a flat in Jersey. Their relationship was described in court as 'stormy' and frequently violent, with D serving a number of prison sentences for violence against V. On the fateful day the pair of them had been drinking heavily both at home and in a nearby pub. In the late afternoon, D made to leave the flat with an axe, apparently to chop some wood. At this point, V said to him 'You haven't got the guts'. At this, D killed V with the axe. The sole issue at the trial was provocation, which was rejected by the jury, and D was convicted of murder. On appeal, however, the Court of Appeal of Jersey allowed his appeal, on the basis that since the trial the House of Lords in *Morgan Smith* had changed the law of provocation, and substituted a manslaughter conviction.

Following an appeal against that decision by the Attorney-General of Jersey, the Privy Council held that the decision in *Morgan Smith* was wrong. Applying the law as re-stated in *Holley*, Lord Nicholls said that:

J 'evidence that [D] was suffering from chronic alcoholism was **not** a matter to be taken into account by the jury when considering whether in their opinion, having regard to the actual provocation and their view of its gravity, a person having ordinary powers of self-control would have done what [D] did'.

The *Holley* decision has created a conflict in the authorities as, strictly speaking, the Privy Council cannot overrule decisions of the House of Lords. However, in *Mohammed* [2005] EWCA Crim 1880, the Court of Appeal preferred to follow *Holley* in preference to *Morgan Smith*. On the precedent value of *Holley*, Baker LJ said:

J 'Although *Holley* is a decision of the Privy Council, and *Morgan Smith* a decision of the House of Lords, neither side has suggested that the law of England & Wales is other than as set out in the majority opinion given by Lord Nicholls in *Holley* and we have no difficulty in proceeding on that basis . . . the objective yardstick against which the effect of provocation falls to be measured has become tighter. Indeed the law is once again as it used to be before the decision in *Morgan Smith* . . . the standard of self-control to be expected of the reasonable man in s 3 is fixed and not variable. Lord Hoffmann's test of excusability introduced an unwarranted development of the law by the courts'.

CASE EXAMPLE

Mohammed [2005] EWCA Crim 1880

D, a devout Muslim father, returned home one night from his local mosque in Manchester. There he discovered a man, Bilal Amin, in his daughter's bedroom. D went to fetch a knife and returned to the bedroom. Amin was by this time escaping through the bedroom window. D went downstairs and stabbed his daughter, Shahida, to death. The pathologist reported 19 knife injuries. D pleaded provocation and the defence adduced medical evidence that D had suffered from depression since the death of his wife in 2000. They also pointed to his strongly held cultural and religious beliefs (which were that sex before marriage brought shame onto the families of both parties); hence, finding a young man in his daughter's bedroom would be particularly provocative to D as a Muslim man and father. However, despite the fact that the trial judge directed the jury in accordance with the principles established in *Morgan Smith*, D was convicted of murder. The Court of Appeal upheld D's conviction, on the basis that the test in *Morgan Smith* was actually more favourable to the accused than that set out in *Holley*.

More recently, in *James, Karimi* [2006] QB 588; [2006] EWCA Crim 14, a five-member Court of Appeal confirmed that the decision in *Holley* had overruled *Morgan Smith*. Giving the judgment of the appeal court, Phillips LJ said:

> J
>
> 'The rule that this court must always follow a decision of the House of Lords and, indeed, one of its own decisions rather than a decision of the Privy Council is one that was established at a time when no tribunal other than the House of Lords itself could rule that a previous decision of the House of Lords was no longer good law. Once one postulates that there are circumstances in which a decision of the Judicial Committee of the Privy Council can take precedence over a decision of the House of Lords, it seems to us that this court must be bound in those circumstances to prefer the decision of the Privy Council to the prior decision of the House of Lords. That, so it seems to us, is the position that has been reached in the case of these appeals.'

The Court of Appeal did certify two questions for decision by the House of Lords, namely:

(i) Can an opinion of the judicial board of the Privy Council take precedence over an existing opinion of the judicial committee of the House of Lords, and if so, in what circumstances?

(ii) Is the majority of the opinion in *Holley* to be preferred to the majority decision in *Morgan Smith*?

Subsequently, the House of Lords' appeal committee refused leave to appeal. That would seem to confirm once and for all that the decision in *Smith (Morgan)* has been overruled.

CASE EXAMPLE

James, Karimi [2006] QB 588; [2006] EWCA Crim 14

Leslie James killed his wife Jennifer in 1979. She had been repeatedly stabbed, punched and finally suffocated, apparently after an argument. At his trial in 1980 D relied, *inter alia*, on provocation. The judge based his directions to the jury on *Camplin*, and D was convicted of murder. Medical evidence regarding D's ability to control his temper was, therefore, not presented to the jury.

Karimi was a member of the Communist Freedom Fighting Movement in Kurdistan in the early 1980s, where he met the woman who later became his wife. Several years later, the couple had relocated to England but the relationship deteriorated. Subsequently, Mrs Karimi began an affair with a man called Sirvan Kabadi, another former freedom fighter from Kurdistan. One day in December 1996, Karimi went to Kabadi's flat and stabbed him to death in what was described as a 'frenzied attack'. At his murder trial, the judge directed the jury according to *Camplin* and *Morhall*, so that evidence that Karimi was suffering post-traumatic stress disorder caused by his years of fighting in Kurdistan was not adduced in order to assess the level of self-control to be expected of the reasonable man. D was convicted of murder.

After the decision in *Smith (Morgan)*, both cases were referred to the Court of Appeal by the Criminal Cases Review Commission (CCRC) but, by the time the cases reached the appeal court, *Holley* had confirmed that *Camplin* was correct all along. The appeals were dismissed.

The latest case in this now lengthy saga is *Moses* [2006] EWCA Crim 1721. D had drowned V, his girlfriend, in the bath. At his murder trial in 1997 he did not deny killing V but relied on provocation, claiming that V had provoked him by making disparaging remarks about his sexual ability and comparing him unfavourably to another man. However, evidence that D was suffering clinical depression, had an 'over-controlled personality' and was 'particularly sensitive about his masculinity' were not attributed to the reasonable man for the purposes of assessing the level of self-control to be expected of D, as the trial judge based his direction to the jury on the law as it was in 1997 (that is, according to *Camplin* and *Morhall*). D was convicted of murder. After the decision in *Morgan Smith*, however, his case (like those in *James, Karimi*) was referred to the Court of Appeal by the CCRC. Of course, by the time his case reached the appeal court the law as it was in 1997 had not only been confirmed to be correct by the Privy Council in *Holley* but also by the Court of Appeal in *James, Karimi*. The Court of Appeal therefore upheld D's conviction of murder. Thus, the *Camplin* distinction has been restored to English criminal law.

Meanwhile, Australian law of provocation, which is based on English law, avoided all of this upheaval and confusion by simply retaining the *Camplin* distinction throughout. Callinan J in the High Court of Australia in *Heron v R* (2003) said that 'In my opinion an *ordinary* person . . . could not have been induced so far to lose self-control as to intend to kill or inflict GBH . . . One particular requirement [of the provocation defence], the possible reaction of the *hypothetical ordinary* person, is not satisfied here' (emphasis in original).

Are *any* characteristics irrelevant?

Prior to *Smith (Morgan)* (2000), certain characteristics were deemed to be irrelevant even when assessing the gravity of the provocation because they were incompatible with the concept of the 'reasonable man'. In *Camplin* (1978), Lord Simon stated that a trial judge may tell a jury that D is not entitled to rely on 'his exceptional excitability (whether idiosyncratic or by cultural environment or ethnic origin) or pugnacity or ill-temper or on his drunkenness'. Despite the other changes made by the majority in *Smith (Morgan)* (2000), this policy, at least, was confirmed. Lord Clyde stated:

> J 'The standard of reasonableness in this context should refer to a person exercising the ordinary power of self-control over his passions which someone in his position is able to exercise and is expected by society to exercise. By position I mean to include all the characteristics which the particular individual possesses and which may in the circumstances bear on his power of self-control . . . Such characteristics as an exceptional pugnacity or excitability will not suffice. Such tendencies require to be controlled.'

Lord Hoffman also said, albeit *obiter*, that 'male possessiveness and jealousy should not today be an acceptable reason for loss of self-control leading to homicide'.

Should a judge draw the jury's attention to specific characteristics?

Does the trial judge have any obligation to draw the jury's attention to specific characteristics? In *Weller* (2003), D had strangled his girlfriend to death following a heated argument about her conduct with other men. There was evidence that he was unusually possessive and jealous but the trial judge did not draw the jury's attention specifically to these as possible characteristics. D was convicted and the Court of Appeal dismissed the appeal. Mantell LJ said that, ideally, the judge <u>should</u> have directed the jury specifically to those issues, but the crucial point was that she had not excluded them. This was confirmed in *Miah* [2003] EWCA Crim 3713. D had been convicted of murder and appealed, arguing, *inter alia*, that the trial judge had failed to draw the jury's specific attention to three characteristics: that he was young, a man and that he was short (about 5 feet 2 inches tall). The appeal was dismissed. The Court of Appeal held that there was no obligation on a trial judge to draw the jury's attention to specific characteristics. Aitkens J said that 'it is clear from *Smith (Morgan)* (2000), in particular Lord Hoffmann's speech, that provided a judge states that these are matters for the jury to decide then it is for a judge to consider precisely how he puts the matter to the jury.'

Would the reasonable man have lost self-control and done as D did?

At common law there was a requirement that the 'mode of resentment must bear a reasonable relationship to the provocation' (*Mancini v DPP* [1942] AC 1). But, in *Camplin* (1978), the House of Lords declared that this rule could not survive s 3 of the 1957 Act, because otherwise the provision that provocation could arise from words alone would be meaningless. The question for the jury to consider is whether the reasonable man, having lost his self-control, would have done as the defendant did. All of D's behaviour is to be considered; not just the immediate act of killing. This is made clear from the facts of *Clarke* [1991] Crim LR 383. D, having been provoked, head-butted and strangled V. She may have still been alive at this point but D, panicking, electrocuted her as well. The Court of Appeal held the judge had rightly allowed the jury to ignore the electrocution. The jury should consider everything which is not 'too remote', which some factors, such as disposal of the body, might be.

A more recent example of this point occurred in *Van Dongen* [2005] EWCA Crim 1728. D had been convicted of murder and appealed, arguing that a possible defence of provocation had not been left to the jury. The Court of Appeal agreed that there was evidence of provocative conduct from V and loss of self-control by D which meant that, in principle, the defence should have been left to the jury to consider. However, the Court nevertheless upheld D's murder conviction on the basis that the reasonable man would not have reacted to the provocation as the appellant did. In the words of May LJ, D had admitted killing V by kicking him in the head as he lay on the ground 'scrunched up in a foetal position' – this was not something the reasonable man would have done.

The objective test in provocation has been in existence since the nineteenth century. However, it has undergone a remarkable metamorphosis in that time. The following table summarises the developments since before the Homicide Act 1957 to the present day.

Key facts: the 'reasonable man' test in provocation

KEY FACTS

Case	Year	Decision	Comment
Bedder (1954)	1954	The reasonable man is an adult, sharing none of D's characteristics.	A 'purely' objective test, this is seen as very harsh now and was overruled by *Camplin* (1978).
Camplin (1978)	1978	The reasonable man 'shares' those characteristics with D which affect the gravity of the provocation. Splits the test into two sub-questions: gravity of the provocation and level of self-control.	First move towards softening the objectivity of the test. The *Camplin* (1978) distinction that the gravity of the provocation and level of self-control are separate issues means that the latter remains 'purely' objective (only sex and age relevant).
Dryden (1995) *Humphreys* (1995)	1995	Characteristics may be psychological as well as physical.	Further softening of the objectivity of the test. Risks confusion with DR.

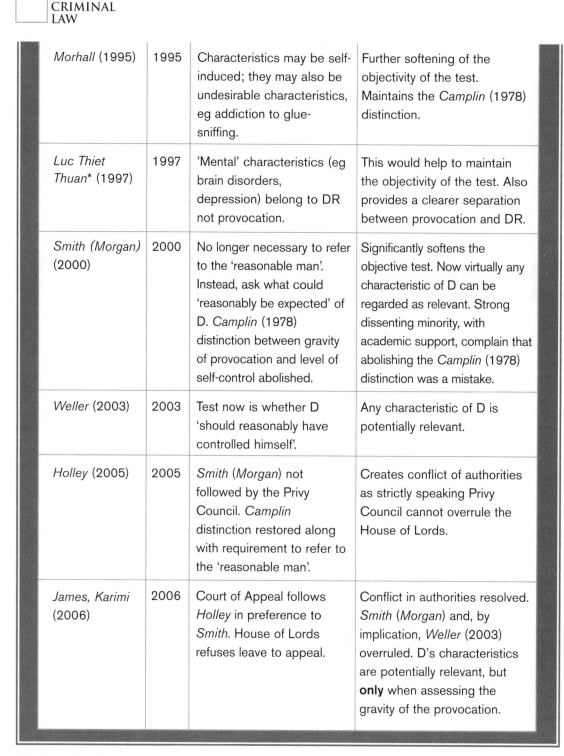

Morhall (1995)	1995	Characteristics may be self-induced; they may also be undesirable characteristics, eg addiction to glue-sniffing.	Further softening of the objectivity of the test. Maintains the *Camplin* (1978) distinction.
Luc Thiet Thuan* (1997)	1997	'Mental' characteristics (eg brain disorders, depression) belong to DR not provocation.	This would help to maintain the objectivity of the test. Also provides a clearer separation between provocation and DR.
Smith (Morgan) (2000)	2000	No longer necessary to refer to the 'reasonable man'. Instead, ask what could 'reasonably be expected' of D. *Camplin* (1978) distinction between gravity of provocation and level of self-control abolished.	Significantly softens the objective test. Now virtually any characteristic of D can be regarded as relevant. Strong dissenting minority, with academic support, complain that abolishing the *Camplin* (1978) distinction was a mistake.
Weller (2003)	2003	Test now is whether D 'should reasonably have controlled himself'.	Any characteristic of D is potentially relevant.
Holley (2005)	2005	*Smith (Morgan)* not followed by the Privy Council. *Camplin* distinction restored along with requirement to refer to the 'reasonable man'.	Creates conflict of authorities as strictly speaking Privy Council cannot overrule the House of Lords.
James, Karimi (2006)	2006	Court of Appeal follows *Holley* in preference to *Smith*. House of Lords refuses leave to appeal.	Conflict in authorities resolved. *Smith (Morgan)* and, by implication, *Weller* (2003) overruled. D's characteristics are potentially relevant, but **only** when assessing the gravity of the provocation.

*Privy Council decision so persuasive only. Not followed in *Smith* (2000).

Criticism of the provocation defence

In October 2003, the Law Commission published a Consultation Paper, *Partial Defences to Murder* (No 173), which identified several criticisms that may be made of the provocation defence. The Commission observed that the issue of the 'reasonable man' has been before the House of Lords or Privy Council four times since 1978, 'culminating in *Smith (Morgan)* (2000) with a 3:2 split. This demonstrates fundamental problems with the concept of the reasonable man'. However, that is not the only problem. The paper states that the 'moral, theoretical and practical difficulties go beyond the reasonable man test . . . its present state is both unclear and unsatisfactory'. Other, specific criticisms made included:

- Provocative conduct now has a very wide meaning. The paper cites *Doughty* (1986) as an authority for the proposition that entirely innocent behaviour can support the defence. This, the Commission says, 'is contrary to one of the fundamental rationales of the defence, which is that [V] contributed to [D]'s lethal loss of temper'.

- Anger is elevated to a status higher than other emotions such as fear, despair, compassion or empathy. According to the paper it is morally questionable that killings following loss of temper should be dealt with as manslaughter but not killings caused by fear, despair and so on.

- The 'sudden and temporary loss of control' criterion is flawed. It makes the defence biased in favour of male defendants, who react to provocation 'in violent anger' as opposed to female defendants, who are more likely to 'kill with premeditation from fear rather than rage'.

- The defence has been stretched by the courts over the last 10 years to accommodate 'slow burn' killings in domestic abuse cases, such that it is now difficult to exclude revenge killings from the scope of the defence.

Reform of the provocation defence

In its 2003 Paper, the Law Commission suggested two broad options for reform: abolition, and modification.

Abolition

The Paper pointed out that the defence of provocation is anomalous because it exists only as a defence to murder. Its original justification was to give judges some discretion in murder cases at a time when the death sentence was inevitable. Although the death sentence was abolished in 1965, it has been replaced with a mandatory life sentence. The rationale for having the defence at all disappears if the mandatory life sentence for murder were to be abolished. It is also objectionable because it results in D being convicted of one offence (manslaughter), despite having the *mens rea* of another offence (murder). Against abolition, the Paper conceded that there is at least one other justification for the defence: fair labelling. D who kills having lost self-control arguably does not deserve to be labelled a murderer alongside those who kill deliberately and in a pre-meditated way.

Modification of the provocation defence

In cl 58 of the Draft Criminal Code (1989), the Law Commission had proposed a new definition of provocation, as follows.

C '58 A person who, but for this section, would be guilty of murder is not guilty of murder if (a) he acts when provoked (whether by things done or said or by both and whether by the deceased person or by another) to lose his self-control; and (b) the provocation is, in all the circumstances (including any of his personal characteristics that affect its gravity) sufficient ground for the loss of self-control.'

The Law Commission's 2003 Paper did not suggest a definition of provocation. Rather, the Paper listed a variety of reforms designed to improve the working of the defence, as follows:

- Tightening up what may amount to provocative conduct. For example, in the Canadian Criminal Code there must have been a 'wrongful act or insult'.

- Abolition of the criterion of sudden and temporary loss of self-control. Instead, the criterion could be that D killed under 'extreme emotional disturbance', which is used in the American Law Institute's Model Penal Code (1985). The Commission conceded that this could be given a 'very wide interpretation. Many, if not most, people who kill are in a heightened emotional state about something'. It could also lead to the defence being extended to 'activists who kill over social issues such as abortion or animal rights, about which they may be passionate and obsessive'.

- Abolition of the objective limb. Given the volume and complexity of the case law generated over the years concerning this limb, it is not surprising that the Commission considered this reform. The paper cited as a supporting authority for this reform the minority judgment of Murphy J in the South Australian case of *Moffa* (1977) 138 CLR 601. He argued that the objective limb was unsuitable in a heterogeneous society, pointing out that 'behaviour is influenced by age, sex, ethnic origin, climatic and other living conditions, biorhythms, education, occupation and, above all, individual differences.' An argument against this reform is that the jury would be left with no choice but to acquit of murder an exceptionally bad-tempered individual who had lost his self-control over some trivial incident and killed; but convict of murder a calm and self-controlled person who had withstood immense pressure before finally killing. For this reason, the Commission cannot support it, because it 'would involve an unjustified lowering of standards'.

- Denial of the defence where D formed an intent to kill (leaving it available in those cases where D formed an intent to do really serious harm). This would remove the 'anomaly' that provocation is not available to attempted murder (for which the *mens rea* is an intent to kill). Against this is the moral difficulty in separating cases where D formed an intent to kill from cases where he 'only' formed an intent to do really serious harm. Also, it ignores the gravity of the provocation: the more extreme the provocation, the more likely that D formed an intention to kill, but also the less likely that he would be entitled to the defence.

- Denial of the defence where the provocation was self-induced. This would reverse the ruling in *Johnson* (1989).

- Reversal of the burden of proof. This would bring provocation into line with diminished responsibility (DR) by placing the burden of proof on D. An alternative reform could be to reverse the burden of proof in cases of DR to bring that defence into line with provocation by placing the burden of proof on the prosecution.

ACTIVITY

Is the Law Commission's 1989 definition of provocation (in the Draft Criminal Code) an improvement on the 1957 definition (in the Homicide Act)? Which (if any) of the 2003 proposals for modification of the defence would you adopt?

The Law Commission's 2003 paper did not actually suggest a definition of provocation but invited feedback on its suggestions for reform. The vast majority of the responses to consultation indicated widespread support for the retention of provocation, albeit not necessarily in its present state. In August 2004, therefore, the Commission proposed a radical new definition of provocation in its Final Report, *Partial Defences to Murder*. The Commission essentially repeated this definition in its paper on homicide, *A New Homicide Act for England & Wales?* (Law Commission Consultation Paper No 177), published in December 2005, and again in its Final Report, *Murder, Manslaughter and Infanticide* (Law Com No 304), published in November 2006. The latest version is as follows:

1. Unlawful homicide that would otherwise be first degree murder should instead be second degree murder if:

(a) D acted in response to

(i) gross provocation (meaning words or conduct or a combination of words and conduct) which caused D to have a justifiable sense of being seriously wronged; or

(ii) fear of serious violence towards D or another; or

(iii) a combination of both (i) and (ii); and

(b) a person of D's age and of ordinary temperament, that is, ordinary tolerance and self-restraint, in the circumstances of the defendant might have reacted in the same or in a similar way.

2. In deciding whether a person of D's age and of ordinary temperament … in the circumstances of D, might have reacted in the same or a similar way, the court should take into account D's age and all the circumstances of D other than matters whose only relevance to D's conduct is that they bear simply on his or her general capacity for self-control.

3. The partial defence should **not** apply where

(a) the provocation was incited by D for the purpose of providing an excuse to use violence, or

(b) D acted in considered desire for revenge.

4. A person should <u>not</u> be treated as having acted in considered desire for revenge if he or she acted in fear of serious violence, merely because he was also angry towards the deceased for the conduct which engendered that fear.

5. A judge should not be required to leave the defence to the jury unless there is evidence on which a reasonable jury, properly directed, could conclude that it might apply.

There are several points to note here.

- **Redefinition of murder.** The Law Commission proposes to divide murder into first and second degree murder, with provocation operating as a defence to first degree murder only, reducing liability, if successful, down to second degree murder. See further section 9.8.

- **Evidence of provocation** (the Law Commission call this the 'trigger') would have to be 'gross' – which would rule out crying babies, as in *Doughty* (1986), or the refusal of retrospective planning permission, as in *Dryden* (1995). 'Gross' means 'serious', as opposed to 'disgusting'.

- **The subjective limb.** In the proposed definition, there is no requirement of a loss of self-control at all, let alone one which is 'sudden and temporary'. The *Duffy* test – confirmed in *Thornton* (1992), *Ahluwalia* (1992), etc – would therefore be abolished. This would clearly benefit victims of domestic violence who undergo a 'slow burn' reaction. The new test would be 'a justifiable sense of being seriously wronged' – presumably a question of fact for a jury, but one which would almost inevitably lead to appeals to clarify its precise meaning and scope.

- **Providing an excuse to use violence.** The defence could not be used where D deliberately set up a situation where V would respond with provocation.

- **Considered desire for revenge.** Similarly, the defence would be disallowed in cases where D acted in 'revenge'. This would mean that the defendants in cases such as *Ibrams & Gregory* (1981) would still have no defence.

- **The objective limb.** The new definition's objective limb was based on the minority view in *Morgan Smith* (2000) and now the majority view in *Holley* (2005), in that it disallows characteristics whose only relevance is in respect of D's self-control. However, 'D's age and all the circumstances of D' could be taken into account in assessing what we presently refer to as the 'gravity' of the provocation. In other words, the *Camplin* distinction is confirmed.

- **Excessive force in self-defence.** The reference to D acting in response to 'fear of serious violence towards D or another' is designed to introduce a partial defence to first degree murder where D used excessive force in self-defence (or in defending another person) – presently the use of excessive force in self-defence is no defence at all to murder as a result of the House of Lords' decision in *Clegg* (1995) – see Chapter 8.

- **Extreme emotional disturbance.** The majority of those who took part in consultation were unhappy with this idea (first suggested in 2003) and the Law Commission now concede that it is too vague and have dropped it from their latest definition.

Key facts on provocation

KEY FACTS

	Law	Section/case
Definition	Evidence on which the jury can find that the person charged was provoked (whether by things done or by things said or by both together) to lose his self control.	s 3 Homicide Act 1957
Examples of provocation	• The continual crying of a 19-day-old baby. • Physical assaults, both on the defendant or on his relatives. • Supplying drugs to the defendant's son. • A denial of stealing the defendant's tools.	*Doughty* (1986) *Pearson* (1992) *Baillie* (1995) *Smith (Morgan)* (2000)
Loss of self-control	There must be a sudden and temporary loss of self-control, so that D is not master of his mind. A time lapse may negative this. It must be sudden but need not be immediate.	*Duffy* (1949) *Ibrams and Gregory* (1981) *Thornton (No 1)* (1992) *Ahluwalia* (1992)
Reasonable man test	Was the provocation enough to make a reasonable man do as D did? Take into consideration age and sex of D and any other relevant characteristics when assessing the gravity of the provocation. Characteristics may be self-induced. Characteristics may be psychological as well as physical.	s 3 Homicide Act 1957 *Camplin* (1978); *Holley* (2005) *Morhall* (1996) *Ahluwalia* (1992); *Dryden* (1995)
Effect of defence	The charge of murder is reduced to manslaughter.	s 3 Homicide Act 1957

9.3.3 Relationship between provocation and diminished responsibility

It is clear from several of the above cases that characteristics may be psychological, as opposed to physical, and yet still relevant in the context of the provocation defence (battered woman syndrome in *Ahluwalia* (1992), obsessiveness in *Dryden* (1995), immaturity and attention-seeking in *Humphreys* (1995), depressive illness in *Smith (Morgan)* (2000)). This raises a potential difficulty concerning the relationship between provocation (where the burden of proof is on the prosecution to disprove the defence beyond reasonable doubt) and DR (where the burden of proof is on the defence to prove the case on the balance of probabilities). However, when Lord Taylor CJ addressed this point in *Thornton (No 2)* [1996] 1 WLR 1174, he was forthright:

> J
> 'What characteristics of a defendant should be attributed by the jury to the notional reasonable person and how far the judge should go in assisting the jury to identify those characteristics are issues which have been clarified in a number of decisions . . . *Ahluwalia*, *Humphreys* and *Morhall* make clear that mental as well as physical characteristics should be taken into account.'

In *Luc Thiet Thuan* (1997), a majority of the Privy Council disagreed with this line of cases and held that mental characteristics should not be relevant in the context of provocation but should be left exclusively to DR. Their reasoning was that to allow D to rely on mental characteristics in the context of provocation undermined DR and subverted Parliament's intention. Lord Goff, giving the majority opinion, stated that, by allowing mental characteristics to be considered in the context of provocation:

> J
> 'the extraordinary result would be that a defendant who failed to establish diminished responsibility on the burden of proof placed upon him by s 2 . . . might nevertheless be able to succeed on the defence of provocation on the basis that, on precisely the same evidence, the prosecution had failed to negative, on the criminal burden, that he was suffering from a mental infirmity affecting his self-control which must be attributed to the reasonable man for the purposes of the objective test.'

In *Smith (Morgan)* (2000), the House of Lords rejected Lord Goff's analysis and decided that mental characteristics could be taken into account in assessing **both** the gravity of the provocation to the reasonable man **and** the level of self-control to be expected. Since then, the Privy Council in *Holley* (2005) has effectively overruled *Smith (Morgan)* and made it clear that no characteristics, whether mental or physical, other than age and sex, are relevant when assessing the level of self-control to be expected of the reasonable man.

However, it is very important to appreciate, even after *Holley*, that characteristics of the accused – both mental and physical – are potentially relevant when assessing the gravity of the provocation. There are two circumstances in which such characteristics may be relevant.

- First, when the characteristics are the target of the provocation. In *Holley* itself, Lord Nicholls stated that 'mental infirmity of the defendant, if itself the subject of taunts by the deceased, may be taken into account as going to the gravity of the provocation'.

- Second, where the characteristics are not the target of the provocation but their very existence exacerbates its gravity. In *Holley*, Lord Nicholls decided that the decisions in cases such as *Ahluwalia* (1992) were correct in allowing psychological characteristics (such as battered woman syndrome) to be attributed to the reasonable man (or woman) for the purposes of assessing gravity, even where those characteristics were not the subject of taunts.

This means that the concerns expressed by Lord Goff in *Luc Thiet Thuan* (1997) are still pertinent – there is a potentially confusing overlap between the defences of provocation and DR. Indeed, in *Holley*, Lord Nicholls did not deny this; if anything he seemed to embrace it. Referring to the 'battered woman syndrome' type of case, he said:

> **J** 'The evidence of the woman's condition may be relevant on two issues: whether she lost her self-control, and the gravity of the provocation for her. The jury will then decide whether, having regard to the actual provocation and their view of its gravity for D, a woman of her age having ordinary power of self-control might have done what D did. More importantly . . . D will in principle have available to her the defence of DR. The potential availability of this defence . . . underlines the importance of not viewing the defence of provocation in isolation from the defence of DR. These two defences must be read together to obtain an overall, balanced view of the law in this field.'

Because of the overlap that undoubtedly exists between the two defences, two leading academics have suggested that it might be sensible to merge them into a single partial defence to murder. Professors Mackay and Mitchell, 'Provoking Diminished Responsibility: Two Pleas Merging into One?' [2003] Crim LR 745 took as their starting point the American Law Institute's Model Penal Code (1985), which states:

> 'A homicide which would otherwise be murder [is manslaughter when it] is committed under the influence of extreme mental or emotional disturbance for which there is reasonable explanation or excuse. The reasonableness of such explanation or excuse shall be determined from the viewpoint of a person in the actor's situation under the circumstances as he believes them to be.'

The Mackay and Mitchell model would allow a partial defence to murder if D killed whilst (a) under the influence of extreme emotional disturbance and/or (b) suffering from unsoundness of mind, either or both of which affected his criminal behaviour to such a material degree that the offence ought to be reduced to one of manslaughter. The Law Commission's Consultation Paper, *Partial Defences to Murder* (Law Com No 173), considered arguments for and against this proposal. They listed several arguments in favour:

1. The provocation defence has expanded to such an extent that it is now practically impossible to disentangle the two defences.

2. When both defences are advanced together (which often happens), it requires trial judges to give complex directions to the jury.

3. Both defences are concerned with those who kill when in a disturbed state of mind.

4. There is 'logic and justice' in allowing a jury to decide whether extreme emotional disturbance and/or abnormality of mind justified reducing D's liability from murder to manslaughter.

The Law Commission also listed a number of arguments against a unified partial defence:

1. DR and provocation are 'fundamentally different' defences with different rationales and elements. Provocation operates as an excuse for those who do wrong but understandably so; DR is a partial denial of responsibility.

2. The fact that a given set of circumstances may support both defences does not mean the two defences should be merged. Rather, it simply demonstrates that the defences are not mutually exclusive.

3. A single defence would 'lack a clear boundary' and be 'unacceptably wide'.

ACTIVITY

> Discuss whether DR and provocation should be merged. If so, should the single partial defence be worded as formulated by Professors Mackay and Mitchell?

In the Law Commission's *Partial Defences to Murder* Final Report, published in August 2004, the Commission stated that it did not support the idea of merging provocation and DR, on the basis that, although the suggestion had 'stimulated a lively debate', the majority of academic comment following the 2003 paper did not support it (see further reading list at the end of this chapter).

9.3.4 Suicide pacts

Section 4(1) of the Homicide Act 1957 provides that the survivor of a suicide pact (where the other party to the pact is killed by D) is not guilty of murder but guilty of voluntary manslaughter. Section 4(3) defines a 'suicide pact' as 'a common agreement between two or more persons having for its object the death of all of them'. The burden of proof is on D on the balance of probabilities.

9.4 Involuntary manslaughter

9.4.1 Constructive manslaughter

D will be guilty of manslaughter if he kills by an unlawful and dangerous act. The following elements must be proven to exist:

- D must commit an unlawful act (in the sense of a crime)
- that act must have caused death
- D must have possessed the mental element for the unlawful act to amount to a criminal offence
- the act must be 'dangerous'.

The requirement of an unlawful act

At one time it was thought that it was sufficient if D committed a civil wrong (a tort), such as in *Fenton* (1830) 1 Lew CC 179, where D was convicted of manslaughter on the basis that he had committed the unlawful act of trespass to property. This approach quickly changed and the law now requires that D commit a criminal offence. In *Franklin* (1883) 15 Cox CC 163, the court stated that 'The mere fact of a civil wrong committed by one person against another ought not to be used as an incident which is a necessary step in a criminal case.' If there is no criminal offence, then there is no possibility of a manslaughter conviction (regardless of how 'dangerous' D's acts may have been). The leading case is *Lamb* [1967] 2 QB 981.

ASE EXAMPLE

Lamb [1967] 2 QB 981

D shot his best friend, V, with a Smith & Wesson revolver. The shooting was accidental; neither D nor V foresaw any risk of the gun firing when D pulled the trigger. Although the gun was loaded, in that there were two bullets in the five-chamber cylinder, there were no bullets in the chamber opposite the barrel. Critically, neither man appreciated that the cylinder revolved before the hammer struck the back of the mechanism. Consequently, V did not apprehend any possibility of injury being caused to himself, and therefore the *actus reus* of assault had not been performed. The Court of Appeal quashed D's conviction. Sachs LJ said that D's act was not 'unlawful in the criminal sense of the word'.

Similarly, in *Jennings* [1990] Crim LR 588, where D had been convicted of manslaughter on the basis that his act of carrying an uncovered knife in the street was unlawful, the Court of Appeal quashed his conviction. Because there was no proof that he had any intent to cause injury (which would have amounted to a crime under s 1 of the Prevention of Crime Act 1953), simply walking along with the knife was 'not a criminal offence which could constitute the unlawful act for this

341

purpose'. The criminal act could, for example, be any of the following:

- assault (*Larkin* [1943] 1 All ER 217; *Lamb* [1967] 2 QB 981; *Mallet* [1972] Crim LR 260)

- battery (*Church* [1965] 2 All ER 72; *Mitchell* [1983] QB 741)

- criminal damage (*DPP v Newbury and Jones* [1977] AC 500)

- arson (*Goodfellow* [1986] Crim LR 468; *Willoughby* [2004] EWCA Crim 3365; [2005] 1 WLR 1880)

- robbery (*Dawson* (1985) 81 Cr App R 150)

- burglary (*Watson* [1989] 2 All ER 865)

- affray (*Carey & Others* [2006] EWCA Crim 17)

- cruelty to a person under 16 (*Gay* [2006] EWCA Crim 820).

In *Gay* [2006] EWCA Crim 820, the Court of Appeal quashed manslaughter convictions against a couple, Angela and Ian Gay, who had been convicted of killing their three-year-old adopted son, Christian, by poisoning him with salt (although a retrial was ordered) after the Court heard medical evidence that the boy may have had an unusual intolerance towards salt. Nowhere in the judgment is it specified which type of manslaughter formed the basis of the conviction, although constructive manslaughter seems the most likely. In the words of Richards LJ: 'The charge of manslaughter was put on alternative bases . . . The second was that the death was caused by the high sodium concentration in Christian's blood, which in turn had been caused by the unlawful administration of salt by the appellants: the evidence was that Christian would have had to ingest 30–40 grams of salt, or at least four-and-a-half teaspoonfuls, to account for such a high level of sodium.' Thus, according to Richards LJ, the administration of salt was 'unlawful'. But why was it unlawful? The Court does not actually explicitly identify what underlying criminal offence was committed by the appellants, although the most likely is cruelty to a person under 16 (s 1 Children and Young Persons Act 1933). This was actually on the indictment as an alternative to manslaughter but no verdict was reached.

A series of cases involving the injection of heroin leading to fatal overdose have caused the courts problems. There are two difficulties, the first of which is identifying the unlawful act. The offence most often used is 'maliciously administering a noxious substance' contrary to s 23 OAPA 1861 (see Chapter 10 for details). If D injects V with heroin, D is guilty of the s 23 offence. If V dies as a result, then D is guilty of manslaughter. This was the case in *Cato* [1976] 1 All ER 260, where D and V had injected each other with a mixture of heroin and water which each man prepared for himself. V subsequently died of an overdose. The Court of Appeal upheld D's manslaughter conviction. The s 23 offence was also used as the basis (or in some cases, one of two possible bases) of manslaughter convictions in these cases:

- *Dalby* [1982] 1 All ER 916 (here the drug was D's prescription diconal tablets)

- *Kennedy* [1998] EWCA Crim 2545; [1999] Crim LR 65 (heroin)

- *Dias* [2001] EWCA Crim 2986; [2002] 2 Cr App R 96 (heroin)
- *Rogers* [2003] EWCA Crim 945; [2003] 1 WLR 1374 (heroin).

In *Kennedy* (1999), the Court of Appeal thought that there was an alternative basis for upholding D's manslaughter conviction. D had provided V with a heroin-filled syringe which V then used to inject himself (and then died of an overdose). The Court described V's self-injection of heroin as an unlawful act, and because D had assisted and encouraged V, then that too was an unlawful act. That view was held to be wrong in *Dias* (2001). This case involved very similar facts to *Kennedy* (1999), and the trial judge had directed the jury to convict if satisfied that D had assisted V to inject himself with heroin. The Court of Appeal quashed the conviction, holding that the self-administration of any substance (including prohibited drugs such as heroin) is not a crime under English law. Thus, simply assisting someone to inject themselves is not an illegal act either and cannot be used to support the crime of manslaughter. D's conviction in *Dias* (2001) was therefore quashed. The decision in *Dias* was then applied by the Court of Appeal in *Richards* [2002] EWCA Crim 3175. D, who had supplied a heroin-filled syringe to V who injected himself and died, had been convicted of manslaughter by a jury after the trial judge directed them, following *Kennedy* (1999), that the self-injection of heroin by V was an unlawful act which D had assisted or encouraged. The Court of Appeal quashed the conviction.

Omissions as unlawful 'acts'

Given that constructive manslaughter requires an unlawful and dangerous 'act', it follows that if D simply omits to act, he cannot be guilty of manslaughter under this head. In *Lowe* [1973] QB 702, Phillimore J said:

> **J** 'If I strike a child in a manner likely to cause harm it is right that if the child dies I may be charged with manslaughter. If, however, I omit to do something, with the result that it suffers injury to its health which results in its death, we think that a charge of manslaughter should not be an inevitable consequence even if the omission is deliberate.'

CASE EXAMPLE

Lowe [1973] QB 702

D was convicted of both neglecting his child so as to cause it unnecessary suffering or injury to its health contrary to s 1(1) of the Children and Young Persons Act 1933 and constructive manslaughter. The trial judge had directed the jury that if they found D guilty of the s 1 offence they had to find him also guilty of manslaughter. The Court of Appeal quashed his manslaughter conviction.

Causation

The second issue which has caused difficulty in the drugs cases above is causation. As a general proposition in constructive manslaughter cases, the normal rules of causation described in Chapter 2 apply (*Pagett* [1983] Crim LR 393). Hence, in *Mitchell* (1983) (the facts of which were described in Chapter 2), there was no break in the chain of causation because it was reasonably foreseeable that pushing an elderly man in a crowded post office could cause him to fall and knock over someone else. Similarly, in *Goodfellow* (1986), where D set fire to his council house (hoping to be rehoused) and ended up killing his wife, two-year-old son and another woman, all of whom were in the house at the time, the Court of Appeal upheld his conviction. The deaths were reasonably foreseeable. There was no problem in *Cato* (1976) on this point, because D's unlawful act of injecting V directly caused V's overdose and death. However, the Court of Appeal quashed D's conviction because of a break in the chain of causation in *Dalby* [1982] 1 All ER 916. D gave some of his prescribed diconal tablets to V, who proceeded to take them in a highly dangerous form and quantity, overdosed and died. D was convicted of manslaughter but the Court of Appeal allowed the appeal. Although the supply of the drugs to V constituted the offence under s 23 OAPA 1861, V's self-administration of the tablets broke the chain of causation.

It would seem that, on the authority of *Dalby* (1982), the conviction in *Kennedy* (1999) based on s 23 OAPA 1861 should have been quashed on the same basis. However, the Court of Appeal found that the chain of causation remained unbroken in *Rogers* (2003). D obtained some heroin for himself and V in two syringes. First V injected D using one syringe, then D held a belt around V's arm to act as a tourniquet while V injected himself with the other syringe. V overdosed and died a few days later. At D's manslaughter trial, D pleaded guilty after the judge ruled that the application of the tourniquet was 'part and parcel' of the administration of a noxious substance (the s 23 offence). D appealed, arguing that, although he had supplied heroin, V had injected himself (thus no chain of causation, as in *Dalby* (1982)). Moreover, V's self-injection was not illegal (following *Dias* (2001)) and so the application of the tourniquet was not a crime either. Therefore, D had committed no unlawful act. However, the Court of Appeal dismissed the appeal, holding that D had played an 'active' part in the 'injection process' and therefore he had committed both the offence under s 23 and manslaughter. The commentary to the case is critical, arguing that the chain of causation was broken by V's self-injection of the heroin: 'the final and overwhelmingly independent act of injection [was] still performed voluntarily by V' ([2003] Crim LR at 556).

In *Kennedy (No. 2)* [2005] 1 WLR 2159; [2005] EWCA Crim 685, the facts of which were given above (see *Kennedy* (1999)), the Court of Appeal dismissed D's second appeal. The issue this time was whether the self-administration of heroin by V had broken the chain of causation. The Court decided that it had been open to the jury to convict D of manslaughter. To convict, the jury had to be satisfied that when the heroin was handed to V 'for immediate injection', D and V were both engaged in one activity of administering the heroin. The appeal judge had been right when he concluded that the critical question for the jury was whether D could be said to be jointly responsible for the carrying out of the act causative of death. In the instant case, the jury were entitled to find that D and V, who were carrying out a combined operation, were jointly engaged in administering the heroin. If D and V were acting in concert in administering the heroin, it was inevitable that the unlawful act of administering a noxious substance contrary to s 23 OAPA 1861 was causative of V's death.

The mental element

While an unlawful act is essential in constructive manslaughter cases, D must also possess the mental element which combines with the unlawful act to constitute a criminal offence. Hence, another ground for allowing D's appeal in *Lamb* (1967), above, was the fact that D (as well as V) did not appreciate that the chamber of the revolver would rotate prior to firing. Therefore, D did not appreciate any risk of the gun firing and, hence, did not possess the mental element of assault (intention or subjective recklessness as to causing force to be applied to V). It appears that this requirement only applies if there is a mental element required for the underlying criminal offence. In *Andrews* [2002] EWCA Crim 3021; [2003] Crim LR 477, the Court of Appeal upheld a manslaughter conviction based on s 58(2)(b) of the Medicines Act 1968, which states that 'no person shall administer any [specified] medicinal product unless he is an appropriate practitioner or a person acting in accordance with the directions of an appropriate practitioner'. This is a strict liability offence; that is, there is no requirement that D be proven to have formed any particular mental element with respect to the elements of the *actus reus*. D had given V, and others, insulin injections to give them a 'rush'. V, who was under-nourished and had been drinking, died. D's appeal was based on the fact that V had consented, but this was dismissed. (You will recall from reading cases such as *Brown and others* [1994] AC 212 in Chapter 8 that, for public policy reasons, consent is restricted in all situations where V runs the risk of suffering at least actual bodily harm, as in this case.) It is important to note that there is no further mental element for constructive manslaughter. In *DPP v Newbury and Jones* (1977), the House of Lords explicitly held that there was no requirement that D foresee that his acts may cause death or even injury.

Dangerousness

In *Church* (1965) (the facts of which appeared in Chapter 3 in the context of the requirement of coincidence of *actus reus* and *mens rea*), the Court of Criminal Appeal laid down a requirement that D's act had to be dangerous (this is in addition to the acts being unlawful). Edmund Davies J, giving judgment for the court, imposed an objective standard for assessing dangerousness:

> J 'An unlawful act causing the death of another cannot, simply because it is an unlawful act, render a manslaughter verdict inevitable. For such a verdict inexorably to follow, the unlawful act must be such as all sober and reasonable people would inevitably recognise must subject the other person to, at least, the risk of some harm resulting therefrom, albeit not serious harm.'

The courts approach this test by asking whether a hypothetical 'sober and reasonable' bystander, who happened to be watching the unlawful act, would regard the act as dangerous. The fact that this is an objective test was emphasised by the Court of Appeal in *Ball* [1989] Crim LR 730.

CASE EXAMPLE

Ball [1989] Crim LR 730

D, who had been involved in a dispute with his neighbour, V, grabbed a handful of cartridges which he loaded into his shotgun and fired at her. V was killed and D was charged with murder. He was acquitted as the jury accepted that he honestly thought the cartridges were blanks. However, his conviction of manslaughter was upheld. The bystander would have regarded D's act of firing a loaded shotgun at V as dangerous. Moreover, the 'sober and reasonable' bystander would not have made D's mistake of thinking the cartridges were blanks.

The jury is entitled to ascribe to the bystander D's pre-existing knowledge about V (if any), including any knowledge which D acquires during the commission of the unlawful act. This is illustrated by the case of *Watson* (1989).

CASE EXAMPLE

Watson [1989] 2 All ER 865

D burgled the house of an 87-year-old man, V. A brick was thrown through a window to gain access and this alerted V, who came down to investigate. There was a confrontation between D and V during which V was verbally abused. D left without stealing anything but V died of a heart attack 90 minutes later. D pleaded guilty to burglary but was also convicted of manslaughter. The Court of Appeal allowed D's appeal against the latter conviction (on causation grounds) but was satisfied that the jury was entitled to find that the burglary was dangerous.

Lord Lane CJ stated:

> 'The judge clearly took the view that the jury were entitled to ascribe to the bystander the knowledge which [D] gained during the whole of his stay in the house and so directed them. Was this a misdirection? In our judgment it was not. The unlawful act in the present circumstances comprised the whole of the burglarious intrusion . . . That being so, D (and therefore the bystander) during the course of the unlawful act must have become aware of [V]'s frailty and approximate age, and the judge's directions were accordingly correct.'

The decision in *Watson* (1989) should be contrasted with that in *Dawson* (1985). D and another man carried out an armed robbery of a petrol station whilst masked and armed with pickaxe handles and replica guns. The attendant, V, was 60 years old. He also had a heart condition and died of a heart attack. The Court of Appeal held this was not manslaughter – neither D nor the 'sober and reasonable' bystander would have been aware of this condition.

ACTIVITY

Do you agree that the convictions in *Dawson* (1985) should have been quashed? How does the approach of the Court of Appeal in this case compare with the decision of the same Court in *Blaue* [1975] 3 All ER 446 (considered in Chapter 2), that D must take their victim as they find them?

In *Carey & Others* [2006] EWCA Crim 17, a 15-year-old girl, Aimee Wellock, had run away from the three defendants after being punched and threatened with further violence, but had collapsed after running about 100 metres and died of an undiagnosed heart complaint aggravated by the running. The defendants were convicted of affray and constructive manslaughter but their manslaughter convictions were quashed on appeal. The Court of Appeal held that the count of constructive manslaughter should have been withdrawn from the jury as the only physical harm to V (a single punch) did not cause her death. Although there were other threats of violence in the course of the affray they were not dangerous, inasmuch as a reasonable person would not have foreseen their causing any physical harm to V.

> 'In considering whether the unlawful act is dangerous in the context of manslaughter, it may be relevant to have regard to the attributes of the victim. Of course, a punch which causes a person to fall will almost inevitably satisfy the test of dangerousness.'

'Harm'

According to the *Church* (1965) test, V must be subjected to 'the risk of some harm'. In *Reid* (1975) 62 Cr App R 109, Lawton LJ thought that 'the very least kind of harm is causing fright by threats', but the court thought that as D was armed, the act was likely to cause death or serious injury and therefore was dangerous. In *Dawson* (1985), Watkins LJ said that 'a proper direction would have been that the requisite harm is caused if the unlawful act so shocks the victim as to cause him physical injury.' Thus, merely frightening or shocking V is insufficient; the trauma must produce some physical injury.

Key facts on unlawful act manslaughter

KEY FACTS

Elements	Comment	Cases
Unlawful act	Must be a crime.	*Lamb* (1967)
	A civil wrong is not enough.	*Franklin* (1883)
	It must be an act; an omission is not sufficient.	*Lowe* (1973)
Examples of unlawful acts	• assault	*Larkin* (1943), *Lamb* (1967)
	• battery	*Church* (1965), *Mitchell* (1983)
	• criminal damage	*Newbury and Jones* (1977)
	• arson	*Goodfellow* (1986)
	• robbery	*Dawson* (1985)
	• burglary	*Watson* (1989)
	• administering noxious substance (heroin)	*Dalby* (1982), *Kennedy* (1999), *Dias* (2002), *Rogers* (2003)

Dangerous act	The test for this is objective – would a sober and reasonable person realise the risk of some harm?	*Church* (1965)
	The risk need only be of some harm – not serious harm.	*Larkin* (1943)
	An act aimed at property can still be such that a sober and reasonable person would realise the risk of some harm.	*Goodfellow* (1986)
	There must be a risk of physical harm; mere fear is not enough.	*Dawson* (1985)
Causes death	Normal rules of causation apply; the act must be the factual and legal cause of death.	*Goodfellow* (1986)
	An intervening act such as the victim self-injecting a drug breaks the chain of causation.	*Dalby* (1982); *Dias* (2001), *Richards* (2002)
	But where D helps with the injection the link is established.	*Rogers* (2003); *Kennedy (No 2)* (2005)
Mens rea	D must have *mens rea* for the unlawful act but it is not necessary to prove that the D foresaw any harm from his act.	*Newbury and Jones* (1977)

9.4.2 Gross negligence manslaughter

The leading case is the House of Lords' decision in *Adomako* [1995] 1 AC 171. The elements of this form of involuntary manslaughter are:

* the existence of a duty of care
* breach of that duty causing death
* gross negligence which the jury consider justifies criminal conviction.

Where manslaughter by gross negligence is raised, it is incumbent upon the judge to direct the jury in accordance with the passage of Lord Mackay's speech in *Adomako* at 187 (*Watts* [1998] Crim LR 833).

Duty of care

The concept of a duty of care is well-known in civil law, but less so in criminal law. The criminal law recognises certain duty situations, as seen in Chapter 2; for example, a doctor owes his patient a duty of care by virtue of his contractual obligations. *Adomako* (1995) itself involved a breach of duty owed by a hospital anaesthetist towards a patient. Similarly, in *Adomako* (1995), the House of Lords approved *Stone and Dobinson* [1977] QB 354 (the facts of which appear in Chapter 2) who were found to have undertaken a duty of care. So the ambit of the offence could be limited to those who, for whatever reason, have either undertaken or had a duty imposed upon them. However, Lord Mackay in *Adomako* (1995) said that 'ordinary principles of law of negligence apply to ascertain whether or not D has been in breach of a duty of care towards the victim . . .'. That being so, it logically follows that those same principles should apply in determining those persons to whom a duty is owed. These principles are to be found in *Donoghue v Stevenson* [1932] AC 562, where Lord Atkin in the House of Lords said:

> J 'You must take reasonable care to avoid acts or omissions which you can reasonably foresee would be likely to injure your neighbour. Who then is my neighbour? The answer seems to be – persons who are so closely and directly affected by my act that I ought reasonably to have them in contemplation as being so affected when I am directing my mind to the acts or omissions which are called into question.'

This clearly goes much further than the traditional duty situations in criminal law, giving this form of manslaughter a very wide scope indeed. Two recent cases illustrate the development of the duty concept.

CASE EXAMPLE

Litchfield [1998] Crim LR 507; [1997] EWCA Crim 3290

D was the master of the *Maria Asumpta*, a sailing ship, which ran aground off the north Cornish coast and broke up, killing three of her 14 crew. D was charged with manslaughter, on the basis that, in sailing on – when he knew that the engines might fail through fuel contamination – he had been in breach of duty serious enough to amount to gross negligence. The jury convicted. On appeal, the Court of Appeal, applying *Adomako* (1995), held that the question had been appropriately left for the jury to decide.

CASE EXAMPLE

Wacker [2003] EWCA Crim 1944; [2003] 4 All ER 295

D was convicted of 58 counts of manslaughter. He was the driver of a lorry found at Dover docks to contain 60 illegal Chinese immigrants – all bar two of them dead. At about 7 pm, while the lorry was waiting at Zeebrugge to board the North Sea ferry, D had closed the only ventilation into the lorry; it could not be opened from the inside. (Presumably this closure was not done with the intent to cause GBH or death, otherwise D would have faced 58 counts of murder.) The journey had taken some five hours, by which time, as Kay LJ described it, 'the dreadful loss of life was discovered'. The Court dismissed D's appeal, which had been based on the premise that, as he and the 60 Chinese immigrants had been jointly engaged on an illegal operation, he did not owe them a duty of care. The Court, following *Adomako* (1995), confirmed that the issue whether a duty of care was owed for the purposes of gross negligence manslaughter was determined by 'the same legal criteria as governed whether there was a duty of care in the law of negligence'. However, this did <u>not</u> include the tortious principle of *ex turpi causa* (according to which the participants in a criminal enterprise did not owe a duty of care to each other).

- In *Willoughby* [2005] 1 WLR 1880; [2004] EWCA Crim 3365, the Court of Appeal followed and confirmed *Wacker*. D, the owner of The Old Locomotive, a disused pub in Canterbury, had hired V to help him burn down the pub (there were financial reasons for doing so). One night the pair of them spread petrol around the pub and started a fire. However, there was an explosion and the building collapsed, killing V. D was charged with gross negligence manslaughter. The prosecution convinced the jury that D had breached his duty of care to V in a grossly negligent way and D was convicted. On appeal, the Court of Appeal accepted that it was possible for the same set of circumstances to give rise to liability for both constructive and gross negligence manslaughter, and that D was almost certainly guilty of constructive manslaughter (based on the unlawful and dangerous act of arson). In terms of gross negligence manslaughter, however, the prosecution had to prove that D breached a duty of care to V. On this point, Rose LJ stated:

> We accept that there could not be a duty in law to look after [V]'s health and welfare arising merely from the fact that [D] was the owner of the premises. But the fact that [D] was the owner, that his public house was to be destroyed for his financial benefit, that he enlisted [V] to take part in this enterprise, and that [V]'s role was to spread petrol inside were, in conjunction, factors which were capable, in law, of giving rise to a duty to the deceased on the part of [D].

Breach of duty

The next issue is at what point D breaches that duty. In civil law, D is judged against the standard of the reasonably competent person performing the activity involved. Hence:

- if D is driving a car, he must reach the standard of the reasonably competent driver (*Andrews v DPP* [1937] AC 576, discussed below)

- if D is sailing a boat, he must reach the standard of the reasonably competent sailor (*Litchfield* (1998))

- if D is a doctor, he is judged against the standard of the reasonably competent doctor (*Bateman* (1925) 19 Cr App R 8)

- if D is an anaesthetist, he is judged against the standard of the reasonably competent anaesthetist (*Adomako* (1995)).

ACTIVITY

> Against what benchmark should the defendants in, respectively, *Stone and Dobinson* and *Wacker* be judged?

In the civil law, no concession is made for inexperience. Thus, a learner driver is judged against the standard of the reasonably competent driver (*Nettleship v Weston* [1971] 3 All ER 581); a junior doctor is judged against the standard of the reasonably competent doctor (*Wilsher v Essex Area Health Authority* [1986] 3 All ER 801). Should the same policy apply in the criminal law?

'Gross negligence'

Simply proving that D has been in breach of a duty owed to another person will not lead inevitably to criminal liability, even though D has been responsible for that person's death. Something more is required to justify imposing punishment. In *Adomako* (1995), the House of Lords confirmed that the correct test for this extra element was 'gross negligence'. This confirmed a line of case law dating back to the nineteenth century (albeit a line which had been temporarily broken by the appearance of objective recklessness in the early 1980s). In one of the early cases, *Doherty* (1887) 16 Cox CC 306, the judge said that 'the kind of forgetfulness which is common to everybody' or 'a slight want of skill' might give rise to civil damages, but for criminal liability there had to 'be culpable negligence of a grave kind'. In *Bateman* (1925), which involved negligent treatment by a doctor which caused the patient to die, Lord Hewart CJ explained the gross negligence test as follows:

> J 'In explaining to juries the test which they should apply to determine whether the negligence, in the particular case, amounted to or did not amount to a crime, judges have used many epithets such as 'culpable', 'criminal', 'gross', 'wicked', 'clear', 'complete'. But whatever epithet be used or not, in order to establish criminal liability the facts must

> be such that, in the opinion of the jury, the negligence of the accused went beyond a mere matter of compensation between subjects and showed such disregard for the life and safety of others as to amount to a crime against the state and conduct deserving punishment.'

This test received approval from the House of Lords in *Andrews v DPP* (1937), which involved manslaughter through negligent driving. Lord Atkin said that 'Simple lack of care as will constitute civil liability is not enough. For purposes of the criminal law there are degrees of negligence, and a very high degree of negligence is required to be proved.' Lord Atkin excluded from the scope of gross negligence manslaughter 'mere inadvertence'. For inadvertence to amount to criminal behaviour, D must have had 'criminal disregard' for others' safety, or 'the grossest ignorance or the most criminal inattention'. In *Stone and Dobinson* (1977), Lane LJ offered the following guidance:

> **J** 'What the prosecution have to prove is a breach of . . . duty in such circumstances that the jury feel convinced that [D]'s conduct can properly be described as reckless, that is to say a reckless disregard of danger to the health and welfare of the infirm person. Mere inadvertence is not enough. [D] must be proved to have been indifferent to an obvious risk of injury to health, or actually to have foreseen the risk but to have determined nevertheless to run it.'

In *Adomako* (1995), however, Lord Mackay stated that the test for the jury to consider was 'whether the extent to which [D]'s conduct departed from the proper standard of care incumbent on him, involving as it must have done a risk of death . . . was such that it should be judged criminal'. But is a 'risk of death' essential? Lane LJ set the standard much lower, with indifference to 'an obvious risk to health' being enough for liability. This issue has now been clarified by the Court of Appeal in *Misra & Srivastava* (2004), discussed below. The test for 'gross negligence' may also be criticised for circularity: it tells the jury to convict if they think D was guilty of a crime. However, in *Adomako* (1995), Lord Mackay said:

> **J** 'It is true that to a certain extent this involves an element of circularity, but in this branch of law I do not believe that it is fatal to its being correct as a test of how far conduct must depart from accepted standards to be characterised as criminal. This is necessarily a question of degree and an attempt to specify that degree more closely is I think likely to achieve only a spurious precision. The essence of the matter, which is supremely a jury question, is whether, having regard to the risk of death involved, the conduct of the defendant was so bad in all the circumstances as to amount in their judgment to a criminal act or omission.'

CASE EXAMPLE

Adomako [1995] 1 AC 171

D was employed as an anaesthetist. One day he was supposed to be supervising the breathing equipment during surgery to repair V's detached retina. During the operation, an essential breathing tube became disconnected. However, D failed to notice anything wrong, until after V went into cardiac arrest nine minutes later, by which time it was too late (V lapsed into a coma and eventually died six months later of hypoxia). The prosecution called two witnesses who described D's failure to notice the problem as 'abysmal' and said that a competent anaesthetist would have recognised the problem 'within 15 seconds'. The jury convicted and D's conviction was upheld by the Court of Appeal and House of Lords.

In *Misra & Srivastava* [2004] EWCA Crim 2375; [2005] 1 Cr App R 21, the Court of Appeal held that the ingredients of gross negligence manslaughter involved no uncertainty which offended against Art 7 of the European Convention on Human Rights. It had been argued that the implementation of the ECHR into British law via the Human Rights Act 1998 meant that the principles set out in *Adomako* (1995) were no longer good law. Judge LJ disagreed with that argument. He said (emphasis added):

> J 'The question for the jury was not whether D's negligence was gross and whether, ***additionally***, it was a crime, but whether his behaviour was grossly negligent and ***consequently*** criminal. This was not a question of law, but one of fact, for decision in the individual case … [Gross negligence manslaughter] involves an element of uncertainty about the outcome of the decision-making process, but not unacceptable uncertainty about the offence itself. In our judgment the law is clear. The ingredients of the offence have been clearly defined, and the principles decided in the House of Lords in *Adomako*. They involve no uncertainty.'

Another issue which arose in *Misra* was whether a risk of death was essential in gross negligence manslaughter cases. On this point, Judge LJ said:

> **J** 'In our judgment, where the issue of risk is engaged, *Adomako* demonstrates, and it is now clearly established, that it relates to the risk of death, and is not satisfied by the risk of bodily injury or injury to health. In short, the offence requires gross negligence in circumstances where what is at risk is the life of an individual to whom the defendant owes a duty of care. As such it serves to protect his or her right to life.'

CASE EXAMPLE

Misra & Srivastava [2004] EWCA Crim 2375; [2005] 1 Cr App R 21

D and E were senior house officers at Southampton General Hospital responsible for the post-operative care of a young man, V, who had undergone surgery to repair his patella tendon on 23rd June 2000. He became infected with staphylococcus aureus but the condition was untreated and he died on 27th June 2000. It was alleged that V died as a result of D and E's gross negligence in failing to identify and treat the severe infection from which he died. The Court of Appeal dismissed their appeals.

Misra was followed in *Yaqoob* [2005] EWCA Crim 2169. D was a partner in the Falcon taxi firm in Aylesbury and had responsibility for making arrangements for the inspection and maintenance of a minibus. However, one night the bus had overturned after its tyre burst on a dual carriageway, killing one of its passengers, V. D was convicted of gross negligence manslaughter and appealed, *inter alia*, arguing that, following *Misra*, what had to be proved was indifference to the risk of death. The trial judge had directed the jury that 'D's conduct has to show such disregard for the life and safety of others that you, the jury, conclude that it amounts to a crime, the crime of criminal inattention'. This, D argued, fell short of the minimum threshold established in *Misra*. However, the Court of Appeal upheld D's conviction. The Court decided that it was 'necessary to consider each direction given to the jury in its context to examine if it accords with the law' as settled by *Misra*. According to Thomas LJ, *Yaqoob* was a case in which it was 'obvious to the reasonable person in the position of the appellant that the minibus would be travelling on very fast dual carriageway roads in the vicinity of Aylesbury at speeds where tyre failure could well result in a fatality; there could be no doubt therefore that the only risk engaged was the risk of death and the reference to the risk to safety was superfluous'.

Key facts chart on gross negligence manslaughter

KEY FACTS

Elements	Comment	Cases
Duty of care	D must owe V a duty of care.	*Adomako* (1995)
	The civil concept of negligence applies.	*Donoghue v Stevenson* (1932)
	The fact that V was party to an illegal act is not relevant.	*Wacker* (2003); *Willoughby* (2004)
Examples of duty situations	• Duty under contract.	*Pittwood* (1902), *Adomako* (1995)
	• Voluntary assumption of care.	*Stone and Dobinson* (1977)
	• Duty of landlord to tenant.	*Singh* (1999)
	• Driver of motor-vehicle to road users and own passengers.	*Andrews* (1937); *Wacker* (2003)
	• Captain of ship to crew.	*Litchfield* (1998)
Breach of duty	This can be by an act or an omission.	*Adomako* (1995)
	Involves falling below the standard of the reasonable person.	
Gross negligence	Going beyond a matter of mere compensation . . . showing such disregard for the life and safety of others as to amount to a crime.	*Bateman* (1925)
	A very high degree of negligence.	*Andrews* (1937)
	Conduct so bad in all the circumstances as to amount to a criminal act or omission.	*Adomako* (1995)
	Gross negligence relates to nothing less than a risk of death	*Misra* (2004); *Yaqoob* (2005)

ACTIVITY

In *Holloway* [1994] QB 302, D was a professional electrician who was prosecuted for manslaughter after wrongly connecting wiring in a new house, with the result that one of the householders was fatally electrocuted. His conviction was quashed by the Court of Appeal because of a misdirection (the trial judge had used the objective recklessness test instead of gross negligence). Imagine you were the presiding judge in a case involving these facts. How would you direct the jury on the meaning of:

a duty of care

b breach of duty

c gross negligence?

9.4.3 Reckless manslaughter

Until recently it was unclear whether this form of manslaughter still existed after *Adomako* (1995). However, in *Lidar* (2000) (unreported), the Court of Appeal dismissed an appeal which was based on an alleged misdirection, the trial judge having referred to recklessness (and not gross negligence) as the criterion for liability. Evans LJ said that 'the judge was correct in his view that this was a case of "reckless" manslaughter and to direct the jury accordingly . . . the recklessness direction in fact given made the gross negligence direction superfluous and unnecessary.' As to the meaning of 'reckless' manslaughter, Evans LJ said that the question was whether D 'was aware of the necessary degree of risk of serious injury to the victim and nevertheless chose to disregard it, or was indifferent to it'.

CASE EXAMPLE

Lidar (2000) (unreported)

D was part of a group that had been asked to leave a public house in Leicester. The group got into a Range Rover with D in the driving seat. D's brother, who was in the front passenger seat, then shouted something at V, a doorman at the pub, who approached the vehicle and put his arms through the open passenger window. At that point, D started to drive off, with V now half-in and half-out of the window. The Range Rover left the car park and 'sped up the road'. After about 225 metres, V was dragged under the rear wheel and suffered fatal injuries. D's manslaughter conviction was upheld on appeal.

9.4.4 Reform

In its paper *A New Homicide Act for England & Wales?* (Consultation Paper No 177), published in December 2005, the Law Commission proposed that reckless manslaughter (defined as occurring where D acted with 'reckless indifference' to causing death) should be upgraded to 'second degree murder' (see further section 9.8 on this point).

The Commission also proposed that the remaining two forms of involuntary manslaughter should be retained, albeit with some changes from the present law. The Commission proposed that D should be guilty of manslaughter when:

- D committed a criminal act, intending to cause physical harm or with foresight that there was a risk of causing physical harm. This would redefine constructive manslaughter. The main difference is that the proposal requires foresight by D of at least a risk of causing harm (a subjective test). The present *Church* test of dangerousness is based on whether 'all sober and reasonable people' would recognise the risk (an objective test).

- Death occurred as a result of D's conduct falling far below what could reasonably be expected in the circumstances, where there was a risk that D's conduct would cause death and this risk would have been obvious to a reasonable person in D's position. D must have had the capacity to appreciate the risk. This essentially describes what is presently gross negligence manslaughter.

The Commission essentially repeated these proposals in their Final Report, *Murder, Manslaughter and Infanticide* (Law Com No 304), published in November 2006, although there are differences in terms of the details. One is that 'second degree murder' would include killings where D:

- was aware that their conduct posed a serious risk of death; and

- had intent to cause either some injury, a fear of injury, or a risk of injury.

The 2006 definition of constructive manslaughter is also slightly different – it is defined as occurring where death was caused by a criminal act:

- intended to cause injury, or

- where there was an awareness that the act involved a serious risk of causing injury.

9.5 Causing death by dangerous driving

Section 1 of the Road Traffic Act (RTA) 1988 (as substituted by s 1 of the RTA 1991) provides that 'A person who causes the death of another person by driving a mechanically propelled vehicle dangerously on a road or other public place is guilty of an offence'. This replaced the previous offence of causing death by reckless driving. The meaning of 'dangerous driving' is set out in s 2A.

'2A(1) For the purposes of section 1 . . . above a person is to be regarded as driving dangerously if (and subject to subsection (2) below), only if:

    (a) the way he drives falls far below what would be expected of a competent and careful driver, and

    (b) it would be obvious to a competent and careful driver that driving in that way would be dangerous.

(2) A person is also to be regarded as driving dangerously . . . if it would be obvious to a competent and careful driver that driving the vehicle in its current state would be dangerous.

(3) In subsections (1) and (2) above dangerous refers to danger either of injury to any person or of serious damage to property; and in determining for the purposes of those subsections what would be expected of or obvious to a competent and careful driver in a particular case, regard shall be had not only to the circumstances which he could be expected to be aware but also to any circumstances shown to have been within the knowledge of the accused.

(4) In determining for the purposes of subsection (2) above the state of a vehicle regard may be had to anything attached to or carried on or in it and to the manner in which it is attached or carried.'

The manner of the driving must be dangerous, or the condition of the vehicle (whether from lack of maintenance or positive alteration) must make it dangerous. It is not enough that the inherent design of the vehicle makes it dangerous to be on a public road, if authorisation has been granted under road traffic regulations. This was vividly demonstrated in *Marchant and Muntz* [2003] EWCA Crim 2099; [2004] 1 WLR 442, involving the use of an agricultural vehicle on public roads.

CASE EXAMPLE

Marchant and Muntz [2003] EWCA Crim 2099; [2004] 1 WLR 442

E, a Warwickshire farmer, owned a Matbro TR250 loading machine, an agricultural vehicle with a grab attached at the front for lifting and moving large round hay bales. The grab consisted of nine spikes each 1 metre in length. E gave instructions to an employee, D, to take the vehicle onto a public road to deliver some hay bales. D was stopped waiting to make a turn onto a farm track when V, a motorcyclist, approached at high speed (estimated at 80 mph) from the opposite direction, collided with the vehicle and was impaled on one of the spikes. He suffered injuries described as 'catastrophic' and died. D and E were convicted, respectively, of causing death by dangerous driving and procuring the offence. The Court of Appeal quashed the convictions. The machine was

authorised for use on public roads by virtue of the Motor Vehicles (Authorisation of Special Types) General Order (SI 1979 No 1198) 1979 and the Court of Appeal held there was nothing dangerous in the way D had driven it. Grigson J said that 'where the state of a vehicle is inherent and the vehicle is authorised for use on the road and is being used in a rural area in which agricultural machinery is frequently driven along country roads, we consider that some reference to these facts should be made to the jury.'

Section 2B of the 1988 Act creates a new offence of causing death by careless, or inconsiderate, driving. Section 2B was inserted by the Road Safety Act 2006. It provides

 '2B A person who causes the death of another person by driving a mechanically propelled vehicle on a road or other public place without due care and attention, or without reasonable consideration for other persons using the road or place, is guilty of an offence.'

Section 3A of the 1988 Act (as inserted by the 1991 Act) creates offences of causing death 'by driving a mechanically propelled vehicle on a road or other public place without due care and attention, or without reasonable consideration for other persons', provided one of three aggravating factors are present:

- D was unfit to drive through drink or drugs
- D was over the prescribed alcohol limit
- D fails to provide a specimen within 18 hours without reasonable excuse.

9.6 Infanticide

Section 1(1) of the Infanticide Act 1938 provides as follows:

 '1(1) Where a woman by any wilful act or omission causes the death of her child being a child under the age of 12 months, but at the time of the act or omission the balance of her mind was disturbed by reason of her not having fully recovered from the effect of giving birth to the child or by reason of the effect of lactation consequent upon the birth of the child, then, notwithstanding that the circumstances were such that but for this Act the offence would have amounted to murder, she shall be guilty of [an offence], to wit of infanticide, and may for such offence be dealt with and punished as if she had been guilty of the offence of manslaughter of the child.'

Infanticide is both a defence to murder and an offence in its own right. The purpose of the defence/offence is to avoid the mandatory life-sentence for murder and allow the judge discretion in sentencing. On a charge of murder, there is an evidential burden on D to produce some

evidence that 'the balance of her mind was disturbed'; it is then for the prosecution to disprove this. Where the prosecution charges infanticide, then it bears the burden of proving that the balance of the mother's mind was disturbed.

In *Kai-Whitewind* [2005] EWCA Crim 1092; [2006] Crim LR 348, the Court of Appeal called for a 'thorough re-examination' of the law of infanticide. After referring to the Law Commission's general review of the law of homicide, Judge LJ stated:

J

'The public interest requires that the problems arising from and connected to the offence of infanticide should be included in any review. We shall highlight two particular areas of concern. The first is whether, as a matter of substantive law, infanticide should extend to circumstances subsequent to the birth, but connected with it, such as the stresses imposed on a mother by the absence of natural bonding with her baby: in short, whether the current definition of infanticide reflects modern thinking. The second problem arises when the mother who has in fact killed her infant is unable to admit it. This may be because she is too unwell to do so, or too emotionally disturbed by what she has in fact done, or too deeply troubled by the consequences of an admission of guilt on her ability to care for any surviving children. When this happens, it is sometimes difficult to produce psychiatric evidence relating to the balance of the mother's mind. Yet, of itself, it does not automatically follow from denial that the balance of her mind was not disturbed: in some cases it may indeed help to confirm that it was. The law relating to infanticide is unsatisfactory and outdated. The appeal in this sad case demonstrates the need for a thorough re-examination.'

CASE EXAMPLE

Kai-Whitewind [2005] EWCA Crim 1092; [2006] Crim LR 348

D had given birth in May 2002 but immediately afterwards suffered post-natal depression. However, she was anxious about the possible implications for her baby, Bidziil, if she were to take anti-depressants. Subsequently, D found it difficult to bond with the child and had problems breastfeeding. In August 2002, Bidziil died, aged three months, and while D claimed that the cause of death was from natural (albeit unexplained) causes, the prosecution alleged murder. D was convicted of murder and the Court of Appeal upheld her conviction. Evidence of D's post-natal depression did not support the defence of infanticide.

9.7 Offences against a foetus

9.7.1 Child destruction

The offence of child destruction, under s 1(1) of the Infant Life (Preservation) Act 1929, makes it a criminal offence for a person to cause a child to die 'before it has an existence independent of its mother'. Section 1(2) adds that 'evidence that a woman had . . . been pregnant for a period of 28 weeks or more shall be *prima facie* proof that she was at that time pregnant [with] a child capable of being born alive'. Section 1(1) imposes a mental element: D must have had 'intent to destroy the life of a child capable of being born alive'. A defence is provided in s 1(1), if the act which causes death of the child was 'done in good faith for the purpose only of preserving the life of the mother'. This can be regarded as a specific example of the necessity defence (see Chapter 8).

9.7.2 Procuring a miscarriage

The crime of procuring a miscarriage is contained in s 58 OAPA 1861. This provides that a pregnant woman who 'with intent to procure her own miscarriage' administers to herself 'any poison or other noxious thing' or uses 'any instrument or other means whatsoever' to carry out that intent commits the offence. Section 58 adds that any person with the same intent who administers poison or uses an instrument to a woman – whether she is in fact pregnant or not – is also guilty of an offence. The offence is now subject to a defence available in s 1 of the Abortion Act 1967 (as amended by s 37 of the Human Fertilisation and Embryology Act 1990). The 1967 Act allows for abortions to be carried out by a registered medical practitioner, subject to various safeguards.

ACTIVITY

1. D has been married for 15 years. Over the last two years he has become increasingly convinced that his wife, V, has been having an affair and this has made him anxious and depressed. For this his doctor has prescribed mildly sedative drugs. D has also taken to drinking, often on his own in pubs after work and at home when V is out, ostensibly working late or with friends. This has led him to put on weight. D and V have argued about the amount of time she spends out of the house. One night they have a particularly heated row, during which V says that if D wasn't such a 'miserable bastard' she wouldn't feel the need to go out so much. She then leaves the room and goes upstairs. D goes into the kitchen to pour himself a whisky. As he drinks he broods on V's behaviour and her comment about him. Eventually he goes upstairs to the bedroom, where V is already in bed reading, and begins to undress. As he does so V looks up and points at D's paunch: 'Not exactly Brad Pitt, are we?', she says. At this, D feels his temper rising. He picks up a pair of scissors from the dressing table and waves them in V's face. 'What the hell are you doing that for?' she cries and tries to grab the scissors. There is a brief struggle during which the scissors end up embedded in V's neck.

At D's trial for murder, he pleads the following defences:

a Lack of intent to kill or cause grievous bodily harm. He admits waving the scissors in V's face but says this was purely out of a desire to frighten his wife and stop her taunting him.

b Provocation.

c Diminished responsibility.

Consider D's liability.

2. Consider whether the Law Commission's proposals to reform involuntary manslaughter should be adopted.

3. D, a 16-year-old schoolboy, has a predilection for playing with matches. One evening he deliberately sets fire to a pile of newspapers that has been left at the back of a newsagent's shop. The fire quickly spreads and, within minutes, the shop itself is in flames. D runs off. A passer-by calls the fire brigade, who arrive soon afterwards and begin to tackle the fire, which has now spread to neighbouring shops. One of the firemen goes inside one of the shops to check for signs of anyone being inside. Tragically, whilst he is inside the roof collapses and the fireman is killed.

Consider D's liability for:

a constructive manslaughter

b gross negligence manslaughter

c reckless manslaughter.

9.8 Reform of the Law of Homicide

In December 2005, the Law Commission published a Paper entitled *A New Homicide Act for England and Wales?* (Consultation Paper No 177). This proposed a sweeping reform of murder, voluntary and involuntary manslaughter – most interestingly, they propose a new idea of a three-tier structure for homicide offences. Unsurprisingly, the Paper attracted considerable academic attention, which was broadly supportive of the new three-tier structure although there were disagreements about the details. Victor Tadros, in *The Homicide Ladder* (2006) 69 MLR 601, was not untypical of the commentators. He said:

> 'Overall, the Commission's proposals are impressive, imaginative and detailed. The range of issues considered is broad, and the technicalities in the area are addressed with vigour. However, there are also some weaknesses both in the offence definitions and the role of defences ... The law at present is, in a sense, the worst of both worlds. Some morally significant elements such as common *mens rea* concepts are

picked out, but poorly defined. A narrow range of partial defences does some work to avoid the worst consequences of that, but not nearly enough to result in a system that is even broadly fair ... The Commission's proposals would remedy some of these defects significantly ... However, some defects still remain ... the range of partial defences would still, in my view, be too narrow ... more importantly, extant partial defences would only operate in relation to first degree murder ... A consequence is that the category difference between second degree murder and manslaughter would reflect moral differences between cases only in the crudest manner.'

After eleven months of consultation, and no doubt cognisant of the academic analysis, the Commission published its Final Report, entitled *Murder, Manslaughter and Infanticide* (Law Com No 304) in November 2006. In it, they retain the idea of a three-tier structure and endorse most of their 2005 proposals. However, there are some differences.

9.8.1 The structure of homicide offences

The Law Commission propose a new three-point structure (penalties on conviction in brackets):

- first degree murder (mandatory life)
- second degree murder (discretionary life)
- manslaughter (fixed term maximum).

9.8.2 First Degree Murder

This would cover all unlawful killings where D was proved to have:

- intent to kill **or**
- intent to do serious injury **and** where D was also aware that their conduct posed a serious risk of death,

unless D could plead a partial defence, of which there would be three (diminished responsibility, provocation and suicide pact). If one of the partial defences was pleaded successfully, it would reduce D's liability to second degree murder (not voluntary manslaughter – this category of homicide would cease to exist). In 2005, the Law Commission had proposed a narrower definition of first degree murder where D had intent to kill only. However, that idea has now been dropped on the basis that the offence would be too narrow and difficult to prove.

9.8.3 Second Degree Murder

This would include all unlawful killings where:

- D had the intent required for first degree murder but pleaded one of the partial defences
- D had intent to do serious injury but was **not** aware of a serious risk of death
- D was aware that their conduct posed a serious risk of death and had intent to cause either:

– some injury, or

– a fear of injury, or

– a risk of injury.

This third category essentially describes what is presently reckless manslaughter, and hence that offence would be upgraded from involuntary manslaughter to murder under the Law Commission's latest proposals.

The Commission did consider the creation of another category of murder, which could be described as 'aggravated murder'. This could include, for example, serial killers (those who kill on more than one occasion) and/or those who kill using torture. Alternatively, it could include those whose killings cause fear amongst a group within society, for example killings with a racist motive. However, the Commission eventually decided that, instead of recommending the creation of a new offence, such killings would remain as murder (whether first or second degree) and their aggravating features would be 'best reflected though an uncompromising approach to the length of the minimum custodial sentence imposed'.

9.8.4 Manslaughter

The Law Commission's proposals to reform involuntary manslaughter have already been examined in detail earlier in this chapter. It should also be noted that, as a consequence of the Commission's proposal to abolish voluntary manslaughter, there would be no need to refer to 'involuntary' manslaughter either. The third tier of homicide would simply be called 'manslaughter'.

9.8.5 Intention

The 2005 Paper proposed two models. Firstly, there could be a **definition of intention**, as follows: 'D acts intentionally with respect to a consequence if he acts (i) to bring it about or (ii) knowing that it will be virtually certain to occur'. This would finally equate foresight of a virtually certain consequence with intention, as opposed to it being merely evidence of intention. Secondly, codification of *Woollin*: this would mean that foresight of a virtually certain consequence would remain as **evidence of intention**, allowing juries to 'find' it. In 2006, the Commission recommended adopting the second model; that is, codification of *Woollin*.

9.8.6 Diminished Responsibility

The Law Commission's proposals to reform DR have already been examined in detail earlier in this chapter. The only point to make here is that DR would only operate as a partial defence to first degree murder, reducing liability to second degree murder.

9.8.7 Provocation

The Law Commission's proposals to reform provocation have also been examined in detail earlier in this chapter. Again, note that provocation would only operate as a partial defence to first degree murder, reducing liability to second degree murder.

9.8.8 Suicide Pact

In 2005 the Law Commission recommended that this defence be repealed but by 2006 had decided against that idea. The survivor of a suicide pact would have a partial defence to first degree murder, reducing liability to second degree murder.

9.8.9 Duress

In 2005, the Law Commission recommended that duress should become a new partial defence to first degree murder – available where D was threatened with 'death or life-threatening harm'. By 2006, however, the Commission's position had changed and they now recommend that duress should be a full defence to murder and attempted murder. In other words, the House of Lords decisions in *Howe* [1986] QB 626 and *Gotts* [1992] 2 AC 412 would be overruled.

9.8.10 A single offence of Criminal Homicide?

Back in 2005, the Law Commission rejected this idea on the basis that it was too wide, as it would include everyone from a hired contract killer to a battered wife to a negligent doctor. The Commission pointed out that the labels of 'murder' and 'manslaughter' serve a function and reflect different levels of culpability.

ACTIVITY

Discuss whether the Law Commission's 2005 and/or 2006 proposals resolve all of the existing defects and problems within the law of homicide. In particular, consider:

- Should murder be split into first and second degrees? If so, how should the different offences be defined?

- Is it right that the partial defences should be available to charges of first degree murder only?

- Should duress be (a) a full defence to murder; (b) a partial defence to murder; (c) no defence to murder at all?

- Should reckless manslaughter be upgraded to second degree murder?

Further reading

Allen, M J, 'Provocation's Reasonable Man: A Plea for Self-Control' [2000] JCL 216.

Ashworth, A, 'The Doctrine of Provocation' [1976] CLJ 292.

Chalmers, J, 'Merging Provocation and Diminished Responsibility: Some reasons for Scepticism' [2004] Crim LR 198.

Dressler, J, 'Provocation: Partial justification or Partial Excuse' (1988) 51 MLR 467.

Edwards, S, 'Abolishing Provocation and Reframing Self-Defence – the Law Commission's Options for Reform' [2004] Crim LR 181.

Elliott, C and De Than, C, 'Prosecuting the Drug dealer when a Drug User Dies' (2006) 69 MLR 986.

Elvin, J, 'The Doctrine of Precedent and the Provocation Defence' (2006) 69 MLR 819.

Gardner, J and Macklem, T, 'Compassion Without Respect? Nine Fallacies in *R v Smith*' [2001] Crim LR 623.

Herring, J and Palser, E, 'The Duty of Care in Gross Negligence Manslaughter' [2007] Crim LR 24.

Horder, J, 'Reshaping the Subjective Element in the Provocation Defence' (2005) 25 OJLS 123.

Horder, J and McGovan, L, 'Manslaughter by Causing Another's Suicide' [2006] Crim LR 1035.

McColgan, A, 'In Defence of Battered Women who Kill' (1993) *Journal of Law and Society* 508.

Mackay, R D, 'Pleading Provocation and Diminished Responsibility Together' [1988] Crim LR 411.

Mackay, R D, 'The Abnormality of Mind Factor in Diminished Responsibility' [1999] Crim LR 117.

Mackay, R D, 'Diminished Responsibility and Mentally Disordered Killers' in *Rethinking English Homicide Law* (2000), edited by Professors Ashworth and Mitchell.

Nicholson, D and Sanghi, R, 'Battered Women and Provocation: The Implications of *R v Ahluwalia*' [1993] Crim LR 728.

Norrie, A, 'From Criminal Law to Legal Theory: The Mysterious Case of the Reasonable Glue Sniffer' (2002) 65 MLR 38.

O'Donovan, K, 'Defences for Battered Women who Kill' (1991) *Journal of Law and Society* 219.

Oremerod, D and Fortson, R, 'Drug Suppliers as Manslaughterers (Again)' [2005] Crim LR 819.

Quick, O and Wells, C, 'Getting Tough with Defences' [2006] Crim LR 514.

Tadros, V, 'The Homicide Ladder' (2006) 69 MLR 601.

Wasik, M, 'Cumulative Provocation and Domestic Killing' [1982] Crim LR 29.

Wells, C, 'Battered Women Syndrome and Defences to Homicide: Where Now?' (1994) 14 Legal Studies 266.

Wilson, W, 'The Structure of Criminal Homicide' [2006] Crim LR 471.

Withey, C, 'Provocation ping-pong' (2006) 156 NLJ 299.

Internet links

Law Commission, *Murder, Manslaughter and Infanticide* (Law Com No 304) (2006), available at www.lawcom.gov.uk.

Law Commission, *A New Homicide Act for England and Wales?* (Consultation Paper No. 177) (2005), available at www.lawcom.gov.uk.

Law Commission, *Partial Defences to Murder* (Final Report) (2004), available at www.lawcom.gov.uk.

Home Office, *Reforming the Law on Involuntary Manslaughter: The Government's Proposals* (2003), available at www.homeoffice.gov.uk/docs/invmans.html.

chapter 10 NON-FATAL OFFENCES AGAINST THE PERSON ■

AIMS AND OBJECTIVES ☐☐☐

After reading this chapter you should be able to:

- Understand the *actus reus* and *mens rea* of common assault

- Understand the *actus reus* and *mens rea* of occasioning actual bodily harm (s 47)

- Understand the *actus reus* and *mens rea* of malicious wounding/inflicting grievous bodily harm (s 20)

- Understand the *actus reus* and *mens rea* of wounding or causing grevious bodily harm with intent (s 18)

- Understand factors which may aggravate an assault

- Analyse critically the law on non-fatal offences against the person

- Apply the law to factual situations to determine whether there is liability for non-fatal offences against the person

The main offences are set out in the Offences against the Person Act 1861 (OAPA). This Act merely tidied up the then existing law by putting all of the offences into one Act. It did not try to create a coherent set of offences and, as a result, there have been many problems in the law. There have been many proposals for reform. In 1980, the Criminal Law Revision Committee made recommendations in its 14th Report, *Offences Against the Person*, Cmnd 7844 (1980). The Law Commission adopted these ideas, first in its Draft Criminal Code (1989) and then in 1993 in its report *Legislating the Criminal Code: Offences against the Person and General Principles*. In February 1998 the Home Office issued a Consultation Document, *Violence: Reforming the Offences against the Person Act 1861*. This pointed out that the 1861 Act 'was itself not a coherent statement of the law but a consolidation of much older law. It is therefore not surprising that the law has been widely criticised as archaic and unclear and that it is now in urgent need of reform'. The consultation document included a draft Bill (see section 10.5 for this draft Bill). Despite all of this, Parliament, as yet, has not reformed the law.

The main offences are based on whether or not the victim was injured; if there were injuries, their level of seriousness; and the intention of the defendant. The main offences, in ascending order of seriousness, are:

- assault – contrary to s 39 of the Criminal Justice Act 1988
- battery – contrary to s 39 of the Criminal Justice Act 1988
- assault occasioning actual bodily harm – contrary to s 47 OAPA
- malicious wounding or inflicting grievous bodily harm – contrary to s 20 OAPA
- wounding or causing grievous bodily harm with intent – contrary to s 18 OAPA.

10.1 Common assault

There are two ways of committing this:

- assault
- battery.

Assault and battery are common law offences. There is no statutory definition for either assault or for battery. However, statute law recognises their existence, as both of these offences are charged under s 39 Criminal Justice Act 1988 which states:

 '39 Common assault and battery shall be summary offences and a person guilty of either of them shall be liable to a fine not exceeding level 5 on the standard scale, to imprisonment for a term not exceeding six months, or to both.'

The definition of both assault and battery, therefore, come from case law. In *Collins v Wilcock* [1984] 3 All ER 374 Goff LJ gave the standard definitions:

> J 'The law draws a distinction . . . between an assault and a battery. An assault is an act which causes another person to apprehend the infliction of immediate, unlawful, force on his person; a battery is the actual infliction of unlawful force on another person.'

As can be seen, the act involved is different for assault and battery. For assault there is no touching, only the fear of immediate, unlawful, force. For battery there must be actual force. There are often situations in which both occur. For example, where the defendant approaches the victim shouting that he is going to 'get him', then punches the victim in the face. The approaching and shouting are an assault, while the punch is the battery. As the act is different for each, it is easier to consider assault and battery separately.

10.1.1 *Actus reus* of assault

An assault is also known as a technical assault or a psychic assault. There must be:

- an act
- which causes the victim to apprehend the infliction of immediate, unlawful, force.

Act

An assault requires some act or words. In *Fagan v Metropolitan Police Commissioner* [1968] 3 All ER 442, where the defendant failed to remove his car from a police officer's foot, the court thought that an omission was not sufficient to constitute an assault. However, they decided that there was a continuing act in this case (see section 10.1.2). In *Lodgon v DPP* [1976] Crim LR 121, D opened a drawer in his office to show another person that there was a gun in it, which D said was loaded. In fact the gun was a fake. The actions of D were held to amount to an assault.

Words are sufficient for an assault. These can be verbal or written. In *Constanza* [1997] Crim LR 576 the Court of Appeal held that letters could be an assault. D had written 800 letters and made a number of phone calls to the victim. The victim interpreted the last two letters as clear threats. The Court of Appeal said that there was an assault, as there was a 'fear of violence at some time, not excluding the immediate future'. In *Ireland* [1997] 4 All ER 225 it was held that even silent telephone calls can be an assault. It depends on the facts of the case.

Apprehend immediate unlawful force

The important point is that the act or words must cause the victim to apprehend that immediate force is going to be used against them. There is no assault if the situation is such that it is obvious that the defendant cannot actually use force. For example, where the defendant shouts threats from a passing train, there is no possibility that he can carry out the threats in the immediate future. It was decided in *Lamb* [1967] 2 All ER 1282 that pointing an unloaded gun at someone who knows that it is unloaded cannot be an assault. This is because the other person does not fear immediate force. However, if the other person thought the gun was loaded then this could be an assault.

Fear of immediate force is necessary; immediate does not mean instantaneous, but 'imminent', so an assault can be through a closed window, as in *Smith v Chief Superintendent of Woking Police Station* [1983] Crim LR 323.

CASE EXAMPLE

Smith v Chief Superintendent of Woking Police Station [1983] Crim LR 323

D got into a garden and looked through the victim's bedroom window on the ground floor at about 11 pm. The victim was terrified and thought that he was about to enter the room. Although D was outside the house and no attack could be made at that immediate moment, the court held that the victim was frightened by his conduct. The basis of the fear was that she did not know what D was going to do next, but that it was likely to be of a violent nature. Fear of what he might do next was sufficiently immediate for the purposes of the offence.

The same line of reasoning was taken in *Ireland* (1997) regarding the fear that a telephone call might generate. Lord Steyn in the House of Lords said:

> J 'It involves questions of fact within the province of the jury. After all, there is no reason why a telephone caller who says to a woman in a menacing way "I will be at your door in a minute or two" may not be guilty of an assault if it causes his victim to apprehend immediate personal violence. Take now the case of the silent caller. He intends by his silence to cause fear and he is so understood. The victim is assailed by uncertainty about his intentions. Fear may dominate her emotions, and it may be the fear that the caller's arrival at her door may be imminent. She may fear the *possibility* of immediate personal violence. As a matter of law the caller may be guilty of an assault: whether he is or not will depend on the circumstance and in particular on the impact of the caller's potentially menacing call or calls on the victim.'

Words indicating there will be no violence may prevent an act from being an assault. This is a principle which comes from the old case of *Tuberville v Savage* (1669) 1 Mod Rep 3, where D placed one hand on his sword and said, 'If it were not assize time, I would not take such language from you'. This was held not to be an assault, but there are other cases where words have not negatived the assault. For example in *Light* (1857) D & B 332, the defendant raised a sword above his wife's head and said, 'Were it not for the bloody policeman outside, I would split your head open'. It was held that this was an assault. These cases are difficult to reconcile, but it could be argued that in *Tuberville* (1669) D did not even draw his sword, while in *Light* D had raised the sword above his wife's head, giving her clear cause to apprehend that immediate unlawful force would be used.

Fear of any unwanted touching is sufficient: the force or unlawful personal violence which is feared need not be serious.

There are many examples of assault; for example:

- raising a fist as though about to hit the victim

- throwing a stone at the victim which just misses

- pointing a loaded gun at someone within range

- making a threat by saying 'I am going to hit you'.

Unlawfulness of the force

The force which is threatened must be unlawful. If it is lawful, there is no offence of common assault. When force is lawful or unlawful is discussed in detail under battery at section 10.1.3.

10.1.2 *Actus reus* of battery

The *actus reus* of battery is the actual infliction of unlawful force on another person. Force is a slightly misleading word as it can include the slightest touching, as shown by the case of *Collins v Wilcock* (1984).

CASE EXAMPLE

Collins v Wilcock [1984] 3 All ER 374

Two police officers saw two women apparently soliciting for the purposes of prostitution. The appellant was asked to get into the police car for questioning but she refused and walked away. As she was not known to the police, one of the officers walked after her to try to find out her identity. She refused to speak to the officer and again walked away. The officer then took hold of her by the arm to prevent her leaving. She became abusive and scratched the officer's arm. She was convicted of assaulting a police officer in the execution of his duty. She appealed against that conviction on the basis that the officer was not acting in the execution of his duty, but was acting unlawfully by holding the defendant's arm as the officer was not arresting her. The court held that the officer had committed a battery and the defendant was entitled to free herself.

Goff LJ said in his judgment:

> **J** 'The fundamental principle, plain and incontestable, is that every person's body is inviolate. It has long been established that any touching of another person, however slight, may amount to battery. . . . As Blackstone wrote in his *Commentaries*, "the law cannot draw the line between different degrees of violence, and therefore totally prohibits the first and lowest stage of it; every man's person being sacred, and no other having a right to meddle with it, in any the slightest manner." The effect is that everybody is protected not only against physical injury but against any form of physical molestation.'

Goff LJ also pointed out that touching a person to get his attention was acceptable, provided that no greater degree of physical contact was used than was necessary, but that while touching might be acceptable, physical restraint was not. He also said that 'persistent touching to gain attention in the face of obvious disregard may transcend the norms of acceptable behaviour'.

Even touching the victim's clothing can be sufficient to form a battery. In *Thomas* (1985) 81 Cr App Rep 331, D touched the bottom of a woman's skirt and rubbed it. The Court of Appeal said, *obiter*, 'There could be no dispute that if you touch a person's clothes while he is wearing them that is equivalent to touching him'.

Hostility

There are conflicting case decisions on whether there needs to be any element of hostility in a battery. In *Faulkner v Talbot* [1981] 3 All ER 468 Lord Lane CJ said that a battery 'need not necessarily be hostile'. However in *Wilson v Pringle* [1986] 2 All ER 440, a civil case, in which one schoolboy sued another for injuries caused when they were fooling around in the corridor at school, it was suggested that the touching must be 'hostile'. Croome-Johnson LJ in the Court of Appeal said:

> **J** 'In our view the authorities lead to the conclusion that in a battery there must be an intentional touching or contact in one form or another of the plaintiff by the defendant. That touching must be proved to be a hostile touching. That still leaves unanswered the question, when is a touching to be called hostile? Hostility cannot be equated with ill-will or malevolence. It cannot be governed by the obvious intention shown in acts like punching, stabbing or shooting. It cannot be solely governed by an expressed intention, although that may be strong evidence. But the element of hostility, in the sense in which it is now to be considered, must be a question of fact for the tribunal of fact . . .'

In a later civil case, *F v West Berkshire Health Authority* [1989] 2 All ER 545, Lord Goff doubted whether there was a requirement that the touching need be hostile. Yet in *Brown* [1993] 2 All ER 75, a case on sado-masochism, (see section 10.2.3) Lord Jauncey in the House of Lords approved the judgment of Croome-Johnson LJ in *Wilson v Pringle* (1986). However, he added that if the defendant's actions are unlawful, they are necessarily hostile. This appears to remove any real meaning from 'hostility' in relation to battery as the key element of a battery is the application of unlawful force.

Continuing act

A battery may be committed through a continuing act, as in *Fagan v Metropolitan Police Commander* (1969).

CASE EXAMPLE

Fagan v Metropolitan Police Commander [1969] 1 QB 439; [1968] 3 All ER 442

D parked his car with one of the tyres on a police officer's foot. When he parked he was unaware that he had done this, but when the police office asked him to remove it, he refused to do so for several minutes. The court described this as 'an act constituting a battery which at its inception was not criminal because there was no element of intention, but which became criminal from the moment the intention was formed to produce the apprehension which was flowing from the continuing act'.

Indirect act

A battery can also be through an indirect act such as use of a booby trap. In this situation the defendant causes force to be applied, even though he does not personally touch the victim. This occurred in *Martin* (1881) 8 QBD 54, where the defendant placed an iron bar across the doorway of a theatre. He then switched off the lights. In the panic which followed, several of the audience were injured when they were trapped and unable to open the door. Martin was convicted of an offence under s 20 of the OAPA 1861. A more modern example is seen in *DPP v K* [1990] 1 All ER 331.

CASE EXAMPLE

DPP v K [1990] 1 All ER 331

D, a 15-year-old schoolboy, without permission took sulphuric acid from his science lesson to try its reaction on some toilet paper. While he was in the toilet he heard footsteps in the corridor, panicked and put the acid into a hot air hand drier to hide it. He returned to his class intending to remove the acid later. Before he could do so another pupil used the drier and was sprayed by the acid. The defendant was charged with assault occasioning actual bodily harm (s 47). The magistrates acquitted him because he said he had not intended to hurt anyone (see section 10.2.2 for the *mens rea* of s 47).

The prosecution appealed by way of case stated to the Queen's Bench Divisional Court. On the point of whether a common assault (remember this includes both an assault and a battery) could be committed by an indirect act, Parker LJ said:

J 'The position was correctly and simply stated by Stephen J in *R v Clarence* (1888) 22 QBD 23 where he said: "If man laid a trap for another into which he fell after an interval, the man who laid the trap would during the interval be guilty of an attempt to assault, and of an actual assault as soon as the man fell in."

In the same way a defendant who pours a dangerous substance into a machine just as truly assaults the next user of the machine as if he had himself switched the machine on.'

Another example of indirect force occurred in *Haystead v Chief Constable of Derbyshire* [2000] Crim LR 758, where the defendant caused a small child to fall to the floor by punching the woman holding the child. The defendant was found guilty because he was reckless as to whether or not his acts would injure the child. It is worth noting that, in this case, the conviction could also be justified by the principle of transferred malice.

Omissions

Criminal liability can arise by way of an omission, but only if the defendant is under a duty to act. Such a duty can arise out of a contract; a relationship; from the assumption of care for another or from the creation of a dangerous situation (see Chapter 2, section 2.3). As the *actus reus* of battery is the application of unlawful force it is difficult to think how examples could arise under these duty situations, but there has been one reported case, *DPP v Santana-Bermudez* [2003] EWHC 2908.

CASE EXAMPLE

DPP v Santana-Bermudez [2003] EWHC 2908

In this case a policewoman, before searching the defendant's pockets, asked him if he had any needles or other sharp objects on him. The defendant said 'no', but when the police officer put her hand in his pocket she was injured by a needle which caused bleeding. The Divisional Court held that the defendant's failure to tell her of the needle could amount to the *actus reus* for the purposes of an assault causing actual bodily harm.

Other scenarios which could make a defendant liable by way of omission are where the defendant has created a dangerous situation which may lead to force being applied to the victim. This can be seen by analogy with *Miller* [1954] 2QB 282, where D accidentally set fire to his mattress but failed to do anything to prevent damage to the building in which he was sleeping. If there had been other people asleep in the room and D had not awakened them to warn them of the danger, and one of them had been hit by plaster which fell from the ceiling as a result of the fire, then there appears no reason why D could not have been charged with battery of that person. It is noticeable that in the draft Bill in 1998 (see section 10.5) it was proposed that only intentionally causing serious injury could be committed by omission; the equivalent of battery would not be able to be committed by omission.

Consent

Where the other person consents to the touching, then there is no battery as there is no unlawful force. This was illustrated by *Slingsby* [1995] Crim LR 570, which was a charged of involuntary manslaughter by an unlawful act.

CASE EXAMPLE

Slingsby [1995] Crim LR 570

The defendant and the victim had taken part in sexual activity which was described as 'vigorous', but which had taken place with the victim's consent. During this a signet ring which the defendant was wearing caused an injury to the victim, and this led to blood poisoning from which she died. The victim's consent meant that there was no battery or other form of assault, and so the defendant was held to be not guilty of manslaughter as there was no unlawful act.

There must, however, be true consent. In *Tabassum* [2000] Crim LR 686, D had persuaded women to allow him to measure their breasts for the purpose of preparing a database for sale to doctors. The women were fully aware of the nature of the acts he proposed to do, but they said they consented only because they thought that D had either medical qualifications or medical training. The Court of Appeal approved the trial judge's direction when he said: 'I should prefer myself to say that consent in such cases does not exist at all, because the act consented to is not the act done. Consent to a surgical operation or examination is not consent to sexual connection or indecent behaviour.'

Implied consent

There are also situations in which the courts imply consent to minor touchings. These are the everyday situations in which there is a crowd of people and it is impossible not to have some

contact. In *Wilson v Pringle* (1986) it was held that the ordinary 'jostlings' of everyday life were not battery. This was also said in *Collins v Wilcock* (1984):

> J
>
> 'Although we are all entitled to protection from physical molestation, we live in a crowded world in which people must be considered as taking on themselves some risk of injury (where it occurs) from the acts of others which are not in themselves unlawful.
>
> Generally speaking, consent is a defence to a battery; and most of the physical contacts of ordinary life are not actionable because they are impliedly consented to by all who move in society and so expose themselves to the risk of bodily contact. So nobody can complain of the jostling which is inevitable from his presence in, for example, a supermarket, an underground station or a busy street; nor can a person who attends a party complain if his hand is seized in friendship, or even if his back is (within reason) slapped.'

This also applies to contact sports. When a person takes part in sports such as rugby or judo, he is agreeing to the contact which is part of that sport. However, if the contact goes beyond what is reasonable then it is possible for an offence to be committed. For example, a rugby player consents to a tackle within the rules of the game, but he does not consent to an opposition player stamping on his head. See Chapter 8 section 8.9 for fuller discussion on consent as a defence.

Unlawful force

For a battery to be committed, the force must be unlawful. As seen above, the force may be lawful if the victim gives a genuine consent to it. Force may also be lawful where it is used in self-defence or prevention of crime (see Chapter 8 section 8.8). If the force used is reasonable in the situation then the person using the force is not guilty of a battery.

Another situation where force may be lawful is in the correction of a child by a parent. English law recognises that moderate and reasonable physical chastisement of a child is lawful. However, in *A v UK* [1998] TLR 578, where a jury had acquitted a father who had beaten his son with a garden cane, the European Court of Human Rights ruled that a law allowing force to be used on children offended art 3 of the European Convention on Human Rights. This article prohibits torture and inhuman or degrading treatment or punishment. Our law is likely to be changed to make it compatible with the Convention, but at the moment force used to correct a child can be lawful. The judge in such a case must direct the jury to take account of the nature, context and duration of the force used by the parent, the physical and mental effect on the child and the reasons for the punishment.

Battery without an assault

It is possible for there to be a battery even though there is no assault. This can occur where the victim is unaware that unlawful force is about to be used on him, such as where the attacker comes up unseen behind the victim's back. The first thing the victim knows is when he is struck; there has been a battery but no assault.

10.1.3 *Mens rea* of assault and battery

The *mens rea* for an assault is either an intention to cause another to fear immediate unlawful personal violence, or recklessness as to whether such fear is caused. The *mens rea* for battery is either an intention to apply unlawful physical force to another, or recklessness as to whether unlawful force is applied. So intention or recklessness is sufficient for both assault and battery.

In *Venna* [1975] 3 All ER 788 the Court of Appeal rejected arguments that only intention would suffice for the mental element of all assault-based offences:

> J 'We see no reason in logic or in law why a person who recklessly applies physical force to the person of another should be outside the criminal law of assault. In many cases the dividing line between intention and recklessness is barely distinguishable.'

The test for recklessness is subjective. For an assault, the defendant must realise there is a risk that his acts/words could cause another to fear unlawful personal violence. For a battery the defendant must realise there is a risk that his act (or omission) could cause unlawful force to be applied to another.

Assault and battery are classed as offences of basic intent. This means that if the defendant is intoxicated when he does the relevant *actus reus* he is reckless. This was considered by the House of Lords in *DPP v Majewski* [1976] 2 All ER 142, where D had consumed large quantities of alcohol and drugs and then attacked people in a public house and also the police officers who tried to arrest him. Lord Elwyn-Jones said:

> J 'If a man of his own volition takes a substance which causes him to cast off the restraints of reason and conscience, no wrong is done to him by holding him answerable criminally for any injury he may do while in that condition. His course of conduct in reducing himself by drink and drugs to that condition in my view supplies the evidence of *mens rea*, of guilty mind certainly sufficient for crime of basic intent. It is a reckless course of conduct and recklessness is enough to constitute the necessary *mens rea* in assault cases.'

This ruling can be criticised, as the point at which the drink or drugs is taken is a quite separate time to the point when the *actus reus* for the offence is committed. It is difficult to see how there is coincidence of the two. It is reasonable to say that the defendant is reckless when he takes drink or other intoxicating substances, but this does not necessarily mean that when he commits an assault or battery three or four hours later he is reckless for the purposes of the offence. The decision can be viewed as a public policy decision.

ACTIVITY

Explain whether there is an assault and/or battery in the following situations.

1. Rick and Sue are having an argument. During the argument, Rick says 'If you don't shut up I'll thump you.' Sue is so annoyed at this that she gets out a penknife and waves it in front of Rick's face.

2. At a party Tanya sneaks up behind William and slaps him on the back.

3. Vince throws a stone at Una, but misses. He picks up another stone and this time hits the loose end of Una's scarf.

4. Grant turns round quickly without realising that Harry is standing just behind him and bumps into Harry. Harry shouts at him 'If you were not wearing glasses, I would hit you in the face'.

10.2 Section 47

We now look at assaults where an injury is caused. The lowest level of injury is referred to as 'actual bodily harm' and it is an offence under s 47 of the Offences against the Person Act 1861, which states:

'47 Whosoever shall be convicted of any assault occasioning actual bodily harm shall be liable . . . to imprisonment for five years.'

The offence is triable either way.

As can be seen from this very brief section, there is no definition of 'assault' or 'actual bodily harm'. Nor is there any reference to the level of *mens rea* required. For all these points it is necessary to look at case law.

10.2.1 *Actus reus* of section 47

This requires:

* a technical assault or a battery, which must

* occasion (ie cause)

* actual bodily harm.

In *Miller* (1954) it was said that actual bodily harm is 'any hurt or injury calculated to interfere with the health or comfort of the victim'. In *R(T) v DPP* [2003] Crim LR 622, loss of consciousness, even momentarily, was held to be actual bodily harm.

So s 47 can be charged where there is any injury. Bruising, grazes and scratches all come within this.

In *DPP v Smith (Michael)* [2006] 2 All ER 16; [2006] 2 Cr App R 1 it was decided that even cutting the victim's hair can amount to actual bodily harm.

CASE EXAMPLE

DPP v Smith (Michael) [2006] 2 All ER 16; [2006] 2 Cr App R 1

D had had an argument with his girlfriend. He cut off her ponytail and some hair from the top of her head without her consent. He was charged with an offence under s 47 of the Offences Against the Person Act 1861. The magistrates found that there was no case to answer as cutting hair could not amount to actual bodily harm. The Divisional Court allowed the prosecution's appeal by way of case stated, holding that cutting off a substantial amount of hair could amount to actual bodily harm. They remitted the case to the justices for the case to continue.

In the judgment, Sir Igor Judge (P), held that physical pain was not a necessary ingredient of actual bodily harm. He said:

'In my judgment, whether it is alive beneath the surface of the skin or dead tissue above the surface of the skin, the hair is an attribute and part of the human body. It is intrinsic to each individual and to the identity of each individual . . .

Even, if medically and scientifically speaking, the hair above the surface of the scalp is no more than dead tissue, it remains part of the body and is attached to it. While it is so attached, in my judgment it falls within the meaning of "bodily" in the phrase "actual bodily harm".'

One area which was less certain was whether psychiatric injury could be classed as 'actual bodily harm'. This was resolved in *Chan Fook* [1994] 2 All ER 552, where the Court of Appeal ruled that psychiatric injury is capable of amounting to actual bodily harm.

> **J** 'The first question on the present appeal is whether the inclusion of the word "bodily" in the phrase "actual bodily harm" limits harm to harm to the skin, flesh and bones of the victim . . . The body of the victim includes all parts of his body, including his organs, his nervous system and his brain. Bodily injury therefore may include injury to any of those parts of his body responsible for his mental and other faculties.'

However, the court stated that actual bodily harm does not include 'mere emotions such as fear, distress or panic', nor does it include 'states of mind that are not themselves evidence of some identifiable clinical condition'.

This decision was approved by the House of Lords in *Burstow* [1997] 4 All ER 225, where Lord Steyn said that 'bodily harm' in ss 18, 20 and 47 must be interpreted so as to include recognisable psychiatric illness.

The matter was considered again by the Court of Appeal in *Dhaliwal* [2006] EWCA Crim 1139; [2006] All ER (D) 236. D was charged with manslaughter of his wife when she committed suicide. The prosecution relied on unlawful act manslaughter (see section 9.1.4). They, therefore, had to prove that D had committed an unlawful act. They tried to prove that D had inflicted psychological harm on his wife over a number of years. However, the prosecution failed because they were unable to prove that V had suffered any recognisable psychiatric illness. This meant that there was no offence under ss 47, 20 or 18 of the Offences Against the Person Act 1861 and so no unlawful act for the purpose of proving manslaughter.

10.2.2 *Mens rea* of section 47

Section 47 makes no reference to *mens rea* but, as the essential element is a common assault, the courts have held that the *mens rea* for a common assault is sufficient for the *mens rea* of a s 47 offence. So the defendant must intend or be subjectively recklessness as to whether the victim fears or is subjected to unlawful force. This is the same *mens rea* as for an assault or a battery and there is no need for the defendant to intend or be reckless as to whether actual bodily harm is caused. In *Roberts* [1971] Crim LR 27 the defendant, who was driving a car, made advances to the girl in the passenger seat and tried to take her coat off. She feared that he was going to commit a more serious assault and jumped from the car while it was travelling at about 30 miles per hour. As a result of this she was slightly injured. He was found guilty of assault occasioning actual bodily harm, even though he had not intended any injury or realised there was a risk of injury. He had intended to apply unlawful force when he touched her as he tried to take her coat off. This satisfied the *mens rea* for a common assault and so he was guilty of an offence under s 47.

This was confirmed by the House of Lords in the combined appeals of *Savage* and *Parmenter* [1991] 4 All ER 698.

CASE EXAMPLE

Savage [1991] 4 All ER 698

A woman in a pub threw beer over another woman. In doing this the glass slipped from the defendant's hand and the victim's hand was cut by the glass. The defendant said that she had only intended to throw beer over the woman. She had not intended her to be injured, nor had she realised that there was a risk of injury. She was convicted of a s 20 offence but the Court of Appeal quashed that and substituted a conviction under s 47 (assault occasioning actual bodily harm). She appealed against this to the House of Lords. The Law Lords dismissed her appeal.

The fact she intended to throw the beer over the other woman meant she had the intent to apply unlawful force, and this was sufficient for the *mens rea* of the s 47 offence. Lord Ackner said:

> J 'The verdict of assault occasioning actual bodily harm may be returned upon proof of an assault together with proof of the fact that actual bodily harm was occasioned by the assault. The prosecution are not obliged to prove that the defendant intended to cause some actual bodily harm or was reckless as to whether such harm would be caused.'

10.2.3 Consent and section 47

There have been arguments as to whether consent could be a defence to a s 47 offence. Originally it was thought that it could be a defence where the injuries were not serious. However, in some cases, such as *Donovan* [1934] 2 KB 498, it was held that an unlawful act 'cannot be rendered lawful because the person to whose detriment it is done consents to it. No person can license another to commit a crime'. This is an area where the courts are prepared to limit the defence on the basis of public policy grounds. It is now accepted that consent is not a defence to a s 47 offence, unless it is one of the exceptions which have been recognised by the courts. Lord Jauncey in *Brown* (1993) pointed out that consent could be a defence to a common assault but not to another more serious assault where there was some injury, even if not serious:

J '. . . [T]he line properly falls to be drawn between assault at common law and the offence of assault occasioning actual bodily harm created by section 47 of the Offences against the Person Act 1861, with the result that consent of the victim is no answer to anyone charged with the latter offence or with a contravention of section 20 unless the circumstances fall within one of the well known exceptions such as organised sporting contests and games, parental chastisement or reasonable surgery. There is nothing in sections 20 and 47 to suggest that consent is either an essential ingredient of the offences or a defence thereto.'

This confirmed the decision by the Court of Appeal in *Attorney-General's Reference (No 6 of 1980)* [1981] 2 All ER 1057, where two young men agreed to fight in the street to settle their differences following a quarrel. The Court of Appeal held that consent could not be a defence to such an action as it was not in the public interest. Lord Lane CJ said:

J 'It is not in the public interest that people should try to cause, or should cause, each other bodily harm for no good reason. Minor struggles are another matter. So, in our judgment, it is immaterial whether the act occurs in private or public; it is an assault if actual bodily harm is intended and/or caused. This means that most fights will be unlawful regardless of consent.'

Lord Lane recognised that there were exceptions where consent might still be a defence, as he went on to say:

J 'Nothing which we have said it intended to cast doubt upon the accepted legality of properly conduct games and sports, lawful chastisement or correction, reasonable surgical interference, dangerous exhibitions, etc. These apparent exceptions can be justified as involving the exercise of a legal right, in the case of lawful chastisement or correction, or as needed in the public interest, in other cases.'

In deciding what was in the public interest the courts have come to decisions which are difficult to reconcile. In *Brown* (1993) the House of Lords held that consent was not a defence to sado-masochistic acts done by homosexuals, even though all the participants were adult and the injuries inflicted were transitory and trifling. But in *Wilson* [1996] Crim LR 573 the Court of Appeal held that where a defendant branded his initials on his wife's buttocks with a hot knife at her request, this was not an unlawful act, even though she had to seek medical attention for the burns which were caused. It held it was not in the public interest that such consensual behaviour should be criminalised.

It is also odd that acts which have caused 'transitory and trifling' injuries are regarded as criminal, whereas very serious injuries can be deliberately inflicted in boxing because it is a recognised sport. This could be seen as showing the bias of the elderly white males, who make up the great majority of judges in our appeal courts. They approve of what they term 'manly sports'.

Consent in organise sport

In *Barnes* [2005] 2 All ER 113, D made a late tackle on V during an amateur football match. V suffered a serious leg injury. D was convicted of an offence contrary to s 20 of the Offences Against the Person Act 1861. On appeal, the Court of Appeal quashed his conviction. They held that criminal prosecutions should be reserved for those situations where the conduct was sufficiently grave to be properly categorised as criminal.

The Court of Appeal set out the following points:

- consent is not normally available as a defence where there is bodily harm, but sporting activities are one of the exceptions to this rule
- the exceptions are based on public policy
- in contact sports, conduct which goes beyond what a player can reasonably be regarded as having accepted by taking part, is not covered by the defence of consent
- however, in a sport in which bodily contact is a commonplace part of the game, the players consent to such contact, even if through an unfortunate accident or serious injury may result.

In deciding whether conduct in the course of a sport is criminal or not the following factors should be considered:

- intentional infliction of injury will always be criminal
- for reckless infliction of injury – did the injury occur during actual play, or in a moment of temper or over-excitement when play has ceased
- 'off the ball' injuries are more likely to be criminal
- the fact that the play is within the rules and practice of the game and does not go beyond it will be a firm indication that what has happened is not criminal.

Mistaken belief in consent

Where the defendant genuinely, but mistakenly, believes that the victim is consenting, then there is a defence to an assault. In this area the decisions of the courts are even more difficult to reconcile with the general principle that 'it is not in the public interest that people should try to cause, or should cause, each other bodily harm for no good reason'. In *Jones* (1986) 83 Cr App R 375 two schoolboys aged 14 and 15 were tossed into the air by older boys. One victim suffered a broken arm and the other a ruptured spleen. The defendants claimed they believed that the two victims consented to the activity. The Court of Appeal quashed their convictions for offences under s 20 of the OAPA 1861 because the judge had not allowed the issue of mistaken belief in consent to go to

the jury. The Court held that a genuine mistaken belief in consent to 'rough and undisciplined horseplay' could be a defence, even if that belief was unreasonable. A similar decision was reached in *Aitken and others* [1992] 1 WLR 1006, where RAF officers poured white spirit over a colleague who was wearing a fire-resistant flying suit, but who was asleep and drunk at the time this was done. He suffered 35 per cent burns. Their convictions under s 20 were quashed, as the mistaken belief in the victim's consent should have been left to the jury.

In *Richardson and Irwin* [1999] Crim LR 494 it was even held that a drunken mistake that the victim was consenting to horseplay could be a defence to a charge under s 20. However, this decision is doubtful, as it is inconsistent with decisions that a drunken mistaken belief that a victim is consenting to sexual intercourse is not a defence to rape. For further discussion, see consent as a defence in Chapter 8, section 8.9.

10.3 Section 20

The next offence in seriousness is commonly known as 'malicious wounding'. It is an offence under s 20 of the Offences against the Person Act 1861:

'20 Whosoever shall unlawfully and maliciously wound or inflict any grievous bodily harm upon any other person, either with or without a weapon or instrument, shall be guilty of an offence and shall be liable . . . to imprisonment for not more than five years.'

The offence is triable either way and the maximum sentence is five years. This is the same as for a s 47 offence, despite the fact that s 20 is seen as a more serious offence and requires a higher degree of injury and *mens rea* as to an injury. For the offence to be proved, it must be shown that the defendant:

- wounded; or
- inflicted grievous bodily harm

and that he did this:

- intending some injury to be caused; or
- being reckless as to whether some injury would be inflicted.

10.3.1 *Actus reus* of section 20

The *actus reus* can be committed by:

* wounding; or
* inflicting grievous bodily harm.

Wounding

For this the defendant must have caused a wound to the victim. Originally it was thought that the wound had to be caused by an assault or a battery. However, in *Beasley* (1981) 73 Cr App R 44 the Court of Appeal held that the narrow view of assault given by the trial judge was not a necessary ingredient of the offence of unlawful wounding under s 20. The trial judge had defined assault as an act which causes the victim to apprehend the infliction of immediate unlawful force. The Court of Appeal held that unlawful wounding can be committed without the victim being frightened or aware of what is going on.

'Wound' means a cut or a break in the continuity of the whole skin. A cut of internal skin, such as in the cheek, is sufficient, but internal bleeding where there is no cut of the skin is not sufficient. In *JCC v Eisenhower* [1983] 3 All ER 230 the victim was hit in the eye by a shotgun pellet. This did not penetrate the eye but did cause severe bleeding under the surface. As there was no cut, it was held that this was not a wound. The cut must be of the whole skin, so that a scratch is not considered a wound. Even a broken bone is not considered a wound, unless the skin is broken as well. In the old case of *Wood* (1830) 1 Mood CC 278 the victim's collar bone was broken but, as the skin was intact, it was held there was no wound.

Inflicting grievous bodily harm

Section 20 uses the word 'inflict'. Originally this was taken as meaning that there had to be a technical assault or battery. Even so it allowed the section to be interpreted quite widely, as shown in *Lewis* [1974] Crim LR 647 where D shouted threats at his wife through a closed door in a second floor flat and tried to break his way through the door. The wife was so frightened that she jumped from the window and broke both her legs. *Lewis* was convicted of a s 20 offence. The threats could be considered as a technical assault. However, it was thought there had to be an assault for s 20 to be committed. The issue was again considered in *Metropolitan Police Commissioner v Wilson* [1984] AC 242 where the House of Lords, following the Australian case of *Salisbury* [1976] VR 452, decided that 'inflict' does not imply an assault.

However, this left a problem because a contrast was drawn between this section and s 18, where the word 'cause' is used. It was thought that the word 'cause' was wider than 'inflict'. It was held that for 'cause', it was only necessary to prove that the defendant's act was a substantial cause of the wound or grievous bodily harm, whereas 'inflict' suggests a direct application of force. However, in *Mandair* [1994] 2 All ER 715 Lord Mackay said there was 'no radical divergence between the meaning of the two words'. In *Burstow* (1997) it was decided that 'inflict' does not require a technical assault or a battery. These decisions mean that there now appears to be little, if any, difference in the *actus reus* of the offences under s 20 and s 18. In *Burstow* [1997] Lord Hope said that for all practical purposes there was no difference between the words, and approved Lord Mackay's judgment in *Mandair* (1994). However, he went on to say:

> **J** 'I would add that there is this difference, the word "inflict" implies that the consequence of the act is something which the victim is likely to find unpleasant or harmful. The relationship between cause and effect, when the word "cause" is used, is neutral. It may embrace pleasure as well as pain. The relationship when the word "inflict" is used is more precise, because it invariably implies detriment to the victim of some kind.'

Grievous bodily harm

It was held in *DPP v Smith* [1961] AC 290 that grievous bodily harm means 'really serious harm'; but this does not have to be life-threatening. In *Saunders* [1985] Crim LR 230 it was held that a direction to the jury which referred only to 'serious harm' was not a misdirection.

In *Bollom* [2003] EWCA Crim 2846; [2004] 2 Cr App R 6 the Court of Appeal held that the age, health or other factors relating to the victim could be taken into consideration when considering what constituted grievous bodily harm.

CASE EXAMPLE

Bollom [2003] EWCA Crim 2846; [2004] 2 Cr App R 6

V, a 17-month-old baby, suffered bruising and abrasions to her body, arms and legs. D, the baby's mother's partner, was found guilty of an offence contrary to s 18 of the Offences Against the Person Act 1861. He appealed against this conviction on several grounds, one of which that the severity of injuries had to be assessed without considering the age, health or other factors relating to V. The Court of Appeal held that the effect of the harm on the particular individual had to be taken into consideration in determining whether the injuries amounted to grievous bodily harm. However, the conviction was quashed on other grounds, and a conviction under s 47 OAPA 1861 substituted.

In *Burstow* (1997), where the victim of a stalker suffered a severe depressive illness, it was decided that serious psychiatric injury can be grievous bodily harm. In October 2003, in *Dica*, there was the first ever conviction for causing 'biological' harm where the defendant had infected two women with HIV when he had unprotected sex with them without telling them he was HIV positive. The Court of Appeal (*Dica* [2004] EWCA Crim 1103) sent the case back for retrial on the issue of consent, but accepted that biological harm came within the meaning of grievous bodily harm.

10.3.2 *Mens rea* of section 20

The defendant must intend to cause another person some harm or be subjectively recklessness as to whether he suffers some harm. The word used in the section is 'maliciously'. In *Cunningham* [1957] 2 All ER 412 it was held that 'maliciously' did not require any ill-will towards the person injured. It simply meant either:

1. an intention to do the particular kind of harm that was in fact done; <u>or</u>

2. recklessness as to whether such harm should occur or not (ie the accused has foreseen that the particular kind of harm might be done, and yet gone on to take the risk of it).

CASE EXAMPLE

Cunningham [1957] 2 All ER 412

D tore a gas meter from the wall of an empty house in order to steal the money in it. This caused gas to seep into the house next door, where a woman was affected by it. Cunningham was not guilty of an offence against s 23 of the Offences Against the Person Act 1861 of maliciously administering a noxious thing, as he did not appreciate the risk of gas escaping into the next-door house. He had not intended to cause the harm, nor had he been subjectively reckless about it.

The joined cases of *Savage* and *Parmenter* (1992) confirmed that *Cunningham* (1957) recklessness applies to all offences in which the statutory definition uses the word 'maliciously'.

This left another point which the courts had to resolve. What was meant by the particular kind of harm? Did the defendant need to realise the risk of a wound or grievous bodily harm? It has been decided that, although the *actus* reus of s 20 requires a wound or grievous bodily harm, there is no need for the defendant to foresee this level of serious injury. In *Parmenter* (1992) the defendant injured his three-month old baby when he threw the child in the air and caught him. Parmenter said that he had often done this with slightly older children and did not realise that there was risk of any injury. He was convicted of an offence under s 20. The House of Lords quashed this conviction but substituted a conviction for assault occasioning actual bodily harm under s 47. Lord Ackner cited the judgment in *Mowatt* [1967] 3 All ER 47, where Lord Diplock said:

> J 'In the offence under s 20 . . . for . . . which [no] specific intent is required – the word "maliciously" does import . . . an awareness that his act may have the consequence of causing some physical harm to some other person. . . . It is quite unnecessary that the accused should have foreseen that his unlawful act might cause physical harm of the gravity described in the section, ie a wound or serious injury.'

389

This decision means that, although there are four offences which appear to be on a ladder in terms of seriousness, there is overlap in terms of the *mens rea*.

Key facts: Different levels of *mens rea* and injury

KEY FACTS

Offence	Mens rea	Injury
s 18	Specific intent to cause GBH or resist arrest etc.	Wound or grievous bodily harm.
s 20	Intention or recklessness as to some harm.	
s 47	Intention or recklessness as to putting V in fear of unlawful force or applying unlawful force assault.	Actual bodily harm.
Common assault.		No injury.

10.4 Section 18

This offence under s 18 of the Offences against the Person Act 1861 is often referred to as 'wounding with intent'. In fact it covers a much wider range than this implies. It is considered a much more serious offence than s 20, as can be seen from the difference in the maximum punishments. Section 20 has a maximum of five years' imprisonment, whereas the maximum for s 18 is life imprisonment. Also s 20 is triable either way but s 18 must be tried on indictment at the Crown Court. The definition in the Act states:

 '18 Whosoever shall unlawfully and maliciously by any means whatsoever wound or cause any grievous bodily harm to any person, with intent to do some grievous bodily harm to any person, or with intent to resist or prevent the lawful apprehension or detainer of any person, shall be guilty of . . . an offence.'

From this it can be seen that the elements to be proved are that the defendant:

• wounded or

• caused grievous bodily harm

and that he did this:

- intending to do some grievous bodily harm or
- intending to resist or prevent the lawful apprehension or detention of either himself or another person and being reckless as to whether this caused injury.

10.4.1 *Actus reus* of section 18

This can be committed in two ways:

- wounding or
- causing grievous bodily harm.

The meanings of 'wound' and 'grievous bodily harm' are the same as for s 20.

The word 'cause' is very wide, so that it is only necessary to prove that the defendant's act was a substantial cause of the wound or grievous bodily harm.

10.4.2 *Mens rea* of section 18

This is a specific intent offence. The defendant must be proved to have intended to:

- do some grievous bodily harm or
- maliciously resist or prevent the lawful apprehension or detainer of any person.

Intent to do some grievous bodily harm

Although the word 'maliciously' appears in s 18, it was held in *Mowatt* (1967) that this adds nothing to the *mens rea* of this section where grievous bodily harm is intended. For this the important point is that s 18 is a specific intent crime. Intention must be proved; recklessness is not enough for the *mens rea* of s 18. Intention has the same meaning as shown in the leading cases on murder. So, as decided in *Moloney* [1985] 1 All ER 1025, foresight of consequences is not intention; it is only evidence from which intention can be inferred or found. And following the cases of *Nedrick* [1986] 3 All ER 1 and *Woollin* [1998] 4 All ER 103 intention cannot be found unless the harm caused was a virtual certainty as a result of the defendant's actions and the defendant realised that this was so. (See Chapter 3 section 3.2 for a fuller discussion on the meaning of intention.)

Intent to resist lawful arrest etc

Where the charge is wounding or causing grievous bodily harm with intent to resist or prevent the lawful apprehension or detainer of any person, then the prosecution have to prove two things for the *mens rea* of the offence. The first is that the defendant had specific intention to resist or prevent lawful arrest or detention. If the arrest or detainer was unlawful then the defendant has not committed any offence. The second point is that the defendant acted 'maliciously' in respect to the wounding or grievous bodily harm. This point was considered in *Morrison* (1989) 89 Cr App Rep 17, where a police officer seized hold of D and told him that she was arresting him. He dived through a window dragging her with him as far as the window so that her face was badly cut by the glass. The trial judge directed the jury that D would be guilty of a s 18 offence if he intended to resist arrest and was *Caldwell* (1982) reckless (ie D either saw the risk or it would have been obvious to an ordinary prudent person) as to whether he caused the officer harm. The Court of Appeal held that this was wrong and that maliciously has the same meaning as in *Cunningham* (1957). This means that the prosecution must prove that defendant realised there was a risk of injury and took that risk. There is still one point unresolved: that is, what degree of harm does the defendant need to foresee? Does he need to foresee that serous harm or a wound will be caused or does he only need to foresee that some harm will be caused? Under s 20 the test is that the defendant should foresee that some physical harm will be caused. For consistency it seems reasonable that the same test should apply to s 18. However, there has been no decision on this point.

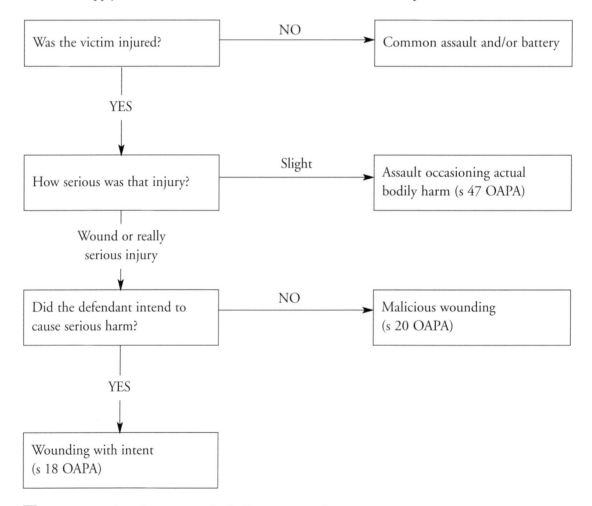

Figure 10.1 Flow chart on non-fatal offences against the person

ACTIVITY

Explain in each of the situations below, what type of offence may have been committed.

1. In a football match Danny is kicked by Victor. This causes bruising to Danny's leg. Danny is annoyed at this and punches Victor in the face causing a cut to his lip.

2. Anish is walking along a canal bank. Kim, who is in a hurry pushes past him, knocking him into the canal. Anish hits his head on the side and suffers a fractured skull.

3. Karl waves a knife at Emma, saying 'I am going to cut that silly smile off.' Emma is very frightened and faints. She falls against Nita, who is knocked to the ground and suffers bruising.

10.5 Reform

This area of the law is in need of reform and, as stated in the opening paragraph of this chapter, recommendations were made as long ago as 1980 by the Criminal Law Revision Committee in its 14th Report, *Offences against the Person*, Cmnd 7844 (1990). This was then adopted in the Law Commission Draft Criminal Code and, as no action had been taken, put forward again by the Law Commission in a modified form in its Report (Law Com No 218) (1993). In 1998 the Home Office issued a Consultation Document, 'Violence: Reforming the Offences against the Person Act 1861', and attached a draft Bill to this document.

The draft Bill published by the Home Office in 1998 proposed the following offences:

Intentional serious injury

1(1) A person is guilty of an offence if he intentionally causes serious injury to another.

(2) A person is guilty of an offence if he omits to do an act which he has a duty to do at common law, the omission results in serious injury to another, and he intends the omission to have that effect.

(3) An offence under this section is committed notwithstanding that the injury occurs outside England and Wales if the act causing that injury is done in England and Wales or the omission resulting in the injury is made there.

(4) A person guilty of an offence under this section is liable on conviction on indictment to imprisonment for life.

Reckless serious injury

2(1) A person is guilty of an offence if he recklessly causes serious injury to another.

(2) An offence under this section is committed notwithstanding that the injury occurs outside England and Wales if the act causing that injury is done in England and Wales.

(3) A person guilty of an offence under this section is liable –

(a) on conviction on indictment, to imprisonment for a term not exceeding 7 years;

(b) on summary conviction, to imprisonment for a term not exceeding 6 months or a fine not exceeding the statutory maximum or both.

Intentional or reckless injury

3(1) A person is guilty of an offence if he intentionally or recklessly causes injury to another.

(2) An offence under this section is committed notwithstanding that the injury occurs outside England and Wales if the act causing that injury is done in England and Wales.

(3) A person guilty of an offence under this section is liable –

(a) on conviction on indictment, to imprisonment for a term not exceeding 5 years;

(b) on summary conviction, to imprisonment for a term not exceeding 6 months or a fine not exceeding the statutory maximum or both.

Assault

4(1) A person is guilty of an offence if –

(a) he intentionally or recklessly applies force to or causes an impact on the body of another, or

(b) he intentionally or recklessly causes the other to believe that any such force or impact is imminent.

(2) No offence is committed if the force or impact, not being intended or likely to cause injury, is in the circumstances such as is generally acceptable in the ordinary conduct of daily life and the defendant does not know or believe that it is in fact unacceptable to the other person.

(3) A person guilty of an offence under this section is liable on summary conviction, to imprisonment for a term not exceeding 6 months or a fine not exceeding the statutory maximum or both.

Assault on a constable

5(1) A person is guilty of an offence if he assaults

(a) a constable acting in the execution of his duty, or

(b) a person assisting a constable acting in the execution of his duty.

(2) For the purposes of this section a person assaults if he commits the offence under section 4.

Causing serious injury to resist arrest etc.

6(1) A person is guilty of an offence if he causes serious injury to another intending to resist, prevent or terminate the lawful arrest or detention of himself or a third person.

(2) The question of whether the defendant believes the arrest or detention is lawful must be determined according to circumstances as he believes them to be.

(3) A person guilty of an offence under this section is liable on conviction on indictment to imprisonment for life.

Assault to resist arrest etc.

7(1) A person is guilty of an offence if he assaults another intending to resist, prevent or terminate the lawful arrest or detention of himself or a third person.

(2) The question of whether the defendant believes the arrest or detention is lawful must be determined according to circumstances as he believes them to be.

(3) For the purposes of this section a person assaults if he commits the offence under section 4.

(4) A person guilty of an offence under this section is liable –

(a) on conviction on indictment, to imprisonment for a term not exceeding 2 years;

(b) on summary conviction, to imprisonment for a term not exceeding 6 months or a fine not exceeding the statutory maximum or both.

Meaning of fault terms

14(1) A person acts intentionally with respect to a result if –

(a) it is his purpose to cause it, or

(b) although it is not his purpose to cause it, he knows that it would occur in the ordinary course of events if he were to succeed in his purpose of causing some other result.

(2) A person acts recklessly with respect to a result if he is aware of a risk that it will occur and it is unreasonable to take that risk having regard to the circumstances as he knows or believes them to be.

Meaning of injury

15(1) In this Act "injury" means –

(a) physical injury

(b) mental injury.

(2) Physical injury does not include anything caused by disease but (subject to that) it includes pain, unconsciousness and any other impairment of a person's physical condition.

(3) Mental injury does not include anything caused by disease but (subject to that) it includes any impairment of a person's mental health.

(4) In its application to section 1 this section applies without the exception relating to things caused by disease.'

This Bill would have tidied up the law and resolved many of the points which have been unclear in case decisions. In particular the *mens rea* of each section is specified. It is also clear that only cl 1 offences could be caused by omission. The more serious offences nominate serious injury rather than wound or grievous bodily harm. A serious wound would be treated as a serious injury while a minor wound would be merely an injury. The difficulty over mental health injury is also tackled with 'any impairment of a person's mental health' being sufficient to prove offences requiring injury, though for clauses 1 and 2 this would have to be serious. It also makes it clear that it would be possible to convict a defendant of a cl 1 offence by infecting a person with HIV. However, an injury through disease was not included for the purposes of any other clause. Although it was sent out for consultation in 1998, this Bill has still not been allocated a place in the Parliamentary timetable and is unlikely to become law.

ACTIVITY

Consider to what extent the draft Bill overcomes the problems in the present law on assaults.

10.6 Racially or religiously aggravated assaults

Under s 29 Crime and Disorder Act 1998, a common assault or an offence under s 47 or s 20 of the Offences Against the Person Act 1861 becomes a racially or religiously aggravated assault if either:

- at the time of committing the offence, or immediately before or after doing so, the offender demonstrates towards the victim of the offence hostility based on the victim's membership (or presumed membership) of a racial or religious group or

- the offence is motivated (wholly or partly) by hostility towards members of a racial or religious group based on their membership of that group.

Where an offence is racially aggravated in this way, the maximum penalty is increased from six months to two years for common assault and from five years to seven years for both s 47 and s 20.

Membership in relation to a racial or religious group includes association with members of that group. 'Racial group' is widely defined in the Act, as it includes a group of persons defined by reference to race, colour, nationality (including citizenship) or ethnic or national origins. In *DPP v Pal* [2000] Crim LR 756 it was held that an Asian defendant was not demonstrating racial hostility because of membership of a racial group when he assaulted a caretaker at a community centre who was of Asian appearance and whom he called a 'white man's arse licker' and a 'brown Englishman'. The Queen's Bench Divisional Court held that the insults were related to the victim's attitude to English people, rather than because he was Asian.

'Religious group' means a group of persons defined by reference to religious belief or lack of religious belief.

10.7 Administering poison

The Offences Against the Person Act 1861 creates two offences under ss 23 and 24:

'23 Whosoever shall unlawfully and maliciously administer to or cause to be administered to or taken by any other person any poison or other destructive or noxious thing, so as to endanger the life of such person, or so as thereby inflict upon such person any grievous bodily harm, shall be guilty of an offence . . .

24 Whosoever shall unlawfully and maliciously administer to or cause to be administered to or taken by any other person any poison or other destructive or noxious thing, with intent to injure, aggrieve, or annoy such person shall be guilty of an offence . . .'

The maximum penalty for s 23 is 10 years' imprisonment and the maximum for s 24 is five years' imprisonment.

For both offences it has to be proved that the defendant:

* unlawfully and maliciously
* administered to or caused to be administered to or taken by any other person
* any poison or other destructive or noxious thing.

The differences are that for s 23 it must be shown that it endangered life or inflicted grievous bodily harm, while for s 24 there is no need to show that it had any effect on the victim, but it must be done with intent to injure, aggrieve, or annoy the victim.

10.7.1 Adminster

In *Gillard* [1998] Crim LR 53 the Court of Appeal held that 'administer' includes 'conduct which not being the direct application of force to the victim nevertheless brings the noxious thing into contact with his body'. In that case the defendant was convicted of conspiring to commit an offence under s 23 when he agreed to spray CS gas into the faces of others.

The sections also make it an offence where the defendant causes the substance to be administered to or taken by the victim. This allows for a conviction where there is no direct administration of the poison or other destructive or noxious thing. An example of causing the administration of a noxious thing is seen in *Cunningham* (1957), where the ripping out of a gas meter caused gas to seep into the next-door house and be inhaled by the victim. In *Kennedy* [1999] Crim LR 65 the Court of Appeal thought that there was an offence under s 23 where the defendant had filled a syringe with heroin and then handed it to the victim who had injected himself. However, in *Dias* [2001] EWCA Crim 2986, where the facts were similar to *Kennedy* (1999), the Court of Appeal left open the question as to whether there might be a conviction in the future for manslaughter on the basis that there was an unlawful act of administering a noxious substance under s 23 of the Offences Against the Person Act 1861.

10.7.2 Noxious thing

The 1861 Act specifically mentions 'poison or other destructive thing', but it also includes any 'noxious thing'. This allows the offences to be wider-ranging than merely administering poison. In *Cato* [1976] 1 All ER 260 the defendant injected another man with heroin. The other had consented to it and was a regular user of heroin. The victim died and Cato was convicted of unlawful act manslaughter and of an offence under s 23. The Court of Appeal considered whether heroin should come within the meaning of 'noxious thing'. Lord Widgery CJ said:

> **J** 'The authorities show that an article is not to be described as noxious for present purposes merely because it has a potentiality for harm if taken in an overdose. There are many articles of value in common use which may be harmful in overdose, and . . . one cannot describe an article as noxious merely because it has that aptitude. On the other hand, if an article is liable to injure in common use, not when an overdose in the sense of accidental excess is used but is liable to cause an injury in common use, should it then not be regarded as a noxious thing for present purposes.
>
> When one has regard to the potentiality of heroin in the circumstances which we read about and hear about in our courts today we have no hesitation in saying that heroin is a noxious thing.'

For s 24 a harmless substance, such as a sedative or a laxative, may become 'noxious' if administered in large quantities. In *Marcus* [1981] 2 All ER 833 a woman put eight sedative and sleeping pills into a neighbour's bottle of milk. The defence relied on the decision in *Cato* (1976) and argued that these could not be a 'noxious thing' because they were harmless in themselves. The Court of Appeal held that for s 24, the quantity could be taken into account in light of the necessary intent to injure, aggrieve, or annoy.

10.7.3 Maliciously

The word 'maliciously' in both sections has the meaning given to it in *Cunningham* (1957). This means that the defendant must intend or be subjectively reckless about the administration of the substance. For s 23 there is no need to prove that the defendant intended or was reckless in respect of the endangering life or inflicting grievous bodily harm. Section 24 has an additional requirement for *mens rea* of intent to injure, aggrieve or annoy. In *Hill* (1985) 81 Cr App R 206 the defendant was a homosexual who gave slimming tablets to two boys intending that it would keep them awake and disinhibit them so they would be more likely to accept his sexual advances. It was held that this was sufficient for an intent to injure.

ACTIVITY

Self-test questions

1. Explain when:

   a words can be sufficient for a technical assault;

   b words will negate an assault.

2. Explain what is necessary for the *actus reus* of a battery.

3. What are the problems in deciding whether consent will be a defence to a battery of a s 47 offence?

4. Explain the difficulties in s 20 using the word 'inflict', while s 18 uses the word 'cause'.

5. Explain the different levels of *mens rea* required for s 47, s 20 and s 18.

Further reading

Bell, B and Harrison, K, '*R v Savage, DPP v Parmenter* and the Law of Assault' (1993) 56 MLR 83.

Gunn, M J and Ormerod, D, 'The Legality of Boxing' (1995) 15 LS 181.

Malik, M, 'Racist crime: racially aggravated offences in the Crime and Disorder Act 1998', Part II (1999) 62 MLR 409.

Smith, J C, 'Offences against the person; the Home Office Consultation Paper' [1998] Crim LR 317.

Weait, M, 'Criminal Law and the transmission of HIV: *R v Dica*' (2005) MLR 121.

SEXUAL OFFENCES ■▬▬

AIMS AND OBJECTIVES ☐☐☐

After reading this chapter you should be able to:

- Understand the law of rape

- Understand the law of assault by penetration, sexual assault, incest, and other sexual offences

- Analyse critically the law on sexual offences

- Apply the law to factual situations to determine whether there is liability for rape or for another sexual offence

The law of sexual offences in England and Wales has recently undergone radical reform. The reform process can be traced back to the then Home Secretary's announcement in January 1999 that a major review of the law governing sex offenders was to take place. An independent review body was set up and its findings, contained in a document entitled *Setting the Boundaries – Reforming the Law on Sex Offenders*, were published in July 2000. The opening paragraphs of the document explain why the review was necessary:

'Why did the law need reviewing? It is a patchwork quilt of provisions ancient and modern that works because people make it do so, not because there is a coherence and structure. Some is quite new – the definition of rape for example was last changed in 1994. But much is old, dating from nineteenth century laws that codified the common law of the time, and reflected the social attitudes and roles of men and women of the time. With the advent of a new century and the incorporation of the European Convention of Human Rights into our law, the time was right to take a fresh look at the law to see that it meets the need of the country today.'

At the time of the review, 'rape' was defined as penetration of the vagina or anus of another person without consent (s 1(1) of the Sexual Offences Act 1956 (as amended by the Criminal Justice and Public Order Act 1994)). Other forms of non-consensual sexual contact were dealt with under an offence called 'indecent assault' (contrary to ss 14 and 15 of the Sexual Offences Act 1956). The *actus reus* of the latter crime covered a very wide range of activities:

- oral sex (*McAllister* [1997] Crim LR 233)

- penetration of the vagina with D's hand (*Boyea* [1992] Crim LR 574)

- spanking (*Court* [1989] AC 28)

- stroking a woman's breasts (*Tabassum* [2000] 2 Cr App R 328)

- stroking a woman's lower leg (*Price* [2003] EWCA Crim 2405; *The Times*, 20th August 2003).

In addition to the width of the offence, there was also sometimes difficulty in establishing that an assault had been 'indecent'. According to Lord Ackner in *Court* (1989), it was a matter for the jury to decide whether 'right-minded persons would consider the conduct indecent or not'. *Setting the Boundaries – Reforming the Law on Sex Offenders* sets out the Review Body's position on the law of sexual offences as follows (paragraph 0.9):

> 'In looking at the law on rape and sexual assault we recommend that these offences should be redefined in the following way:
>
> - that **rape** be redefined to include penetration of the mouth, anus or female genitalia by a penis;
>
> - a new offence of **sexual assault by penetration** to deal with all other forms of penetration of the anus and genitalia;
>
> - rape and sexual assault by penetration should be seen as equally serious, and both should carry a maximum sentence of life imprisonment;
>
> - a new offence of **sexual assault** to replace other non-penetrative sexual touching now contained in the offence of sexual assault.'

After a consultation period culminating in March 2001, in November 2002 the Government published a White Paper called *Protecting the Public – Strengthening Protection against Sex Offenders and Reforming the Law on Sexual Offences* setting out its proposals for reform. The Government clearly endorsed the findings of the independent review body, as this extract shows (Overview, paragraphs 8–9):

> 'The law on sex offences, as it stands, is archaic, incoherent and discriminatory. Much of it is contained in the Sexual Offences Act 1956, and most of that was simply a consolidation of nineteenth-century law. It does not reflect the changes in society and social attitudes that have taken place since the Act became law and it is widely considered to be inadequate and out of date. While some piecemeal reform has taken place over the years, we have now undertaken a comprehensive review of the law so that it can meet the needs of today's society.'

The proposed reforms were put to Parliament and in due course the Sexual Offences Act 2003 was passed, the main provisions of which entered into force on 1st May 2004.

11.1 Rape

Section 1(1) of the Sexual Offences Act 2003 defines 'rape' in the following terms.

S '1(1) A person (A) commits an offence if −

(a) he intentionally penetrates the vagina, anus or mouth of another person (B) with his penis,

(b) B does not consent to the penetration, and

(c) A does not reasonably believe that B consents.'

Section 1(2) provides that 'whether a belief is reasonable is to be determined having regard to all the circumstances, including any steps A has taken to ascertain whether B consents'. The new definition replaces that found in s 1(1) of the Sexual Offences Act 1956 (as amended by the Criminal Justice and Public Order Act 1994), which stated that 'it is an offence for a man to rape a woman or another man'. Section 1(2) added that a man committed rape if he had 'sexual intercourse with a person (whether vaginal or anal) who at the time of the intercourse does not consent to it; and (b) at the time he knows that the person does not consent to the intercourse or is reckless as to whether that person consents to it.'

Actus reus elements

- Penetration of the vagina, anus or mouth of another person, V, with the penis.
- Lack of consent by V.

Mens rea elements

- Intent to penetrate V's vagina, anus or mouth.
- Lack of reasonable belief in V's consent.

Summary of changes

- Penetration of the mouth becomes rape.
- Genuine belief that V was consenting is no longer a good defence. The belief must be reasonable.

11.1.1 Penetration of the vagina, anus or mouth of another person, with the penis

Prior to the 1994 Act, rape could only be committed by penetration of V's vagina (it followed that only women could be the victims of rape). The definition of 'rape' was expanded in 1994 to include penetration of the anus, which meant that prosecution for male rape was possible for the first time (prior to 1994, the non-consensual anal penetration of either a man or woman would have been charged as buggery). Following the 2003 Act, the non-consensual penetration of either the vagina, anus or mouth amounts to the *actus reus* of rape. The one constant feature over this time has been the requirement that the penetration be by D's penis. The non-consensual penetration of V's vagina or anus by some other body part, or anything else, may now be charged under s 2 of the 2003 Act, as 'assault by penetration' (see section 11.2 below). Section 79(3) of the 2003 Act states that 'references to a part of the body include references to a part surgically constructed (in particular, through gender reassignment surgery).' This would allow:

- a post-operative female-to-male transsexual to commit rape using an artificially created penis
- a post-operative male-to-female transsexual to be the victim of rape if her artificially created vagina were to be penetrated by D's penis.

One of the first cases under s 1 to reach the Court of Appeal under the 2003 Act involved the extended definition of rape, that is, penetration of V's mouth with D's penis. In the case, *Ismail* [2005] EWCA Crim 397, Lord Woolf CJ noted that 'the fact that this was oral rape does not mean that it is any less serious than vaginal or anal rape'.

CASE EXAMPLE

Ismail [2005] EWCA Crim 397

D, aged 18, approached V, aged 16 and a virgin, who was standing near a phone box in Sheffield. V decided to walk to her friend's house and D accompanied her. When they reached a deserted path through grass verges D suddenly grabbed V from behind and pulled her onto the verge. He touched her vagina (which led to a separate conviction of sexual assault under s 3, see below) and then forced V to suck on his penis. He threatened to stab her if she did not comply and slapped and punched her about the face until he ejaculated into her mouth. Afterwards he stroked her hair and apologised. After D was arrested and charged he claimed consent but V had recorded the whole incident on her mobile phone. D changed his plea to guilty and his appeal (against sentence) was dismissed.

Penetration

Section 79(2) of the Sexual Offences Act 2003 states that 'penetration is a continuing act from entry to withdrawal'. This gives statutory effect to the Privy Council ruling in *Kaitamaki* [1984] 2 All ER 435, where the Court held that D commits rape if, having penetrated with consent, or believing he has consent, declines to withdraw on consent being revoked, or on realising that V does not consent. This was confirmed by the Court of Appeal in *Cooper and Schaub* [1994] Crim LR 531. V had allegedly been raped by the two defendants, whom she had met in a pub and later had sex with. After retiring to consider a verdict, the jury asked the judge: 'If we find that initially there was consent to intercourse and this was subsequently withdrawn and intercourse continued, does this by law constitute rape?' The judge answered in the affirmative and the jury convicted. Although the convictions were quashed on appeal, the Court of Appeal confirmed the correctness of the judge's direction on the point of law.

11.1.2 The absence of consent

An essential element in rape is the absence of consent to penetration. As rape is an indictable offence, this is a matter for the jury to decide. Early authorities emphasised the use of force; that the penetration had to be against V's will. However, it is now clear that the lack of consent may exist with or without force being used. In *Olugboja* [1982] QB 320, D contended that rape required the submission of the victim, induced by force or the threat of force. He had been convicted of raping a 16-year-old girl who had not offered resistance nor cried for help, because she was too frightened. The Court of Appeal dismissed the appeal. Dunn LJ said:

> **J** 'It is not necessary for the prosecution to prove that what might otherwise appear to have been consent was in reality merely submission induced by force, fear or fraud, although one or more of these factors will no doubt be present in the majority of cases of rape . . . [The jury] should be directed that consent, or the absence of it, is to be given its ordinary meaning and if need be, by way of example, that there is a difference between consent and submission.'

This is made explicit in the new Act. Section 74 states that a person 'consents if he agrees by choice, and has the freedom and capacity to make that choice'. V may appear to be consenting – perhaps through fear that physical resistance, struggling, screaming or shouting for help may provoke D into violence – and yet not actually be doing so. This was demonstrated vividly in *McFall* [1994] Crim LR 226. D kidnapped his former girlfriend, V, at gunpoint and had driven her from Leeds to a hotel in Hull, where they had sex. V faked orgasms throughout the intercourse, so that it may have appeared that she was consenting. However, D's rape conviction was upheld. Taking into account the fact that D had kidnapped V with a gun (although in fact an imitation, it looked real, and he had told her that it was loaded), there was sufficient evidence that V's apparent consent was not genuine in order for the jury to convict.

Presumptions about consent

Sections 75 and 76 of the Sexual Offences Act 2003 apply to the offences in s 1 (rape), s 2 (assault by penetration), s 3 (sexual assault) and s 4 (causing a person to engage in sexual activity without consent).

Evidential presumptions

Section 75 of the 2003 Act is headed 'Evidential presumptions about consent'.

'75(1) If in proceedings for an offence to which this section applies it is proved –

    (a) that [D] did the relevant act,

    (b) that any of the circumstances specified in subsection (2) existed, and

    (c) that [D] knew that those circumstances existed,

[V] is to be taken not to have consented to the relevant act unless sufficient evidence is adduced to raise an issue as to whether he consented, and [D] is to be taken not to have reasonably believed that [V] consented unless sufficient evidence is adduced to raise an issue as to whether he reasonably believed it.

(2) The circumstances are that –

    (a) any person was, at the time of the relevant act or immediately before it began, using violence against [V] or causing [V] to fear that immediate violence would be used against him;

    (b) any person was, at the time of the relevant act or immediately before it began, causing [V] to fear that violence was being used, or that immediate violence would be used, against another person;

    (c) [V] was, and [D] was not, unlawfully detained at the time of the relevant act;

    (d) [V] was asleep or otherwise unconscious at the time of the relevant act;

    (e) because of [V]'s physical disability, [V] would not have been able at the time of the relevant act to communicate to [D] whether [V] consented;

    (f) any person had administered to or caused to be taken by [V], without [V]'s consent, a substance which, having regard to when it was administered or taken, was capable of causing or enabling [V] to be stupefied or overpowered at the time of the relevant act.'

One of the evidential presumptions in s 75 is the situation where V is 'unlawfully detained' (s 75(2)(c)), although the Court of Appeal did not need to refer to that section in the recent case of *B* [2006] EWCA Crim 400. In the words of Swift J, D forced V to 'put her wrists into some dog leads, which he secured to the bed posts. He tied her ankles with a belt and forced open her legs. He pulled down her pyjama bottoms and her thong to her ankles. He then took off his own clothes and said, "You have a choice, either up the front or up the back". He turned her over and committed an act of anal rape.'

Section 75(2)(d) refers to the situation in cases such as *Larter and Castleton* [1995] Crim LR 75. There, D had sexual intercourse with V, a 14-year-old girl, who was asleep at the time. He was charged with rape and argued that it had to be proved that V had demonstrated lack of consent. The Court of Appeal upheld D's conviction, confirming that it is not necessary to prove a positive dissent by V, it is enough that he/she did not <u>assent</u>. On these facts, there would now be an 'evidential presumption' that V was not consenting, requiring D to prove that she was consenting.

A similar situation arose in *Blacklock* [2006] EWCA Crim 1740, where D was convicted of rape after having sex with a sleeping girl. The Court of Appeal did not actually refer to the presumption in s 75(2)(d), although it would appear to have been relevant. Mitting J simply stated that 'The facts disclose that the appellant had to go into the victim's bedroom, remove her knickers and his own clothes and *rape her whilst she was asleep*' (emphasis added).

Section 75(2)(f) refers to the situation in cases such as *Camplin* (1845) 1 Den 89, where D was convicted of rape after rendering a woman insensible by plying her with alcohol before having intercourse. On these facts, there would now be an 'evidential presumption' that V was not consenting, requiring D to prove that she was consenting. This situation is all too familiar in the early twenty-first century, with incidents involving the use of 'date rape' drugs. Powerful sedatives designed to alleviate sleeping disorders are available in tablet form and can be easily crushed and dissolved in liquid. Because they are usually tasteless and odourless, they can be slipped into V's drinks in a bar or nightclub without her knowledge, in order to render her unconscious or semi-conscious during sex.

The evidential presumption does not apply where V has become drunk or drugged or otherwise intoxicated of his/her own free will, as opposed to though use of force or some subterfuge on the part of D. Nevertheless, if D takes advantage of V whilst he/she is in this condition, this could still be rape, although the burden of proof would remain on the prosecution. For example, in *Malone* [1998] EWCA Crim 1462; [1998] 2 Cr App R 447, V, a 16-year-old girl, got so drunk when out with friends that she was incapable of walking and had to be given a lift home. D, a neighbour, was asked to help carry her into her house where her friends undressed her and put her to bed. Thereafter D stayed, ostensibly to make sure she did not vomit and choke. However, V claimed that he then climbed on top of her and had intercourse before she could kick him off. D was convicted of rape and appealed on the ground that, in this sort of case involving neither force nor fraud, a lack of consent had to be demonstrated either by speech or physical conduct. The Court of Appeal disagreed and dismissed the appeal.

Conclusive presumptions

Section 76 of the Act is headed 'Conclusive presumptions about consent'.

'76(1) If in proceedings for an offence to which this section applies it is proved that [D] did the relevant act and that any of the circumstances specified in subsection (2) existed, it is to be conclusively presumed –

(a) that [V] did not consent to the relevant act, and

   (b) that [D] did not believe that [V] consented to the relevant act.

(2) The circumstances are that –

   (a) [D] intentionally deceived [V] as to the nature or purpose of the relevant act;

   (b) [D] intentionally induced [V] to consent to the relevant act by impersonating a person known personally to [V].'

Rape through fraud and deception

Where D deceives V as to the very nature of the act which he is performing, there is now a 'conclusive' presumption that V did not consent and that D did not believe that V was consenting (s 76(2)(a)). The new presumption would, presumably, apply to the situations which arose in the following cases:

- *Flattery* (1877) 2 QBD 410. V had sex with D – although she was under the impression that he was performing a surgical operation which would cure her fits.

- *Williams* [1923] 1 KB 340. V (a 16-year-old choirgirl) had sex with D (the choirmaster) – although she was under the impression that he was performing exercises to help her breathing (she did not, apparently, even realise she was actually having sex).

However, the presumption will not apply in cases such as arose in *Linekar* [1995] 3 All ER 69, where D's deception does <u>not</u> go to the 'nature or purpose' of the act. For example, misrepresentations by D as to his wealth or professional status would not render sex obtained thereby rape. In *Linekar* (1995), Morland J stated: 'An essential ingredient in the law of rape is the proof that the woman did not consent to [the act of penetration] with the particular man who penetrated her.'

CASE EXAMPLE

Linekar [1995] 3 All ER 69

V, a prostitute, agreed to have sex with D in return for £25 after he approached her outside the Odeon cinema in Streatham. They duly had sex on the balcony of a block of flats. Afterwards D made off without paying. V complained that she had been raped. D was convicted of rape on the basis that he had never had any intention of paying and hence V's consent was vitiated by his fraud. The Court of Appeal quashed the conviction. It was the absence of consent, not the presence of fraud, which made otherwise lawful sexual intercourse rape.

The Court of Appeal in *Linekar* (1995) approved an Australian case, *Papadimitropoulos* (1958) 98 CLR 249, in which V was deceived into thinking that she was married to D. In fact the marriage was a sham. The High Court of Australia held that this consent was a defence to rape. A very similar case to that of *Linekar* (1995) is the British Columbia Court of Appeal judgment in *Petrozzi* (1987) 35 CCC (3d) 528. D had agreed to pay V $100 for sexual services but did not intend to make that payment. The Court held that this type of deception could not be said to relate to the nature and quality of the act and was insufficient to vitiate V's consent.

Rape through impersonation

Where D impersonates V's husband, fiancé or boyfriend (or some other person known to V), then again the conclusive presumption applies (s 76(2)(b)). This would apply to the type of situation that arose in *Elbekkay* [1995] Crim LR 163. D had deceived V into thinking that he was her boyfriend. He was convicted of rape after the trial judge directed the jury that there was no difference between impersonating a husband and impersonating a boyfriend or fiancé: both cases amount to rape. The Court of Appeal upheld the conviction.

11.1.3 Intent to penetrate

The meaning of 'intention' is the same throughout the criminal law. Refer to Chapter 3 for discussion.

11.1.4 Lack of reasonable belief

It must be proved that, at the time of the penetration, D did not reasonably believe that V was consenting. It will no longer be a defence to plead that D honestly (but unreasonably) believed that V was consenting. The House of Lords' judgment in *DPP v Morgan and others* [1976] AC 182 has therefore been overruled. If D's belief that V was consenting was mistaken, and this mistake was due to alcohol or other intoxicants, then it would seem to follow that such belief would be regarded almost automatically as unreasonable (unless there are other factors to explain D's mistake). The defendant in *Woods* (1981) 74 Cr App R 312 committed the *actus reus* of rape but pleaded in his defence that he mistakenly thought the victim was consenting (the mistake being caused by intoxication). He was convicted after the jury was directed that evidence of intoxication was irrelevant. Following the 2003 Act, the jury would be directed to consider whether D's belief was reasonable. It is submitted that they would convict.

In *Fotheringham* (1989) 88 Cr App R 206, D had been out with his wife and had been drinking heavily (7–8 pints of lager). When they returned home, he climbed into the marital bed where the baby-sitter, V, was asleep. Under the mistaken impression that V was his wife, he had sex with her without her consent. At the time, the fact that D was married meant he could not be convicted of rape if he genuinely believed V was his wife. However, the judge directed the jury to ignore the effects of drink in considering whether there were reasonable grounds for his belief that he was having lawful intercourse: 'The reasonable grounds are grounds which would be reasonable to a

sober man'. He was convicted and the Court of Appeal upheld the conviction. Watkins LJ said that: 'in rape self-induced intoxication is no defence, whether the issue be intention, consent or, as here, mistake as to the identity of the victim . . .'. This decision would certainly be the same today.

In *Taran* [2006] EWCA Crim 1498, the Court of Appeal considered the provision in s 1 that D is not guilty if he reasonably believed that V was consenting. In the case D had been convicted of raping a girl in his car; her version of events was that throughout the incident she had been struggling to escape. Hughes LJ stated (emphasis added):

> **J** 'A direction upon absence of reasonable belief clearly falls to be given when, *but only when*, there is material on which a jury might come to the conclusion that (a) the complainant did not in fact consent, but (b) the defendant thought that she was consenting. Such a direction does not fall to be given unless there is such material ... we are, in the circumstances, unaltered in our conclusion that a misunderstanding as to whether or not the complainant consented was *simply not a realistic possibility* on the evidence before this jury.'

11.1.5 The marital exception to rape

At common law, it was formerly the case that rape did not apply to married couples. The rule that a man could not rape his wife survived until the later years of the twentieth century (*Jones* [1973] Crim LR 710). This rule was finally removed by the Lords in *R* [1992] 1 AC 599.

11.1.6 Women as defendants

Before the 2003 Act, it was explicit that only a man could commit rape. Although the 2003 Act changes the wording of the offence from 'man' to 'person', it then makes clear that only a man can commit rape because there has to be penetration by a penis. Thus, that aspect of the law is unchanged. However, despite the fact that only a man may commit rape as a principal, a woman may be convicted of rape as a secondary party (refer back to Chapter 5, section 5.3, if necessary, for a reminder of these terms). This was demonstrated in *DPP v K and C* [1997] Crim LR 121, when two girls were convicted of procuring the rape of a girl by an unknown youth (the girls had ordered V to remove her clothing and have sex). This is surely right: without the girls' actions the rape might never have taken place; and in terms of liability as a secondary party, the girls' gender was irrelevant to their liability.

11.2 Assault by penetration

This is a new offence created by the Sexual Offences Act 2003. Section 2(1) of the Act states:

 '2(1) A person (A) commits an offence if (a) he intentionally penetrates the vagina or anus of another person (B) with a part of his body or anything else; (b) the penetration is sexual; (c) B does not consent to the penetration; and (d) A does not reasonably believe that B consents.'

Section 2(2) repeats the wording of s 1(2). (See section 11.1.)

Actus reus elements

* Penetration of the vagina or anus of another person, V.

* With a body part or anything else.

* Penetration must be 'sexual'.

* V does not consent.

Mens rea elements

* Intent to penetrate V's vagina or anus.

* Lack of reasonable belief in V's consent.

'Sexual'

This word is defined in s 78 of the Sexual Offences Act 2003 as follows.

 '78 Penetration, touching or any other activity is sexual if a reasonable person would consider that (a) whatever its circumstances or any person's purpose in relation to it, it is because of its nature sexual, or (b) because of its nature it may be sexual and because of its circumstances or the purpose of any person in relation to it (or both) it is sexual.'

An early case involving s 2 is *Coomber* [2005] EWCA Crim 1113. D had penetrated the anus of V, a sleeping boy (D had drugged V with sleeping tablets) with his finger. D was convicted after footage which D had taken himself using his own digital camera was seized. In *Cunliffe* [2006] EWCA Crim 1706, D was convicted of a s 2 assault after attacking a 14-year-old girl on a deserted field and inserting one or more of his fingers into her anus. In both of these cases it is clear that D's penetration was sexual 'because of its nature'.

The relationship between s 1 and s 2 of the 2003 Act was considered in *Lyddaman* [2006] EWCA Crim 383. Openshaw J noted that on the evidence 'plainly there had been some sexual interference and indeed penetration. The question for the jury was whether it was *penile* penetration to make

the appellant guilty of rape ... or *digital* penetration to render him guilty of sexual assault by penetration' (emphasis added). Upholding the conviction, the Court of Appeal noted that the jury had convicted D under s 2, which was described as 'the lesser offence'.

11.3 Sexual assault

This is another new offence created by the Sexual Offences Act 2003, although it clearly replaces that of indecent assault. This development is described by Simester and Sullivan, in the second edition of their book *Criminal Law Theory and Doctrine* (2003) as 'very welcome'. They criticised the old offence as 'an anachronism', the emphasis on 'indecency' being 'beside the point in a modern law focused on sexual violence'. Section 3(1) of the Act states that:

 '3(1) A person (A) commits an offence if (a) he intentionally touches another person (B); the touching is sexual; (c) B does not consent to the touching, and (d) A does not reasonably believe that B consents.'

Section 3(2) repeats the wording of s 1(2). (See section 11.1.)

Actus reus elements

* Touching of another person, V.
* Touching is 'sexual' (see the definition in s 78 above).
* V does not consent to the touching.

'Touching'/'sexual touching'

This is a new concept for English criminal law. Previously, it was necessary to establish an 'assault'. Clearly any physical contact between D and V will suffice, but is not necessary. Section 79(8) provides a definition of what is <u>included</u> in the concept of 'touching' – in other words, this is not an exhaustive but an illustrative definition. It states that 'touching' includes touching (a) with any part of the body; (b) with anything else; (c) through anything. Finally, 'touching amounting to penetration' is included 'in particular'. This means that there is deliberate overlap between the offences in ss 2(1) and 3(1). Under the definition of 'sexual' in s 78, certain 'touchings' are automatically 'sexual' (paragraph (a)), whereas other touchings are ambiguous and whether they are 'sexual' or not depends on the circumstances and/or D's purpose (paragraph (b)).

Since the 2003 Act entered into force in May 2004 the Court of Appeal has dealt with several cases under s 3, mostly appeals against sentence. Nevertheless these cases illustrate the wide range of circumstances in which the offence may be committed (as you read through this list consider which of these touchings are automatically sexual because of their 'nature' and which are only sexual because of the circumstances and/or D's purpose):

- Touching V's breasts (*Bamonadio* [2005] EWCA Crim 3355; *Burns* [2006] EWCA Crim 1451; *Ralston* [2005] EWCA Crim 3279).

- Touching V's private parts (*Elvidge* [2005] EWCA Crim 1194; *Forrester* [2006] EWCA Crim 1748).

- Kissing V's private parts (*Turner* [2005] EWCA Crim 3436).

- Kissing V's face (*W* [2005] EWCA Crim 3138).

- Pressing D's body against V's buttocks (*Nika* [2005] EWCA Crim 3255).

- Rubbing D's penis against V's body (*Osmani* [2006] EWCA Crim 816).

- Sniffing V's hair while stroking her arm (*Deal* [2006] EWCA Crim 684).

- Ejaculating onto V's clothes while dancing close together (*Bounekhla* [2006] EWCA Crim 1217).

Section 3(1) requires that D 'touches another person', although s 79(8)(c) provides that it can be 'through anything'. This was considered in *R v H* (2005), *The Times*, 8th February, where the Court of Appeal held that the touching of V's clothing was sufficient to amount to 'touching' for the purposes of an offence under s 3(1).

Mens rea elements

- Intent to touch another person.

- Lack of reasonable belief in V's consent.

11.4 Rape and other offences against children under 13

Prior to the 2003 Act, there was a crime of unlawful sexual intercourse with a girl under 13 (s 5, Sexual Offences Act 1956). The new Act replaces this crime with a new offence, rape of a child. Other new offences are also created.

- **Rape of a child under 13** (s 5(1)). This offence shares some *actus reus* elements with the crime of rape in s 1 – penetration of V's vagina, anus or mouth with D's penis – but there are two crucial differences. First, V must be under 13. Second, lack of consent is not an element of the *actus reus*. Thus, for example, D will not be able to argue that V, a 12-year-old girl, was unusually precocious and gave consent to sex.

  The only *mens rea* element stated is that D intended to penetrate V's vagina, anus or mouth. Liability is intended to be strict with regard to V's age; that is, if D is charged with the new offence under s 5 after having sex with a 12-year-old girl (for example) he will not be able to argue that he honestly thought that she was older than she was.

This scenario – used as an example in the first edition of this book – duly occurred in fact shortly afterwards. *Corran & Others* [2005] EWCA Crim 192 involved four different cases, in one of which D, a 20-year-old man, was deceived by V, aged 12, into thinking that she was in fact 16.

CASE EXAMPLE

Corran & Others [2005] EWCA Crim 192

D, aged 20, and V, aged 12, lived in Connah's Quay near Chester. They met when V was accompanied by a number of 15- or 16-year-old girls. V apparently looked and behaved like a 16-year-old. She told D that she was 16, in year 11 at school and that she would be soon leaving school. They began a relationship which lasted several weeks. It was V who actually initiated sex with D, by removing her clothes, and they used a condom. Subsequently, however, when V told her mother what had happened she contacted the police. D admitted that sex occurred but told police that he thought V was 16 and said that he would never have become involved with her had he known her real age. He felt 'disgusted and ashamed'. Nevertheless, D was convicted of raping a girl under 13, as the trial judge held that both V's consent as to intercourse and D's belief in her age were both irrelevant. The Court of Appeal upheld the conviction.

In *G* [2006] EWCA Crim 821; [2006] 1 WLR 2052, the Court of Appeal held that the offence of rape of a child under 13, contrary to s 5(1), was one of strict liability. The elements of the offence are that D (a) intentionally penetrates the vagina, anus or mouth of another person with his penis and (b) the other person is under 13. Although D must have the intention to 'penetrate', there is no *mens rea* as to V's age, nor is there any *mens rea* as to whether or not V is consenting. In other words, the prosecution simply have to prove that D intentionally had sex with V. If it turns out that she is under 13 years of age, D is guilty. In the case, D, a 15-year-old boy, had consensual sex with a 12-year-old girl although he honestly (and, apparently, reasonably) believed that she was, in fact, 15. However, after being told that these factors were irrelevant, G pleaded guilty and appealed. The Court considered whether imposing strict liability under s 5(1) would amount to a breach of Article 6(1) of the ECHR (the right to a fair trial), and decided that it would not.

In *D* [2006] EWCA Crim 111, the Court of Appeal confirmed that 'absence of consent is not an ingredient of the offence' under s 5(1), although the Court went on to hold that 'presence of consent is . . . material in relation to sentence, particularly in relation to young defendants. The age of the defendant, of itself and when compared with the age of the victim, is also an important factor'. The case involved a 14-year-old boy having consensual sex with his 12-year-old sister. D was convicted and sentenced to three years' detention.

- **Assault of a child under 13 by penetration** (s 6(1)). The *actus reus* elements are that D must penetrate V's vagina or anus with a body part or anything else and the penetration must be 'sexual'. V must be under 13. Lack of consent is not an element of the crime.

  The only *mens rea* element stated is that D intended to penetrate V's vagina or anus. Liability is intended to be strict with regard to V's age.

Early cases to have reached the Court of Appeal involving s 6(1) include *RC* [2005] EWCA Crim 3160, where D inserted his fingers inside the vagina of his own 12-year-old daughter while she was asleep; and *C* [2006] EWCA Crim 768, where D, in the words of McKinnon J, 'attempted to penetrate V's anus with his penis and actually penetrated her anus with a vibrator on two occasions. All the while the victim was aged only 5'.

- **Sexual assault of a child under 13** (s 7(1)). The *actus reus* elements are that D touches V, the touching is 'sexual' and V is under 13. Lack of consent is not an element of the crime.

  The only *mens rea* element stated is that D intended to touch V. Liability is intended to be strict with regard to both (a) the 'sexual' nature of the touching and (b) V's age. That is, D will not be able to argue that he honestly thought that a particular touching was not 'sexual' if the reasonable person would regard it as 'sexual'.

Several cases have already reached the Court of Appeal involving s 7(1). Early examples where convictions have been upheld include *Vatcher* [2006] EWCA Crim 1381, where D admitted touching and kissing a 7-year-old boy's penis, and *Mackney* [2006] EWCA Crim 1202, where D kissed an 11-year-old girl on the lips.

The situation in *Davies* [2005] EWCA Crim 3690, was unusual in that, unlike the cases cited above, D was a woman. Lynne Davies was aged 21 when, at a friend's house party, she kissed two young girls, one aged 11, and the other aged 8, on the lips.

ACTIVITY

> D, an adult man, often talks to V, a 12-year-old girl, whom he sees every day at the same bus stop. D thinks that she looks at least 14. He asks her age and she replies that she is 15. One day D asks V if she would like to have sex. V readily agrees and they walk to D's house, where they have sex. That night, V tells her parents what happened and they call the police. D is arrested and charged with rape of a child under 13, contrary to s 5(1) of the 2003 Act. Consider D's liability.

11.5 Sexual activity with a child

Section 9(1) of the 2003 Act creates a new offence of 'sexual activity with a child'. This replaces the offence under s 6 of the Sexual Offences Act 1956, unlawful sexual intercourse with a girl under 16.

Actus reus elements

- D must be aged 18 or over.
- D must touch another person, V.
- The touching must be 'sexual' (see the definition in s 78 above).
- V must be under 16.

The touching need not necessarily involve D's penis nor is it necessary that V's vagina, anus or mouth be penetrated. However, if the touching involves any of the following:

- penetration of V's anus or vagina with a part of D's body or anything else
- penetration of V's mouth with D's penis
- penetration of D's anus or vagina with a part of V's body
- penetration of D's mouth with V's penis,

then the offence is indictable, that is, any trial would take place in the Crown Court (s 9(2)). Other touchings (not involving penetration) are triable either way (s 9(3)).

If D is aged under 18, then D would not escape liability. Instead, the charge would be brought under s 13(1) of the 2003 Act instead, the only other difference being that the maximum sentence on conviction is reduced.

Mens rea elements

- D must intend to touch V.
- D must have no reasonable belief that V is 16 or over.

Liability is therefore intended to be strict with regard to the 'sexual' nature of the touching. If V is, in fact, under 13 then the only *mens rea* requirement is an intent to touch. Liability will be strict with regard to (a) the 'sexual' nature of the touching and (b) V's age.

Several cases have also reached the Court of Appeal involving s 9(1). The cases include the following (in each case the conviction was upheld):

- *Eitreri* [2005] EWCA Crim 935. D, aged 24, had consensual sex with a 13-year-old girl on the living room sofa in her mother's home.
- *Couch* [2005] EWCA Crim 1309. D, aged 18, and V, a 14-year-old girl, engaged in 'some oral sex and various other sexual touchings which included a degree of penile penetration', according to the Court of Appeal.
- *Gardner* [2005] EWCA Crim 1399. D used his fingers to penetrate a 14-year-old girl's vagina.
- *Elliot* [2005] EWCA Crim 2835. D, aged 35, had consensual sex with V, a 14-year-old girl, on several occasions.

- *Monks* [2006] EWCA Crim 54. D admitted performing oral sex on a 15-year-old boy on 'about 20 occasions' and performing an act of anal sex on the same boy 'between 30 and 40 times'.
- *Greaves* [2006] EWCA Crim 641. According to Burnton J in the Court of Appeal: 'There were two victims. The first . . . was aged 14 . . . The second was 12-years-old . . . he licked the first victim's vagina and digitally penetrated it and he touched the second victim's breasts.'

In each case the Court of Appeal upheld the convictions despite suggestions in several of them that V was consenting. In *Gardner*, the Court of Appeal ruled that even a reasonable belief in V's consent was irrelevant. In other words, children under the age of 16 are incapable of consenting to sexual activity for the purposes of s 9(1). Walker J stated that D 'admitted digital penetration and accepted that he knew that [V] was under 16 years of age. He reasonably believed that she was consenting to digital penetration . . . [The trial judge] accepted that what the appellant did was consensual. *It was nonetheless still a serious offence*' (emphasis added).

11.6 Incest

The old offence of incest (under ss 10 or 11 of the Sexual Offences Act 1956) has been replaced, under the 2003 Act, with new offences under s 25 of 'Sexual activity with a child family member', under s 64 of 'Sex with an adult relative: penetration' and under s 65 of 'Sex with an adult relative: consenting to penetration'.

11.6.1 'Sexual activity with a child family member'

Actus reus elements

- D touches V.
- The touching is 'sexual' (as defined in s 78, described above).
- D is related to V (as defined in s 27).
- V is under 18.

Mens rea elements

- D intended to touch V.
- D knew, or could reasonably be expected to know, that his relation to V was 'of a description falling within' s 27.
- D had no reasonable belief that V was over 18.

Liability is therefore intended to be strict with regard to the 'sexual' nature of the touching. If V is, in fact, under 13 then the only *mens rea* requirements are an intent to touch and knowledge pertaining to the relationship between D and V. Liability will be strict with regard to (a) the 'sexual' nature of the touching and (b) V's age.

The first Court of Appeal case involving s 25 is *AT* [2006] EWCA Crim 1232, involving D, a man in his late 30s, having consensual sex on a number of occasions with his 13-year-old stepdaughter. The Court of Appeal was primarily concerned with the appropriate sentence, but did offer the following general guidance for future incest cases:

> J 'The sexual activity was procured by someone in the position of a parent. That is not only a gross breach of trust but is likely to add very substantially to the psychological impact on the child. [Although] the case would have been still more serious if force or violence had been used, we must emphasise that "consent" in the case of sexual intercourse with a child of 12 or 13 and a family member is a limited concept.'

'Family relationships': s 27

Section 27(1)(a) provides that the relationship between D and V constitutes one of the *actus reus* elements in a variety of situations. Certain relationships automatically satisfy the relationship element of the offence. Under s 27(2) it is enough if one party is the other's:

- parent
- grandparent
- brother or sister
- half-brother or half-sister
- aunt or uncle
- foster parent (here it is enough that D is <u>or has been</u> V's foster parent).

There are few incest cases reported, but reference will be made to one case under the old law which may prove important under the new law. In *Pickford* [1995] 1 Cr App R 420, the Court of Appeal held that the purpose of s 10 of the 1956 Act (which made it unlawful for a man to have sex with, *inter alia*, his mother) was to protect boys under 14 from their mothers. The Court therefore held that a boy under 14 could not commit the offence. Professor Sir John Smith did not agree. In the 10th edition of *Smith and Hogan's Criminal Law* (2001), he wrote that 'that does not seem to be the purpose of the offence of incest. If Parliament had wanted to protect young boys from predatory women, it would surely have created a general offence, not limited to particular relationships'. Under s 27(3) another set of relationships is provided, but there is a precondition: <u>either</u> that D and V live or have lived in the same household <u>or</u> that D is or has been regularly involved in caring for, training, supervising or being in sole charge of V. The relationships are that D and V are cousins or D is or has been V's:

- step-parent
- stepbrother or stepsister.

A final category involves the situation where the parent or present or former foster parent of one of them is or has been the other's foster parent. Under s 27(4) if D and V live or have lived in the same household <u>and</u> D is or has been regularly involved in caring for, training, supervising or being in sole charge of V, then that is sufficient relationship for the purposes of the offence. This would most obviously (but not necessarily exclusively) catch relations between an adopted child and his or her adopted parents.

Relations between adopted children and their natural parents

Section 27(1)(b) provides that it is sufficient for the offence if a relationship would have fallen within s 27(2), (3) or (4) 'but for s 67 of the Adoption and Children Act 2002'. This provides that 'An adopted person is to be treated in law as if born as the child of the adopters or adopter' (s 67(1)). Section 27(1)(b) means that the relationship between adopted children and their natural parents continues to subsist for the purposes of the criminal offence in s 25.

Defences

Two defences are provided for: marriage and pre-existing sexual relationships.

* Section 28 provides a defence where D and V are lawfully married and V is aged 16 or over. The burden of proving that D and V were lawfully married at the time is on D.

* Section 29 provides a defence where D and V were in a sexual relationship immediately before falling within s 27(3) or (4).

11.6.2 'Sex with an adult relative'

Section 64(1) provides that it is an offence for D to have sex with an adult relative in certain circumstances.

Actus reus elements

* D must be aged 16 or over.
* D must penetrate V's vagina or anus with a part of his body or anything else, or penetrate V's mouth with his penis.
* The penetration must be 'sexual' (as defined in s 78, above).
* V must be aged 18 or over.
* D and V must be related as parent, grandparent, child, grandchild, brother, sister, half-brother, half-sister, uncle, aunt, nephew or niece.

Note: despite the reference to 'his body' in s 64(1)(a), it is clear from the list of relatives in s 64(1)(e) that the offence could be committed by a female relative.

419

Mens rea elements

- Penetration must be intentional.

- D knows or could reasonably be expected to know that he is related to V in that way.

11.6.3 Sex with an adult relative: consenting to penetration

The above provisions relate to the offence committed by the relative who performs the penetration. However, s 65(1) creates a criminal offence committed, in certain circumstances, by a relative who consents to penetration by an adult relative. It is inappropriate to refer to the other party as 'V' here as it is quite likely that the other party will also be liable for the offence under s 64. Hence the other party will be referred to as E.

Actus reus elements

- E penetrates D's vagina or anus with a part of E's body or anything else, or penetrates D's mouth with E's penis.

- D consents to the penetration.

- The penetration is 'sexual' (as defined in s 78, above).

- E is aged 18 or over.

- The relationship between them is that E may be related to D are as parent, grandparent, child, grandchild, brother, sister, half-brother, half-sister, uncle, aunt, nephew or niece.

Mens rea elements

- D knows or could reasonably be expected to know that he is related to E in that way.

Incest: analysis

The 2003 Act does not explain why incest continues to be a crime. As Professor Sir John Smith observed in the 10th edition of *Smith and Hogan's Criminal Law* (2001), incest was not a crime until 1908 (previously it was dealt with by the ecclesiastical courts). He suggested that 'probably a significant reason' for its existence is 'the horror and disgust that the idea of it arouses'. Another possible justification was 'that the genetic risks of incest appear to be very high'.

ACTIVITY

> Should incest be a criminal offence? If so, do you agree that the 2003 Act defines appropriately the familial relationships that must exist? If you think that incest should not be a crime, would you nevertheless agree with Professor Sir John Smith when he wrote in *Criminal Law* (2001) that 'if the offence of incest . . . were to be abolished, it would probably be thought necessary to provide protection for persons under 21 from the lustful attentions of other members of the family'?

11.7 Other crimes under the Sexual Offences Act 2003

Space precludes giving detailed coverage to all the offences contained in the 2003 Act. The following table provides a summary of a selection of the other crimes.

KEY FACTS

Offence	Definition
Grooming (s 14)	Intentionally arranging or facilitating something that D intends to do if doing it will involve the commission of an offence under any of ss 9–13.
Meeting a child (s 15)	D (being 18 or over) intentionally meeting (or travelling with the intention of meeting, in any part of the world) V (being under 16), the pair having met or communicated with each other on at least two earlier occasions. D must intend to do something to or in respect of V, during or after the meeting, which will involve the commission of a 'relevant offence' (defined as any offence in Part 1 of the Act).
Abuse of position of trust (s 16)	Sexual touching by D of a person, V, to whom D was in a 'position of trust'. V must be under 18 and D must not reasonably believe that V was aged 18 or over, unless V was under 13, in which case liability is strict as to V's age.
Trespass with intent to commit a sexual offence (s 63)	Trespassing 'on any premises' with intent to 'commit a relevant sexual offence on the premises'. D must know or be reckless as to the trespass. This replaces the offence in s 9(1)(a) of the Theft Act 1968, whereby D is guilty of burglary if he enters a building (or part of a building) with intent to rape anyone therein. The s 63 offence is wider in two respects: (1) D need not necessarily intend to commit rape (sexual assault, for example, would suffice); (2) 'premises' is a more flexible concept than 'building'.
Exposure (s 66)	Intentionally exposing D's genitals with intent that 'someone will see them and be caused alarm or distress'.

Voyeurism (s 67)	Observing, for the purposes of obtaining sexual gratification, 'another person doing a private act' if D knows that the other person, V, does not consent to being observed. The offence can be committed in other ways, eg operating equipment with the intention of enabling someone else to observe V; recording V doing a private act; or installing equipment with the intention of enabling himself or another person to observe V doing a private act. A 'private act' is defined in s 68(1) as one done in a place which 'would reasonably be expected to provide privacy' and where (a) V's 'genitals, buttocks or breasts are exposed or covered only with underwear'; or (b) V is using a lavatory; or (c) V is 'doing a sexual act that is not of a kind ordinarily done in public'.
Intercourse with an animal (s 69)	Intentionally 'performing an act of penetration' with D's penis into the vagina or anus, or 'any similar part', of 'a living animal'. D must know or be reckless as to whether that is what is being penetrated.
Sexual penetration of a corpse (s 70)	Intentionally 'performing an act of penetration' with a part of D's body or anything else into 'a part of the body of a dead person'. D must know or be reckless as to whether that is what is being penetrated. The penetration must be sexual (liability is strict in this respect).

ACTIVITY

1. The Sexual Offences Act 2003 was designed to bring 'coherence and structure' to the law. Consider the extent to which it has succeeded in achieving this purpose.

2. The appeal courts in cases such as *Morgan* (1976) (on belief in consent), *Williams* (1987), *Owino* (1996) and *Martin (Anthony)* (2002) (on belief in the need to use force) and *Cairns* (1999) (on belief in circumstances creating a threat of death or serious injury) have emphasised that D is entitled to be assessed on the basis of what he or she <u>genuinely</u> believed. The Sexual Offences Act 2003 goes against that trend in establishing that a belief in consent for the purposes of the Act must be <u>reasonable</u>. Do you agree with Parliament's decision? What are the arguments for and against the use of an objective standard for assessing D's belief in whether V consented?

Further reading

Finch, E and Munro, V E, 'Intoxicated Consent and the Boundaries of Drug-Assisted Rape' [2003] Crim LR 773.

Gardner, J, 'Appreciating *Olugboja*' (1996) 16 Legal Studies 275.

Herring, J, 'Mistaken Sex' [2005] Crim LR 511.

Lacey, N, 'Beset by Boundaries: The Home Office Review of Sex Offenders' [2001] Crim LR 3.

Rumney, P, 'Review of Sex Offenders and Rape and Law Reform: Another False Dawn?' (2001) 64 MLR 801.

Sullivan, G R, 'The Need for a Crime of Sexual Assault' [1989] Crim LR 331.

Tadros, V, 'Rape Without Consent' (2006) 26 OJLS 515.

Internet links

Independent Review, 'Setting the Boundaries – Reforming the Law on Sex Offenders' (2000), available at www.homeoffice.gov.uk/docs/vol1main.pdf.

Home Office, *Protecting the Public,* White Paper (2002), available at www.protectingthepublic.homeoffice.gov.uk/default.asp.

Sexual Offences Act 2003, available at www.hmso.gov.uk.

chapter 12 THEFT ■

12.1 Background

The law relating to theft, robbery, burglary and other connected offences against property (see Chapters 13 and 14) is contained in two Acts:

• Theft Act 1968

• Theft Act 1978.

The Theft Act 1968 was an attempt to write a new and simple code for the law of theft and related offences. It made sweeping and fundamental changes to the law that had developed prior to 1968. The Act was based on the Eighth Report of the Criminal Law Revision Committee, *Theft and Related Offences*, Cmnd 2977 (1966). Previous Acts were repealed and the 1968 Act was meant to provide a complete code of the law in this area.

The Act is intended to be:

> **J** 'expressed in simple language, as used and understood by ordinary literate men and women. It avoids as far as possible those terms of art which have acquired a special meaning understood only by lawyers in which many of the penal enactments were couched.'
>
> Lord Diplock in *Treacy v DPP* [1971] 1 All ER 110.

Despite this, the wording of the Theft Act 1968 has led to a number of cases going to the appeal courts. The decisions in some of theses case are not always easy to understand. In particular there have been complex decisions on the meaning of the word 'appropriates'. Another problem is that, as the wording uses ordinary English, the precise meaning is often left to the jury to decide. This can lead to inconsistency in decisions. As Professor Sir John Smith pointed out:

> 'Even such ordinary words in the Theft Act as "dishonesty", "force", "building" etc. may involve definitional problems on which a jury require guidance if like is to be treated as like.'
>
> D. Ormerod, *Smith and Hogan Criminal Law* (11th edn, Butterworths, 2005), p 646

Amendments to the Theft Act 1968

It soon became apparent that the law was defective in the area of obtaining by deception and, following the Thirteenth Report by the Criminal Law Revision Committee, Cmnd 6733 (1977), the Theft Act 1978 was passed. This repealed part of s 16 of the 1968 Act and instead created four new offences. The 1978 Act also added another offence, of making off without payment, to fill a gap in the law.

Despite this amendment, it was held in the case of *Preddy* [1996] 3 All ER 481 that the law still did not cover certain deception frauds in obtaining mortgages and money transfers. The Law Commission was asked to research this area of law and following their report *Offences of Dishonesty: Money Transfers*, Law Com No 243, the Theft (Amendment) Act 1996 was passed to fill these gaps. This Act made amendments to both the Theft Act 1968 and the Theft Act 1978 so that those amendments now form part of those Acts.

12.1.1 Theft

Theft is defined in s 1 of the Theft Act 1968 which states that:

> '1 A person is guilty of theft if he dishonestly appropriates property belonging to another with the intention of permanently depriving the other of it.'

The Act then goes on in the next five sections to give some help with the meaning of the words or phrases in the definition. This is done in the order that the words or phrases appear in the definition, making it easy to remember the section numbers. They are:

- s 2 – 'dishonestly'
- s 3 – 'appropriates'
- s 4 – 'property'
- s 5 – 'belonging to another'
- s 6 – 'with the intention of permanently depriving the other of it'.

Remember that the offence is in s 1. A person charged with theft is always charged with stealing 'contrary to section 1 of the Theft Act 1968'. Sections 2 to 6 are definition sections explaining s 1. They do not themselves create any offence.

12.1.2 The elements of theft

The *actus reus* of theft is made up of the three elements in the phrase 'appropriates property belonging to another'. So to prove the *actus reus* it has to be shown that there was appropriation by the defendant of something which is property within the definition of the Act and which, at the time of the appropriation, belonged to another. All these seem straightforward words, but the effect of the definitions in the Act together with case decisions means that there can be some surprises. For example, although the wording 'belonging to another' seems very clear, it is possible for a defendant to be found guilty of stealing his own property. (See section 12.4.1.)

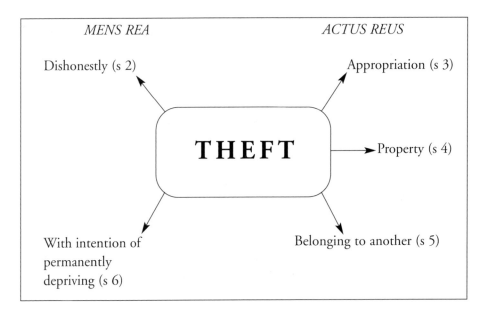

Figure 12.1 The elements of theft

There are two elements which must be proved for the *mens rea* of theft. These are that the appropriation of the property must be done 'dishonestly', and there must the intention of permanently depriving the other person of it.

We will now go on to consider each of the elements of theft in depth.

12.2 Appropriation

The more obvious situations of theft involve a physical taking, for example a pickpocket taking a wallet from someone's pocket. But appropriation is much wider than this.

Section 3(1) states that:

'3(1) Any assumption by a person of the rights of an owner amounts to an appropriation, and this includes, where he has come by the property (innocently or not) without stealing it, any later assumption of a right to it by keeping or dealing with it as owner.'

12.2.1 Assumption of the rights of an owner

The first part to be considered is the statement that 'any assumption by a person of the rights of an owner amounts to appropriation'. The rights of the owner include selling the property or destroying it as well such things as possessing it, consuming it, using it, lending it or hiring it out.

In *Pitham v Hehl* [1977] Crim LR 285, CA, D had sold furniture belonging to another person. This was held to be an appropriation. The offer to sell was an assumption of the rights of an owner and the appropriation took place at that point. It did not matter whether the furniture was removed from the house or not. Even if the owner was never deprived of the property, the defendant had still appropriated it by assuming the rights of the owner to offer the furniture for sale.

In *Corcoran v Anderton* (1980) Cr App Rep 104 two youths tried to pull a woman's handbag from her grasp, causing it to fall to the floor. The seizing of the handbag was enough for an appropriation (the youths were found guilty of robbery which has to have a theft as one of its elements), even though they did not take the bag away.

The wording in s 3(1) is '*any* assumption by a person of the rights of an owner'. One question which the courts have had to deal with is whether the assumption has to be of *all* of the rights or whether it can just be of *any* of the rights. In *Morris* [1983] 3 All ER 288, D had switched the price labels of two items on the shelf in a supermarket. He had then put one of the items, which now had a lower price on it, into a basket provided by the store for shoppers and taken the item to the check-out, but had not gone through the check-out when he was arrested. Lord Roskill in the House of Lords stated that:

> **J** 'It is enough for the prosecution if they have proved . . . the assumption of any of the rights of the owner of the goods in question.'

So there does not have to be an assumption of all the rights. This is a sensible decision since in many cases the defendant will not have assumed all of the rights. Quite often only one right will have been assumed, usually the right of possession.

Later assumption of a right

Section 3(1) also includes within the meaning of appropriation situations where a defendant has come by the property without stealing it, but has later assumed a right to it by keeping it or dealing with it as owner. This covers situations where the defendant has picked up someone else's property, eg a coat or a briefcase, thinking that it was his own. On getting home the defendant then realises that it is not his. If he then decides to keep the property this is a later assumption of a right and is an appropriation for the purposes of the Theft Act 1968.

However, under s 3(1) if the person has stolen the item originally, then any later keeping or dealing is not an appropriation. This was important in *Atakpu and Abrahams* [1994] Crim LR 693. The defendants had hired cars in Germany and Belgium using false driving licences and passports. They were arrested at Dover and charged with theft. The Court of Appeal quashed their convictions because the moment of appropriation under the law in *Gomez* (1993) (see section 12.2.3) was when they obtained the cars. So the theft had occurred outside the jurisdiction of the English courts. As they had already stolen the cars, keeping and driving them could not be an appropriation. This meant that the theft was completed in the country where they hired the cars, and there was no theft in this country.

12.2.2 Consent to the appropriation

Can a defendant appropriate an item when it has been given to them by the owner? This is an area which has caused major problems. Nowhere in the Theft Act does it say that the appropriation has to be without the consent of the owner. So, what is the position where the owner has allowed the defendant to take something because the owner thought that the defendant was paying for it with a genuine cheque? Or where the item was hired (as in *Atakpu and Abrahams*), but unknown to the owner the defendant intended to take it permanently? This point was addressed in *Lawrence* [1972] AC 626; (1971) Cr App R 64.

CASE EXAMPLE

Lawrence [1972] AC 626; (1971) Cr App Rep 64

An Italian student, who spoke very little English, arrived at Victoria Station and showed an address to Lawrence who was a taxi driver. The journey should have cost 50p, but Lawrence told him it was expensive. The student got out a £1 note and offered it to the driver. Lawrence said it was not enough and so the student opened his wallet and allowed Lawrence to help himself to another £6. Lawrence put forward the argument that he had not appropriated the money, as the student had consented to him taking it. Both the Court of Appeal and the House of Lords rejected this argument and held that there was appropriation in this situation.

Viscount Dilhorne said:

> J 'I see no ground for concluding that the omission of the words "without the consent of the owner" was inadvertent and not deliberate, and to read the subsection as if they were included is, in my opinion, wholly unwarranted. Parliament by the omission of these words has relieved the prosecution of the burden of establishing that the taking was without the owner's consent. That is no longer an ingredient of the offence.'

This view of Viscount Dilhorne is supported by the fact that under the old law in the Larceny Act 1916 the prosecution had to prove that the property had been taken without the consent of the owner.

However, in *Morris* (1983) the House of Lords did not take the same view. This was the case where the defendant had switched labels on goods in a supermarket. Lord Roskill said 'the concept of appropriation involves not an act expressly or impliedly authorised by the owner but an act by way of adverse interference with or usurpation of [the rights of an owner]'.

In fact this part of the judgment in *Morris* (1983) was *obiter*, since the switching of the labels was clearly an unauthorised act. But the judgment in *Morris* (1983) caused confusion since it contradicted *Lawrence* without the Law Lords saying whether *Lawrence* (1972) was overruled or merely distinguished.

In subsequent cases, matters became even more complicated. In *Dobson v General Accident Fire and Life Insurance Corp* [1990] 1 QB 354, a civil case, Dobson made a claim on his insurance policy for theft of some jewellery after he had agreed to sell the jewellery to X, who gave as payment a building society cheque which unknown to Dobson was stolen. The insurance company refused to

pay on the basis that, although there had been an offence of obtaining property by deception (s 15 Theft Act 1968), there was no theft and the policy only covered theft. The Court of Appeal held that there had been a theft, on the basis that the property was not intended to pass to X except in exchange for a valid cheque, so the property still belonged to Dobson and X had appropriated it at the moment he took delivery of it.

Parker LJ pointed out that in *Lawrence* (1972) the student had merely allowed or permitted the taxi driver to take the extra money. This was consistent with the concept of consent but differed from situations where the owner had authorised the taking as in *Skipp* [1975] Crim LR 114 and *Fritschy* [1985] Crim LR 745. In *Skipp* (1975), a lorry driver posing as a haulage contractor was given three loads of oranges and onions to take from London to Leicester. Before reaching the place for delivery he drove off with the loads. The Court of Appeal held that the collecting of the loads was done with the consent of the owner and that the appropriation had only happened at the moment he diverted from his authorised route.

Parker LJ considered this case in his judgment in *Dobson* (1990) and pointed out that at the time of loading the goods on to the lorry there was more than consent: there was express authority. The same had happened in *Fritschy* (1985) where D, the agent of a Dutch company dealing in coins was asked by the company to collect some krugerrands (foreign coins) from England and take them to Switzerland. He collected them and went to Switzerland but then went off with them The Court of Appeal quashed his conviction for theft because all that he did in England was consistent with the authority given to him. There was no act of appropriation within the jurisdiction: this only occurred after Fritschy had got to Switzerland.

12.2.3 The decision in *Gomez*

The point as to whether the appropriation had to be without the consent of the owner was considered again by the House of Lords in *Gomez* [1993] 1 All ER 1.

CASE EXAMPLE

***Gomez* [1993] 1 All ER 1**

Gomez was the assistant manager of a shop. He persuaded the manager to sell electrical goods worth over £17,000 to an accomplice and to accept payment by two cheques, telling the manager they were as good as cash. The cheques were stolen and had no value. Gomez was charged and convicted of theft of the goods.

The Court of Appeal quashed the conviction, relying on the judgment in *Morris* (1983) that there had to be 'adverse interference' for there to be appropriation. They decided that the manager's consent to and authorisation of the transaction meant there was no appropriation at the moment of taking the goods. The case was appealed to the House of Lords with the Court of Appeal certifying, as a point of law of general public importance, the following question:

'When theft is alleged and that which is alleged to be stolen passes to the defendant with the consent of the owner, but that has been obtained by a false representation, has (a) an appropriation within the meaning of section 1(1) of the Theft Act 1968 taken place, or (b) must such a passing of property necessarily involve an element of adverse interference with or usurpation of some right of the owner?'

The House of Lords decided, by a majority of four to one, in answer to (a) 'yes' an appropriation had taken place and in answer to (b) 'no' there was no need for adverse interference with or usurpation some right of the owner. Lord Keith giving the majority decision referred back to the case of *Lawrence* (1972), pointing out the effect of judgment in that case:

> J 'While it is correct to say that appropriation for purposes of section 3(1) includes the latter sort of act [adverse interference or usurpation], it does not necessarily follow that no other act can amount to an appropriation and, in particular, that no act expressly or impliedly authorised by the owner can in any circumstances do so. Indeed *Lawrence v Commissioner of Metropolitan Police* is a clear decision to the contrary since it laid down unequivocally that an act may be an appropriation notwithstanding that it is done with the consent of the owner.'

Lord Keith also stated that no sensible distinction could be made between consent and authorisation. Lord Browne-Wilkinson who agreed with Lord Keith put the point on consent even more clearly when he said:

> J 'I regard the word "appropriate" in isolation as being an objective description of the act done irrespective of the mental state of the owner or the accused. It is impossible to reconcile the decision in *Lawrence* (that the question of consent is irrelevant in considering whether this has been an appropriation) with the views expressed in *Morris* which latter views, in my judgment, were incorrect.'

This judgment in *Gomez* (1993) resolved the conflicts of the earlier cases as the judgment in *Lawrence* was approved while the dictum of Lord Roskill in *Morris* (1983) was disapproved. The cases of *Skipp* (1975) and *Fritschy* (1985) were overruled.

The decision widens the scope of theft but it can be argued that it is now too wide. It has made s 15 of the Theft Act 1968 (obtaining property by deception) virtually unnecessary as situations of obtaining by deception can now be charged as theft. The facts in *Gomez* (1993) were clearly obtaining by deception as he persuaded the manager to hand over the goods by telling him the cheques were as good as cash when he knew they were worthless.

This factor was one of the reasons for Lord Lowry dissenting from the decision of the majority in *Gomez* (1993). He also thought that extending the meaning of appropriation in this way was contrary to the intentions of the Criminal Law Revision Committee in their Eighth Report. Lord Lowry thought that the Law Lords should have looked at that report in deciding the meaning of appropriation. However, the majority accepted Lord Keith's view that it served no useful purpose to do so.

It can be argued that the effect of the decision in *Gomez* (1993) has been to redefine theft. This point of view was put by a leading academic, Professor Sir John Smith, who wrote:

> 'Anyone doing anything whatever to property belonging to another, with or
> without his consent, appropriates it; and, if he does so dishonestly and with intent
> by that, or any subsequent act, to permanently deprive, he commits theft.'

D. Ormerod, *Smith and Hogan Criminal Law* (11th edn, Butterworths, 2005), p 653

Key facts on appropriation

KEY FACTS

Law on appropriation	Section/case	Comment
Definition is 'any assumption of the rights of an owner'.	s 3(1) Theft Act 1968	Includes a later assumption where D has come by the property without stealing it.
No need to touch property for an appropriation.	*Pitham v Hehl* (1977)	An offer to sell property was appropriation of the rights of the owner.
No need for the assumption of all of the rights of an owner.	*Morris* (1983)	An assumption of any of the rights is sufficient (label swapping on goods in supermarket).
There can be an assumption even though there is apparent consent.	*Lawrence* (1972)	Irrelevant whether owner consents to appropriation or not.
Where consent is obtained by fraud there can still be appropriation.	*Gomez* (1993)	An assumption of any of the rights is sufficient. No need for adverse interference with or usurpation some right of the owner.
There can still be appropriation even though the owner truly consents to it.	*Hinks* (2000)	Appropriation is a neutral word. No differentiation between cases of consent induced by fraud and consent given in any other circumstances. All are appropriation, even gifts.
Where property is transferred for value to a person acting in good faith, no later assumption of rights can be theft.	s 3(2) Theft Act 1968 *Wheeler* (1990)	When sale is complete before the seller knows the items are stolen, the later completion of the sale when the facts are known does not make it theft.

12.2.4 Consent without deception

So does the decision in *Gomez* (1993) extend to situations where a person has given property to another without any deception being made? This was the problem raised in the case of *Hinks* [2000] 4 All ER 833.

CASE EXAMPLE

Hinks [2000] 4 All ER 833

Hinks was a 38-year-old woman who had befriended a man who had a low IQ and was very naïve. He was, however, mentally capable of understanding the concept of ownership and of making a valid gift. Over a period of about eight months Hinks accompanied the man on numerous occasions to his building society where he withdrew money. The total was about £60,000 and this money was deposited in Hinks' account. The man also gave Hinks a television set. She was convicted of theft of the money and the TV set. The judge directed the jury to consider whether the man was so mentally incapable that the defendant herself realised that ordinary and decent people would regard it as dishonest to accept a gift from him.

On appeal it was argued that if the gift was valid the acceptance of it could not be theft. The Court of Appeal dismissed the appeal and the following question was certified for the House of Lords to consider:

> 'Whether the acquisition of an indefeasible title to property is capable of amounting to an appropriation of property belonging to another for the purposes of section 1(1) of the Theft Act 1968?'

In the House of Lords the appeal was dismissed on a majority of three judges to two with four of them giving the answer 'Yes' to the question. Lord Hobhouse dissented and answered the question in the negative. Lord Hutton, although agreeing with the majority on the point of law, dissented on whether the conduct showed dishonesty.

Lord Steyn gave the leading judgment. He pointed out that in the case of *Gomez* (1993) the House of Lords had already made it clear that any act may be an appropriation regardless of whether it was done with or without the consent of the owner. They had also rejected a submission that there could be no appropriation where the entire proprietary interest in property passed. Lord Steyn summarised the law in *Gomez* (1993) as follows.

> **J** '. . . it is immaterial whether the act was done with the owner's consent or authority. It is true of course that the certified question in *R v Gomez* referred to the situation where consent had been obtained by fraud. But the majority judgments do not differentiate between cases of consent induced by fraud and consent given in any other circumstances. The ratio involves a proposition of general application. *R v Gomez* therefore gives effect to s 3(1) of the 1968 Act by treating "appropriation" as a neutral word comprehending "any assumption by a person of the rights of an owner".'

A major argument against the ruling in *Hinks* (2000) is that in civil law the gift was valid and the £60,000 and the TV set belonged to the defendant. Lord Steyn accepted that this was the situation, but he considered that this was irrelevant to the decision.

> **J** 'The purposes of the civil law and the criminal law are somewhat different. In theory the two systems should be in perfect harmony. In a practical world there will sometimes be some disharmony between the two systems. In any event it would be wrong to assume on *a priori* grounds that the criminal law rather than the civil law is defective. Given the jury's conclusions, one is entitled to observe that the appellant's conduct *should* constitute theft, the only charge available. The tension which exists between the civil and the criminal law is therefore not in my view a factor which justifies a departure from the law as stated in *Lawrence*'s case and *R v Gomez*.'

Lord Hobhouse dissented for three main reasons:

- That the law on gifts involves conduct by the owner in transferring the gift and once this was done, the gift was the property of the donee. It was not even necessary that the donee should know of the gift, for example, money could be transferred to the donee's bank account without the donee's knowledge. In view of this it was impossible to say, as the Court of Appeal had, that a gift may be clear evidence of appropriation.

- That, as a gift transfers the ownership in the goods to the donee at the moment the owner completes the transfer, the property ceased to be 'property belonging to another' unless it could be brought within the situations identified in s 5 of the Theft Act 1968 (see section 12.4.2).

- If the acceptance of a gift is treated as an appropriation this creates difficulties under s 2(1)(a) of the Act which states that a person is not dishonest if he appropriated property in the belief that he had in law a right to deprive the other person of it. The donee does indeed have a right to deprive the donor of the property.

He also pointed out that there were further difficulties under the Theft Act 1968 as under s 6 (which defines intention to permanently deprive – see section 12.6) the donee would not be acting regardless of the donor's rights as the donor has already surrendered his rights. Further it was difficult to say that under s 3 the donee was 'assuming the rights of an owner' when she already had those rights under the law on gifts.

Despite these arguments put forward by Lord Hobhouse, the majority ruling means that even where there is a valid gift the defendant is considered to have appropriated the property. The critical question is whether what the defendant did was dishonest.

12.2.5 Appropriation of credit balances

Another area which has created difficulty for the courts is deciding when appropriation takes place where the object of the theft is a credit balance in a bank or building society account. In such cases the thief may be in a different place (or even country) to the account. In *Tomsett* [1985] Crim LR 369, $7m was being transferred by one bank to another in New York in order to earn overnight interest. The defendant, an employee of the first bank in London, sent a telex diverting the $7m plus interest to another bank in New York for the benefit of an account in Geneva. The Court of Appeal accepted, without hearing any argument on the point, that the theft could only occur where the property was. This meant that D was not guilty of theft under English law, as the theft was either in New York or Geneva. The money had never been in an account in England. So even though D's act occurred in London, the matter was outside the jurisdiction of the English courts.

This does not seem a very satisfactory decision and in fact it was not followed by the Divisional Court in *Governor of Pentonville Prison, ex parte Osman* [1989] 3 All ER 701 when deciding whether Osman could be deported to stand trial for theft in Hong Kong. Osman had sent a telex from Hong Kong to a bank in New York instructing payment from one company's account to another company's account. If *Tomsett* (1985) had been followed then the theft would have been deemed to have occurred in New York. However, the Divisional Court held that the sending of the telex was itself the appropriation, and so the theft took place in Hong Kong.

> **J** 'In *R v Morris* . . . the House of Lords made it clear that it is not necessary for an appropriation that the defendant assume all rights of an owner. It is enough that he should assume any of the owner's rights . . . If so, then one of the plainest rights possessed by the owner of the chose in action in the present case must surely have been the right to draw on the account in question . . . So far as the customer is concerned, he has a right as against the bank to have his cheques met. It is that right which the defendant assumes by presenting a cheque, or by sending a telex instruction without authority. The act of sending the telex instruction is therefore the act of theft itself.'

The most surprising point about this decision is that two of the judges (Lloyd LJ and French J) had also decided the case of *Tomsett* (1985) but then refused to follow their own decision.

In the judgment in *Osman* (1989) the court had mentioned presenting a cheque as one of the rights of an owner, and this was the situation which occurred in *Ngan* [1998] 1 Cr App Rep 331.

CASE EXAMPLE

Ngan [1998] 1 Cr App Rep 331

D had opened a bank account in England and been given an account number which had previously belonged to a debt collection agency. Over £77,000 intended for the agency was then paid into D's bank account. Because of s 5(4) of the Theft Act 1968 (see section 12.4.4) this money was regarded as belonging to the agency. D realised there was a mistake but signed and sent blank cheques to her sister (who also knew of the circumstances) in Scotland. Two cheques were presented in Scotland and one in England.

The Court of Appeal applied the principle in *Osman* (1989) that the presentation of a cheque was the point at which the assumption of a right of the owner took place. They quashed D's conviction for theft in respect of the two cheques presented in Scotland, as they were outside the jurisdiction of the English courts, but upheld her conviction for theft in respect of the cheque presented in England. They took the view that signing blank cheques and sending them to her sister were preparatory acts to the theft and not the actual theft.

However, it should be noted that in *Osman* (1989) the court had also stated that appropriation took place when the defendant dishonestly issued a cheque. So, it could be argued that the decision in *Ngan* was wrong as sending the cheques to her sister was 'issuing' them.

The problems of when and where appropriation takes place in banking cases has become even more difficult with the use of computer banking. In *Governor of Brixton Prison, ex parte Levin* [1997] 3 All ER 289 the Divisional Court distinguished the use of a computer from the sending of a telex or the presentation of a cheque. D had used a computer in St Petersburg, Russia to gain unauthorised access to a bank in Parsipenny, America and divert money into false accounts. The court ruled that appropriation took place where the effect of the keyboard instructions took place.

J
'We see no reason why the appropriation of the client's right to give instructions should
not be regarded as having taken place in the computer [in America]. Lloyd LJ [in *Osman*]
did not rule out the possibility of the place where the telex was received also being
counted as the place where the appropriation occurred if the courts ever adopted the
view that a crime could have a dual location . . . [T]he operation of the keyboard by a
computer operator produces a virtually instantaneous result on the magnetic disc of the
computer even though it may be 10,000 miles away. It seems to us artificial to regard the
act as having been done in one rather than the other place. But, in the position of having
to choose . . . we would opt for Parsipenny. The fact that the applicant was physically in
St Petersburg is of far less significance than the fact that he was looking at and
operating on magnetic discs located in Parsipenny. The essence of what he was doing
was there. Until the instruction is recorded on the disc there is in fact no appropriation.'

These cases leave the law on where and when appropriation takes places in banking cases a little
uncertain, but the principles appear to be:

* telex instructions – appropriation at place and point of sending telex
* presenting a cheque – appropriation at place and point of presentation
* computer instructions – appropriation at place and point of receipt of instructions.

Key facts on the law on appropriation of credit balances

		KEY FACTS		
Type of transaction	**Case**	**Where does the appropriation take place?**		
		Place where thief does act	**Place where instructions are received**	**Place where transfer is complete**
Cheque	*Ngan* (1998)	No. Signing cheque and sending it to sister not appropriation.	Yes. The point of presenting cheque at bank.	N/A
Telex	*Tomsett* (1985)	No.	Either here	Or here

| Telex | *Osman* (1989) | Yes. | No. Unless it could occur at two places. | No. |
| Computer | *Levin* (1997) | No. Unless it could occur at two places. | Yes. As the operation of the keyboard produced a 'virtually instantaneous' result. | |

12.2.6 Protection of innocent purchasers

As appropriation has been ruled to be a 'neutral word comprehending any assumption by a person of the rights of an owner', it is important to protect people who innocently acquire a right in property for value from a charge of theft. This is done by s 3(2) of the Theft Act 1968:

'3(2) Where property or a right or interest in property is or purports to be transferred for value to a person acting in good faith, no later assumption by him of rights which he believed himself to be acquiring shall, by reason of any defect in the transferor's title, amount to theft of the property.'

This section was included by the Criminal Law Revision Committee because without it a purchaser who bought goods for the market value not knowing they were stolen, but who later discovered they were stolen, would be guilty of theft if he then decided to keep the goods. The CLRC thought that, while there might be a case for making such conduct criminal, 'on the whole it seems to us that, whatever view is taken of the buyer's moral duty, the law would be too strict if it made him guilty of theft'.

Under s 3(2), not only is the original acquisition not theft, but also any later dealing in the property by the innocent purchaser cannot be theft. This was illustrated in *Wheeler* (1990) 92 Cr App Rep 279.

CASE EXAMPLE

Wheeler (1990) 92 Cr App Rep 279

D purchased some military antiques which, unknown to him, were stolen. Before he knew they were stolen he agreed a sale of some of the items to another person. The arrangement was that the items would be left with D while the new purchaser arranged for payment. By the time the new purchaser returned to collect and pay for the items, D had been told by the police that they were stolen. D could not be guilty of theft by keeping them for himself or by selling them.

Wheeler was charged with obtaining property by deception, but was also found not guilty of this. This point is discussed in Chapter 14, section 14.4.1.

APPLYING THE LAW

□ □ □

Discuss whether there has been an appropriation in each of the following situations.

1. Jasper has an argument with his neighbour. When his neighbour is out, Jasper holds an auction of the neighbour's garden tools and patio furniture. The neighbour returns before any of the furniture is taken away.

2. Poppy goes shopping at the local supermarket and takes her three-year-old daughter, Selina, with her. While at the check-out, Selina takes some bars of chocolate and puts them in the pocket of her pushchair. Poppy does not realise Selina has done this until she finds the chocolate when they get home. Poppy decides that she will not take the chocolate back to the supermarket.

3. The owner of a shop asks Carry, who is a lorry driver, to pick up a load of DVD equipment and take it to a warehouse. Carry agrees to do this, but after collecting the equipment decides that she will not take it to the warehouse but will instead sell it.

4. Brendan, aged 19, is infatuated with Hannah, a married woman aged 30. Brendan uses his student loan to buy expensive presents for Hannah. She knows he is a student and has very little money but she accepts the gifts from him.

5. Adam buys some motor-cycle parts from a small garage. Three days later he is told by one of his friends that the garage has just been raided by the police and much of their stock of spare parts has been identified as stolen goods. Adam decides to keep the parts he has and not to say anything about them.

6. Mike, who lives in England, goes on holiday to Poland. While there he uses a computer to get unauthorised access to his company's English bank accounts and arranges for money to be transferred to an account he has in Switzerland. While in Poland he is asked by a colleague to drive a car to Switzerland. Mike agrees to do this although he has already decided to take the car to England and sell it.

□ □ □

12.3 Property

For there to be theft, the defendant must have appropriated 'property'. Section 4 gives a very comprehensive definition of property which means that almost anything can be stolen. The definition is in s 4(1) of the Theft Act 1968:

'4(1) "Property" includes money and all other property real or personal, including things in action and other intangible property.'

This section lists five types of items which are included in the definition of 'property'. These are:

- money
- real property
- personal property
- things in action
- other intangible property.

In this list, money is self-explanatory. It means coins and banknotes of any currency. Personal property is also straightforward as it covers all movable items. Books, CDs, jewellery, clothes, cars are obvious examples, but it also includes very large items such as aeroplanes or tanks and very small trivial items such as a sheet of paper. It has even been held that body parts from dead bodies can be personal property, for the purposes of theft.

CASE EXAMPLE

Kelly and Lindsay [1998] 3 All ER 741

Kelly was a sculptor who asked Lindsay to take body parts from the Royal College of Surgeons where he worked as a laboratory assistant. Kelly then made casts of the parts. They were convicted of theft and appealed on the point of law that body parts were not property. The Court of Appeal held that, though a dead body was not normally property within the definition of the Theft Act, the body parts were property as they had acquired 'different attributes by virtue of the application of skill, such as dissection or preservation techniques, for exhibition or teaching purposes.'

12.3.1 Things which cannot be stolen

However there are some exceptions which cannot be stolen. These are set out in s 4(3) and s 4(4) of the Theft Act 1968. The first of these concerns plants and fungi growing wild.

 '4(3) A person who picks mushrooms growing wild on any land, or who picks flowers, fruit or foliage from a plant growing wild on any land, does not (although not in possession of the land) steal what he picks, unless he does it for reward or sale or other commercial purpose.

For the purposes of this subsection "mushroom" includes any fungus, and "plant" includes any shrub or tree.'

This only applies to plants etc growing wild, so it is possible to steal cultivated plants. Taking apples from trees in a farmer's orchard would be theft, but picking blackberries growing wild in the hedgerow around the field would not be theft unless it was done for sale or reward or other commercial purpose. Similarly, picking roses from someone's garden would be theft, but picking wild flowers in a field would not (unless for sale or reward). However, it should be noted that it is an offence to pick, uproot or destroy certain wild plants under the Wildlife and Countryside Act 1981.

Where picking fungi, flowers, fruit or foliage is done with the intention of selling them or for reward or any commercial purpose, then they are considered property which can be stolen. An example of this would be picking holly to sell at Christmas time.

The other exception of personal property which is not 'property' for the purpose of theft concerns wild creatures.

 '4(4) Wild creatures, tamed or untamed, shall be regarded as property; but a person cannot steal a wild creature not tamed nor ordinarily kept in captivity, or the carcase of any such creature, unless it has been reduced into possession by or on behalf of another person and possession of it has not since been lost or abandoned, or another person is in course of reducing it into possession.'

The effect of this subsection is that it is not theft if a wild creature such as a deer is taken from the grounds of a large estate (though there is an offence of poaching) but it is theft if a deer is taken from a zoo, as in this case it is ordinarily kept in captivity.

12.3.2 Real property

Real property is the legal term for land and buildings. Under s 4(1), land can be stolen, but s 4(2) states that this can only be done in three circumstances:

 '4(2) A person cannot steal land, or things forming part of land and severed from it by him or by his directions, except in the following cases, that is to say –

    (a) when he is a trustee or personal representative, or is authorised by power of attorney, or as liquidator of a company, or otherwise, to sell or dispose of land belonging to another, and he appropriates the land or anything forming part of it by dealing with it in breach of the confidence reposed in him: or

    (b) when he is not in possession of the land and appropriates anything forming part of the land by severing it or causing it to be severed or after it has been severed; or

    (c) when, being in possession of the land under a tenancy, he appropriates the whole or any part of any fixture or structure let to be used with the land.'

So there is only one category of person who can be charged with stealing any land iself. These are trustees etc. who act in breach of confidence. The second circumstance only applies where something has been severed from the land. This makes it theft to dig up turfs from someone's lawn or to dismantle a wall and take the bricks. In 1972 a man was prosecuted for stealing Cleckheaton railway station by dismantling it and removing it. He was in fact acquitted by the jury as he said he acting under a claim of right, but there was no doubt that the station could be property under the Theft Act definition. Section 4(2)(b) also covers situations where the owner of the land has legitimately severed something, such as stone from a quarry, but another person then appropriates the stone. This person will be guilty under s 4(2)(b).

The final part of s 4(2)(c) applies only to tenants of land, who can be guilty of theft if they appropriate fixtures or structures from the land. As tenants they are in possession of the land and so cannot be guilty under s 4(2)(b). However, if a tenant appropriates an item such as a door handle or a washbasin, then this can be theft. This subsection only requires appropriation; it does not require the item to be severed from the land. As appropriation means 'any assumption of the rights of an owner', this could include a situation where the tenant sold a fireplace to a dealer on the basis that the dealer would dismantle it later. The act of selling is an assumption of the rights of an owner so the theft occurs even if the dealer never does dismantle the fireplace.

12.3.3 Things in action

A thing in action is a right which can be enforced against another person by an action in law. The right itself is property under the definition in s 4. An example is a bank account. The bank does not keep coins or banknotes for each customer's account in a separate box! Instead the customer has a right to the payment of the amount in his account. Even an overdraft facility is a thing in action as the customer who has the facility has a right to withdraw money from the bank up to the limit of the overdraft.

So if D causes the bank to debit another person's account he has appropriated a thing in action. If he does this dishonestly and with the intention permanently to deprive the other of it, then D is guilty of theft.

CASE EXAMPLE

Kohn (1979) 69 Cr App R 395

Kohn was an accountant authorised by a company to draw cheques on the company's account to pay the company's debts. The company had an overdraft facility and was sometimes overdrawn. When Kohn drew cheques on the company's account to meet his own personal liabilities he was guilty of theft, as the bank account was a thing in action. This was so whether it was a credit balance or the overdraft facility.

A cheque itself is a thing in action, but it is also a piece of paper which is property which can be stolen, and it is a 'valuable security' which can also be stolen under the definition of 'property'.

12.3.4 Other intangible property

This refers to other rights which have no physical presence but can be stolen under the Theft Act. In *Attorney-General of Hong Kong v Chan Nai-Keung* [1987] 1 WLR 1339 an export quota for textiles was intangible property which could be stolen. A patent is also intangible property which can be stolen.

However, there are some types of intangible property which have been held not to be property within the Theft Act definition. In *Oxford v Moss* [1979] Crim LR 119, knowledge of the questions on an examination paper was held not to be property.

Electricity is another sort of intangible property which cannot be stolen, but there is a separate offence under s 13 of the Theft Act 1968 of dishonestly using electricity without due authority, or dishonestly causing it to be wasted or diverted.

ACTIVITY

Explain whether the items in each of the following situations would be property for the purposes of theft.

1. Arnie runs a market stall selling flowers. Just before Christmas he picks a lot of holly from a wood, intending to sell it on his stall. He then digs up a small fir tree for his own use. On his way home he sees some late flowering roses in a garden and picks them to give to his girlfriend.

2. Della finds the examination papers she is to sit next week in the next-door office. She writes out the questions from the first paper on to a note pad of her own. The second paper is very long, so she uses the office photocopier to take a copy, using paper already in the machine.

3. Gareth and Harry go out poaching pheasants. Gareth successfully shoots one pheasant and picks up the dead bird. Harry fails to hit any. As they are going home Harry sees an unattended Land Rover. He looks inside it and sees that in the back are two dead pheasants. He takes them.

12.4 Belonging to another

For the purposes of theft, the property must belong to another. However, s 5(1) of the Theft Act 1968 gives a very wide definition of what is meant by 'belonging to another'.

'5(1) Property shall be regarded as belonging to any person having possession or control of it, or having in it any proprietary right or interest (not being an equitable interest arising only from an agreement to transfer or grant an interest).'

From this it can be seen that possession or control of the property or any proprietary interest in it is sufficient. One reason for making it wide is so that the prosecution does not have to prove who is the legal owner.

12.4.1 Possession or control

Obviously, the owner of property normally has possession and control of it, but there are many other situations in which a person can have either possession or control of property. Someone who hires a car has both possession and control during the period of hire. If the car is stolen during this time then the thief can be charged with stealing it from the hirer. Equally, as the car hire firm still own the car (a proprietary right), the thief could be charged with stealing it from them.

The possession or control of the item does not have to be lawful. Where B has stolen jewellery from A and subsequently C steals it from B, B is in possession or control of that jewellery and C can be charged with stealing it from B. This is useful where it is not known who the original owner is, as C can still be guilty of theft. This wide definition of 'belonging to' has led to the situation in which an owner was convicted of stealing his own car.

CASE EXAMPLE

Turner (No 2) [1971] 2 All ER 441

Turner left his car at a garage for repairs. It was agreed that he would pay for the repairs when he collected the car after the repairs had been completed. When the repairs were almost finished the garage left the car parked on the roadway outside their premises. Turner used a spare key to take the car during the night without paying for the repairs. The Court of Appeal held that the garage was in possession or control of the car and so Turner could be guilty of stealing his own car.

The decision in this case has been criticised. The garage clearly had a lien (a legal right to retain the car until payment was made) and it could have been held that this gave the garage control of the car. However the judge had directed the jury to ignore any question of a lien. On appeal to the Court of Appeal the judges simply based their decision to uphold the conviction on the fact that the garage had possession and control. In fact, if the question of lien is ignored, the garage were bailees of the car and under the law of bailment Turner had the right to end the bailment at any time and take the car back. The point also involved whether Turner was acting dishonestly and this is discussed at section 12.6.1.

In a subsequent case, *Meredith* [1973] Crim LR 253, a Crown Court judge directed a jury differently. In this case D's car had been impounded by the police because it was causing an obstruction. D removed it without the police knowing and without paying the charge to get it out of the pound. It was held that D could not be convicted of theft even though the car was apparently in the possession and control of the police. Although the police had a right to enforce the charge for its removal, they had no right to keep the car.

It is possible for someone to be in possession or control of property even though they do not know it is there. In *Woodman* [1974] 2 All ER 955 a company, English China Clays, had sold all the scrap metal on its site to another company which arranged for it to be removed. Unknown to English China Clays, a small amount had been left on the site. There was no doubt that they were in control of the site itself as they had put a barbed wire fence round it and had notices warning trespassers to keep out. D took the remaining scrap metal. He was convicted of theft and the Court of Appeal upheld the conviction.

12.4.2 Proprietary right or interest

Clearly, legal ownership comes within this, but a proprietary right or interest is much wider than just ownership. There are also equitable rights to property, for example the trustees of a trust fund have the legal ownership of the fund, but the beneficiaries have the equitable interest.

Co-owners

If there are co-owners of property, then each can be guilty of stealing from the other, as each has a proprietary interest in the property. This happened in *Bonner* [1970] 2 All ER 97, where D was a partner who was found guilty of stealing partnership property. In partnership law each partner is joint owner of all the partnership property, but he can be guilty of theft if he appropriates the property intending to permanently deprive the other partners of their rights in the property.

Lost or abandoned property

Where property has been lost, the owner still has a proprietary right in it. It is only if the property has been completely abandoned that it is ownerless and so does not belong to another for the purposes of theft. However, the courts are reluctant to reach the conclusion that property has been abandoned, or may decide that ownership has passed to the owner of the land on which it was abandoned. For example, where a golfer hits a golf ball into a lake and decides to leave it there, he has abandoned it, but it becomes the property of the owner of the golf course.

Special situations

Section 5 goes on to make it clear that in certain situations a defendant can be guilty of theft even though the property may not 'belong to another'. These are situations in which the defendant is acting dishonestly and has caused a loss to another or has made a gain. These are:

- trust property
- property received under an obligation
- property received by another's mistake.

Trust property

Normally both trustees and beneficiaries have proprietary rights or interests in the trust property. So if a trustee takes the trust property for his own he can be charged with theft as it also belongs to the beneficiaries. But to make sure that any dishonest appropriation of trust property by a trustee could be theft, s 5(2) sets out:

'5(2) Where property is subject to a trust, the persons to whom it belongs shall be regarded as any person having a right to enforce the trust and an intention to defeat the trust shall be regarded accordingly as an intention to deprive of the property any person having that right.'

In particular this avoids problems with theft by a trustee from a charitable trust as there are no specific beneficiaries with a right to enforce the trust. However, charitable trusts are enforceable by the Attorney-General, making him a 'person having a right to enforce the trust' for the purposes of this subsection.

12.4.3 Property received under an obligation

There are many situations in which property (usually money) is handed over to D on the basis that D will keep it for the owner or will deal with it in a particular way. Section 5(3) tries to make sure that such property is still considered as 'belonging to the other' for the purposes of the law of theft.

'5(3) Where a person receives property from or on account of another, and is under an obligation to the other to retain and deal with that property or its proceeds in a particular way, the property shall be regarded (as against him) as belonging to the other.'

Under this subsection there must be an obligation to retain and deal with the property in a particular way. So, where money is paid as a deposit to a business, the prosecution must prove that there was an obligation to retain and deal with those deposits in a particular way. If the person paying the deposit only expects it to be paid into a bank account of the business, then if that is what happens there cannot be theft, even if all the money from the account is used for other business expenses and the client does not get the goods or service for which he paid the deposit. This is what happened in *Hall* [1972] 2 All ER 1009.

CASE EXAMPLE

Hall [1972] 2 All ER 1009

Hall was a travel agent who received deposits from clients for air trips to America. D paid these deposits into the firm's general account, but never organised any tickets and was unable to return the money. He was convicted of theft, but on appeal his conviction was quashed because when D received the deposits he was not under an obligation to deal with them in a particular way. The Court of Appeal did stress that each case depended on its facts.

In *Klineberg and Marsden* [1999] Crim LR 419 there was a clear obligation to deal with deposits in a particular way. The two defendants operated a company which sold timeshare apartments in Lanzarote to customers in England. Each purchaser paid the purchase price on the understanding that the money would be held by an independent trust company until the apartment was ready for the purchaser to occupy. Over £500,000 was paid to the defendants' company, but only £233 was actually paid into the trust company's account. The defendants were guilty of theft as it was clear that they were under an obligation to the purchasers 'to retain and deal with that property or its proceeds in a particular way' and that they had not done this.

There can be an obligation in less formal situations. This was the case in *Davidge v Bunnett* [1984] Crim LR 297

CASE EXAMPLE

Davidge v Bunnett [1984] Crim LR 297

D was guilty of theft when she was given money by her flatmates to pay the gas bill but instead used it to buy Christmas presents. There was a legal obligation in this situation, as there was an intention to create legal relations under contract law. It is not clear whether there would be a legal obligation (and so theft) if the situation happened between members of the same family or whether this would be a domestic arrangement without the intention to create legal relations.

Another problem area can occur when D collects money from sponsors for charity but then does not pay the money over. In *Lewis v Lethbridge* [1987] Crim LR 59 D was sponsored to run the London Marathon for charity. His sponsors paid the money to him but he did not hand it over to the charity. The Queen's Bench Divisional Court quashed the conviction since the magistrates had not found that there was any rule of the charity which required him to hand the actual cash over or

to set up a separate fund for it. This meant that as against the charity he was not under an obligation to 'to retain and deal with that property' in a particular way. He was merely a creditor of the charity. This decision was criticised by the late Professor Sir John Smith and this criticism was adopted by the Court of Appeal in *Wain* [1995] 2 Cr App R 660 when it disapproved of the decision in *Lewis v Lethbridge* (1987).

CASE EXAMPLE

Wain [1995] 2 Cr App R 660

D had organised various event to raise money for The Telethon Trust, a charity created by Yorkshire Television Company. He paid the money, totalling £2,833.25, into a special bank account, but then, with permission of a representative of the TV company, transferred the money to his personal bank account. He then spent the money from his own account and was unable to pay any money to the charity.

The Court of Appeal considered the point of whether the defendant was obliged to hand over the actual coins and notes or whether there was a more general principle that he was under an obligation to hand over an amount equal to the money he had raised. It quoted from Professor Sir John Smith in its judgment when it said:

J
'Professor Smith . . . in his *Law of Theft* (6th ed.) at p. 39 [states]
". . . In *Lewis v Lethbridge* . . . no consideration was given to the question whether any obligation was imposed by the sponsors. Sponsors surely do not give the collector (whether he has a box or not) the money to do as he likes with. Is there not an overwhelming inference . . . that the sponsors intend to give the money to the charity, imposing an obligation in the nature of a trust on the collector?"

It seems to us that the approach of the court in the *Lethbridge* case was a very narrow one based, apparently, on the finding by the justices that there was no requirement of the charity that the appellant hand over the same notes and coins … it seems to us that by virtue of section 5(3), the appellant was plainly under an obligation to retain, if not the actual note and coins, at least their proceeds, that is to say the money credited in the bank account which he opened for the trust with the actual property.'

This decision is preferable to that in *Lewis v Lethbridge* (1987). Any person giving money to a person collecting for charity, whether it is by sponsoring him or by some other donation, is only

doing this because they want to support the charity. They intend that amount to be paid to the charity.

12.4.4 Property got by a mistake

The final subsection of s 5 deals with situations where property has been handed over to D by another's mistake and so has become D's property. If there were no special provision in the Act then this could not be 'property belonging to another' for the purposes of the law of theft.

 '5(4) Where a person gets property by another's mistake, and is under an obligation to make restoration (in whole or in part) of the property or its proceeds or of the value thereof, then to the extent of that obligation the property or proceeds shall be regarded (as against him) as belonging to the person entitled to restoration, and an intention not to make restoration shall be regarded accordingly as an intention to deprive that person of the property or proceeds.'

In *Attorney-General's Reference (No 1 of 1983)* [1985] 3 All ER 369, the facts were that D's salary was paid into her bank account by transfer. On one occasion her employers mistakenly overpaid her by £74.74. She was acquitted by the jury of theft, but the prosecution sought a ruling on a point of law, namely, assuming that she dishonestly decided not to repay the £74.74, would she have been guilty of theft? The Court of Appeal held that s 5(4) clearly provided for exactly this type of situation. She was under an 'obligation to make restoration' and if there was an intention not to make restoration, then the elements of theft were present.

There must be a legal obligation to restore the property. In *Gilks* [1972] 3 All ER 280 D had placed a bet on a horse race. The bookmaker made a mistake about which horse D had backed and overpaid D on the bets he had placed. D realised the error and decided not to return the money. The ownership of the money had passed to D, so the only way he could be guilty of theft was if s 5(4) applied. It was held that as betting transactions are not enforceable at law, s 5(4) did not apply and D was not guilty.

Key facts on 'belonging to another'

KEY FACTS

Theft Act 1968	Rule	Comment/case(s)
s 5(1)	Property is regarded as belonging to any person having possession or control or having any proprietary right.	Not limited to owner – *Turner (No 2)* (1971) stole own car. One co-owner can steal from another – *Bonner* (1970).
s 5(2)	Trust property 'belongs' to any person having right to enforce the trust.	
s 5(3)	Property belongs to the other where it is received under an obligation to retain and deal with it in a particular way.	Must have to deal with it in a specific way. *Hall* (1972) not guilty because no specific way. *Klineberg and Marsden* (1999) guilty because should have been placed in special account.
s 5(4)	Where D gets property by another's mistake then it 'belongs' to the other. But there must be a legal obligation to make restoration.	*Att-Gen's Reference (No 1 of 1983)* (1985). *Gilks* (1972).

12.5 Dishonestly

There are two points which need to be proved for the *mens rea* of theft. These are:

- dishonesty
- intention permanently to deprive.

Apart from these the Act also states in s 1(1) that it is immaterial whether the appropriation is made with a view to gain, or is made for the thief's own benefit. In other words, if all the elements of theft are present, the motive of D is not relevant. So a modern-day Robin Hood stealing to give to the poor could be guilty of theft. D does not have to gain anything from the theft, so destroying property belonging to another can be theft, although it is also, of course, criminal damage. Theft can also be charged where D does not destroy the other's property but throws it away. For example, if D threw a waterproof watch belonging to another into the sea, this could be theft.

12.5.1 Dishonesty

The 1968 Theft Act does not define 'dishonesty', though it does give three situations in which D's behaviour is not considered dishonest. These are in s 2 of the 1968 Act.

'2(1) A person's appropriation of property belonging to another is not to be regarded as dishonest –

(a) if he appropriates the property in the belief that he has in law the right to deprive the other of it, on behalf of himself or of a third person; or

(b) if he appropriates the property in the belief that he would have the other's consent if the other knew of the appropriation and the circumstances of it; or

(c) (except where the property came to him as trustee or personal representative) if he appropriates the property in the belief that the person to whom the property belongs cannot be discovered by taking reasonable steps.'

All three situations depend on D's belief. It does not matter whether it is a correct belief or even whether it is reasonable belief. If D has a genuine belief in one of these three then he is not guilty of theft.

Belief in a right at law

Section 2(1)(a) was considered in the case of *Turner (No 2)* (1971) (see section 12.4.1). Turner claimed that he believed he had the right to take back his car from the garage. The Court of Appeal pointed out that the judge had dealt fully and correctly with the law on this point, saying:

> '[The judge] went on to give [the jury] a classic direction in regard to claim of right, emphasising that it is immaterial that there exists no basis in law for such belief. He reminded the jury that the appellant had said categorically in evidence: "I believe that I was entitled in law to do what I did." At the same time he directed the jury to look at the surrounding circumstances. He said this:
>
>> "The Prosecution say that the whole thing reeks of dishonesty, and if you believe Mr Brown that the [appellant] drove the car away from Carlyle Road, using a duplicate key, and having told Brown that he would come back tomorrow and pay, you may think the Prosecution right."
>
> The whole test of dishonesty is the mental element of belief.'

Belief of owner's consent

Section 2(1)(b) covers situations where D does not have the chance to get permission from the person to whom the property belongs, but D believes he would have been given permission. For example, if you are baby-sitting at a friend's house and while there you cut your finger, you take a plaster from your friend's first aid box believing that they would consent if they knew about it.

Belief that owner cannot be found

This appears to be aimed at situations where D finds property such as money or other personal items in the street. If D genuinely believes that he cannot find out who the owner is by taking what he thinks are reasonable steps, then D's appropriation of the property is not dishonest and he cannot be guilty of theft. D's belief does not have to be reasonable. However, the more unreasonable it is, then the more likely a jury will not accept that he actually held that belief.

In *Small* [1987] Crim LR 777 D took a car. He said he believed it was abandoned. It had been parked in the same place without being moved for two weeks. Also it appeared abandoned because the doors were unlocked, the keys were in the ignition, there was no petrol in the tank, the battery was flat, one of the tyres was flat and the windscreen wipers did not work. D put petrol in the tank and managed to start it. When he was driving it he suddenly saw police flashing their lights at him. At that point he panicked and ran off, but he claimed that until he saw the police he had never thought that it might be a stolen car. He was convicted, but the Court of Appeal quashed the conviction because the question was whether D had (or might have had) an honest belief that the owner could not be found and there was evidence that he might have believed the car was abandoned.

Willing to pay

In some situations D may say that he is willing to pay for the property or may, on taking property, leave money to pay for it. This does not prevent D's conduct from being dishonest, as s 2(2) states that:

'2(2) A person's appropriation of property belonging to another may be dishonest notwithstanding that he is willing to pay for the property.'

At first this may seem severe, but it prevents D taking what he likes, regardless of the owner's wishes. For example, D likes a painting which is hanging in a friend's home. He asks the friend how much it is worth and is told that it is only a copy, worth less than £100, but it was painted by the friend's grandmother and is of sentimental value. A few days later D takes the painting without the friend's consent but leaves £200 in cash to pay for it. D's taking of the painting may be considered dishonest, even though he left more than the cash value of it.

12.5.2 The *Ghosh* test

As can be seen, s 2 only applies in specific circumstances. It does not create a general rule or definition about dishonesty. In its Eighth Report, the Criminal Law Revision Committee stated that it had used the word 'dishonestly' in preference to the word 'fraudulently' because:

> 'The question "Was this dishonest?" is easier for a jury to answer than the question "Was this fraudulent?" Dishonesty is something which laymen can recognise when they see it, whereas "fraud" may seem to involve technicalities which have to be explained by a lawyer.'

It appears that, since they took the view that dishonesty was something laymen could recognise, there was no need for a definition. Not surprisingly, the early cases on the Theft Act took the view that whether the defendant's state of mind was dishonest was a matter for the jury to decide. In *Brutus v Cozens* [1972] 2 All ER 1297 the House of Lords held that the meaning of an ordinary word such as dishonestly was not a question of law for the judge, but one of fact for the jury.

In *Feely* [1973] 1 All ER 341 the Court of Appeal did at least give a standard of dishonesty to be applied by the jury. Feely was the manager at a branch of bookmakers. The firm notified all branches that the practice of borrowing from the till was to stop. D knew this, but still 'borrowed' £30. When it was realised there was a shortfall in the till, D immediately said what he had done and offered an IOU. In addition, he was owed more than twice the amount by the firm. At his trial the judge directed the jury that what Feely had done was dishonest and he was convicted of theft. He appealed on the ground that the question of dishonesty should have been left to the jury. The Court of Appeal allowed the appeal, stating:

> **J** 'Jurors, when deciding whether an appropriation was dishonest can reasonably be expected to, and should, apply the current standards of ordinary decent people. In their own lives they have to decide what is and what is not dishonest. We can see no reason why, when in a jury box, they should require the help of a judge to tell them what amounts to dishonesty.'

This does give a guideline to the jury of the 'current standards of ordinary decent people'. However, a criticism of this is that different juries might well have different standards, even though they are notionally applying the 'current standards of ordinary decent people'. Another criticism is that it is too objective. It does not take into account whether the defendant believed he was being honest. In *Boggeln v Wiliams* [1978] 2 All ER 1061 a subjective test was used of the defendant's belief as to his own honesty was used. The defendant's electricity had been cut off, but he had reconnected it without authorisation. He notified that electricity board that he was doing this and he believed that he would be able to pay the bill. The court decided that his belief was the most important factor.

This left a conflict of whether the test should be objective (standards of ordinary decent people) or subjective (whether the defendant believed that what he was doing was honest). This was finally resolved in *Ghosh* [1982] 2 All ER 689, which is now the leading case on the matter.

CASE EXAMPLE

Ghosh [1982] 2 All ER 689

Ghosh was a doctor acting as a locum consultant in a hospital. He claimed fees for an operation he had not carried out. He said that he was not dishonest as he was owed the same amount for consultation fees. The trial judge directed the jury that they must apply their own standards to decide if what he did was dishonest. He was convicted and appealed against the conviction.

The Court of Appeal considered all the previous cases on the matter and decided that the test for dishonesty should have both objective and a subjective elements. It put it in this way:

> J 'In determining whether the prosecution has proved that the defendant was acting dishonestly, a jury must first of all decide whether according to the ordinary standards of reasonable and honest people what was done was dishonest. If it was not dishonest by those standards, that is the end of the matter and the prosecution fails. If it was dishonest by those standards, then the jury must consider whether the defendant himself must have realised that what he was doing was by those standards dishonest.'

So this means that the jury have to start with an objective test. Was what was done dishonest by the ordinary standards of reasonable and honest people? If it was not the defendant is not guilty. However, if the jury decide that it was dishonest by those standards then they must consider the more subjective test of did the defendant know it was dishonest by those standards.

This second test is not totally subjective as the defendant is judged by what he realised ordinary standards were. This prevents a defendant from saying that, although he knew that ordinary people would regard his actions as dishonest, he did not think that those standards applied to him. This was made clear in the judgment in *Ghosh* [1982] 2 All ER 689.

J 'It is dishonest for a defendant to act in a way which he knows ordinary people consider to be dishonest, even if he asserts or genuinely believes that he was morally justified in acting as he did. For example, Robin Hood or those ardent anti-vivisectionists who remove animals from vivisection laboratories are acting dishonestly, even though they may consider themselves to be morally justified in doing what they do, because they know that ordinary people would consider these actions to be dishonest.'

ACTIVITY

Self-test questions on dishonesty in theft

1. Explain the three situations in s 2(1) of the Theft Act 1968 in which D is not regarded as dishonest.

2. Explain why D may be dishonest even though he is willing to pay for the goods he appropriates.

3. The Theft Act 1968 does not define 'dishonesty'. What different approaches have the courts used in deciding what is meant by 'dishonesty'?

4. Explain the *Ghosh* (1982) test.

5. Is it necessary to have an objective element in deciding whether D's conduct was dishonest?

12.6 With intention to permanently deprive

The final element which has to be proved for theft is that the defendant had the intention to permanently deprive the other of the property. In many situations there is no doubt that the defendant had such an intention. For example, where an item is taken and sold to another person, or where cash is taken and spent by the defendant. This last example is true even when D intends to replace the money later, as was shown in *Velumyl* [1989] Crim LR 299 where D, a company manager, took £1,050 from the office safe. He said that he was owed money by a friend and he was going to replace the money when that friend repaid him. The Court of Appeal upheld his conviction for theft as he had the intention of permanently depriving the company of the banknotes which he had taken from the safe, even if he intended replacing them with other banknotes to the same value later.

Another situation where there is a clear intention to permanently deprive is where the defendant destroys property belonging to another. This can be charged as theft, although it is also criminal damage.

There are, however, situations where it is not so clear and to help in these s 6 of the Theft Act 1968 explains and expands the meaning of the phrase.

'6(1) person appropriating property belonging to another without meaning the other permanently to lose the thing itself is nevertheless to be regarded as having the intention to permanently deprive the other of it if his intention is to treat the thing as his own to dispose of regardless of the other's rights; and a borrowing or lending of it may amount to so treating it, if, but only if, the borrowing or lending is for a period and in circumstances making it equivalent to an outright taking or disposal.'

Intention is to treat the thing as his own

So the basic rule is that there must be an intention to treat the thing as his own to dispose of regardless of the other's rights. One problem for the courts has been the meaning of 'dispose of' and what, if anything, it adds to ' treat the thing as his own'.

In *Cahill* [1993] Crim LR 141 the Court of Appeal accepted that the meaning of 'dispose of' should be that given by the *Shorter Oxford Dictionary*. This was 'To deal with definitely: to get rid of; to get done with, finish. To make over by way of sale or bargain or sell'.

However, in *DPP v Lavender* [1994] Crim LR 297 the Divisional Court did not refer to *Cahill* (1993) but ruled that the dictionary definition of 'dispose of' was too narrow as a disposal could include 'dealing with' property.

CASE EXAMPLE

DPP v Lavender [1994] Crim LR 297

D took doors from a council property which was being repaired and used them to replace damaged doors in his girlfriend's council flat. The doors were still in the possession of the council but had been transferred without permission from one council property to another. The Divisional Court held that the question was whether D intended to treat the doors as his own, regardless of the rights of the council. The answer to this was yes, so D was guilty of theft.

A similar decision was reached in *Marshall* [1998] 2 Cr App Rep 282, where the defendants obtained day tickets to travel on London Underground (LU) from travellers who had finished with them, and the defendants then sold the tickets to other travellers. They were convicted but appealed on the ground that, as each ticket would be returned to (LU) when they had been used by the second traveller, there was no intention to permanently deprive LU of the tickets. The

Court of Appeal upheld their convictions on the basis that the men were treating the tickets as their own to dispose of, regardless of LU's rights. It was not relevant that the tickets would eventually be returned to LU.

12.6.1 Borrowing or lending

Another difficulty with s 6 is the point at which 'borrowing or lending' comes within the definition. Normally borrowing would not be an intention to permanently deprive. Take the situation of a student taking a textbook from a fellow student's bag in order to read one small section and then replace the book. This is clearly outside the scope of s 6 and cannot be considered as an intention to permanently deprive. But what if that student also took a photocopying card, which had a limit placed on its use, used it, then returned it. The photocopy card has been returned, but it is no longer as valuable as it was. So is there an intention to permanently deprive so far as the card is concerned?

Section 6 states that borrowing is not theft unless it is for a period and in circumstances making it equivalent to an outright taking or disposal. In *Lloyd* [1985] 2 All ER 661 it was held that this meant borrowing the property and keeping it until 'the goodness, the virtue, the practical value . . . has gone out of the article'. In this case a film had been taken for a short time and copied, then the original film replaced undamaged. This was not sufficient for an intention to permanently deprive.

Lord Lane CJ said:

> **J** '[s 6(1)] is intended to make clear that a mere borrowing is never enough to constitute the guilty mind unless the intention is to return the thing in such a changed state that it can truly be said that all its goodness or virtue has gone.'

From this it appears that in the example of the photocopy card, there would an intention to permanently deprive if all the value of the card had been used up, but if it still had value then there is no intention to permanently deprive.

Another difficulty is where D picks up property to see if there is anything worth stealing. What is the position if he decides it not worth stealing and returns it? This is what happened in *Easom* [1971] 2 All ER 945. D picked up a handbag in a cinema, rummaged through the contents and then replaced the handbag without having taken anything. He was convicted of theft of the handbag and its contents, but the Court of Appeal quashed this conviction. They held that even though he may have had a conditional intention to deprive, this was not enough. Note that he could now probably be charged with attempted theft under the Criminal Attempts Act 1981. (See Chapter 6, section 6.4.)

12.6.2 Conditional disposition

The final part of s 6 covers situations where D parts with property, taking the risk that he may not be able to get it back.

> '6(2) Without prejudice to the generality of subsection (1) above, where a person, having possession or control (lawfully or not) of property belonging to another, parts with the property under a condition as to its return which he may not be able to perform, this (if done for purposes of his own and without the other's authority) amounts to treating the property as his own to dispose of regardless of the other's rights.'

The first point to note is that this subsection applies even if D is lawfully in possession or control of the property. The second point is that the act must be done for D's own purpose and without the other's authority. The common example given to illustrate this is where D has been lent an item and then pawns it, but hopes he will have enough money to redeem it before he is due to give it back to the owner. This is a condition as to its return which he may not be able to perform and so he is treating it as his own to dispose of regardless of the other's rights.

Key facts on theft

KEY FACTS

Section of Theft Act 1968	Definition	Comment/Cases
s 1	A person is guilty of theft if he dishonestly appropriates property belonging to another with the intention of permanently depriving the other of it.	Full definition of theft. D is charged under this section.
s 2	(1) Not dishonest if believes: • has right in law • would have the other's consent • owner cannot be discovered. (2) Can be dishonest even if intends paying for property.	No definition of dishonesty in the Act. *Ghosh* two-part test: • is it dishonest by ordinary standards? • if so, did D know it was dishonest by those standards?
s 3	Appropriation (1) 'Any assumption of the rights of an owner'. (2) *Bona fide* purchaser has not appropriated.	Held to be assumption of any of the rights of an owner – *Gomez* (1993). Given 'neutral' meaning, so consent irrelevant – *Lawrence* (1971); *Hinks* (2000).
s 4	(1) 'Property' includes money and all other property real or personal, including things in action and other intangible property. (2) Land cannot be stolen except by trustee or tenant or by severing property from land. (3) Wild mushrooms, fruit, flowers and foliage cannot be stolen unless done for commercial purpose. (4) Wild animals cannot be stolen unless tamed or in captivity.	

s 5	(1) Property is regarded as belonging to any person having possession or control or any proprietary right. (2) Trust property belongs to any person having a right to enforce the trust.	Not limited to owner – *Turner (No 2)* (1971).
	(3) Property belongs to the other where it is received under an obligation to retain and deal with it in a particular way.	Must be a particular way – *Hall* (1972), *Klineberg and Marsden* (1999).
	(4) Property received by a mistake where there is a legal obligation to make restoration belongs to the other.	*Att-Gen's Reference (No 1 of 1983)* (1985). Must be a legal obligation – *Gilks* (1972).
s 6	(1) Intention to permanently deprive includes to treat the thing as his own to dispose of regardless of the other's rights and includes a borrowing or lending for a period and in circumstances making it equivalent to an outright taking or disposal. (2) Includes disposing of property under a condition as to its return which he may not be able to perform.	Conflicting views on 'dispose of' – *Cahill* (1993); *Lavender* (1994). The ' goodness or practical value must have gone from the property *Lloyd* (1985).

ACTIVITY

In each of the following situations, explain whether the elements of theft are satisfied.

1. Denise comes from a country where property placed outside a shop is meant for people to take free of charge. She sees a rack of clothes on the pavement outside a shop and takes a pair of jeans from it.

2. Katya is given a Christmas cash bonus in a sealed envelope. She has been told by her boss that the bonus would be £50. When she gets home and opens the envelope she finds there is £60 in it. She thinks her employer decided to be more generous and so keeps the money. Would your answer be different if (a) Katya realised there had been a mistake but did not return the money or (b) the amount in the envelope was £200?

3. Engelbert is given permission by his employer to borrow some decorative lights for use at a party. Engelbert also takes some candles without asking permission. When putting up the lights Engelbert smashes one of them. He lights two of the candles so that by the end of the evening they are partly burnt down. One of the guests admires the remaining lights and asks if he can have them to use at a disco at the weekend. Engelbert agrees to let him take the lights.

Further reading

Beatson, J and Simester, A P, 'Stealing one's own property' (1999) 115 LQR 372.
Gardner, S, 'Property and Theft' [1998] Crim LR 35.
Griew, E, 'Dishonesty: the objections to *Feely* and *Ghosh*' [1985] Crim LR 341.
Shute, S, 'Appropriation and the Law of Theft' [2002] Crim LR 445.
Smith, A T H, 'Gifts and the Law of Theft' [1999] CLJ 10.
Smith, A T H, 'Theft as Sharp Practice: Who Cares Now?' [2001] CLJ 21.
Smith, J C, 'Obtaining Cheques by Deception or Theft' [1997] Crim LR 396.

ROBBERY, BURGLARY AND OTHER OFFENCES IN THE THEFT ACTS ■────

AIMS AND OBJECTIVES □□□

After reading this chapter you should be able to:

■ Understand the *actus reus* and *mens rea* of robbery

■ Understand the *actus reus* and *mens rea* of burglary and related offences

■ Understand the *actus reus* and *mens rea* of taking a conveyance

■ Understand the *actus reus* and *mens rea* of blackmail

■ Understand the *actus reus* and *mens rea* of handling stolen goods

■ Understand the *actus reus* and *mens rea* of making off without payment

■ Analyse critically all the above offences

■ Apply the law to factual situations to determine whether robbery, burglary or other offences under the Theft Acts have been committed

In the last chapter we focused on the offence of theft. This chapter discusses other offences contained in the Theft Act 1968, together with one offence from the Theft Act 1978. Some of these have theft as an essential element, such as robbery. Others are connected to theft, such as going equipped for theft or handling stolen goods.

13.1 Robbery

Robbery is an offence under s 8 of the Theft Act 1968 and is, in effect, theft aggravated by the use or threat of force.

'8 A person is guilty of robbery if he steals, and immediately before or at the time of doing so, and in order to do so, he uses force on any person or puts or seeks to put any person in fear of being then and there subjected to force.'

So the elements which must be proved for robbery are:

- theft

- force or putting or seeking to put any person in fear of force.

There are two conditions on the force, and these are that it:

- must be immediately before or at the time of the theft; and

- must be in order to steal.

13.1.1 Theft as an element of robbery

There must be a completed theft for a robbery to have been committed. This means that all the elements of theft have to be present. If any one of them is missing then, just as there would be no theft, there is no robbery. So there is no theft in the situation where D takes a car, drives it a mile and abandons it because D has no intention permanently to deprive. Equally there is no robbery where D uses force to take that car. There is no offence of theft, so using force cannot make it into robbery.

Another example is where D has a belief that he has a right in law to take the property. This would mean he was not dishonest and one of the elements of theft would be missing, as seen in *Robinson* [1977] Crim LR 173.

CASE EXAMPLE

Robinson [1977] Crim LR 173

D ran a clothing club and was owed £7 by I's wife. D approached the man and threatened him. During a struggle the man dropped a £5 note and D took it claiming he was still owed £2. The judge directed the jury that D had honestly to believe he was entitled to get the money in that way. This was not the test. The jury should have been directed to consider whether he had a belief that he had a right in law to the money which would have made his actions not dishonest under s 2(1)(a) of the Theft Act. The Court of Appeal quashed the conviction for robbery.

Where force is used to steal, then the moment the theft is complete, there is a robbery. This is shown by *Corcoran v Anderton* [1980] Crim LR 385.

CASE EXAMPLE

Corcoran v Anderton [1980] Crim LR 385

One defendant hit a woman in the back and tugged at her bag. She let go of it and it fell to the ground. The defendants ran off without it (because the woman was screaming and attracting attention). It was held that the theft was complete so the defendants were guilty of robbery.

However, if the theft is not completed, for instance if the woman in the case of *Corcoran v Anderton* had not let go of the bag, then there is an attempted theft and D could be charged with attempted robbery.

13.1.2 Force or threat of force

Whether D's actions amount to force is something to be left to the jury. The amount of force can be small. In *Dawson and James* (1976) 64 Cr App R 170, one of the defendants pushed the victim, causing him to lose his balance, which enabled the other defendant to take his wallet. The Court of Appeal held that 'force' was an ordinary word and it was for the jury to decide if there had been force.

It was originally thought that the force had to be directed at the person, and that force used on an item of property would not be sufficient for robbery. In fact this was the intention of the Criminal Law Revision Committee when it put forward its draft Bill. It said in its report that it would:

'. . . not regard mere snatching of property, such as a handbag, from an unresisting owner as using force for the purpose of the definition [of robbery], though it might be so if the owner resisted'.

This point was considered in *Clouden* [1987] Crim LR 56.

CASE EXAMPLE

Clouden [1987] Crim LR 56

Court of Appeal held that D was guilty of robbery when he had wrenched a shopping basket from the victim's hand. The Court of Appeal held that the trial judge was right to leave to the jury the question of whether D had used force on a person.

It can be argued that using force on the bag was effectively using force on the victim, as the bag was wrenched from her hand. However, if a thief pulls a shoulder bag so that it slides off the victim's shoulder, would this be considered force? Probably not. And it would certainly not be force if a thief snatched a bag which was resting (not being held) on the lap of someone sitting on a park bench.

The definition of 'robbery' makes clear that robbery is committed if D puts or seeks to put a person in fear of force. It is not necessary that the force be applied. Putting V 'in fear being there and then subjected to force' is sufficient for robbery. This covers threatening words, such as 'I have a knife and I'll use it unless you give me your wallet', and threatening gestures, such as holding a knife in front of V.

CASE EXAMPLE

Bentham (2005), *The Times*, 11th March 2005

D put his fingers into his jacket pocket to give the appearance that he had a gun in there. He then demanded money and jewellery. He was charged with robbery and pleaded guilty. He was also charged with having in his possession an imitation firearm during the course of the robbery contrary to s 17(2) of the Firearms Act 1968. His conviction for this was quashed by the House of Lords.

It was clear that D was guilty of robbery as he had sought to put V in fear of being then and there subjected to force. The fact that it was only his fingers did not matter for the offence of robbery. However, for the offence of possessing an imitation firearm there had to be some item and not just a part of D's body. This was because what had to be possessed had to be a 'thing' and that meant something which was separate and distinct from oneself. Fingers were therefore not a 'thing'. In addition, the House of Lords pointed out that if fingers were regarded as property for the purposes of s 143 of the Powers of Criminal Courts (Sentencing) Act 2000 then this created the nonsense that a court could theoretically make an order depriving D of his rights in them!

Robbery is also committed even if the victim is not actually frightened by D's actions or words. If D seeks to put V in fear of being then and there subjected to force, this element of robbery is present. So if V is a plain clothes policeman put there to trap D and is not frightened, the fact that D sought to put V in fear is enough.

On any person

This means that the person threatened does not have to be the person from whom the theft occurs. An obvious example is an armed robber who enters a bank, seizes a customer and threatens to shoot that customer unless a bank official gets money out of the safe. This is putting a person in fear of being then and there subjected to force. The fact that it is not the customer's property which is being stolen does not matter.

13.1.3 Force immediately before or at the time of the theft

The force must be immediately before or at the time of stealing. This raises two problems. First, how 'immediate' does 'immediately before' have to be? What about the situation where a bank official is attacked at his home by a gang in order to get keys and security codes from him? The gang then drive to the bank and steal money. The theft has taken place an hour after the use of force. Is this 'immediately before'? It would seem right that the gang should be convicted of robbery. But what if the time delay were longer, as could happen if the attack on the manager was on Saturday evening and the theft of the money not until 24 hours later. Does this still come within 'immediately before'? There have been no decided cases on this point. The second problem is deciding the point at which a theft is completed, so that the force is no longer 'at the time of stealing'.

CASE EXAMPLE

Hale [1979] Crim LR 596

Two defendants knocked on the door of a house. When a woman opened the door they forced their way into the house and one defendant put his hand over her mouth to stop her screaming while the other defendant went upstairs to see what he could find to take. He took a jewellery box. Before they left the house they tied up the householder and gagged her.

They argued on appeal that the theft was complete as soon as the second defendant picked up the jewellery box, so the use of force in tying up the householder was not at the time of stealing. However, the Court of Appeal upheld their convictions. The Court of Appeal thought that the jury could have come to the decision that there was force immediately before the theft when one of the defendants put his hand over the householder's mouth. In addition, the Court of Appeal thought that the tying up of the householder could also be force for the purpose of robbery as it held that the theft was still ongoing.

J 'We also think that [the jury] were also entitled to rely upon the act of tying her up provided they were satisfied (and it is difficult to see how they could not be satisfied) that the force so used was to enable them to steal. If they were still engaged in the act of stealing the force was clearly used to enable them to continue to assume the rights the owner and permanently to deprive Mrs Carrett of her box, which is what they began to do when they first seized it . . .

To say that the conduct is over and done with as soon as he laid hands on the property . . . is contrary to common-sense and to the natural meaning of words . . . the act of appropriation does not suddenly cease. It is a continuous act and it is a matter for the jury to decide whether or not the act of appropriation has finished.'

So, in this case for robbery, appropriation is viewed as a continuing act or a course of conduct. However, *Hale* (1979) was decided before *Gomez* (1993), which is the leading case on appropriation in theft. *Gomez* (1993) rules that the point of appropriation is when D first does an act assuming a right of the owner. This point was argued in *Lockley* [1995] Crim LR 656. D was caught shoplifting cans of beer from an off-licence, and used force on the shopkeeper who was trying to stop him from escaping. He appealed on the basis that *Gomez* (1993) had impliedly overruled *Hale* (1979). However, the Court of Appeal rejected this argument and confirmed that the principle in *Hale* (1979) still applied in robbery.

But there must be a point when the theft is complete and so any force used after this point does not make it robbery. What if in *Lockley* (1995) D had left the shop and was running down the road when a passer-by (alerted by the shouts of the shopkeeper) tried to stop him? D uses force on the passer-by to escape. Surely the theft is completed before this use of force? The force used is a separate act to the theft and does not make the theft a robbery. The force was, of course, a separate offence of assault.

Finally it should be noted that the threat of force in the future cannot constitute robbery, although it may be blackmail.

13.1.4 Force in order to steal

The force must be used in order to steal. So if the force was not used for this purpose, then any later theft will not make it into robbery. Take the situation where D has an argument with V and punches him, knocking him out. D then sees that some money has fallen out of V's pocket and decides to take it. The force was not used for the purpose of that theft and D is not guilty of robbery, but guilty of two separate offences: an assault and theft.

13.1.5 *Mens rea* for robbery

D must have the *mens rea* for theft, that is, he must be dishonest and he must intend to permanently deprive the other of the property. He must also intend to use force to steal.

Key facts on robbery

KEY FACTS

Element	Law	Case
Theft	There must be a completed theft if any element is missing there is no theft and therefore no robbery.	*Robinson* (1977)
	The moment the theft is completed (with the relevant force) there is robbery.	*Corcoran v Anderton* (1980)
Force or threat of force	The jury decide whether the acts were force, using the ordinary meaning of the word.	*Dawson and James* (1976)
	It includes wrenching a bag from V's hand.	*Clouden* (1987)
Immediately before or at the time of the theft	For robbery, theft has been held to be a continuing act.	*Hale* (1979)
	Using force to escape can still be at the time of the theft.	*Lockley* (1995)
In order to steal	The force must be in order to steal. Force used for another purpose does not become robbery if D later decides to steal.	
On any person	The force can be against *any* person. It does not have to be against the victim of the theft.	

ACTIVITY

Explain whether or not a robbery has occurred in each of the following situations.

1. Arnie holds a knife to the throat of a one-month-old baby and orders the baby's mother to hand over her purse or he will 'slit the baby's throat'. The mother hands over her purse.

2. Brendan threatens staff in a post office with an imitation gun. He demands that they hand over the money in the till. One of the staff presses a security button and a grill comes down in front of the counter so that the staff are safe and Brendan cannot reach the till. He leaves without taking anything.

3. Carla snatches a handbag from Delia. Delia is so surprised that she lets go of the bag and Carla runs off with it.

4. Egbert breaks into a car in a car park and takes a briefcase out of it. As he is walking away from the car, the owner arrives, realises what has happened and starts to chase after Egbert. The owner catches hold of Egbert, but Egbert pushes him over and makes his escape.

5. Fenella tells Gerry to hand over her Rolex watch and, that if she does not, Fenella will send her boyfriend round to beat Gerry up. Gerry hands over the watch.

13.2 Burglary

This is an offence under s 9 of the Theft Act 1968.

'9(1) A person is guilty of burglary if –

    (a) he enters any building or part of a building as a trespasser and with intent to commit any such offence as is mentioned in subsection (2) below; or

    (b) having entered a building or part of a building as a trespasser he steals or attempts to steal anything in the building or that part of it or inflicts or attempts to inflict on any person therein any grievous bodily harm.

  (2) The offences referred to in subsection (1) (a) above are offences of stealing anything in the building or part of a building in question, of inflicting on any person therein any grievous bodily harm, and of doing unlawful damage to the building or anything therein.'

As can be seen by reading these subsections, burglary can be committed in a number of ways and the following chart shows this.

Key facts on different ways of committing burglary

KEY FACTS

Burglary	
Section 9(1)(a)	**Section 9(1)(b)**
Enters a building or part of a building as a trespasser.	Having entered a building or part of a building as a trespasser.
With intent to: • steal • inflict grievous bodily harm • do unlawful damage NB used to include intention to rape but this is now covered by s 63 Sexual Offences Act 2003.	• steals or attempts to steal; or • inflicts or attempts to inflict grievous bodily harm.

Although ss 9(1)(a) and 9(1)(b) create different ways of committing burglary they do have common elements. These are that there must be:

• entry

• of a building or part of a building

• as a trespasser.

The distinguishing feature between the subsections is the intention at the time of entry. For s 9(1)(a) the defendant must intend to do one of the three listed offences (known as ulterior offences) at the time of entering. However, there is no need for the ulterior offence to take place or even be attempted. For s 9(1)(b), what the defendant intends on entry is irrelevant, but the prosecution must prove that he actually committed or attempted to commit theft or grievous bodily harm.

13.2.1 Entry

'Entry' is not defined in the 1968 Act. Prior to the Act, common law rules had developed on what constituted entry. The main rules were that the entry of any part of the body (even a finger) into the building was sufficient and also that there was an entry if D did not physically enter but inserted an instrument for the purpose of theft. For example, where D used a fishing net to try pick up items. Initially when the courts had to interpret the word 'enters' in the Theft Act 1968, they took a very different line to the old common law rules.

The first main case on this point was *Collins* [1972] 2 All ER 1105 (see section 13.2.3 for the facts of *Collins*). In this case the Court of Appeal said that the jury had to be satisfied that D had made 'an effective and substantial entry'. However, in *Brown* [1985] Crim LR 167 this concept of 'an effective and substantial entry' was modified to 'effective entry'.

CASE EXAMPLE

Brown [1985] Crim LR 167

D was standing on the ground outside but leaning in through a shop window rummaging through goods. The Court of Appeal said that the word 'substantial' did not materially assist the definition of entry and his conviction for burglary was upheld as clearly in this situation his entry was effective.

However, in *Ryan* [1996] Crim LR 320 the concept of 'effective' entry does not appear to have been followed.

CASE EXAMPLE

Ryan [1996] Crim LR 320

D was trapped when trying to get through a window into a house at 2.30 am. His head and right arm were inside the house but the rest of his body was outside. The fire brigade had to be called to release him. This could scarcely be said to be an 'effective' entry. However, the Court of Appeal upheld his conviction for burglary, saying that there was evidence on which the jury could find that D had entered.

13.2.2 Building or part of a building

The Theft Act 1968 does not define building but does give an extended meaning to it to include inhabited places such as houseboats or caravans, which would otherwise not be included in the offence. This is set out in s 9(4).

'9(4) References . . . to a building shall apply also to an inhabited vehicle or vessel, and shall apply to any such vehicle or vessel at times when the person having a habitation is not there as well as at times when he is.'

The main problems for the courts have come where a structure such as a portacabin has been used for storage or office work. In a very old case decided well before the Theft Act 1968, *Stevens v Gourley* (1859) 7 CB NS 99, it was said that a building must be 'intended to be permanent, or at least to endure for a considerable time'.

This means that the facts of each case must be considered. There are two cases on whether a large storage container is a building. In these cases the court came to different decisions after looking at the facts.

- In *B and S v Leathley* [1979] Crim LR 314 a 25 foot long freezer container which had been in a farmyard for over two years was used as a storage facility. It rested on sleepers, had doors with locks and was connected to the electricity supply. This was held to be a building.

- In *Norfolk Constabulary v Seekings and Gould* [1986] Crim LR 167 a lorry trailer with wheels which had been used for over a year for storage, had steps provided access and was connected to the electricity supply was held not to be a building. The fact that it had wheels meant that it remained a vehicle.

Part of a building

The phrase 'part of building' is used to cover situations in which the defendant may have permission to be in one part of the building (and therefore is not a trespasser in that part) but does not have permission to be in another part. A case example to demonstrate this is *Walkington* [1979] 2 All ER 716. D went into the counter area in a shop and opened a till. He was guilty of burglary under s 9(1)(a) because he had entered part of a building (the counter area) as a trespasser with the intention of stealing. Other examples include storerooms in shops where shoppers would not have permission to enter or where one student entered another student's rooms in a hall of residence without permission.

13.2.3 As a trespasser

In order for D to commit burglary he must enter as a trespasser. If a person has permission to enter he is not a trespasser. This was illustrated by the unusual case of *Collins* (1972). NB Since May 2004, Collins would be charged with an offence under s 63, Sexual Offences Act 2003.

CASE EXAMPLE

Collins [1972] 2 All ER 1105

D, having had quite a lot to drink, decided he wanted to have sexual intercourse. He saw an open window and climbed a ladder to look in. He saw there was a naked girl asleep in bed. He then went down the ladder, took off all his clothes except for his socks and climbed back up the ladder to the girl's bedroom. As he was on the window sill outside the room, she woke up, thought he was her boyfriend and helped him into the room where they had sex. He was convicted of burglary under s 9(1)(a), ie that he had entered as a trespasser with intent to rape. (He could not be charged with rape, as the girl accepted that she had consented to sex.) He appealed on the basis that that he was not a trespasser as he had been invited in. The Court of Appeal quashed his conviction, pointing out:

J '. . . there cannot be a conviction for entering premises "as a trespasser" within the meaning of s 9 of the Theft Act 1968 unless the person entering does so knowing he is a trespasser and nevertheless deliberately enters, or, at the very least, is reckless whether or not he is entering the premises of another without the other party's consent.'

So to succeed on a charge of burglary, the prosecution must prove that the defendant knew, or was subjectively reckless, as to whether he was trespassing.

Going beyond permission

However, where the defendant goes beyond the permission given, he may be considered a trespasser. In *Smith and Jones* [1976] 3 All ER 54, Smith and his friend went to Smith's father's house in the middle of the night and took two television sets without the father's knowledge or permission. The father stated that his son would not be a trespasser in the house; he had a general permission to enter. The Court of Appeal referred back to the judgment in *Collins* (1972) and added this principle.

J 'It is our view that a person is a trespasser for the purpose of s 9(1)(b) of the Theft Act 1968 if he enters premises of another knowing that he is entering in excess of the permission that has been given to him to enter, or being reckless whether he is entering in excess of [that] permission.'

This meant that Smith was guilty of burglary. This decision was in line with the Australian case of *Barker v R* (1983) 7 ALJR 426, where one person who was going away asked D, who was a neighbour, to keep a eye on the house and told D where a key was hidden should he need to enter. D used the key to enter and steal property. He was found guilty of burglary. The Australian court said:

> **J** 'If a person enters for a purpose outside the scope of his authority then he stands on no better position than a person who enters with no authority at all.'

The late Professor Sir John Smith argued that this would mean that a person who enters a shop with the intention of stealing would be guilty of burglary as he only has permission to enter for the purpose of shopping. However, it would be difficult in most cases to prove that the intention to shoplift was there at the point of entering the shop.

There are many situations where a person has permission to enter for a limited purpose. For example, someone buys a ticket to attend a concert in a concert hall, or to look round an historic building or an art collection. The ticket is a licence (or permission) to be in the building for a very specific reason and/or time. If D buys a ticket intending to steal one of the paintings from the art collection, this line of reasoning would suggest that he is guilty of burglary. However, in *Byrne v Kinematograph Renters Society Ltd* [1958] 2 All ER 579, a civil case, it was held that it was not trespass to gain entry to a cinema by buying a ticket with the purpose of counting the number in the audience, not with the purpose of seeing the film. This case was distinguished in *Smith and Jones* (1976) on the basis that the permission to enter a cinema was in general terms and not limited to viewing the film and was very different from the situation where D enters with the intention to steal (or cause grievous bodily harm or criminal damage).

If a person has been banned from entering a shop (or other place), then there is no problem. When they enter they are entering as a trespasser. This means that a known shoplifter who is banned from entering a local supermarket would be guilty of burglary if he or she entered intending to steal goods (s 9(1)(a)) or if, having entered, he then stole goods (s 9(1)(b)).

The law is also clear where D gains entry through fraud, such as where he claims to be a gas meter reader. There is no genuine permission to enter and D is a trespasser.

13.2.4 Mental element of burglary

There are two parts to the mental element in burglary. These are in respect of:

* entering as a trespasser
* the ulterior offence.

First, as stated above, the defendant must know, or be subjectively reckless, as to whether he is trespassing. In addition, for s 9(1)(a) the defendant must have the intention to commit one of the offences at the time of entering the building. Where D is entering intending to steal anything he

can find which is worth taking, then this is called a conditional intent. This is sufficient for D to be guilty under s 9(1)(a). This was decided in *Attorney-General's References Nos 1 and 2 of 1979* [1979] 3 All ER 143. For s 9(1)(b), the defendant must have the *mens rea* for theft or grievous bodily harm when committing (or attempting to commit) the *actus reus* of these offences.

13.2.5 Burglary of a dwelling

This carries a higher maximum sentence than burglary of other types of building as a result of an amendment to the Theft Act 1968 by the Criminal Justice Act 1991. Section 9(3) now reads:

 '9(3) A person guilty of burglary shall on conviction on indictment be liable to imprisonment for a term not exceeding −

(a) where the offence was committed in respect of a building or part of a building which is a dwelling, fourteen years;

(b) in any other case, ten years.'

This reflects the public view that burglary of someone's home is more serious (and more frightening for the victim) than burglary of another type of building such as a shed or an office or a warehouse. The word 'dwelling' includes an inhabited vehicle or vessel.

Key facts on burglary

KEY FACTS

Elements	Comment	Case/section
Entry	This has changed from • 'effective and substantial' entry: to • 'effective' entry: to • evidence for the jury to find D had entered.	*Collins* (1972) *Brown* (1985) *Ryan* (1996)
Building or part of a building.	Must have some permanence.	*B and S v Leathley* (1979) *Norfolk Constabulary v Seekings and Gould* (1986)
	Includes inhabited vehicle or vessel.	s 9(4) Theft Act 1968
	Can be entry of part of an building.	*Walkington* (1979)

As a trespasser	If has permission is not a trespasser.	*Collins* (1972)
	If goes beyond permission then can be a trespasser.	*Smith and Jones* (1976)
Mens rea	Must know or be subjectively reckless as to whether he is a trespasser **PLUS EITHER** intention at point of entry to commit: • theft or • grievous bodily harm or • criminal damage **OR** *mens rea* for theft or grievous bodily harm at point of committing or attempting to commit these offences in a building.	s 9(1)(a) Theft Act 1968 s 9(1)(b) Theft Act 1968

ACTIVITY

In each of the following, explain whether or not a burglary has occurred, and if so whether it would be an offence under s 9(1)(a) or s 9(1)(b).

1. Jonny has been banned from a local pub. One evening he goes there for a drink with a friend. While he is waiting for the friend to get the drinks at the bar, Jonny sees a handbag under one of the chairs. He picks it up and takes a £10 note from it. He then puts the handbag back under the chair.

2. Ken and his partner, Lola, have split up and Ken has moved out of the flat he shared with Lola, taking most of his belongings with him. One evening he goes back there to collect the rest of his belongings. Lola is out so Ken asks the neighbour to let him have the spare key which the neighbour keeps for emergencies. While Ken is packing his clothes, Lola returns. They have an argument and Ken beats up Lola causing her serious injuries.

3. Mike works as a shelf-filler in a DIY store. One day when he is putting packs of batteries out on to a shelf, he slips one in his pocket. He does not intend to pay for it. Later in the day he sees the manager leave her office. Mike goes in and takes money from the desk. The door to the office has a notice saying 'Private'.

4. Nigella, who is a pupil at the local comprehensive, goes to the school buildings late in the evening after school. She intends to damage the science lab as she hates the teacher. She gets in through a window but is caught by the caretaker before she does any damage.

13.3 Aggravated burglary

This is where a burglary is made more serious by the carrying of an article which could be used to inflict injury. The Criminal Law Revision Committee in its Eighth Report pointed out that 'burglary when in possession of the articles mentioned [in s 10] is so serious that it should in our opinion be punishable with imprisonment for life. The offence is comparable with robbery . . . It must be extremely frightening to those in the building, and it might well lead to loss of life'.

The offence is set out by s 10 of the Theft Act 1968:

'10 A person is guilty of aggravated burglary if he commits any burglary and at the time has with him any firearm or imitation firearm, any weapon of offence, or any explosive, and for this purpose –

(a) "firearm" includes an airgun or air pistol and "imitation firearm" means anything which has the appearance of being a firearm, whether capable of being discharged or not; and

(b) "weapon of offence" means any article made or adapted for use for causing injury to or incapacitating a person, or intended by the person having it with him for such use; and

(c) "explosive" means any article manufactured for the purpose of producing a practical effect by explosion, or intended by the person having it with him for that purpose.'

These articles cover a wide range of things, especially 'weapon of offence', which is much wider than the definition of 'offensive weapon' in the Prevention of Crime Act 1953. In s 10 it includes any article intended by D to cause injury or to incapacitate a person. This appears to include such items as rope or masking tape which D intends to use to tie up the householder.

13.3.1 Has with him

A key part of the offence of aggravated burglary is that D has the article with him at the time of the burglary. So for a s 9(1)(a) burglary, he must have it at the moment of entry, but for a s 9(1)(b) burglary he must have at the point when he commits or attempts to commit the ulterior offence. These points are illustrated by the case of *Francis* [1982] Crim LR 363.

CASE EXAMPLE

Francis [1982] Crim LR 363

The defendants, who were armed with sticks, demanded entry. Having been allowed to enter, they then put down the sticks. Later they stole items from the house. Their convictions for aggravated burglary were quashed because although they had the weapons with them on entry, there was no evidence that they intended to steal at that point. Then, when they did actually steal, they did not have the weapons with them, so the condition for s 9(1)b was not satisfied.

Conversely the fact that D has no weapon when he enters does not prevent him from being guilty of aggravated burglary if he picks up an article in the house and has it with him when he then steals or causes grievous bodily harm. This was the position in *O'Leary* (1986) 82 Cr App R 341. D did not have a weapon when he entered a house as a trespasser, but while in the house he picked up a knife from the kitchen. He then went upstairs and threatened the occupants with the knife so that they gave him property. He had the knife with him when he stole and, as this was the point at which he committed a s 9(1)(b) burglary, he was guilty of aggravated burglary. It also worth noting that, as D had the knife with him at the point at which the burglary was committed, he would have been guilty of aggravated burglary even if he had not used the knife.

Joint burglars

Where there are two or more offenders participating in the burglary, but only one of them has a weapon, all of them may be guilty of aggravated burglary. The key fact is that those without a weapon must know that one of the others has a weapon. However, in *Klass* (1998) 1 Cr App Rep 453 it was decided that if the accomplice with one of the aggravating articles remains outside the building, then the person entering will not have committed aggravated burglary.

13.4 Removal of items from a place open to the public

This offence was included in the Theft Act 1968 to cover situations where an item is removed from a museum, art gallery or historic house etc, but where it might not be possible to prove an intention to deprive permanently for a charge of theft. The offence is set out in s 11 of the Theft Act 1968:

'11(1) . . . where the public have access to a building in order to view the building or any part of it, or a collection or part of a collection housed in it, any person who without lawful authority removes from the building or its grounds the

whole or part of any article displayed or kept for display to the public in the building or that part of it shall be guilty of an offence.

For this purpose "collection" includes a collection got together for a temporary purpose, but references in this section to a collection do not apply to a collection made or exhibited for the purpose of effecting sales or other commercial dealings.'

So it has to be proved that an article was taken in the following circumstances:

- it must be from a place where the public have access; this can be a building or part of a building or its grounds

- the article must be displayed or kept for display; so this includes items which are not at the time on display, eg those in a storeroom or which restoration work is being carried out

- the display must not be for a commercial purpose.

Section 11(2) makes it clear that where there is a permanent display, such as in a museum or art gallery, then, even if the taking is on a day when the public do not have access to the building, this offence is committed. However, where the display is temporary the taking must be on a day when the public have access.

Mens rea

The only requirement is an intention to take the item. However, s 11(3) does qualify this as it states that 'a person does not commit an offence under this section if he believes that he has lawful authority for the removal of the thing in question or that he would have it if the person entitled to give it knew of the removal and the circumstances of it'.

ACTIVITY

Self-test questions

1. Explain the amount of force needed to prove robbery.

2. How does the ruling in *Lockley* (1995) appear to conflict with the ruling in *Gomez* (1993) on appropriation?

3. Explain the different tests the courts have used for 'entry' in burglary.

4. How do the courts define trespasser for the purposes of burglary?

5. Why is it necessary to have an offence of removal of items from a public place (s 11 Theft Act 1968) when there are offences of theft and burglary?

13.5 Taking a conveyance without consent

This is another offence which does not require proof of an intention permanently to deprive. There are instances where the taking of a vehicle is theft and can be charged as that; for example, where an expensive car is stolen and then sold to an innocent third party. This section is not intended for that type of situation. It is meant to cover situations which are commonly referred to as 'joy-riding'; in other words, where D temporarily takes or drives a vehicle and then abandons it.

The rationale for the offence is to cover temporary use of a conveyance, since it is often difficult to prove that there was the intention permanently to deprive which is necessary for proving theft.

The basic offence is set out in s 12(1) of the Theft Act 1968.

 '12(1) Subject to subsections (5) and (6) below, a person shall be guilty of an offence if, without having the consent of the owner or other lawful authority, he takes any conveyance for his own or another's use or, knowing that any conveyance has been taken without such authority, drives it or allows himself to be carried in or on it.'

Subsection (5) states that s 12(1) does not apply to pedal cycles, but instead it creates a separate offence of taking a pedal cycle.

Subsection (6) goes to D's *mens rea* and states that 'a person does not commit an offence under this section by anything done in the belief that he has lawful authority to do it or that he would have the owner's consent if the owner knew of his doing it and the circumstances of it'.

13.5.1 Taking for his own or another's use

There are three ways in which the offence can be committed:

- taking
- driving
- allowing oneself to be carried.

Each of these needs to be further explained.

Taking

There have been several cases on what is meant by taking. In *Bogacki* [1973] 2 All ER 864 the three defendants had got onto a bus in a depot and tried, unsuccessfully, to start it. The Court of Appeal quashed their conviction because there was no 'taking'. They explained the decision by saying:

> **J** '[It must] be shown that he took the vehicle, that is to say, that there was an unauthorised taking possession or control of the vehicle by him adverse to the rights of the true owner, coupled with some movement, however small . . . of that vehicle following such unauthorised taking.'

In *Bogacki* (1973) the defendants could have been guilty of attempting to take the bus, but not of the completed offence under s 12. In *Bow* [1977] Crim LR 176 D, his brother and father, were stopped by a gamekeeper, who suspected they were poaching. The gamekeeper parked his Land Rover blocking the way so that they could not drive off in their own car. D got into the Land Rover, released the handbrake and sat in it while it rolled about 200 yards, so that their escape route was no longer blocked. He did not start the engine.

It was accepted that if D had not been in the vehicle while it rolled down the road, then he would not have been guilty of an offence, as he had not taken it for his own or another's use. The Court of Appeal referred to Smith and Hogan's *Criminal Law* (3rd edn, 1973) and quoted the following passage:

> 'But subject to the requirement of taking, the offence does seem, in essence, to consist in stealing a ride. This seems implicit in the requirement that the taking be for "his own or another's *use*". Thus if D releases the handbrake of a car so that it runs down an incline, or releases a boat from its moorings so that it is carried off by the tide this would not as such be an offence within the section. The taking must be for D's use or the use of another and if he intends to make no use of the car or the boat there would be no offence under section 12. But it would be enough if D were to release the boat from its moorings so that he would be carried downstream in the boat.'

The taking does not need to involve driving or being in the conveyance, provided it is intended for use later. This was shown in *Pearce* [1973] Crim LR 321 where D took a boat away on a trailer.

Drive or allow himself to be carried

Where a person did not 'take' the conveyance, he can still be guilty under this section, if he:

- drove it knowing that it had been taken without consent or
- allowed himself to be carried in it knowing that it had been taken without consent.

13.5.2 Without consent

The usual situation in cases charged under this section is where D has taken a car from the street or a car park. In this type of situation there is no question that D did not have the consent of the owner. However, there are cases where the owner has given consent for some use of the conveyance but D has gone beyond the permission given. In these cases it is still possible for D to be guilty.

An example is *McGill* (1970) 54 Cr App Rep 300.

CASE EXAMPLE

McGill (1970) 54 Cr App Rep 300

D was given permission to use a car to drive another person to the station, on the condition that D then returned the car immediately. D drove to the train station but then continued to use the car and did not return it for some days. It was held that he was guilty under s 12. The taking without permission occurred from the moment he used the car for his own purpose after leaving the station.

This situation can also happen where an employee has permission to drive a company vehicle for work but if he uses it for his own purposes, then that is a taking without consent of the owner. In *McKnight v Davies* [1974] RTR 4 the Queen's Bench Divisional Court upheld the conviction of a lorry driver who had not returned a lorry at the end of his working day but had used it for his own purposes, only returning it in the early hours of the following morning.

In both these cases there was a clear limit on the permission given to D and when D went beyond that permission he was guilty under s 12. However, in *Peart* [1970] 2 All ER 823 it was held that D was not guilty of an offence under s 12 when he obtained the use of a van by pretending that he had a urgent appointment in Alnwick and would return the van by 7.30 pm. In fact, he drove to Burnley and was found there with the van by the police at 9 pm. The Court of Appeal took the view that the owner had merely been deceived as to the purpose for which the van was to be used and this did not vitiate the owner's consent to the taking of the van at the start of the journey. The Court of Appeal could not consider whether there was a taking at a later point (either when D diverted from the route to Alnwick or when he continued to use the van after 7.30 pm), because this point had not been left to the jury.

In *Whittaker v Campbell* [1983] 3 All ER 582 the Queen's Bench Divisional Court came to the decision that D was not guilty of a s 12 offence where D, who did not hold a driving licence, hired a van using a driving licence belonging to another person. The fraud went only to the hiring of the van and not its use. The actual use that D made of the van was within the terms of the hiring.

13.5.3 Conveyance

What can be taken? The word used is 'conveyance' and this is defined very widely in s 12(7)(a):

'12(7)(a) "Conveyance" means any conveyance constructed or adapted for the carriage of a person or persons whether by land, water or air, except that it does not include a conveyance constructed or adapted for use only under the control of a person not carried in or on it, and "drive" shall be construed accordingly.'

So this does not cover just road vehicles: it also includes trains, boats and aircraft. There are only two conditions placed on this wide definition. The first is that the conveyance must have been constructed or adapted for carrying people. The second is that the operator (or person in control) must also be carried in it or on it. This excludes radio-operated vehicles.

13.6 Aggravated vehicle-taking

This offence was added to the Theft Act 1968 by the Aggravated Vehicle-Taking Act 1992 because of the number of cases under s 12 where cars, having been taken, were driven dangerously, causing injury or damage. It was clear that a higher penalty was needed for such cases. The new section states:

'12A(1) Subject to subsection (3) below, a person is guilty of aggravated taking of a vehicle if –

    (a) he commits an offence under section 12(1) above (in this section referred to as a 'basic offence') in relation to a mechanically propelled vehicle; and

    (b) it is proved that, at any time after the vehicle was unlawfully taken (whether by him or another) and before it was recovered, the vehicle was driven, or injury or damage caused in one or more of the circumstances set out in paragraphs (a) to (d) of subsection (2) below.

(2) The circumstances referred to in subsection (1)(b) above are –

    (a) that the vehicle was driven dangerously on a road or other public place;

    (b) that, owing to the driving of the vehicle, an accident occurred by which injury was caused to any person;

    (c) that, owing to the driving of the vehicle, an accident occurred by which damage was caused to any property, other than the vehicle;

    (d) that damage was caused to the vehicle.'

So in order to prove this offence the prosecution must show that:

1. the basic offence was committed; and

2. that this was in relation to a mechanically propelled vehicle; and

3. one of the following:

- dangerous driving
- injury owing to the driving
- damage to other property owing to the driving
- damage to the vehicle.

13.6.1 Dangerous driving

There is a two-part test for dangerous driving set out in s 12A(7). First, the way D drives must fall 'far below what would be expected of a competent and careful driver', and second, 'it would be obvious to a competent and careful driver that driving the vehicle in that way would be dangerous'. This imposes an objective standard on D.

13.6.2 Injury or damage

For the three situations set out in ss 12A(2)(b), 12A(2)(c) and 12A(2)(d), it is not necessary to prove any fault in the driving of the defendant. The prosecution need only show that D committed the basic offence and that one of the three things then occurred. This was shown in the case of *Marsh* [1997] Crim LR 205, where a pedestrian ran out in front of the car and was slightly injured. The Court of Appeal held that D was guilty even though there was no fault in his driving.

Section 12A(3) allows for a person to be not guilty in two situations. These are:

- if the driving, accident or damage occurred before the basic offence was committed
- if he was not in or on the vehicle or in the immediate vicinity when the driving, accident or damage occurred.

13.7 Abstracting electricity

It is necessary to have a separate offence for this, since electricity does not come within the definition of property for the purposes of theft.

Section 13 of the Theft Act 1968 makes it an offence where a person 'dishonestly uses without due authority, or dishonestly causes to be wasted or diverted, any electricity'.

The concept of dishonesty is that in the *Ghosh* [1982] 2 All ER 689 test (see Chapter 12, section 12.5.2) so the first question is, was what was done dishonest by the ordinary standards of reasonable and honest people? If it was not the defendant is not guilty. However, if the jury decide that it was dishonest by those standards, then they must consider the more subjective test of did the defendant know it was dishonest by those standards.

13.8 Blackmail

This is an offence under s 21 Theft Act 1968 which states:

'21(1) A person is guilty of blackmail if, with a view to gain for himself or another or with intent to cause loss to another, he makes any unwarranted demand with menaces; and for this purpose a demand with menaces is unwarranted unless the person making it does so in the belief –

(a) that he has reasonable grounds for making the demand; and

(b) that the use of the menaces is a proper means of reinforcing the demand.

(2) The nature of the act or omission demanded is immaterial, and it is also immaterial whether the menaces relate to action to be taken by the person making the demand.'

So, from this it can be seen that there are four elements to be proved:

- a demand
- which is unwarranted; and
- made with menaces
- with a view to gain or loss.

13.8.1 Demand

There must be a demand, but that demand may take any form, for example it may be by words, conduct, in writing or by e-mail. It need not even be made explicitly to the victim. In *Collister and Warhurst* (1955) 39 Cr App Rep 100 two police officers discussed the chances of them dropping a charge against the defendant in return for payment. They did this in circumstances where the defendant could easily overhear them and they meant him to overhear them. Even though they did not make a direct demand, this was held to be a demand for the purpose of blackmail.

Making the demand is the *actus reus* of the offence. It does not have to be received by the victim. So, if a demand is sent through the post then the demand is considered made at the point the letter is posted. This was decided by the House of Lords in *Treacy* [1971] 1 All ER 110, when D posted a letter containing a demand with menaces posted in England to someone in Germany. The offence of blackmail was therefore committed in England. However, Lord Diplock thought that the demand continues until it reaches the victim. So, if the reverse had happened, ie a letter posted in Germany to someone in England, the demand can also be considered as occurring at the point when the victim reads it and, again, the offence would have been committed in England.

13.8.2 Unwarranted demand

Section 21 explains that any demand made with menaces is unwarranted unless the two tests set out in s 21(1)(a) and s 21(1)(b) are fulfilled. This means that D has to show that he believed:

- he had reasonable grounds for making the demand
- the use of the menaces was a proper means of reinforcing the demand.

These tests focus on D's belief and so give a subjective element to what is an unwarranted demand. They also mean that where D has a genuine claim, he can still be guilty of blackmail if he does not believe that the use of the menaces was a proper means of reinforcing the demand. This was clearly the intention of the Criminal Law Revision Committee, which wrote in its Eighth Report:

'The essential feature of the offence will be that the accused demands something with menaces when he knows either that he has no right to make the demand or that the use of the menaces is improper. This, we believe, will limit the offence to what would ordinarily be thought to be included in blackmail. The true blackmailer will know that he has no reasonable grounds for demanding money as the price of his victim's secret: the person with a genuine claim will be guilty unless he believes that it is proper to use the menaces to enforce his claim.'

The fact that menaces was *not* a proper means of reinforcing a demand was essential in *Harvey* (1981) 72 Cr App R 139.

CASE EXAMPLE

Harvey (1981) 72 Cr App R 139

D and others had paid the victim £20,000 for what was claimed to be cannabis. In fact it was, as D put it, 'a load of rubbish'. The defendants wanted their money back as they felt they had been 'ripped off' to the tune of £20,000. In fact, as the deal was an illegal contract, there was no right in law to recover the money. However, it could be accepted that the defendants believed they had 'reasonable grounds for making the demand'. But the defendants reinforced their demand by kidnapping the victim, his wife and child, and threatened to cause them serious physical injury if the money was not repaid. They were guilty.

13.8.3 View to gain or loss

The *mens rea* of blackmail is that D must be acting with a view to gain for himself or another or with intent to cause loss to another. The interpretation section in the Theft Act 1968, s 34(2)(a) defines 'gain' and 'loss'. This states that:

'34(2) For the purposes of this Act –

(a) "gain" and "loss" are to be construed as extending only to gain or loss in money or other property, but as extending to any such gain or loss whether temporary or permanent; and –

(i) "gain" includes a gain by keeping what one has, as well as a gain by getting what one has not; and

(ii) "loss" included a loss by not getting what one might get, as well as a loss by parting with what one has.'

So the gain or loss must involve money or other property, but need not be permanent, it can be temporary.

An unusual case on view to a gain or a loss was *Bevans* [1988] Crim LR 236 where D, who was suffering from severe osteoarthritis, pointed a gun at his doctor and demanded a morphine injection for pain relief. The doctor gave him the injection. It was held that the morphine was property and, also, that it was both a gain for the defendant and a loss to the doctor from whom it was demanded.

13.8.4 Menaces

The demand must be made with menaces. Menaces have been held to be a serious threat, but are wider than just a threat. In *Thorne v Motor Trade Association* [1937] 3 All ER 157, Lord Wright said:

> **J** 'I think the word "menace" is to be liberally construed and not as limited to threats of violence but as including threats of any action detrimental to or unpleasant to the person addressed. It may also include a warning that in certain events such action is intended.'

In *Clear* [1968] 1 All ER 74 it was said that the menace must either be 'of such a nature and extent that the mind of an ordinary person of normal stability and courage might be influenced or made apprehensive by it so as to unwillingly accede to it'. It is not necessary to prove that the victim was actually intimidated. So if the menaces would affect an ordinary person, this is sufficient, but if they would not, then blackmail cannot usually be proved. However, in *Garwood* [1987] 1 All ER 1032 the Court of Appeal said that where a threat is made which would not affect a normal person, this can still be menaces if the defendant was aware of the likely effect on the victim.

CASE EXAMPLE

Harry [1974] Crim LR 32

D, who was the treasurer of a college rag committee, sent letters to 115 local shopkeepers asking them to buy a poster, with the money to go to charity. The poster contained the words: 'These premises are immune from all Rag 73 activities whatever they may be'. The letter sent out indicated that paying for a poster would avoid 'any rag activity which could in any way cause you inconvenience'. Of the 115 shopkeepers who received that letter, only about five complained. The trial judge pointed out that as a group, the shopkeepers who had received the letter were unconcerned about the supposed 'threat'. He, therefore, ruled that according to the definition given in *Clear* (1968), blackmail was not proved. There had not been any 'threat' which influenced or made them apprehensive so as to unwillingly accede to the demand.

13.9 Handling stolen goods

This is an offence under s 22 Theft Act 1968, which states that:

'22 A person handles stolen goods if (otherwise than in the course of stealing) knowing or believing them to be stolen goods he dishonestly receives the goods, or dishonestly undertakes or assists in their retention, removal, disposal or realisation by or for the benefit of another person or he arranges to do so.'

So to prove a charge of handling it must be shown that:

- the property comes within the definition of 'goods' in s 34(2)(b)

- those goods were stolen at the time of the handling

- the handler received or undertook or assisted in their retention, removal, disposal or realisation

- where the allegation is that D undertook or assisted in their retention, removal, disposal or realisation, this must be by another person or for another person's benefit

- D knew or believed the goods to be stolen

- D was dishonest.

The first four points are the *actus reus* of the offence, the last two points are the *mens rea*.

13.9.1 Goods

The definition of goods set out by s 34(2)(b) is:

'34(2)(b) "goods" . . . includes money and every other description of property except land, and includes things severed from the land by stealing.'

This definition does not specifically mention 'a thing in action' but the Court of Appeal, in *Attorney-General's Reference (No 4 of 1979)* [1981] 1 All ER 1193, was prepared to take the view that it could be included in the wide definition of ' every other description of property'. The only exception to what can be handled is land. Things which have been severed from land can be handled but the land itself (even though it is possible to steal land in some circumstances) cannot be handled.

13.9.2 Stolen

The goods must be stolen for the full offence of handling to be committed, but where the defendant believes the goods are stolen there can be an attempt to handle them, even though they are not stolen. This was decided in *Shivpuri* [1986] 2 All ER 334 which, although not a case on handling, overruled *Anderton v Ryan* [1985] 2 All ER 355 on the point of attempting to commit the impossible. (See Chapter 6, section 6.4.)

Section 24(4) states that as well as goods obtained by theft (and remember that theft is an element of robbery and can also be an element of burglary), stolen goods for the purposes of the Theft Act 1968 include those obtained by deception under s 15(1) and those obtained by blackmail.

Section 24(2) extends the definition of stolen goods to include other goods which represent the stolen goods:

'24(2) . . . references to stolen goods shall include, in addition to the goods originally stolen and any parts of them (whether in their original state or not)–

(a) any other goods which directly or indirectly represent the stolen goods in the hands of the thief as being the proceeds of any disposal or realisation of the whole or part of the stolen goods or of goods representing the stolen goods; and

(b) any other goods which directly or indirectly represent or have at any time represented the stolen goods in the hands of a handler of the stolen goods or any part of them as being the proceeds of any disposal or realisation of the whole or part of the stolen goods handled by him or of goods so representing them.'

This means that if the original goods are sold for cash, the money obtained for them is proceeds, and is also regarded as stolen. This was accepted by the Court of Appeal in *Attorney-General's Reference (No 4 of 1979),* where it was stated that:

J
'. . . where . . . a person obtains cheques by deception and pays them into her bank account, the balance in that account may, to the value of the tainted cheque, be goods which "directly . . . represent . . . the stolen goods in the hands of the thief as being the proceeds of any disposal or realisation of the . . . goods stolen" . . . within the meaning of section 24(2)(a).'

Also note that it is sufficient if D handles part of the goods. This could apply where a car is stolen and broken up to be used in other cars. If D buys one of these cars (knowing or believing that it or part of it is stolen), then he is guilty of handling.

A thief cannot be charged with handling for anything done in the course of the theft. The correct charge against him is theft. However, if he steals, passes the goods on to an accomplice and then later receives them back, at this point he can be guilty of handling those goods, even though he stole them originally.

Goods ceasing to be stolen

Section 24(3) states that, where stolen goods have been restored to the person they were stolen from, or to other lawful possession or custody, they are not considered stolen goods for the purposes of handling. This has been important in cases where it is discovered that goods have been stolen and a plan has been made to trap the handler as, if the plan involves the goods returning into lawful possession, they will no longer be stolen goods and D will not be guilty of handling. If the owner or person from whom they were stolen (or the police) merely follows the thief to catch the handler, then the goods have not been 'restored to the person they were stolen from or to other lawful possession or custody'. For example, in *Greater London Metropolitan Police v Streeter* (1980) Cr App R 113, the goods were marked in order to trap the handler, but they were still considered to be stolen goods. It was made clear in *Attorney-General's Reference (No 1 of 1974)* [1974] 2 All ER 899 that the facts of each case have to be carefully considered.

CASE EXAMPLE

Attorney-General's Reference (No 1 of 1974) [1974] 2 All ER 899

A police officer suspected that goods in the back of a parked car were stolen, so he removed the rotor arm of the car to prevent it being driven away and kept watch. When D returned to the car the officer questioned him about the goods and arrested him because he could not give a satisfactory account. The jury acquitted the defendant and the Attorney-General referred the point of law to the Court of Appeal. The Court held that the jury should have been asked to consider the officer's intention. If he had not made up his mind to take possession of the goods before questioning D, then the goods would have remained stolen goods. If he had already decided to take possession of the goods, then, by removing the rotor arm he had reduced them into his possession. The police officer's state of mind was something which should have been left to the jury to find as a fact.

13.9.3 Handling

Section 24 creates a number of ways in which the *actus reus* of handling may be committed. These are:

- receiving or arranging to receive stolen goods
- undertaking or assisting or arranging their
  - retention
  - removal
  - disposal
  - realisation.

These last four must be by another person or for the benefit of another person.

Each word used in s 24 to describe handling has a separate meaning. Receiving means taking possession or control. As arranging to receive is sufficient for guilt, D does not have to be in possession or control if he has arranged to be so in the future.

'Retention' means 'keep possession of, not lose, continue to have'. This was demonstrated by the case of *Pitchley* [1972] Crim LR 705.

CASE EXAMPLE

Pitchley [1972] Crim LR 705

D was given £150 in cash by his son who asked him to take care of it for him. D put the money into his Post Office savings account. At the time of receiving the money D was not aware that it was stolen. His son said he had won it betting on horse races. Two days later D found out that it was stolen, but did nothing, leaving the money in the account. He was convicted of handling. By leaving the money in the account he had retained it on behalf of another person.

'Removal' is literally moving goods from one place to another. So this covers carrying the goods from one house to the next-door house, up to arranging for the goods to be flown out of the country. 'Disposal' is getting rid of them. This can be by destroying the goods, giving them away or doing another act such as melting down silver items. 'Realisation' means selling.

As already stated, the retention, removal, disposal and realisation must be done for the benefit of another. In *Bloxham* [1982] 1 All ER 582 D purchased a car which he later came to believe was stolen. He sold the car very cheaply to another person and was charged with handling on the basis that he had disposed of or realised the car for another's benefit; the prosecution alleging that this was for the benefit of the purchaser. The House of Lords held that he had been wrongly convicted. The disposal was for his own benefit. It was the purchase which benefited the purchaser; and a purchase was not a disposal or realisation of the car by the purchaser.

13.9.4 Undertaking or assisting

To be an offence the undertaking or assisting must be done in relation to retention, removal, disposal or realisation of the goods. To be considered as assistance, something must be done by the offender towards one of those four things. Knowing that stolen items are being kept in your neighbour's garage is not enough. Even using them does not come within the offence. This was decided in *Sander* (1982) Cr App R 84, where D used a stolen heater and battery charger in his father's garage. By using them he had not assisted in retaining or removing them (nor, of course, had he assisted in disposing of or realising them). If he had allowed the items to be stored in his own garage, then that would have been assisting in retaining them.

Although the undertaking or assistance is often by a physical act, for example, helping to carry goods, it can also take the form of verbal or written representations. In addition, the assistance need not be successful in achieving the retaining, removal, disposal or realisation of the goods. Both these points were illustrated in *Kanwar* [1982] 2 All ER 528.

CASE EXAMPLE

Kanwar [1982] 2 All ER 528

D's husband had used stolen goods to furnish their home. D was aware that the items were stolen. When the police called and made inquiries about them, she gave answers which were lies. The Court of Appeal in their judgment gave two specific examples. These were first that in relation to a painting which was hanging on their living room, she said that she had purchased it at a shop and had a receipt for it. She was unable to produce any receipt and tacitly admitted that no such receipt existed. The second example was when she told the police that she had bought a mirror in the market. Again this answer was a lie. Her conviction for handling stolen goods was upheld on the basis that her lies were aimed at assisting the retention of the stolen goods.

The Court of Appeal explained the offence in this way:

J 'To constitute the offence, something must be done by the offender, and done intentionally and dishonestly, for the purpose of enabling the goods to be retained. Examples of such conduct are concealing or helping to conceal the goods, or doing something to make them more difficult to find or identify. Such conduct must be done knowing or believing the goods to be stolen and done dishonestly and for the benefit of another.

We see no reason why the requisite assistance should be restricted to physical acts. Verbal representations, whether oral or in writing, for the purpose of concealing the identity of stolen goods may, if made dishonestly and for the benefit of another, amount to handling stolen goods by assisting in their retention . . . The requisite assistance need not be successful in its object.'

The court went on to explain that if the assistance had to be successful, it would lead to the absurd situation that D would be not guilty of assisting in the retention of goods when caught in the act of doing something such as hiding them. D could argue that, as the police had recovered the goods, his effort at hiding them had not succeeded and he should be not guilty.

13.9.5 *Mens rea* of handling

The defendant must know or believe the goods to be stolen at the time he does the act of handling. In *Pitchley* (1972) D was not guilty when he received the money from his son because at that time

he did not know or believe it to be stolen. He only became guilty when he knew the money was stolen and he then assisted by keeping the money. This was why the charge related to the 'retention of' the money, as D did retain the money after he had the knowledge that the money was stolen.

The test is subjective. It is what D knows or believes, and not what he ought to have known or realised. 'Know' is where D has first-hand information about the fact the goods are stolen, eg he has been told by the thief that this is so. 'Believe' is the state of mind where D says to himself 'I cannot say I know for certain that these goods are stolen, but there can be no other reasonable conclusion in the light of all the circumstances.' This definition of 'believe' was given in *Hall* [1985] Crim LR 377. The Court of Appeal went on to say that 'What is not enough, of course, is mere suspicion'. This part of the judgment was held later in *Forsyth* [1997] Crim Law 846 to be confusing because of the use of the word 'mere'. This might lead juries to consider that although 'mere' suspicion was not enough, 'great' suspicion was enough to convict, when in fact suspicion is never enough to convict.

Professor Sir John Smith puts forward the theory that the Criminal Law Revision Committee thought 'believe' would in fact cover a high level of suspicion. The Committee pointed out in its Eighth Report that there was a 'serious defect' in the law pre the 1968 Act, as the prosecution had to prove actual knowledge that the goods were stolen and this was often impossible. It said:

> 'In many cases indeed guilty knowledge does not exist, although the circumstances of the transaction are such that the receiver ought to be guilty of an offence. The man who buys goods at a ridiculously low price from an unknown seller whom he meets in a public house may not *know* that the goods are stolen, and he may take the precaution of asking no questions. Yet it may be clear on the evidence that he believes that the goods were stolen.'

Cmnd 2977 (1966), para 64

Professor Sir John Smith said that this showed they intended to include what is known as 'wilful blindness', which has been held in some offences to be included in the word 'knowing'. In other words, D could be guilty of handling where he had great suspicion that the goods were stolen, and chose to shut his eyes to the fact. However, the decision in *Forsyth* (1997) means that even a very high level of suspicion does not come within the definition of 'believe'.

Dishonestly

The handling must be done dishonestly. The test for dishonesty is the same *Ghosh* (1982) test as for theft. Was what was done dishonest by the ordinary standards of reasonable and honest people? If it was not, the defendant is not guilty. However, if the jury decide that it was dishonest by those standards, then they must consider the more subjective test of whether the defendant knew it was dishonest by those standards.

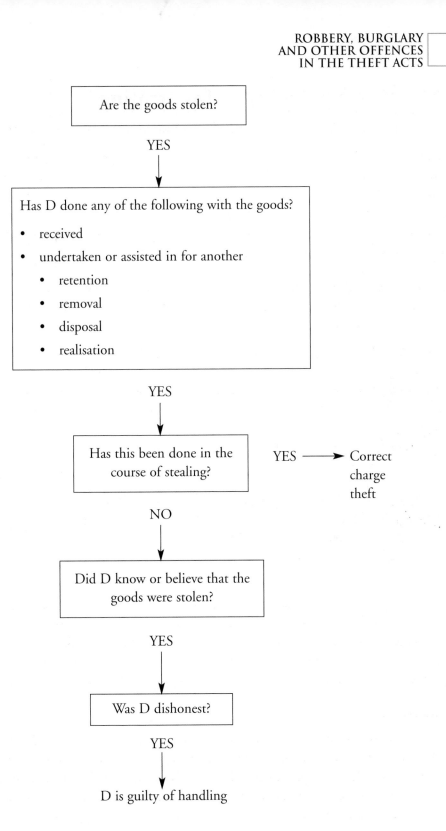

Figure 13.1 *Flow chart on handling stolen goods*

13.10 Going equipped for stealing

This is an offence under s 25(1) Theft Act 1968, which states:

> '25(1) A person shall be guilty of an offence if, when not at his place of abode, he has with him any article for use in the course of or in connection with any burglary, theft or cheat.'

For the purposes of this section, 'theft' includes taking a conveyance under s 12(1) of the Theft Act 1968, and 'cheat' refers to any offence under s 15.

13.10.1 *Actus reus* of going equipped

From s 25 it can be seen that the requirements for the *actus reus* of this offence are:

- D has with him
- any article
- for use in the course of or in connection with any burglary, theft or cheat; and
- D must not be at his place of abode.

Has with him

This, of course, includes items which D physically has on his person, such as car keys which are in his pocket or gloves which he is wearing. But it also includes situations where D can be thought of as being in possession or control of an article, such as a car he has parked down the street. The items do not need to belong to him. It can be something which he has just picked up. This point of view is supported by *Minor v DPP* [1988] Crim LR 55, where D and another man were seen getting ready to siphon petrol from a car. They had two empty petrol cans and a tube with them. There was no evidence that they had brought these from their homes, but they clearly had them with them when the police stopped them, and this was enough to make them guilty under s 25.

Any article

The Criminal Law Revision Committee made it clear that any article could come within this section if it was intended for use in committing a burglary, theft or obtaining by deception. In its Eighth Report it said:

> '[T]he offence under the [section] applies to possessing articles of any kind. There is no reason for listing particular kinds of articles . . . anything intended for use in committing any of the offences referred to should be included. The offence will apply for example, to firearms and other offensive weapons, imitation firearms, housebreaking implements, any articles for the purpose of concealing identity (for example, face masks, rubber gloves and false car number-plates) and . . . [a variety

of] car keys and confidence tricksters' outfits. The reference to the offender having
the article for use "in the course of or in connection with" any of the offences
mentioned will secure that the offence under the clause will apply to having an
article (for example a motor car) for getting to the place of the crime.'

Cmnd 2799 (1966), para 148

The word 'article' has indeed been interpreted very widely by the courts, so that as well as the type
of items mentioned in the extract above, such articles as bottles of wine and clothing with fake
brand names have been included.

CASE EXAMPLE

Doukas [1978] 1 All ER 1061

D was a wine waiter in a hotel. He took bottles of wine into the hotel, intending to sell
them to people dining at the hotel, so that he could pocket the money. There was no
doubt that the bottles of wine were articles for the purpose of s 25. The main point on
appeal was whether they were for use in a s 15 offence of obtaining money by deception.
In the earlier case of *Rashid* [1977] 2 All ER 237, where a British Railways waiter had
taken his own tomato sandwiches to sell on board a train, Bridge LJ had suggested,
obiter, that there would be no obtaining by deception. It was thought that customers on
the train would be indifferent as to whether their sandwiches were 'genuine' British
Railways sandwiches or from another source, so the deception would not have any effect
on their actions.

The Court of Appeal in *Doukas* (1978) disagreed with the *obiter dicta* statements in
Rashid (1977). It thought that any diner in the hotel would refuse to have the wine if they
knew that it was brought in by D for his own profit.

For use

In *Minor v DPP* (1988) it was held that it did not matter when D had come into possession of the
cans and tube. The important point was that the 'having with' must be before the theft or other
offence. This was also seen in *Ellames* [1974] 3 All ER 130 where D was stopped and he had with
him articles which had been used in a robbery (masks, guns, gloves) and which he was trying to get
rid of. He was not guilty of having with him these articles 'for use', as the robbery was in the past.
The court did, however, say that D could commit the offence if he had the items for future use by
another person.

Under s 25(3) Theft Act 1968, proof that a person had with him any article made or adapted for use in committing a burglary, theft or cheat shall be evidence that he had it with him for such use. Where the item has an innocent use, such as a pair of gloves, then it is for the prosecution to prove that the defendant intended to use it for a burglary, theft or cheat.

Not at his place of abode

In *Bundy* [1977] 2 All ER 382 D argued that he used his car as his 'place of abode', as he had nowhere to live. However, when he was arrested he had been driving the car and was not at the site where he usually parked it to sleep. It was accepted that a car could be a 'place of abode', but in the circumstances he was not there and so was guilty under s 25.

13.10.2 *Mens rea* of going equipped

The prosecution must prove that D:

- knew he had the article and
- intended to use it in the course of or in connection with one of the listed crimes.

The intention to use must be for a future crime. See *Ellames* above.

13.11 Making off without payment

This offence was created as it became obvious that the Theft Act 1968 left gaps in the law where D was not guilty of any offence, even though his conduct would be seen as 'criminal' by most people. The Criminal Law Revision Committee in its Thirteenth Report, *Section 16 of the Theft Act 1968*, Cmnd 6733 (1977) recommended a new Act to fill those gaps. This was done by the Theft Act 1978.

One of the gaps had become apparent in *Greenburg* [1972] Crim LR 331, where D had filled his car up at a garage and then driven off without paying. He was not guilty of theft because at the moment he appropriated the petrol it belonged to him. This is because the civil law rules on the transfer of ownership in a sale of goods state that the goods become D's the moment that the petrol is put into the tank of his car. It was also not possible to prove an offence of obtaining the petrol by false pretences because he claimed he had gone into the garage intending to pay, and so made no deception about his conduct. He only decided not to pay when he had filled up the tank.

This situation is now covered by s 3(1) of the Theft Act 1978 (remember this is a different Act from the Theft Act 1968), which makes it an offence, stating:

'3(1) Subject to subsection 3 below, a person who, knowing that payment on the spot for any goods supplied or service done is required or expected from him, dishonestly makes off without having paid as required or expected and with intent to avoid payment of the amount due shall be guilty of an offence.

The goods supplied or service done must be lawful. If the supply of goods is unlawful (eg cigarettes to someone under 16) or the service is not legally enforceable (eg prostitution), then under s 3(3) no offence has been committed.

The offence covers a wide range of situations which include making off without paying for a haircut or a taxi ride. It can also apply to customers in restaurants who leave without paying for their meal or hotel guests who leave the hotel without paying for their room.

13.11.1 Payment on the spot

It has to be proved that payment on the spot was required or expected. In *Vincent* [2001] Crim LR 488 D had stayed at two hotels and not paid his bills. He said that he had arranged with the proprietors of each to pay when he could, so payment on the spot was not required or expected. At his trial the judge directed the jury that D could not rely on a dishonestly obtained agreement to avoid payment. His conviction was quashed, as s 3 merely states that payment on the spot must be required or expected. If there had been an agreement not to expect payment on the spot, it was irrelevant for the purposes of s 3 that that agreement had been dishonestly obtained. In fact D could have been charged with an entirely different offence under s 2(1)(b) of the Theft Act 1978. (See section 14.6.)

13.11.2 Makes off

A key ingredient of the offence is that D 'makes off'. In other words, he leaves the scene where payment was expected. In *McDavitt* [1981] Crim LR 843 D had an argument with the manager of a restaurant and refused to pay his bill for a meal. He got up and started to walk out, but was advised not to leave as the police had been called. He then went into the toilet and stayed there until the police came. The judge directed the jury to acquit D at the end of the prosecution case, as he had not 'made off'.

13.11.3 *Mens rea* of making off without payment

The *mens rea* of the offence involves:

- dishonesty (this is the same test as for theft; see Chapter 12, section 12.1.5)
- knowledge that payment on the spot is required
- an intention to avoid payment.

The Act only states 'with intent to avoid payment of the amount due', but in *Allen* [1985] 2 All ER 641 the House of Lords held that there must be an intent permanently to avoid payment. D owed £1,286 for his stay at a hotel. He left without paying, but his defence was that he genuinely intended to pay in the near future, as he was expecting to receive sufficient money to cover the bill. The House of Lords agreed with the decision of the Court of Appeal, who had said:

'[T]he phrase "and with intent to avoid payment of the amount due" adds a further ingredient: an intention to do more than delay or defer, an intention to evade payment altogether.'

It has been argued that this decision in *Allen* (1985) allows defendants to put forward fictitious defences of what they hoped to be able to do about payment in the future. But there have been no further cases on this point, so presumably the law is working satisfactorily.

ACTIVITY

The following scenarios involve offences covered in this chapter. In each situation, explain what offences have or may have been committed.

1. Aziz rides his own bicycle to college and leaves it in the cycle park available for students. When he leaves to go home he takes Ben's bicycle, which is the same model, by mistake. The next morning he realises his mistake but he decides to keep the bicycle for a few days. Two days later he abandons the bicycle near the college.

2. Cate takes several skeleton keys out with her as she intends to break into a house to steal money. She goes round to the back of one house and manages to open the back door. In the house she finds a wallet which she takes. She then hears the front door being opened and realises that the householder, who is an elderly woman, has come home. Cate is unable to leave without being seen, so she punches the woman and knocks her out, causing her a serious head injury. Cate then leaves the house.

3. Dylan, who is a known shoplifter, has been banned from entering his local supermarket. He is very annoyed about this and persuades Errol to come to the shop with him in order to cause damage to the displays. On entering the shop Dylan goes to the magazine stand and sprays paint over the magazines on it. Errol goes through a door marked 'staff only' and takes a bottle of whisky he finds in the room there. He is caught in there by Frankie. Frankie tells Errol that he will call the manager unless Errol gives him all the money he has on him.

4. Gina knows that her boyfriend has stolen some television sets from a warehouse. Two weeks later he brings a set round to her house and asks her if can leave it there. Gina is suspicious that it may be one of the ones he stole, and tells him she will not have it in the house but he can put it in the garage.

Further reading

Ashworth, A, 'Robbery Reassessed' [2002] Crim LR 851.

Pace, P J, 'Burglarious Trespass' [1985] Crim LR 716.

Spencer, J, 'Handling, theft and the *mala fide* purchaser' [1985] Crim LR 92 and 440.

Spencer, J, 'The Aggravated Vehicle-Taking Act 1992' [1992] Crim LR 699.

Williams, G, 'Temporary appropriations should be theft' [1981] Crim LR 129.

chapter 14 DECEPTION OFFENCES ■

Originally ss 15 and 16 in the 1968 Theft Act contained the only offences of obtaining by deception. However, it was quickly apparent that part of s 16 was difficult to interpret and created major problems for the courts, so s 16(2)(a) was repealed and replaced by ss 1 and 2 of the Theft Act 1978. In 1996, the decision in the case of *Preddy* [1996] 3 All ER 481 (see section 14.2 below) left a gap in the law on money transfers, and the Law Commission was asked to report on this. Following the Law Commission's recommendations in *Offences of Dishonesty: Money Transfers* (Law Com No 243), the Theft (Amendment) Act 1996 was passed. This Act inserted a new s 15A into the Theft Act 1968.

So now the Theft Acts of 1968 and 1978 contain five sections which create offences of dishonestly obtaining (or in one case evading) something by deception. These are:

• s 15 Theft Act 1968 – obtaining property

• s 15A Theft Act 1968 – obtaining a money transfer

• s 16 Theft Act 1968 – obtaining a pecuniary advantage

- s 1 Theft Act 1978 – obtaining services
- s 2 Theft Act 1978 – evading a liability.

NB The new Fraud Act 2006 repeals all these sections and creates new offences in their place. (See section 14.9 for the provisions of the Fraud Act 2006.)

Common elements

For each of the sections listed above there are common elements of:

- a deception
- obtaining (or evading) because of that deception
- dishonesty.

These elements will be examined first. Remember that they apply to all the offences discussed in this chapter.

14.1 The common element of deception

There is a basic definition of deception in s 15(4) Theft Act 1968. This states that it is:

'15(4) ... any deception (whether deliberate or reckless) by words or conduct as to fact or as to law, including a deception as to the present intentions of the person using the deception or any other person.'

This applies to ss 15, 15A and 16 of the Theft Act 1968 and also (because it is specifically stated in s 5 of the 1978 Act) to the offences in ss 1 and 2 of that Act. Although s 15(4) makes clear that the deception can be by words or conduct and it can be about fact or law or intention, it does not actually say what deception is. As a result, the courts have had to try to explain what is meant by deception. In *DPP v Ray* [1973] 3 All ER 131 Lord Reid approved of a definition given in the old case of *Re London and Globe Finance Corporation Ltd* [1900–03] All ER Rep 891 at 893, where it was said:

> J   'To deceive is to induce a man to believe that a thing is true which is false, and which the person practising the deceit knows or believes to be false.'

There have also been decisions on the factors mentioned in s 15(4) and these are considered next.

14.1.1 Deliberate or reckless

Any deception has to be made deliberately or recklessly. A deliberate deception is where the defendant knows that what he is representing is false. To decide whether a deception has been made recklessly there is a subjective test. The defendant must be aware that the representation may be false. In *Goldman* [1997] Crim LR 894 the Court of Appeal affirmed that it had to be a subjective test because otherwise it would be inconsistent with the requirement for dishonesty. If the defendant believes that what he is saying is true then this is not a reckless deception. This is so even if the defendant's belief is unreasonable, provided it is what the defendant genuinely believes. In *Staines* (1974) 60 Crim App Rep 160 it was held that the level of recklessness must be more than carelessness or negligence.

14.1.2 Words or conduct

Words can deceive the other person. Such words can be spoken or written. In *Silverman* [1987] Crim LR 574 D gave an excessive quotation to two elderly sisters for work to be done on their flat. He had done work for them previously and had built up a situation of mutual trust. By giving an exorbitant quotation he was deceiving them as to the true cost of the repairs and the amount of profit he was making. The Court of Appeal, however, quashed his conviction because of an inadequate summing-up to the jury.

The Act makes it clear that conduct can also be relied on to prove a deception. Conduct covers a very wide range of activities, including showing a false identity card or wearing a uniform. In the old case of *Barnard* (1837) 7 C & P 784, D went into a shop in Oxford wearing the cap and gown of a fellow commoner of the university. He also said he was a fellow commoner and as a result the shopkeeper agreed to sell him goods on credit. The court said, *obiter*, that he would have been guilty even if he had said nothing. The wearing of the cap and gown was itself a false pretence. A more modern example would be standing on a street corner with a collecting box labelled 'Guide Dogs for the Blind'. This is implying that D is collecting on behalf of the charity. If D intends to pocket the money then he is guilty under s 15 of the Theft Act 1968 of obtaining property by deception.

Where conduct of the defendant is relied on, there is an implied representation through that conduct. In *DPP v Ray* (1973), where D had ordered a meal and then run off without paying for it, Lord Reid stated that:

> J 'In my view, where a new customer orders a meal in a restaurant, he must be held to make an implied representation that he can and will pay for it before he leaves.'

An unusual case where deception by way of conduct was relied on is *DPP v Stonehouse* [1977] 2 All ER 909, where D faked his death by leaving clothes on a beach in Miami so that it would be presumed

that he had drowned. He had transferred all his money to Australia, where he started a new life with his mistress under an assumed name. He had taken out life insurance policies so that his wife would not be left without money. He was held to be guilty of attempting to obtain money by deception.

It has also been held that using a cheque card or credit card is conduct which implies that the user has authority to use it. The problems in cheque and credit card cases are considered more thoroughly below.

Silence

Normally, saying or doing nothing would not amount to words or conduct from which a deception can be implied, but staying silent can be deception in certain circumstances. These include where the silence implies an intention to pay as in *DPP v Ray* (1973).

CASE EXAMPLE

DPP v Ray [1973] 3 All ER 131

D went to a restaurant with three friends. He did not have enough money to pay for a meal, but one of his friends agreed to lend him enough to pay for the meal. After eating the meal they all decided not to pay for it. Ten minutes later when the waiter went into the kitchen all four ran out of the restaurant without paying. The Court of Appeal had quashed D's conviction for obtaining a pecuniary advantage under s 16(2)(a) of the Theft Act 1968 (this section has now been repealed but the point of law is still valid). The House of Lords reinstated the conviction. The problem was whether D could be guilty when his original representation that he would pay was genuine. Did the change of mind produce a deception? The House of Lords held that it did. Lord MacDermott explained it by saying:

J '. . . it did falsify the representation which had already been made because that initial representation must, in my view, be regarded not as something then spent and past but as a continuing representation which remained alive and operative and had already resulted in the [defendant] and his defaulting companions being taken on trust and treated as ordinary, honest customers. It covered the whole transaction up to and including payment and must therefore, in my opinion, be considered as continuing and still alive at the time of change of mind. When that happened, with the [defendant] taking (as might be expected) no step to bring the change to notice, he practised to my way of thinking a deception just as real and just as dishonest as would have been the case if his intentions all along had been to go out without paying.'

Silence can also be conduct for the purposes of deception where circumstances have changed and the defendant does not inform the other person of the change. This was seen in *Rai* [2000] Crim LR 192, where D applied for a grant from the local council towards installing a downstairs bathroom for his elderly mother. A grant of £9,500 was approved by the council, but two days later his mother died. He carried on with the improvement and did not tell the local council of his mother's death. The Court of Appeal upheld his conviction for obtaining property by deception under s 15 of the 1968 Act. It held that 'conduct' included a 'positive acquiescence in knowingly letting the work proceed'.

Silence can also be deception where the defendant is under a duty to disclose information. In *Firth* [1990] Crim LR 326 D was a doctor who failed to inform the NHS hospital where he worked that some of the patients he had seen there were private patients. This meant that he avoided paying charges to the hospital for the private patients. The Court of Appeal upheld his conviction under s 2 of the Theft Act 1978. It held that it did not matter whether the conduct was an act or an omission (as in this case) by the defendant.

Use of cheques

When a person draws a cheque, they are implying to the other person that:

- they have an account with that bank

- the existing state of facts is such that in the ordinary course the cheque will be honoured.

If D writes a cheque on a non-existent account or on someone else's account, then there is a clear deception. The problems come where D writes a cheque on his own account but there is not enough money in that account to meet it. Has D made a deception? The answer is that D has only deceived the other person if D knows that there is not (or will not be) enough money in the account to meet the cheque or is reckless as to whether there is or will be. D is in effect making a representation that either:

a there are sufficient funds in the account to meet the cheque; or

b he intends paying in sufficient funds; or

c he believes a third party will pay in sufficient funds (eg monthly pay from his employers will be going into the account).

All these are representations of fact and if none of them is true then the act of drawing the cheque is a misrepresentation.

In *Gilmartin* [1983] 1 All ER 829, D, a stationer, paid for supplies with post-dated cheques which he knew would not be met. This was held to be a deception. By drawing the cheques he was representing that there would be funds in the account to meet the cheques on the dates they were due to be presented.

A more difficult case to understand is *Greenstein* [1976] 1 All ER 1 where D applied for large numbers of shares and enclosed a cheque to cover the purchase price. He knew he did not have enough money in the bank to cover this full purchase price, but he knew from past experience that he would only be allocated a proportion of the shares he had applied for. He also knew that when the shares were allocated he would be sent a cheque for the difference between the full purchase price and the amount he actually had to pay. He would be able to pay this cheque into his account in time to meet the cheque he had drawn for the full purchase price, either on its first presentation or at worst on its second presentation. The Court of Appeal held that the drawing of the cheque for the full purchase price was a deception. D had no authority to draw a cheque for such a large amount when he knew that the cheque would only be met if the share company were deceived into thinking that his application for the full amount was genuine. Also D was reckless as he knew there might not be funds in his account in time to meet the cheque the first time it was presented.

Use of cheque guarantee cards

A cheque guarantee card is one which is issued by the bank with which a current account is held. The card will have a limit, usually £50 or £100. The bank guarantees that a cheque for up to the amount of the limit will be met by the bank. The leading case on the use of cheque guarantee cards is *Metropolitan Police Commissioner v Charles* [1976] 3 All ER 112.

CASE EXAMPLE

Metropolitan Police Commissioner v Charles [1976] 3 All ER 112

D had a bank account with an overdraft facility of £100. The bank had issued him with a cheque card which guaranteed that any cheques he wrote up to £30 would be honoured by the bank. D wrote out 25 cheques for £30 in order to buy gaming chips and backed each cheque with the cheque card. He knew that the bank would have to pay the gambling club the money so there was no deception in respect of the fact that the cheques would be honoured. However, he knew that he did not have enough money in his account to meet the cheques and also that the amount would exceed his overdraft limit. He had also been told by the bank manager that he should not use the card to cash more than one cheque of £30 a day.

The House of Lords held that there was a false representation that he had the bank's authority to use the card in the way he did and upheld his conviction under s 16 of the 1968 Act of obtaining a pecuniary advantage by deception. Lord Diplock considered the relationship with simply drawing a cheque and said:

J   'When a cheque card is brought in to the transaction, it still remains the fact that all the payee is concerned with is that the cheque should be honoured by the bank. I do not think that the fact that a cheque card is used necessarily displaces the representation to be implied from the act of drawing the cheque which has just been mentioned. It is, however, likely to displace that representation at any rate as the main inducement to the payee to take the cheque, since the use of the cheque card in connection with the transaction gives to the payee a direct contractual right against the bank itself to payment on presentment, provided that the use of the card by the drawer to bind the bank *to pay the cheque* was within the actual or ostensible authority conferred on him by the bank.' (Emphasis added.)

By exhibiting to the payee a cheque card containing the undertaking by the bank to honour cheques drawn in compliance with the conditions endorsed on the back and drawing the cheque accordingly, the drawer represents to the payee that he has actual authority from the bank to make a contract with the payee on the bank's behalf that it will honour the cheque on presentment for payment.

Use of credit cards

Where a credit card is used to pay for goods there are representations that the user of the card is the person in whose name the card is issued and that he has the authority of the card company to use the card.

This was seen in *Lambie* [1981] 2 All ER 776 where D had a credit card (Barclaycard) with a £200 limit. She exceeded this limit and the bank which had issued the card wrote asking her to return the card. She agreed that she would return the card on 7th December 1977, but she did not do so. On 15th December 1977 she purchased goods worth £10.35 in a Mothercare shop with the card. She was convicted of obtaining a pecuniary advantage by deception, contrary to s 16(1) of the Theft Act 1968. The Court of Appeal allowed her appeal but the House of Lords reinstated the conviction. Lord Roskill quoted from the judgment in *Metropolitan Police Commissioner v Charles* (1976) and said that if the words 'to honour the voucher' were substituted for the words 'to pay the cheque' (see italics in the judgment above), the entire passage was equally applicable to the dishonest misuse of cheque cards.

A rather different situation arose in *Fizeal Nabina* [2000] Crim LR 481 where D had obtained credit cards in his own name by false pretences. He then used those cards to make a number of purchases from different shops and sales outlets. He was charged with obtaining property by deception, contrary to s 15 Theft Act 1968. The deception relied on in the charge was that he had represented to the various shops that he was the legitimate holder of the cards. The judge directed the jury that they must be sure that the defendant had obtained the cards by deception from the

credit companies. However, the judge did not direct the jury that they must also be satisfied that the defendant had deceived the sales outlets as to the fact that he was the legitimate holder of the cards. The defendant was convicted, but the Court of Appeal quashed his conviction. This was because there is a general rule in civil law that the contract between the banks issuing the cards to the defendant would be voidable. That means that the banks could, because of his false representations to him, cancel the contract but until they did so the contract (and the right to use the cards) remained. There was no evidence that the banks had withdrawn his authority to use the cards. Nor was there any evidence that the contract might include a clause automatically cancelling the contract when there was fraud. Bingham CJ compared the case with *Lambie* (1981) and said:

> **J** 'In that case [*Lambie*] the customer did not have the actual authority of the bank to warrant that the bank would honour the voucher upon presentation because she was in excess of her limit, and her authority to use the card had been revoked by the bank's request for its return and her agreement to return it. Here, so far as the evidence went, the appellant did have the actual authority of the issuing institutions to warrant that they would honour the vouchers upon presentation because the cards had been issued to the appellant and, even if the banks would have been entitled to revoke his authority to use the cards, they had not done so.'

The prosecutor had argued that the civil law rule was not relevant because this was a criminal case involving dishonesty. The Court of Appeal felt they could not rule on this point as there was no evidence of what the contracts between the defendant and the issuing banks actually contained. They decided that the judge's failure to direct the jury that they must be satisfied that the defendant had deceived the sales outlets as to the fact that he was the legitimate holder of the cards was 'a fatal omission'. As a result they, reluctantly, felt compelled to allow the appeal.

14.1.3 Deception as fact, law or intention

The Act makes it clear that a false statement about the law can be a deception. For example, this could be making a false representation about the effect of a legal document in order to obtain property.

Equally any deception about a fact can be the basis for a conviction under the relevant sections of the Theft Acts. In *King and Stockwell* [1987] 1 All ER 547 the defendants falsely represented to a 68-year-old widow that they were from a reputable firm of tree surgeons. They then falsely claimed that two trees were in danger of damaging her gas supply and house foundations. She agreed to pay £470 in cash for the removal of the two trees. When she went to the building society to withdraw the money she told the cashier about it and the police were informed. The defendants argued that they were going to cut the trees down and the payment would be for the work done. This would mean that the false representations were not the cause of the payment. The Court of Appeal upheld their convictions for attempting to obtain property by deception (s 15 of the 1968 Act) on the basis that there was 'ample

evidence on which the jury could come to the conclusion that had the attempt succeeded the money would have been paid over by the victim as a result of the lies told to her by the appellants'.

The present intentions of the defendant can also form the basis of the deception. So, if the intentions of a diner when ordering a meal in a restaurant are to leave without paying, then he is deceiving the waiter from whom he is ordering. The main problem is in being able to prove what those intentions are.

14.2 The common element of the obtaining being induced by the deception

As well as proving that there was a deception, it must be shown that a person was deceived. This is the second common element to all deception offences. If no person is deceived, then the full offence is not committed but the defendant may be liable for an attempt. As a person has to be deceived, it is not possible for there to be a deception offence by obtaining from a machine, eg by typing in someone's PIN to obtain cash or by using a fake coin. However, this conduct could amount to theft.

In *Collis-Smith* [1971] Crim LR 716 D filled up his car with petrol. This meant that at that moment ownership of the petrol had passed to him. He then falsely claimed that his company would pay for the petrol. His conviction under s 15 was quashed as the property had not been obtained by that deception. Ownership had passed to him before he made his false statement. This (and other cases) revealed a gap in the law and led to the passing of the 1978 Act. Now anyone doing the same as *Collis-Smith* (1971) could be charged with evading a liability by deception under s 2 of the 1978 Act.

However, there are other cases in which the problem of whether the deception caused the obtaining has been the key point of the case. In *Laverty* [1970] 3 All ER 432 D changed the registration number plates and the chassis number on a car and sold the car to P. The changing of the numbers was a representation that the car was the original car to which these numbers had been allocated. However, the conviction was quashed as P had merely said in evidence that he thought that D was the owner of the car. There was no evidence that the deception regarding the number plates had influenced P to buy the car, so there was no proof that D had obtained the purchase money from P as a result of the particular deception.

A different decision was reached in *Etim v Hatfield* [1975] Crim LR 234 where D produced a false declaration to a Post Office clerk that he was entitled to supplementary benefit. The clerk gave him £10.60. At his trial no evidence was given by the clerk or anyone else from the Post Office. However, the conviction was upheld as the court distinguished it from *Laverty* on the basis that there was no other conceivable reason why the payment would have been made.

The problem was also considered in *Doukas* [1978] 1 All ER 1061 where the defendant was charged with going equipped to cheat contrary to s 25 of the Theft Act 1968 (see section 13.10).

D was a wine waiter who intended serving his own wine to customers in the hotel restaurant where he worked, instead of the hotel's wine. He was going to keep the money the customers paid for the wine. The deception was that when a wine waiter serves wine, he is implying that the wine is the hotel's. The critical element in this case was whether there was proof that the obtaining would have been, wholly or partially, by virtue of the deception. A similar situation had occurred in *Rashid* [1977] 2 All ER 237 where a British Railways waiter had substituted his own tomato sandwiches and sold them implying that they were BR sandwiches. The Court of Appeal had quashed his conviction because the summing-up to the jury had been inadequate, but they had said, *obiter*, that the obtaining of the customers' money would not have been a result of the deception. They thought that a BR customer would have been indifferent as to whether the sandwich was a 'genuine' BR sandwich or one home-made by the waiter. In fact it is quite likely that they might have preferred the home-made ones!

In *Doukas* (1978) the Court of Appeal upheld his conviction. They considered the *obiter* comment in *Rashid* (1977) and came to a different conclusion, saying:

> J
>
> 'Of course each case of this type may produce different results according to the circumstances of the case and according, in particular, to the commodity which is being proffered. But, as we see it, the question has to be asked of the hypothetical customer: why did you buy this wine? or, if you had been told the truth, would you or would you not have bought the commodity? It is . . . for the jury in the end to decide that question. . . . The hypothetical customer must be reasonably honest as well as being reasonably intelligent and it seems to us incredible that any customer, to whom the true situation was made clear, would willingly make himself a party to what was obviously a fraud by the waiter on his employers. If that conclusion is contrary to the *obiter dicta* in *Rashid*, then we must respectfully disagree with those *dicta*.'

This judgment ignores the reality of whether the customers in a restaurant would actually be influenced by the deception when they paid for the wine. As the Court of Appeal recognised in *Rashid* (1977), it may well be that customers would only be interested in getting a good wine and the deception as to whose wine it was would be irrelevant to them. Instead the Court of Appeal have applied their own standards to the 'hypothetical customer'.

The question of whether the defendant's deception induced the obtaining was also considered in *Metropolitan Police Commander v Charles* (1976) and in *Lambie* (1981). In both cases the House of Lords had held that the deception was that the defendant had the authority of the bank to use the card. However, this point did not appear to matter to the victims in those cases. This is shown by what was said in evidence. In *Charles* (1976) the manager of the gambling club said that it was 'totally irrelevant' to him whether the defendant had authority to draw the cheque. In *Lambie* (1981), the departmental manager in Mothercare made it perfectly plain that she made no assumption about the

defendant's credit standing at the bank. She stated that 'We will honour the card if the conditions are satisfied whether the bearer has authority to use it or not'. In the two cases the important conditions to the victims were that D's signature matched that on the card and the card was not on a 'stop list'.

The Court of Appeal in *Lambie* (1981) had quashed the conviction because they thought that there was no proof that the deception had induced the obtaining. The House of Lords, however, took a different view. They held that it was not necessary to have direct evidence of the reliance on a particular deception if the facts were such that 'it is patent that there was only one reason which anybody could suggest for the person alleged to have been defrauded parting with his money'. They thought that in the case of credit cards it would make the law unworkable if there had to be direct evidence that the deception induced the obtaining in every case. Lord Roskill said:

> J
>
> 'Credit card frauds are all too frequently perpetrated, and if conviction of offenders against ss 15 and 16 of the Theft Act 1968 can only be obtained if the prosecution are able in each case to call the person on whom the fraud was immediately perpetrated to say that he or she positively remembered the particular transaction and, had the truth been known, could never have entered into that supposedly well-remembered transaction, the guilty would often escape conviction. . . . [W]here, as in the present case, no one could reasonably be expected to remember a particular transaction in detail, and the inference of inducement may well be in all the circumstances quite irresistible, I see no reason in principle why it should not be left to the jury to decide, on the evidence in the case as a whole, whether that inference is in truth irresistible as to my mind it is in the present case.'

This decision shows that the Law Lords preferred to use a 'common-sense' approach rather than apply the law strictly. This is in contrast with the Court of Appeal's approach in *Lambie* (1981), where they did apply the law strictly and quashed the conviction because they thought that there was no proof that the deception had induced the obtaining. Both the Court of Appeal and the House of Lords were aware that quashing the conviction would open a 'gateway to successful fraud'. In these circumstances the House of Lords used what can be described as 'necessary fantasy' of an irresistible inference that the victim had been induced by deception. As the departmental manager in *Lambie* (1981) had stated that 'We will honour the card if the conditions are satisfied whether the bearer has authority to use it or not', this inference was indeed a fantasy.

The difficulties in *Lambie* (1981) could be resolved by creating a new offence, as suggested by the Law Commission in its Consultation Paper, *Legislating the Criminal Code: Fraud and Deception* (Law Com No 155) (1999). In this it suggested an offence of 'dishonest imposition of liability':

'A person commits an offence if he intentionally causes a legal liability to pay money to be imposed on another, knowing that the other does not consent to his doing so and that he has no right to do so.'

This would cover situations such as *Lambie* (1981) without the need to prove any deception or that the deception induced the victim to part with goods or even the need to prove dishonesty. However, it would not cover situations where a credit card transaction is carried out over the telephone or on the Internet. This is because in these cases the rules of the credit system mean that the transaction is carried out at the risk of the retailer. If the person ordering by phone or on the Internet does not pay then no legal liability to pay the retailer is imposed on the credit card company.

ACTIVITY

There are many decisions, particularly regarding the fraudulent use of cheques, cheque cards and credit cards, which are difficult to reconcile. The following questions require discussion of some of these points.

1. Discuss whether the conviction in *Greenstein* (1976) is justified in law.

2. Is there any offence of which *Fizeal Nabina* (2000) could have been convicted?

3. Is the decision in *Laverty* (1970) in conflict with decisions in *Etim v Hatfield* and *Lambie*?

4. Discuss whether *Fizeal Nabina* (2000) would be guilty of the offence of 'dishonest imposition of liability' suggested by the Law Commission.

14.3 The common element of dishonesty

The same test for dishonesty is applied to deception offences as to theft. This is the *Ghosh* (1982) test which poses two questions. First, was what was done dishonest by the ordinary standards of reasonable and honest people? If it was not, the defendant is not guilty. However, if the jury decide that it was dishonest by those standards, then they must consider the more subjective test of did the defendant know it was dishonest by those standards. (See Chapter 12, section 12.5.2 for further discussion of the *Ghosh* (1982) test.)

ACTIVITY

Explain in each of the following situations whether or not there is a deception, an obtaining by that deception and dishonesty.

1. Annabel, who owns a shop, puts a collecting box on the counter with a label 'Cancer Research' on it. She keeps all the money which customers put in the box.

2. Brian takes Candy to a local restaurant. Candy expects Brian to pay for the meal, but Brian has decided that he will leave without paying. They both order a meal and at the end of the meal, Brian gets up to leave. Candy asks him about paying and he says 'Come on, there's no one looking, we can just go', and he walks out of the door. Candy waits a few minutes and then decides to leave without paying.

3. Donna has discovered that fake coins provided with one of her child's toys fit into a slot machine selling cigarettes. She uses one of the fake coins to obtain a packet of cigarettes from the machine. Later that day she uses two more fake coins to pay for a magazine in a newsagent's shop.

4. Elvis has a credit card. He has not paid his debt on the credit card for three months and the card company have written to him saying that he must make a minimum payment or else they will ask him to return the card. Elvis does not pay anything off the debt but continues using the card. A month later he receives a letter from the card company. He does not open it, but goes out and buys a new pair of trainers using the card. When he gets home he opens the letter and finds out that the card company have withdrawn his right to use the card and asked him to return it.

Key facts on the common elements for deception offences

KEY FACTS

Common element	Law	Comment	Cases
Deception	1. Must be deliberate or subjectively reckless.	'Reckless' must be a subjective test otherwise inconsistent with the requirement of dishonesty.	*Goldman* (1997)

	2. Can be words or conduct	eg wearing a uniform	*Barnard* (1837)
	(a) Conduct can include silence	This can be where intentions change or circumstances change or where there is a duty to disclose information.	*DPP v Ray* (1973) *Rai* (2000) *Firth* (1990)
	(b) Use of cheques	Implies they have an account with that bank; *and* the cheque will be met.	*Metropolitan Police Commander v Charles* (1976)
	(c) Use of cheque guarantee and credit cards.	Implies have authority to use card.	*Lambie* (1981)
	3. Can be about fact, law or present intention.		*King and Stockwell* (1987)
Effect of deception	The deception must be the cause of the obtaining.	If ownership passes before the deception then there is no offence.	*Collis-Smith* (1971)
		If the deception is about an fact which is irrelevant to the victim there is no offence.	*Laverty* (1970)
Dishonesty	The same two-part test as for theft.	Objective test – is it dishonest by ordinary standards of reasonable and honest people? If so Subjective test – did D know it was dishonest by those standards?	*Ghosh* (1982)

14.4 Section 15: Obtaining property by deception

We now go on to look at the individual offences in the Theft Acts 1968 and 1978. Remember that the common elements explained in the first part of the chapter apply to all these offences. The first offence to be considered is s 15 of the Theft Act 1968 which creates the offence of obtaining goods by deception. Section 15 states that it is an offence where:

'15(1) A person who by any deception dishonestly obtains property belonging to another, with the intention of permanently depriving the other of it, shall on conviction on indictment be liable to imprisonment for a term not exceeding ten years.

(2) For purposes of the section a person is to be treated as obtaining property if he obtains ownership, possession or control of it, and "obtain" includes obtaining for another or enabling another to obtain or retain.'

The phrases used in this offence are very similar to those used in theft. The main difference between this offence and theft is the fact that the property must be obtained as result of a deception whereas in theft the property must be appropriated. However, since the judgment in *Gomez* [1993] 1 All ER 1 (see Chapter 12, section 12.2.3) there is a very large overlap between s 15 and theft and most offences of obtaining by deception could also be charged as theft.

14.4.1 *Actus reus* of obtaining property by deception

The defendant must:

- obtain
- property
- belonging to another
- because of a deception.

Obtain

Section 15(2) of the Theft Act 1968 states that obtaining property means obtaining ownership, possession or control of it. Any one of these three will be sufficient. For example, D may have deceived the other person into making a contract giving D ownership of some goods, but they have not yet been delivered to D. In this case D has ownership and can be charged with the offence even though he has not yet got possession of the goods. Subsection (2) also makes it clear that the obtaining can be for another or to enable another to obtain or keep property. An example of this could occur where D pays for goods with a stolen credit card and asks for those goods to be delivered to another person.

Property

By virtue of s 34(1) property has the same meaning as for theft. It includes money and all other property, real or personal, including things in action and other intangible property (see Chapter 12, section 12.3). There is a difference, however, in that there are no restrictions on the obtaining by deception of land, whereas for theft s 4(2) places limitations on when land can be stolen. This means that land can be obtained by deception. An example could be where someone falsely claimed to be the heir to an estate which includes a house or other land.

Belonging to another

Section 34(1) also states that s 5(1) on belonging to another in theft (see Chapter 12, section 12.4) applies to s 15. So it has the same meaning for s 15 as for theft and property belonging to another 'shall be regarded as belonging to any person having possession or control of it, or having in it any proprietary right or interest'. As with theft, this means that the person from whom the property is obtained does not have to be the owner. In fact, it is even possible for a person to obtain his own property by deception if another person has possession or control of it or a right or interest in it.

There must, however, be something which belonged to the victim before the deception occurred. This caused a major problem in *Preddy* (1996), where the defendants made false representations in order to obtain a number of mortgage advances from building societies to purchase houses. They intended to repay the mortgages when they sold the houses, as they hoped, at a profit. The mortgage advances were paid to them in three different ways: cheque, telegraphic transfer and CHAPS. The House of Lords quashed their convictions on the basis that no property *belonging to another* had been obtained. Lord Goff said:

> **J** 'I do not see for myself how this can properly be described as obtaining property belonging to another. In truth, the property which the defendant has obtained is the new chose in action constituted by the debt now owed to him by his bank, and represented by the credit entry in his own bank account. This did not come into existence until the debt so created was owed to him by his bank, and so never belonged to anyone else. True, it corresponded to the debit entered in the lending institution's bank account; but it does not follow that the property which the defendant acquired can be identified with the property which the lending institution lost when its account was debited. In truth, s 15(1) is here being invoked for a purpose for which it was never designed, and for which it does not legislate.'

So, where the payment was by cheque, the cheque belonged to the payee (the defendants) and not the drawer. Where payments were made by electronic means there was no identifiable property which passed from the lending institutions to the defendants. A new thing in action was created in the defendant's bank account. So, even though as a result the credit in the payer's bank account was

reduced, the defendant had not obtained property belonging to the payer. This decision revealed a very large gap in the law and led to the passing of the Theft (Amendment) Act 1996 which inserted s 15A into the Theft Act to cover such situations in future. (See section 14.5.)

The obtaining must be because of a deception

The general rules on the deception having to be the cause of the obtaining apply to a s 15 offence (see section 14.2). If the obtaining is not because of a deception there is no offence under s 15. For example, where the property is obtained before the deception is made as in *Collis-Smith* (1971) or where the deception is about a matter which is irrelevant to the victim, as in *Laverty* (1970), there is no offence.

A more unusual situation occurred in *Wheeler* (1990) 92 Cr App R 279, where the defendant was a market stall holder who made a contract with a regular customer to sell him a medal for £150. The customer became the owner of the medal once that contract was completed. It was agreed that D should keep possession of the medal until the customer returned with the payment for it. On his return the customer, who had heard that some medals had been stolen, checked with D that D was the owner and was entitled to sell it. By this time D knew that the medal was stolen but he falsely represented that it was his to sell. He was convicted of obtaining the £150 purchase price by deception. His conviction was quashed because the customer was already the owner of the medal when the statement was made. In this case the title (or ownership) of the medal had passed to the customer even though the medal was stolen, because this was a sale in a market where special rules apply to sales. If the sale had been in a shop then the normal rule in sale of goods cases would have applied and, as the seller did not have a good title himself (because the goods were stolen) he could not have passed the title to the customer. This would have meant that the offence of obtaining the £150 by deception would have been committed.

14.4.2 *Mens rea* of obtaining property by deception

The defendant must:

- be dishonest

- intend permanently to deprive the other of the property

- make the deception deliberately or be reckless as to whether they are deceiving the other.

All these three points have already been discussed. For dishonesty the test is the same as for theft (see section 14.3). So far as intention permanently to deprive is concerned, s 15(3) states that s 6 of the Theft Act which applies to theft (see Chapter 12, section 12.6) shall apply for the purposes of s 15 with the appropriate amendments. This means that the word obtaining has to be read into it instead of appropriation. So again the law is the same as for theft.

The point that the defendant has to make the deception deliberately or recklessly is covered earlier in this chapter in the general principles at section 14.1.1.

14.5 Obtaining a money transfer by deception

As we have seen, *Preddy* (1996) highlighted a gap in the law of obtaining by deception. In order to fill this gap s 15A was inserted into the Theft Act 1968 by the Theft (Amendment) Act 1996. This section states:

'15A(1) A person is guilty of an offence if by any deception he dishonestly obtains a money transfer for himself or another.

(2) A money transfer occurs when –

(a) a debit is made to one account,

(b) a credit is made to another, and

(c) the credit results from the debit or the debit results from the credit.

(3) References to a credit and to a debit are to a credit of an amount of money and to a debit of an amount of money.

(4) It is immaterial:

(a) whether the amount credited is the same as the amount debited;

(b) whether the money transfer is effected on presentation of a cheque or by another method;

(c) whether any delay occurs in the process by which the money transfer is effected;

(d) whether any intermediate credits or debits are made in the course of the money transfer;

(e) whether either of the accounts is overdrawn before or after the money transfer is effected.'

'Deception' is given the same meaning as in s 15.

Where the obtaining is by cheque rather than electronic means, the full offence is only committed when the cheque is honoured by the bank. If the defendant obtains a cheque but then decides not to pay it in to a bank, he has not committed an offence under s 15A. However, the defendant can be charged under s 15 with obtaining the actual cheque itself by deception. The piece of paper the cheque is written on is property for the purposes of that section.

At the point when the defendant presents the cheque to the bank that is an attempt to commit an offence under s 15A, but the full offence is only committed when a debit is made to one account and a credit is made to another.

14.6 Obtaining a pecuniary advantage by deception

Section 16 provides:

'16(1) A person who by any deception dishonestly obtains for himself or another any pecuniary advantage shall on conviction on indictment be liable to imprisonment for a term not exceeding five years.

(2) The cases in which a pecuniary advantage within the meaning of this section is to be regarded as obtained for a person are where –

(a) [*Repealed.*]

(b) he is allowed to borrow by way of overdraft, or to take out any policy of insurance or annuity contract, or obtains an improvement of the terms on which he allowed to do so; or

(c) is given the opportunity to earn remuneration or greater remuneration in an office or employment, or to win money by betting.'

Since the repeal of s 16(2)(a), this section covers only a very limited range: overdrafts, insurance, annuities and opportunities to earn or win money.

14.6.1 Section 16(2)(b)

Where the charge relates to allowing the defendant to borrow by way of overdraft, it was held in *Watkins* [1976] 1 All ER 578 that the defendant does not need to use the overdraft facility. The offence is committed when the bank grants him the facility. It was also held in *Waites* [1982] Crim LR 369 that a defendant who has a cheque guarantee card is 'allowed' to borrow by way of overdraft if he uses the card to back cheques for an amount which is greater than the amount he has to his credit in the account. So a defendant can be convicted of a s 16(2)(b) offence if he has obtained this facility by a deception.

Examples of how the offence could be committed for insurance purposes include:

• a smoker falsely declaring that he is a non-smoker when he takes out a health insurance policy

• a traveller falsely claiming that he has no existing illnesses when taking out a holiday insurance

• lying about one's age in order to obtain cheaper car insurance

• falsely stating that an HIV test has proved negative in order to obtain an endowment policy.

14.6.2 Section 16(2)(c)

This relates only to the opportunity to earn money through employment or to win money by betting. The meaning of 'employment' has been considered by the courts. In *Callender* [1992] 3 All ER 51 D was a self-employed accountant who obtained work by falsely claiming to hold certain qualifications. Even though he was self-employed the Court of Appeal upheld his conviction under s 16(2)(c). Employment was to be given its natural meaning, not a technical one.

However, in *McNiff* [1986] Crim LR 57 it was held that the tenant of a public house was not employed by the brewery nor did he hold an office. It was also held that the tenant did not have the opportunity to earn remuneration, as no remuneration was paid by the brewery. The tenant would only earn money by his own efforts.

14.6.3 *Mens rea* for s 16

The same elements of dishonesty and making the deception deliberately or recklessly apply to this section as to all other deception offences. For s 16 offences the defendant must also intend to obtain the pecuniary advantage for himself or another. However, in *Clarke (Victor)* [1996] Crim LR 824 it was held that where the defendant maintains that, even though he lied in order to get employment, he was not dishonest as he intended to give his employer value for money, the question of whether he was dishonest or not must be left to the jury.

It must be noted that it is *not* necessary to prove for a s 16 offence that the defendant had an intention permanently to deprive.

14.7 Obtaining services by deception

The last group of offences to be considered are those in the Theft Act 1978. The first of these is under s 1 Theft Act 1978, which provides:

'1(1) A person who by any deception dishonestly obtains services from another shall be guilty of an offence.

(2) It is an obtaining of services where the other is induced to confer a benefit by doing some act, or causing or permitting some act to be done, on the understanding that the benefit has been or will be paid for.'

So, for there to be an obtaining of services, the other person must be induced to confer a benefit by:

- doing some act; or
- causing some act to be done; or
- permitting some act to be done.

In each situation there must be an act. This offence cannot be committed if the other is induced not to do something (ie an omission). The act must confer a benefit. Finally there must be an understanding that the benefit 'has been or will be paid for'. This means that if the service is free then an offence is not committed even if the defendant lies to obtain it. Although there must be an understanding that the benefit has been or will be paid for, it is not necessary for the victim to suffer economic loss. The deception will generally relate to payment but it can be over any other

matter which induces the other to confer a benefit. For example, if a boy aged 14 claims to be 15 years old in order to buy a ticket for entry to see a film with a 15 rating, then he has induced the cinema employees to allow him the service of viewing the film. The fact that he has paid for the ticket and the cinema has not suffered any financial loss does not prevent it from being an offence under s 1 Theft Act 1978. However, it may be difficult to prove that he was being dishonest by this conduct.

14.7.1 Services

This covers a wide range of activities, including having a haircut, staying in a hotel, any social or entertainment activity such as a dance or a disco, or being allowed to see a film or use leisure facilities. It also covers situations where the other person is induced to repair goods or to do decorating or cleaning. In *Widdowson* [1986] Crim LR 233 it was held that the obtaining of hire purchase in order to buy a car was services.

However, in *Halai* [1983] Crim LR 624 the Court of Appeal held that a mortgage advance was not services. Halai was convicted of three offences. First, that he had obtained services by deception from the agent of a building society when he induced that agent to instruct a surveyor to prepare a report on a house. He had paid with a postdated cheque for £40 when he knew that he had only £28 in his bank account. The Court of Appeal upheld this conviction. Second, that he had obtained services by deception from the building society when they permitted him to open a savings account with them on the false basis that he could pay in a cheque for £500. The Court of Appeal quashed the conviction on this count as there was no understanding about payment for this benefit. Third, that he had obtained services by deception from the building society when he got a mortgage advance on the false basis that he had been in a particular job for 18 months. This conviction was quashed because the Court of Appeal held that a mortgage was not a service.

It is interesting to note that in *Widdowson* (1986) the Court of Appeal distinguished *Halai* (1983) and said, *obiter*, that a hire-purchase agreement was not to be treated in the same way as a mortgage advance. It rejected the suggestion 'that the obtaining of a hire-purchase agreement cannot amount to the obtaining of services'.

The decision that a mortgage was not 'services' within the meaning of s 1 of the 1978 Act was widely criticised. Eventually, in order to overturn this part of the decision in *Halai* (1983), subs (3) was inserted into s 1 by the Theft (Amendment) Act 1996. It applies to all cases where the defendant's deception occurs after 18th December 1996. This subsection reads:

 '1(3) Without prejudice to the generality of subsection (2) above, it is an obtaining of services where the other is induced to make a loan, or to cause or permit a loan to be made, on the understanding that any payment (whether by way of interest or otherwise) will be or has been made in respect of the loan.'

So now if the defendant obtains a loan or mortgage for himself or for another person by a deception, this is an offence under s 1 of the Theft Act 1978. In *Sofroniou* [2003] EWCA Crim 3681 it was held that obtaining loans through a bank account or by way of overdraft was now, with the amending addition of s 1(3), clearly within the meaning of services. The Court of Appeal also held in *Sofroniou* (2003) that the subsection meant that opening a bank account or obtaining a credit card was also obtaining services.

Obtaining a bank account or a credit card involves obtaining access to the whole structure of 'financial services' which are normally associated with them. However, to be an offence under s 1 it also has to be shown that these were benefits which had been or would be paid for.

14.7.2 The understanding that the benefit has been or will be paid for

In order for an offence to be committed under s 1 of the Theft Act 1978 there must be an understanding that the benefit which the other is induced to confer has been or will be paid for. One query is whether the opening of a bank account is a benefit for which there is an understanding that it has been or will be paid for. If there is no such understanding then no s 1 offence is committed in respect of the opening of the account.

However, there can be an offence if a bank account or a credit card account is operated dishonestly where charges are likely to be incurred. This was decided in *Sofroniou* (2003).

CASE EXAMPLE

Sofroniou [2003] EWCA Crim 3681

The defendant operated two bank accounts under false names. There was no evidence as to who had opened them. He arranged for loans from both banks and also caused both bank accounts to become overdrawn. He also applied for a store credit card and exceeded the credit limit placed on the card. He was convicted of an offence under s 1 of the Theft Act 1978 in respect of both bank accounts and the credit card. The Court of Appeal upheld these convictions.

The Court of Appeal's reasoning was that s 1(2) refers to an understanding in respect of payment, not an agreement. It held that this covered situations where nothing was specifically said about payment, but there was a common understanding that the service was not going to be provided free of charge. In banking, although no charges are usually made on an account which remains in credit, there is a common understanding that bank loans and overdrafts are paid for. So, both when the defendant applied for loans and when he became overdrawn in respect of the bank accounts the bank was conferring a benefit on the understanding the benefit had been or would be paid for.

Similarly for the credit card, opening such an account where the defendant's intention was to exceed the limit so that charges would be payable meant that the defendant was inducing the card company to confer a benefit on the understanding that the benefit has been or will be paid for.

It is also interesting that initially *Sofroniou* (2003) also appealed against another conviction under s 1 which involved the obtaining services by deception from American Express when he used a false identity to obtain a credit card from them. However, he withdrew his appeal on this point as it was accepted that the benefit had been or would be paid for, as the agreement with American Express specifically provided for an annual charge of £12.

14.7.3 *Mens rea*

As with all the other deception offences, the prosecution must prove dishonesty and that the deception was made intentionally or recklessly. However, there is no need to prove any intention permanently to deprive.

14.8 Evasion of a liability

Section 2 of the Theft Act 1978 creates three different offences by which evasion of a liability can be committed.

'2(1) Subject to subsection (2) below, where a person by any deception –

(a) dishonestly secures the remission of the whole or any part of any existing liability to make a payment, whether his own liability or another's; or

(b) with intent to make permanent default in whole or in part on any existing liability to make a payment, or with intent to let another do so, dishonestly induces the creditor or any person claiming on behalf of the creditor to wait for payment (whether or not the due date for payment is deferred) or to forgo payment; or

(c) dishonestly obtains any exemption from or abatement of liability to make a payment; he shall be guilty of an offence.'

For all of these liability is limited to legally enforceable liability and in s 2 the Act specifically states that 'subsection (1) shall not apply in relation to a liability that has not been accepted or established to pay compensation for a wrongful act or omission'.

These sections were enacted following the Law Commission's Thirteenth Report. The view of the Law Commission was that:

> 'Para 13 . . . Subsection 1 (a) covers the deception which dishonestly secures the remission of the whole or part of an existing liability to make payment. An example would be where a man borrows £100 from a neighbour and, when

repayment is due, tells a false story of some family tragedy which makes it impossible for him to find the money; this deception persuades the neighbour to tell him that he need never repay the loan.

Para 14 Clause 2(1)(b) is concerned with the stalling debtor. It provides that a creditor who by deception dishonestly induces his creditor to wait for payment or to forgo payment is guilty of an offence if, and only if, he intends to make permanent default in whole or in part of his liability to pay. This final limitation makes the offence narrower than the [original] offence in s 16(2)(a). We recognise that the practical difficulties of proving an intention never to pay will have the consequence that there will be few prosecutions under this head, but this is consistent with our view that the criminal law should not apply to the debtor who is merely trying to delay making a payment.

Para 15 Clause 2(1)(c) is concerned with a type of fraud which can conveniently be brought within the scope of the offence of obtaining relief from liability by deception although it differs from the other cases covered by the offence in that it can include frauds where the offender has been acting dishonestly from the outset of the transaction … Another example of the application of this part of clause 2 is the case where a person by deception obtains services at a reduced rate (for example, air travel at a special rate for students when the traveller is not a student).'

Each of these subsections creates a different offence, even though it can be argued there is a degree of overlap, and it is necessary to look at each of them separately.

14.8.1 Securing remission of a liability

As seen in the extract from the Law Commission's report, it was intended that this subsection should cover situations where, by deception, the defendant persuades his creditor to let him off repaying all or part of his debt. This may be through D telling the creditor an untrue hard luck story, or any other deception. In *Jackson* [1983] Crim LR 617 D paid for petrol with a stolen credit card. As the petrol had been put into his tank and the ownership of if had passed to him (because it is inextricably mixed with the petrol already in there), it was decided that he had an existing liability to pay for it. By using a stolen credit card he had deceived the garage into letting him off paying for the petrol.

14.8.2 Inducing a creditor to wait for or forgo payment

As with s 2(1)(a) there must be an existing liability to make a payment, but for this offence it is enough if D induces the creditor to wait for payment. The offence is also committed if the creditor

is induced to forgo payment. This seems very similar to s 2(1)(a) but there is a key difference in that for s 2(1)(b), the defendant must intend to make permanent default. An interesting application of this section was seen in the case of *Holt and Lee* [1981] 2 All ER 854.

CASE EXAMPLE

Holt and Lee [1981] 2 All ER 854

The two defendants had had a meal in a pizza restaurant. After they finished the meal they made a plan to tell their waitress that payment had already been made to another member of staff, so that they could leave without paying. Their conversation was overheard by another diner who was an off-duty policeman and he arrested them for attempting to induce a creditor to forgo payment. The Court of Appeal upheld their convictions.

This subsection also includes the situation where the defendant uses a cheque to pay, knowing that the cheque will not be met. This is specifically stated in s 2(3):

'2(3) For purposes of subsection (1)(b) a person induced to take in payment a cheque or other security for money by way of conditional satisfaction of a pre-existing liability is to be treated not as being paid but as being induced to wait for payment.'

The use of this provision is illustrated by the case of *Turner* [1974] 3 All ER 124. D owed money for some work done. When his creditor pressed him for payment, D said he had no ready cash and persuaded the creditor to accept a cheque. D knew that this cheque would not be met by the bank. This conduct comes within the section, provided D intended to make permanent default.

Mens rea

For this subsection, as well as proving dishonesty and that the deception was made intentionally or recklessly, it must also be proved that the defendant had an intention to make permanent default.

14.8.3 Obtaining an exemption from or an abatement of liability

This offence covers many every day situations where people use invalid tickets or claim discount that they are not entitled to. The leading case on this section is *Silbartie* [1983] Crim LR 470.

CASE EXAMPLE

Silbartie [1983] Crim LR 470

D, who was a law student, bought two Underground season tickets for his daily journey to college. One ticket covered the beginning of his journey for two stations and the other covered the end of his journey on another line for two stations. He had no valid ticket for the middle part (some 14 stations) of his journey. He had to change from one line to the other, and on passing a ticket inspector D flashed an invalid season ticket so quickly that the inspector could not see what was on it. He was convicted of attempted evasion of a liability contrary to s 2(1)(c) of the Theft Act 1978 and the conviction was upheld by the Court of Appeal.

The basis for this was that D by flashing the ticket was, in effect, saying that he was the holder of a correct ticket and was entitled to travel and not liable to pay any more. This was dishonestly obtaining an exemption from the liability to pay the excess fare for the stations for which he had no valid ticket. It was accepted that there might also be an offence committed under s 2(1)(b) but this was irrelevant to D's guilt under s 2(1)(c).

On the point of the overlap between subss (a), (b) and (c), the following points were made in the commentary on the case in the *Criminal Law Review*.

> 'When the defendant "flashed" his wallet he was, it appears, attempting to avoid having to pay the proper fare for the journey which he was in fact undertaking. Payment was due at the outset of the journey and he was trying to deceive the inspector into believing that the fare had been paid by the purchase of a season ticket covering the whole journey. Section 2(1) of the Theft Act probably creates three offences and a case may be made for saying that he was guilty of an attempt to commit all of them.
>
> Assuming he had succeeded –
>
> **a** Did he secure the remission of part of an existing liability to make a payment (section 2(1)(a))?
>
> **b** Did he induce the creditor to forgo payment of part of an existing liability, with intent to make permanent default (section 2(1)(b))?
>
> **c** Did he obtain an exemption from liability to make a payment (section 2(1)(c))?
>
> If he was guilty of three offences, does this not look like a case of overkill on the part of the legislator? Some overlap of offences is reasonable and to be expected;

but it must surely be assumed that Parliament intended each offence to have some function. If the broadest construction is put upon each offence there seems to be nothing for paragraph (b), in so far as it relates to forgoing payment, to do.

Paragraphs (a) and (c) do not require proof of an intent to make permanent default and, if they cover cases of forgoing payment, Parliament's evident intention that one who merely induces a creditor to forgo payment should not be guilty unless he has an intent to make permanent default, is defeated. It is no answer to this argument that there was evidence of an intent to make permanent default in the present case. Such an intent was no part of the offence of which the appellant was convicted.'

ACTIVITY

Answer the questions put in the article as to whether the defendant had committed each of the three offences in s 2 of the Theft Act 1978.

A more straightforward case is *Firth* [1990] Crim LR 326, in which a consultant who did both NHS work and private work did not inform the hospital that two of his patients were private patients. This meant that neither he nor the patients were billed for services provided for them. The Court of Appeal upheld his conviction for obtaining an exemption from or abatement of liability.

These three subsections are confusing with their different *actus reus* and *mens rea*. To help make it clear what has to be proved for each offence a key facts chart of these three subsections is set out on next page.

Key facts on Theft Act 1978 s 2 offences

Subsection	Actus reus	Mens rea	Cases
2(1)(a)	• secures • remission • whole or part • own or other's • existing liability.	• deliberate or reckless deception • dishonesty.	*Jackson* (1983)
2(1)(b)	• induces • creditor or other • to wait for or forgo payment • including by paying a cheque (s 2(3)).	• deliberate or reckless deception • dishonesty AND • intent to make permanent default.	*Holt and Lee* (1981) *Turner* (1974)
2(1)(c)	• obtains • exemption from or • an abatement of • liability.	• deliberate or reckless deception • dishonesty.	*Silbartie* (1983)

ACTIVITY

Discuss the criminal liability, if any, in each of the following situations.

1. Julie, aged 57, goes to her local DIY store on the day when they have a special 10 per cent discount for people over 60. Julie buys goods worth £70 and at the check-out she falsely claims to be over 60 and is given a discount of £7.

2. Ken fills his car up at a petrol station. He knows he has not got enough money on him to pay so he uses his credit card, although he knows he has exceeded his limit and the credit card company have asked him to return the card. In the shop he uses a fake coin to obtain some chocolate from a machine.

3. Leonora stays at a health spa for two nights. While there she uses the leisure facilities and has a beauty treatment. She also has meals in the restaurant. When she checks out at the end of her stay she uses a stolen credit card to pay for everything.

4. Melvyn borrows £50 from Norbert. It is agreed that Melvyn will pay it back when he receives his pay cheque at the end of the month. Two days before the end of the month Melvyn falsely tells Norbert that he has been made redundant and cannot afford to pay the money back. Norbert is sorry for Melvyn and tells him he need not repay the loan.

5. Rosa obtains a part-time job as a lifeguard by falsely claiming that she has passed the national lifeguard qualification. When travelling to work Rosa shows an out of date season ticket which she has altered so that it appears to be current.

14.9 Fraud Act 2006

In 2002 the Law Commission issued a report on the law of fraud (Law Com No 276 Cm 5560 (2002)) with recommendations for a complete reform of the law. A draft Bill was attached to the report. The Government consulted on this in 2004 and the Fraud Bill 2006 was presented in Parliament. This Bill was based on the Law Commission's recommendations, but the Government made changes and added new offences. The Bill received Royal Assent in November 2006. The Act came into effect in January 2007.

The Act repeals ss 15, 15A, 15B, 16 and 20(2) of the Theft Act 1968 as well as ss 1 and 2 of the Theft Act 1978. The previous offences are replaced by four new offences under the Fraud Act 2006. These are:

- fraud by false representation (s 2)
- fraud by failing to disclose information (s 3)
- fraud by abuse of position (s 4)
- obtaining services dishonestly (s 11).

14.9.1 Fraud by false representation

Under s 2 of the Fraud Act 2006, this will be committed if D:

'2(1)

(a) dishonestly makes a false representation, and

(b) intends, by making the representation:

(i) to make a gain for himself or another, or

(ii) to cause loss to another or to expose another to the risk of loss.'

A representation is false if:

'2(2)

    (a) it is untrue or misleading, and

    (b) the person making it knows that it is, or might be, untrue or misleading.'

Section 2(3) states that a representation means any representation as to fact or law, including making a representation as to the state of mind of the person making the representation or any other person.

Section 2(4) states that a representation may be express or implied. The original Bill included that a representation covered conduct as well as words. This does not appear in the final Act. The explanatory notes published with the original Bill gave an example of conduct at paragraph 13. This stated:

'An example of a representation by conduct is where a person dishonestly misuses a credit card to pay for items. By tendering the card, he is falsely representing that he has the authority to use it for that transaction. If he knows that he does not, or might not, have that authority, then he is committing an offence under this clause. It is immaterial whether the merchant accepting the card for payment is deceived by the representation.'

This clearly showed that the offence was intended to be wide enough to cover the situation in the case of *Fitzeal Nabina* [2000] Crim LR 481 where D had obtained credit cards in his own name by false pretences. His conviction of obtaining property contrary to s 15 of the Theft Act 1968 was quashed as the judge had not directed the jury they must be satisfied that D had deceived the sales outlets as to the fact that he was the legitimate holder of the cards. Although there is no mention of conduct in the Act, D would now presumably be guilty on the facts in *Fitzeal Nabina*. This is because the offence under s 2 of the Fraud Act 2006 does not require any proof that the seller was deceived.

The explanatory notes made it clear that the *Ghosh* test for dishonesty (see section 12.5.2) applies to this new offence.

'1 The law on deception includes where D makes a statement being reckless as to its truth. The wording here is that D knows the representation "might be untrue or misleading". Is this narrower than being reckless as to its truth?

2 Would *DPP v Ray* [1973] 3 All ER 131 [silence when changing one's mind about paying for a meal – see section 14.1.2] be covered by this new offence? Or could that behaviour now only be charged under making off without payment?

3   The wording of the offence means that it is not necessary for the fraud to succeed. There will no longer be any requirement for there to be an obtaining or for 'deception' to be the cause of obtaining. The problems in *Collis-Smith* [1971] Crim LR 716 and *Laverty* [1970] 3 All ER 432 would no longer arise [see section 14.2]!

14.9.2 Fraud by failing to disclose information

Under s 3 of the Fraud Act 2006 this offence will be committed where a person:

 '3

(a) dishonestly fails to disclose information to another person which he is under a legal duty to disclose; and

(b) intends by failing to disclose the information:

(i) to make a gain for himself or another, or

(ii) to cause loss to another or to expose another to the risk of loss!

This was changed from the Law Commission's draft Bill. That included where there was a legal duty, but also included any situation where:

* the information is the kind that V trusts D to disclose

* D knows this

* any reasonable person would disclose the information.

The omission of this means that there the prosecution will have to prove there was a legal obligation on D. Consider the cases of *Rai* [2000] Crim LR 192, and *Firth* [1990] Crim LR 326 (see section 14.1.2). Would they be covered by this new offence?

However, the explanatory notes published with the Act make it clear that the Law Commission's definition of 'legal duty' is relevant. The Law Commission's Report on *Fraud* (Law Com No 276 Cm 5560 (2002)) stated:

'7.28   Such a duty may derive from statute (such as the provisions governing company prospectuses), from the fact that the transaction in question is one of the utmost good faith (such as a contract of insurance), from the express or implied terms of a contract, from the custom of a particular trade or market, or from the existence of a fiduciary relationship between the parties (such as that of agent and principal).

7.29   For this purpose there is a legal duty to disclose information not only if the defendant's failure to disclose it gives the victim a cause of action for damages, but also if the law gives the victim a right to set aside any change in his or her legal position to which he or she may consent as a result of the non-disclosure.

For example, a person entering into a contract with his or her beneficiary, in the sense that a failure to make such disclosure will entitle the beneficiary to rescind the contract and to reclaim any property transferred under it.'

14.9.3 Fraud by abuse of position

Under s 4 of the Fraud Act 2006 the offence of fraud by abuse of position will be committed where a person:

'4(1)

(a) occupies a position in which he is expected to safeguard, or not to act against, the financial interests of another person;

(b) dishonestly abuses that position, and

(c) intends by means of abuse of that position:

(i) to make a gain for himself or another, or

(ii) to cause loss to another or to expose another to the risk of loss.'

Subsection 4(2) states that this offence can be committed by an omission as well as by an act.

The original Law Commission draft added the word 'secretly' so that it read in (b) 'dishonestly and secretly abuses that position'. As the Act does not include the word 'secretly', s 4 will apparently cover situations where V knows what is going on. Is this an extension by analogy with *Hinks* [2000] 4 All ER 833 (see section 12.2.4) where it was held that theft could be committed even though V had given the property to D?

'Gain' or 'loss'

The three offences all require that D intends to make a gain for himself or another, or to cause loss to another or to expose another to the risk of loss. Section 5 defines 'gain' and 'loss'. The definition in this section is very similar to that in s 34 of the Theft Act 1968. Both 'gain' and 'loss' extend only to gain or loss in money or other property. Property for this purpose is defined in the same way as in s 4(1) of the Theft Act 1968. It means any property whether real or personal including things in action and other intangible property. The gain or loss can be temporary or permanent.

14.9.4 Obtaining services dishonestly

This is clearly intended to replace ss 1 and 2 of the Theft Act 1978 and also s 15A of the Theft Act 1968. Section 11 of the Fraud Act 2006 states:

'11(1) A person is guilty of an offence under this section if he obtains services for himself or another:

(a) by a dishonest act, and

(b) in breach of subsection (2).

11(2) A person obtains services in breach of this subsection if:

(a) they are made available on the basis that payment has been or will be made for or in respect of them,

(b) he obtains them without any payment having been made for or in respect of them or without payment having been made in full, and

(c) when he obtains them he knows:

(i) that they are being made available on the basis of described in paragraph (a), or

(ii) that they might be, but intends that payment will not be made, or will not be made in full.'

The explanatory notes to the Act give examples of situations which will be covered. These include using false credit card details to obtain services on the Internet. The offence is also intended to cover situations such as climbing over a wall to watch a football match. There is no deception here in this behaviour but it is obtaining a service which is provided on the basis that people will pay for it. As there will no longer be any need to show that 'deception' was the cause of the obtaining, it is possible for such situations to be covered.

14.9.5 Other offences

The Act also creates other offences. These include:

- possession etc of articles for use in frauds (s 6)

- making or supplying article for use in frauds (s 7)

- participating in fraudulent business carried on by sole trader (s 9)

- participating in fraudulent business carried on by company etc (s 10).

Further reading

Law Commission, *Fraud* (2002) (Law Com 276) Cm 5560.
Law Commission, *Offences of Dishonesty: Money Transfers* (1996) (Law Com No 243).
Shute, S and Horder, J, 'Thieving and Deceiving: What is the Difference?' (1993) 56 MLR 548.
Smith, A T H, 'The Idea of Criminal Deception' [1982] Crim LR 721.
Smith, J C, 'Obtaining Cheques by Deception or Theft' [1997] Crim LR 396.
Spencer, J R, 'The Theft Act 1978' [1979] Crim LR 24.
Yeo, N, 'Bull's-eye', *New Law Journal*, 9 February 2007 and 16 February 2007

Internet Links

www.lawcom.gov.uk for Law Commission Reports
www.parliament.gov.uk for Bills before Parliament
www.opsi.gov.uk for new Acts of Parliament

chapter
15 CRIMINAL DAMAGE ■

AIMS AND OBJECTIVES □□□

After reading this chapter you should be able to:

■ Understand the *actus reus* and *mens rea* of the basic offence of criminal damage

■ Understand the *actus reus* and *mens rea* of the offence of endangering life when committing criminal damage

■ Understand the *actus reus* and *mens rea* of arson

■ Understand other offences related to criminal damage

■ Analyse critically all offences in the Criminal Damage Act 1971

■ Apply the law to factual situations to determine whether there is criminal liability for an offence under the Criminal Damage Act 1971

The law on criminal damage is contained in the Criminal Damage Act 1971. This created a complete code for this area of the law, just as the Theft Act 1968 did for the law on theft. The Criminal Damage Act was the result of a report by the Law Commission, *Offences of Damage to Property* (Law Com No 29) (1970). As well as codifying the law on criminal damage, one of the aims of the Law Commission was to bring the law in line with the law on theft, so far as was practicable. For this reason some of the words used in the Act are the same as the words used the Theft Act 1968.

The Criminal Damage Act creates four offences which are:

• the basic offence of criminal damage

• aggravated criminal damage

• arson

• aggravated arson.

15.1 The basic offence

The basic offence is set out in s 1(1) of the Criminal Damage Act 1971:

 '1(1) A person who without lawful excuse destroys or damages any property belonging to another intending to destroy or damage any such property or being reckless as to whether any such property would be destroyed or damaged shall be guilty of an offence.'

The *actus reus* is made up of three elements. These are that D must:

•   destroy or damage

•   property

•   belonging to another.

15.1.1 Destroy or damage

This phrase is not defined in the 1971 Act. However, the same phrase was used in the law prior to 1971 (the Malicious Damage Act 1861), and old cases ruled that even slight damage was sufficient to prove damage. For example, in *Gayford v Chouler* [1898] 1 QB 316, trampling down grass was held to be damage. The cases prior to the Criminal Damage Act 1971 are, of course, no longer binding, but they may still be used as persuasive precedent.

Destroy

'Destroy' is a much stronger word than 'damage', but it includes where the property has been made useless even though it is not completely destroyed.

Damage

Damage covers a wide range and in *Roe v Kingerlee* [1986] Crim LR 735 the Divisional Court said that whether property has been damaged was a 'matter of fact and degree and it is for the justices to decide whether what occurred was damage or not'. In that case D had smeared mud on the walls of a police cell. It had cost £7 to have it cleaned off and it was held that this could be damage even though it was not permanent.

In an Australian case, *Samuels v Stubbs* [1972] SASR 200 it was stated that:

> **J** '[I]t is difficult to lay down any very general rule and, at the same time, precise and absolute rule as to what constitutes "damage". One must be guided in a great degree by the circumstances of each case, the nature of the article and the mode in which it is affected or treated . . . [T]he word is sufficiently wide in its meaning to embrace injury, mischief or harm done to property, and that to constitute "damage" it is unnecessary to establish such definite or actual damage as renders property useless, or prevents it from serving its normal function.'

In *Samuels v Stubbs* (1972) D had jumped on a policeman's cap, denting it. There was no evidence that it was not possible to return the cap to its original shape without any cost or real trouble. Even so the judge ruled that there was damage, as there was a 'temporary functional derangement' of the cap.

In English cases under the Criminal Damage Act 1971, although it has been held that non-permanent damage can come within the definition of 'damage', the courts' approach seems to be based on whether it will cost money, time and/or effort to remove the damage. If so, then an offence has been committed, but if not then there is no offence. This is illustrated in the following case.

CASE EXAMPLE

Hardman v Chief Constable of Avon and Somerset Constabulary [1986] Crim LR 330 CND

Protesters, to mark the fortieth anniversary of the dropping of the atomic bomb on Hiroshima, painted silhouettes on the pavement with water soluble paint. The local council had the paintings removed with water jets. The defendants argued that the damage was only temporary and the paintings would have quickly been erased by the weather and by people walking on them and there was no need for the local council to go to the expense of having the paintings removed by high-pressure water jets. The court held that this was damage.

Similar decisions were made in *Blake v DPP* [1993] Crim LR 586. D wrote a biblical quotation on a concrete pillar. This needed to be cleaned off and so was held to be criminal damage. The same decision was reached in *Roe v Kingerlee* (1986) where it cost £7 to remove mud from a cell wall.

The 'temporary impairment of value or usefulness' was the key factor in *Fiak* [2005] EWCA Crim 2381.

CASE EXAMPLE

Fiak [2005] EWCA Crim 2381

D was arrested on suspicion of being in charge of a vehicle when he was over the limit for alcohol and for assault on a police officer. He was taken to a police station and placed in a cell. He put a blanket in the toilet in the cell and flushed the toilet several times. This caused water to overflow and flood the cell and two adjoining cells. The blanket was not visibly soiled but it had to be cleaned and dried before it could be used again. The cells had to be cleaned. This was held to be criminal damage.

However, in *A (a Juvenile) v R* [1978] Crim LR 689, spit which landed on a policeman's uniform was not damage as it could be wiped off with a wet cloth with very little effort. But what if the spit had landed on a light coloured T-shirt and left a stain, so that the T-shirt needed washing or dry cleaning? It seems that could be enough to constitute damage.

The type and purpose of the property may be relevant, as in *Morphitis v Salmon* [1990] Crim LR 48, DC, where it was held that a scratch on a scaffolding pole was not damage. Scaffolding poles are likely to get quite scratched in the ordinary course of use and it does not affect their usefulness or integrity. However, a scratch on a car would almost certainly be considered damage.

Computer disks and programs

Altering computer programs was held to be within the definition of criminal damage in *Whiteley* (1991) 93 Cr App R 25, when a computer hacker had altered and deleted files and changed some passwords. It was held that there was damage to the magnetic particles on the hard disk which made the computer inoperable. However, it was recognised that there were problems in proving damage in some cases of computer hacking and the Computer Misuse Act 1990 was passed to clarify the law. This Act creates an offence of 'unauthorised modification of computer material'. It also makes it clear that the Criminal Damage Act no longer applies as s 3(6) provides that '[F]or the purposes of the Criminal Damage Act 1971 a modification of the contents of a computer shall not be regarded as damaging any computer or computer storage medium unless its effect on that computer or computer storage medium impairs its physical condition'.

ACTIVITY

Explain whether or not there is 'damage' within the meaning of the Criminal Damage Act 1971 in each of the following situations.

1. Aisha throws a bucket of clean water over Bess. The water thoroughly wets Bess's jacket and skirt. Would it make any difference to your answer if the water was muddy?

2. Conrad writes on the brick wall of the local town hall with white chalk.

3. Dan is working on a construction site. He throws a spanner down. It hits a wall which is being constructed and causes a small piece of brick to chip off. The spanner also hits a scaffolding post and causes a small dent in it.

15.1.2 Property

'Property' is defined in s 10(1) of the Criminal Damage Act 1971:

'10(1) In this Act "property" means property of a tangible nature, whether real or personal, including money and –

(a) including wild creatures which have been tamed or are ordinarily kept in captivity, and any other wild creatures or their carcasses if, but only if, they have been reduced into possession which has not been lost or abandoned or are in the course of being reduced into possession; but

(b) not including mushrooms growing wild on any land or flowers, fruit or foliage of a plant growing wild on any land.'

The wording of this is similar to the Theft Act 1968 but there are two main differences. First, land is property which can be damaged although it cannot normally be stolen and secondly, intangible rights cannot be damaged, though they may be stolen.

15.1.3 Belonging to another

Again, the definition of 'belonging to another' set out in s 10(2) is similar to the definition which is used for the purposes of theft.

'10(2) Property shall be treated for the purposes of this Act as belonging to any person –

(a) having the custody or control of it;

(b) having in it any proprietary right or interest (not being an equitable interest arising only from an agreement to transfer or grant an interest); or

(c) having a charge on it.

539

> (3) Where property is subject to a trust, the person to whom it belongs shall be
> so treated as including any person having a right to enforce the trust.'

This gives the same wide definition of 'belonging to' as in theft. It is not restricted to the owner. In fact a co-owner can be guilty of criminal damage as the other co-owner has a proprietary right in the property, as shown in *Smith* [1974] 1 All ER 632.

CASE EXAMPLE

Smith [1974] 1 All ER 632

D removed some electrical wiring, which he had earlier fitted in the flat which he rented. In doing this he damaged some of the fixtures he had put in. In civil law these fixtures belong to the landlord and this was property 'belonging to another'. However, D was found not guilty because he lacked the necessary *mens rea* (see section 15.1.5).

It is important to note that for the purposes of the basic offence the property affected must belong to another. A person cannot be guilty of the basic offence if the property he destroys or damages is his own. But for the aggravated offence a person can be guilty even though it is his own property (see section 15.2).

15.1.4 *Mens rea* of the basic offence

The defendant must do the damage or destruction either intentionally or recklessly. For the meanings of intention and recklessness the Law Commission meant the previous principles of *mens rea* used in criminal damage cases to apply. So far as intention is concerned the courts have done this, but the meaning of the word 'reckless' has caused problems and debate.

Prior to the passing of the Criminal Damage Act 1971 the law on criminal damage was contained in the Malicious Damage Act 1861 and amending Acts. These used the phrase 'unlawfully and maliciously'. Maliciously was taken to have the meaning of either intending the damage or knowing there was a risk of damage and taking that risk. This type of risk taking is known as subjective recklessness. When the Law Commission recommended reform of the law they identified the essential mental element in the malicious damage offences as 'intent to do the forbidden act or recklessness in relation to its foreseen consequences'. They suggested replacing the old-fashioned word of maliciously with the phrase 'intending or being reckless'. This was meant to have the same meaning as the courts had given to the word 'maliciously'.

Intention

D must intend to destroy or damage property belonging to another. As Professor Sir John Smith pointed out:

> 'It is not enough that D intended to do the act which caused the damage unless he intended to cause the damage; proof that D intended to throw a stone is not proof that he intended to break a window. Nor is it enough that D intends to damage property if he does not intend to damage property of another.'

Smith and Hogan Criminal Law (11th edn, Butterworths, 2005), p 897

The first point made by Professor Sir John Smith that proving the act is not enough, there must be intention to do the damage, was seen in the old case of *Pembliton* [1874-80] All ER Rep 1163 where D threw a stone at some men whom he had been fighting with. The stone missed them but hit and broke a window. D was not guilty of causing damage to the window as he had no intention to damage the window (or any other property), even though he intended to throw the stone. (But note that under the Criminal Damage Act 1971 he may have been reckless if he aimed at a person standing in front of a window.)

The second point on the need to intend to damage property belonging to another was illustrated in *Smith* [1974] 1 All ER 632. Smith mistakenly believed that the property he was damaging was his own. His conviction was quashed by the Court of Appeal, who said:

> **J** 'The element of *mens rea* relates to all the circumstances of the criminal act. The criminal act in the offence is causing damage to or destruction of "property belonging to another" and the element of *mens rea*, therefore, must relate to "property belonging to another". Honest belief, whether justifiable or not, that the property is the defendant's own negatives the element of *mens rea*.'

Reckless

This word has caused problems. In *Stephenson* [1979] 2 All ER 1198, D was a tramp who sheltered in a hollow in a haystack and, because he was cold, lit a fire there. The haystack caught fire and was destroyed. The Court of Appeal quashed D's conviction on the grounds that, although an ordinary person would realise the risk of the haystack catching fire, he did not as he suffered from schizophrenia and this point should have been left to the jury to decide. The Court of Appeal was using the subjective test for reckless.

However, in *Caldwell* [1981] 1 All ER 961 the House of Lords stated that a person is reckless if he did an act which in fact created an obvious risk that property will be destroyed and, when he did the act he either:

• had not given any thought to the possibility of there being any risk (objective)

or

• had recognised that there was some risk involved, and has nonetheless gone on to take it (subjective).

This became known as *Caldwell* (1981) recklessness and, as can be seen, it included both subjective and objective recklessness. The objective test considered whether the risk was obvious to an ordinary prudent person. If so, then the fact that the defendant did not give any thought to the possibility of there being any risk was enough to make the defendant guilty.

This objective test was harsh in its application, particularly where the defendant was young or mentally backward. This was seen in *Elliott v C* [1983] 2 All ER 1005, where the defendant was incapable of appreciating the risk but was still guilty under this test. D was a 14-year-old girl with severe learning difficulties who had been out all night without food or sleep. She got into a garden shed and in an effort to get warm, poured white spirit on to the carpet and set light to it. The magistrates found that she had given no thought to the possibility that the shed might be destroyed. They also found that in the circumstances the risk would not have been obvious to her and they acquitted her. The prosecution appealed by way of case stated to the Queen's Bench Divisional Court which ruled that as the risk would have been obvious to a reasonably prudent man, the magistrates had to convict the girl. A similar decision was reached by the Court of Appeal in *Gemmell and Richards* [2002] EWCA Crim 192, but was later reversed by the House of Lords (*G and another* [2003] UKHL 50).

CASE EXAMPLE

Gemmell and another [2003] UKHL 50; [2002] EWCA Crim 192

The defendants were two boys aged 11 and 12 years. During a night out camping, they went into the yard of a shop and set fire to some bundles of newspapers which they threw under a large wheelie bin. They then left the yard. They expected that as there was a concrete floor under the wheelie bin the fire would extinguish itself. In fact the bin caught fire and this spread to the shop and other buildings, causing about £1 million damage. The boys were convicted under both s 1 and s 3 of the Criminal Damage Act 1971.

The trial judge directed the jury that whether there was an obvious risk of the shop and other buildings being damaged should be decided by reference to the reasonable man, ie the reasonable adult. He said: 'the ordinary reasonable bystander is an adult . . . He has got in mind that stock of everyday information which one acquires in the process of growing up' and 'no allowance is made by the law for the youth of these boys or their lack of maturity or their own inability, if you find it to be, to assess what was going on'.

The Court of Appeal held that this direction was in line with the law in *Caldwell* (1981) and dismissed the appeal on the basis that *Caldwell* (1981) was binding on it. However, it certified the following point of law of general public importance:

> J   'Can a defendant properly be convicted under section 1 of the Criminal Damage Act 1971 on the basis that he was reckless as to whether property was destroyed or damaged when he gave no thought to the risk but, by reason of his age and/or personal characteristics the risk would not have been obvious to him, even if he had thought about it?'

The House of Lords ruled that a defendant could not be guilty unless he had realised the risk and decided to take it. It overruled the decision in *Caldwell* (1981), holding that in that case the Law Lords had 'adopted an interpretation of section 1 of the 1971 Act which was beyond the range of feasible meanings'. It emphasised the meaning that the Law Commission had intended and which Parliament must also have intended. Lord Bingham said:

> J   '[S]ection 1 as enacted followed, subject to an immaterial addition, the draft proposed by the Law Commission. It cannot be supposed that by "reckless" Parliament meant anything different from the Law Commission. The Law Commission's meaning was made plain both in its Report (Law Com No 29) and in Working Paper No 23 which preceded it. These materials (not, it would seem, placed before the House in *R v Caldwell*) reveal a very plain intention to replace the old expression "maliciously" by the more familiar expression "reckless" but to give the latter expression the meaning which *R v Cunningham* [1957] 2 QB 396 had given to the former. . . . No relevant change in the *mens rea* necessary for the proof of the offence was intended, and in holding otherwise the majority misconstrued section 1 of the Act.'

Lord Bingham also quoted from the Law Commission's Draft Criminal Code when he said that he would answer the certified question. He gave cl 18(c) of the Draft Bill for the Criminal Code (Law Com No 177, 1989) as his answer:

'18(c) A person acts recklessly within the meaning of section 1 of the Criminal Damage Act 1971 with respect to −

(i) a circumstance when he is aware of a risk that it exists or will exist;

(ii) a result when he is aware of a risk that it will occur;

and it is in the circumstances known to him, unreasonable to take the risk.'

This judgment by the House of Lords in *G and another* (2003) affects the meaning of reckless for all the offences created by s 1.

15.1.5 Without lawful excuse

The Act defines two lawful excuses in s 5. These are available only for the basic offence.

'5(2) A person charged with an offence to which this section applies shall whether or not he would be treated for the purposes of this Act as having a lawful excuse apart from this subsection, be treated as having a lawful excuse −

(a) if at the time of the act or acts alleged to constitute the offence he believed that the person or persons whom he believed to be entitled to consent to the destruction of or damage to the property in question had so consented, or would have so consented to it if he or they had known of the destruction or damage and its circumstances; or

(b) if he destroyed or damaged or threatened to destroy or damage the property in question ... in order to protect property belonging to himself or another or a right or interest in property which was or which he believed was vested in himself or another, and at the time of the act or acts alleged to constitute the offence he believed −

(i) that the property was in need of immediate protection; and

(ii) that the means of protection adopted or proposed to be adopted were or would be reasonable in all the circumstances.

(3) For the purposes of this section it is immaterial whether a belief is justified or not if it is honestly held.'

There is therefore a defence under s 5 in two circumstances. D must honestly believe either that:

- the owner (or another person with rights in the property) would have consented to the damage; or

- other property was at risk and in need of immediate protection and what he did was reasonable in all the circumstances.

Belief in consent

In *Denton* [1982] 1 All ER 65, D, who worked in a cotton mill, thought that his employer had encouraged him to set fire to the mill so that the employer could make an insurance claim. The Court of Appeal quashed his conviction as he had a defence under s 5(2)(a).

The combination of s 5(2)(a) and s 5(3) allows a defence of mistake to be used, even where the defendant makes the mistake because they are intoxicated. In *Jaggard v Dickinson* [1980] 3 All ER 716 D, who was drunk, went to what she thought was a friend's house. There was no one in and so she broke a window to get in as she believed (accurately) her friend would consent to this. Unfortunately in her drunken state she had mistaken the house and had actually broken into the house of another person. The Divisional Court quashed her conviction, holding that she could rely on her intoxicated belief as Parliament had 'specifically required the court to consider the defendant's actual state of belief, not the state of belief which ought to have existed'. They pointed out that a belief may be honestly held whether it is caused by intoxication, stupidity, forgetfulness or inattention.

Belief that other property was in immediate need of protection

Section 5(2)(b) could give a defence in situations where trees are cut down or a building demolished to prevent the spread of fire. A case in which the defence was successfully pleaded in a jury trial was in April 2000 when Lord Melchett and several other members of Greenpeace damaged genetically modified (GM) crops in order to prevent non-GM crops in neighbouring fields being contaminated with pollen from the GM crops. The judge allowed the defence to go to the jury, but they were unable to agree on a verdict. A retrial was ordered and this time the jury acquitted the defendants.

If D has another purpose in doing the damage, then the court may rule that the defence is not available to him. In *Hunt* (1978) 66 Cr App R 105 D helped his wife in her post as deputy warden of a block of old people's flats. He set fire to some bedding in order, as he claimed, to draw attention to the fact that the fire alarm was not in working order. The judge refused to allow a defence under s 5(2)(b) to go to the jury as his act was not done in order to protect property which was in immediate need of protection. The Court of Appeal upheld his conviction, despite the very subjective wording of s 5(2)(b).

In the case of *Blake v DPP* [1993] Crim LR 586, the defendant put forward defences under both s 5(2)(a) and s 5(2)(b).

CASE EXAMPLE

Blake v DPP [1993] Crim LR 586

D was a vicar who believed that the Government should not use military force in Kuwait and Iraq in the Gulf War. He wrote a biblical quotation with a marker pen on a concrete post outside the Houses of Parliament. He claimed that:

*   he was carrying out the instructions of God and this gave him a defence under s 5(2)(a), as God was entitled to consent to the damage of property and

*   the damage he did was in order to protect the property of civilians in Kuwait and Iraq and so he had a defence under s 5(2)(b).

He was convicted and appealed, but both the claims were rejected. The court held that God could not consent to damage and that what the vicar had done was not capable of protecting property in the Gulf judged objectively, again despite the apparent subjective wording of both s 5(2)(a) and (b).

Oddly enough the Act does not provide a defence where D believes he is acting to protect a person from harm. In *Baker and Wilkins* [1997] Crim LR 497 the two defendants believed that Baker's daughter was being held in a house. They tried to enter the house, causing damage to the door. They were convicted and their conviction was upheld on appeal as s 5(2)(b) only provides a defence where other property is in immediate need of protection.

15.2 Endangering life

This is an aggravated offence of criminal damage under s 1(2) Criminal Damage Act 1971, which states:

'1(2) A person who without lawful excuse destroys or damages any property, whether belonging to himself or another –

(a) intending to destroy or damage any property or being reckless as to whether any property would be destroyed or damaged; and

(b) intending by the destruction or damage to endanger the life of another or being reckless as to whether the life of another would be thereby endangered; shall be guilty of an offence.'

This offence is regarded as much more serious than the basic offence and it carries a maximum sentence of life imprisonment.

CRIMINAL
DAMAGE

15.2.1 Danger to life

The danger to life must come from the destruction or damage, not from another source in which damage was caused. In *Steer* [1987] 2 All ER 833 D fired three shots at the home of his former business partner, causing damage to the house. The Court of Appeal quashed his conviction as it held the danger came from the shots, not from any damage done to the house through those shots. It certified the following question to go to the House of Lords:

> 'Whether, upon a true construction of s 1(2)(b) of the Criminal Damage Act 1971, the prosecution are required to prove that the danger to life resulted from the destruction of or damage to the property, or whether it is sufficient for the prosecution to prove that it resulted from the act of the defendant which caused the destruction or damage.'

The House of Lords ruled that as the Act used the phrase 'by the destruction or damage', it could not be extended to mean 'by the damage or by the act which caused the damage'. It also pointed out that if it did include the act (as opposed to the damage), then there would be an anomaly which Parliament could not have intended, which it illustrated in the following way:

> **J** 'If A and B both discharge firearms in a public place, being reckless whether life would be endangered, it would be absurd that A, who incidentally causes some trifling damage to the property, should be guilty of an offence punishable with life imprisonment, but that B, who causes no damage, should be guilty of no offence. In the same circumstances, if A is merely reckless but B actually intends to endanger life, it is scarcely less absurd that A should be guilty of the graver offence under s 1(2)(b) of the 1971 Act, B of the lesser offence under s 16 of the Firearms Act 1968.'

In the later conjoined cases of *Webster and Warwick* [1995] 2 All ER 168 the Court of Appeal strained to distinguish the decision in *Steer* (1987). In *Webster* (1995) three defendants pushed a large stone from a bridge on to a train underneath. The stone hit the roof of one coach and caused debris to shower the passengers in that coach, although the stone itself did not fall into the carriage. In *Warwick* (1995), D rammed a police car and threw bricks at it causing the rear window to smash and shower the officers with broken glass. The Court of Appeal quashed the conviction in *Webster* (1995) because the judge had misdirected the jury that an intention to endanger life by the stone falling was sufficient for guilt, but it substituted a conviction based on recklessness. In *Warwick* (1995) it upheld the conviction. Lord Taylor CJ stated:

> J '[I]f a defendant throws a brick at a windscreen of a moving vehicle, given that he causes some damage to the vehicle, whether he is guilty under s 1(2) does not depend on whether the brick hits or misses the windscreen, but whether he intended to hit it and intended that the damage therefrom should endanger life or whether he was reckless as to that outcome. As to the dropping of stones from bridges, the effect of the statute may be thought strange. If the defendant's intention is that the stone itself should crash through the roof of a train . . . and thereby directly injure a passenger or if whether he was reckless only as to that outcome, the section would not bite. . . . If, however, the defendant intended or was reckless that the stone would smash the roof of the train or vehicle so that metal or wood struts from the roof would or obviously might descend upon a passenger, endangering life, he would surely be guilty. This may seem a dismal distinction.'

It is of interest to note that the Court of Appeal's decision in these cases is contrary to *obiter* statements in the judgment in *Steer* (1987), where Lord Bridge specifically considered this type of situation:

> J 'Counsel for the Crown put forward other examples of cases which he suggested ought to be liable to prosecution under s 1(2) of the 1971 Act, including that of the angry mob of striking miners who throw a hail of bricks through the window of a cottage occupied by the working miner and that of people who drop missiles from motorway bridges on passing vehicles. I believe that the criminal law provides adequate sanctions for these cases without the need to resort s 1(2) of the 1971 Act. But, if my belief is mistaken, this would still be no reason to distort the plain meaning of that subsection.'

15.2.2 Life not actually endangered

Life does not actually have to be endangered. In *Sangha* [1988] 2 All ER 385, D set fire to a mattress and two chairs in a neighbour's flat. The flat was empty at the time and, because of the design of the building, people in adjoining flats were not at risk. The Court of Appeal applied the now discredited test from *Caldwell* (1982) when it said that:

> J   'The test to be applied is this: is it proved that an ordinary prudent bystander would have perceived an obvious risk that property would be damaged and that life would thereby be endangered? The ordinary prudent bystander is not deemed to be invested with expert knowledge relating to the construction of the property, nor to have the benefit of hindsight. The time as which the perception is relevant is the time when the fire started.'

This decision took the objective test to a ridiculous degree. It meant that if D was an expert and knows there is no risk of endangering life by his actions, he would not have been judged by that but by whether an uninformed ordinary prudent bystander would think there was a risk. This objective interpretation must now be taken to be superseded by the use of subjective recklessness in *G and another* (2003). So, the test is whether the defendant realised that life might be endangered. If he did then he would be guilty even if there was no actual risk.

15.2.3 Own property

Section 1(2) applies where the property damaged is the defendant's own. This can be justified in most situations, as the aim of the section is to make D guilty where he has intended or been reckless as to whether life is endangered by the damage he does. It does not matter whether the damage is to his property or someone else's. However, the case of *Merrick* [1995] Crim LR 802 shows how the section can be extended to absurd lengths.

In *Merrick* (1995), D was employed by a householder to remove some old television cable. While doing this D left the live cable exposed for about six minutes. His conviction under s 1(2) of the 1971 Act was upheld by the Court of Appeal. In this case the householder was using *Merrick* (1995) as an agent, but if the householder had done the work personally it seems that he would equally have been guilty. The other anomaly shown by this case is that *Merrick* (1995) was guilty only because he was removing old cable and 'damaging' it by this process. If he had been installing new wiring and left that exposed for six minutes it would have been difficult to argue that there was any damage and so he would have been not guilty. Yet the action and the danger in both situations is the same.

15.2.4 *Mens rea*

There are two points which the prosecution must prove. These are:

1. intention or recklessness as to destroying or damaging any property

2. intention or recklessness as to whether the life is endangered by the destruction or damage.

Intention and recklessness have the same meaning as for the basic offence (see section 15.1.4.) This means that the *Caldwell* (1982) test for recklessness has been overruled and the prosecution must

prove that the defendant was aware both that there was a risk the property would be destroyed or damaged and that life would be endangered.

The decision in *R (Stephen Malcolm)* (1984) 79 Cr App Rep 334, where the Court of Appeal followed the decision in *Elliott v C* (1983), even though they were reluctant to do so, must be taken as overruled. In that case the defendant was a 15-year-old boy who, with two friends, had thrown milk bottles filled with petrol at the outside wall of a neighbour's ground-floor flat. These had caused sheets of flame which flashed across the window of the flat, endangering the lives of the occupants. D argued that he had not realised the risk, but the Court of Appeal held that the test was whether an ordinary prudent man would have appreciated the risk that life might be endangered. The decision following *G and another* (2003) would be whether the defendant had realised the risk.

This was confirmed in *Cooper* [2004] EWCA Crim 1382 and *Castle* [2004] EWCA Crim 2758.

CASE EXAMPLE

Cooper [2004] EWCA Crim 1382

D, who lived in a hostel for people needing support for mental illness, set fire to his mattress and bedding. There was no serious damage. When asked by the police if it had crossed his mind that people might have been hurt, he replied 'I don't think, it did cross my mind a bit but nobody would have got hurt.' He was charged with arson being reckless as to whether life would be endangered. The trial judge directed the jury in accordance with *Caldwell*. D was convicted but the conviction was quashed as the Court of Appeal held that the *Caldwell* test was no longer appropriate. The test for recklessness was subjective.

Rose LJ made it clear that *G and R* (2003) had affected the law in respect of the level of recklessness required for all criminal damage offences when he said:

> J
>
> 'In the light of the House of Lords speeches in *G and R*, the *Caldwell* direction was a misdirection. It is now, in the light *G and R*, incumbent on a trial judge to direct a jury, in a case of this kind, that the risk of danger to life was obvious and significant to the defendant. In other words, a subjective element is essential before the jury can convict of this offence.'

A similar decision was reached in *Castle* [2004] EWCA Crim 2758 where D broke into some offices at night to burgle them. On leaving he set fire to the premises. There were two flats above the offices but neither of the occupants were at home. These flats were smoke and soot damaged by the fire. The trial judge directed the jury in accordance with *Caldwell*. As in *Cooper* the Court of Appeal quashed D's conviction stating that the *Caldwell* test was no longer appropriate. The test for recklessness was subjective.

15.3 Arson

Under s 1(3) Criminal Damage Act 1971, where an offence under s 1 Criminal Damage Act 1971 is committed by destroying or damaging property by fire, the offence becomes arson. The maximum penalty is life imprisonment.

The basic offence of criminal damage must be destruction or damage by fire. All the other ingredients of the offence are the same as for the basic offence. Where aggravated arson is charged then it is necessary for the prosecution to prove that the defendant intended or was reckless as to whether life was endangered by the damage or destruction by fire.

In *Miller* [1983] 1 All ER 978 the House of Lords held that arson could be committed by an omission where the defendant accidentally started a fire and failed to do anything to prevent damage from that fire.

Key facts on criminal damage

			KEY FACTS	
Criminal Damage Act 1971	*Actus reus*	**Comment/case**	*Mens rea*	**Comment/ case**
s 1(1) Basic offence.	Destroy or damage	Damage need only be slight and non-permanent *Roe v Kingerlee* (1986)	Intending or	Normal principles of intention apply.
		but must need some effort to remove it *A (a Juvenile)* (1978).	being reckless as to destruction or damage.	*Cunningham* (1957) recklessness applies.
	property	Any tangible property including land can be damaged.		*G and another* (2003).
	belonging to another.	Having a proprietary right.		
s 1(2) Endangering life.	Basic offence and intending or being reckless as whether life was endangered.	Danger must come from destruction or damage *Steer* (1987) *Webster and Warwick* (1995). Can commit offence by damaging own property.	*Mens rea* for basic offence and intention or recklessness as to whether life was endangered.	Intention and recklessness have the same meaning as for the basic offence. *Castle* (2004)
s 1(3) Arson Arson offence.	Committed by fire. Aggravated offence committed by fire.	Can be committed by omission *Miller* (1983).	The intending or being reckless as to destruction or damage must be by fire.	

15.4 Threats to destroy or damage property

This is an offence against s 2 of the Criminal Damage Act 1971:

'2 A person who without lawful excuse makes to another a threat, intending that that other would fear it would be carried out –

(a) to destroy or damage any property belonging to that other or a third person; or

(b) to destroy or damage his own property in a way which he knows is likely to endanger the life of that other or a third person; shall be guilty of an offence!

The threat is, therefore, of conduct which would be an offence under s 1 of the Act. However, there is a key difference in that the defendant must intend that the other would fear the threat would be carried out. Section 2 does not give any alternative of being reckless as to whether the other would fear the threat would be carried out.

In *Cakman and others, The Times,* 28th March 2002, the defendants had occupied two of the 'pods' of the London Eye, demonstrating against human rights abuses in Turkey. They used an intercom to contact the operator of the wheel. They threatened to set fire to themselves if any attempt was made to storm the pods. Some of the protestors were seen to pour liquid over themselves. They were convicted of an offence under s 2(b).

The Court of Appeal quashed the convictions as they held that it was not enough to prove that the threatener was reckless as to whether the person threatened feared that the threats would be carried out. It had to be proved that the person making the threat intended that the person threatened would fear that the threat would be carried out. There is no mention of 'recklessly' in s 2, whereas in s 1, for the basic offence, 'recklessly' is expressly included. The Court of Appeal also pointed out that the nature of the threat of damage to the property had to be considered objectively. It does not matter what the person threatened thought.

15.5 Possessing anything with intent to destroy or damage property

Section 3 of the Criminal Damage Act 1971 sets out;

'3 A person who has anything in his custody or under his control intending without lawful excuse to use it or cause or permit another to use it –

(a) to destroy or damage any property belonging to some other person; or

(b) to destroy or damage his own property in a way which he knows is likely to endanger the life of some other person;

shall be guilty of an offence!

The *actus reus* is having the item in one's custody or control. The possession must be for the purpose of committing an offence under s 1. There is no time limit on when the offence will be committed, so there is no need to prove that it was imminent. The *mens rea* is the intention of using the item to commit a s 1 offence. This can be a conditional intention where the defendant only intends to use the item if he has to or in a certain event.

15.6 Racially aggravated criminal damage

This is an offence under s 30(1) of the Crime and Disorder Act 1998. An offence under s 1 of the Criminal Damage Act 1971 must have been committed, but in the special circumstances set out in s 28 of the Crime and Disorder Act 1998. These are that:

- at the time of the offence, or immediately before or after doing so, the offender demonstrates towards the victim of the offence hostility based on the victim's membership (or presumed membership) of a racial group or

- the offence is motivated by hostility towards members of a racial group based on their membership of that group.

APPLYING THE LAW

Discuss what offences, if any, have been committed in the following situations.

1. Anwal, aged 10, stands at the side of a country road and throws stones at passing cars. One stone hits the door of a car and causes a slight mark on the door. Another stone hits the side window of the car causing it to smash, showering the driver with glass. The driver swerves but manages to stop the car safely. Would your answer be different if Anwal was aged 20 and throwing stones onto cars from a bridge across a busy motorway?

2. Charlene has had an argument with her flatmate, Louisa, Charlene decides to teach Louisa a lesson by setting fire to some of her clothes. Charlene hangs an expensive dress out of the window and sets it alight. She then goes out. The flames from the dress set the window curtains alight and the fire spreads to the rest of the flat.

3. Donovan writes racially abusive words in chalk on the pavement outside a neighbour's house. The next day it rains and the chalk is washed away.

4. Errol and Fred are demolition workers for a local council. They are given instructions to demolish houses owned by the council in Green Street. The house numbers they are given are 1, 3, 5, 7, 9, and 11. When they arrive in Green Street they find that the houses are semi-detached in pairs, 1 and 3, 5 and 7, 9 and 11. They start by demolishing the pair of numbers 1 and 3. They then use heavy machinery to knock down the side wall of number 5. At this point Hannah comes out from number 7 and tells them to stop as she owns number 7 and if they continue to demolish number 5 it will damage her house. Errol and Fred insist they have the right to demolish both number 5 and number 7. While Hannah is arguing with them, her son, Ian, aged 14, removes some wiring from the engine of their demolition machinery. This means they are unable to do any more work. However, they have so weakened the structure of number 5 that it collapses and causes damage to number 7.

Further reading

Elliott, D W, 'Endangering Life by Destroying or Damaging Property' [1997] Crim LR 382.
Haralambous, N, 'Retreating from *Caldwell*: restoring subjectivism' (2003) NLJ 1712.

chapter 16 PUBLIC ORDER OFFENCES ◼

The main public order offences are now contained in the Public Order Act 1986, though there are other offences, for example wearing a uniform for a political purpose under the Public Order Act 1936, and aggravated trespass under s 68 of the Criminal Justice and Public Order Act 1994.

The Public Order Act 1986 abolished the old common law offences of riot, rout, unlawful assembly and affray and created three new offences in their place. These are riot, violent disorder and affray. The law has been made more coherent, with common themes of using or threatening unlawful violence, and conduct which would cause a person of reasonable firmness present at the scene to fear for his personal safety.

Although these offences are aimed at maintaining public order, the Act states that all three offences can be committed in private as well as in a public place.

16.1 Riot

This is an offence under s 1 of the Public Order Act 1986:

'1(1) Where twelve or more persons who are present together use or threaten unlawful violence for a common purpose and the conduct of them (taken together) is such as would cause a person of reasonable firmness present at the scene to fear for his personal safety, each of the persons using unlawful violence for the common purpose is guilty of riot.

(2) It is immaterial whether or not the twelve or more use or threaten unlawful violence simultaneously.

(3) The common purpose may be inferred from conduct.

(4) No person of reasonable firmness need actually be, or likely to be, present at the scene.

(5) Riot may be committed in private as well as public places.'

16.1.1 The *actus reus* of riot

This has several elements. It requires:

- at least 12 people to be present together with a common purpose

- violence to be used or threatened by them

- so that the conduct would cause a person of reasonable firmness present at the scene to fear for his personal safety.

The 12 or more people need not have agreed to have assembled together; the fact that they are there together is the key point. The common purpose need not have been previously agreed. As s 1(3) states, the common purpose can be inferred from the conduct of the 12 or more people. This covers situations where a number of people come to the scene (whether together or one by one) and then because of an incident involving one person (perhaps being arrested by the police), 12 or more of the people there start threatening the police. All those threatening or using violence will then be guilty of riot.

The offence of riot can be committed even if the common purpose is lawful, for example employees want to discuss redundancies with their employer. But if 12 or more of them use or threaten unlawful violence they may be guilty of riot.

Violence

The meaning of 'violence' is explained in s 8 of the Act:

'8 . . . (i) except in the context of affray, it includes violent conduct towards property as well as violent conduct towards persons, and

(ii) it is not restricted to conduct causing or intended to cause injury or damage but includes any other violent conduct (for example, throwing at or towards a person a missile of a kind capable of causing injury which does not hit or falls short).'

Only unlawful violence can create riot. If the violence is lawful, for example in prevention of crime, or self-defence, then there is no offence.

16.1.2 *Mens rea* of riot

Section 6(1) states the mental element required for the offence:

 '6(1) A person is guilty of riot only if he intends to use violence or is aware that his conduct may be violent.'

So from this it can be seen that intention or 'awareness' is the mental element. Intention has the normal meaning in criminal law. However, awareness is a new concept. It has some similarity to *Cunningham* (1957) recklessness (see Chapter 3, section 3.3) as it is a partly subjective test: the defendant must be aware that his conduct may be violent. But it is not fully subjective as it does not require the defendant to be aware that it is unreasonable to take the risk that his conduct may be considered violent or threatening.

Section 6 also has a subsection specifically on the effect of intoxication on a defendant's *mens rea*. Section 6(5) states that:

 '6(5) For the purposes of this section a person whose awareness is impaired by intoxication shall be taken to be aware of that which he would be aware if not intoxicated, unless he shows either that his intoxication was not self-induced or that it was caused solely by the taking or administration of a substance in the course of medial treatment.'

This makes riot a basic intent offence. However, unlike other basic intent offences, it puts the onus of proving that the intoxication was involuntary on the defendant.

Intoxication is defined in s 6(6) as 'any intoxication, whether caused by drink, drugs or other means, or by a combination of means'.

16.1.3 Trial and penalty

Riot is viewed as a serious offence and has to be tried on indictment at the Crown Court. The maximum penalty is imprisonment for 10 years. It is the fact that there is criminal behaviour by a large group of persons which makes riot regarded as serious.

16.2 Violent disorder

This is an offence under s 2 Public Order Act 1986:

 '2(1) Where three or more persons who are present together use or threaten unlawful violence and the conduct of them (taken together) is such as would cause a person of reasonable firmness present at the scene to fear for his personal safety, each of the persons using or threatening unlawful violence is guilty of violent disorder.

(2) It is immaterial whether or not the three or more use or threaten unlawful violence simultaneously.

(3) No person of reasonable firmness need actually be, or likely to be, present at the scene.

(4) Violent disorder may be committed in private as well as public places.'

16.2.1 Comparison with riot

Most of the elements are the same as for riot. The similarities are that:

- the people must be present together
- they must use or threaten unlawful violence so that their conduct would cause a person of reasonable firmness present at the scene to fear for his personal safety
- the violence can be to a person or to property
- it can be in either a public or a private place
- there must be intention to use violence or awareness by D that his conduct may be violent. This is specifically stated in s 6(2) of the Act
- s 6(5) applies to both riot and violent disorder, so violent disorder is also a basic intent offence and D has to prove that any intoxication was involuntary.

The differences are:

- there need only be three people involved (although it can be charged where there is a greater number of persons involved – even where there are 12 or more)
- there is no need for a common purpose.

16.2.2 Trial and penalty

Violent disorder is regarded as less serious than riot. It is intended to be used where fewer people are involved or for less serious happenings of public disorder. This can be seen by the fact that it is triable either way (though in most cases it is tried on indictment). Where it is tried on indictment the maximum penalty is imprisonment for five years.

16.3 Affray

This is an offence under s 3 Public Order Act 1986:

'3(1) A person is guilty of affray if he uses or threatens unlawful violence towards another and his conduct is such as would cause a person of reasonable firmness present at the scene to fear for his personal safety.

(2) If two or more persons use or threaten unlawful violence, it is the conduct of them taken together that must be considered for the purposes of subsection (1).

(3) For the purposes of this section a threat cannot be made by the use of words alone.

(4) No person of reasonable firmness need actually be, or likely to be, present at the scene.

(5) Affray may be committed in private as well as public places.'

The threat cannot be made by words alone, even if the words are very threatening and the tone of voice aggressive. There must be some conduct. In *Dixon* [1993] Crim LR 579 the Court of Appeal upheld D's conviction for affray where the police had been called to a domestic incident. When they got there D ran away, accompanied by his Alsatian-type dog. The police officers cornered him and he encouraged the dog to attack them. Two officers were bitten before extra police arrived and D was arrested. Encouraging the dog to attack was held to be conduct.

16.3.1 Person of reasonable firmness

Section 3(4) states that it is not necessary for a person of reasonable firmness to have been at the scene. This point was illustrated in *Davison* [1992] Crim LR 31, where the police were called to a domestic incident. D waved an eight-inch knife at a police officer saying 'I'll have you'. The Court of Appeal upheld his conviction for affray. It was not a question of whether the police officer feared for his personal safety. The test was whether a hypothetical person of reasonable firmness who was present at the scene would have feared for his personal safety.

However, there must be someone present at the scene, as the use or threat of unlawful violence must be against a person. (This is different to riot and violent disorder.) The point was decided in *I, M and H v DPP* [2001] UKHL 10.

CASE EXAMPLE

I, M and H v DPP [2001] UKHL 10

All three Ds were members of a gang. They had armed themselves with petrol bombs which they intended to use against a rival gang. Before the rival gang came on the scene, the police arrived and the group (including the three Ds) threw away their petrol bombs and dispersed. The stipendiary magistrate found that there was no one present apart from the police. There was no threat to the police because the moment they arrived, the gang dispersed. Their conviction was quashed by the House of Lords, as affray can only be committed where the threat was directed towards another person or persons actually present at the scene.

Lord Hutton in his judgment pointed out that the defendants should have been charged under s 1 of the Prevention of Crime Act 1953 or s 4 of the Explosive Substances Act 1883.

16.3.2 *Mens rea* of affray

The defendant is only guilty if he intends to use violence or is aware that his conduct may be violent. This is the same rule as for riot and violent disorder (s 6(2) of the Act). The same rule also applies of the onus being on the defendant to prove that any intoxication was involuntary (s 6(5)).

16.3.3 Trial and penalty

Affray is triable either way but it is usually tried summarily at the Magistrates' Court. If it is tried on indictment then the maximum penalty is three years' imprisonment.

Key facts on riot, violent disorder and affray

KEY FACTS

	Riot	Violent disorder	Affray
Public Order Act 1986	s 1	s 2	s 3
Number needed	12	3	1
Use or threaten unlawful violence	Yes	Yes	Yes, but not words alone (s 3(3)).
Common purpose required	Yes Can be inferred from conduct (s 1(3))	No	No
Can be in public place or in private	Yes (s 1(5))	Yes (s 2(4))	Yes (s 3(5))
Can include violent conduct towards property	Yes (s 8(a))	Yes (s 8(a))	No
Must intend violence or be aware conduct might be violent	Yes (s 6(1))	Yes (s 6(2))	Yes (s 6(2))

16.4 Fear or provocation of violence

Section 4 of the 1986 Act states:

'4(1) A person is guilty of an offence if he:

(a) uses towards another person threatening, abusive or insulting words or behaviour, or

(b) distributes or displays to another person any writing, sign or other visible representation which is threatening, abusive or insulting, with intent to cause that person to believe that immediate unlawful violence will be used against him or another by any person, or to provoke the immediate use of unlawful violence by that person or another, or whereby that person is likely to believe that such violence will be used or it is likely that such violence will be provoked.

(2) An offence under this section may be committed in a public or private place, except that no offence is committed where the words or behaviour are used, or the writing, sign or other visible representation is distributed or displayed, by a person inside a dwelling and the other person is also inside that or another dwelling.'

This is a summary offence, triable only in the Magistrates' Court and carrying a maximum sentence of six months' imprisonment.

16.4.1 *Actus reus* of a s 4 offence

This offence can be committed in four different ways:

- using threatening, abusive or insulting words towards another person
- using threatening, abusive or insulting behaviour towards another person
- distributing to another person any writing, sign or other visible representation which is threatening, abusive or insulting
- displaying to another person any writing, sign or other visible representation which is threatening, abusive or insulting.

The offence can be committed in a public or private place, but s 1(2) specifically excludes events that occur within a dwelling. In *Atkin v DPP* [1989] Crim LR 581, D used threatening words while in his own home. This could not be an offence under s 4 of the Act.

16.4.2 Threatening, abusive or insulting

The common element of the four ways of committing this offence is the phrase 'threatening, abusive or insulting'. These words are not defined in the Act, but they were previously used in the Public Order Act 1936. Cases on that Act held that these words should be given their ordinary meaning. In *Brutus v Cozens* [1972] 2 All ER 1297 it was even stated that it was not helpful to try to explain them by the use of synonyms or dictionary definitions, because 'an ordinary sensible man knows an insult when he sees or hears it'. In this case the House of Lords held that whether something was 'threatening, abusive or insulting' was a question of fact.

CASE EXAMPLE

Brutus v Cozens [1972] 2 All ER 1297

D made a protest about apartheid in South Africa by running onto the court during a tennis match at Wimbledon and blowing a whistle and distributing leaflets. The protest lasted about two or three minutes. The magistrates acquitted him of an offence under s 5 of the Public Order Act 1936 (since repealed) and found as a fact that his behaviour was not insulting. The House of Lords held that this finding of fact was not unreasonable and the acquittal could not therefore be challenged.

Although it was said that 'an ordinary sensible man knows an insult when he sees or hears it', there have been some convictions under s 4 which appear strange. In *Masterson v Holden* [1986] 3 All ER 39, intimate cuddling by two homosexual men in Oxford Street at 1.55 am in the presence of two young men and two young women was held capable of being insulting.

16.4.3 Towards another person

Section 4(1)(a) provides that the threatening, abusive or insulting words must be towards another person. In *Atkin v DPP* (1989) it was held that this means 'in the presence of and in the direction of another person directly'. In *Atkin* (1989), D knew that a bailiff was in a car outside his house. He told customs officers who entered his house that if the bailiff came in, he was 'a dead un'. The bailiff was informed of this and felt threatened. However, because he was not present and the words were not used at him, D was not guilty.

16.4.4 *Mens rea* of s 4

Section 6(3) states:

 '6(3) A person is guilty of an offence under section 4 only if he intends his words or behaviour, or the writing sign or other visible representation, to be threatening, abusive or insulting, or is aware that it may be threatening, abusive or insulting.'

The first point is that D must intend, or be aware, that his words or behaviour towards the other person might be threatening, abusive or insulting. Then, for an offence under this section to be proved, it must also be shown that:

- D intends that the other person will believe that immediate unlawful violence will be used against him or
- D intends to provoke the immediate use of unlawful violence by the other person or
- the other person is likely to believe that immediate unlawful violence will be used against him or
- it is likely to provoke the immediate use of unlawful violence.

16.5 Intentionally causing harassment, alarm or distress

Section 4A was added to the Public Order Act 1986 by the Criminal Justice and Public Order Act 1994. It creates a more serious version of the offence in s 5 of the 1986 Act, as D must act intending to cause harassment, alarm or distress. There are also similarities with s 4, as there must be:

- threatening, abusive or insulting words or behaviour or distribution or display of writing, sign or other visible representation which is threatening, abusive or insulting; (although there can also be a charge where there is disorderly behaviour)
- this can be in a public or private place, but not a dwelling.

Section 4A states:

'4A(1) A person is guilty of an offence if, with intent to cause a person harassment, alarm or distress, he

(a) uses threatening, abusive or insulting words or behaviour, or disorderly behaviour, or

(b) displays any writing, sign or other visible representation which is threatening, abusive or insulting,

thereby causing that or another person harassment, alarm or distress.'

Like s 4, this is a summary offence triable only in the Magistrates' Court.

It must be proved both that D intended to cause a person harassment, alarm or distress and that D's behaviour did in fact cause someone harassment, alarm or distress. This was shown by *R v DPP* [2006] All ER (D) 250 (May). The facts of the case were that the defendant, aged 12, was with his sister when she was arrested for criminal damage. D made masturbatory gestures towards the police and called them 'wankers'. One police officer, who was over six feet in height and weighed over 17 stones, arrested D and he was charged with an offence contrary to s 4A. The officer gave evidence that he was not personally annoyed by D's behaviour but that he found it distressing that a boy of D's age was acting in such a manner. The Divisional Court quashed D's conviction as there was no evidence that D intended to cause real emotional disturbance or upset to the police officer. Also the

Youth court could not properly have concluded on the evidence of the police officer that he was distressed by D's behaviour.

In *Dehal v DPP* [2005] EWHC 2154 (Admin) it was held that there should be a threat to public order for a prosecution to be the method of dealing with behaviour. If not, then there could be a breach of the right to freedom of speech under Art 10 of the European Convention on Human Rights.

CASE EXAMPLE

Dehal v DPP [2005] EWHC 2154 (Admin)

D entered a temple and placed a notice stating that the preacher at the temple was 'a hypocrite'. D was convicted of an offence under s 4A of the Public Order Act 1986. D argued that his right to freedom of expression was infringed by being prosecuted for his action. The Divisional Court quashed his conviction. They held that the criminal law should not be invoked unless the conduct amounted to such a threat to public order that it required the use of the criminal law and not merely the civil law.

16.5.1 Defences

The Act specifically provides that:

'4A(3) It is a defence for the accused person to prove –

   (a) that he was inside a dwelling and had no reason to believe that the words or behaviour used, or the writing, sign or other visible representation displayed would be heard or seen by a person outside that or any other dwelling, or

   (b) that his conduct was reasonable.'

16.6 Harassment, alarm or distress

Section 5 of the 1986 Act provides that:

'5(1) A person is guilty of an offence if he –

   (a) uses threatening, abusive or insulting words or behaviour, or disorderly behaviour, or

   (b) displays any writing, sign or other visible representation which is threatening, abusive or insulting, within the hearing or sight of a person likely to be caused harassment, alarm or distress thereby.'

The person who is likely to be caused harassment, alarm or distress can include a police officer who is called to deal with a domestic incident. This was shown in the case of *DPP v Orum* [1988] 3 All ER 449.

CASE EXAMPLE

DPP v Orum [1988] 3 All ER 449

D had an offensive and public argument with his girlfriend. The police intervened and he was abusive to them. They arrested him for breach of the peace. When he was put in the back of a police van he assaulted a police officer. He was charged with and found guilty of an offence under s 5 and assaulting a police office in the execution of his duty.

The Divisional Court held that a police officer may be a person who is likely to be harassed, alarmed or distressed for the purpose of s 5(1).

In this case, the use of a public order offence seems inappropriate. There were other offences the defendant could have been charged with. Indeed, he was also charged, far more appropriately, with assaulting a police office in the execution of his duty.

In *Taylor v DPP* (2006), *The Times*, 14th June, it was held that proving there was someone near enough to hear the words was sufficient. It was not necessary to prove that any person actually heard. In *Taylor v DPP* a police officer gave evidence that D had shouted, screamed and sworn using racist language. There were a number of people on the scene near enough to hear the abusive language. The Divisional Court held that this was sufficient to uphold D's conviction.

16.7 Racially aggravated public order offences

Section 31 of the Crime and Disorder Act 1998 created racially aggravated versions of the offences under s 4, s 4A and s 5 of the Public Order Act 1986.

These involve the offences above committed in the special circumstances set out in s 28 of the Crime and Disorder Act 1998. These are that:

- at the time of the offence, or immediately before or after doing so, the offender demonstrates towards the victim of the offence hostility based on the victim's membership (or presumed membership) of a racial group or
- the offence is motivated by hostility towards members of a racial group based on their membership of that group.

It is clear that if a defendant uses words identifying specific nationalities or races, then this can make the offence an aggravated one within the definition of s 28. It has also been held that more general words such as 'foreigners' or 'immigrants' come within the scope of s 28.

566

CASE EXAMPLE

Rogers (Philip) [2006] EWCA Crim 2863; [2006] 1 Cr App R 14

D encountered three Spanish women. D, who was in a wheelchair, called them 'bloody foreigners' and told then to go back to their own country. He then pursued them to a kebab house in an aggressive manner. He was convicted of using racially aggravated abusive or insulting words contrary to s 31(1)(a) of the Crime and Disorder Act 1998. He appealed on the basis that his words were not capable of demonstrating hostility based on membership of a racial group. 'Foreigners' did not constitute a racial group as defined in s 28(4) of the Act. The Court of Appeal upheld his conviction. They held that a racial group within the definition of s 28(4) did not have to be distinguished by particular racial characteristics. The definition was sufficiently wide to embrace within a single racial group all those who were 'foreign'.

The Court of Appeal approved the judgment of the Divisional Court in *DPP v M (minor)* [2004] EWHC 1453 (Admin); [2004] 1 WLR 2758 where D had used the same phrase 'bloody foreigners' and the Divisional Court had decided that this was capable of describing a racial group.

In *Attorney-General's Reference (No 4 of 2004)* [2005] EWCA Crim 889; [2005] 2 Cr App R 26 the Court of Appeal held that using the words 'an immigrant doctor' was capable of demonstrating hostility based on the doctor's membership of a racial group.

ACTIVITY

Self-test questions

1. Explain the differences between riot and violent disorder.

2. What is unusual about the effect of s 6(5) of the Public Order Act 1986?

3. Explain the rules on what has to be proved about the presence and/or effect on a person of reasonable firmness in the offence of affray.

4. Is the fact that riot, violent disorder and affray can be committed in private satisfactory?

5. Why is the offence under s 4A of the Public Order Act 1986 regarded as more serious than the offence under s 4 of the same Act?

APPLYING THE LAW

☐☐☐

Explain what offences, if any, have been committed in the following situation.

Sonya and Tex are against the use of animals for testing drugs. They agree to demonstrate outside a local drugs company who use animals for this purpose. They have a banner which reads 'Death to those who do tests on animals'. They stand outside the entrance to the company holding up this banner and shouting. Wilbur and Zoe, who have been drinking, see them and think that it will be amusing to join the protest. They stand opposite Sonya and Tex, shouting and making it difficult for workers to get past them on their way into work.

☐☐☐

appendix 1 PROBLEM-SOLVING QUESTIONS ■

The following scenarios require you to apply the law from different areas:

1. Annika and Britney are the directors of a small company, Bustit Ltd, which is unable to pay its debts. Annika and Britney decide to spend the weekend in a luxury hotel to discuss the financial problems. The hotel reservations are made by the company secretary. After reviewing the company accounts, Annika and Britney leave the hotel without paying the bill.

   Consider the criminal liability, if any, of Annika, Britney and Bustit Ltd.

2. Craig and Del are next-door neighbours and workmates. Some of Craig's work tools, including a powerdrill, have gone missing and he suspects that Del has taken them. One evening, when Del is out, Craig enters Del's garden and goes into a garden shed to look for his possessions. He finds two screwdrivers which he mistakenly believes are his and takes them. He also finds a powerdrill which he suspects is his. He decides to teach Del a lesson and he alters the wiring in the drill so that it will give Del an electric shock when he next uses it. In fact the two screwdrivers and the powerdrill are Del's own.

   The next day Del lends the powerdrill to a friend, Elmer. When Elmer switches the drill on, he gets a massive electric shock which kills him.

   Discuss the criminal liability, if any, of Craig.

3. Fiona meets a friend, Grant. Fiona knows that Grant is a drug dealer and has convictions for violence. Grant threatens Fiona that he will 'mark' her two-year-old son unless Fiona agrees to take some crack cocaine to another friend, Hayley and bring back £200 which Hayley owes Grant. Fiona reluctantly agrees to do this. She goes to Hayley's house and tells her she has the cocaine for her, but that she must have the £200 before she will hand it over. Hayley refuses to give her the money, so Fiona grabs Hayley's purse from her hand. Hayley tries to stop her and Fiona pushes her hard, causing her to fall and cut her head.

   Discuss the criminal liability, if any, of Fiona.

4. Ian's car has broken down on a country road. He finds that he has left his mobile phone at home, so he decides to walk to a cottage which he had passed a mile back down the road to get help. When he gets to the cottage he knocks on the door, but no one answers. Ian can see that there is a telephone in the hallway and so he uses a penknife to open a window catch and climbs into the house. He phones a local garage who say they cannot come out for at least an hour. As it is cold, Ian decides to wait in the house and make himself a cup of tea. When he is sitting in the kitchen, the householder, Jamal, returns.

Jamal sees Ian's penknife with the blade open on the table and, thinking Ian will attack him, Jamal seizes the knife. Ian tries to stop him and both Ian and Jamal suffer cuts to their hands. Ian then pushes Jamal away from him, causing Jamal to hit his head on a shelf. Jamal falls to the floor, unconscious. Ian runs out of the house, leaving Jamal there. Jamal suffers bleeding to the brain. He is not discovered for two days and dies as a result.

Discuss the criminal liability, if any, of Ian.

5. Kate and her friend, Lennox, decide to demonstrate against the visit of a foreign politician from a country in which there are human rights abuses. They stand silently outside a hotel where he is staying. After half an hour, Malcolm who has been watching them starts shouting abuse at them. Kate and Lennox ignore this to start with but when Malcolm starts making racist remarks about Lennox, Kate rushes at him and threatens to hit him. Two women who are walking past are afraid that there will be a fight.

Discuss the criminal liability, if any, of Kate, Lennox and Malcolm.

6. Naomi, Olga and Peter are drug addicts. At Olga's flat Naomi fills a syringe with heroin and gives it first to Olga who injects herself. Naomi then injects herself and then hands the empty syringe to Peter who refills it and injects himself. Naomi is HIV positive but does not tell Peter, nor warn him not to use the needle she has just used. All three lapse into unconsciousness after taking the heroin. When Naomi and Peter come round they realise that Olga's breathing is very bad and they cannot rouse her. They both leave the flat, leaving Olga still unconscious. Olga is found dead the next day. Some weeks later, Peter discovers that he is HIV positive.

Discuss what offences, if any, have been committed by Naomi.

7. Robert belongs to a teenage gang. One day they all decide to 'see off' a rival gang. Fourteen of them arm themselves with sticks and drive to a street where they know the other gang often meet. They park their vehicles and join up at the end of the street. Before they can start walking down the road, they see a police car coming towards them. They all drop their sticks and run away.

Discuss what criminal offences, if any, have been committed.

appendix 2 HOW TO ANSWER QUESTIONS ▪━━━

When studying law you will be expected to write essays and you will also have to apply the law in legal problems based on scenarios. This appendix gives some hints on the skills you need for both of these.

Legal problem solving

There are four essential ingredients to answering problem questions. You need to:

1. identify the important facts in the questions and from these identify the area of law you need to apply

2. define the area of law

3. expand your definition including relevant sections and cases to show that you know and understand the area of law thoroughly

4. apply the law to the problem and reach a conclusion.

The initial letters of this list give IDEA: a simple idea to remember!

Consider the following situation.

Ella and Gary agree to steal electrical goods from a local shop. Ella takes a car belonging to her next-door neighbour without the owner's permission, so that the number plate cannot be traced to either Ella or Gary. She drives Gary to the shop and waits around the corner in the car while he goes in.

In the shop Gary takes a basket and selects several expensive small items, placing them in the basket. He notices that only two check-outs are staffed and he goes to one of the empty check-outs at the far end of the line. He leans into the cashier's area and tries to open the till, but is unable to do so. Unknown to him, the till has just been emptied. As he is doing this, a store attendant notices him and walks over to the till. Gary runs out of the shop and is chased by the store attendant, who catches him. Gary punches the man hard in the face, breaking his jaw. Gary then runs round the corner and jumps into the car. He shouts at Ella to drive off fast. Ella does this but a mile down the road she loses control of the car and it crashes into a barrier. Gary and Ella get out of the car and run off.

Answering the question

Identifying the facts

The tutor or examiner who sets the question will make sure that most of the facts are relevant. So work your way through, looking at what both Ella and Gary do. Where there are two or more people involved in the criminal activity it is often easier to tackle one person at a time. So, starting with Gary, the main facts are:

1. an agreement to steal

2. being a passenger in a car which has been taken without the owner's consent

3. places items in a basket provided by the store and eventually leaves the store without paying for these

4. leans into the cashier's area and tries to open a till

5. assaults the store attendant who is chasing him

6. encourages Ella to drive fast.

From these, now identify the areas of law involved. Some of them are very clear from writing down these facts.

1. Wherever there is an agreement to do a criminal act, the law on conspiracy is relevant.

2. Being a passenger in a car which has been taken without the owner's consent brings s 12 of the Theft Act 1968 into play.

3. For the goods in the shop the offence of theft (s 1 Theft Act 1968) is relevant.

4. Trying to open the till makes the law on attempt relevant. Also, as he has leant into the cashier's area, consider burglary as a possibility.

5. The assault is an offence against the person, but it is also linked to the theft so robbery must also be considered.

6. Is there participation by encouraging dangerous driving?

Having identified the areas of law you must now explain them in more detail, especially where there is some doubt on the point. So now look at the relevant law in detail and apply it.

1 Conspiracy

The definition of 'conspiracy' is in s 1 of the Criminal Law Act 1977: agreeing a course of conduct which will necessarily amount to or involve the commission of an offence by one or more of the parties to the agreement. The agreement to commit theft is clearly within this definition of 'conspiracy'.

2 Section 12

Under s 12 of the Theft Act 1968 it is an offence to allow oneself to be carried in a conveyance knowing that it has been taken without the consent of the owner. The scenario does not state whether Gary knew that Ella had taken the car without her neighbour's consent. If he does (and this includes where he wilfully shuts his eyes to the obvious), he is guilty of this offence. If he does not then he is not guilty of the offence.

3 Theft

The definition of 'theft' is in s 1 of the Theft Act 1968: dishonestly appropriating property belonging to another with the intention of permanently depriving that other of it. The only point for discussion in this scenario is exactly when the appropriation took place. This is at the point when Gary puts the goods in the basket: *Morris* [1983] 3 All ER 288, *Gomez* [1993] 1 All ER 1.

4 (a) Attempted theft

The Criminal Attempts Act 1981 s 1(1) defines an attempt as where 'with intent to commit an offence a person does an act which is more than merely preparatory to the commission of the offence'. As Gary has tried to open the till, this is clearly more than merely preparatory. However, there is nothing in the till so the law on attempting the impossible must be considered. Under s 1(2) of the Criminal Attempts Act 1981 person may be guilty of attempting to commit an offence even though the facts are such that the commission of the offence is impossible. This subsection makes Gary guilty of attempted theft even though there is nothing in the till to steal.

(b) Burglary

Under s 9(1)a of the Theft Act 1968 one of the ways of committing burglary is where the defendant enters as a trespasser with intent to commit theft. Has Gary entered as a trespasser? He intends to steal, so is going beyond the purpose for which he is permitted to enter: *Smith and Jones* [1976] 3 All ER 54. He therefore enters as a trespasser. Also, he has leant into a private area of the shop where shoppers do not have permission to go. In *Walkington* [1979] 2 All ER 716 the defendant was held guilty of burglary where he walked behind the counter in a shop and opened the till. To be a trespasser there must be effective entry. Is leaning in an effective entry? *Brown* [1994] 1 AC 212 was guilty of burglary by leaning through a window, so by analogy Gary is likely to be guilty.

5. (a) Assault

Under s 47 of the Offences against the Person Act 1861 it is an offence to occasion actual bodily harm: under s 20 it is an offence to inflict grievous bodily harm: under s 18 it is an offence to cause grievous bodily harm with intent to do so. Applying this to the punch by which Gary breaks the store attendant's jaw, at the least Gary is guilty of s 47. The points for discussion are: is a broken jaw capable of being grievous bodily harm? and, if so: has Gary the necessary *mens rea* for s 18?

(b) Robbery

Section 8 of the Theft Act 1968 says that robbery is committed where a person steals, and immediately before or at the time of doing so, and in order to do so, he uses force on any person or puts or seeks to put any person in fear of being then and there subjected to force. The points which need exploring are whether the force was 'at the time' of the theft and was it used 'in order to' steal. In *Hale* [1979] Crim LR 596 it was held that the act of appropriation can be a continuing one, so that any force used in order to steal while the appropriation is continuing would make this robbery. This contrasts with *Gomez* (1993) where it was decided that the point of appropriation in theft is when D first does an act assuming a right of the owner. So which decision should be applied to Gary? A similar situation to Gary's occurred in *Lockley* [1995] Crim LR 656 where D was caught shoplifting cans of beer from an off-licence and used force on the shopkeeper who was trying to stop him from escaping. In that case the Court of Appeal rejected an argument that *Gomez* (1993) had impliedly overruled *Hale* and confirmed that the principle in *Hale* (1979) still applied in robbery. As Gary has left the shop before he uses force the *Hale* principle is not likely to apply.

6. Participation

To be a secondary party the defendant must 'aid, abet' counsel or procure' the commission of an offence (s 8 Accessories and Abettors Act 1861). Abetting has been held to be any conduct which instigates, incites or encourages the commission of the offence, including shouting encouragement or paying for a ticket for an illegal performance as in *Wilcox v Jeffrey* [1951] 1 All ER 464. As Gary shouts encouragement, this could make him liable as a secondary party for any offence of dangerous driving committed by Ella as principal.

Now move on to consider Ella. The relevant facts for Ella are:

1. An agreement to steal.

2. Takes a car without consent of the owner.

3. Get away driver for Gary.

4. Drives too fast, crashes car.

The first point on conspiracy has already been identified and dealt with under Gary. The same law will apply to Ella. For the other points the areas of law which need to be identified are s 12 taking a conveyance without consent (and possibly theft of the car), secondary participation in the theft from the shop, the burglary, assault and robbery and, finally, aggravated vehicle-taking through the possibility of dangerous driving and/or the damage to the car.

Section 12 Theft Act 1968

Section 12 makes a person guilty of an offence if, without having the consent of the owner or other lawful authority, he takes any conveyance for his own or another's use. The only possible point for discussion is whether Ella believed she would have her neighbour's consent, giving a defence under s 12(6) which states that 'a person does not commit an offence under this section by anything done in the belief that he has lawful authority to do it or that he would have the owner's consent if the owner knew of his doing it and the circumstances of it'. However, it is highly unlikely that consent would be given to use of the car to commit a crime.

Theft of car

Theft requires that there is an intention permanently to deprive the owner. Applying this to the scenario, it is unlikely that Ella has committed theft.

Secondary participation

As already stated in relation to Gary, to be a secondary party it is necessary to prove that D aided, abetted counselled or procured the commission of an offence (s 8 Accessories and Abettors Act 1861). Aiding is giving help, support or assistance. This can be before the offence or during the time it is being committed, for example acting as look-out, as in *Betts and Ridley* (1930) 22 Cr App R 148. By driving Gary to the shop and waiting outside as get away driver, Ella is a secondary participant in the theft of the goods in the shop. The point which needs more detailed examination is whether she is also a secondary participant in the burglary, the assault or the robbery.

In *Chan Wing-Siu* [1985] 1 AC 168 and also in *Powell* [1999] AC 1; [1997] 4 All ER 545; [1997] UKHL 45 it was held that contemplation or foresight that the principal might commit a certain type of offence is sufficient to a make a secondary party liable for the offence committed by the principal offender. Ella knows that Gary is going to steal so clearly she is a secondary party to that. Is burglary sufficiently close to be within the range of possible offences, as in *Maxwell v DPP of Northern Ireland* [1978] 1 WLR 1350? Almost certainly. However, the plan did not involve any violence. Ella can only be liable as a secondary party for these if she contemplated or foresaw that Gary might use violence if he was challenged by anyone in the shop. So, if she knows he has used violence in such situations in the past she may be a secondary party to both the assault and robbery.

Aggravated vehicle-taking

Finally, Ella crashed the car, bringing in aggravated vehicle-taking (s 12A Theft Act 1968). Under s 12A the basic offence must be committed plus an aggravating factor. Two of these factors are that the vehicle was driven dangerously on a road or other public place, or that damage was caused to the vehicle. The test for 'dangerous' is objective, in that 'the driving must far below what would be expected of a competent and careful driver' and that 'it would be obvious to a competent and careful driver that driving the vehicle in that way would be dangerous'. Discuss Ella's losing control of the car because of excessive speed in the light of these tests.

General hints

Where the potential defendant is involved in more than one situation, make a list of the relevant facts. Where there is more than one person's criminal liability involved, always make a list of the

facts relevant to each one separately. Doing this will help to identify the different aspects of law relevant to the scenario.

Legal essay writing

Consider the following essay title:

> 'Critically discuss the way in which the courts have interpreted the meaning of "appropriation" in the definition of theft.'

Answering the question

There are nearly always two key elements in answering essays in law. These are:

1. setting out certain factual information on a particular area of law with supporting statutes and cases

2. answering the actual question set which usually takes the form of some sort of critical element. This may be discussing development of law or analysing case decisions or comment on an area of law or evaluating the contribution of a case or the need for reform of an area, etc.

The first element is the easiest to do, but you must be careful to explain only relevant areas of law. Usually the question will be quite specific on the area required. In the question above the area is limited to 'appropriation' in the definition of theft. This means that there is no requirement to set out the law on the other elements of theft.

The second part involving analysis, criticism, evaluation etc is more demanding, but needs to be based on the law you have set out. Arguments must be supported with reference to relevant decisions. Where the judges have given different reasons for a decision or where there is a dissenting judgment then the differences need to be explored and commented on.

Putting this into practice

When explaining the law for the above title, start with the definition of appropriation in s 3(1) of the Theft Act 1968 which states 'any assumption by a person of the rights of an owner amounts to an appropriation, and this includes, where he has come by the property (innocently or not) without stealing it, any later assumption of a right to it by keeping or dealing with it as owner'. Then it is necessary to cover the following points:

1. Discuss what is meant by 'the rights' in particular, whether the assumption has to be of *all* of the rights or whether it can just be of *any* of the rights: *Morris* (1983).

2. Explain what the courts have decided where the defendant has taken the item with the consent of the owner: *Lawrence* [1972] AC 626; *Gomez* (1993).

3. Explain the decision in *Hinks* [2000] 4 All ER 833 on there being appropriation even though the consent was genuine and the goods were gifts.

4. Explain the problem of when appropriation takes place in appropriation of credit balances: *Tomsett* [1985] Crim LR 369; *Governor of Pentonville Prison, ex parte Osman* [1989] 3 All ER 701; *Governor of Brixton Prison, ex parte Levin* [1997] 3 All ER 289.

5. Explain the decisions in cases of robbery that appropriation is a continuing act, *Hale* (1979); *Lockley* (1995).

Remember that simply writing out the decisions is not enough. The question demands that you critically discuss these various decisions. There is plenty of material for discussion and comment. The points which can be raised include:

1. The fact that if appropriation had to be of *all* the rights of an owner, then there would be far fewer successful prosecutions for theft. The decision in *Morris* (1983) can be regarded as sensible and pragmatic.

2. The fact that cases where consent is obtain by fraud could be charged under s 15 Theft Act 1968 as obtaining by deception and the problem the judges faced when this charge had not been brought in the cases of *Lawrence* (1972) and *Gomez* (1993). The decisions can be criticised as an endeavour to ensure that the convictions for theft were upheld, because the actions of the defendants were 'criminal'.

3. Is the extension of this principle in *Hinks* (2000) to a situation where the victim had genuinely consented pushing the definition of 'appropriation' beyond what was meant in the Theft Act? The comments by Lord Hobhouse in his dissenting judgment can be useful explored on this point.

4. The conflicting decisions in *Tomsett* (1985) and *Governor of Pentonville Prison, ex parte Osman* (1989) on when appropriation took place. Is it necessary that appropriation takes place in only one location?

5. Are decisions in the two robbery cases in conflict with the decision in *Gomez* (1993)? Can the judgment of the Court of Appeal in *Lockley* (1995) that *Gomez* (1993) had not impliedly overruled *Hale* (1979) be justified?

Conclusion

Having discussed all your points, you must then end with a conclusion in which you briefly summarise your arguments, showing where decisions are justified and where a decision is open to criticism.

INDEX

Page numbers in *italics* refer to diagrams.